Additional Dialogue

Additional Dialogue

Letters of Dalton Trumbo, 1942-1962

Edited by Helen Manfull

Published by

M. Evans and Company, Inc.
New York
and distributed in association with
J. B. Lippincott Company,
New York and Philadelphia

Several of the letters in this book were previously
published in *Esquire* magazine.

Contents

Foreword
by
Dalton
Trumbo

Several years ago an eccentric publisher suggested an autobiography and offered a large enough advance against royalties to excite both the larcener who dwells inside my skin and that other tenant who lusts for acclaim and insists that no one is better qualified to bestow it than himself. Since autobiography is the only vocation on earth that guarantees a man two lives—the one he has lived and the one he thinks he lived—a chance to paint the lily at someone else's expense was not to be rejected out of hand.

Determined not to betray the eagerness that clamored so shamefully for a quick yes, I said I'd think about it and immediately did. I understood as well as the next practitioner that the recipe for true autobiographical *haute cuisine* calls for eight cups of quietly understated virtue craftily spiced with half a *soupçon* of small sins, reluctantly confessed and far too human to be condemned. Wart-preening, the latter is called; before you're through with it each wart not only resembles a pearl but is.

Since virtues homogenize perfectly with pearls, all that remains is to fatten the mix with one misdeed—one, and no more—so heartless that its memory will haunt the autobiographer to the end of his days; a dereliction described with such remorse, such self-loathing, that the reader is driven at once to passionate intervention—no, no, forgive yourself, it wasn't that bad, you're too splendid a chap to suffer so much for something so small! Once they've swallowed *that* chunk of suet they're gastronomically psyched: they'll eat anything.

The whole feast, of course, to be preceded by an apéritif called the dedication, which must without fail commemorate that wonderful woman without whose agile footwork from kitchen to laundry to nursery to sickbed to market to dog-vomit on the living-room rug the author couldn't possibly have become what he certainly is, God bless those shriveled old dishwater hands, thrice bless those fluting bird-like little cries—*Yes, yes, right away, coming up!*—with which she has filled his heart, home, life, world, universe. With this down the hatch all that follows translates as the poetry of a life so richly lived, so candidly revealed, so . . .

At this point my soaring hopes collided in midair with the tardy realization that I was too old even then to play the autobiographical game with a generation that makes it at forty, stops just long enough to celebrate the wonder in twenty-two ounces of hard-cover prose and then, starting fast to make up for lost time, stampedes toward volume two—or three—or even four, mere existence itself become medium, message, motive, means, marker and muse.

What to do? What, indeed, to do? In a game that disqualifies you for a twelve-second rest, I paused to pray on the matter for two nights and three dingy days. On the afternoon of the third day I was delivered from evil by Helen Manfull's request for permission to select a volume of letters from the mass I had on file at the University of Wisconsin, and offer them for publication.

It didn't take much blocking or tackling to bring me around. I was, after all, a writer, or at least I call myself one, and while writers dearly love to work, they stand with parsons and painters and philosophers in loving just as dearly to be paid for it. What were all those letters entombed in Madison, Wisconsin, but the accumulated residue of past work thrown into the pot for nothing and by now almost forgotten? The idea of being paid for them so many years later in real money (one of the most prodigious academic and political swells of our time recently sold publication rights to a seventy-nine-word letter for $25) was too staggering for a mere journeyman-outsider to resist. Instant autobiography, so to speak. And on the cheap. *C'est fini!* Also she promised to correct the spelling. *Voilà!* I am yours, Helen Manfull, forever and only yours.

A year later I received and began to read eleven pounds of ancient, annotated correspondence. It was all my own doing. Guided by greed, I had actually *wanted* to view this austere, wart-hummocked landscape in the exact center of which, I'd been told, at precisely five o'clock in the afternoon, every pilgrim confronts at last his moment of truth. Surely these pages, obsessed with money, filled with endlessly reiterated objects, lost clauses, metaphors not merely mixed but macerated, trivial grievances, contradictions, false prophesies, unkept resolutions, high purposes brought low and low ones here and there brought high—surely these letters weren't the me I knew so well and remembered so differently.

For two years I pretended I hadn't yet found time to read them through to the end. I wrote cunningly evasive notes from London, Rome, Budapest, Lausanne, Munich and Mexico City as I roamed the world, working on other projects to be sure, but actually hoping to leave behind me so dim a trail and so faint a scent that Manfull would tire of the hunt or have another baby (which she did) or go off somewhere to rest and not come back. I began to delay reading her letters for months after their receipt. I absurdly calculated which of them were most likely to contain the hottest reproaches, and put them aside unopened. Some I have not opened yet. On Christmas Day, 1968, the burden of those unopened letters grown too large to bear, I telephoned her in the hope of negotiating an armistice. Sensing the instability of my position and the weakness of my character, she held out for unconditional surrender and got it.

Once the issue was settled, I sank gratefully into that state of euphoric stupor which marks the defeated. The die was cast, the

Rubicon crossed. That part of me which wanted the project to go through had triumphed over the part which didn't, for the very good reason—and here lay the truth of it—that some of those letters I *liked*. I liked them a great deal. If publication of those I didn't like was the price for those I did—well, better men had made poorer bargains and survived without too many 'scars.

By now, of course, with the dance ended and the dancers going home and what we call the custodial personnel already at work on the floor, there's nothing for it but to pay the fiddler. That thin, soft-wheedling whine—*gee-dee-aee-eee*—approaching from the wings may sound like the fiddler's bitch but it's not; it's the fiddler himself. Welcome, brother. *L'addition.*

Dalton Trumbo

Los Angeles, California
March 1, 1970

Editor's
Preface

In the early sixties, while I was working at the Wisconsin Centre for Theatre Research, I had the task of organizing the newly acquired scripts, records and papers of Dalton Trumbo. I knew very little about the man; I was in elementary school when Trumbo's best-known screen plays—*Kitty Foyle, A Guy Named Joe, Thirty Seconds over Tokyo,* and *Our Vines Have Tender Grapes*—were written; and I knew the reputation of his novel *Johnny Got His Gun.* I was just approaching my very unaware teens when a group of directors, producers, and writers (including Trumbo), who later called themselves The Hollywood Ten, were summoned before the House Committee on Un-American Activities in 1947 and indicted for contempt of Congress for refusing to state whether or not they were or ever had been members of the Communist Party. The name Dalton Trumbo meant little to me until years later.

Then suddenly I was confronted with carton upon carton of his papers, a major portion of which was the voluminous correspondence dating from the mid-thirties to the early sixties. As I began to examine the letters, my attention was arrested here by a flippant or vitriolic remark and there by an expression of eloquent tenderness and compassion. I began to read more and more of the letters; I could not stop reading them. They seemed too brilliantly composed, too trenchant in their wit, too wise to be withheld from anyone who might wish to read them. Soon the idea for a book materialized, and Trumbo promptly answered my request for permission to begin the edition, saying:

Any man who'd plead modesty in rejecting a letter such as yours would have to be a liar or an idiot, and probably both. You'd need to be much older to understand how delightful it is to be told that a young and obviously educated woman, living amidst the urgent turmoil of 1963, still finds interest in letters written long ago, in circumstances so strikingly different.

In his concluding paragraph, Trumbo quipped, "My letters—! What will they think of next? It's like the day I sold my seventh novel and called it the first."

What was there in these letters by a man who declares that he is "not a literary figure of any distinction" that so compelled my attention and led me to compile this edition? In the first place, the letters tell the story of a Hollywood personality struggling against the machinations of that wily community in an extraordinary era in America's political history. The Hollywood blacklist, the workings of the subsequent black market, and the unwritten, unproclaimed demise of the blacklist—all this was experienced by one man who was intrinsically involved in the maneuvering of the Congressional investigations and Hollywood house cleaning, and who suffered a complete loss of professional name and fortune by refusing to compromise or to sacrifice principle or personal integrity. Trumbo articulated his own struggle in a letter to Ralph Newman at the time he submitted his papers to the research centre.

I've always thought of my life as a sequence of conflicts, each separate battle segregated in my mind under the heading, "My fight with these guys" or "My fight with those guys." In thinking back I now realize I have regarded each fight as distinct and unrelated to the other, and have sometimes marveled how one man could have so many of them. I now realize it was all one fight; that the relation of each to the other was very close; and that I am really no more combative than any other man. It just happened in my case that the original fight once undertaken, expanded marvelously into what seemed like many fights and that the most recent in a sequence of fights is actually no more than the current phase of the primary engagement. Since all men have at least one fight in their lives, and are not considered professional troublemakers because of it, the longer view reveals in me a citizen no less peaceful than his neighbors.

It is a curious and fortunate accident that Trumbo has spent most of his professional life either geographically or professionally cut off from friends and business associates. The prime of his pre-blacklist career found him at a mile-high ranch in the mountains, eighty-five miles from Hollywood; prison and self-exile in Mexico isolated him again. Still, if presented with the alternative, and regardless of his protestations to the contrary, Trumbo would undoubtedly prefer to pen his reactions to problems and situations rather than to deliver them in conversation.

Juxtaposed are letters from the writer trying to shape a scene or a poem, from the unswerving but witty friend, the venomous and outraged enemy, the loving and devoted father and husband, the compassionate humanitarian, the seasoned philosopher, the discontented customer, the liberal, and the moralist.

What emerges most strongly from these diversified aspects of his make-up is a kind of American ideal: a man who knows what he believes and who is willing to speak out and fight for those beliefs frankly and fearlessly no matter what the cost; a man to whom principles and honor are not just words but integral parts of his being and way of life. Trumbo ably expressed his philosophy in a speech for the Teachers' Union of New York on April 9, 1960:

The Right to express ideas, good ideas, bad ideas, wicked ideas, crazy ideas, impossible ideas—this is the most precious right the individual can have. And the interesting thing is that in the course of securing it for himself he must inevitably guarantee it to his enemy. Otherwise, there can be no freedom for anyone.

There are going to be wider areas of freedom in this country and in the world as the Cold War diminishes. But no matter how pleasant the relaxation of governmental interference with the writer and the teacher may seem, it will be wasted if we do not use it to revive the old American custom of fighting City Hall.

Upon your shoulders, particularly upon the shoulders of teachers and education, lies the noble burden of encouraging the habit of inquiry once more. Inquiry into everything. That is where the secret of freedom is found: to inquire, to question, to doubt, to dispute, to challenge. These are the rights we have compromised for ourselves and which we must re-establish for our children.

The convictions set down in the correspondence may well be at odds with those of the reader, yet every word, action and attitude emanates from his own basic honesty and sense of right. Some of the letters were never mailed, others never developed beyond rough draft, some were hastily dictated into a machine, and still others were carefully and methodically drafted and re-drafted until he achieved a precise result. Certainly none were intended for publication.

Most of the letters—whether rough draft, final draft, or dictated notes—are presented as Trumbo wrote them. Occasionally, however, repetitions or obscure references are deleted, and unintentional errors of spelling or punctuation have been corrected. Names of black market films have occasionally been eliminated to protect both the writer and the producer; names of the men who helped Trumbo— writers who allowed their names to be used by him, as well as the independent producers who knowingly accepted black market work —have similarly been deleted.

Each section, introduced by brief biographical or background information, hinges upon a major event in Trumbo's career. Many letters are included for their humor, literary excellence, information about Hollywood, or insight into the man's character. Footnotes provide identifications and explanations, but the letters tell their own story—of a man, an industry, an era, and a principle.

Helen Manfull

Pennsylvania State University
January 2, 1970

1.
"How Gaily
I Blossomed
Forth"

Within the confines of a single decade, Dalton Trumbo advanced from a reader in the story department of Warner Brothers' Studios to one of Metro-Goldwyn-Mayer's most influential and highly paid screen writers. After the sale of his first novel, *Eclipse,* in 1936, Warner Brothers' hired the young script reader as a writer at $60.00 a week. From Warners he went to Columbia at $250.00 a week and then briefly to Metro-Goldwyn-Mayer in 1937. When Trumbo returned to MGM five years later, he had built a solid reputation as a craftsman and had written pictures for a number of studios including Twentieth-Century Fox, RKO, and Paramount.

By 1946 Trumbo had obtained from Metro the best contract ever held by a writer in the motion picture industry to that time: a straight five-year contract, without option on the part of the studio, in which he could choose a salary of $3,000 per week for as long as was necessary to complete a job, or $75,000 per script, the latter probably being his choice for hurried or pressured assignments; complete freedom in the selection or rejection of subject material; the opportunity to invoke vacation privileges as he wished although the studio had no lay off privileges; and finally no morality clause. This contract was the first in the history of Hollywood in which the morality clause had been specifically excluded—a unique deletion that was to cause considerable technical difficulty when the Hollywood Ten brought civil suits against the studios that had employed them.

Trumbo's personal success, however, did not prevent him from championing the cause of writers less fortunate than himself. He became vitally active in the Screen Writers' Guild which, after a crushing defeat by the counterorganization and company union, Screen Playwrights, Inc., had secretly reformed in 1936 under the auspices of the Authors' League of America. The Guild, as a collective bargaining organization for screen writers, was dedicated to securing recognition and adequate remuneration for writers in a producer-centered industry.

The reorganized Guild had, in 1936, petitioned the National Labor Relations Board for an election to determine which of the two unions should represent the writers of Hollywood. The Guild, the producers, and the Screen Playwrights presented their cases to the NLRB, Trumbo appearing as the first witness in behalf of the Guild; an election materialized, and the Screen Writers' Guild won by a large majority. Many supporters of the management controlled Screen

Playwrights later banded into a powerful, conservative organization called the Motion Picture Alliance for the Preservation of American Ideals, founded in 1943, which perpetuated attacks on Hollywood trade unions and began the cries against subversion and communism that ultimately culminated in the 1947 House Committee on Un-American Activities hearings. Many were even to serve as witnesses friendly to HUAC.

When the liberal Guild began publishing a magazine, *The Screen Writer,* in June of 1945, Trumbo was selected as its first editor. He and others of his staff found the new periodical a suitable vehicle for venting anger against particular producers, the MPA, and extreme right groups in Hollywood. As a result, under Trumbo's two term editorship, conflict between factions intensified; moreover, friction developed within the Guild itself as members of the executive board reacted negatively to the alleged leftist views expounded in the magazine.

Approaching storms are hinted at in Trumbo's 1942 rough draft letter to the FBI, and in the revelation of the alleged Communist front organizations to which Trumbo and others of the Ten presumedly offered their support. The list is a long one: American League for Peace and Democracy, Americans against War and Fascism, American Peoples' Mobilization, American Peace Mobilization, American Youth for Democracy, Civil Rights Congress, Committee of 1000, the United Negro and Allied Veterans of America, Joint Anti-Fascist Refugee Committee, National Federation for Constitutional Liberties, Sleepy Lagoon Defense Committee, United American Spanish Aid Committee, Veterans of the Abraham Lincoln Brigade, and many others.

Having written for such magazines as *The North American Review, Forum, Vanity Fair, Liberty, McCall's* and *The Saturday Evening Post,* Trumbo was now writing for *New Masses* and *Masses & Mainstream.* His novel, *Johnny Got His Gun,* had been serialized in the *People's World.* He was rich, presumedly having earned in excess of $95,000 in 1945 and $71,000 in 1946 from his work at Metro alone. He was outspoken and had made many enemies. His career was, indeed, at a high point, and as the final letter of the section suggests, Trumbo had no indication that he was soon to be jobless, penniless, and professionally untouchable.

1. To Elsie McKeogh[1]

Los Angeles, California
[c. October, 1942]

Dear Elsie:

It occurs to me that I may not have written you for some time. Our life has been highly irregular, what with moving back and forth from town to country;[2] my work at the studio[3] has become so stupendously dull that it moves with difficulty; the uncertainty and the continual consciousness of the war—all these have combined to make me even a worse correspondent than usual.

Things go well with us. Nikola and Christopher[4] grow larger and wiser; Cleo[5] tolerates me with remarkably good will; and I, you may be pleased to know, am stirring restlessly. Gas rationing has forced us back to town. The address is 1439 Stone Canyon Road, Bel Air, Los Angeles. But it might be better to write me at the studio (MGM)—if, indeed, you do write—because the mailbox here is a distance from the house, and people don't seem to pick up the mail as often as I might wish them to.

I am, as you perhaps know, in the middle of my first picture on a two picture deal for Metro. My raise went in just before salary freezing, as if that makes much difference. Ring Lardner, Jr. and I have just finished a screenplay based on a story by another guy, which we are going to put on the market Monday.[6] Johnny Hyde of the [Wil-

---

[1] Elsie McKeogh, of Barbour and McKeogh, had been Trumbo's literary agent since 1934. Mrs. McKeogh, widow of Arthur McKeogh, who had edited *Good Housekeeping,* had managed Trumbo's first important literary sale: *Eclipse,* Trumbo's first novel to be published, to Lovat Dickson Limited in London.

[2] In 1938, with a total of $1,250 in the bank, Trumbo made a $750 down payment on a 320-acre ranch in Lockwood Valley. The investment—ultimately worth over $80,000—consisted of five rooms with kerosene lamps, a wood burning stove, and no telephone. The Trumbos' first year at the ranch (hopefully but inappropriately titled the "Lazy T"), resulted in the creation of his most successful novel, *Johnny Got His Gun,* of one of his finest films, *A Man to Remember,* and of a first child and daughter, Nikola.

[3] Metro-Goldwyn-Mayer.

[4] Born January 26, 1939, and September 25, 1940, respectively.

[5] Mrs. Trumbo. Trumbo had signed with MGM in the fall of 1937. That winter found Trumbo engaged in a courtship so hectic as to be almost a full-time job. "One of my problems," Trumbo says, "was a rival who was constantly threatening to shoot me, and who, on two occasions, very nearly succeeded." Since there was not time for both wooing and screen writing and since the girl was more important than the studio, Trumbo married Cleo Fincher on March 13, 1938, and almost simultaneously was fired by Sam Zimbalist—later a close friend—for whom he had been writing a film titled *Two in the Snow.*

[6] Trumbo refused Metro's bid of $25,000 in order to put this script, *The Fishermen of Beaudrais,* on the open market. It did not sell.

liam] Morris office, representing Lardner and the other guy, will handle it. It's good. He's going to ask a hundred thousand, and take what he can get. If the price is good, I'm going to take a small piece of it after the first of the year and go to the ranch and try some writing for a change. In other words, see what I can do for myself off a studio payroll.

I begin to realize why people believe the legend that Hollywood corrupts writers. But they're quite wrong. All Hollywood does is give them enough money so they can get married and have kids like normal people. But it's the getting married and having kids that really corrupts them. They haven't got time to hold down a studio job and write at the same time because all their off-studio hours are taken up, by choice, wondering at their children and enjoying the company of their wives. I realize that's why I haven't written in the last year or two. Considering the fact that everything I've ever published has been tossed off, so to speak, after hours—and further considering that there are no more after hours—I'm curious to see what I could do if I devoted myself to the single task of writing with a serious purpose in view. I might be good.

There have been strange symptoms. For the past two months I've scarcely had a drink. I didn't swear off—just lost my appetite for it. At first I was alarmed. Now I don't mind. It seems pleasant not to be fuzzy-headed most of the time. I do not think it is a permanent thing, for I have no intention of growing old and eccentric along such lines. But at least it has happened and I am surprised, as you should be. Cleo is the least bit worried, for I have become vain and proud in my abstinence, and refuse those before dinner highballs which are her particular delight. She suspects dyspepsia or another woman.

Then again, I've been doing some reading. O'Brien and O. Henry prize stories, and such. Since I am, as you know, practically illiterate, I was surprised at how feeble most of them are, and have become convinced that I can do as well. I have about twenty in mind. Not *Post* stuff, in the main, but to hell with the *Post.*[7] I'm hungry for a little prestige, and the prestige stuff looks easier to me than the *Post* anyhow. Besides, I do my duty to the mass mind in pictures, and wouldn't dislike thumbing my nose at it for a while.

Then I have a fine idea for a novel, a serious novel. It would be short and, I hope, passionate and powerful. Then I have one or two other ideas for books. I thought maybe we might hawk a few of the stories to the highbrows, and then combine them with one or two things out of *Johnny,*[8] and have a volume of short stories. Then

[7] *The Saturday Evening Post* had published two Trumbo short stories, one, "Darling Bill—", also appeared in *Post Stories of 1935.*

[8] *Johnny Got His Gun* was published by the J. B. Lippincott Company in 1939 and won one of the four American Booksellers' Awards for that year.

I would be a real artist with a proper scorn for money; I could walk around muttering lofty things about to hell with plot and form: it's the sensitive moment sensitively etched that counts. . . .

I'm very serious about it. Cleo and I sat down and figured it out. We've made and got rid of around $300,000 in less than five years of marriage. That's enough money to prove to yourself that you can get it if you want it; and it isn't enough money to force oneself to do the kind of work I have to do to get it. There's only one way for me to live on less, and that is to earn less. Otherwise I seem to spend it or give it away or something. Taxes don't bother me because you always have enough to live on after paying them anyhow. Only they mount up the way I handle things. Of course, I'll quit owing money, but that seems natural. If the Lardner script and another I have in mind for sale before the first of the year go over, I'll be in the clear except for 1942 taxes, and they will just have to lie in the lap of the gods.

. . . .

Nikola has discovered superlatives. She says: "That's the biggest cow I ever saw," or "That's the meanest spider I ever saw." The other day, Adele, our nurse, came home with the picture of the infant son of a friend of hers—a three month old youngster lying naked on his back. Nikola inspected it gravely, came over to me. "Isn't he a nice boy?" she said. I agreed. "This," she pointed out, "is his penis." And she was right. Then, after a moment of profound consideration, she turned to me and declared: "He's the penisest boy I ever saw!"

And so it goes. Anyway it's a long letter!

Affectionately,
DALTON, et al.

After seven Lippincott editions, Trumbo bought the plates from Lippincott in 1944. Later editions have been brought out by Monogram Publishers, 1946; The Liberty Book Club, 1952; Ace Books, 1960; Lyle Stuart, 1959 and 1970; and Bantam Books, 1967 and 1970. The novel has also been published in England, Denmark, Norway, Italy, West Germany and Brazil.

Of *Johnny* Trumbo wrote Elsie McKeogh in 1939, "Granting the fact that I'm usually wrong, I have very definite ideas about this book. I think it is damned good. I think it is a cinch to be a best seller. I think it will do me more good than anything or everything I'll ever do."

2. Rough draft of a letter to FBI agents[9]

Los Angeles, California
[c. 1944]

Recently you were kind enough to call at my house to read certain letters I have been receiving which indicate that the writers are (1) anti-war, (2) anti-Semitic, (3) in the process of organizing politically, (4) distributing pamphlets to further their cause and corresponding with persons detained by the Federal government, and (5) of the opinion that the Commander in Chief of the American forces is "the greatest criminal incendiary in history."

In the course of the conversation you expressed considerable interest in my own views and attitudes toward the war. In the end, you asked me to mail you the evidence I had to offer and to include with it a written summary of my position on various matters which you brought up. Although I find this an odd request, I hasten to comply with it.

I am of native ancestry dating back to 1731.[10] I have never trav-

[9] This undated draft is explained in Trumbo's introduction to the 1959 Ace Book edition to *Johnny Got His Gun:*

The book has a weird political history. Written in 1938 when pacifism was anathema to the American left and most of the center, it went to the printers in the spring of 1939 and was published on September third—ten days after the Nazi-Soviet pact, two days after the start of World War II.

As the conflict deepened, and *Johnny* went out of print altogether, its unavailability became a civil liberties issue with the extreme American right. Peace organizations and "Mothers'" groups from all over the country showered me with fiercely sympathetic letters denouncing Jews, Communists, New Dealers and International bankers who had suppressed my novel to intimidate millions of true Americans who demanded an immediate negotiated peace.

My correspondents, a number of whom used elegant stationery and sported tidewater addresses, maintained a network of communications that extended to the detention camps of pro-Nazi internees. They pushed the price of the book above six dollars for a used copy, which displeased me for a number of reasons, one of them fiscal. They proposed a national rally for peace-now, with me as cheer leader; they promised (and delivered) a letter campaign to pressure the publisher for a fresh edition.

Nothing could have convinced me so quickly that *Johnny* was exactly the sort of book that shouldn't be reprinted until the war was at an end. The publishers agreed. At the insistence of friends who felt my correspondents' efforts could adversely affect the war effort, I foolishly reported their activities to the FBI. But when a beautifully matched pair of investigators arrived at my house, their interest lay not in the letters but in me. I have the feeling that it still does, and it serves me right.

[10] Dalton Trumbo has always been very proud of his ancestral background: the fact that French-Swiss Jacob Trumbo settled in Virginia in 1736 and that his forebears fought in the Revolutionary War, the Indian Wars, and in both the Union and Confederate armies of the Civil War. He boasts descent from real pioneer stock, his maternal grandfather having built one of the first houses in what is now Montrose, Colorado, and his father, Orus Trumbo, having

eled abroad. I am a writer of novels, motion pictures and pamphlets.[11] I subscribe to and read about thirty periodicals and newspapers ranging from the *Foreign Affairs* Quarterly through *Fortune* and the Sunday *New York Times* to the *New Masses.* I wrote a pamphlet on Harry Bridges inspired by his incorruptible record as a labor leader and his high sense of patriotism in condemning and trying to halt such practices as the sale of oil and steel to Japan. I wrote a book called *Johnny Got His Gun,* which was published within three days of the outbreak of the war in Europe. No one who has carefully read its concluding chapters has called it pacifist. I myself have never been a pacifist. I have been, at various times, called a communist—a label which few conscientious Americans from the President down have managed to escape.

You were especially interested in my attitude toward the European war and our entry into it, and how my attitude toward the war had changed—if it had changed—and why. This question requires a certain recapitulation of history, and hence a somewhat longer answer than would usually be embodied in a communication of this sort, but I shall do my best to answer it fully.

1. It seemed to me that there were some suspicious characters in the French governments revolving around Flandin, Daladier, Chautemps, Bonnet, Laval, and Pétain. These men seemed to admire and

---

also migrated from the civilized east to the vast expanses of space and opportunity in the west.

James Dalton Trumbo, born on December 9, 1905, was the first child of Maud and Orus Trumbo. When Trumbo was a year old, his father, variously a shoe salesman and a beekeeper, moved to Grand Junction, Colorado, where Trumbo's two sisters—Catherine and Elizabeth—were born and where the writer attended school and first developed an interest in journalism working as a cub reporter on the Grand Junction *Daily Sentinel.*

Just after Trumbo's graduation from high school, his parents completed the western journey begun two hundred years before and moved to Los Angeles. Their son remained behind to attend the University of Colorado in the year 1924–25, but a spirit of adventure, and a yen for some hard cash, caused him to join his parents after his freshman year.

[11] Trumbo's novels were *Eclipse* in 1934, *Washington Jitters* in 1936, *Johnny Got His Gun* in 1939, and *The Remarkable Andrew* in 1941.

His credits in the first ten years of screen writing included *Prison Farm,* Warner Brothers, 1936; *The Devil's Playground,* Columbia, 1937; *A Man to Remember,* RKO, 1938 (Ten Best Films); *Five Came Back,* RKO, 1939; *Heaven with a Barbed-Wire Fence,* Twentieth Century-Fox, 1939; *A Bill of Divorcement, Kitty Foyle* (Academy Award nomination), *We Who Are Young,* MGM, 1940; *The Remarkable Andrew,* Paramount, 1941; *A Guy Named Joe,* MGM, 1943 (*Boxoffice* Magazine Award); *Thirty Seconds over Tokyo,* MGM, 1943 (*Boxoffice* Magazine Award, *Parents* Magazine Medal, Ten Best Films); *Tender Comrade,* RKO, 1943; and *Our Vines Have Tender Grapes,* MGM, 1945 (*Boxffice* Magazine Award, *Parents* Magazine Medal).

His pamphlets to date were "Harry Bridges" in 1939 and "An Open Letter to the American People," which advocated a second front in 1942.

trust the Germans so greatly that I doubted their ability to make with us an honest and effective alliance *against* the Germans. There was, for example, the instance of Marshal Pétain giving the contract for the electrification of the Maginot Line to a subsidiary of the German firm of Siemans. I thought this irregular. I didn't see how such men could fight a very successful war. I thought we would be better off if they were against us rather than for us. I hated to think of the lives of American boys being in any way tied up with such men. All of this is now changed. The men in question *didn't* fight a very successful war. And all of them who are not now in jail for treason, are openly against us and actively collaborating with Hitler.

2. I was alarmed by the behavior of Chamberlain. At Munich he seemed determined to make Germany the most powerful nation in Europe. This appeared to me both stupid and foolish; and stupid and foolish men make bad allies. I couldn't understand why he decided *not* to fight for Czechoslovakia, which had a democratic government and a fine army—and why he decided he would fight for Poland, which wasn't a democracy and had an army that fought mostly on horses. Then, too, he seemed surrounded by men who, from their speeches, thought a little too highly of the German government, even to the point of making a secret naval treaty permitting the Germans to make more battleships than the Convention of Versailles permitted them. Of course, since then Chamberlain has been thrown out, and most of his collaborators with him, and many of the German ships built under that treaty have been sunk by the English fleet. So that situation has changed, too.

3. Finland was quite a problem for me also. For a time it appeared that England and France, and even the United States, were ready to spring to Finland's defense. This seemed unnatural to me, since Finland was established as an independent country by the Germans, and during the last war offered her throne to a son of the German Kaiser, and ever since has been under German influence, and had an army chieftain in Mannerheim who has never deviated from his devotion to Germany. It therefore seemed to me that in any war Finland would have to be Germany's ally, and I couldn't understand the concern for her safety which so many people so passionately expressed at that time. And then when the English and French began stripping their armies to send guns and munitions to Finland, and even sent Weygand with 600,000 men out of France into Syria to assist the Finns by an attack on the Russians when the time came— when these things happened, it seemed to me that the English and French, if they were really at war with the Germans, might be wiser to save those guns and munitions and men against the time when they might need them to withstand the German assault. It almost looked as if the French and British governments couldn't make up their minds whether they were going to fight the Germans or the

Russians. To fight *both* Germany and Russia appeared somewhat more than they could undertake, so I assumed they were planning to fight only one. But it was my idea that before the United States jumped into the struggle, we should first find out *which* one because to declare war on one and end up fighting the other would be confusing, and would require a shift in plans, and might hopelessly bewilder the home front. This, of course, is all changed. We know that our enemy is Germany. We know that Finland is allied with Germany. A lot of American seamen have been killed off the North Finnish coast, and the British long since have declared war against the Finns.

4. And finally, it seemed clear to me that before we went into the war, we should come to some understanding with the Russians about the war and about the peace. I thought it would cost many years of struggle and millions upon millions of American and British lives for us to defeat the Germans unless the Russians were on our side, or we on theirs, or however one wishes to put it. As it now turns out, the President and the Chief of Staff and Wendell Willkie and Eddie Rickenbacker and a number of other well-informed Americans seem pretty much agreed on this point. So that, too, has changed. But I still ask myself occasionally: What would have happened had the United States entered the war prior to June 22, 1941?

This was the way I felt about the war. From 1939 onward there were many excited, passionate, honest American men and women who would have had us leap into the fray at the earliest possible moment. This seemed to me a disastrous course, so I opposed it. I opposed, as you suggested, Lend-Lease on the general principle that if you are trying to keep a hot-headed man out of a fight, you don't hand him a gun. Some have been unkind enough to say that such a course was not idealistic of me. I am inclined to wait and see. Idealists are worthy or unworthy people only in relation to what their ideals *are*. Ignorant or purely emotional idealists frequently bring on great tragedies which culminate in the defeat of the very ends toward which their ardor led them.

So you see, in answer to your question as to why I "changed" in my attitude toward the war, I must leave it up to your more objective judgment as to whether it was I or events that changed. By the time Pearl Harbor was attacked—all the conditions which had seemed to me to make for an honest and effective and successful war against the Axis had been fulfilled. And when the Vice-President began his brilliant series of interpretations of the war and its aims, I was delighted to note that it was precisely the kind of war which the maimed hero of *Johnny Got His Gun* had declared to be a good and worthy battle—a war for the liberation of people, a war to make the slogans into realities. And the Atlantic Charter, as a slogan, is good enough for me.

That is why I wrote the pamphlet advocating a second front in which you professed some interest. At that time certain ex-isolationists and defeatist elements had combined in a violent press campaign against the opening of a second land front in Europe. It was their contention that air power alone would defeat the enemy, and that our enormous armies being assembled were foolish waste, and that the draft should immediately be emasculated. This campaign became a rallying point for a good many shabby and sinister forces. At the request of several Los Angeles unions I wrote a pamphlet quoting competent authorities that a second land front *was* necessary. "Be assured," I wrote, "that no amount of popular agitation will precipitate the President into a foolish military venture. The military facts are secrets of the general staff, and of right should be, and will remain so. But no leader of a democratic country would dare open a second front—with its inevitable tragic loss of life—without the knowledge that his country supported him in such a venture." However even this is no longer an issue. For apparently the Chief of Staff has maintained from the first that a second front in Europe was necessary; and such a front is shortly to be opened. And the very newspapers which clamored so loudly against a second front are those which today anticipate it with the greatest enthusiasm.

I have, in the past, signed various petitions, of which you are no doubt aware. One urged that Bridges not be deported. He has not been. Another requested the release of the anti-fascist political prisoners in North African concentration camps. They have been released. Still another protested the installation of Peyrouton to the Governor Generalship of French North Africa. He has been ejected from office and imprisoned for dealing with the enemy.

So you see, the things in which I have believed along with hundreds of thousands of other Americans, and the petitions I have signed—they have been generally successful, and apparently in the best interests of the country. The war—aside from its horrifying loss of life—goes well; and like all other patriotic citizens, I support it by war bond purchases, subscription to war charities, and the contribution of my time and whatever talent I have to enterprises approved by the government for the furtherance of the war.

And last but not least, I share with the men of your organization a sincere desire to see an end to all such seditious propaganda as criminal slander of the Commander in Chief, defeatism, pacifism, anti-Semitism and all similar deceits and stratagems designed to assist the German cause. Which, of course, was why I called on you when I possessed evidence of such activity.

I was, perhaps, somewhat startled to discover that your interest in me was greater than your interest in the small evidence I had to offer. Considering the nature of the Nazi enemy, and your concern about my attitude toward the war, and the deep aversion we both feel toward all who would impede the successful prosecution of the war, I might have been tempted to ask even more questions had I been in your place. For example: Are you sympathetic to the Christian Front? The Ku Klux Klan? The German-American Bund? America First? Gerald Smith? Winrod? Coughlin? Are you anti-Semitic? Anti-Catholic? Anti-Negro? Are you opposed to the Moscow Agreement? The Teheran Conference? Did you agree with Charles A. Lindbergh that "the British, the Jews and the Roosevelt administration" were pushing this country into war? Did you approve of the Chicago *Tribune* when it stole from the War Department and actually published secret plans for the defense of the United States?

To all of them my answer would have been "No." I take your failure to ask them as a compliment to me which you will withhold from the people whose correspondence I enclose.

Yours very truly,
DALTON TRUMBO

3. To Ring Lardner, Jr.[12]

Los Angeles, California
October 28, 1945

Dear Ring:

About two years ago I was having dinner and a few drinks at the Players with Hugo [Butler],[13] and he happened to mention that

---

[12] Ring Lardner, Jr., one of the original Hollywood Ten, has maintained a close friendship with Trumbo over the years and is addressed and mentioned frequently in the letters. This son of the famous American humorist was a successful screen writer until the blacklist of 1947, his screenplays including *Cross of Lorraine, Tomorrow the World, Cloak and Dagger, Forever Amber* and *Woman of the Year* (Academy Award). During the blacklist he turned anonymously to television (*Robin Hood,* with another blacklisted writer, Ian Hunter) and published a critically acclaimed novel, *The Ecstasy of Owen Muir.* His latest screen credits have been *The Cincinnati Kid* and *M*A*S*H,* the latter of which won the 1970 Grand Prix at the Cannes Festival.

[13] Hugo Butler, also a blacklisted screen writer, met Trumbo while employed as a junior writer at MGM in the mid-thirties. The two men and their families moved to Mexico together in 1951 and remained close friends until Butler's death at the age of 53 in 1968. His pre-blacklist credits included *Lassie Come Home, Young Tom Edison, Edison the Man, A Christmas Carol* and *Huckleberry Finn.* During the blacklist he wrote *Robinson Crusoe* and *The Young One* for Luis Bunuel, and wrote and directed *How Tall Is a Giant* and *Torero,* all pseudonymously, as well as *Eve* for Joseph Losey in London.

He was the son of the late Frank Butler, a Hollywood writer known for you looked sallow, and I said you weren't. I told Hugo flatly that I thought it was a hell of a thing to say about somebody you were pretending to be friendly with, and that I had never thought you were sallow, and that a lot of people who were running around whispering and giggling about how sallow you are could occupy their time much better by staying home and paying their bills. I also told him that I was your friend, that I didn't care whether you were sallow or not, and that sallowness was something like having a club foot: if a man had it he had it, and it didn't help matters any by going around and blabbering about it behind his back.

I also pointed out that even if you had seemed to him to be sallow, that wasn't any sign you had always been sallow or would necessarily continue to be. I told him for example that liver trouble might cause a man to be sallow, and that a little spell of clean living generally fixed a liver up, and what the hell business was it of Hugo or anybody else about the state of your liver. I likewise told him liver trouble was no joke, with a lot of pain attached to it, and anybody who had it deserved more pity than censure. We parted friends, but that night I got to thinking about all the things Hugo had said, and I sent him a note by hand in which I repeated everything I had said to him just for the record. I'm glad now that I did, too.

About six to eight months later I was having dinner and a few drinks at the Players with Lester Cole,[14] and quite suddenly Lester said to me wasn't it a shame the way Ring was running around drinking himself to death and ruining his liver and not paying his bills. He said that Hugo said that I had said that this was because you were so callow. Lester said this, for him, hit the nail right on the head. I saw right then what was happening—in fact, I foresaw this whole situation coming up as far back as that—so I set Lester straight right then and there. I told him I'd much rather have a dirty mind than a dirty liver, and that if you wanted to drink yourself to death, who had a better right?

I also told him that when your eyes slide up under your forehead like they do sometimes when you're goat drunk, why it wasn't intentional because it was something you couldn't avoid under the circumstances, and probably didn't come from the liquor at all but rather from a sudden fit of depression. I also told him I didn't know

---

some of the Hope-Crosby *Road* series and such comedies as *Going My Way.* Butler's wife, Jean, has appeared in films and was heard in the radio serial, "One Man's Family," for many years.

[14] Lester Cole, one of the Hollywood Ten, was also a writer at MGM. At one time president of the Writers' Guild, his pre-blacklist screenplays included *None Shall Escape, Blood on the Sun, Fiesta, Romance of Rosy Ridge, The High Wall.* His most recent screenplay was *Born Free* for producer Carl Foreman, although his name did not appear on the screen.

anything about your bills. I said you were my friend and your not paying your bills didn't lessen my liking and loyalty one iota. I denied that I had ever said you were callow. I said you were young, naturally, but has a man got to be callow just because he is young? I said your callowness had never made the slightest difference in our relationship, and that you would straighten up as soon as you had broadened and deepened, and that in the meanwhile I didn't want to talk any more about the matter. That night I wrote him a note by hand and delivered it myself to make sure he got it. Now he probably still has that letter, and if you want to get in touch with him one reading of it will clear a great deal of our current misunderstanding, and perhaps show you who is your true friend.

Now not so long ago I was having dinner and a few drinks at the Players with Bob Rossen,[15] and Bob said he'd been talking to Lester, and that Lester had said he believed I had doped Lardner just about right when I said that he was too shallow to care whether his liver rotted away and his bills were paid or not, and that all this boozing and liver trouble had given him fits. Bob wanted to know whether it was epileptic fits or just kind of stomach fits. Naturally I denied all this, and went into a great deal of detail to get the story straight again.

I said to him, how should I know what kind of fits they are? I said you were a friend of mine and I didn't like everybody in town talking about your having fits. I told him I saw no connection between you being shallow and having fits, and I named him eleven people who are shallower than you and don't have fits at all. I also told him that epileptics are normally harmless if you just stick a piece of rubber or something between their teeth to stop them from biting their tongues off. I told him if I didn't mind fits, why the hell should he? I said that regardless of what kind of fits you had, dieting and a wholesome life would steady them down quite a bit and maybe even eventually cure them entirely.

I got so sore about Bob talking like this about a friend of mine that I didn't even wait to get home to write. I grabbed two menus and a pen and wrote him a letter on the spot. Now I don't know whether or not he still has it, and I didn't make a carbon, but I'm writing him a note by hand tonight asking him to send it to you by hand if he still has it, and after you've seen what I really said, you can drop me a note by hand if you still care to keep me as your friend.

Now I suppose a lot of this has got back to you, twisted and dis-

---

[15] Bob Rossen was a writer-director and producer, and in 1943 chairman of the Hollywood Writers Mobilization. A writer turned director, his pre-blacklist directorial credits included *Body and Soul* and *All the Kings' Men*. His post-blacklist films were *The Brave Bulls, Alexander the Great, Island in the Sun, The Hustler* and *Lilith*. He died in 1966.

torted as usual, and that you are sore. Paul Trivers [16] wrote me a note by hand saying you had written a note by hand to Ranald MacDougal [17] asking him to stop writing falsehoods about you. I've written Randy a note by hand asking him to explain himself, and I expect an answer by hand before evening. Now I'll send you a note the minute I hear from him, together with a copy of my note to him and Trivers and Trivers' note to me, together with any other notes that may arrive in the meantime, and then maybe we can compare notes and try to straighten this thing out. Until then, I don't see any reason for you getting so hysterical about it as indicated in your note by hand of yesterday.

On the other hand, maybe you don't want to straighten it out, and if you don't, why that's okay with me too. The goddamned doorbell is ringing all hours of the day or night, waking the kid up every time it rings, and the kid is bawling and notes are coming in by hand from people I never even bothered to make enemies of, and I think you might remember once in a while that I've got a job to take care of and a wife and children who are dependent on me. Or I guess maybe you figure I've knocked out four novels, three short stories, twenty motion picture scripts, and speeches and pamphlets too numerous to mention by just sitting around writing notes in your defense. Now I want you to understand this very clearly:

When this whole thing first came up, and Hugo said to me you were sallow, I knew goddamned well you were sallow. You may have thought you had deceived me, but you didn't. I thought you were sallow from the first day I met you. I have often said to Cleo, "Christ, he's sallow!" It was only my loyalty to you that caused me to deny something that every loose-lipped son-of-a-bitch in town has been talking about for years. Now if this is the reward I get, then okay.

About your bills, why hell, they're not my responsibility. But just to stop your yapping, I'll pay them if it'll make you feel any better. Just send them into the Roberts office and I'll see they're taken care of so we won't for Christ's sake have to hear any more of your talk about them.

About your liver, I don't see how you can hold me responsible for its condition at all. *I* didn't teach you to drink—you were a dipso long before I met you.

About your eyes the way they roll up on you, why I haven't known whether you were looking at me or the inside of your forehead for

[16] Paul Trivers was a playwright and screen writer, who later became a story editor and production assistant. Inactive in films since the blacklist, he died in 1965.

[17] Ranald MacDougal, a writer and director, is known for such films as *Objective Burma, Mildred Pierce,* and *The Hasty Heart.*

seven years, and now with the attitude you're taking, I frankly don't give a good goddamn.

God knows I've tried to be a good friend, and loyal, and stop all the talking about you. But I may as well tell you that I think you bring a lot of it on yourself by the way you go around acting all the time. And while I'm at it, I might as well tell you that I'd rather you didn't drop by the house all the time any more. If you have anything to take up with me, just drop me a note by hand. I don't mind you being around, and certainly Cleo doesn't, but I'm not going to have you scaring the kids half to death in one of your goddamned fits.

Sincerely your friend,
DALTON TRUMBO

4. To Elsie McKeogh

Los Angeles, California
[probably late 1945 or early 1946]

Dear Elsie:

Enclosed is the Danish thing signed.[18] About the English royalties [19] you mentioned some time ago, let them for this time remain for the Lord Mayor's Fund, if you have not already arrived at that conclusion by reason of my silence.

All royalties that come in the future I shall take, and I wish you would cooperate with me by letting me play a trick on myself. You know the hostility which seems to arise between me and a dollar. Very well. Please from now on deposit whatever comes in for me in some bank in New York, and send the statement on to R. B. Roberts, 1052 Carol Drive, Los Angeles (that's West Los Angeles). He's my business manager, and the statement will permit him to register it as income and pay taxes on it. Then perhaps sometime I may accumulate as much as $50 or $60 in some New York bank against a rainy day.

My high fever of last spring has, as perhaps you suspected it would, subsided. The trip overseas [20] took a lot of cash, and by the

[18] Contract for a Danish edition of *Eclipse.*
[19] Probably royalties for *Eclipse.*
[20] In the summer of 1945 Trumbo was one of eight writers selected by the Army Air Force as war correspondents for the Pacific area. Rather than going in search of current news stories, these particular men—representatives of leading publishing firms, magazines like *The Saturday Evening Post* and *Reader's Digest,* and newspapers such as the New York *Herald Tribune*—were sent in

time I returned it was fall, and Cleo was pregnant and close to delivery,[21] and Nikola was ready to begin a school term, and it seemed foolish to sell the house and invite turmoil at such a point. I believe I would have done it in June, if the trip hadn't come up.

I have consoled myself by quarreling with the studio. Have been on pay, off pay, ever since. Object being that I still intend to write, and want to finagle some freedom. They're about convinced now, and are drawing up a new contract which gives them only one right— my exclusive services in the writing of screenplays. I have the privilege of writing none or as many as I wish, taking as long or as short a time on each as I wish. They guarantee a constant supply for the next four years at $75,000 per script. Since I am a hell of a lot faster than I've led them to suspect, this seems to offer the reasonable possibility of earning 150 gs in the first four or five months of each year, after which there is absolutely no incentive (you see how precisely a radical reacts to the income tax?) for me to do anything but what I really wish to do—which, perhaps, shall be some novels.

The trip was extraordinarily interesting. . . . I got ashore at Balikpapan 15 minutes after the first wave, and spent three days and nights with the advance patrols and saw some shooting and learned some things. Two correspondents were killed within 100 yards of me,[22] which convinced me of course that I was a hero. The raid over Kyushu was fairly disastrous—the second of the B-25 raids out of Okinawa, and seven planes were lost, and again there was shooting and I didn't like it. The captain in charge of our party

order that their future work in film, novel, or journalism might yield greater authenticity. Trumbo, affiliated with the J. B. Lippincott Co., was over draft age and was eager for the experience.

When Trumbo returned he wrote "Notes on a Summer Vacation," for *The Screen Writer,* September, 1945. In an introduction to that article, he summarized the itinerary:

The route lay from Hamilton Field to Oahu, Johnston, Kwajalein, Guam, Tinian, Iwo Jima; then back to Guam and on to Manila; thence with the Royal Australian Air Forces to Tawi Tawi at the tip of the Sulu Archipelago where part of an American invasion fleet was gathering for the assault on Balikpapan; from Tawi Tawi with the Navy through Macassar Strait to South Borneo and from there back to Manila. Out of Clark Field on Luzon and Kadena Field on Okinawa two of our number went on raids over Formosa and Kyushu. We returned by way of Leyete, Morotai, Biak, Finchaven, Guadalcanal, Kwajalein, Oahu and Hamilton Field. Aside from the invasion of Balikpapan—the last of the war as it has turned out— we traveled by air, mostly on bucket seats, in C-54s, C-46s, C-47s, B-24s, B-25s, PBYs and an EOA-10. Thus we were enabled to see action with the land, sea and air forces.

Although the novel planned from these letters and hundreds of pages of notes is still unfinished, Trumbo has drawn amply both in later correspondence and in his writings upon the events he witnessed and participated in.

[21] Melissa Trumbo was born October 4, 1945.

[22] The correspondents were Australian, not members of Trumbo's party.

was killed when his plane received a direct hit, so we came home alone, convinced that things were dangerous.[23]

I learned a great deal. I have never been anywhere in my life, and I needed the experience. I let my beard grow, and it turned out to be quite gray, and the G.I.'s marveled that so old a customer could move about so nimbly. I think I am not vain in saying that I made an astonishing number of friends, from whom I hear constantly. I was pleased that effete living had not removed me from the possibility of enjoying the companionship of non-artists (curse that word!) —and that I was able to think and behave and speak in their terms which are, after all, my own, but which by constant association with phonies I had half-way come to believe might have left me.

In the two weeks preceding the trip I went to San Francisco and ghosted Stettinius's Report to the Nation on the Conference.[24] There I saw the real seamy underside of life, things I'd read but never believed, feeling them to be the distortions of left-wing propaganda. But they were all true. And when, six days later, I was talking to wounded soldiers on Guam and hearing their deep interest in the Conference, and trying to answer their questions honestly, I began to realize I had been enabled to observe a unique slant on war and peace. I came back with 300 pages of notes, as they typed up, and I have perhaps a hundred on the Conference. It was in that hospital I saw the sergeant from Okinawa, who had just arrived the day before after encountering a land mine and losing all four extremities. He also had punctured lungs and abscessed ears. His father had lost both legs in the last war, and the boy himself had deliberately chosen the army as a career, being wounded in his eighth year of service. All the doctors were pleased with him because, in the midst of such ghastly mutilation, he had managed to preserve one of the worst tempers they'd ever encountered.

So I sat around with my notes and wondered what to do with

[23] In his article "Notes on a Summer Vacation," Trumbo wrote:

Captain Robert Reeves who had organized our mission and was in command of it had one idea in mind: that we should travel as working correspondents rather than as tourists. But for his intercession at every point we would have been relegated to routine inspections and dreary lectures. Whatever is accomplished by us would have been impossible had it not been for his assistance. On July 10 Captain Reeves flew as an aerial observer on a B-25 assigned to the barge sweep over Formosa. The mission was completed successfully and the plane was returning to Luzon when it spotted an enemy concentration. The ship went in low for strafing, and received a direct hit from 40 mm. AA fire. It exploded into the sea with the loss of all six aboard.

[24] Edward R. Stettinius, Secretary of State and Chairman of the United States delegation to the United Nations Conference on International Organization. In gratitude for Trumbo's services, Stettinius presented the writer with an inscribed photograph. Later, when Trumbo came under the attack of HUAC, Stettinius denied ever knowing him.

them. I was dead set against a correspondent's report, because after seeing real correspondents at work, I knew it would be pretentious and false. As for a book of personal impressions, I rejected that as trivial. Very well, I said, then fiction. And I must say here that the juxtaposition of the conference and the trip make a perfect frame for an excellent design for a novel. But the problem became complex: my reactions to what I saw are the reactions of a man of forty whose past experience has encompassed certain conditions and resulted in certain attitudes. But are those attitudes and that background comprehensible, believable in a soldier of twenty-two? What do I do—report the attitudes I saw and heard in fiction? Or do the thing from the point of view of my own? Obviously I must do the latter. But then, who is my character? It can't be just the character in war, it must reveal the character as he was before the war, the character as his life molded him to have my attitudes and reactions. Very well, but this becomes a novel in which the war is simply the climax. You see?

Anyhow, I realized I must face the problem I've always deferred. The bakery. I have seven—wrong, six—novels on the bakery,[25] all n.g. In the twenty-one years that have passed since I first went to work there, many things have happened to the many characters I knew there. They've exploded out in all directions, all over the world, and I am one fragment. There were 600 there, and the turnover was 80% per year and I was there eight years, so you can see there were lots of us. And among that welter of characters, there must be a man with a son. And the son, in a later novel—the son we know now because we know his background, his family, his circumstances—becomes the hero of the war book I shall write one day based upon the trip and the conference. And he, like all the others, will be simply one of the many, many characters that must be dealt with all over the country if the bakery novel is to become valid and real. But the bakery must come first, then the stories of later on, the continuation of the bakery saga into other fields, efforts, communities until finally it becomes a part of history and of the world. That sounds vague enough, doesn't it?

Anyhow I have done a great deal of work, and the enterprise I have in view becomes very ambitious. It lines up into six novels, as follows:

(1)—1925–1929 (depression begins)

[25] A year before his father Orus Trumbo died, young Trumbo went to work as a bread wrapper at the Davis Perfection Bakery in Los Angeles. He began in 1925 at a salary of $27.50 a week and ended, eight and one-half years later, at a salary of $18. During this time Trumbo wrote eighty-eight short stories and six novels (all rejected), attended the University of Southern California, repossessed motorcycles, and reviewed pictures for a motion picture trade magazine.

(2)—1929–1933 (Roosevelt begins)
(3)—1933–1941 (war begins)
(4)—1941–1945 (the war, home front)
(5)—1945   (the conference, trip novel)
(6)—1945–194? (the conclusion of the mess)

I have a great deal of research accomplished, much more to do: 161 characters charted through the six-novel action (many of them minor, of course): and a first chapter done. I shall not be able to get down to serious work until summer. I don't think there's any point in telling Lippincott about it, because I'd kinda like to spring this one full-blown and unexpected. I'm pretty sure I'll embark on this enterprise, although you have more than a perfect right to put it down to another of my fantasies. When I get a first draft, you'll get it. And on this enterprise I am now old enough and serious enough to want forthright criticism, not only from you but from the editors. George Stevens (is that his name, the Lippincott editor?) was dead right about those two chapters in *Andrew*. They were a disgrace to me as a novelist, and a worse disgrace to me as a man who thinks logically, or pretends to. But then the whole damned book was a fake anyhow, and I shall never be similarly trapped. When I think that those two chapters were published simultaneously in the *Daily Worker* and the Chicago *Tribune,* I am ashamed of myself for selling to the latter, and ashamed of the *Daily Worker* for falling for such slop. It's a mistake I don't propose to repeat.

Things otherwise go well. We have a dining room but no furniture, so I've fixed it up as a work room and it's excellent. Melissa is a fine kid, and I believe we enjoy her more than the others when they were babies because we're more experienced and not so afraid of her as we were of them. Chris fell today from some great height at school and has an egg on his forehead. Nikola fell from a bicycle and has the skin of half her knee gone. Cleo spent too much time under the sunlamp and fried herself. Our dog was run over and recovered after an operation for ruptured stomach. I am quite broke. Everything normal.

Salutations,
DALTON

P.S. For my money those Danes are the most literate tribe in Europe!

5. Letter to Sam Sillen, editor of Masses & Mainstream Magazine

Los Angeles, California
[1946]

For a long while now it has been fashionable in all circles, both left and right, to howl Hollywood down with charges of corruption, and to proceed at once to analysis of more respectable media: that is, the novel and the theatre.[26]

The answer to the problem, of course, lies in Hollywood's mode of production. No one here, I believe, would care to challenge the idea that the freedom of the artist to express himself decreases in proportion to the increase of capital investment required for the production of his work. The freest art form is the pamphlet—and I insist that a fine pamphlet *is* art—because a pamphlet costs very little to produce. A novel can be published for $2,000, a play produced for $15,000. It is not, therefore, difficult to understand why the theatre deals less frequently with progressive subject matter than the novel. But when we deal with motion pictures we touch such stratospheric figures as half a million dollars for a cheap film to three million dollars for a genuine, 14-karat A. And the problem of the artist conscientiously employing his art as a weapon for the advancement of all mankind becomes correspondingly more acute.

It would seem unrealistic in the extreme specifically to condemn Hollywood producers on a moral basis for their reluctance to place their product at the disposal of the peoples of the world without regard to the profit involved. They are perfectly normal, healthy, intelligent American capitalists—economic brothers to the Fords, the Du Ponts, the Pews and the Morgans. They are directly responsible to the great banking houses of Wall Street. They respond sensitively to the stimuli of the society they have helped to create and presently help to control. They entertain the idea that their companies exist to earn profits at a constantly increasing rate, and no amount of persuasion or cajolery will wean them from this conviction. The less passion spent in denouncing them, and the more time devoted to studying their methods and necessities, the better.

The motion picture industry represents monopoly capital in control of an art form and developed to a very high degree. Five major producing companies control practically all the stage space in Hollywood. They also control the 2,800 key theatres of the country. Two companies produce ninety percent of the raw film which goes into the making of pictures. The upsurge of independent production in Hollywood affects the basic structure of the industry very little. For the so-called "independent" production—that is, presently, a com-

---

[26] Trumbo, here, gives preliminary airing to his thoughts for a proposed symposium on the arts and the expression of ideas.

pany in which the actors, directors and writers function as owners—is dependent upon the banks for its capital, upon the major studios for its stage space, and upon those same majors for its theatre release. The present vogue for independent production units mainly represents the drive of highly-paid creative talent to participate in the profits of production; in other words, to become producers, capitalists, themselves.

The growth of this illusory "independent" production in Hollywood may result in a realignment of competitive capital forces within the industry; but granting an exception here and there—an exception which occasionally crops up even among the major studios —it appears doubtful that independent production will materially influence the social content of motion pictures; first, because the independents exist by sufferance and within the capital structure of the industry, and second, because the artist turned capitalist invariably develops a strange sensitivity to his rate of profit, without which he cannot continue to function in his new capacity.

The Playwrights Company did not produce a renaissance in the theatre, nor does it seem at all likely that the independents will revolutionize motion pictures. The industry remains what it has been —the first instance, aside from radio, that so powerful an artistic weapon has been organized industrially under the structure of a monopoly capital which begins with the manufacture of the film and ends with the final exhibition of the picture in a company-owned theatre.

The result of this highly organized capital structure is a changed relationship between the creative artist—that is the writer, the originator and translator of ideas—and his employer: a relationship which sharply differs from that of the novelist to his publisher or the playwright to his producer. It is not accidental that Hollywood workers speak always of the industry, never of the medium. For motion picture writers are purely industrial workers, subject to a great many of the economic ills of industrial workers in other industries. There are 1,200 writers in Hollywood, but permanent year-round employment exists only for 350 of them. In an average year perhaps 700 will work part of the time, 500 not at all. Two-fifths of the 700 will earn less than $5,000 for annual income. Over half will earn less than $10,000. Last year six of the most talented, or the luckiest, or the shrewdest, earned over $100,000 each. Competition exists in proportion to the size of the largest possible income: it is understandably intense, and at times unscrupulous. But the argument that Hollywood writers are more surfeited with riches than writers in other media—and therefore necessarily more corrupt—is a formulation based upon ignorance, contrary to the facts and inadmissible to any thoughtful discussion of the problem.

Screen writers, because of their position as industrial workers under a monopoly capital set-up, have organized to advance their interests on what amounts to a trade union basis. The Screen Writers' Guild, in practical terms, is a union of writers, much more closely united and hence generally more progressive than members of the Authors' League, for example, or the Dramatists' Guild—for the excellent reason that their employers are much more closely united in the Motion Picture Association than publishers and theatrical producers.

How, then, does the writer as industrial employee achieve a more comprehensive guarantee of his right of free speech? How does he use his art as a weapon for the destruction of fascism, of racial bigotry, of economic oppression, of the drive toward war? First, of course, there comes the primary battle of the individual writer to defend his individual stories and their development into a finished screenplay. This is fundamental—and for the purposes of this discussion, its absolute necessity is assumed. Every screen writer worth his salt wages the battle in his own way—a kind of literary guerilla warfare. But very rarely does victory for the individual writer raise the freedom-level of his fellow writers, just as the individual who achieves a very high salary does not raise the general wage level of the group.

The fight for the freer use of the screen as a weapon for human decency rests fundamentally upon an organizational basis—specifically that organization of Hollywood writers which functions as their union. The fight for freedom of expression in Hollywood is inextricably tied up with the fight for economic security. This dual battle takes the form of demands by the writer for ownership of his ideas, for free development of his scripts, for greater control of his material. It is the common fight of all labor and progressive organizations, just as their fight for peace and security is likewise the fight of all screen writers.

There are, of course, those who declare that because of the enormous capital agglomeration invested in motion pictures, the medium itself is hopeless, and can never be employed for progressive purposes. To accept this view is tantamount to abandoning the struggle altogether. Such specious and defeatist reasoning would resign the most influential medium in the world to the exclusive use of reactionaries and, in certain instances, of conscious fascists. It is, moreover, based upon a false assumption: for motion pictures have improved in content and can, under proper conditions, continue to improve.

The Screen Writers' Guild achieved recognition during the great struggles of the thirties.[27] It was precisely during this period that

---

[27] Trumbo refers to the 1936 conflict between the Screen Writers' Guild and the Screen Playwrights, Inc. The studios in violent opposition to the liberal Guild formed the Playwrights, a company union, recognized by the producers

motion pictures underwent a sharp decline in the use of reactionary themes, in the slander of minority groups and in general vilification of organized labor. The organized writers of Hollywood contributed very greatly to this improvement, but it would be a mistake to assume that they accomplished it alone. Their rising prestige—and with it their rising influence over the content of films—corresponded to the great upsurge of the CIO, the general organizational advance of workers all over the country, the developing struggle against fascism and the confirmation of labor rights by federal legislation. Hollywood writers, by participating in the general struggle for social advancement, achieved greater effectiveness for their art as a weapon. They achieved it not as talented Galahads jousting individually, but as organized industrial workers.

A second forward move in screen content came with the war. Here again it was the tremendous mass pressure of the anti-fascist masses of the world, the direct intervention of the federal government through the OWI [Office of War Information] and affiliated agencies, and the formation by writers themselves of the Hollywood Writers' Mobilization, which caused motion pictures—temporarily at least—to give voice to the democratic aspirations of the great coalition. Without the war, without the tremendous upsurge of anti-fascist feeling that came with it, no writer—even the most talented—would have had the opportunities then made available to him to affect so decisively the social content of the screen.

Many of Hollywood's war films were superficial, uncritical and frankly opportunistic. A few were deeply searching in their implications and in their contribution to the morale of the embattled democracies. Symbols of racial, political, economic and religious prejudice practically vanished from the screen. But something else, something significant, also happened: sustained by the tremendous anti-fascist feelings of the great masses of people, a few motion pictures went over to the offensive. In such films as *Confessions of a Nazi Spy, Joe Smith, American, Watch on the Rhine, Sahara, The Great Dictator* and *Action in the North Atlantic,* screen writers took the point of view that it was much more desirable and honorable and dramatic to attack evil than simply to refrain from evil. A fundamental change of viewpoint was involved in this process; and since it occurred under the impact of one historical phase of the war against fascism, there is no reason to believe that it cannot develop and deepen in the succeeding phase of that same war.

---

as the representative body of all screen writers in spite of the fact that the Screen Playwrights numbered approximately one hundred in contrast to the six or seven hundred members of the Screen Writers' Guild. Unable to withstand the power of the producers, the ranks of the Guild dwindled to some thirty members, of which Trumbo was one. As has already been mentioned, the Guild later reformed and regained its former influence.

But the job will not be accomplished in solitude by even the most gifted individual—great as his contribution may be—nor by the concept of the artist above and beyond the struggle admiring his virtue through the perfumed and poisonous fog of cultural isolation. It will be done by organized writers, striving individually and organizationally and politically in the closest possible relationship with the great masses of workers who represent the only decent, democratic, anti-fascist force in the world today. Through them, and as a part of them, we shall be enabled to use art as a weapon for the future of mankind, rather than as an adornment for the vanity of aesthetes and poseurs.

DALTON TRUMBO

6. Extract of a letter to Bob Coryell of the Berg-Allenberg Agency

Los Angeles, California
February 6, 1947

I hasten to assure you that I find only superficial parallels between then and now.[28] I was distressed with [H. N.] Swanson [29] because it seemed clear he was perfectly able to lend me the money and was being backward about it through an excess of that fearful caution which parades among the unimaginative as "good business." Such a relationship between agent and client is, of course, intolerable, and I hastened at once to put an end to the sick and feeble thing.

[28] Trumbo had asked his Hollywood agents Berg-Allenberg for a loan of $2,000. When he received a letter from Robert Coryell of the Agency explaining that office decorations prevented extending the desired loan, Trumbo penned this cheerful response—ironic in view of the forthcoming Congressional hearings and subsequent blacklist.

[29] Trumbo felt that it was an agent's natural function to lend money to his clients. His first Hollywood agent had been the late Arthur M. Landau. When Landau was forced to liquidate his business in 1940, the contracts of all his clients automatically lapsed. Landau asked Trumbo's permission to sell his own lapsed contract for $3,500 to the H. N. Swanson Agency. Trumbo agreed, but inserted a clause in the sales contract which permitted him to buy the contract back, if he wished, for the same sum Swanson had paid for it. Shortly thereafter he asked Swanson to lend him $1,500 to pay for a fur coat he wished to give his wife. Swanson offered to cosign a bank loan, which was not at all what Trumbo had been thinking of. He retaliated by selling himself and his agency contract to Berg-Allenberg for $5,000, which, after repaying Swanson's $3,500, left him the exact sum he needed. He tested the new association almost immediately by asking for and receiving a $2,500 loan, which he promptly repaid.

But toward Berg-Allenberg I feel quite differently. I have been through your redecorated quarters, and I know enough about the world to realize that such sumptuous surroundings cost more money than any business firm can reasonably afford. I could see on every hand evidences of the most wanton expenditure. Thus I wasn't surprised when Mrs. Roberts informed me of the wolf which had come to live with you: I was only saddened, somehow, and full of sympathy.

Mind you, as a friend I cannot *condone* the profligacy which has brought you to such low estate; I cannot pretend that I think it was shrewd of you to jump in beyond your depth for the sake of a bit of silk and a splash of paint; but at least I understand, and to understand is to forgive. It simply is not in my heart to blame you. I know what you are going through.

Pondering your present situation, I think back upon my own period of folly—how gaily I blossomed forth in a handsome house all filled with downy furniture. I remember too well the heartaches that come when a man realizes he has paid too much for his whistle. You told me at the time how foolish I was: little did either of us know that fate had marked you for the next! I could stop right here and compose a full essay on the tragic fallibility of human nature which never learns from the mistakes of others and only rarely from its own! I *could* write the essay, but I haven't in me the cruelty to do it. For I know too well those anxious days and sleepless nights when the pale horses of regret gallop endlessly through weary minds and there is no hope in sight.

In such moments a man wants neither advice nor sympathy. He wants help! Understanding this so well, I have been ridden with guilt when I think back upon my slothful moments, when I consider the modest commissions I have brought in to you. "If I had only worked more diligently," I tell myself. "If I had only thought more of them and less of me, then my commissions would have been larger, and then perhaps my agents would not at this very moment be suffering the agonies of crucifixion upon a cross of gold!"

Those are strong, meaty thoughts, and they have wracked me from end to end. But idle guilt is not enough; it is, in the last consideration, the resort of weaklings and of fools. Men have actually starved to death in this world while other men stood by feeling guilty. "No!" I tell myself over and over again, "Guilt is not enough!" Therefore I have resolved that I shall no longer remain passive during your hours and perhaps years of need. To prove my intentions I hereby pledge upon my honor that during the next six years I have a plan, and that this six-year plan shall be to *double* those commissions I have paid to you during the past six. I am so eager to do this I would have made it a five-year plan, except that it might sound like you know what.

But this is not all. With the receipt of my next check from Metro I shall be in excellent financial shape. That is, for me. It is not right that I should be comfortably situated at the very moment when you people are struggling to keep your heads above water. You have been generous with me in the past: very well, I shall be generous with you in the future. You need only call on me and I shall lend you any sum in my possession. More it is not in my power to offer; less would place upon me the brand of ingrate.

Meanwhile, to *all* of you—chins up! The Republicans are in, and that always means—as I have discovered!—a period of tight money. But by closing ranks we shall be able to weather the storm. . . . A man never had finer representation than you have given me. I shall stand with you during your lean years as you have stood with me during your fat ones. A little restraint in the future when Bill Haines [30] drops in to work his wiles, and we shall live to see the time when we'll laugh—actually *laugh*—at those privations which afflicted us during the first gloomy months of 1947. "For after all," we shall say as we lift our glasses in happy, prosperous friendship, "how should we ever learn anything—except by making mistakes?"

---

[30] William Haines, the interior decorator for the Berg-Allenberg offices, had been a popular motion picture star of the twenties.

2.

"Broke as a
Bankrupt's Bastard"
or
"The Hope of
Succeeding Elsewhere"

In October of 1947, Trumbo, along with eighteen others, was summoned before the House of Representatives Committee on Un-American activities under the chairmanship of J. Parnell Thomas of New Jersey, with Karl E. Mundt of South Dakota, John McDowell of Pennsylvania, Richard M. Nixon of California, Richard B. Vail of Illinois, John S. Wood of Georgia, John E. Rankin of Mississippi, and J. Hardin Peterson of Florida as members and with Robert E. Stripling as clerk and chief investigator. This hearing in Washington, D.C., lasting two weeks, was the follow-up of a March 1947 preliminary meeting during which the House Committee had announced its intention of holding ". . . a secret investigation of Communism in motion pictures." Just why the first national attack on alleged Communists—which culminated in the early 1950s with the investigations of the late Senator Joseph McCarthy of Wisconsin—focused on Hollywood is a point open to conjecture: the outspokenness of liberal vs. conservative factions has already been mentioned; moreover the Committee may well have believed that the glamour concomitant with Hollywood, coupled with mounting Cold War tension, was sure to draw world-wide publicity.

The first witnesses to appear before the Committee—Rupert Hughes, James K. McGuinness, Richard Macaulay, Adolphe Menjou, John Charles Moffitt, Fred Niblo, Ayn Rand, Lela Rogers, Morrie Ryskind, Sam Wood and others—largely represented the Motion Picture Alliance for the Preservation of American Ideals and came to be known as the witnesses who were "friendly" to the Committee. They were permitted to read statements, refer to notes, and ramble at length as they hurled accusations that the motion picture industry was infested with Communists and that those Communists were using the film medium to spread propaganda to the American people.

Of the nineteen subpoenaed witnesses who were "unfriendly" to the Committee, only eleven were actually called to the stand. The eleventh, German playwright Bertolt Brecht, completely bewildered the committee. The other ten—directors Herbert Biberman and Edward Dmytryk, producer Adrian Scott, and writers Alvah Bessie, Lester Cole, Ring Lardner, Jr., John Howard Lawson, Albert Maltz, Samuel Ornitz, and Trumbo—were branded as the "unfriendly ten" (a title they later changed to the Hollywood Ten over Trumbo's objections) and cited for contempt of Congress for refusing to answer the questions, "Are you a member of the Screen Writers' Guild?" and "Are you now, or have you ever been, a member of the Communist party?" Actually, as Trumbo's testimony of October 28 indi-

50

cates, he did not specifically refuse to answer the questions but rather refused to answer them in a manner that was satisfactory to the Committee:

MR. STRIPLING: The first witness, Mr. Chairman, will be Mr. Dalton Trumbo.

THE CHAIRMAN: Mr. Trumbo, take the stand. Raise your right hand, please. Mr. Trumbo, do you solemnly swear that the testimony you are about to give is the truth, the whole truth, nothing but the truth, so help you God?

MR. TRUMBO: I do.

THE CHAIRMAN: Sit down, please.

MR. TRUMBO: Mr. Chairman, I have a statement I should like to read into the record, if you please—

MR. STRIPLING: Mr. Trumbo, just a moment, please. We want to conduct the hearing as orderly as possible, and I am sure you desire to cooperate.

MR. TRUMBO: I do, indeed.

MR. STRIPLING: You have counsel with you?

MR. TRUMBO: I have.

MR. STRIPLING: And would you identify your counsel?

MR. TRUMBO: Mr. Bartley Crum and Mr. Robert Kenny. May I request of the Chair the opportunity to read a statement into the record?

THE CHAIRMAN: Yes. May we see your statement?

MR. TRUMBO: Yes.

THE CHAIRMAN: To determine whether it is pertinent to the inquiry. (*The Committee then inspected the statement of the witness.*) Mr. Trumbo, we have looked over this statement very carefully. It has been our practice to permit witnesses to read statements that are pertinent to the inquiry, that is, the alleged infiltration of communism in the moving picture industry. We have read your statement here. We have concluded, and unanimously so, that this statement is not pertinent to the inquiry. Therefore, the Chair will rule that the statement will not be read.*

---

*STATEMENT BY DALTON TRUMBO TO THE HOUSE COMMITTEE ON UN-AMERICAN ACTIVITIES

Mr. Chairman:

As indicated by news dispatches from foreign countries during the past week, the eyes of the world are focused today upon the House Committee on Un-American Activities. In every capital city these hearings will be reported.

MR. TRUMBO:	The Chair has considered a statement from Gerald L. K. Smith to be pertinent to its inquiries.
THE CHAIRMAN:	That statement is out of order.
MR. TRUMBO:	(*continuing*) And where is mine different from that, sir?
THE CHAIRMAN:	As a witness, if you conduct yourself like the first witness yesterday [John Howard Lawson],

---

From what happens during the proceedings, the peoples of the earth will learn by precept and example precisely what America means when her strong voice calls out to the community of nations for freedom of the press, freedom of expression, freedom of conscience, the civil rights of men standing accused before government agencies, the vitality and strength of private enterprise, the inviolable right of every American to think as he wishes, to organize and assemble as he pleases, to vote in secret as he chooses.

The quality of our devotion to these principles will be weighed most thoughtfully by all who have been urged to emulate the American way of life. Whether we wish it or not, the committee and its witnesses appear here before the world as a living test of American democracy in action. By reason of this we have all been committed to a very heavy responsibility.

I shall therefore pass quickly over the hearsay and slander of witnesses classified as friendly to this committee, as well as over other evidence already established as perjury. I call your attention only briefly to political coincidence that nearly all friendly witnesses summoned by the committee have violently opposed the ideals of Wendell Willkie and Franklin Roosevelt, while without exception the unfriendly witnesses have supported such ideals. I shall make no comment at all on the petty professional jealousies, the private feuds, the intra-studio conflicts which have been elevated to the dignity of the record. And only with reluctance and shame do I find it necessary to recall how fulsomely this committee has complimented witnesses who have proposed that all who disagree with them be deprived of citizenship and handed over to the mercy of mobs.

There are three principal points I wish to stress in my statement to this committee:

First: In the course of these hearings your committee has launched a direct attack upon the constitutional rights of property and of management and of that system which we call private enterprise. You have attempted to compel management to hire and fire at your own dictation, without any regard for rights and agreements already established between management and labor within the motion picture industry. But even beyond this, you have attempted to dictate to industry what kind of product it *shall* make and what kind it shall *not* make.

Let every businessman in America clearly understand that if this committee can usurp the rights of management in *one* industry, it has establish[ed] the precedent by which it can usurp the rights of management in *all* industries. Modern history reveals many instances abroad where workers in private industry have resolutely defended the rights of management against the encroachments of a corporate state. I am certain they will make such a defense in this country against the attempt with which this committee is presently engaged.

Second: The committee in its hearings has consistently attacked the con-

	you won't be given the privilege of being a witness before a Committee of Congress, before this Committee of Congress. Go ahead, Mr. Stripling.
MR. STRIPLING:	Mr. Trumbo—
MR. TRUMBO:	I would like to know what it is that is in my statement that this Committee fears be read to the American people?

stitutional guarantees of a free press, which encompass the guarantee of a free screen. The American film, as a medium of communication, as a purveyor of ideas, is completely beyond the investigatory powers of this committee. No committee of the Congress can dictate to the motion picture industry what ideas it shall and shall not incorporate into films, nor can it dictate to the American people what ideas they may and may not see upon the screens of their neighborhood theatres.

But you have not exclusively attacked the principle of a free screen. In the past, you have sought to intimidate workers in the radio industry. And during these hearings you have thanked witnesses who have testified against the theatre, the publishing business and the press itself. This constant attempt to interfere with the rights of every medium of free expression provides the consistent brown thread which binds together all testimony thus far presented by friendly witnesses. It clearly reveals your intention to establish a slave screen, subservient to the cultural standards of J. Parnell Thomas and the humanitarian precepts of John E. Rankin.

Third: The committee throughout its hearings has approved even the grossest attacks upon the right of the artist to express his ideas freely and honestly in his work. Similarly, you have sought testimony attacking his right to function in craft organizations and trade unions for the advancement of his interests. You are now attacking his right to think, and seeking by public inquisition to ferret out his innermost ideas and his most private and personal convictions. No institution on earth possesses this power over American citizens. You violate the most elementary principles of constitutional guarantees when you require anyone to parade for your approval his opinions upon race, religion, politics, or any other matter.

We must furthermore remember always that the defense of constitutional rights is not simply a convenience to be invoked in time of need, but a clear and continuous obligation imposed equally upon all of us at all times. We are, as citizens, literally commanded by its implications to defend the constitution against even the slightest encroachment upon the protective barrier it interposes between the private citizen on one hand and the inquisitors of government on the other.

Already the gentlemen of this committee and others of like disposition have produced in this capital city a political atmosphere which is acrid with fear and repression; a community in which anti-Semitism finds safe refuge behind secret tests of loyalty; a city in which no union leader can trust his telephone; a city in which old friends hesitate to recognize one another in public places; a city in which men and women who dissent even slightly from the orthodoxy you seek to impose, speak with confidence only in moving cars and in the open air. You have produced a capital city on the eve of its Reichstag fire. For those who remember German history in the autumn of 1932 there is the smell of smoke in this very room.

THE CHAIRMAN:	Go ahead, Mr. Stripling, ask a question—
MR. TRUMBO:	I have some evidence to introduce—
THE CHAIRMAN:	(*pounding gavel*) Ask one question, Mr. Stripling—
MR. TRUMBO:	I should like to introduce evidence—
THE CHAIRMAN:	(*pounding gavel*) You are out of order.
MR. STRIPLING:	State your name, please.
MR. TRUMBO:	Dalton Trumbo.
MR. STRIPLING:	What is your present address?
MR. TRUMBO:	329 South Rodeo Drive, Beverly Hills, California.
MR. STRIPLING:	When and where were you born, sir?
MR. TRUMBO:	I was born in Montrose, Colorado, on December 9, 1905.
MR. STRIPLING:	What is your occupation?
MR. TRUMBO:	My occupation is that of a writer.
MR. STRIPLING:	How long have you been in the motion picture industry as a writer?
MR. TRUMBO:	I believe since 1934 or '35.
MR. STRIPLING:	Are you a member of the Screen Writers' Guild?
MR. TRUMBO:	At this point, sir, I should like to introduce certain evidence bearing upon this case—
MR. STRIPLING:	Mr. Chairman—
MR. TRUMBO:	I—
MR. STRIPLING:	Just a moment, please—
MR. TRUMBO:	I should like to introduce statements—
THE CHAIRMAN:	(*pounding gavel*) Just a minute—
MR. TRUMBO:	—about my work—
THE CHAIRMAN:	What was the question—
MR. TRUMBO:	—from General Arnold of the Army Air Forces—
THE CHAIRMAN:	(*pounding gavel*) Now, just a minute—
MR. TRUMBO:	—from a municipal judge—
THE CHAIRMAN:	(*pounding gavel*) Just a moment. The Chair wants to find out what the question was and to see whether your answer is pertinent to the question. What was the question?
MR. STRIPLING:	Mr. Trumbo, I shall ask various questions, all of which can be answered "yes" or "no." If you want to give an explanation after you have made that answer, I feel sure that the Committee will agree to that. However, in order to conduct this hearing in an orderly fashion, it is necessary that you be responsive to the ques-

	tion, without making a speech in response to each question.
MR. TRUMBO:	I understand, Mr. Stripling. However, your job is to ask questions and mine is to answer them. I shall answer "yes" or "no," if I please to answer. I shall answer in my own words. Very many questions can be answered "yes" or "no" only by a moron or a slave.
THE CHAIRMAN:	The Chair agrees with your point, that you need not answer the questions "Yes" or "No"—
MR. TRUMBO:	Thank you, sir.
THE CHAIRMAN:	But you should answer the questions.
MR. TRUMBO:	Thank you, sir.
THE CHAIRMAN:	Go ahead, Mr. Stripling.
MR. TRUMBO:	May I, if the Chair please, I am not going to make a speech. I simply have evidence from responsible people as to the nature of my work. I have twenty scripts which I propose and wish to introduce into the record so that it may be known what my work is, and what this Committee may seek to prevent the American people from seeing in the future.
MR. STRIPLING:	Mr. Chairman—
THE CHAIRMAN:	Now, don't make a statement like that. That is not correct. May I ask how long one of these scripts may be?
MR. TRUMBO:	I am sorry to say that they average from one hundred fifteen to one hundred sixty or seventy pages, with very few of them of the latter type.
THE CHAIRMAN:	And how many do you want to put in the record?
MR. TRUMBO:	I have twenty. They are not quite all that I have written.
THE CHAIRMAN:	I think the Chair will have to rule—
MR. TRUMBO:	But, sir—
THE CHAIRMAN:	They are too long—
MR. TRUMBO:	My work has been under attack.
THE CHAIRMAN:	Too many pages.
MR. TRUMBO:	Then may I introduce into evidence statements of responsible people concerning my work?
THE CHAIRMAN:	All right, you let the investigator ask his questions, and then you answer them the best you can.
MR. STRIPLING:	I will be glad to cover all of your works, Mr. Trumbo.

MR. TRUMBO:	I realize that, but yesterday a man's work [Lawson's] was covered after he left the stand. I should like to discuss my work now.
MR. STRIPLING:	Well, Mr. Trumbo, I will repeat the question: Are you a member of the Screen Writers' Guild?
MR. TRUMBO:	I shall answer that question in just a moment. I want only to protest the fact that I have been denied the right to introduce evidence, to introduce statements of General Arnold, of Juvenile Court judges, of the head of the Motion Picture Division of the UNRRA, of the Naval Chaplain in charge of motion picture projects for the United States Navy. These I consider pertinent. And with that protest, I shall go to your question.
MR. STRIPLING:	Are you a member of the Screen Writers' Guild?
MR. TRUMBO:	Mr. Stripling, the rights of American labor to inviolably secret membership lists have been won in this country by a great cost of blood and a great cost in terms of hunger. These rights have become an American tradition. Over the Voice of America we have broadcast to the entire world the freedom of our labor.
THE CHAIRMAN:	Are you answering the question, or are you making another speech?
MR. TRUMBO:	Sir, I am truly answering the question.
THE CHAIRMAN:	Because if you want to make another speech we can find a corner right up here where you can make some of these speeches.
MR. TRUMBO:	I would be willing to do that, too.
THE CHAIRMAN:	All right, now what was the question, Mr. Stripling?
MR. STRIPLING:	The question, Mr. Chairman, is—I asked Mr. Trumbo if he is a member of the Screen Writers' Guild.
MR. TRUMBO:	You asked me a question which would permit you to haul every union member in the United States up here to identify himself as a union member, to subject him to future intimidation and coercion. This, I believe, is an unconstitutional question.
THE CHAIRMAN:	Now, are you making another speech, or is that the answer?
MR. TRUMBO:	This is my answer, sir.

THE CHAIRMAN:	Well, can't you answer: Are you a member of the Screen Writers' Guild, by saying "Yes" or "No," or "I think so," or "Maybe," or something like that?
MR. TRUMBO:	Mr. Chairman, I should like to accommodate you. May I try to answer the question again?
THE CHAIRMAN:	Well, we would certainly like to have you accommodate us.
MR. TRUMBO:	If there were a committee of Congress all the members of whom had voted in favor of the Taft-Hartley Bill—
MR. MCDOWELL:	Oh, that isn't answering the question.
THE CHAIRMAN:	(pounding gavel) —
MR. TRUMBO:	—it might be considered that committee was hostile to labor.
THE CHAIRMAN:	(pounding gavel) Now, Mr. Trumbo—
MR. MCDOWELL:	It is no disgrace, you know, to identify yourself as a member of a labor union in the United States. Most of us belong to something.
THE CHAIRMAN:	Now the question is, Mr. Trumbo: Are you a member of the Screen Writers' Guild?
MR. TRUMBO:	Mr. Chairman, I would not consider it a disgrace to be a member of a labor union.
MR. MCDOWELL:	Of course he wouldn't.
MR. TRUMBO:	But labor unions have the right to secrecy of their membership lists.
THE CHAIRMAN:	I am getting back to the question: Are you a member of the Screen Writers' Guild?
MR. TRUMBO:	Mr. Chairman, this question is designed to a specific purpose. First—
THE CHAIRMAN:	(pounding gavel) Do you—
MR. TRUMBO:	First, to identify me with the Screen Writers' Guild; secondly, to seek to identify me with the Communist party and thereby destroy that Guild—
THE CHAIRMAN:	(pounding gavel) Are you refusing to answer the question?
MR. TRUMBO:	I will refuse to answer none of your questions, sir.
THE CHAIRMAN:	Well, you are refusing to answer this question.
MR. TRUMBO:	I am, indeed, not refusing to answer the question.
THE CHAIRMAN:	I will ask you the question—
MR. TRUMBO:	You ask me.
THE CHAIRMAN:	Are you a member of the Screen Writers' Guild?

MR. TRUMBO:	I repeat—
THE CHAIRMAN:	(*pounding gavel*) Excuse the witness—
MR. STRIPLING:	Just a moment, Mr. Chairman—
MR. TRUMBO:	Am I excused?
MR. STRIPLING:	I have more questions—
MR. TRUMBO:	Am I excused or not?
THE CHAIRMAN:	No. Just a minute. The chief investigator wants to ask some questions.
MR. STRIPLING:	Just a moment. I have some other questions, Mr. Trumbo, that I would like to ask you. Are you now, or have you ever been, a member of the Communist party?
MR. TRUMBO:	Mr. Chairman, first I would like to know whether the quality of my last answer was acceptable, since I am still on the stand?
THE CHAIRMAN:	This hasn't got anything to do with your answer to the last question.
MR. TRUMBO:	I see.
THE CHAIRMAN:	This is a new question now.
MR. TRUMBO:	I see. Mr. Stripling, you must have some reason for asking this question—
MR. MCDOWELL:	Yes, we do.
MR. TRUMBO:	You do. I understand that members of the press have been given an alleged Communist party card belonging to me—is that true?
MR. STRIPLING:	That is not true.
THE CHAIRMAN:	You are not asking the question—
MR. TRUMBO:	I was.
THE CHAIRMAN:	The chief investigator is asking the questions.
MR. TRUMBO:	I beg your pardon, sir.
THE CHAIRMAN:	Are you now, or have you ever been, a member of the Communist party?
MR. TRUMBO:	I believe I have the right to be confronted with any evidence which supports this question. I should like to see what you have.
THE CHAIRMAN:	Oh. Well, you would!
MR. TRUMBO:	Yes.
THE CHAIRMAN:	Well, you will, pretty soon. (*Laughter and applause.*) The witness is excused. Impossible.
MR. TRUMBO:	This is the beginning—
THE CHAIRMAN:	(*pounding gavel*) Just a minute—
MR. TRUMBO:	—of an American concentration camp.
THE CHAIRMAN:	This is typical Communist tactics. This is typical Communist tactics (*pounding gavel*).

The Ten maintained that the Committee was challenging man's

right to political opinion and his right to speak freely upon any controversial issue; indeed they maintained that the hearings were witch hunts that challenged the very foundations of democracy and immunities guaranteed by the Bill of Rights. They asked, and were denied, permission to read prepared statements or to introduce scripts and films as evidence. Interestingly enough, the hearings proved nothing to support the charge that communist propaganda had ever reached the motion picture screen.

Hundreds of Hollywood personalities, many of whom went to Washington or formed organizations such as the Committee for the First Amendment, were outraged and protested the hearings. Moreover it appeared that Hollywood officials were outraged. Eric Johnston, president of the Motion Picture Association of America, answered Parnell Thomas's advice that the industry "clean house" by saying that for producers "to join together and to refuse to hire someone or some people would be a potential conspiracy" and that the industry would not countenance blacklisting.

When the hearings ended, Trumbo retired to the ranch to finish the script of *Angel's Flight* for Metro knowing only that he and his colleagues had been charged with contempt for their behavior toward the Committee's authority and that he faced trial. His Metro contract was, he knew, irrevocable, and Eric Johnston's statement assured his position in Hollywood.

On Thanksgiving morning of 1947, as Trumbo was making mincemeat pies for the family dinner, Sam Zimbalist drove to the ranch with the news that further complications seemed inevitable: at a two-day conference at the Waldorf Astoria Hotel in New York, top Hollywood executives representing the Motion Picture Association of America, the Association of Motion Picture Producers, and the Independent Motion Picture Producers, met with the New York film executives and industry overlords, and agreed to issue on December 3, what has come to be known as the Waldorf Manifesto—the first clear intimation of the blacklist—composed by the same Eric Johnston who had stalwartly held out against a blacklist only weeks before:

Members of the Association of Motion Picture Producers deplore the action of the ten Hollywood men who have been cited for contempt. We do not desire to prejudge their legal rights, but their actions have been a disservice to their employers and have impaired their usefulness to the industry.

We will forthwith discharge or suspend without compensation those in our employ and we will not re-employ any of the ten until such time as he is acquitted or has purged himself of contempt and declares under oath that he is not a Communist.

On the broader issues of alleged subversive and disloyal elements in Hollywood, our members are likewise prepared to take positive action.

We will not knowingly employ a Communist or a member of any party or group which advocates the overthrow of the Government of the United States by force or by illegal or unconstitutional methods. In pursuing this policy, we are not going to be swayed by hysteria or intimidation from any source. We are frank to recognize that such a policy involves dangers and risks. There is the danger of hurting innocent people. There is the risk of creating an atmosphere of fear. Creative work at its best cannot be carried on in an atmosphere of fear. We will guard against this danger, this risk, this fear. To this end we will invite the Hollywood talent guilds to work with us to eliminate any subversives, to protect the innocent, and to safeguard free speech and a free screen wherever threatened.

The impact of the statement was immediately felt in Hollywood. A producers' delegation composed of Dore Schary, Walter Wanger, and Eddie Mannix appeared at a meeting of the Screen Writers' Guild and pleaded for support of the Association of Motion Picture Producers decree, resolving that the industry would not hire a Communist or anyone suspected of being a Communist.

So it was that Trumbo, along with his colleagues, found himself facing trial for contempt, suspended from work, and blacklisted. A smashed career, coupled with a maze of litigations soon found the writer in critical and perpetual financial difficulties. Yet his sense of humor remained intact and, in many ways, he felt relieved to be barred in Hollywood. His interests and abilities were turned away from the consuming task of film writing and toward establishing a new career and a new name for himself.

1. To W. R. Wilkerson (possibly never sent)

Lazy T Ranch
Frazier Park, California
[*c. mid-1947*]

Dear sir:

Illness has prevented an earlier response to your editorial dealing with my activities as a "Red Commissar." [1]

My last three films (*A Guy Named Joe, Thirty Seconds over Tokyo, Our Vines Have Tender Grapes*) have been highly recommended by your journal. By soliciting and publishing advertisements calling attention to their merits you have assisted in the dissemination of the ideas which they express.

If these films contained any elements of communist propaganda, I cannot believe that you lack either the intelligence to detect them or

---

[1] Wilkerson was the editor and publisher of *The Hollywood Reporter*.

the courage to denounce them. Your failure to do so indicates that your professed alarm about communist propaganda on the screen is insincere and without basis in truth. Your real concern is the growing strength of the Screen Writers' Guild as it moves toward its legitimate objectives, not one of which is political nor ever has been.

We live in a country founded upon the principle that a man's race, his religion and his politics are his private concern, protected as such by law. Any answer to your "questions," either positive or negative, would constitute an admission on my part of your right to assume the function of industry inquisitor. I deny that right, and have no intention of collaborating with you to establish it.

Your piece on me is, in the main, a melange of inaccuracies, distortions and inventions. Coming from one who has testified in open court that he does not necessarily believe the editorials to which he affixes his name, this should surprise no one.

. . . .

From such a one, to quote the prophet, "Open rebuke is better than secret love."

Very truly,
DALTON TRUMBO

2. To W. F. K.

Lazy T Ranch
Frazier Park, California
December 2, 1947

Mr. W. F. K.
St. Clairsville, Ohio

My dear sir:

You have favored me with a letter, thus obliging me to pay you the courtesy of an answer. It is nevertheless an unfair exchange, since I customarily receive money for my writing while you, I surmise, have retained an amateur standing.

If you are genuinely interested in the Hollywood investigation conducted by the House Committee on Un-American Activities, I suggest that you write the Committee and they will be glad to send you the official transcript of my testimony which, as you will discover, differs considerably from that reported in *Life* Magazine.

Although I do not know you and have never heard of you, still you provide me with a great deal of information about your pedigree and the gallantry of your family, none of which I care to question. I lay no such claims to antiquity, my family on both sides being parvenus who settled in Virginia a scant fifty years before the Revolution. Neither had I grandchildren in the war, although as a highly nervous correspondent I have dodged snipers in Luzon, ducked bombs on Okinawa, ridden through AA fire over Japan and hit the beach with the Australians in Borneo.

I have, additionally, come under the fire of the Thomas Committee, of innumerable crackpots and pests, and finally of your esteemed self. I grant you the right to demand my hanging if you wish; and you in your turn must concede to the Supreme Court the final decision as to whether I or the Committee and its supporters stand on the side of Americanism in this issue.

Good health to you, sir. Long life to your progeny and honor to your forebears.

DALTON TRUMBO

3. To William B. Barnes

Lazy T Ranch
Frazier Park, California
December 2, 1947

Mr. William B. Barnes
Buffalo, New York

My dear sir:

I understand your grief for your son, for I too have a son. I also understand something of what your son went through, for as a war correspondent I have been bombed on Okinawa, and sniped at on Luzon; I have ridden through AA fire over Japan, been with the fleet in Macassar Straits and hit the beach at Balikpapan.

I must dispute with you the idea that Americans died for any country but their own. Declarations of war were simultaneously made against us by the Japanese, the Germans and the Italians. The Russians had nothing whatever to do with it. At the time I advocated a second front, President Roosevelt, General Marshall and General Eisenhower were also advocating it to Churchill. Every military leader in the world understood that we must invade Europe or lose the war. The only question was: when? If the front had been opened at the time I wrote favoring it, your son would quite possibly have been alive today; for at that time there were far fewer German divisions defending France than when the invasion was finally and belatedly engaged upon.

The above facts may be verified by consulting the *War Reports of Marshall, Arnold and King,* published by Lippincott; *My Three*

Years with Eisenhower published by Simon and Schuster; Commager's history of the war published by Little, Brown and Company; Root's history of the war published by Scribner's; and McInnis's five-volume history of the war published by the Oxford University Press.

I write this not to change your violent antipathy toward me, but simply to correct your errors of fact.

Yours very truly,
DALTON TRUMBO

4. To Elsie McKeogh

Lazy T Ranch
Frazier Park, California
December 4, 1947

Dear Elsie:

Your wonderful old friend (and his wonderful old friends) [2] have accomplished through the Thomas Committee what they were never able to do in open competition—to bring an end to my career in pictures.

When I come back for trial, I hope very much to be able to have an hour or so with you to discuss the advisability of building up another name for myself. I don't know just how such things are done, but I suspect they will be necessary.

Meanwhile let me pester you to reduce the bank account to minimum token strength by withdrawing the sum indicated in the attached check.

I shall never be able to complain that my middle years were dull. They grow livelier and hotter by the minute!

Yours in Christ,
DALTON

[2] One of the witnesses friendly to the Committee's purposes, Rupert Hughes, was an old friend of Elsie McKeogh.

5. To Charles Katz

Lazy T Ranch
Frazier Park, California
December 4, 1947

Dear Charley: [3]

By now I presume you have in your possession a copy of my contract from Berg-Allenberg. I do not remember having read it in great detail, but I do remember that I made a great point about it having no morals clause; and Phil Berg and Bob Coryell both assured me that the clause had been eliminated.

Here is a short history of the contract. It went into effect about a year ago. I accepted the assignment to do a script on a novel called *The House Above the River* for Sam Zimbalist.[4] I also signed a separate agreement that *Lust for Life* would follow *House Above the River* as my next assignment.

We held a few conferences on *House,* and I came down with diphtheria and damned near died. I wasn't able to get back to work on *House* until after the first of the year. It was a terrible assignment, and I gave them far more conference time than the contract called for between each draft, as well as more drafts than the contract called for. Sam and I chewed at it for approximately eight months. At any time I could have invoked the protective clauses in my contract, and declared the job finished.

However I continued on, out of regard for Sam and respect for my own work, finally turning in the final draft around September 1, 1947. This draft was based upon the line approved by Sam. I received final payment for it, and the job was completed in all its legalities.

I took a couple of weeks off before starting on my next assignment, which Sam and I had agreed should be a script based on a novel called *Angel's Flight* for Clark Gable. I checked in at the studio for the new assignment on Monday, September 15, 1947.

At this point I discovered that many conferences had been going on over *House,* parts of which were not liked. Remember that this was legally finished, and the line had been approved by Sam Zimbalist. Sam and I conferred about the script, and then I conferred with Sam, Mannix, Thau, and Joe Cohn and Larry Weingarten [5] en masse. It was agreed certain changes should be made.

Examining the contract, you will see it stipulates that after I have finished a script, any further work done by me shall be paid for by

---

[3] Trumbo's good friend and one of his lawyers during the HUAC hearings and subsequent trials for contempt of Congress.

[4] Sam Zimbalist, Metro producer and close personal friend.

[5] Edward Mannix, Benjamin Thau, Joseph Cohn, Lawrence Weingarten— all producers or executives at MGM.

the studio at the rate of $3,000 per week. However, out of pride in my work, I waived verbally any such payment. I worked on *House* free of charge from September 15 through October 12—four full weeks—turning in a new draft of the script on Monday, October 13.

During the four weeks I was engaged on the free re-write of *House,* the studio paid me my first $14,000 on the new assignment, *Angel's Flight.* On Monday, October 13, I went into conferences on *Angel's Flight* and continued conferences through Thursday, October 16. Thursday night I flew east with the boys. I returned to the studio the morning of Thursday, November 6, and immediately went into conferences on *Angel's Flight* which were carried through Friday, November 21.

On Friday afternoon I left the studio to come to the ranch and start writing. Eddie Mannix had urged upon Sam that I should go away in order to get the work done quickly, since there was a Gable script crisis. Sam agreed I should work on it at the ranch. Mr. Mayer inquired of Sam how quickly I could get the script done.

Accordingly, I started writing at the ranch on Saturday, November 22, working at emergency speed because it had been impressed upon me that this was terribly important. On December 2, I received through the mail a telegram from Bert Allenberg, mis-addressed and dated November 26. . . .

I had a hell of a time finding a typist to help me with the script, and probably shall not be in town with it until Monday, December 8. At that time I shall consult with you.

Contentions: doesn't the studio stand legally obliged to pay me the $14,000 due for the first draft of this script? Doesn't the studio, in view of its abrupt and illegal treatment of me, stand morally to pay me $12,000 for the free job I did on *House,* bearing always in mind that if I had stood by my contract I would have the $12,000—and that if I had not done the work, I would have gone much earlier onto *Angel's Flight,* would have by now been into a second draft, and would have received a great deal more money.

The rest I leave up to you for study. It seems to me I want: (1) $12,000 for work done on *House*; (2) $14,000 for the first draft of *Angel's Flight*; (3) some arrangement for the remainder of the *Angel's Flight* deal; (4) some arrangement for the *Lust for Life* deal which was postponed by the studio but for which I am still committed; (5) some settlement for the balance of the contract beyond those enterprises specifically undertaken.

Perhaps negotiations between the studio and Berg-Allenberg could best obtain the $26,000 in items 1 and 2. We shall naturally have to go over the whole thing very carefully, which I shall be ready to do on Monday, coordinating you, Berg-Allenberg and myself into some efficient plan for getting dough. Hell of it is—as always—I *need* money, and can prove (if such proof is helpful) commitments undertaken and expenditures made based upon the thoroughly legal expectation of the *Angel's Flight* deal going through to its completion.

Now to get down to some personal considerations which I hope you will consider very seriously. For several years I have disliked pictures and planned tentatively to get out of them. Now I am apparently out, and in a way very glad of it. I never want to work in them again. I hope we can honestly arrange a cash settlement and deal me out. The money would be a backlog—because it should be considerable—and I could get about the job of building up a new career for myself, which I am eager to do. I hope I shall not be obliged to put up a big legal fight to retain my job and serve out the contract. I don't want the job and I don't want to finish the contract. I want the only thing I ever really wanted out of pictures—the money which would be due me were the contract fulfilled. I hope very much we can try to settle on this basis. Each of the guys, I know, has an individual problem. Please consider this as mine: an overpowering desire never again to have anything to do with this depraved industry, and an equally overpowering desire to get what cash I can and blow. My feelings about pictures now are such that I doubt if, during the next year or two, I could write them well anyhow. The restrictions and suspicions would be too great.

Question: if it were possible to make a cash settlement and get out, could I still sue the Producers Association on the basis that regular applications for work submitted to all studios had over a considerable period of time indicated blacklist? Because I would naturally like a million dollar law suit in addition to the cash settlement.

Again, maybe the cash settlement is out of the question: perhaps I'm talking through my hat. In which event, I'm in trouble, but then hell, who isn't?

Phil Berg and Bert Allenberg are very skillful negotiators, and they have a good moral case in terms of me, and I naturally think we should all think the thing through, with this principal objective in mind: cash!

I will be in touch with you at least by Monday. Goodness gracious, old boy, but we are an unpopular little crew! Until I see you, these are my final instructions as client to counsel: defend my interests with all your intelligence and, if necessary, with your last dollar.

Yours in Christ,
DALTON

6. To William Denels

Lazy T Ranch
Frazier Park, California
December 15, 1947

Dear Mr. Denels: [6]

I am at a complete loss to understand the reason for your discourtesy toward me. For over ten years I have dealt exclusively with you—not only in terms of two pianos, over a thousand dollars worth of records, but all the small miscellany that one needs from time to time. I am not aware that I have ever swindled or cheated you.

You promised delivery of the sink unit some three weeks ago. I came up here expecting it. After two weeks I wrote you a courteous note about it. A week went by without even the civility of a reply. I went to town to telephone you.[7] You pointed out you were unable to get a plumber to install it—something you might have told me at least two weeks before. You promised it for Sunday.

I accordingly arranged to have a plumber come up on Monday. He arrived this morning at eight o'clock. But you had failed to keep your word, and I was obliged to pay him $25.00 for nothing.

Now I wish you could do me one favor, which doesn't appear to me to be too difficult: write me a letter and let me know the precise day on which you propose to deliver the unit. It seems a business-like procedure, and I beg you to do it.

I am not angry; but I feel that my long status as a customer of yours entitles me to a little more courtesy than you thus far have been willing to pay me.

Yours very truly,
DALTON TRUMBO

7. To William Denels

Lazy T Ranch
Frazier Park, California
December 27, 1947

Dear Mr. Denels:

Forget and forgive my quibbling little note. The only thing that still perplexes me is that we are waiting for a porcelain top, whereas you had told us some time ago that none was available, and asked

[6] This letter and the second to Denels on December 27, 1947 (#7) take on an interesting dimension in relation to Trumbo's letter to Sam Zimbalist on February 5, 1948 (#15 below, page 74).

[7] The ranch was twelve miles from the nearest telephone.

us if we would accept stainless steel instead, which you said you had on hand at the moment. We agreed stainless steel would be fine.

Would appreciate it if you could let us have some idea of when we might get delivery. You have no idea how chapped my hands are getting over the sink—I've inherited the dishwashing job, although I swear to my wife it's your fault and you should be taking the punishment instead of me.

Incidentally, I haven't received any schedule of payments yet. Surely one must be due by now. How about letting me in on the deal?

Best wishes for a prosperous New Year, and stacks of sink tops, both porcelain and stainless steel.

Yours,
DALTON TRUMBO

8. Extract of a letter to William Pomerance[8]

Lazy T Ranch
Frazier Park, California
December 27, 1947

And in the same vein, you couldn't interest me in motion pictures if you gave me a whole fucking studio. But—and this is quite confidential and for your own information—I hear that Chaplin has made certain overtures in the way of studio space and capital to Adrian Scott. I haven't talked to Adrian about it, but you might find a way to get in touch with Dymytrik (how the hell does he spell it?) [Edward Dmytryk] or Adrian or Herbert Biberman, and see what you can find out.

Basically I think your idea is a good one, and the boys might be interested in it. Undoubtedly would be. But count me out, old boy, I never did like that racket and although I'm not especially fond of the *way* I got out of it, still and all I'm glad I *am* out. I may steal a little now and again on a piece of shit, but I'll never work for them again. Life's too short and movies are too long.

[8] William Pomerance, then executive secretary of the Screen Writers' Guild, had been with the national administration of the National Labor Relations Board. After leaving the Guild, he went to New York and established a highly profitable studio for television cartoon commercials. When Pomerance was investigated by HUAC, many of his best clients threatened to withdraw; hence, he was forced to sell at a tremendous loss.

9. To a motion picture associate

Lazy T Ranch
Frazier Park, California
December 30, 1947

Dear ————:

I am told you take it badly that I have not yet answered your note, and that you consider my original letter to you insulting.[9]

I am astonished to find you still so sensitive: for I have grown quite accustomed to abuse lately—not only the quietly slanderous kind which impels you to raise political bars against me in my trade union, but also that which comes from your less genteel colleagues and obliges me to hide my mail lest the children see letters addressed quite openly to "Traitor Trumbo," "Bolshevik Dalt T.," "Jew-lover Trumbo," "Red Rat Trumbo" and other epithets of like nature. No criminal, no murderer nor rapist can safely be called the names which with impunity are now applied to me: there lives no man so foul or so low that he may not elevate himself a little in the esteem of society by spitting upon my name and proscribing my work.

I say this to you because for long years you have been a political hermaphrodite, lifting your voice in the defense of no man, espousing no principle which smells of danger. But now you are a politico. You have found a faith to fight for. You have embarked upon a crusade—not *for* something, to be sure, but at least against something. Hence you must prepare yourself for a certain amount of recrimination. You must callous yourself and harden your heart a little, for there is much work to be done before your objective is fully achieved.

Your crusade isn't a very new one. Its first disciples felt the call in Germany immediately after the Reichstag fire, when hundreds of thousands rushed forth to sanctify political discrimination a good four years before it blossomed at Nuremberg into racial and religious discrimination. You belong to the legion of men who traditionally sacrifice their brothers to gain a little more time for themselves—the shuddering, exquisite, sensitive men who quietly deplore injustice while dining upon its victim. This is your right, ————, and your choice and your destiny.

But you should not, in your letter to me, assume a whore's virtue at confession by using the word "affection." My affection caused me to assert your ability to producers when you were out of favor; yours impelled you to cry out against me in the most fatal hour of my career. Mine persuaded me to spend long hours in discussion of your story problems when you sought to re-establish yourself; yours led

[9] This former friend wrote Trumbo in the fall of 1947, enclosing a check to help fight the blacklist and telling Trumbo of his great affection in spite of political differences. Trumbo returned the check.

you to organizational meetings calculated to deprive me of my rights within the [Screen Writers'] Guild, to destroy my good name and to make it impossible for me to work in my profession. Give me no more such affection, _____: I stagger beneath that already conferred. Give me rather your hatred and let me console myself by the exchange of a weak friend for a strong enemy.

And do not attribute, as you did in your letter, the destruction of our friendship to political differences. Political opposition I have freely given and taken both in victory and in defeat. But I have never advocated the savagery of second-class citizenship for anybody, nor sought to impose it, nor tolerated its suggestion. There can be no real political differences between you and me because you have no politics but expediency, no standard of conduct but deceit, no principle but self-love.

I did not wish to write this letter, and would not have done so but for your characteristically widespread complaints. With it—and with your last kiss still hot upon my cheek—I bid you farewell.

DALTON TRUMBO

10. To W. F. K.

Lazy T Ranch
Frazier Park, California
January 12, 1948

My dear Mr. K.:

I responded to your first letter out of courtesy. I ignored the second as a hint that I did not intend to become your permanent pen pal. The arrival of still a third obliges me to be a little more explicit.

I have always been interested in the morbid aberrations which drive persons like yourself so pompously to seek correspondence with strangers. In this respect your letters have been illuminating. But they also reveal you as a witless and meddlesome old ass, self-deluded and full of vapors.

I must, therefore, urge you in the future to address yourself to your own affairs rather than to mine. As an incentive toward this healthy goal, I promise that your future correspondence will be returned to you unopened.

Cordially,
DALTON TRUMBO

11. To Elsie McKeogh

Lazy T Ranch
Frazier Park, California
January 12, 1948

Dear Elsie:

I haven't answered your most recent letter, and the wire about Mr. [Lee] Sabinson, because I thought I would be able to see you while in the east for arraignment. But a series of missed connections and forced flights prevented my even reaching New York, so, back home once more, I take up the things to which you referred.

1. *Johnny.* I am, more than ever before, interested in seeing my stuff published in other countries, and would be delighted with a French translation. I don't have any spare copies of *Johnny,* but the reprint presently is in the hands of Monogram Publishers in New York. I enclose $10.00 as a petty cash fund to buy what copies you need. God bless anybody anywhere abroad who will publish my work! And incidentally, is there any chance of getting a copy of the Danish translation of *Eclipse* for my records? And did anything come of the other foreign contracts we signed? Perhaps we could launch a foreign campaign on *Eclipse* and *Johnny.* The other two [*Washington Jitters* and *The Remarkable Andrew*] should have been smothered at birth.

2. *Mr. Sabinson and the play.*[10] I am very pleased and touched by Mr. Sabinson's offer, and I propose to accept it at once. Fortuitously enough, I have for the past several weeks been at work on a play. I am not disposed to outline it, for to do so would only water down whatever dramatic virtues it may possess. But herewith is certain specific information on it which you might transmit to Mr. Sabinson:

a. It is called *The Aching Rivers* from Walt Whitman's line:
   From pent-up aching rivers,
   From that of myself without which I were nothing . . .
b. It is in three acts with one set.
c. It has eleven characters: seven males aged 89, 55, 54, 50, 49, 39, 24: four females aged 70, 51, 48, 18.
d. To the degree that I can make it so, it will be a thoughtful and serious drama into which I am putting the most earnest effort. In the sense that no thoughtful work can escape having social point, it will have a certain import in line with my convictions. But it will contain no exhortations, no social declamations, no obvious political demands. Whatever meaning the audience carries home I hope shall come from their interpretation of events which occurred on the stage, rather

---

[10] First mention of Trumbo's play (later called *The Emerald Staircase* and finally *The Biggest Thief in Town*) which Lee Sabinson produced on Broadway in the spring of 1949. Herman Shumlin directed. Sabinson's earlier productions included *Counter Attack* in 1943, *Trio* in 1944, *Home of the Brave* in 1945, and *Finian's Rainbow* with W. P. Katzell in 1947.

than from any blue-print formula predigested for them by the author. I see nothing in the theme and its treatment which would place the play outside the main stream of general serious drama and into the specifically radical category.

e. I propose to have a tolerable first draft ready by the middle of March, and there is just a bare possibility that I may be able to bring some of it back with me when I stand trial on February 16 or shortly thereafter. Then you and Mr. Sabinson and I could discuss it fully and very critically. I shall have a great deal at stake in this enterprise, and I shall seek and accept advice in carrying it out.

I hope that Mr. Sabinson in making this (to me) most heartening offer understands (a) that he is dealing with a man who is a total novice in the theatre, and (b) that motion picture money might never be forthcoming on a play which bears my name. Both of these handicaps, however, *might* be overcome by a first-rate piece of work.

I am telling no one here, outside of Cleo, that I am working on a play—and I should like for it similarly to be a secret in the east, shared only by you and Mr. Sabinson . . . until such time as we mutually agree it should be revealed.

If, after considering all that I have written here, Mr. Sabinson still wants to carry his kind offer through, please conclude a deal at once on whatever terms you and he agree are fair. I need not be consulted by you, for you know more about these matters than I do and I trust you implicitly . . .

Incidentally, please tell Mr. Sabinson that I have strong loyalties, that I am genuinely grateful for his implied expression of confidence in a dark hour, and that if this play is no good I shall keep on writing plays for him until we *do* get a good one.

And needless to say, I shall also be happy for the money—and that as quickly as possible. Telegrams do not reach me here at the ranch any more quickly than regular air mail.

Regards,
DALTON

12. Extract of a letter to Sheridan Gibney[11]

Lazy T Ranch
Frazier Park, California
February 2, 1948

I should also like to commend the entire board upon the new department in *The Screen Writer* entitled "Unemployment: I." I

---

[11] President of the Screen Writers' Guild.

look forward eagerly to "Unemployment: II" et seq. I am following Mr. Longstreet's recommendations to the best of my ability. I have no talent at horoscopes, but I am deep in greeting card verse. It's tricky work, but I shall get the hang of it soon.

13. To Harry Tugend

Lazy T Ranch
Frazier Park, California
February 2, 1948

Dear Harry:

I have received a notice, presumably from you as treasurer of the [Screen Writers'] Guild, warning that I am now in jeopardy of being placed in bad standing for non-payment of dues.

Please be informed that my contract with MGM has been abrogated, my work has been proscribed and that I myself have been banned from employment in my profession until such time as I perform an act of political purification hitherto characteristic of fascist states.

I am sure you understand the situation in which I find myself, since you may take credit for being one of its architects by reason of your advocacy of the same political test for Guild officership which the producers have taken over as a test for employment.

In consequence, my income has ceased and I have no money with which to pay dues. After thirteen years of membership—years during which some members of the present board resigned in terror lest they displease the producers—I am therefore obliged to go into bad standing.

Attached herewith my card.

Cordially,
DALTON TRUMBO

14. To Elsie McKeogh

Lazy T Ranch
Frazier Park, California
February 4, 1948

Dear Elsie:

I feel like a deflowered girl, full of confusion and yet liking it a little and hoping my ineptitude will not prevent a continuation of the affair. I am sending you herewith the first draft of the first act of the first play I have ever tried.

I propose at the outset to make every possible excuse for it. I saw *Six Cylinder Love* in high school and it was swell. I saw *Bombo* in college and loved it. I saw *Strange Interlude* when I came to Los Angeles and have never forgotten it. Some three years later I beheld *Autumn Crocus* which gave me a violent start. I didn't stop quivering until you took Cleo and me to see *You Can't Take It with You* (or was it *The Man Who Came to Dinner?*) which I had read, and *Two on an Island* which sent me skittering so fast I've never returned.

On the basis of this experience with the theatre, it is presumptuous for me even to try a play, and downright foolhardy of poor Mr. Sabinson to lay out cash without looking at least this far into the poke before he closes for his pig. Let him see it at your own discretion.[12]

Do with this what you will. Be as critical as you can be. If it is quite hopeless, it will be kinder to tell me now, for necessity makes me dauntless and I am only too ready to launch a second craft onto the only dramatic seas remaining open to me. Specifically: is it too windy? Does it need more action—or a lot more or just a little? Is the dialogue too stilted? Are the characters interesting? Do you think you could have sat through it in a theatre? Do you have any curiosity about Act II? What else? If there's a ghost of virtue in it, I shall rewrite gladly until it comes to life.

Here is the reason I prefer to keep this enterprise quiet for the time being. Berg-Allenberg stare at me with melancholy eyes and address me in the past tense. Something has made me less attractive to them than formerly. They have done nothing about stirring up prospects in any other field. I propose to let two more months slip by without action on their part, and then commit an incision on them. They shall share in any recovery from my present contract—I am prosecuting the suit at my own expense—and they may, if they choose, handle any personal employment in the future if it is offered and I want it. But I do not want them to share in projects such as this one, in which they have taken no part; and only under certain conditions do I want them to handle the sale of future material to films. They are first-rate people, and if one has an agent here at all, they would be my choice. But I am so revolted with their present god-forsaken resignation that I wish my ties with them to be fragile. I must perform this operation on them in quietude and stealth, and therefore want no rumors of plays to reach their ears.

About the Sabinson deal: I think of nothing specific I should like included, since I know so little about what is customary. I should

---

[12] On February 25 Mrs. McKeogh wrote Trumbo that Sabinson had read and was enthusiastic about the play.

naturally like all the advantages that decently may be got. If I have any money at the time, I might like to buy in on the production. I might also like to raise some of the production money out here, with a proportionate share of the producer's percentage going to me for my efforts.

Mr. Sabinson must understand that I am not discharged from Metro: merely suspended and prohibited from working elsewhere in pictures until such time as I bellow to the moon or a federal judge that I certainly am not and never never was a communist. This will be a considerable while, during which certain standard movie contract features operate in my case. I am free to write a play, but Metro must be given the customary first opportunity to back it. I doubt that they will feel impelled to do so. But they have the standard rights of reading, etc.

My trial has been postponed until approximately the first week in March, which is pleasant. I shall let you know well in advance and we can all get together—provided, of course, the enclosed copy does not impel you both to wash your hands of me. I am moving ahead into the rest of the play, and should have more pages in a reasonable time. . . .

Regards,
DALTON

15. To Sam Zimbalist

Lazy T Ranch
Frazier Park, California
February 5, 1948

Dear Sam:

It is four A.M. I have been working since ten last night—back at last to the hours I love—and all night it has been snowing. I just flashed the spots on, and the sight is wonderfully soothing and beautiful, no corners anywhere in the world, everything rounded and smooth and immaculate. The kids and Cleo are asleep, the house is in order, the machines all function smoothly, the larder is full (we could be incommunicado for two months and eat handsomely)— and I feel, for the moment at least, that I am the luckiest and most contented man in the world. If you were here we would break a bottle and light the fire and watch the falling snow—through glass, of course!—and I would tell you all about it. That being impossible, I shall write.

First I shall tell you something which would embarrass us both greatly if I were to speak it. Separated from people as I have been for the past three months, I have had a great deal of time to think about them. I have observed their reactions to the present troubled times; I have had a chance to see how their actions square with their principles. I do not refer to what their principles *are*—but to whether or not they are lived by, whether or not they are proved in action. I have seen many betray themselves, I have seen many fail in any decent test of conduct, some of them my friends—and I have shucked them off with as little feeling as I would toss away a nail paring, and have experienced no sense of loss in the process. Only loathing and contempt and, I must confess—being human and as vindictive as the next—a resolution not to forget and never to forgive.

But through this whole interesting experience, my respect for you has deepened and my affection has grown more profound. Not only for the money you lent me—although that was a life-saver and a great demonstration of faith—but for your attitude toward me and other persons and toward life itself: for your willingness to grant me any belief I cherish so long as it is not harmful to others, even when you disagree with it—and for your personal sense of outrage when that right is denied. This and this alone makes decent men and decent societies, and it is rare, and it is why I feel warm in the knowledge that we are friends.

To get to less interesting things: you are a very lucky man that I have not been working for you since Christmas. For we have been going through one of our customary cycles of minor catastrophes which delay work to the point where the man who's waiting for copy is bound to say to himself at least once or twice, "Oh no, it can't be, the sonofabitch *must* be lying!" We have, if you remember, had such periods in the past while on the payroll. It may interest you to know that they also occur on my time, to wit: the trip to Washington simply to be arraigned; Christopher getting bucked off a horse and knocked colder than a mackerel; virus X for Cleo, Chris and Nikola in rapid sequence (Melissa and I escaping); threatened t.b. on the part of my married sister [Elizabeth Baskerville], necessitating her coming to live with us for a period and the trial coming up in March. Altogether a busy time, and one during which you would have received a lousy script—if at all.

To a degree this accounts for my rude failure to thank you for the Christmas things. The package from Blum's arrived and was admired and eaten. However the coffee maker went to Bakersfield, and was not picked up until several days after Christmas. Many of the children's packages had been similarly diverted, so we had a second Christmas on New Year's morning. May I tell you that if I die of coffee heart you are responsible? I read the directions carefully, and have never deviated from them, even to the fine point of pouring the

water at 185 degrees rather than 212. I make ten cups at a time and
—again according to the instructions—keep it hot all night by placing it in a skillet of simmering water. It makes the best coffee I have
ever drunk, and is used constantly. It serves a further purpose with
guests, since the elaborate ceremony involved in using it impresses
them and raises me greatly in their esteem. All in all a fine gift which
receives from us the highest possible tribute—constant use.

Now as to how I am existing: very well, I am surprised to say.
The crisis has brought out all my craftiness and guile: I am like a
shrewd old fox, keeping one eye on the pursuing hounds and the
other on my vixen and her whelps—back-tracking and scampering,
and snorting a little with pleasure when I squeak through a narrow
one and hear the hounds in the distance, temporarily frustrated and
baying mournfully.

I have developed a fine technique of dealing with the large creditors—those I told you about, which amount to several thousand
dollars in each account. I concluded at the outset I had two choices:
either to beg them for terms and rely on sympathy to get them, or
to snap at them angrily and set the terms myself. I chose the latter
course, and they follow like lambs. For example, I am dealing with
the electrical contractor. I owe him eight thousand dollars. I cannot
pay him. So I write him a letter in which I make certain complaints
about the work. In order to do this I have gone carefully over his
itemized statement and found those discrepancies which occur in
any transaction. Then I ask him what we are going to do about making the job a satisfactory one. I tell him I do not intend to be unreasonable; that as a matter of fact I am concerned lest he be put
to too great an expense in rectifying his mistakes, which are, after
all, likely to occur among the most efficient and conscientious electrical contractors. I ask him to reply as quickly as possible. And I
enclose a check for $1,000, noting as if by afterthought that it is at-
tached, and that I shall pay off the balance in similar installments
each month. The result is interesting. Our correspondence gets so
involved with the bad work I have received that the terms are never
questioned; and once established, *that* account is taken care of much
better than by notes or bank loan or any other method. And so down
the line. They all feed out of my hand, and doff their hats when
they speak to me, and we have so focused their interest that their
principal concern no longer is whether they shall get paid, but
whether I shall in the end be pleased. I pass this information on to
you in case you overextend yourself at Malibu and find yourself in
the fending-off-tradesmen department.

I have taken things away from the [Bob] Roberts office—no task
since there was nothing for them to do—and now I hoard money in
cashier's checks and currency, and deal directly out of pocket. I have
got the [John] Garfield trust deed in my possession, so the ranch is

clear and in a moment of dire necessity I can hock it for an adequate sum. It shall have to be genuine necessity, however, for I am almost superstitious about the place, and shall beg and borrow and steal with great energy before I put it in soak.

Again, our expenses are down so greatly that what money I lay fist upon goes an astonishingly long way. And money *does* drift in. I have one under the counter job which I start tomorrow—only five thousand (how the mighty have fallen!)—but on the other hand only a week's work. I daresay I could come by others if I put feelers out, but I don't intend to do so. Just as I do not wish to hock the ranch, neither do I wish to fall into the trap of getting money by anonymous work in which there is no merit, no satisfaction and no real gain. I have my eye on other goals.

One of the nicest things that has happened is the discovery that I have a reputation outside Hollywood. Although I am as full of vanity and arrogance as the next one, still I had never realized it. I have been approached by two top New York producers, which astounded and delighted me. They appear to have no fear about my name driving the customers away, or how it may affect movie sales. One of them offered me an advance sight unseen on anything I wished to do. I took him up. Lawyers are now framing things, and the deal is set. I have finished a first act even. The second offered an advance for me to dramatize a specific property—a very fine and famous novel— I am vague here because I just don't trust the mails—and I am in the course of taking him up too.[13] The third I turned down, because two projects seemed enough.

You better than most—and certainly better than the gentlemen who have sought my services—know how little I understand about the theatre; you know the six plays I have seen in my life. However I set to work in the long night hours trying to learn. Instead of going to Norman Krasna, Garson Kanin and F. Hugh Herbert, I began an intensive reading of Ibsen, Shaw, Chekhov and the Irish playwrights. First it was stimulating, and secondly it was instructive. Granted the ability to write dialogue and to construct plot, I believe that the most perplexing problem of the theatre—as differentiated from the screen —is that on the screen we are able to show progression of time, action occurring in relation to time, a steady advancement of the story through the use of time by reason of our flexibility and our dissolves; but in a play time moves ahead only as the clock moves through the course of any single act. Thus the progression can no longer be principally a movement through time, as on the screen, but it must be a dramatic movement ahead in terms of events, characters and ideas functioning in the same time element which governs the audience

---

[13] An adaptation of Henry James's *The Turn of the Screw* for George Brandt. The project did not materialize.

from the opening to the end of the act. This, I believe, is the principal difference and the thing I have got to learn.

I cannot tell you how much pleasure it gives me to be writing on something which is mine, something over which I possess complete control, and something which is new to me and fraught with danger and speculation. I am transported back to the time when I was trying to write novels—the same nervous interest, continuing and mounting from day to day; the same wonderment as to whether it is good or whether it stinks; the same trepidation at the thought of failure and the same dreaming of success. My mind is actually *working*—I am on my own—hammering at the doors of an entirely new way of writing. And I must say—whether I win, lose or draw—I have the feeling of living and of pitting myself against the best that others are able to do. I had forgotten how it felt, and it feels good.

Perhaps I should not be as angry as I am against the weaklings, cravens and liars who have succeeded in banning me from motion pictures. For I feel a sense of relief and a sense of buoyancy at no longer being an employee, at no longer being under the absolute necessity of earning, say, $75,000 a year. I'm sure I should never have had the courage—or perhaps one should say the foolhardiness—to have left it voluntarily. My feeling now—as of today, that is, with the hope of succeeding elsewhere still strong in me—that I shall never return to films, that if Metro asked me back tomorrow with all forgiven, I should refuse. Hunger, of course, could in time alter that decision. But for the present it stands.

Well, now, enough! I hope all things go well with you. Cleo and I send you our best, and the children have just risen and started shouting through the house at the discovery of the snow. I shall have to try to keep them quiet until Cleo and Melissa get a little more sleep.

Say hello to my friends and piss on my enemies. And incidentally, no one in town, not even my friends or my agent, knows of my New York deals or of my plans.

Salutations!
DALTON

16. To Bert Allenberg

Lazy T Ranch
Frazier Park, California
February 12, 1948

Dear Bert:

I haven't answered your letter of December 17th rejecting my request for a loan because I was too busy trying to keep alive and hadn't the time for a reply. However since I now want to take up something else with you, I shall touch first upon the money thing.

Your letter shocked me for two reasons: first, it sounded as if you were the one buffeted by fate rather than I; and second, it was not forthright. You stated you couldn't lend me money because of the firm's policy, overlooking the obvious fact that you yourself make that policy, and that three times in the past year Phil [Berg] has specifically asked me if I needed money, has urged me to ask for it any time I did, and has assured me that last year's incident was a temporary expedient invoked at a special time and had no application to me. This was the reason I asked you for a loan. I considered, in view of the above facts, that I was well within my rights in doing so, just as I consider that you were within yours in refusing.

You then stated that "you didn't see where I could find that you had any obligation to make me a loan." Of course you hadn't any such obligation. My letter neither stated nor implied that such an obligation existed. When a man's work has been proscribed, when he has been banished from his profession, he immediately thinks of his family and his children, and he seeks to borrow money to tide him over into some new line of work. He goes to those who have money and who might lend it to him. He asks them for it. He doesn't put it as an obligation. If he is a gentleman he doesn't wish to, just as he doesn't like to have a refusal based upon the denial of an obligation which he had never suggested. What he wants is a painless yes or no.

You stated: "Our obligation is to serve you well which we have done . . ." Since it is you who brought the matter of obligation into discussion, may I also add that it is your obligation to continue to serve me well until the expiration of our contract? What does that involve? It involves getting me employment. Can you do it? It involves collecting moneys due me from the studio. Can you do it? It involves at least collecting your own percentage of what is due me. Can you do it? Of course you can't. Have I complained, or do I now complain, because you are incapable of performing your functions? I have not and do not intend to.

The obligations, as they turn out, are quite the reverse of what you have stated them to be: i.e., I am obliged to take over your functions and to serve you as well as I can. It is my obligation to find work for myself in order that I may live. It is my obligation to fight a lawsuit for recovery from the studio and to finance court costs out of my own pocket. Once recovery has has been made, it is my obligation to pay you ten percent of the contract-settlement sum. I do not complain about this. I simply state it, so that you may understand the facts as they are, and not confuse my situation with your own.

You continue, in reference to your obligations: ". . . and to stand by your side in any fight you may be involved in whether we are sympathetic to it or not." Now I am truly shocked at the fundamental immorality of this statement.

If you believe my suit against Metro is a just one, then you certainly should be sympathetic to it and you should stand by my side, even if only in spirit as at present. But if you believe it to be an unjust suit, then you should oppose it. This is only sound human honesty—and good business ethics into the bargain. I would not want you associated with me in any enterprise to which you were unsympathetic because such association would be worthless to me and degrading to you. I think we should clearly understand this, and that you should decide at once whether you are sympathetic or unsympathetic to my present civil suit against Metro.

Now none of the foregoing has anything to do with a fresh effort to get money out of you. That project was finished with the receipt of your letter, and I do not intend to reopen it. I have commented on the letter itself because of my feeling that our relationship is such that you owed me a short and merciful "no" rather than an evasive and pitiful justification of the "no."

Now to the real purpose of this letter: will you give me a release from our present contract, covered by a stipulation to be drawn up by Martin Gang to the effect that you are to share in ten percent of any money derived from a settlement of my Metro contract after deduction of legal fees? I frankly do not see why you are entitled to share in moneys when the entire burden of collection devolves upon me, but I daresay it is legal and I am willing to accept it.

I have three principal reasons for suggesting a dissolution of our contract:

First: I feel that you regard the whole studio situation as hopeless, and have been intimidated by the ferocious onrush of fascism in this country—I use the term advisedly, for its parallel can be found in prewar Germany in precisely such cases as my own. I base this estimate of your reaction on what you told X about lending me money. This showed me clearly that you consider any written connection with me to be dangerous, and that you view my situation as hopeless. This, I think, would disqualify you for any really aggressive work in my behalf. And in the years to come, I shall really need aggressive work.

Second: During the two months I have been idle, you have made no effort of any kind to secure me work or money out of other lines of writing. I consider this indicative of your hopeless attitude. Mrs. MeKeogh in New York has, in the meanwhile, been working very hard, and has found two top producers who are willing to advance money sight-unseen on any play by me about any subject I choose. These deals are presently being concluded. The advances are, I may add, far more generous than the minimum. Frankly, I feel that Mrs. McKeogh should receive all the fees resulting from her initiative— initiative taken at a time when it was badly needed by me and very difficult for her. That is the kind of representation I shall need in the future—someone who feels that my career is beginning rather than ending, someone who has the courage to go out and find people who will openly purchase my work, under my own name, without subterfuges of any kind.

Third: in terms of Hollywood work—originals, and such—I feel that you are the finest agents an established writer can have. But I do not feel that you are equipped to handle unknowns such as I shall be. If I re-enter the Hollywood lists, it will be as a new man with a new name, and in the beginning my stuff will command small prices, will be sold on small lots and to small producers. There will necessarily have to be a lot of chiseling and really petty stuff on the part of the agent who handles my material, and you people can't afford to do that, and haven't the taste for it if you could.

Let me, to recapitulate, make myself perfectly clear. I do not make this suggestion out of pique. I do not make it out of ill will or resentment. You know my opinion of you too well for it to be reiterated here. I simply feel that in this new situation my best interests will be served by a severance of our relationship. Perhaps you will feel so too. If not, we can have a fuller discussion of it. But please let me know at once what your reactions are.

Cordially,
DALTON TRUMBO

17. To Harry Tugend

Lazy T Ranch
Frazier Park, California
February 18, 1948

Dear Harry:

I have received your letter and read it with the liveliest interest.[14] I thought it rather loud and more than ordinarily witless, but to deny you those qualities would be to silence you altogether; and that, for constitutional reasons alone, I should not like to see happen. I can't clearly make out whether your main quarrel is with me or the Mother Tongue, you have damaged us both almost beyond repair.

Your questions about my finances would, I believe, be perfectly proper had I requested credit arrangements permitting me to retain my voting status while deferring payment of dues. Since I made no such request, you exceed your treasurer's authority in propounding them. If, however, you pose them merely as an inquisitive citizen, I'm sure we can arrange for you to browse through my accounts and my wife's wardrobe whenever you find that time. In relation to your interest in the latter, I think a sense of delicacy and a consideration of your own excitable nature might indicate it were wiser for you to examine only the outer garments.

When I cease living on borrowed capital, which I hope shall be soon, and manage a little income of my own in some other field, be assured I shall pay my dues. And when and if I recover from Metro on my voided contract, I shall reimburse the membership—always remember it is the membership, Harry, and not the board—for my proportionate share of the expenses of the amicus curiae brief.

I was temporarily saddened to learn that I am unloved in your set. But fuller consideration persuaded me that not even J. Parnell Thomas can accuse me of any act which could possibly merit your esteem. Since I do not intend to alter my behavior in the future, I'm afraid you'll just have to go on hating.

Cordially,
DALTON TRUMBO

[14] Tugend had responded hotly to Trumbo's letter of February 2 concerning non-payment of Guild dues, stating that Trumbo had been billed *before* the HUAC hearings and therefore before financial difficulties had set in. Tugend made several allusions to Trumbo's squandering wealth on furs for Mrs. Trumbo; hence this angry reply.

18. To William Denels

Lazy T Ranch
Frazier Park, California
February 27, 1948

Dear Bill Denels:

You are probably the worst businessman in the world. I don't mind, but I think you should know it. On the other hand, I should be grateful for your slothfulness, for otherwise I would never have managed to get into you as substantially as I have. When you have a man on the hook as solidly as I have you, you can afford to insult him occasionally.

Herewith a few items I should like to hear from you about whenever you can distract your attention from liquor, women and screwing the public. To wit:

1. I haven't the faintest idea what I owe you. I am now taking care of all accounts myself, which means bills should no longer be sent to the Roberts office. Will you, for the sake of my own peace of mind and curiosity, send me an itemized statement of all swindles you have thus far perpetrated upon me, together with cost of same, plus a notation of what I have paid against same, plus the monthly date on which that hundred bucks is due?

2. Per your instructions, I have paid the piano off in full, for which you should be both surprised and grateful. Would you now mind shoving this lovely instrument up your ass? It is only a spinet size, and should fit there comfortably.

3. The sink arrived and has been installed. Surprisingly enough, it works.

4. The plumber, however, could not install the garbage disposal system. For one thing, it requires about ten feet of electrical cable to achieve a connection. Will you, therefore, send a henchman up to install and connect it, or shall I have to write the manufacturer and file a bill of complaint against you?

5. Upon two different occasions you took note of the space measurements in which the sink was to fit, and were to send us two cabinets to go on either side of it, making the unit complete. Yet when your men arrived with the sink and I asked them where the cabinets [were], they just looked dreamy and shrugged and made gestures toward the sky. The present installation is inconvenient as hell, because water drips to the floor through the cracks on either side of the sink installation. Therefore I give you the measurements again: total space available for sink and two side cabinets or whatever you call them—91 ⅞ inches. I think a total of 92 inches can be fitted in. Therefore deduct length of sink from total available space, divide result by two, and you have the size of the two cabi-

nets we want installed. Let the henchman who comes to install the garbage disposal also bring the cabinets.

6. Now for the stinger: why don't you send me the total cost (itemized) of the Gibson stove, the 50 or 60-gallon water heater and the electric griddle? Calculate thereon the least sum you will take down for the three, plus the least monthly sum which the payments would add to my hundred buck installment. Then we shall begin dickering.

7. Treat me nicely, for I shall soon have lots of money, and I intend to equip six guest apartments up here, and I shall remember merchants who behaved handsomely during my period of exile, and I shall discriminate against those who in any way betrayed concern. After all, isn't my friendship worth more than money? No. You are quite right.

In Christ's name,
DALTON TRUMBO

19. To Elsie McKeogh

Lazy T Ranch
Frazier Park, California
March 2, 1948

Dear Elsie:

This thing grows too complicated. You probably by now have the clauses in my contract relating to plays. I have just talked to my lawyer. I have the right to write plays when on leave of absence; but being presently under suspension, I do not have that right. It is inadvisable to ask Metro for a leave of absence from the point of view of my civil case against them, which will come up here in Federal Court in the next two months. I am asking for declaratory relief.

It would, it seems to me, be very simple to sign a contract with Sabinson [15] and receive an advance from him, based upon the written understanding that I would do the work, i.e., write the play as soon as I receive a leave of absence from Metro. I am confident that this would delay nothing in terms of getting the play done. But if Mr. Sabinson feels it would, and if he insists upon a reiteration from Metro of the terms of their contract, or if he wished his attorneys in any way to get in touch with Metro, then I cannot permit it, and we shall have to call things off.

---

[15] For *The Biggest Thief in Town:* $1,000 upon signing and $1,000 upon agreement to make revisions; the producers would then have six months to produce the play; other terms of the basic minimum agreement with the Dramatists' Guild of the Authors' League of America.

In any event, I shall have to put the play temporarily aside and get a little money together before I continue work on it. It should not, incidentally, be known that I am working on it. It can, of course, be known wherever necessary that I am going to do a play for Mr. S. or anyone else who contracts for one, as soon as I am legally able.

The trial has been postponed until about May 1st.[16] I am, however, coming east in a couple of weeks to talk in Boston, and at Dartmouth and Yale. It may be that I shall be able then to come on to New York and discuss this personally with you, which would be better. I'll let you know. But for the present, the hideous complexities of trying to do a piece of work and get money for it are too great.

Regards,
DALTON

20. To Hy Kraft[17]

Lazy T Ranch
Frazier Park, California
March 3, 1948

Dear buddy-pal:

An explosive thought has just occurred to Cleo and me. March heralds your wedding anniversary. And the Hunters'.[18] And ours. Why not, therefore, a party this Saturday night? Cleo and I will be in town for the martyrdom dinner; and a party the following evening would take the taste of charity out of our mouths. I shall be leaving about the 20th for a ten-day series of important public pronounce-

[16] The two court cases mentioned in this letter should not be confused as one. In the first paragraph Trumbo refers to his civil suit against Metro-Goldwyn-Mayer Studios and in the final paragraph to his forthcoming trial for contempt of Congress.

[17] Hy Kraft, a friend of Trumbo's for many years, is both a screen writer (blacklisted) and a playwright, probably best known for his Broadway success, *Cafe Crown*.

[18] Ian McLelland Hunter and his wife, Alice, are close friends and correspondents in subsequent sections. Hunter was a prolific screen writer whose last pre-blacklist credit was *Roman Holiday,* for which he received an Academy Award. During the blacklist he became the first editor of the *Diners' Club News,* collaborated with Ring Lardner, Jr., on the *Robin Hood* and *Lancelot* TV series, and became a studio executive in England. His post-blacklist work includes the 1964 Bert Lahr musical *Foxy* (with Ring Lardner, Jr.), the two-hour ABC television special, *Dr. Jekyll and Mr. Hyde,* which won the Mystery Writers' Award for 1969, and *A Dream of Kings,* starring Tony Quinn.

The other friends mentioned in this letter have been previously identified.

ments; and thereafter the trial will occur, and this appears a fine time for a bust.

We have here an enormous smoked turkey which we will bring. We have a handsome tenderized ham which we shall bring. Will or shall? Anyhow, we are also going to bring the liquor and the works. I'll do the cooking. It will give us all a feeling of well-being.

Now if there are reasons why it can't be at your house, could you not try the Butlers and the Lardners to see if their mansions are available? For ourselves we should like to see the Butlers, Hunters, Lardners, Trivers, Roberts and Katz's. And for yourselves, whomever you like. Who or whom?

Now obviously there will be no sense in you answering this note, because we shall be in town by the time your answer could come. Therefore we shall bring the booty in for consumption, hoping that if your household can't accommodate us, you will have found someone else's that will.

Voilà! Alors! Celebrando! Yours in the spirit of William Vaughn Moody,

TRUMBO

21. To Elsie McKeogh

Lazy T Ranch
Frazier Park, California
March 8, 1948

Dear Elsie:

Here is the situation. I have received no earned money since September 18. Metro suspended me five days before $61,000 was due me for work turned in. They refused to pay this sum. I had certain accounts and taxes which I planned to pay from this sum.[19] I have since my suspension paid off some $10,000 in debts, spent $7,500 on the Washington case, stood our family expenses and those of my numerous dependents. I am now nearing the end of my resources.

[19] To summarize the frequently mentioned suit against Metro: Because *Angel's Flight* was a rush job, Trumbo had elected the $75,000 flat payment instead of the usual $3,000 a week. He had been paid $14,000 at the time of suspension. Since the first draft script was in its final stages, Trumbo argued that he was owed a balance of $61,000 for that screenplay alone, not to mention the fact that he held a $3,000 a week irrevocable contract until 1950. It should be added that Metro was forced to suspend, rather than fire, Trumbo, because of the fact that the charges against him were moral but there was no morals clause in his contract. For further details of the various suits filed by the Hollywood Ten and their outcomes, see #35, p. 142.

I feel there is no hazard in Mr. Sabinson drawing up a contract with me on the terms outlined, namely $1,000 immediately, $1,000 upon agreement on changes, subject of course to the stipulation that I shall violate no part of my Metro contract. Mr. Katz, my attorney, is so confident of the legality of such a procedure that he will advance me $2,000 tomorrow and dispose of the play to Herman Shumlin. This I would not do until you and I had discussed it. But if I have to wait two or three more weeks while legalities are being discussed and papers drawn, I shall be obliged to take the Katz offer. I do not mean this in ill temper; but I simply must have some money, and I see no reason why, if Mr. Sabinson is willing to make a deal with me at all, he can't, upon my assuming responsibility for the legality of my action, forward the first $1,000 at once while we straighten the rest out. It will, I promise you, be a very simple matter.

Perhaps showing him this letter, which is a forthright statement of my position and an honest one, might clarify the situation in his mind and break the dam of negotiations which keeps him from paying me and me from working.

Incidentally, is there any chance, in your opinion, of getting an advance out of Lippincott on a novel to be delivered one year from date?

Cordially,
DALTON

22. To Philip Berg

Lazy T Ranch
Frazier Park, California
March 8, 1948

Dear Phil:

Here is the situation, and I'll try to explain it without rhetoric. It is just ten days short of six months since I received my last check from Metro. During that time I have managed to pay off $9,954 in debts; I have laid out slightly over $7,500 on the Washington case; I have managed to care for my dependents (two groups) [20] plus my own family at 75% reduction in living costs accomplished by no servants, no spending, no rent (and me doing the cooking!).

I have held off the big and menacing accounts referred to in my

[20] Trumbo refers to his mother, Maud Trumbo, and to Mrs. Trumbo's mother, Elizabeth Fincher, both widows.

money letter to Bob [Coryell] [21] very nicely. But I have not been able properly to attend to the small accounts which are many. In the last week I have discovered that no bank will lend on my cars, although they are both late models and in excellent condition; that no bank or insurance company will lend a penny on my ranch, although it is clear. I cannot accept money for work while presently under suspension, and technically I cannot even work.

There is simply no way I can get money unless it is by borrowing; and no one will lend to me because the publicity has, apparently, placed me outside the pale. My ranch represents an investment of $80,000, which figure is after 6% annual depreciation for the last seven or eight years. My furniture and equipment, as appraised on July 16, 1946, by the United Appraisal Company, stands at $56,544 reproductive value, or $52,126 total sound value. Both ranch and contents are all clear, paid for, mine. Yet I cannot raise a dime on anything.

I enclose, just that you may see my situation clearly, an itemized list of my open accounts long past due. If these people should ever get impatient, which they give natural signs of doing now, they could not only snowball me under with small suits; but they could, if they had any idea of my clear assets, throw me quickly into involuntary bankruptcy which would, of course, accomplish my complete ruin.[22]

---

[21] On March 1, 1948 Trumbo wrote Coryell at Berg-Allenberg saying, "Those Berg and Allenberg are wonderful! Here I am, flat on my ass—a 'hold' on my bank account invalidating checks I sent out last week to creditors—arranging to borrow on one car and sell another—trying to work out a mortgage on the ranch in order to save the $80,000 I have in it—and Phil and Bert want me to drop by for a nice cozy chat! Man, I haven't got time to talk about anything but money, and unless that's what's on their minds (which I know it ain't), we'll have to defer conversations until I put out the fire these boys are setting under my bottom."

[22] Shortly after his marriage, Trumbo had applied for relief under Section 77-B of the Federal Bankruptcy Act, a procedure which enabled financially troubled corporations to enjoin their creditors from legal action for a stipulated period of corporate reorganization, after which the debts were paid or the corporation was thrown into involuntary bankruptcy. A few days after he had appeared on the stand before the Thomas Committee, the following item appeared in the Los Angeles *Daily News* (October 31, 1947):

All this [HUAC hearing and contempt charges] seems odd in the light of what happened here in [*sic*] August 2, 1938. Trumbo on that date appeared in bankruptcy court and petitioned for relief from his creditors. He owed $10,593 to a host of merchants for food, furniture and what not.

He was advised that for approximately $35 he could declare himself bankrupt, pay his creditors a fraction on the dollar and get a fresh start. It was, he was told, *standard practice.* "No," said Trumbo, "I want to pay *them off in full.*" He merely wanted them not to bother him at the moment so he could work.

Thereafter a stream of checks came into the bankruptcy office, and in about a year he *paid every cent* of the $10,593.

Now what does a man do in a situation in which nothing he possesses has any value? His assets will not secure him a loan; his suit against Metro cannot be hypothecated, although it is popularly presumed to be a good one; his future work is worthless as security; he has been forever banned from the profession for which he has trained himself; he cannot accept money from any other form of writing so long as he is under suspension; and he cannot, technically, write at all. Just what does he do?

What I should like to do is to ask you to pay these attached accounts—with none of the money going to me—just to issue checks for them all, since I have closed my bank account for safety's sake—and to trust me to repay you. I am in town today, but I want you to have time to digest this, and shall call tomorrow for an appointment. I literally know of nothing else to do.

Regards,
DALTON

23. To Elsie McKeogh

Lazy T Ranch
Frazier Park, California
March 11, 1948

Dear Elsie:

I have just received a copy of the letter Miss Brown of the [Martin] Gang office sent you relative to the contract. First, let me explain who everybody is. The firm of Gang, Kopp & Tyre, . . . of which Miss Brown is a member, represents me in my civil suit against Metro. Charles Katz . . . is my friend and one of the attorneys representing us in the criminal case in Washington.

Now: I was alarmed by Miss Brown's letter which, while stating the cold legal facts, did not present them in any way advantageous to me. I have therefore asked Gang to send you another letter explaining a clear and obvious legal point: that I have the full right to accept advances at this moment against any kind of work to be done in the future, at such a time as it is legal for me to do the work. This can be stipulated in any advance, and can enable me to draw advance moneys. I take full responsibility for this being the legal truth of the matter.

Second: we are now making application to Metro for sixty days

---

Hugh Dickson, referee in bankruptcy, doesn't know whether Trumbo is a Communist either, but he has a high regard for him. *As far as he knows,* this is the only case on record where this has happened.

leave of absence.[23] This would enable me legally to write and present the play to Mr. Sabinson during that period, or to present it to him even after the expiration of the leave of absence period. If it is not granted, I shall not presently be able to offer Mr. Sabinson a completed play until such time as it has legal clearance. My civil suit will come up within six weeks, and should resolve this problem. Criminal case still as of the last time I informed you.

Third: I have a deadline of the most urgent necessity: March 17th. If there is any advance forthcoming on the play, I simply must have it by that time, even though the legal papers are not completed.

Yours,
DALTON

24. Extract of a letter to Charles Katz

Lazy T Ranch
Frazier Park, California
March 29, 1948

One more thing: I have written an original screenplay, and it hits the market this week. I want this to be the darkest kind of secret between us, not only so that Metro won't discover this violation of their contract, but also to protect the guy under whose name it is being sent out, since the faintest rumor might harm his career in the sense that whatever good work he has done in the past or might [do] in the future could, by such rumor, be attributed to me, hence spoiling his own reputation. I think this thing will sell: I know it would under my own name; but there are slip-ups, and there is always the chance it won't. Anyway, the possibility of it selling throws me into a fury when I think of slipping into the paws of good old X for lack of time.[24]

---

[23] The leave was ultimately granted by Metro; however, there was considerable difficulty in drafting a suitable agreement, and Trumbo, although he was advanced his first $1,000, was prevented from signing with Sabinson until August of 1948.

[24] X is identified in the following letter (#26) to Martin Gang, Trumbo's first lawyer in the civil suit against Metro. Gang, as attorney for Berg-Allenberg, had negotiated the Trumbo MGM contract.

25. To Martin Gang (probably never sent)

Lazy T Ranch
Frazier Park, California
March 29, 1948

Dear Martin:

I have just received the terms under which Jack Nerdrum has finally been able to negotiate a loan. The lender is X, a vice-president of the _____ bank . . . I am to put up the ranch ($80,000) plus its furnishings and equipment as itemized in the inventory ($52,000), plus certain items which X saw on his inspection of the place and added to the inventory without consulting me, such as, for example, my childrens' saddle blankets. I am to receive $12,500, minus $1,250 bonus, minus $750 interest in advance, minus surveyor's fees, minus costs. In other words, everything I own in the world, everything which spells any kind of security for my family, is to be put into the hands of a deceitful and avaricious man: and I must pay it all back in three years.

Nerdrum has done the best he can; and so also, I presume, has Phil Berg. Phil has explained to me that it is against his business interests and not "compatible with his principles" for any money to pass from him to me, whether by direct loan, by secured loan or mortgage, or by his guaranty of my note. It is not, however, against either his business interests or his principles for money to pass from me to him, such as his percentage of the sum I manage ultimately to collect from Metro, or of any other sums I may earn during the life of his contract with me.

Even isolated as I am from the normal courtesies and considerations of what we call civilized society, I am *not* going to take the X loan, for the man is dishonest and would ultimately destroy me. I am, rather, going to sell things on the streets piece by piece before permitting this particular vulture to fatten on me. For this purpose, incidentally, I wish you would secure for me the name of a respectable pawnbroker, since I have a watch and one or two items of my wife's which I want to pledge while in town to stall off by small payments certain creditors who must be appeased by Thursday morning, which is the first of the month.

I have thought this whole matter over for three days, and I have come to definite conclusions. On the one hand I have in my possession a home and furnishings and equipment in the sum of about $140,000. They are clear, and represent security to me. I stand in immediate danger of losing them for want of a small sum of cash. On the other hand, I have a suit against Metro which *may* bring me a net sum of, say, $100,000. But this is only a possibility. I must therefore balance the positive possession against the possible acquisition. I find real and present value only in the positive possession.

Therefore, if the question should arise—and it does arise now, this moment—whether in an emergency I should risk the positive possession or the possible acquisition, good sense indicates I should retain the positive and sacrifice the possible.

Therefore the course by which I stand to lose least is as follows: you mentioned vague murmurs from Metro about why not settle matters. Let us, therefore, instead of going about our depositions, spend our time with Mr. Selvin discussing an immediate settlement. The total sum of the possible acquisition does not interest me, so long as it serves to protect the positive possession. I am therefore willing to settle the whole matter for $25,000 which, after deduction and costs, will leave me with sufficient to save what I now have and start out on a new career. The *only* important thing is immediate security and peace of mind for work: for with them, I can, under a half a dozen names, earn as much money as a victory in the suit would deliver into my hands.

Let us, then, at our luncheon tomorrow, go over the specifics of how to accomplish this as quickly as possible. I realize I must be a most difficult client to you, but then when you enter into relationship with a man who corrupts the screen with subversion, who plots to overthrow his government, who acts constantly as the agent for a foreign power (I *do* wish they'd pay off!)—what can you expect?

Ad astra per aspera!
DALTON

26. To Cleo Trumbo

Washington, D.C.
Friday, May 7, 1948

Dear Cleo:

I know my non-letter writing habit must be irritating. But literally, there is so much to write that I cannot think of where to start, and I am unable to write it sketchily; and I have been busy and under constant pressure, from seven or eight in the morning until three or four the next. But that, fortunately, is practically all over. I have had many nice experiences, and a few bad ones.

It is a curious thing, this business I have been through.[25] As you get into it, you begin to disassociate yourself from it. You are there, in that chair, before that tribunal, only in body. The rest of you has

[25] Written from Washington, D.C., at the time of the contempt of Congress trial. On May 21, 1948, Trumbo was found guilty on two charges of contempt of Congress, a misdemeanor, fined $1,000 and sentenced to one year in prison.

become remote. You watch the stately, formal little dance of legality as if it were someone else involved. You become so scornful of it you can no longer take it seriously. So all that is left is a detached interest, polite and very cool.

I am told—and I was pleased to hear it—that during the fiercest denunciation of me in that room, and during the hottest defense of me, I gave no visible reaction at all. I even began to draw friendly comments from the Washington press, which is a little unbelievable. In a word, I have observed everything with interest, and have not once, either alone or with others, permitted my emotions the slightest outlet. And this is good. It is the way I hoped to do it.

As you can see from the other letters, I don't know exactly when I shall be home. I shall have to return for one hour—flying both ways in a day and a half—for sentence. But that is some time away. There is absolutely no doubt about our case as far as appeal goes. Rex [26] tells me, in a nice letter, that he has money and you are to call on him if you need anything. And I tell you that I have been the lonesomest man in America during these past ten days, staring with open envy at men on the streets and in railroad stations who have their wives at their side, and a child or two in tow.

They tell me you looked wonderful at the Butlers' house the night you were there. I shall return as quickly as the good Lord permits to verify this for myself.

All love,
TRUMBO

27. To Charles Katz

Lazy T Ranch
Frazier Park, California
May 29, 1948

Dear Charley:

Well, this is the letter I've been holding out on and hating to write, mainly because I don't like to bite friends. But once into it, I'll bang away to my point. As you know, I mortgaged the ranch, paid up every penny in current debts I owed, left enough for Cleo and the kids and my mother and my mother-in-law during the Washington siege: and now have nothing left.

I turned down—rashly, I suppose—another black market venture,

[26] J. C. Rex Cole, Trumbo's newly appointed business manager and financial adviser. He quickly negotiated a $10,000 mortgage on the ranch on favorable terms.

because I see no profit in putting in time and whatever talent I have on such projects, when I feel that my big gamble and my main chance lies in the play, which simply must be finished by the end of June if it is to make Lee's proposed mid-September opening date. So I've decided, if possible, to do the work on borrowed money rather than earned, to get enough to last through September. After that, if the play's a flop and the Metro suit doesn't pay off, I'll simply liquidate, pay off and start over again. If either of the above two hit, then of course I'll have no trouble paying off.

The point is: I'm asking you for two thousand. I don't like to do it, because goddam it, a man who's put in the time you have for free shouldn't be asked to pay the client's grocery bill in addition. If you can't do it, the hell with it, no explanations are necessary. And if you can do it, my affection for you will not increase one degree, because it can't.

When the play's done, I want you up for a reading. . . . I know a fella in Bakersfield wants to go in contempt of something if he can get a good lawyer. Should I recommend you?

Life here is good. It's nice to be back on fatback and chickory after that rich eastern food. Only trouble is, how the hell do you break kids from eating red clay?

Yours in Marx, Engels, Lenin,
Stalin,
D.T.

28. To Charles Katz

Lazy T Ranch
Frazier Park, California
June 3, 1948

Dear Charley:

I lied to you.

I said that even if you were able to assist me, it would be impossible for me to like you more for it. Yet as the rich organ tones of your letter seeped through my consciousness, I felt myself suffused with something which upon analysis proved to be the increased affection for you that I had sworn was impossible.

It seems incredible that I could be so base, but there it is. I am corruptible. I can be bought. It's just as I've often said to Cleo (who, womanlike, has pretended not to understand what I meant)—"My dear, that I love you is beyond question. But it's the most deplorable kind of nonsense to contend that I couldn't love you a little more if you had a little more."

I enclose the delightful piece of paper you sent me, autographed by us both as a mark of our esteem. I also have a scheme by which you, who have upon several occasions snatched the Lazy T from the grip of my creditors, might at last see that troublesome piece of real estate.

I am finishing the play sometime between the 14th and the 20th of this month, and shall be in the mood for a let-down. I will let you know a week in advance, and we two old foxes shall foregather here with our vixens and their whelps and read it aloud for the first time. I think it goes well: but if not well, then as Christ is my witness it goes fast.

Shabbily,
D.T.

29. Extract of a letter to Katie Roberts (Mrs. Robert B.)

June 6, 1948

Yep. Second act already finished, and I'm into the third act like a hungry leopard in pursuit of a striped-assed ape. My aunt in Bakersfield is typing it, and the kids stand by in shifts to remove cigarette butts from the study.

I read the [Hollywood] box office is down. What a shame! I hear writers aren't working. That's terrible! I don't see why all these people who are in trouble don't retire to a nice ranch somewhere and live on borrowed money and write plays. It's an extremely pleasant life, if the fools could only be made to see it.

Joseph and Mary be with you!
TRUMBO

30. Extract of a note to Martin Gang

Lazy T Ranch
Frazier Park, California
June 6, 1948

Up here in the breath-taking mountain spring, I can but feel a twinge of sympathy for all you money-grubbing bastards in Hollywood as you struggle against falling box office and recalcitrant studio treasuries. It's much simpler to borrow money and live graciously.

Joseph and Mary attend you!
DALTON

31. To Lee Sabinson

Lazy T Ranch
Frazier Park, California
July 1, 1948

Dear Lee:

I finished the play approximately when I indicated to you in my last note I would. Then I took it into town and read it to three friends whose judgment I value highly.[27] They felt the first act and a half was superb, and the second act and a half terrible. I had made the unforgivable error of shifting all emphasis, midway in the play, from the undertaker, his family and his friends to the dead magnate [Troybalt] and his retinue. The result was a disastrous dichotomy of feeling, and a complete letdown of interest. What is essentially a humane comedy turned at its halfway point into an angry, heavy-handed revelation of Troybalt in relation to those about him. The structure, however, is well conceived and dramatically sound, and I am now engaged in what is really the pleasant and not too difficult task of returning the last half of the play to the people to whom it belongs. I think it will be good, and that two more weeks will complete the job.

You may wonder why I didn't send the completed piece on to you. I think I was right in not doing so. Your enthusiasm is very important to me, and to send you something which was not basically right would necessarily diminish your enthusiasm. Furthermore, the distance between us would have greatly aggravated and complicated the problem of correcting the errors. In a word, I want you to think well of me, and with confidence; and some of that would have been destroyed had you witnessed the alarming botch I had contrived. Now I feel good about it, and will send the next version directly on to you, by-passing local criticism, because I am confident that the conception will be right.

Regards,
DALTON

[27] Before *The Biggest Thief in Town* was completed, Trumbo had held several of these reading sessions and received criticism from Charles Katz, Ring Lardner, Jr., Hy Kraft, Paul Trivers, Hugo Butler, Bob Roberts, and Ian Hunter.

32. To Elsie McKeogh

Lazy T Ranch
Frazier Park, California
July 1, 1948

Dear Elsie:

Enclosed copy of letter to Sabinson is self-explanatory.

The Gang office has arrived at a tentative agreement with Metro, not yet signed, which would, from March 15th onward until (a) dissolution of my contract, (b) decision by a court of law, or (c) my return to work under the contract, permit me to write novels, plays, short stories, without prejudice to my contract or to any legal action deriving therefrom, subject only to Metro's natural right to first refusal, or, in case of a play, to participate in financing. This arrangement would untie my hands and permit me once more to earn a living, and I am going to town tomorrow to discuss it more fully and perhaps to conclude the business. But in any event, a successful conclusion is now assured, and we shall be able to sign with Sabinson in the near future. You might explain the above to him.

Cretin that I am, I have lost the royalty statement—not the one which paid off in stamps, but the one which had a check, as I recall it, for fourteen bucks or thereabouts. I can't find it anywhere, so you might check at your bank to see if a forger has risked twenty years to swindle me out of so small a sum.

The kids are at camp, praise God, and life here is conducive to work.

Regards,
DALTON

3.
"Nameless, Faceless, Voiceless"

In an article for the May 4, 1957, *Nation,* titled "Blacklist=Black Market," Trumbo wrote:

> It is not alone the loss of income or of property that hurts: the more terrible wound is the loss of a profession to which one's entire life has been dedicated. A director must have the facilities of a studio: denied them, he sells real estate. A violinist must appear in person for the concert: barred from admittance, he becomes a milkman and practices six hours a day against the unrevealed time when his music once more may be heard. The actor's physical personality, which is his greatest asset, becomes his supreme curse under the blacklist; he must be seen, and when the sight of him is prohibited he becomes a carpenter, an insurance salesman, a barber.
>
> A writer is more fortunate. Give him nothing more than paper, a pencil and a nice clean cell, and he's in business. Dante, Cervantes, Rousseau, Voltaire, Ben Jonson, Milton, Defoe, Bunyan, Hugo, Zola and a score of others have long since proved that in jail or out, writing under their own names or some one else's or a pseudonym or anonymously, writers will write; and that having written, they will find an audience. Only fools with no knowledge of history and bureaucrats with no knowledge of literature are stupid enough to think otherwise.
>
> And so it chanced in Hollywood that each blacklisted writer, after swiftly describing that long parabola from the heart of the motion-picture industry to a small house in a low-rent district, picked himself up, dusted his trousers, anointed his abrasions, looked around for a ream of clean white paper and something to deface it with, and began to write. Through secret channels, and by means so cunning they may never be revealed, what he wrote was passed along until finally it appeared on a producer's desk, and the producer looked upon it and found it good, and moneys were paid, and the writer's children began contentedly to eat. Thus the black market.

Trumbo had spent over thirteen years practicing and mastering a craft. Now he needed money badly. In the first place, he had inestimable legal fees: the civil suit against Metro was pending; and in the spring of 1948 he was tried in Washington, D.C., convicted and sentenced to a $1,000 fine and a year in prison; he remained free on bail during the processes of appeal and refusal of the Supreme Court to review the case on April 10, 1950. Secondly, he had a family to support and to see through the inevitable prison term. For all his professed hopes of building a reputation in a new form of writing, Trumbo naturally turned back to what he was sure he could do.

Work, however, was not so easy as it had been in the days when Trumbo had commanded $3,000 a week: for one thing, as he wrote a friend in September of 1948, "It simply requires that I work three times as fast for about one-fifth of my former price"; for another, the cautiousness, craftiness, and secrecy requisite to work in the black market demanded almost as much energy and art as the writing itself. While the letters, tracing Trumbo's career from his early black market activities to his imprisonment, depict the hazardous demands of "bootleg" writing, they also suggest that Trumbo, whose whole career had been charged with drama, rather enjoyed the intricacy and intrigue of his professional maneuvers.

1. Extract of a letter to Bob Coryell at Berg-Allenberg

Lazy T Ranch
Frazier Park, California
July 17, 1948

Second: I'm again broke as a bankrupt's bastard. I have stayed out of the black market because I wanted to get the play done. With it finished, I am sniffing about. Do any of your clients have a quick polish job or a sick script they'd like to have a coat of rouge put on? I'm their boy. I'd hate to take a project from scratch for the kind of money they're paying but I presume I'd even do that if I had to. Anyhow, I thought you might have an idea.

2. Extract of a letter to an unidentified correspondent addressed simply as "Beloved friend"

Lazy T Ranch
Frazier Park, California
July 17, 1948

Things go well. The trout jump. Melissa swears. Cleo is thirty-two years old today. And we're all terribly glad we're Methodists.

3. To George Willner

Lazy T Ranch
Frazier Park, California
July 17, 1948

Dear George:[1]

I am broke as a bankrupt's bastard. I am finishing a play in the next five or six days, and then I shall be on the hunt for a little black market money. . . .

I only want a few thousand—although naturally I would take a handsome sum if possible. Basically, I want a polish job—or a story that's well figured out—or at least that a producer knows what he needs. I'd like a sick script with an early shooting date—you know.

I'm terribly anxious to arrange something, because I am wanted in New York on the Wallace campaign, and hope to spend all of September and October there—but must needs finance the home folks, etc., etc. If the play's any good, we'll put it on at the same time.

This deal would have to be darker than dark—nothing in writing, no correspondence, toilet-meetings, etc. I shall be in town probably Friday, Saturday, Sunday and Monday—the 23rd to the 26th. On one of these days I'll get in touch with you, and see if you have any prospects, or if you think it possible.

Destroy this letter, too. Too goddam many things are getting subpoenaed these days. And mention it, when you solicit, as darkly and roundaboutly as possible—even in your own cozy little agency.

Aside from this, how the hell are you? I hear it's very chilly for anti-fascists down there.

Love————DT

4. To Frank Butler

Lazy T Ranch
Frazier Park, California
July 17, 1948

Dear Frank:

Things are awfully broke up here at the moment and I am writing like a striped-assed ape. But we are coming down soon to see you.

We hear with regret that it took a good shaking up to convince you you'd made too much money for Paramount, and sufficient for

[1] A Hollywood agent who was to handle a large number of Trumbo's early black market enterprises. Willner himself was later called before the Committee and blacklisted.

yourself, and should slow down.[2] It will add twenty years to your life and is, in reality, a great stroke of fortune.

With both of us at least temporarily banned from the movie business, we can look forward to peaceful old ages in this pleasanter land. We shall sit through the summer evenings on the front porch —you with your *London Times* and I with my *Pravda*—in comfortable disagreement on every subject in the world save our respect for each other and our admiration of our wives.

Affectionately,
DALTON

5. To George Willner

Lazy T Ranch
Frazier Park, California
October 2, 1948

Dear George:

Those fellows are hooked, I think. They have a good script, and they appear to respect me.[3] The final draft goes to them in the same mail that this letter goes to you. Which brings up the matter of credit. They are willing for A——————— B———— to have credit, and I think he should take it. It will be no great shakes, but it will be a good production of its kind, and might lead to better things. The KB[4] say that the writer who gets credit on it will go out and get himself $2,500 a week as a result. I doubt their optimism, but it might be a good idea to introduce your boy to them, and have him take the credit.

In relation with the above, I have sent with the script a letter asking them to turn the final payment over to you immediately. They understand and have my word for it that I will do any further changes they want. Then I wish A——————— B———— could cash the check as he did last time at the California Bank at Hollywood and Vine. It is inconvenient for him, I know, but I know of no other way to keep my name out of it. Once he has come that far, I wish he could put the cash in the enclosed envelope and take it upstairs in the same building and leave it with Rex Cole, my busi-

---

[2] Frank Butler, Hugo's father, had suffered a heart attack. He owned a ranch in Lebec, California, twenty miles from the Lazy T. He died in 1968, twenty years later.

[3] Trumbo refers to the sale of one of his first black market scripts.

[4] King Brothers Productions, frequent producers of Trumbo's black market screenplays.

ness manager. Then he will have saved me a trip into town, and put money in my account which I sorely need, all in the same trip.

Enclosed is a carbon (the only one I have) of a novelette by Emmett Doyle. This is presently in the hands of Mrs Elsie McKeogh in New York for magazine sale. If it does not sell to magazines fairly quickly, perhaps you should consider sending it out without a sale. In any event you have it, can read it, and decide what would be the best way to handle it.

The whole point of this is that Emmett Doyle is a nom de plume of Beth Fincher.[5] Beth Fincher writes either under it or her own name. Beth Fincher wants you to handle her on the regular business-like basis. I believe KB are ready to sign her up for another picture. She has turned down one story, and they are going to offer her another. They like the last job so well that I am sure they will come up in price, together with a piece of the picture. Miss Fincher would like to have you handle this for her; and other things in the future. I think of nothing else, except to say thank you.

DR. ABBOTT[6]

6. To Lee Sabinson

Lazy T Ranch
Frazier Park, California
October 2, 1948

Dear Lee:

I bow to no one in my distaste for writing letters, but I now am afraid we must come to some understanding about correspondence. It has been five weeks since I sent you the play, and two and one half weeks since our chance telephone conversation, yet I have not had a word from you.

I have no idea whether your conversations with Shumlin[7] are go-

---

[5] Beth Fincher, Mrs. Trumbo's given middle and maiden name, came to be a favorite of Trumbo's many pseudonyms. In this case he has a pseudonym for a pseudonym. It should be noted, incidentally, that Trumbo sent this story to Elsie McKeogh and that she left the name Emmett Doyle on the manuscript; however, she wrote Trumbo on September 9, 1948, that, while she was willing to submit the story under the pseudonym, she felt honor bound to reveal its true authorship to a purchasing editor.

[6] Dr. John Abbott was another favorite pseudonym. John Abbott was the central character in Trumbo's 1934 novel, *Eclipse;* Dr. Abbott was also the name of a character in Trumbo's first successful film, *A Man to Remember.*

[7] Herman Shumlin, it will be remembered, was engaged to direct *Thief.* He also co-produced with Sabinson.

ing forward, have resulted in an agreement, or have fallen through. I have no idea whether you are going to produce the play or whether you are not. I have no idea whether you plan it for winter or spring or for next fall. I have no concrete ideas upon which to ponder for changes. I have nothing upon which I can base any plans for the future.

Aside from sheer curiosity—which I admit I have—there are more practical reasons why I should be taken into your confidence. I am the sole support of three households. I must estimate my income very carefully to provide for them. I therefore must contract to do certain pieces of work. I have been trying to hold off, hoping to hear something from you. If you go ahead without letting me in on your plans, it may very likely turn out that I shall not be available to you when you want me because of prior commitments: and you may be delayed in production a month or two months or even a whole season. I have been vainly waiting—and at considerable cost to myself—to hear what your general plans or hopes are. I shall wait no more. I cannot afford to. I have three deals available, and I am going in to make them Monday.

Beyond this, there is the play itself. It seems to me it would be very simple for you to dictate in general what you consider wrong with it, what changes you deem necessary. By receiving this, I could not only be setting my mind to work on the problems, but I might also be able to do some practical work toward solving them. This would be much better than being confronted with them suddenly, and with a time limit involved. I am more than willing to work earnestly on this project, but I must have your cooperation.

Here is what I want: (1) information on approximately when you hope to put the play on, if you put it on; (2) some word about the negotiations with Shumlin; (3) a general summary of what is wrong with the play and what you think might be done to help it. Please understand, I will not hold you to any of this information, for I well understand the uncertainties of life in general as well as those of the theatre in particular. But I must have something to go on—I must have a hunch—a hint—a suspicion—a rumor—a whisper of what might happen.

If you find yourself too busy to write yourself, why not get in touch with Mrs. McKeogh once a week, and I am sure she will be glad to relay to me whatever information you have. But really, for the good of our relations and the good of the play, I must find some means of opening channels of communication with you. The telephone is no good: I am twelve miles from one, and I do not make regular trips into Hollywood. The telegraph is no good—it comes to me via the mail. Racing camels and carrier pigeons, while fundamentally sound, are not entirely dependable and their forage costs money. A letter is the only practical thing.

In all good will, but with a certain emphasis, I remain your pro-
tégé, your discovery, your slave, and the most mystified neophyte in
the history of the theatre.

DALTON TRUMBO

7. To Larry Parks

Lazy T Ranch
Frazier Park, California
October 4, 1948

Dear Larry: [8]

Mary Rolphe, who has generally taken over the job of coordinat-
ing work for the [Hollywood] Ten, has tried unsuccessfully to get
you to come to one of our Tuesday night meetings; and I myself
have called your house and left my name and number and received
no answer.

Here is the problem: we found that we needed a total of $49,000
to carry the criminal cases through to their last appeal. We found
that among the Ten our homes were mortgaged, our incomes nothing, our careers destroyed. We do not have the money. One printing
bill alone comes to $6,500, and if it isn't paid our appeal is dropped
and we go to jail. We were and still are in a state of acute crisis.

We started a series of Tuesday night meetings—quiet meetings of
a few interested and uninvolved people at Bob Kenny's [9] apartment.
They were not public, and the names of those who came were not
publicized, and they were not asked to act for us in a public manner. They were merely asked for money, after a detailed explanation
of the budget and of our own financial conditions. In four meetings
we gathered $14,000. That is good, but not good enough, and we
have to keep at it persistently and everlastingly.

That is why we wanted to have you come. A number of people—
seven or eight—have given as much as $1,000 at the meetings. We
felt that you might give us a similar sum. I know it is presumptuous
to state the sum one asks for. But presumption bows to necessity. I
have been on the giving end myself for ten years, and I assure you
that it is much pleasanter than asking.

[8] Larry Parks, a film actor, was one of the original nineteen "unfriendly"
witnesses. Although he was not summoned to the stand at that time, he was
subsequently blacklisted.

[9] Robert Kenny, a former Attorney General of California and an unsuccessful candidate for the governorship of that state, was principal defense lawyer
for the Hollywood Ten. He is now a Superior Court Judge in Los Angeles.

Let me make myself perfectly clear. A month ago I was approached by the American Socialist Party and asked to get in touch with you and urge you to speak with Wallace at the Yankee Stadium. It was felt that our friendship might influence your decision favorably. I refused to do it. I said that I did not think that personal pressure should be exerted in a political matter, and particularly upon a person whose career was at an extremely delicate turning point.

But I do not feel that way about the request contained in this letter. I feel that I have the right to ask it, and that you ought to and will want to give it. It can be in cash, or it can be made out to Bob Kenny and represent a legally deductible expense since Bob represented you at the hearings. It can be kept confidential if you wish. I should not write so frank a letter as this if the need were not so desperate. Will you drop me a note right away, telling me how you feel about it?

. . . . Cleo joins me in sending our best to you and Betty.

DALTON

8. To Lee Sabinson

Lazy T Ranch
Frazier Park, California
October 9, 1948

Dear Lee:

We have overcome time, distance, geography: we are triumphantly in touch with each other!

I was, needless to say, interested in all you had to tell me, and shall await Mr. Shumlin's coming with impatience. I am glad you feel that we shall move right ahead; and to that end I shall work as rapidly as possible on the changes.

Of course I think [Walter] Huston perfect for the part; [10] I have admired both him and his son [John] for a long while.

If this damned thing goes over—which, judging by the mortality rate this season, is doubtful—I have a number of other ideas I have cuddled through the years, and I shall do nothing but sit up here in my mile high beauty and isolation and hammer them out.

I don't know whether I have told you how pleased I am that you originally approached Elsie McKeogh to get me to write. I have always said I would one day write a play, but I doubt that I would

---

[10] Ultimately the leading role was filled by Thomas Mitchell with Walter Abel in support.

have without the stimulus of a specific request, and also the thousand bucks. That, in itself, when you have lived the prodigal life to which I have been accustomed for the past ten years, is a hell of an incentive. Because, you see, at the time I didn't have a thousand dollars.

Best,

DALTON

P.S.   After this glorious start, don't forget to write to me now and again. I await your letters as I would a lover's.

9. To George Willner

Lazy T Ranch
Frazier Park, California
Sunday night
[c. October 1, 1948]

Dear George:

The enclosed copy of a letter which went out with this one to the K[ing] B[rother]s is self-explanatory. The part about the dough is especially urgent. I think I have proven to them that I am a straight-shooter, and can be depended upon to do what I say I will. To do this, I took very small dough, which I considered good tactics.

This brings us to the consideration of deal #2. I think I should get more dough. $6,000 minimum. This is a job no one has worked on, so their previous objections to independent contractor status for me should not hold—in a word there should be no withholding tax. Another thing, I want the three payments to be in equal sums—not a lesser sum for the start, and two greater sums for first and second draft respectively. Reason? I need dough badly.

Beth Fincher will agree to do the deal, and will sign the contract.

Whatever price you decide upon, emphasize to them the fact I need dough at once—today—and that if a little matter like papers not signed and contracts not yet drawn up intervenes, they should be good guys and good gamblers and give the dough at once without waiting, relying on me to fulfill the proper forms, and your guarantee I will. They are going to be out of town Wednesday, so if we could get on it Tuesday, that would be good.

Finally, try for whatever sum you think possible. Negotiate and close without consulting me. If we get only $6,000 I think a piece of the picture would be in order. But your judgment is final.

Beth Fincher will be willing at any time to sign an agency contract with you. Also, should she join the Guild, and how?

The KBs and I were at lunch at Beecher's last Friday, and Mr. Nat

Goldstone [11] walked over to the table, leering knowingly. I had a script and a pen in my hand at the time. It was an amusing encounter.

Benisons!
ABBOTT

10. To Elsie McKeogh

Lazy T Ranch
Frazier Park, California
November 8, 1949

Dear Elsie:

Herman and Lee and I have satisfactorily concluded our conferences, and I am now at work on the agreed changes. . . .

Things go well. That item . . . we couldn't find a name for found a name out here,[12] and has been sold for thirty-five thousand, of which, after paying some bonuses to my fronts, as well as agent's fee, I still have a little more than twenty thousand for myself. It's a very handsome relief, and puts me in fine shape again—that is, for a short while. I also feel smug about being able to command such a price under the name of a new writer. They're going to have to figure out new ways of blacklisting before they starve me out entirely. And with that boasting note—which I am sure will bring me bad luck—I had better close.

If you hear anything about the play, etc., I'll be all ears.

Regards,
DALTON

P.S. Did you notice Thomas stood on his Constitutional rights? Ha! [13]

[11] A Hollywood agent in whose office Willner was employed.

[12] Mrs. McKeogh had written on October 7, 1948, stating again her refusal to deceive her good friends in editorial offices. (Mrs. McKeogh's husband, Arthur, it will be remembered, had been editor of *Good Housekeeping.*) Shortly thereafter she returned the unsold manuscript and magazine citiques.

[13] J. Parnell Thomas was found guilty of embezzling government funds and was sentenced to three years at Danbury, Connecticut, federal prison where fellow inmates were Lester Cole and Ring Lardner, Jr. Mr. Thomas, pleading *nolo contendere* avoided taking the witness stand in his trial.

11. To Los Angeles Telephone Signal Company

Lazy T Ranch
Frazier Park, California
November 8, 1948

Dear burglars:

Our baby sleeps in one bedroom and we sleep in another. When she yelps at night we cannot hear her. A man said you were the people to see about such things.

Can you install a speaker in her room and one in ours, so we can gossip back and forth with her during the wee small hours? Not one of your solid gold outfits. Something sensible and serviceable. I am not a rich man any more.

The distance along the floorboards from her room to ours is no more than seventy-five feet: and if you go through the roof, it will be much less.

Now let's all get together and see if we can arrange a decent, modest little outfit for an old customer without screwing him to death in the process.

Irritably yours,
DALTON TRUMBO

12. To G. Fourness of Los Angeles Telephone Signal Company

Lazy T Ranch
Frazier Park, California
November 15, 1948

My dear Mr. Fourness:

Your letter has arrived and been put to the only sensible use I could think of. When we Reds come into power we are going to shoot merchants in the following order: (1) those who are greedy, and (2) those who are witty. Since you fall into both categories it will be a sad story when we finally lay hands on you.

I had hoped time might have improved your character, but the prices you quote convince me otherwise. You still cannot imagine a happy moment which does not find your fist in somebody else's pocket. Since I have very little choice in the matter, I must yield.

Send the set described and with it a man for installation. I have no intention of creeping about the house on all fours with a wire in one hand, a hammer in the other and my larynx clogged with tacks. Besides, I want the wire to go through the ceiling, and unlike your associates I am no second-story man. Also, let's arrange for a weekday job. There is no urgency about the matter, and I have little taste for that weekend overtime racket.

The bill should be sent to my new business manager, whose name is Rex Cole. . . . I have employed him because he hates creditors and does not pay them too promptly. You will feel better over Thanksgiving and Christmas if you have something to look forward to during the hangover period which follows: and I tell you quite frankly that it will probably be sixty days before you get your money. Considering what you've done to me, I ought to make you wait the full nine months.

Naturally I hope this will be the last time I shall be obliged to do business with you, although I daresay the junk you've pushed off on me will soon begin to wear out and we shall have to start the whole weary routine over again. Please extend my good wishes for the holiday season to everyone in the thuggery.

Cordially,
DALTON TRUMBO

13. To Mrs. Meta Reis of the Berg-Allenberg Agency

Lazy T Ranch
Frazier Park, California
December 17, 1948

Dear Meta:

Our foreman broke through a foot of snow in his jeep, and by a miracle of luck received your wire in Lebec by telephone. It will be two or three days before I shall be able to get through, but in the meanwhile I have certain doubts about the firm of Berg-Allenberg which I feel you should know. As a matter of fact, I have five specific doubts, and for the sake of clarity I shall enumerate them below.
(1)

The last time Mr. Berg granted me a private audience—I believe it was during the first week of April in 1948—he spoke fully and frankly to me, and I have remembered what he said, as I always remember the words of people who have got on in the world. He spent considerable time criticizing me for "making long speeches" when I was on the Congressional carpet before that rascal—now happily indicted for defrauding his government—the Hon. J. Parnell Thomas. I was stunned by this accusation from Mr. Berg, and asked him if he had read the committee testimony as published in the record: because, I said, if he had read it he would realize that it was the friendly witnesses and not the ten unfriendly ones who made the "long speeches." Mr. Berg replied that he had indeed read the testimony, and that I had made speeches "this long"—and to illustrate how long he held his hands out in a widespread gesture of measurement.

This statement, coming from an employee of mine, from an employee whose job it was to keep my best interests constantly in mind, gave me considerable pause. For according to the record he said he had read, my testimony before the Committee on Un-American Affairs comprised only four and a half pages, and my longest "speech" —as Mr. Berg and later the prosecuting attorney at my trial insisted on calling those brief statements I was able to get into the record— my longest "speech" counted exactly 75 words.

What caused me especially to think upon the matter was the fact that Mr. Samuel Grosvenor Wood, at the time of the hearings a client of Berg-Allenberg, testified for 14 pages, and his longest speech counted 148 words; that Mr. James Kevin McGuinness, at the time of the hearings a client of Berg-Allenberg, testified for 18 pages, and his longest speech counted 400 words; that Mr. Adolphe Menjou, at the time of the hearings a client of Berg-Allenberg, testified for 17 pages, and his longest speech counted 671 words; that Miss Ayn Rand, at the time of the hearings a client of Berg-Allenberg, testified for 9 pages, and her longest speech counted 1,636 words.

It therefore seemed odd to me that Mr. Berg should contend that those clients of his who were my opponents at the hearings, clients who had rehearsed their testimony with the convict Thomas—that these clients did not make "long speeches," and that I with my 75 word interjection did make them. I have addressed myself prayerfully to this problem, and I have reached the conclusion that either Mr. Berg lied when he said he had read the record (and not having read it had no right to offer judgment on the matter), or that he did read the record and was so befogged with prejudice that he was incapable of recognizing the truth when it lay clearly before him on the printed page.

In either event—that is, whether Mr. Berg in this instance was a deliberate liar or was simply possessed of an inability to perceive the truth—it seemed to me then, and it still seems to me, that he offers extremely dubious assets as an agent, for the ability to tell the truth and to recognize it are important qualities, and the lack of them is a sad thing to contemplate. I do not believe that Mr. Berg or his organization can possibly represent me honestly and without prejudice unless Mr. Berg has since been cured of these faults. And I doubt that, at his age in any event, a permanent cure of such a large ethical deficiency is possible.

(2)

During this same conversation Mr. Berg suggested to me a scheme whereby I and my nine colleagues, if they agreed to it, might be received back into the motion picture industry. He stated to me that

Mr. Westbrook Pegler, a journalist of the fascist lunatic fringe, was a good friend of his; and that he would pay Mr. Pegler's expenses to the coast and arrange a meeting between him and the ten, or him and me alone; and that by talking freely to Mr. Pegler and revealing to him the motives which prompted us to behave as we did before the indictee Thomas, we would deliver ourselves from the onus allegedly attached to our names and make possible our return to our jobs.

I held my silence while this went on, for I was so nauseated that to speak would have been to lose my temper, and to lose my temper is to become completely incoherent. I never again took the matter up with Mr. Berg for a reason which he should understand as well as I —namely, that Westbrook Pegler is one of the most dangerous, malicious, and outspoken anti-Semites in the country. His constant reference to men with Jewish names such as Hillman, Frankfurter, Potofsky and dozens of others, combined with his gleeful tracing back of Americanized names to their original Jewish sources and his enthusiastic approval of lynching bees is evidence enough of his depravity for most sensitive men.

I am fully aware—albeit with sadness—that there are men in this country so wanting in self-esteem that they are perfectly willing, for a matter of money, to deal with anti-Semites. But neither I nor any other of the ten is such a man. Two of our number lost their jobs solely because they made a picture against anti-Semitism, and we take a certain pride in the fact that neither cash nor contract can tempt us into any kind of relationship with an anti-Semite—not even if he be sponsored by Mr. Berg, and referred to affectionately as "Peg."

Moreover, even from an opportunistic point of view, I can imagine no more damaging advice from agent to client; for Westbrook Pegler, as five successive national elections have proved, is the representative of a discredited minority whose espousal of our cause not only would have shamed us in the eyes of the community and of the world, but also would have destroyed our careers, our usefulness and our possibilities for decent work in the future. How, then, will it be possible for me in the future to pay the slightest heed to the advice of a man capable of the monstrous idiocy outlined above? (3)

In the course of this same conversation I brought my financial condition to Mr. Berg's attention. Three times during the previous six months Mr. Berg had assured me that if I needed money I had only to ask for it. Moreover, part of the fee I had been paying Mr. Berg over the years was in consideration of business management—a fact which both Mr. Berg and Mr. Allenberg had called to my attention at various intervals. They had even gone so far as to urge me to discharge my business manager and avail myself of the business service for which I was paying them. So it was also in his capacity as my business manager that I approached Mr. Berg about money.

I had previously sent him a statement of the $80,000 investment in my ranch, together with an inventory of chattels prepared for insurance purposes by the United Appraisal Company, listing them at $40,000 current value. I asked Mr. Berg either to lend me $10,000 outright; or to take a $10,000 trust deed on the ranch; or, if he found himself unable to do either, to guarantee a first mortgage at the bank against both ranch and chattels in the sum of $15,000.

Mr. Berg replied that for business reasons and for reasons of his reputation he could not possibly afford to appear to be sponsoring me or backing me or guaranteeing me in any way, no matter how large the security nor how safe the investment. He did, however, authorize his associate, Mr. Jack Nerdrum, to look around for private money against ranch and chattels, with the clear understanding that in so doing Mr. Nerdrum did not represent Berg-Allenberg, and that the firm had no interest or connection with the transaction.

Mr. Nerdrum, thus deprived of the sponsorship of his firm, found a vice-president of the _____ Bank who was canny enough to reject the loan for his bank, yet shrewd enough to accept it for himself in the name of his mother-in-law. When papers finally were drawn, I discovered that both ranch and chattels were to be pledged for the sum of $12,000, less a $1,200 bonus to be paid by me, less approximately $300 expenses to be paid by me—and that the balance was to be discharged in three years at 6% interest.

The more I pondered this kind of business management—for which I had been paying but luckily had never used before—the more disastrous it appeared. In the end I refused to enter into the illegal conspiracy which my new business management had cooked up. Instead I employed myself a competent business manager, and without any difficulty negotiated a trust deed on the ranch alone without inclusion of chattels, at no bonus and no expense, bearing the legal rate of 5% interest. And already I have paid off slightly over one-third of the sum borrowed.

Now the point of this grimy little narrative is this: that for reasons of business Mr. Berg could not afford to be the medium by which money flowed into my pocket, no matter how firm the security or how legitimate the transaction. Such a connection with me would somehow be harmful to him in the conduct of his affairs. But this brings us even a larger question, and one which greatly perplexes me and has caused me sleepless nights. If money flowing through Mr. Berg to me would injure him, is it not true that money flowing through me to Mr. Berg would be equally injurious to him? The stain would be on it, and no amount of rationalization can wash it off. You can understand, then, why I shrink from the responsibility of placing him and his firm in such jeopardy.

As for Mr. Berg's reputation—and he spoke of it lovingly—it appeared in some way to hinge on the matter of patriotism. He explained to me that this was the finest country in the world because in it I had been able to rise from poverty to a high-salaried position, and because he, from similar poverty, had been able to accumulate a million dollars. This seemed a little curious, for if the virtues of America are made apparent to Mr. Berg primarily by the money he has accumulated, how much more virtuous a country must Hyderbad be, where one man has been able to accumulate well over a billion? And contrariwise, how dreadful it is to think that my father, who died poor, had no reason at all to love his country; and how wrong he was in teaching me to cherish America for her beauty, her institutions and her people, rather than equating her glories in terms of my personal bank account!

Let us, however, pass quickly over the above as a mere philosophical digression, and get back to Mr. Berg's reputation, which he cherishes and which association favoring my cause would tarnish. I must, to make the record complete, point out that there are men in this country whose reputations are almost as great in the eyes of the world as Mr. Berg's, and as precious to them as his to him, and whose patriotism measures up to any standard—Dr. Albert Einstein, Dr. Harlow Shapley, Mr. Thomas Mann to mention only three of thousands were moved to lend their names, their reputations and their best efforts to smash the blacklist and defend its victims. They were doing this while Mr. Berg—my employee whose job it was to advance my interests—hung shyly in the shadows and preserved the lustre of his name.

Now in view of the fact that association with me or advocacy of my cause or involvement in a mortgage or business deal with me would be harmful to Mr. Berg's reputation, I am moved to ask what kind of people are not harmful to his reputation? Would he, for example, hesitate to enter into a legitimate deal with . . . any of the dozens of perverts, homosexuals and lesbians who work prominently in motion pictures, or any of that legion of men—some of them even Mr. Berg's own associates for all I know—who perjure themselves in their marriage vows by later acquisition of concubines? I doubt that Mr. Berg would hesitate to deal with any of these people. I am quite sure that he has, at one time or another, dealt with practically all of them. As a matter of fact I believe that even now he represents an aging actor who, in the full glare of the public prints, is seeking to avoid payment for the support of an illegitimate child. His reputation curiously survives association with such people; he does not find them offensive or dangerous. But I am dangerous to his reputation, perhaps because I do not sin in a way that Mr. Berg understands.

In view of all this, and understanding the delicacy of Mr. Berg's feelings and the quality of his reputation, I fail to see how it is possible for him to sponsor me, to back me, to accept the incriminating dollar from me, unless he publicly admits a close economic association with me and begins to fight vigorously for my right to work. I don't see how this is possible for him unless he is willing, at this late date, to make a moral compromise; and I should hate to think him the sort of man to whom moral compromise comes easily; and, regardless of how difficult the struggle, if it came at all, then he would not be the kind of person I should wish to employ as my representative.

In a word, now that the battle is practically over, I should not wish to be responsible for blotting the escutcheon of so lofty a house as that of Berg-Allenberg; nor is it in me to see Mr. Berg's own proud plumes dragged in the mire of publicity which has attended my life during the past year. Not even if—as it now appears—there might one day be a dollar in it for him.

(4)

There is still another matter which puzzles me, and concerning which I suspect that Mr. Berg cherishes naive illusions. I employ him for two purposes: (1) to find employment for me—which he has not been able to do for over a year; and (2) to collect payment for my work—which he has been conspicuously unable to do in, for example, the case of *Angel's Flight*. I have therefore been compelled to employ an attorney, Mr. Martin Gang, to enforce my contract and to collect the funds which Berg-Allenberg were unable to collect.

The expense of filing the various suits, of court fees and what not, have run into a considerable cash sum, all of which I myself have paid out of pocket. At the outset I suggested to the firm of Berg-Allenberg that they participate in this expense, since their normal ten percent commission was involved. But they thriftily refrained from sharing any of the costs—not even ten percent to protect their own interest in the suit. Apparently they believed that some deeply charitable impulse on my part would cause me to advance cash for the legal costs of their percentage as well as my own. Unfortunately, they overestimated my benevolence. Having refused to protect their interest in the case by sharing their proportionate part of its cost, they no longer have any interest at all. And I, having assumed all of the financial risk, shall retain for myself all of the financial gain. I'm sure this will come as no surprise to them, for they are good businessmen and must have considered the consequences at the time they decided it would be shrewder to allow me the privilege of bearing the whole burden of the suit.

(5)

There is only one more major point, and then this letter shall come to an end. It's been *so* long since I've heard either from Mr. Berg or Mr. Allenberg. In the old days when they were the two most highly paid men in my employ, I heard from them very often. From every spa between Miami and Rio de Janeiro came their cheerful little wonderful-vacation-wish-you-were-here postal cards. One such even came from Mr. Berg amidst the storm and stress of seagoing life aboard his yacht as it plowed its way through the Caribbean waves. But I have not heard from them lately. I have not heard from them at all. My last letter from Mr. Berg was mailed March 3rd, 1948, and the most recent from Mr. Allenberg was dated June 1, and even then was in answer to a letter of my own. During all these intervening months—nothing. No more vacation notes. No more photographs of tropic splendors.

I worry about this, Meta. I worry, and then I wonder: aren't they taking vacations any more? What can be wrong? And then a hopeful thought comes to me: why obviously if they're not flying down to Rio or challenging the peril of the tropic seas, then it must mean that they are too busy for relaxation, that they are working. And then the gnawing thought: busy with what? working for whom? For you see, Meta, I receive no word from them about the state of employment in the motion picture industry. They have made no suggestions about how I might proceed to get work. They have given me no hint of the story market, of what stories are needed by what stars, of the general trends of the market. I have received no advice from them whatever, business or otherwise. They tell me nothing of their ceaseless efforts to get me a job. They render me no account of the rebuffs, the heartbreaks and the high resolution which attends their efforts in my behalf. In fact they do not write me at all. Just . . . silence. Six long months of silence. I thought I had been forgotten, I assumed that our relationship was over, that I was on my own, that this sensitive pair were addressing themselves to other and higher matters. And then your wire—!

Which, of course, brings us back to the present. Well, as you can readily see, I am perplexed, and I have tried in my faltering fashion to communicate my perplexity to you. I think in view of all that has happened, Mr. Berg and Mr. Allenberg and their friends and associates should consider very carefully their relationship with me. I don't think there is a relationship, although I should be glad to discuss the matter with any or all who hold contrary opinions. If you think it wise, you might communicate the general trend of my thinking to them.

In the meanwhile, Meta,[14] please be assured of my very best wishes, and extend them also to Bob Coryell and Jack Nerdrum and all the girls there who, apparently having no reputations to consider, dealt with me during bad fortune exactly as they had dealt with me during good. And to Mr. Berg and Mr. Allenberg I add my wishes for a

---

[14] Three years later Mrs. Reis was subpoenaed by HUAC and gave names.

thoughtful Christmas, a contemplative New Year and a re-dedication to those high principles and gleaming reputations which are associated with them wherever men and women of good will foregather during this holiday season.

Cordially,
DALTON TRUMBO

14. To Charles Katz

Lazy T Ranch
Frazier Park, California
December 27, 1948

My dear Charles:

Did God smile on you this Christmas? Did he smile on your spouse and little one? He smiled on me.

Nature up here is in one of her more savage moods, and it has been snowing, and is still snowing, and apparently intends to continue. Through a plate glass window this winter wonderland is very fine to look at; but it certainly isn't anything for a civilized man to leave the house for. Daddy does not pull the children about on sleds; the little bastards pull themselves or go shank's mare.

. . . .

It is very late, and I am going to bed. The electric blanket is already turned on, and a solid silver tray beside the bed is cleaned and polished by underlings, ready to receive ashes from my last contemplative cigarette.

Good night, sweet gladiator. May the Lord splatter you hugely with goodnesses during the glad New Year. May peace attend your dreams, and may they always be dry.

Your friend, disciple and
least profitable client,
DT

15. To Martin Gang

Lazy T Ranch
Frazier Park, California
January 22, 1949

Dear Martin:

After considerable meditation and consultation with my nine colleagues, I am forced to the conclusion that we should, to borrow from John L. Lewis, cease our disaffiliation.

I think we have fallen into a couple of errors which closer collaboration with the others might have avoided—errors, I hasten to add, in which I concurred with you, and to which I attach no blame whatsoever.

First, our strategy of going before a judge alone, taking an adverse decision and winning an appeal is obviously not so good as the [Lester] Cole strategy of fighting the issue before a jury, winning and forcing the studios to appeal. We are now in the position of protecting a victory in the lower courts, rather than hoping for one on appeal.

Second, our confidence in my lack of a morality clause caused me to permit the studios to inquire much more deeply into my political activities and beliefs than they were permitted to inquire in the cases of the other nine. Although the theory upon which we admitted such questions is fool proof, it was based upon a purely legal issue rather than upon a contemplated appeal to a jury, and I am inclined to think we may find it disadvantageous to our cause in the lower courts.

Beyond this, the unexpected victory in the Cole case alters the entire situation, making every move on the part of every plaintiff of the most critical importance to the remaining nine. The only way the ten can proceed as one, so to speak, in guarding the present victory and assuring future ones, is for all counsel to collaborate as one. A clear victory means much more than reinstatement for the ten: it means calling a halt everywhere to arbitrary discharge on political grounds, and as such has great political significance for every person who works.

Finally, it is the mixed legal and political aspects of these cases—aspects which are inseparable—which actually compel us to associate our case with the others. You are the industry expert on frying producers; Kenny-Katz-Margolis are the industry experts on frying red-baiters. In my case we have both jobs to do, and hence we shall need both talents. Bob [Kenny] and his associates have devoted the better part of fifteen months almost exclusively to the study of the political and criminal aspects of the cases in relation to the civil issue—indeed, of the inseparability of the political and criminal from the civil—and I think we would be most unwise not to avail ourselves of the experience they have gained and the thousands of dollars worth of research they have accumulated.

Therefore I have concluded that the time has come for you, as my counsel, to enter into full, public and legal association with the other attorneys under Bob Kenny as chief counsel. I think you know me well enough to understand from the very tone of this letter itself that my decision involves not the slightest change in my very high opinion of you as an attorney, as a man and as a friend.

I have just received an urgent summons to New York on the play, and I dash this off just before leaving the ranch to catch the Saturday noon train. I shall be gone about three months . . .

Wish me luck on the play!

Regards,
DALTON

16. Extract of an undated letter to Herman Shumlin

Lazy T Ranch
Frazier Park, California
[*c. January 22, 1949*]

Anyhow, I shall be your complete and undistracted slave for the next two months, and you shall produce a hit which shall make me rich—although it won't do me any permanent good, for I seem to stay rich only a day or two.

17. To Cleo Trumbo

New York, New York
[*February 12, 1949*]

Darling:

In forty-eight hours it will be Valentine's day. I shall send you no memento upon this tender occasion, for I find myself quite unable to love you any more on Monday than I do on Sunday or Tuesday. Hence a valentine would, in any event, be an understatement.

The play is now in the period of vast uncertainty. The actors are entirely wrong in their lines and characterizations. The director is scared out of his wits, and wobbling for changes to cover his own inadequacy. The first flush of enthusiasm has departed, and those who were unreasonably enthusiastic at the outset now become unreasonably pessimistic. The fear of failure operates like a sleeping pill on Herman, seeping gradually through everything he does.[15] Therefore we are headed for a sharp collision which I calculate shall

[15] Trumbo wrote: "Mr. Shumlin's assistant on *Thief* was a young attorney from St. Louis serving his apprenticeship in the theatre." Trumbo describes him as "a quiet, courteous young man with perhaps the most intelligent eyes I have ever seen. I felt that he recognized every mistake in the play and its production and would remember it. His kindness to Cleo and me extended to Nikola and Christopher, whom he occasionally shepherded when we could not. His name was David Merrick."

come on Monday or Tuesday. Someone must say: success or failure is beside the point, let us stop our wavering, let us make our decision and set upon it, even if it is wrong. That person, I fear, shall have to be me, and I am ready for it.

Death of a Salesman has taken the cream off the season. It is an excellent play which is called great by reason of comparison with two weak seasons. Miller, the author, is an extraordinarily nice, talented and modest man. The result is to reduce our play to the status of, at the best, a modest and pleasant satire with possibilities of considerable success. And this is perfectly fine with me, although it throws Herman into fits of depression.

I enclose proof of an ad and a couple of luggage stickers, to establish to your satisfaction that this shadowy enterprise has assumed at least the outward forms of reality, and to convince you that I am here engaged in an actual project rather than merely bloviating. More than ever, watching these tormented people, am I convinced that the act of decision—whether it be a right or a wrong decision—is the most important part of any enterprise.

. . . . As for the problem of your children, I have no solution, except that I will adapt myself to any solution which you conclude is reasonable. It is your problem. They are, after all, the fruit of your own unbridled lust, and if they now appear inconvenient, remember the joy of their conception. With this bit of sagacity, let me tell you that I am working almost constantly, that I love you all very dearly, that I would not live on this troubled little island for all the gold in its bowels, and that I enjoy the letters from your heatless community more than our limited 26-letter alphabet can spell out.

DALTON

18. To Wolcott Gibbs

Lazy T Ranch
Frazier Park, California
April 11, 1949

Dear Mr. Gibbs:

I have just read your obstinately wrong-headed review of *The Biggest Thief in Town*.[16]

[16] The review appeared in *The New Yorker*. After a moderately successful tryout in New Haven under the title of *The Emerald Staircase*, the play went to Boston. Here reviews were poor. Trumbo began frantic rewrites, and the title was changed to *The Biggest Thief in Town*. Reviews were again favorable in Philadelphia. The comedy opened in New York at the Mansfield Theatre on March 30, 1949; it survived thirteen performances.

I call to your attention the sentence, "Unfortunately, Mr. Trumbo, whatever his gifts as a political thinker may be" is a dull dog, etc.

The very wording of the comment indicates that here I have you on unfamiliar ground. Please, therefore, be informed that my gifts as a political thinker are of a very high order.

Yours,
DALTON TRUMBO

19. Extract of a letter to George Willner

Lazy T Ranch
Frazier Park, California
April 18, 1949

If these boys [the King Brothers] haven't got anything, has anybody else? I shall sit up here and grind out originals until I starve to death, but God knows it's an unwholesome way to die. Do you have any idea of a specific market for a specific kind of original? I might do that. Or then again, I might go jump in the lake. I have one, you know. It's my personal property. Come up and I'll show it to you. Maybe we can jump in together.

20. Extract of a letter to Charles Katz

Lazy T Ranch
Frazier Park, California
July 19, 1949

Just a mile across the valley, they drill night and day. This damned rig looks like a Christmas tree after sunset, shattering the placid darkness of our valley, and the grinding comes to us and permeates our beings. They will discover oil everywhere here except on our place, and all the farmers will be millionaires, and we alone shall remain impoverished and forgotten—we who once were the lords of the valley. Curse modern industry and its disregard for rustic scenery and habits!

21. To the Editor of the *Saturday Review of Literature*

Lazy T Ranch
Frazier Park, California
July 20, 1949

Sir:

Mr. Arthur M. Schlesinger, Jr., whose popularity with the slick magazines is perhaps too great to permit him the luxury of calling other writers hacks, notes in the *Saturday Review* of July 16 that "Like Maltz, John Howard Lawson, Alvah Bessie and Dalton Trumbo, the fellow-traveling ex-proletarian writers go to Hollywood and become film hacks. Until, that is, they refused to own up to their political beliefs before a committee of Congress—in response to which the film industry, rearing itself in an unwonted spasm of moral nobility, turned them out into the storm."

Quite aside from the fact that I, for one, worked in motion pictures before I became an "ex-proletarian writer," this business of refusing to answer questions relating to political and trade union affiliations is one which has deeply and unnecessarily agitated the Luce intellectuals of late. I say unnecessarily because I do not think it possible for a committee of the Congress to ask Mr. Schlesinger a question which would do violence to his conscience. He takes his stand squarely in the tradition of chronic confessors who have plagued the earth since the first establishment of orthodoxy.

Wherever inquisitorial courts have been set up, Mr. Schlesinger and his breed have appeared in eager herds to proclaim: "I do not wish to imply approval of your questions, but I am not now nor have I ever been a dissenter. I am not now nor have I ever been a Communist. I am not now nor have I ever been a trade unionist. I am not now nor have I ever been a Jew. Prosecute those who answer differently, O masters, silence them, send them to jail, make soap of them if you wish. But not of me, for I have answered every question you chose to ask, fully, frankly, freely—and on my belly." [17]

DALTON TRUMBO

Note: If you find it impractical to publish this note in toto, kindly drop it altogether. DT

---

[17] Trumbo's distaste for Schlesinger reached its climax twenty years later in their exchange of correspondence published in the January, 1970, issue of *Esquire*.

22. To Albert Maltz

Lazy T Ranch
Frazier Park, California
August 6, 1949

Dear Albert:

Ring [Lardner, Jr.] has reported to me his conversation with you about the always disagreeable matter of finances. . . .

I know there have been rumors that I have made millions during the past couple of years, and since you are the current angel of our enterprise. [18] I feel a report is in order to set matters straight and to give some idea of what may be expected from me during the rest of the year.

Just prior to the Washington trip—in September of 1947—I let contracts for a great deal of work here at the ranch: a mile of paving, an irrigation reservoir, electrification, landscaping, etc., to the total of about $23,000. The work was in progress when the summons arrived, and there was no way of stopping it. It had been my intention to pay this sum and also my 1947 income taxes out of the $61,000 due on the current Metro project. As you know, the project was completed and the money was not paid. When I returned from Washington and received the suspension, I therefore had to borrow $35,000 at uncomfortable terms to care for the short-term obligations. Since then my task has been to pay back on this sum and support the three households for which I am accountable. The fact that the ranch and equipment represent an investment of $150,000 makes prompt payment of money borrowed doubly necessary, for the vultures would like nothing better than an excuse to see me out.

Ring tells me you are under the impression that the Spiegel [19] assignment, which you told him you assisted me in getting, involves considerable money. I don't know what Spiegel told you when you saw him and _____ that day, but I had been wrangling with him by mail, telegram and in person about money for some ten days previously; and the final fee, decided upon between us the morning of the day you saw him, turned out to be $2,500 down for a first draft against $5,000 ninety days from the date of completion. It is now completed, and we are wrangling over terms for a second draft, for which I hope to make approximately the same deal.

So, as you can see, I am an impoverished fellow. I have now resolved to have no more of these little deals, of which there is always a plethora, since they are no real solution to my truly heroic needs. I therefore intend, during the next three months, to gamble recklessly on original screenplays. I have only written three in my life.

[18] Financial support of the cause of the Hollywood Ten.
[19] Hollywood producer, Sam Spiegel.

but they have all sold, and my record of sales on straight originals has always struck a tolerable average, so that I feel I am not unduly optimistic in thinking that at least one of the present three will find a home.

When and if it does I shall be in a position to make a substantial payment, either directly to you as a way of sharing your present burden, which I know is very great, or into the general fund [Holly-wood Ten], whichever you think fitter. Meanwhile, in the unlikely event that we should not collect on our civil suits, I would consider it a moral obligation of the first order to get together with you and work out an arrangement whereby I would share with you the wholly disproportionate expense to which you have thus far been put.

In Jesus' Name!
DALTON

23. To Lee Sabinson

Lazy T Ranch
Frazier Park, California
August 15, 1949

Dear Lee:

I did get the books, and I did read them, and I am presently in the course of reading Jack Lawson's book.[20]

But I think you should count it among your blessings that there will be no Trumbo play this season. Good God, lad, the first one damned near ruined the most promising man on Broadway—and I don't refer to Trumbo or Shumlin. You've had quite enough punishment for the moment.

Seriously, when I returned I had to turn in hot pursuit of the Yankee dollar. It was elusive and I was tired, and not until about a week ago did I finally catch up with it. It would be much too late to think of doing a play for this season. But I do have serious hopes for next.

My idea of perfection would [be] to spend the winter doing a play (which I think my finances will once again permit); to have a version with which I am fairly satisfied in your hands by April; to have a version with which we are both pleased by May; to spend June with the director, July casting, August thinking and September

[20] Trumbo was studying playwriting. Sabinson had sent him several books. The reference here is to John Howard Lawson's *Theory and Technique of Playwriting* published by G. P. Putnam's Sons, 1936.

in rehearsal; thereafter to have only one week tryout in a town which is not New Haven, Boston or Philadelphia, and which is sufficiently removed from New York to keep the local sharpies out; to decide on the basis of that week whether to go ahead or not, and if decision favorable, to go to New York cold and let her ride. Above plan might even call for me to direct. Who can tell? Could I be worse than the last?

All the above is serious, for my ass is sore burned by your big city word mongers parading as critics. You behaved splendidly. I was reminded by your conduct of those who went proudly down with the *Lusitania* (or was it the *Titanic?*) singing God Save the King and knowing damned well if the king were there He couldn't. Cleo and I call benisons down upon your head. We burn candles for Billy [Mrs. Sabinson] and the kids. We bow east whenever the muezzin calls the hour in our desolate but well-loved little mountain meadow.

Now write, you bastard. . . . Tell me I am a shit for not this instant being engaged in a play. You will, of course, be right. But the little ones eat, and the Yankee dollar was scarce, and pappy had to screw the producers under a phony name, which he did. But it took time.

Yours in Jesus!
DALTON

24. To Sam Spiegel

Lazy T Ranch
Frazier Park, California
September 17, 1949

Dear Sam:

At long last patience and friendship must give way to necessity. I am as sympathetic as a man can be to financial embarrassments of all kinds, and have tried—at my own cost—to be understanding of yours.

In order to finish your work, I was obliged to hock my watch and a ring of my wife's. I violated a standing rule I have always found to be a good one: no money, no work. I relied on your personal promise. Twice you assured me money was being sent to my dependents; once you swore it had been sent; it has not been sent yet. George [Willner] now tells me he finds it impossible to get you on the telephone.

Certain complications have rendered useless a piece of work I was going to submit for sale, and I cannot submit it. My wife and my various families are therefore totally dependent upon the $2,000 you owe me. It is right and necessary that I take every means to protect them from hardship, particularly when I have done honest work which should receive its prompt reward.

I must therefore insist that the moneys you owe me be paid over to George Willner within twenty-four hours of your receipt of this letter. No excuses will suffice. No promises can be accepted. There must be absolutely no delay, or the consequences will be serious for both of us.

Regards,
DALTON TRUMBO

25. To Elsie McKeogh

Lazy T Ranch
Frazier Park, California
September 17, 1949

Dear Elsie:

By all means penetrate the iron curtain with anything they wish. My feeling about all foreign sales is this: while I would sooner get the money, I would prefer publication with *no* money to no publication. Let that rule therefore guide us in all our dealings with outlanders.

Regards,
DALTON

26. To John Garfield

Lazy T Ranch
Frazier Park, California
[*c. November 1, 1949*]

Dear Julie:

I read, of course, about your illness,[21] but being canny of newspapers paid no heed until I talked to John Huston and Sam [Spiegel], who told me you had been through a really serious thing. Of all the lousy actors around, why did it have to happen to you?

Cleo and I want you to know we are concerned, and that we urge you to go easily and live to be eighty. Any time you and Robbie and

---

[21] Garfield, the noted actor and film star, had suffered a heart attack.

the kids would like to get away from things, come up to the ranch and rest. I will personally cook for you, and guarantee no disturbances. If Robbie and the children are in New York, come up yourself, and we can at least horseshit each other into happy frames of mind.

If there is anything in the world I can do—script doctoring or spiritual advice or a personal massage—holler and it's yours.

Affectionately,
DALTON

27. To Ted Riner

Lazy T Ranch
Frazier Park, California
[c. November 1, 1949]

Dear Uncle: [22]

Have received your letter of the 25th, and note by sly implication in one paragraph that you are one of those silly fellows who believe everything they read in the newspapers,[23] which is, of course, all right with me, except it leaves a guy so ignorant of what really goes on about him.

For your information I therefore will set you straight on several misapprehensions you might have come under as a result of your addiction to the press. Get set then, for the truth, to which you have always been an almost complete stranger.

On three o'clock of the day in question I leave Hugo Butler's house, having had no drink. I go to Equitable Investment Corporation to get some money, no drink. I go to Zandt Carpet, buy a bathroom rug, no drink. I go to bookstore and buy library for two older kids for which they have been screaming, no drink. I go to Beverly Citizen plant and order stationery, no drink. I go to electrical shop, buy some bulbs, no drink. I go to drug store, buy some candy, no drink. I go to floral shop, buy some chrysanthemums, no drink. I go to the Hunters' house, give flowers to Alice. Ian is not home yet. I look for liquor. There is maybe quarter inch wash over bottom of bottle. I drink it. Some drink.

[22] Ted Riner is the husband of Maud Trumbo's younger sister; hence the salutation "Uncle." Riner, a warm friend of Trumbo's, was an infantry man in France during World War I, a roughneck in Texas and California oil fields, and is now a retired manufacturer of fishing lures.

[23] Trumbo was arrested in front of the home of Ian Hunter and charged with drunkenness on October 19, 1949. He was booked in the Venice (California) jail and released on $20 bail.

Ian arrives, and we sit and talk until 8:15, when the baby sitter comes. No drink because there ain't none. Baby sitter arrives, we go out to dinner. I want to go to the Marquis Cafe, take my own car and separate from the Hunters there and go to the Butlers' and to bed. But they think drive to Marquis too far for them. We settle on Italian eating place in Santa Monica called Lizari's or Reachi's or some such name, I forget at the moment. Anyhow, Ian has known this man when he had a big restaurant in the city. He went broke and opened small eatery in Santa Monica, and Ian wishes to confer patronage on him. We therefore go in Ian's car.

We are unnerved when we get to the restaurant to discover man has come so far down in the world he owns no liquor license, can serve no stimulants. No drink at all. This is first time in twenty-seven years no drink with dinner. Am distressed and deeply sober. We stay late, because there are many courses, and we talk. We get back to Hunter's about 11:30. Dismiss baby sitter. Alice goes to bed. During our absence drug store has delivered bottle of scotch. We sit down with bottle, but being very stuffed with food are not nearly so thirsty as would have been earlier. Conduct conversation with each other and consume two highballs. Two. Some drunk.

It is now 1:35 in morning. Decide to go to bed there. Hunter goes into bedroom to undress. I need to urinate. I don't want to urinate in the only toilet, because thing goes dribble-drabble for hours afterward unless one jiggles handle violently. Violent jiggling invariably awakens baby in next room. I go outside to curb. Very remote little residential section, a G.I. community. No moon. No streetlights. No lights in any houses except ours. No traffic. No people. Haul out and urinate as my father taught me to. Car turns corner, catches me like moth in powerful light. Try quickly to insert penis back in pants. Car stops. Am trapped while still buttoning.

Police want identification. I give. Want to know what am doing. I say urinating in gutter, pardon the expression. They say why. I say toilet jammed, dribble-drabble, jiggle, child, disturbance, innate courtesy, here I am. They say drinking? I say yes. They say when last. I say two minutes ago. They say drunk! I say no. Then I say, with anger, the way they talk would think I'd been drinking since six-thirty in morning. (This choice quote comes out in one paper as saying boasted of capacity, said had been drinking since six-thirty a.m.) They say climb in car. I do. Hunter comes flapping out in bathrobe crying outrage, snatch, violation of rights. I tell him not to worry, I'll take sobriety test, be back in twenty minutes.

Arrive at station. Ask for sobriety test. One cop phones papers, other divests me of everything including glasses. Am booked. While this goes on newspapermen arrive. I repeat story wearily to them, repeat demands for sobriety test. Newspaper guys leave. Desk sergeant says now I can bail myself out. Twenty bucks please. He knows I have that much because has carefully gone through wallet. The charge is "drunk in public place." Some public. Some place. I say if I'm drunk it's their duty to hold me until I'm sober, that no man could possibly sober up in twenty minutes, twenty dollars or no twenty dollars, and that I will not bail out until have sobriety test. I am taken behind bars where I prepare to wait it out. Hunter arrives, dressed by now, saying shocking conduct of police, kidnaping, miscarriage of justice. Gets in touch with attorney. Attorney says if they won't give me sobriety test, there is no way I can force them to; and since I've made the stand, now to please give them twenty bucks and come out. I give them twenty bucks and come out.

I drive rapidly to Los Angeles and waken Bob Riemer at his house. There he gives me sobriety test. I walk straight line in normal stride, then heel and toe.; I close eyes, clasp hands, touch nose easily with both hands, or rather both forefinger-tips. I take speech test a man ordinarily couldn't pass when sober. Lights in room are turned out, and eyes are probed for dilation of pupils with stabbing little light. No dilation. Lights go on. Blood pressure is taken (it goes down from normal when drunk), pulse is taken, temperature is taken. Blood is drawn from left arm into bottle, send to laboratory for chemical analysis of alcoholic content. Result: every test perfect. I am one of the soberest men in the community. I am almost too sober.

Next morning am in fighting mood, particularly after I see how press has murdered me. With lawyers I make plans for trial and acquittal, which is a cinch. Prosecution lets it be known if I testify in court I was urinating in gutter in defense of drunk charge, they will then file charges of indecent exposure. This is a nasty charge, generally associated with waving genitals at young children. Can't stand trial on that too. Publicity not good. Attorneys go to judge. Judge is both amused and angry about situation. Judge says thing simply proves man hasn't same right as horses. However judge can only mediate between me and cops.

Cops remain adamant on second charge if I defend self on first. They are taken aback, however, by sobriety test. They do not want a trial and acquittal. I am not eager for publicity attending a trial, even one I would win. It never reaches as far as the original story. I finally resolve to make only one stand: I will not plead guilty to being drunk, come hell or high water. Cops on their part agree not to prosecute. When matter came up in court, neither defense nor prosecution appeared in court. Bail was forfeited. I am not guilty of any misdemeanor. On the records I am guilty neither of being drunk nor of urinating in gutter. Seemed best solution to get thing out of headlines, keep my aging puss out of pictorial section.

Am now waiting for some enemy, including you if necessary, to make snide public remark or to put in writing I am convicted drunk, or guilty of drunkenness. Will then sue for million dollars and win.

Come up some time and have a drink with me, and I will show you how nicely our toilets work.

Your nephew,
DALTON

28. To Maud Trumbo

Lazy T Ranch
Frazier Park, California
November 1, 1949

Dear mother:

I have been meaning to write you ever since my latest burst in the headlines, but I have been desperately busy with an assignment, and am preparing to leave for a two-week lecture tour, and have put it off from day to day. Ted [Riner], however, wrote me a very amusing letter, and I replied to him in kind with a full report of my misadventures. It occurred to me that the simplest way of telling what happened would be to send you a copy of my letter to Ted, and then Catherine,[24] if she wishes, can strike off copies and mail to whichever relatives she thinks may be interested. The important thing, of course, is that my record is clear, as the letter will show you, and that the newspapers played it up simply because I am me.

I enclose also a pamphlet entitled "Time of the Toad"[25] which was published about a week before the incident. Upon reading it, you will see there is nothing in it which would endear me to the press or the police. Originally scheduled for publication in 10,000 copies, the pamphlet has caused a moderate sensation, is now coming out in second edition of 15,000, and a third edition of 25,000 is on the way. It is aimed mainly at intellectuals, the universities, the churches, the professions, and has already achieved nation-wide circulation. A physicist at the Princeton Institute for Advanced Studies sent in money for thirty, with addresses of thirty professors to whom it should be sent. A minister from the Midwest has ordered a hundred copies, and wrote the Ten, "God bless Dalton Trumbo." One man writes me: "In my opinion, which is at least that of a fellow writer, 'The Time of the Toad' is the finest American political pamphleteer-

[24] Trumbo's sister, Mrs. Catherine Baldwin.
[25] "The Time of the Toad," subtitled "A Study of Inquisition in America," published in October, 1949.

ing since Tom Paine. It is very likely that your pen has struck the mightiest blow yet against democracy's besworded enemies." Another says: "I have just finished reading 'The Time of the Toad.' God, what a magnificent job! Certainly one of the best pamphlets I've ever read. An awful lot of words are being turned out in this town but I doubt very much that any of them will be as long remembered as yours. Dorothy Parker gave me her copy, and in case you don't hear from her personally, I think you should know she shares my enthusiasm. So does everyone I've talked to who's had a chance to read it. A fine, fine piece of work." A woman writes: "I have just finished reading 'The Time of the Toad' and feel that I must write you and tell you how truly excellent it is. In your hand the pen becomes a sword, or should I say the typewriter becomes a machine gun? Too often pamphlets are written with fervor, from facts, but without skill. To say that your writing is skillful would be presumptuous, but may I praise the passion, the irony, and above all, the scope of your pamphlet? The only other document I have read which has had a similar impact for me, and which I urge you to read if you have not already done so, is a communication to the American Historical Association from Henry Adams, dated December 12, 1894, which you can find on page 125 of *The Degradation of the Democratic Dogma*. I am purchasing a large quantity of your pamphlet, and will distribute them to close friends, casual acquaintances and business contacts. Thank you again, Dalton Trumbo." Rev. Stephen H. Fritchman of the First Unitarian Church in Los Angeles, in writing me to address his congregation—which I can't do because I shall be east— says: "I would like you and Mrs. Trumbo to have a buffet supper with us before we go to the church. I will then tell you personally my great delight in reading 'The Time of the Toad.' I shall be using it in a hundred ways the next few months, I hope with due credits."

I quote so extensively only to show you that there are persons who do not make the calumnies of the newspapers the basis of their judgment. I am leaving about the tenth of November for a speaking tour, which interests me because it covers a part of the country I don't know very well. St. Louis, Minneapolis, Milwaukee, Madison, mainly university and professional groups. Then to Chicago for a big Progressive Party rally, where I speak with Wallace, Robeson and Marcantonio. Then home.

The status of our case is this: we are waiting for the Supreme Court to decide whether or not they will accept the case for review. We shall hear November 14th. If they refuse to take it, there is a certain amount of legal stalling permissible before we actually go to jail. If they do take it, the issue will be postponed for months. More briefs have been filed on our behalf with the court, urging it to take the case, than for any case in the history of the country. Groups like the Methodists, Episcopalians, Unitarians, Civil Liberties Union, Congress of Civil Rights, Authors' League of America, several Jewish groups, the National Association for the Advancement of Colored People—altogether an astonishing outpouring of support, which we hope will have some influence upon the court.

I enclose also a copy of the published playing edition of *The Biggest Thief in Town*. I don't know whether I mentioned to you that *Theatre Arts* Magazine has purchased the play for publication in its January issue. In addition they asked me for a preface which I wrote, and for which they not only paid me—something they don't do—but as a result of which they have asked me to contribute whenever I have anything to say about the theatre, which is breaking down the magazine barrier in terms of the blacklist.

I also, about a week ago, wrote my first short story in twelve years. I enclose a copy, which I shall need returned. Elsie likes it very much, and is now trying to peddle it. We shall see how much resistance there is to my name in fiction. I send it because I think it is a story you will probably like. Additionally, in the last three months I have earned $50,000, finished a diet and taken off ten pounds, and bought a jeep to shoot the kids to school in this winter— a station wagon with heater. The record, I think, will not bear out the contention that so much work can have been done in so short a time by a chronic alcoholic.

Cleo and the kids are fine. I invented a Hallowe'en costume for Nikola and rehearsed her in her portrayal of character, and she walked off with the prize at school, which delighted her and distressed Chris. Ethel and Frank Butler visited here today, and Ethel tells me that Mrs. Smailes, the principal, says Chris is the brightest child in school—which would comfort him for the loss of the prize, although we shan't tell him.

I am now working to finish an assignment, for which I shall be paid next year. Then I have another to do before Christmas, which will also be paid for next year. Thus I shall have enough funds, in the event of disaster, to take care of every responsibility for a full year, and have a little left over. Debts are non-existent, and if the good luck of a [court] reversal should occur—which I don't plan on—I shall be in a position to do whatever I wish for a year or two and live comfortably at the same time.

All in all, things are not so bad. They are, in fact, very good. When something nasty happens, I always think of you and suffer for you, as I am sure someday I shall feel pain because of Chris or Nikola or Mitzi. But I reassure myself with this thought; your friends admire you, not for me, but for yourself, and then I know you will ride through.

When I look back on my own convictions and rebellion, I find nothing remarkable in it. For I am reminded that at a younger age than I my mother, too, rebelled, left her church, joined an unpopular and ridiculed faith,[26] insisted upon the immunity of her children from supervision of medical authorities; and that the church she joined was fighting for its life before various legislatures, and that its founder was in the newspapers, falsely and outrageously, and fought them off to the end. How, then, could a rebellious mother produce anything but a rebellious son?

Disagreeing as we do and have, we have finally struck a relationship which I am sure pleases us both—one of mutual respect. I love you very much, but I respect you even more, and that is what I hope to earn from my own children, after suitable conflicts and disagreements. Instead of regrets for my present plight, I have only renewed confidence, and a joy in writing that five years ago I thought would never come to me.

My God, I've given you enough reading material for a month. Enough, then! One would think I was trying to sell it to you.

DALTON

29. To the Editor of the *Saturday Review of Literature*

Lazy T Ranch
Frazier Park, California
[c. late fall, 1949]

Dear sir:

I know how tedious controversy can become, especially when it is reduced to the calibre of Mr. [Arthur] Schlesinger's "whew" for rebuttal.[27] But I live in the country and pick up my mail only rarely, and have just come across the *Saturday Review* for August 20th, in which Mr. Schlesinger insists that I answer certain questions.

"But I would be naive, of course," writes Mr. Schlesinger, who is too young to be naive and too old to find nourishment in such sophistry, "to suppose that Mr. Trumbo thinks that Trotskyites and Klansmen, for example, should be accorded the same rights as Communists and fellow-travelers."

I have always thought my stand on this issue quite clear. I deny the right of Congress, or of any agent of government, or of any other group or person to call American citizens to account for their political affiliations or sympathies. I affirm the basic constitutional principle that men may be questioned and prosecuted for their acts, never for their thoughts.

[26] Mrs. Trumbo became a Christian Scientist in 1912. All her children regularly attended the Christian Science Sunday school and church services.
[27] See letter #21 above, p. 124.

Trotskyites sponsor a political organization called the Socialist Workers' Party, which offers a political program to the electorate. Members of this party and its sympathizers are endowed with all the constitutional immunities which apply to other parties. This is the law, and I support it.

The Ku Klux Klan is not a political party, nor does it offer a political program to voters. Its members are murderers, arsonists and floggers. Their acts are subject to legal processes which derive from criminal law. Congress has the power and, indeed, the obligation to investigate such criminal acts—an obligation which I regret it does not fulfill.

If, in the improbable event that either of these organizations is brought before the House Committee on Un-American Activities, I do not spend my time and money in their defense, it will not be because I deny their civil rights or value them less; it will be because I value more the violated civil rights of their victims, and choose to engage my energies in their behalf.

By victims I mean men on picket lines who are subjected to Trotskyite violence as a result of the National Association of Manufacturers' directive to its members to seek out and work with Trotskyites for employer ends in periods of labor strife. I also refer to those countless Negro citizens who have been murdered outright or railroaded to their deaths by the Klan mentality—specifically to the Trenton Six, who were saved from electrocution by the efforts of the "subversive" Civil Rights Congress in a fight which found Americans for Democratic Action lolling as always in the summer sun of liberal indolence.

My concept of civil liberties and constitutional immunities derives from the law as it has been conceived and guarded in this country for a hundred and sixty years. Unless Mr. Schlesinger and his fellow Eisenhower-Douglas-Truman-or-anybody theoreticians of A[mericans for] D[emocratic] A[ction] yield more than lavender lip service to this doctrine, the country they lust to lead will not be worth the tiny candle they presently burn for it.

Very truly,
DALTON TRUMBO

30. Rough draft of a letter to Herbert Biberman

Lazy T Ranch
Frazier Park, California
[c. December, 1949]

Dear Herbert:

I cannot tell you how seriously we have been harmed by the unauthorized use of the name "Cleo Fincher Trumbo" on the petition to the Supreme Court,[28] and its subsequent publication in the *People's World*. Her name, for all future records, is *CLEO TRUMBO*. It is in this name that she owns the ranch, signs checks, possesses her driver's license, has listed her relationship to the children on their birth certificates, becomes a beneficiary of my insurance, will exercise her power of attorney when I am gone.

Why was she not consulted on *how* her name should be signed. Certainly Helen Clare Nelson Bessie must have been consulted as to her signature, for who can remember so many names? Certainly Gale Sondergaard must have been consulted about eliminating the Biberman from her name. Why should not the same courtesy be extended to Cleo?

You may ask why I am upset. For eighteen months I have been carefully building up the name "Fincher" in the motion picture industry as a legitimate writer. Today by telegraph I have received (1) a cancellation of a screen credit in that name, and (2) the abrogation of a job for which the contracts had been made out but not yet signed. Men have paid moneys to that name on the assurance it would not become known. It is a name that in six months would have had real value, and which, when I came out, was ready to become a vehicle through which, without depending on plotting with others, I might have earned a legitimate living. Now it is destroyed, and the hell with it.

I say that we are a special kind of people, operating under special conditions, and that each of us should recognize this fact in relation to the other, and that *nothing* like this should occur without consultation. Even if it appears harmless. No one has the right to sign either of our names. And if they are determined to change the accustomed use of our names, then by Jesus Christ they should discuss it with us before witlessly proceeding on their own.

This letter is only for your eyes, and for transmission to the person who committed this unauthorized act. I want it to go no farther because there are three uses of this name in the past which may possibly go unnoticed by those who paid. My experience has been that

---

[28] Petitions as Friends of the Court (Amici-Cuciae) by individuals and organizations backing the Hollywood Ten. The purpose of the petitions was to appeal the lower courts' conviction and affirmation of that conviction.

if the full Ten know it, a paid ad in the *Hollywood Reporter* could not achieve half the coverage in twice the time.

Sore? You're goddamned right we're sore. Recriminations? What is the use? It's done, and it was done innocently. But here is the rule from now on:

No one is ever again to issue *any* statement about *anything* over *either* of our names without those names being signed by us *in person*. No quotation, no statement, no signature, no nothing. This is the only way we can protect ourselves from such damnably foolish mistakes in the future.

My name is Dalton. Hers is Cleo. The last name is Trumbo. None of the children has three names. Those are simple names to remember, and let your research department save its efforts to elaborate them or to make them elegant sounding.

Finally, I want a list of every publication to which this petition was sent, so that Cleo can write and tell them they are in error about the name Fincher, and request, not that they correct what was printed, but that they do not use it again in future copy. Otherwise the goddamned name will lie in morgues and be used and reused for years.

You think this is drastic? I tell you it isn't. It will take me two years to correct the blunder. I say it is loose, inefficient, presumptuous—and since the trouble of recalling her maiden name served no purpose whatsoever, it also was pointless and foolish. We really must have more respect for each other and each other's private lives and problems, and consult, consult, *consult* before we blossom out changing common usages for God knows what obscure and ineffective purpose.

Aside from that, dear lad, I send you and Gale and the kids our real affection—but an affection which does not in one single degree diminish the emphasis of what has preceded it.

DALTON

31. To Sally Deutsch of *Theatre Arts* Magazine

Lazy T Ranch
Frazier Park, California
March 2, 1950

Dear Sally Deutsch:

I'll be very pleased to do the Academy article.[29] However the investigations I made originally suggest certain difficulties. First, I

[29] "The Graven Image," *Theatre Arts*, July, 1950. The magazine requested the article after the success of Trumbo's introduction to the published text of *The Biggest Thief in Town*, in its January, 1950 issue.

cannot find evidence that studio pressure has ever affected decisions on the Oscars. Second, the method of selection—by groups of workmen within the various arts and crafts affected—appears to be as sound as possible. Third, the awards themselves are no sillier than most other honors.

However, there *is* an amusing job to be done on the general situation of awards in Hollywood. Rivaling the academy now are *Look, Redbook,* the New York Critics, and a dozen other foundations, sodalities, clubs and professional groups. Directors, writers, cinematographers also give *their* awards. Some of these affairs are considerably plushier than the Academy's own.

Now how would this be:

1. Develop the idea that no moderately competent hack in *any* field of Hollywood endeavor can spend ten years in the community without winning a wide assortment of plaques, medals and certificates of merit.

2. Develop the theme that an award actually glorifies the donor much more than the recipient—hence the frantic competition to *give* awards, which even exceeds the frenzy to receive them.

3. And finally—that if you haven't got one of the several hundred awards given by the presumably legitimate groups, you can, at small cost through a good publicity man, receive a good many extracurricular testimonials, scrolls, etc., at will. For instance, at the premier of *Battleground* here, the producer, writer, and director took to the stage *before* the picture was shown, and received from high brass a large sheaf of commendations and certificates, and made appropriate speeches of response, after which [a large portion of the] audience was appalled at this method of getting awards not otherwise available.

What do you think?

DALTON TRUMBO

32. To Elsie McKeogh

Lazy T Ranch
Frazier Park, California
April 16, 1950

Dear Elsie:

Theatre Arts liked the article very much apparently, and will publish it either in the June or July issue, at which time they will pay over to you $75.00.

The papers have doubtless informed you that at least one of your clients will shortly become a number. We consider the chances excellent that we shall be in jail within ten days, and a thousand to one that we shall be in by June 1.

Once the doors spring upon me, whatever business occurs will have to be transacted with Cleo, who will continue to live at the ranch. She possesses complete power of attorney for me, and is authorized to sign anything which you advise her to. You will find her an agreeable person with whom to do business, in the unlikely event that any shows up.

Regards,
DALTON

33. To George Willner

Lazy T Ranch
Frazier Park, California
April 21, 1950

Dear George:

Enclosed with this letter is an original entitled _____.[30] It is not as well done as it might be, for I was able to allow myself only four days on it. I don't know whether you will like it or not, but I *do* know that if it were given to me as an assignment, I would make one of the best pictures ever filmed out of it.

In selecting a form in which to tell it, I considered the fact that many of *The New Yorker* Roving Reporter articles are now being purchased, such as "Old 888" and Joel Sayre's story of the guy who jumped out of the Gotham Hotel window. So I decided to try to lend an air of added reality to this yarn by doing it as if a *New Yorker* man were reporting an actual incident.

I will not go into my finances with you, for I am the only one in the world who can do anything about them. But I can tell you that the urgency is so great that I have worked day and night to get this finished, and have sent a man into town with it, so that no time will be lost. If you like it, I beg you to get it to the mimeographers *tomorrow*—even if it means extra cost for weekend work. For it would be a great comfort to me to know before I leave what happens to it. I hate to push you in this fashion, but if you think it a possibility, I must urge you to do everything possible to get it out on Monday, or Tuesday at the latest.

I am now, like a fiendish machine, starting on another one, and if

[30] Although this original sold for $40,000, it was never filmed.

God is good and time lasts for me, I shall have three in your hands before I leave.[31] Please forgive the sound of urgency in this note—I love you well despite the way I push you. I may try to telephone you tomorrow for your reaction. Or, better still, could you send me a wire saying "Good" or "Bad"? Then my man could get it in the morning.

A thousand apologies, ten thousand banzais, and a little affection to boot!

DALTON

34. To Dr. Robert Riemer[32]

Lazy T Ranch
Frazier Park, California
April 23, 1950

Dear Bob:

To save me from dipping into that liquid material you gave me for sleeping, will you please send me fifty Seconals? Also, since I am engaged in a prodigious program of work and have no time to waste, either in waking up or going to sleep, send me also fifty Benzedrine and a hundred Dexedrine.

Would you also do me the favor of calling Dr. Miller and telling him we have decided to cancel our reservation at Cedars [of Lebanon Hospital] for April 25th? I do not have his name and initials, hence find it awkward to write him myself. We have concluded to wait until after I go and the children are adjusted to one parent before depriving them of the other, even for a few brief days of hospitalization. The possibility of me going at the same time Cleo is in the hospital is too great to gamble on, and we think such a coincidence would not be good for them. Cleo will rely on Dr. Miller for such affective palliative as he already has given her, and at a later date will have the job done.[33]

Jesus attend you,
DALTON

[31] Trumbo managed to complete two of the proposed three originals before going to jail.

[32] Trumbo's personal physician.

[33] Minor surgery.

35. To William Pomerance

Lazy T Ranch
Frazier Park, California
April 24, 1950

Dear Bill:

The chances are, according to our most optimistic attorneys, better than a thousand to one that I at least shall be in jail within three weeks. For the first few days there was actual danger of being picked up prior to our filing of petition for rehearing, which occurs tomorrow. The case, barring an absolute miracle, is utterly hopeless.

This, of course, bars any work on the play for the time being. With my three households et al. I am in a last-minute series of legal and financial arrangements, and am, of course, trying as desperately as possible, to scrape up a little cash in the way of earnings before I leave. Jim and Adele Martin [34] are returning to the ranch, which will be a comfort to Cleo; and the Hugo Butlers plan to move up and spend the summer here with her, which will provide friendship during the first three—and emotionally, probably the most important—months.

If the miracle should occur and the court should dally until the summer recess, I would have until autumn. The delay itself would be the biggest victory possible, for there isn't a chance this court will ever rule in our favor. If the above unexpected good fortune came to pass, I would do the play during the summer (perhaps even under another name, who knows at this moment what would be best?) and at least have it in someone's hands before I went off.

In the long run, the sooner the better. It's a wearying routine, and I am fed up with it. The kids are wonderful. Said Chris, with a malicious glint in his eye, when I told him I would shortly be on my way: "And what are they going to do with us—send us to the reform school?" He was immensely pleased with this crack, although he confessed later and privately to Cleo that when I went "it *would* be a bit of a shock."

Things will either get better or they will get worse. With this profound statement, and love to Edwina, I subscribe myself.

Yours in Christ,
DALTON

[34] Adele Zimple became Christopher's nurse in 1940 and remained with the Trumbos until her marriage to James Martin, with whom she had three children. The Martins, who had previously worked at the Lazy T as manager and housekeeper, returned to the ranch for the period of Trumbo's incarceration and remained until it was sold. On the Trumbos return from Mexico in 1955, Mrs. Martin became their part-time housekeeper while completing her college education. She now teaches in a Los Angeles school for handicapped children. When Melinda, the eldest Martin child, was married in 1968, Trumbo stood as surrogate for her deceased father.

36. To Herbert Biberman

Lazy T Ranch
Frazier Park, California
April 26, 1950

Dear Herbert:

The chances are that I may get to jail twenty-four hours before the rest of you, hence that my time is that much shorter. I have the immediate problem of figuring out enough cash to provide for a wife and three children for nine months, plus the total support of two elderly women living in separate Hollywood apartments.

The only way I have figured out how to solve this purely practical and, to me at least, absolutely urgent problem, is to spend 12 to 14 hours each night at my typewriter, *and to continue this routine without break until the day I have to leave*. In order to maintain it, I take drugs to put me to sleep without loss of time, and other drugs to awaken me promptly.

In the past week I have received five different requests from various well-intentioned persons commanding me to "telephone the minute you get this letter." Each one of these—had I obeyed, which I did not in a single instance—would have sent me on a 24 mile trip, with no positive assurance the person called would even be in at the time I called. To get a picture of what it means, let me reverse it: let's assume that I had sent five demands to people in Hollywood, telling each to jump out of bed at three o'clock in the morning, travel to South Pasadena and there gamble on the possibility of being able to reach me by phone. This, I am sure, would be regarded as unreasonable of me, particularly when matters of such nature can well be dealt with by mail. When there is a real emergency I shall of course want to know and will telephone at once. But no more wolf cries, in God's sweet name.

I am making the television show [35]—at what may be a considerable financial cost to my family—because the reasons you give are reasonable. I am disturbed that the subject has been changed, think it a mistake, but still will come. I shall, as I told Albert [Maltz] by

[35] Trumbo refers to a television debate for which he was selected to represent the Hollywood Ten. Trumbo and Carey McWilliams debated a newspaper columnist and a lawyer. Looking back on the incident, Trumbo says: "As I recall that particular program, I was practically mute and poor Carey had to carry the burden of our argument. The reason was that I had never been at such close quarters with such people as our opponents, and I was absolutely bowled over by the quality of their minds. Later on, and particularly after I emerged from the pokey, I grew somewhat more blasé about such people, and handled myself rather well against them. Indeed, I tangled with them on TV so frequently and so successfully that I began to like it, which, of course, is a danger signal. I was becoming a pro and a ham, entirely too slick for my own good. The result is I gave it up, and wild horses couldn't drag me back onto TV in my present civilized frame of mind."

letter, be at the Globe Theatre Sunday at 2:30 p.m. and no earlier. I shall not go into the reasons which prevent me from coming sooner, but they are important ones. I am astonished at a shooting schedule which, because the film begins with a group shot, must itself open with that group shot. However if the schedule is so inelastic, the group will not have me in it.[36] I shall be at your disposal from Sunday 2:30 p.m. through Monday night. Immediately after the television, I shall return home.

God bless you, lad, and forgive the firm tone of this missive. I may be around another two weeks, and I simply want to explain my situation and stop the frantic imperatives of "phone at once."

DALTON

37. To George Willner

Lazy T Ranch
Frazier Park, California
April 27, 1950

Dear George:

Here is number two—the comedy, so called, of which you have already read the first twenty-two pages. I have done it so rapidly that I am in no position to pass sensible judgment on it. Offhand, I would at least say that better have been written and worse have been sold.[37]

The basic idea of the girl who invented Toni-Wave is Hugo's, and many months ago we agreed that if I ever sold it, I would pay him $2,500 for the idea. Thus, in a way, he has first claim on the thing. *If* you think it saleable—and *if* you think submission of it will not destroy his reputation—and if he thinks it okay to do so—then that would be fine with me. But I want to be certain that nothing is done that will hurt his reputation in any way. This is of paramount importance to all of us.

If, however, you think the yarn hasn't much chance but might just sneak by with a sale, I suggest _____. The dialogue here, whether as dialogue or as comment, is sometimes amusing, and can do no harm to a man who has as yet had no big credits. There is a story of a kind, there are characters (although admittedly done here so hastily they are caricatures instead)—there is a situation, a back-

[36] A two-reel film directed by John Berry and produced in Hollywood by Friends of the Hollywood Ten, which was used extensively at meetings to raise funds for court battles. As none of the Ten found sufficient spare time to work on the script, it was done by outsiders.
[37] This original apparently did not sell.

ground and an amusing scene or two. I don't think it would hurt him, do you?

As always, I must rely on you. Any speed (provided you decide to submit it) will be appreciated. For I never, in a situation like the present one, like to gamble everything on one throw of the dice. First throw has been made. Here is second, which I view with equal urgency.

The third, a frank love-action-melodrama, is now in the works.

God, old boy, what an affliction I must be to you. But then comfort yourself that I am even a worse affliction upon myself. Time bears heavily upon me, and whatever you can do in the way of speed and pressure will be most gratefully accepted. And if you miss—this lad is not the one who will ever blame you.

Selah!
D.T.

38. To George Willner

Lazy T Ranch
Frazier Park, California
April 28, 1950

Dear George:

I cannot resist writing to tell you how superbly you handled that matter, and how deeply grateful to you we all are.[38] I am absolutely certain anyone else would have fluffed it. Only your deep knowledge of what this town really is carried you through. I am more aware than you think of what it must have done to your nerves, your emotions and your stomach.

Beyond my immense sense of relief, I also derive another kind of pleasure from a deal like this. Part of it is the pure joy one gets from a feeling of professional competence, which I must admit is close to conceit, and yet which I still feel. And secondly, I look forward to the time when, despite being nameless, faceless, voiceless—as has been the case for the past two and a half years—I shall still achieve a place on your lists of clients of which—purely in dollars and cents—you can say with truth that I am among your top ten.

I verily believe that if you and I were pitched alone against this town, we could figure out a way to live very comfortably off of it. Which is to say, with forthright egotism, that I think both of us are awfully good.

[38] Trumbo refers to the $40,000 sale of the first original.

I shall check with you Sunday or Monday. But I want this much at least down in writing: thanks again and again—and again!

Affectionately,
DOC

39. To Rexroth & Rexroth, Bakersfield, California

Lazy T Ranch
Frazier Park, California
May 15, 1950

Gentlemen:

It appears that any Monday I shall go to jail. I am therefore clearing up all of what I consider my imperative obligations before I go. Among them I naturally place your balance of $600.00, and enclose the final check for that amount.

I should like also to tell you how very much I appreciate your extreme patience in this matter. To do eight or nine thousand dollars worth of work on a sixty-day basis, and then to wait for over two and a half years to have the debt finally cleared is really extraordinary. Your kindness has enabled me to extricate myself from what appeared to be an impossible financial situation, to save my assets from a mass assault of creditors, and to care for my family.

I hope some day to be in a position to repay my obligation to you —an obligation which I consider goes far beyond the simple act of finally cleaning up my cash debt. The moral debt I still owe.

Sincerely,
DALTON TRUMBO

4.

#7551

On June 21, 1950, after eleven days in a Washington, D.C., jail, Trumbo took up residence at the Federal Correctional Institute in Ashland, Kentucky, where he was to remain for ten months—the actual time of his one-year maximum penalty sentence for contempt of Congress. Trumbo was a model prisoner, uncomplaining and obedient, who quickly made friends with both the staff and his fellow inmates, many of whom wrote him affectionate letters after his release on April 8, 1951. Most of his prison acquaintances were at a loss to understand this strange offense called contempt and even more bewildered when, upon hearing of the HUAC hearings again in full swing in Hollywood, they observed that "buddies were stooling"—the most despicable breach of trust in their peculiarly rigid code of honor.

The results of the 1947 hearings seem insignificant compared with those of the investigations of early spring 1951. When the question of the constitutionality of the Congressional hearings—which had prevented continuation of the investigations during the intervening period—had been answered by the Supreme Court's refusal to review the case of the Ten in 1950, the House Committee resumed its attack with vigor. Ninety industry personalities gave evidence, and the policy of informing became firmly established as a primary technique of personal clearance. One writer, admitting to former communist party membership, established something of a record by naming 162 individuals he claimed to have known as communists. Thus, when the hearings were over, the Congressional Committee's annual report listed 324 undesirable names.

The requisites for clearance were largely established by Edward Dmytryk, the only one of the original Hollywood Ten to purge himself in order to return to work. During his six-month prison term, Dmytryk had issued a statement attacking the communist party; upon release, he gave secret testimony before the committee, later repeated at the public hearings, naming names and renouncing the party; finally he wrote a sympathetic exposé of himself as a communist for *The Saturday Evening Post* in May of 1951. Still another project to ensure clearance was speech making for those organizations that considered themselves the guardians of Americanism in Hollywood: the Motion Picture Alliance for the Preservation of American Ideals and the American Legion. These things accomplished, the writer, actor, or director was free to return to work.

While this storm raged in Hollywood, Trumbo, unable to help, unable even to comment, was rapidly "building time" in the Ashland prison. He spent his days working: early in his term, unloading truckfuls of foodstuffs, and later as an office clerk, organizing and updating files. Evenings were passed reading the large number of newspapers and magazines to which he was permitted subscription, working on the Pacific novel, and writing to his wife and those few friends whose names were approved by the prison authorities. To one always so active and energetic, the change of pace must have been disquietting, though not altogether miserable. Details of daily existence—showering, personal hygiene, problems of diet—replaced legal battles, political fights, and problems of earning a living, assuming almost ritualistic importance.

In these letters the lash and bite so typical of the total correspondence is replaced by gentleness and simplicity. Trumbo becomes a very ordinary men separated from his loved ones: marking off days on his calendar, reminiscing and planning for the future, inflating trivia, and worrying about things at home he is powerless to control.

1. To Cleo Trumbo

Washington, D.C.
[c. June 9, 1950]

Darling—

I write this in a cab on the way to court. . . . I lost your note before I read it, probably when I presented my plane ticket at the gate. We are going to try for Danbury, Conn.[1] We are fine—I love you very much and you will hear from me soon. Tell the kids they were wonderful at the airport [2] and made me very proud of them—as I have always been of you!

DALTON

[1] Of the Ten, Lester Cole and Ring Lardner, Jr. were sent to Danbury, where they were fellow inmates of ex-Congressman and Chairman of HUAC, J. Parnell Thomas.

[2] At the Los Angeles airport, Trumbo's children had proudly joined demonstrators and carried a banner of protest stating, "Dalton Trumbo is going to jail. Free the Hollywood Ten."

2. To Cleo Trumbo and the children

Washington, D.C.
Sunday, June 11, 1950

My darling—in fact, *all* my darlings!

As you perhaps know by now, I had a pleasant plane trip, arriving in New York Thursday at about 11:30 a.m. Jack [Lawson] and Lee and Billie [Sabinson] and Dr. Henry Pratt Fairchild met me at the plane, along with the usual photographers and reporters, both hunting bad angles. Went to Lee's, bathed, napped for a couple of hours, made a wire recording of an interview, recorded the poem,[3] and back to Lee's again for dinner with Lee, Billie, Bill and Edwina [Pomerance]. Then to Leila Hadley's—whose pictures I showed you in *Look*—for a farewell party. Saw Bart Crum[4] there, who is just recovering from a nervous breakdown, occasioned, I am told, by his abrupt dismissal from F.D.R. Jr's law firm. Said F.D.R. Jr.—"I don't need you any more for Jewish business. I have my own influence with the Jews now." A number of other partnerships in the firm were also dissolved, leaving F.D.R. Jr. all the business his colleagues had amassed.

There were over a thousand people to see us off at Penn Station, and Jack [Lawson][5] and I had the rather grotesque experience of being carried aloft through the crowd like a pair of startled, sacrificial bullocks on their way to the altar. There were speeches and FBI's and harried Pennsylvania officers, the latter as eager as we to have us downstairs in quieter surroundings. Slept the slumber of exhaustion, awakening in Washington. To the Raleigh Hotel for a press conference and horrible pictures, then to court, then to the district jail, Washington, D.C., where I presently reside, clean, well-fed, and getting lots of sleep. I expect a transfer by Wednesday, so I suggest you not write me until you know where I am going to be. I shall let you know the minute I am settled, and then you can tell me all about yourself, your fine children, mother, the ranch, the rye crop, the trees and the news.

Looking back over the years I find only a few things to regret. One of them is the money I pitched in to hire the Shrine for Truman when he was campaigning for the vice-presidency. Another, perhaps,

[3] *Masses & Mainstream* Magazine issued a professional recording of Trumbo reading his poem "Confessional."

[4] One of the defense lawyers for the "unfriendly" nineteen at the October, 1947 HUAC hearings.

[5] John Howard Lawson, a leading playwright of the thirties (*Processional, Success Story*), was founding president of the Screen Writers' Guild and author of such screenplays as *Blockade, Algiers, Action in the North Atlantic, Counter-Attack*. During the blacklist he wrote a number of films anonymously, as well as his critical works: *Film in the Battle of Ideas, Film: The Creative Process,* and *The Hidden Heritage.*

is my financial carelessness—the thousands of dollars I gave away, or contributed, or lent; with them, we would be much more comfortable economically. But perhaps they should not be regretted when one considers the stout friends who pitched in when the going got rough. The bread cast upon the waters came back—but of course it will take three years at least after I am out of here to repay what has been lent. All in all, from October in 1947 it will probably have taken seven long years even to begin to recover from the blow dealt by the blacklist. But the discovery of friends who would rally round with such incredible generosity perhaps makes the whole experience worthwhile.

The weather here is warm, but not at all unbearably so. Late yesterday afternoon there was a wonderful thunder storm. I could smell the rain in the air, and wished you had it at the ranch, and that I were with you in it, which, of course, I shall be in not too long a time. I think of men I met in the Pacific who had been separated from their families for four years and realize how lucky I am. I send you all kisses—

DALTON TRUMBO DCDC #85297

3. To Cleo Trumbo

Washington, D.C.
June 14, 1950

Well, darling—!

I am still here in D.C. awaiting the day of transfer which, I think, draws very near. My last—or first—letter to you was delayed in leaving here because of technical instructions about correspondence which I overlooked. I hunger for news of you, but shall now have to wait until I send you a third letter from my permanent domicile.

Today's *Times-Herald* has a preposterous double-column lead editorial, headed by photos of Stettinius, Hiss and me, entitled "A Ghost Goes to Jail," labelling me an advisor to Stettinius at San Francisco —"Trumbo advised him at S.F. where the Soviet Union's insistence on three votes and the veto in the United Nations were honored"— forgetting the three votes for the U.N. were agreed upon at Yalta (together with three votes for the U.S.A. if we wanted them)—and forgetting also that the veto was proposed by the U.S.A. at Dumbarton Oaks, and steadfastly insisted upon thereafter by the U.S.A. delegation. Thus do liars distort history, and, I presume, thus also do fools believe them.

Having much time to think here, I can remember innumerable

things I intended to do before I left and didn't get around to doing. Thus, in relation to personal debts on personal loans (as apart from business or ranch obligations, which are in excellent shape)—the following.

I wrote Eddie, Yip,[6] and Sam [Zimbalist] explaining that repayment would begin upon my release. I also made arrangements for Bob [Roberts] to be paid (out of funds due me in 1951). I did not, however, get in touch with Earl [Felton]. He moves so frequently no one can keep up with him, and, knowing he was rather alarmed by all the fuss and furor, I didn't wish to embarrass him by writing him at the studio. I then planned to see him that last day in town, but it was so hectic I completely forgot. I wish therefore that you would get in touch with Bob [Roberts] and ask him to do the following:

Get in touch with Earl [7] and tell him we haven't forgotten him, and intend to begin repaying him (in driblets of necessity) early next year. . . . Also, Bob should find out how Earl is doing, because if things go badly for him, we might squeeze out a little emergency money for him right now. Please ask Bob to explain to Earl how it came about that I didn't see him before I left.

Now, to the more agreeable subject of money due *us!* Has the Sam Spiegel check come through? [8] Do John's [9] payments continue? (Note: I paid the Katz loan off in full, so we don't have to think about *that* one!)

How are our lovely children? And their beautiful mother? And their courageous and lovely paternal grandmother? My letters, I suspect, will grow more philosophical and less specific as time goes on. Keep them all for me as you did my Pacific letters, in their own envelopes, so that one day I may read them as a record of my adventures in the cold war as contrasted to the hot one. I am reading that greatest and most serene of all novels, *War and Peace,* with as much joy as the first time. A kiss for you all!

DALTON TRUMBO DCDC #85297

---

[6] Lyricist E. Y. Harburg, nicknamed Yip or Yippur, and his wife, Eddie, were friends of Trumbo and are referred to occasionally in subsequent correspondence. Harburg wrote the lyrics and book for *Bloomer Girl, The Happiest Girl in the World, Flahooley, Jamaica,* and *Finian's Rainbow.* Among his films are *Meet the People, Cabin in the Sky,* and *The Wizard of Oz.*

[7] Earl Felton is one of Trumbo's oldest friends. The two were readers at Warner Brothers together and became screen writers at approximately the same time. Felton is one of Trumbo's few screen writer friends who was not blacklisted.

[8] See Section 3, #22, pp. 125-126. During his entire prison term Trumbo was intent on collecting moneys due him from this producer.

[9] John Bright was a screen writer who made his reputation writing gangster pictures that starred James Cagney.

4. To Cleo Trumbo

Washington, D.C.
June 18, 1950

A surprise for you, darling!—I am still here. It has been longer than I was led to expect, but the place is agreeable, my habits would delight you by their regularity, and I haven't had such a rest in years. I expect to be on the move by tomorrow or the next day.

I have the exact dates of my sentence now. I shall be eligible for parole (for which a campaign will have to be planned) on October 8, 1950. Counting my time off for good behavior, I shall be released on April 9, 1951. I have now very complacently served 10 days, and have earned additionally 1⅔ days off for good behavior. Physically I tingle with good health, am full of ideas and naturally eager to go to my permanent place and get organized.

Has the new stove come? Did Geller come to place the house phones in shape? And Luth to repair the radio? Have the Butlers arrived? How absurd it is to ask questions which you cannot possibly answer! My next letter for sure will contain my address, and a list of the rules you must follow in writing to me.

Here, I think, is the last piece of business which will occur to me. I wish you'd tell Bob [Roberts] to tell Julie [Garfield] that the present trust deed which Hepburn holds on the ranch is now down to $3,000—and that as soon as it is paid off, which at the outermost will be a year from now, we shall at once give Julie a trust deed to replace the one he so generously lifted in order to permit us to borrow the Hepburn money. I would have written Julie myself, but he was in New York during my last two weeks, and I didn't have his address.

I had a delightful dream two nights ago. I was in a theatre. The orchestra pit was flooded with water, and across it floated a canoe carrying Groucho, Benny, and one or two other comedians, with Chaplin sitting in the stern. As the boat drifted by, Chaplin took a club and knocked his colleagues senseless, one by one. Then he got out of the canoe, tipped it over, and his competitors at once sank. Chaplin pulled himself up on to the stage apron, shook the water from his clothes, faced the audience and shrugged with an innocent smirk curling his lips. At this moment I was awakened by the sound of loud laughter—my own. The dream isn't funny, though the laughter was very pleasant to me, and caused certain comment. What sort of criminal is this, who laughs in the night in his dreams?

I read with amusement Drew Pearson's strictures upon Congressman Wood,[10] and of [Senator Joseph] McCarthy's successful literary sales. Is it possible that all of these men are thieves? They look like it, of course, but to have it proved is more delightful than one had any right to anticipate.

[10] John S. Wood of Georgia, a member of HUAC.

I have some fine ideas for work—and when they come into my mind I start up, on the verge of telling them to you—and then, of course, you're not here and I'm obliged to keep them to myself. Which shows that I am only half of myself without you. The usual felicitations to all the people I love.

DALTON TRUMBO DCDC #85297

5. To Cleo Trumbo

Federal Correctional Institute
Ashland, Kentucky
June 21, 1950

At last, sweetheart, I have arrived at the Federal Correctional Institute in Ashland, Kentucky, in the midst of beautiful wooded hills and the greenest grass you have ever seen. From what I have seen of the institution and its personnel, one could not wish for a pleasanter place, granted that one must be imprisoned in the first instance. I may write three letters per week, one page, using both sides of the page. I may receive seven letters per week of no more than four pages each, one side of the page only. My address is as . . . on the envelope, namely: Dalton Trumbo, Box No. P.M.B. 7551, Ashland, Kentucky. All who write me, including you, must sign their names in full, together with their address. You could use my ranch stationery, which gives you large pages, and write small. The letterhead contains your address by placing "Mrs." before my name. All incoming and outgoing mail is, of course, censored.[11] I imagine all my letters from now on will go to you regular mail, while it would be nice if yours came air mail. I haven't lined up exactly who will be on my correspondence list, but I think I shall make you the only family member. If you wrote me three letters a week, I could still receive letters from four other persons, whose names I must submit here first. By writing you one letter one week and two the next, and so on, I could also keep the other correspondence going. I think perhaps I would put Hy [Kraft], Hugo [Butler], [Bill] Pomerance, and Ian [Hunter] down as my other correspondents, so if you will send me their addresses I can make the arrangements.

Did *Theatre Arts* come out with my article? Did the departure

[11] Trumbo wrote, "It should be explained that all mail sent or received by inmates was opened, read and occasionally censored. Like all censorship, this knowledge of constant snoopery produces self-censorship, inhibits spontaneity, limits the areas in which truth can be spoken, and tempts the inmate to manufacture small, cheerful lies about prison life to please the warden. You're really not writing to your wife, you're writing to *him*."

merit any local newspaper space? How did the children react to the demonstration? Have you any quotable reactions on the poem ["Confessional"]? It was read last night at a New York meeting for the Eight [12] in Town Hall. Forget the information I gave you about parole and the October 8 date. Apparently the whole thing was an error on the part of the Washington jail authorities, and, although we shall check with our attorneys, we probably are totally ineligible. I understand a national broadcast has been arranged for next month in our behalf, with a dazzling array of names.

I presume you found my glasses in the glove compartment. I also presume that by this time Superior Optical Co. has sent you or Rex [Cole] [13] the two other new pair. I need, in all, the three new pair— one bifocal, one distance, and one reading. Send them with your return address when you can, and insure them. And also, as a special favor, drop mother a note that I send her greetings on her birthday tomorrow.

I cannot tell you, after 11 days in the Washington jail, what a pleasure it is to be in this new place. I had a fine train ride overnight, arriving in Ashland at 1:00 p.m. today, after a morning of lovely hill and river scenery. I hope quickly to get work to do here, which will make the time pass much more swiftly. My reading progresses ravenously, and I shall surely be in better physical shape when I come out than when I came in.

Well—that must do for today. Write me three letters quickly in the three days after you have received this, giving me all the news in a great gush. Then I shall be caught up again. Kiss the children soundly and send them to bed without any dinner. Tell Adele [Martin] to watch those two newcomers [the Butlers], and reserve for yourself as much of my love as you can absorb.

DALTON TRUMBO – #7551

[12] In order to avoid the expense of trials for each member of the Hollywood Ten, the group made an agreement with the Deputy U.S. District Attorney and the Court that only two formal trials would be held—those of Lawson and Trumbo—and that the remaining eight would abide by the decisions rendered in the two governing cases. Hence, while Trumbo and Lawson were already imprisoned, the remaining eight were awaiting sentence.
[13] Cole took charge of business and finances during Trumbo's prison term.

6. To Cleo Trumbo

Federal Correctional Institute
Ashland, Kentucky
June 22, 1950

Hello, darling—!

First to business, then to pleasure. We are permitted here to have newspapers and magazines sent to us directly from their publishers. I wish, therefore, you would rush a letter to Rex, telling him to subscribe for me, immediately, for a period of nine (9) months, to the following newspapers: the Los Angeles *Times,* Louisville *Courier-Journal,* and *The New York Times.* I want both daily and Sunday editions on each. I would like *The New York Times* and the Los Angeles *Times* to be sent air mail. I would like the subscriptions to be rushed to the publishers air mail also. As to magazines, I should like him to air mail change of address from the ranch to here for: *Harper's, Atlantic Monthly, The New Yorker, Saturday Review of Literature, Time, Newsweek, Life, The Nation, Partisan Review, Masses & Mainstream, Variety, New Republic, Fortune* and *Theatre Arts.* He probably hasn't the addresses of these magazines in his files, so it may be necessary for you to find the Circulation Department address in the front of each magazine and send them to him. . . . If you wish to keep any of the above magazines for yourself, by all means do so, and have Rex simply enter a new nine month subscription for me for those you keep. Also, on your next trip to town, I wish you would take one of my tan English oxfords in to the Morris Bootery next door to Rothchilds in Beverly Hills, and pick out for me the finest pair of weejuns (or whatever those loafer-moccasin type oxfords are which have no laces and simply slip on). Then hold them at the ranch until I write you that I have authorization to receive them here, at which time you can mail them to me.

Life here is something like life in a sanitarium. The place is airy, immaculate and most attractive, with wide expanse of lawns, and views of green country-side in every direction. The food is good, the attitude is friendly, and the restrictions are not onerous. The regularity of food, sleep—and later, I hope—work is most relaxing. Looking at myself in the mirror, I am persuaded that the wrinkles of work and tension are vanishing, and that I appear much younger than I did two weeks ago. After some twenty-five years of the most intensive work, the sudden shucking off of all responsibility gives one a sense of almost exhilarating relief—a total resignation of personal responsibility and a peaceful acceptance of the regulations and requirements of the institution, none of which I have thus far found to be unreasonable.

As I told you, my release date is April 9. But I am informed that there are certain kinds of work here which give one an additional two days off per month. If I were so fortunate as to secure such work in the next week or two, I could possibly cut another eighteen to twenty days off my time, which, of course, would be wonderful.

I do hope, darling, that you are well and happy. I say that because of the responsibilities suddenly thrust upon you in addition to your regular responsibility to the children. This sentence is more severe upon you than upon me. You have no idea how comforting it is to me—and how proud I feel—to have you for my wife. I embrace the children, and salute all our friends.

DALTON TRUMBO – #7551

7. To Cleo Trumbo

Federal Correctional Institute
Ashland, Kentucky
June 23, 1950

Salutations!

Since I have one more letter allowed to me this week, I naturally address it to you. I have just returned from the dentist, who filled, quite painlessly, two small cavities which showed up on my examination. I have not been assigned to work yet, but anticipate it momentarily. Once established in a regular routine of work, the time will pass much more swiftly.

Already I engage in the pleasant fantasies of release day. As perhaps you know, the government pays the bus fare of released prisoners to their homes. Out of natural thrift they therefore, in the last weeks of one's term, begin to shift a man from prison to prison, aiming for his release date to find him in the institution nearest his final destination. The only way, I am told, in which one can avoid the discomforts of the final migration is to have one of one's closest relatives appear and sign the inmate out. Thus, if I were released on April 9, you would come to Ashland, rent hotel rooms, and pick me up at midnight, April 8. Then I envision a week in New York before heading westward for the ranch. It would be fun, wouldn't it? And, of course, if I were successful in getting time-off work, release date would be approximately three weeks earlier. What pleasures await that day!

It has been extremely hot today. I sweat freely, but don't mind it at all because we are permitted showers every evening, clean socks and handkerchiefs daily, complete wardrobe changes twice weekly, and fresh linen weekly. I think I shall soon have to begin watching my diet, for I eat too heavily. We have all the fresh vegetable salad we wish each day, raised here on the prison farm. I am still in quarantine, which is a necessary health procedure, and thus have not got down to doing anything yet. But when I am assigned my permanent quarters I shall. I hear from other inmates that Ashland is much newer and considerably superior to Danbury.

Did you communicate my message to Bob? I presume that Nikola left for camp yesterday, and that Mike [14] and Chris will soon be off. That should relieve household pressure considerably. Does Hugo [Butler] find the path an easy way to the lake, and does he find the table and chairs I had set up by the water's edge relaxing enough? Tell Jean [Butler] that in the Washington jail I heard "One Man's Family" drifting up from the ground floor to my high cell on the upper range—and found my dislike for it increased, if possible. But the sound of her voice was very pleasant.[15] How is Adele—still swelling? [16] And how is my little Mitzi. And you? A flood of kisses for all of you.

DALTON TRUMBO – #7551

8. To Cleo Trumbo

Federal Correctional Institute
Ashland, Kentucky
June 27, 1951 [17]

Again—hello.

I haven't heard from you, but calculating the mails and the time required for censorship, I realize I shall not hear until tomorrow or Thursday at the earliest. Affairs here go well. I am still in quarantine, but expect to be out and assigned to work any day now. I am pleased to tell you that at medical inspection today I weighed only 153 pounds, which is fine; and that, as a result of having my teeth cleaned, they gleam like pearls. If you were here I would flash them at you and you would swoon at their beauty. Under the heading of Good and Welfare, I have the honor to report that I have finished *War and Peace, The Decline and Fall of the Roman Empire* and *Huckleberry Finn* and now am racing through *Gulliver's Travels.* Consider that but for the beneficence of the Honorables Clark and

[14] One of Hugo Butler's children, the only son; Christopher Trumbo's contemporary and colleague.

[15] Mrs. Butler, it will be remembered, was a regular on "One Man's Family."

[16] Mrs. Martin, housekeeper at the ranch, was pregnant.

[17] Although in other instances I have corrected the error, it is interesting and even amusing that Trumbo frequently and unintentionally dated his prison letters not by the actual year but by the year of his release.

McGrath, it might have been years before I had the leisure to go through them again. I was particularly drawn to the following passage, referring to the oppressions of Julian the Apostate against the Christians in *Decline and Fall*: "But the will of the legislator was not exempt from prejudice and passion; and it was the object of the insidious policy of Julian to deprive the Christians of all the temporal honors and advantages which rendered them respectable in the eyes of the world. A just and severe censure has been reflected on the law which prohibited the Christians from teaching the arts of grammar and rhetoric. The motives alleged by the emperor to justify this partial and oppressive measure, might command, during his lifetime, the silence of slaves and the applause of flatterers." I like it so much I am using it in my appeal for presidential pardon. And from *Huck* I have chosen the following gem for your delight: ". . . and sometimes I lifted a chicken that warn't roosting comfortable, and took him along. Pap always said, take a chicken when you get a chance, because if you don't want him yourself you can easy find somebody that does, and a good deed ain't never forgot."

Why don't you make up a small album of family pictures, place them back to back in cellophane and send them to me labeled "photographs," for they are, I discover, permitted to us. Also, if you have the loafers or weejuns ready, I have the permission to receive them, and my feet cry out for their softness. Are the glasses on the way? In jail your sentence is your "time." And you don't "put in" time; you "build" your time. And of all the various ways to build your time, sleeping is accounted to be the best. Because when you're asleep you have escaped, you are utterly free. Another excellent way to build time, I find, is to attend in the greatest detail to matters of personal hygiene. Thus I give myself a daily manicure and pedicure, and as a result both toes and talons are things of beauty.

Please let me know what, if any, plans go forward for the Ten, and also what you hear of the Eight, for I have heard nothing. If Melinda [Martin] says "up" tell her "no, no, no!" for me. Keep my Mitzi from changing too much, and preserve yourself against my return as lovely and beautiful as only you can be.

DALTON TRUMBO — #7551

9. To Cleo Trumbo

Federal Correctional Institute
Ashland, Kentucky
June 29, 1950

Greetings!

What a wonderful letter, and how fine to know things go well with all of you. By this time I presume we know whether it was a boy or a girl or a mixed pair or two of a kind for Adele [Martin]. I am delighted to hear of your speech, and very proud.[18] I knew that once my stifling influence was removed you would flower!

Today I was removed from quarantine under minimum custody (we have three classes, close, medium and minimum) and was assigned to work in the supply room, which receives and disburses all materials used here at the institution. Because of the beginning of a new fiscal year, I am told we shall be very busy for the next three or four weeks. We had a rush of incoming trucks this afternoon, and I found myself heaving 100 pound sacks of sugar solo. The officer in charge, seeing the wind grew short, told me to slow down and break in easily. Our crew is composed of very nice people (one of them thought I was thirty-five, bless him!) and I expect soon to be well-hardened. Also to replace fat with muscle, which will be all to the good. I am living in a dormitory, have leisure time to wander outside on the grass, or watch the evening ball games, and all in all can think of nothing to complain of, except, of course, the mere fact I'm here.

My list of correspondents must be trimmed somewhat, so for the present. I have only you, Hugo, Bob [Roberts] and the attorneys on it. Later I may be able to add one or two friends. Don't hold yourself to an arbitrary number of letters—just write when you feel like it, and at whatever length under four pages (or from four down) you find convenient. It mustn't become a burden to you, although I must say, you write so well you will never again deceive me into writing for you!

About Bob, I think the message to him rather urgent, so as soon as possible I would like him to have an exact copy of them. About *Theare Arts*: you may not send one to me, but if you will ask *Theatre Arts* to send that particular number direct (aside from the change of address) to me it will be accepted here. Please have Rex eliminate *Masses & Mainstream* from my list, and have it continue at the ranch. About the 1947 tax records,[19] they might be in my lower dresser drawer, or they might have been in one of the two deep drawers of the desk you took over, or above or below my shoe shelves in

[18] Cleo Trumbo had made a speech at a fund-raising dinner for the Ten.
[19] Mrs. Trumbo had been notified that the government wished to check Trumbo's 1947 tax records and was unable to locate them.

closet opposite the bar. And—I'm ashamed even to suggest this—
they might still be in the tire compartment of the sedan. I imagine
the government wants to check my 1947 deductions to Robert W.
Kenny, trustee, since they have challenged all such deductions on the
others of the Ten. Let me know if, or when, you find them. I send
you as much love as I have lifted sugar today!

DALTON TRUMBO – #7551

10. To Cleo Trumbo

Federal Correctional Institute
Ashland, Kentucky
July 3, 1950

Hello, sweetheart!—

Not having heard since your first letter three days ago, I assume
Saturday or Sunday caught you without mailing facilities, or they
are stacked up here in censorship. Thus, I don't know whether or not
you have found the records yet; and if not, I can only suggest that
someone check with the garage where the sedan was repaired to see
if by any chance they might have been taken from the car there (if,
indeed, they were *in* the car at the time, which I can't for the life of
me recall) and still be around the garage. You don't suppose some
idiot could have packed them away from the ranch at the same time
the bed, tools, and other things were stolen, do you? Or could it be
possible that Summers, the mover, has them around his place? I remember once he *did* have several boxes of stuff for a year or two before notifying us, and that several books out of our volume sets never
did show up again. Please keep me informed about this, because
with no records to back us up, we may be in the position of having
to pay, willy-nilly, any sum which any second guesser chooses to
name. I am thus naturally quite concerned about it.

Has Bob returned from New York yet? And if so, have you got in
touch with him about the messages? If not, I suggest that you give
them at once to Katy [Roberts], who should, of course, not act upon
them. Then when Bob arrives, see him too, and give them to him
exactly. If Bob is still in New York I would like very much for him
to visit me here on his return. Wednesdays, Saturdays and Sundays
are visiting days, and in view of the fact I shall receive no visits from
my family during my whole term, I believe they would let me see a
friend, if I were given advance notification of when to expect him, to
enable me to make proper arrangements.

Another matter: Has Sam Spiegel paid the $4,500 yet (4,050 net to you)? If not, it was due June 6, and I think you should write George [Willner] at once, ordering him to take action immediately to collect.

1. If the Spiegel money *has* come in, I wish you would have Rex at once draw up the following checks in the following sums, to the following persons: (1) E. F[elton], $200.00—(2) E[dward] G. Robinson, 150.00—(3) S. Zimbalist, 100.00—(4) Y. Harburg, 75.00—(5) J. Garfield, 50.00. Each check should be marked *"Installment on loan."* Each check should be sent by Cole to you, *retained by you,* and *sent out by you* to the person due. But turn the $200.00 check and $50.00 check directly over to *Bob* for him to deliver personally, since these were the two I did not see before I left. I like the idea of continuing to pay off while in jail. It seems somehow in character.

2. If the 4,500 has *not* come in, then have Rex draw only the $200.00 check and the $50.00 check, turn them over to Bob yourself, and have him deliver them.

I hope the above isn't too complicated, and that you will be able to attend to it at once. In all such matters, keep in close and constant personal touch with Bob [Kenny] and Katz.

Did you know that the "Toad" was run in the *New York Daily Compass* in twenty-one installments, ending last Friday? That probably gives it another 100,000 readers. It has also been translated into French under the title, "L'heure du Crappaud." I am reminded that five years ago Saturday I went in at Balikpapan, Borneo, and that five years ago July 4th, I flew back from Borneo to Tawi-Tawi. What a change! What would you think, after this is over, of headquartering somewhere in Asia with the family, while I covered the doings there as a correspondent? It might be fun—and again, it might not.

How go things with you, darling? I presume Nikola, too, is now gone, and that you are totally surrounded by little girls. Tell Mitzi that when she is naked she is *still* a little fish, whether I am there or not. Tell mother I send her my love. I saw a picture of Ring [Lardner, Jr.], Albert [Maltz], Herbert [Biberman] and Lester [Cole] being led off to jail. I am terribly interested in the two six-month sentences [Dmytryk and Biberman], and wonder if it gives us a wedge for cutting down the other sentences. But I have heard nothing from the attorneys. Have you? Will you send me mother's, Catherine's and Elizabeth's addresses? And will you, beyond anything and everything else, be cute? All night long?

DALTON TRUMBO – #7551

11. To Cleo Trumbo

Federal Correctional Institute
Ashland, Kentucky
July 4, 1950

My dear:

I received your second letter yesterday, and was, of course, delighted to get it. It will be helpful to me if you date your letters: then I will know exactly the time of the news you send. Also, please tell me when this letter, date July 4, reaches you, so I can have some idea of how long it takes my letters to reach you.

I have a cold today, and feel otherwise dejected—a condition I hope shall be only temporary. One doesn't have much to think of here, so it is only natural that my mind should go back hourly, daily and constantly to our conversation after leaving the Players, and it is, of course, maddening that my best efforts apparently have been unable to cope with it.[20]

I am, furthermore, shocked that George [Willner] has permitted the Sam Spiegel matter to go so long without action. It is a foolish attitude on his part which will cost us money. There is no excuse for dalliance, and if he does not take immediate and vigorous action, he serves me very badly, both as agent and friend.

I was also saddened to find that your last letter makes no mention of Bob. Is there nobody on earth who knows when he will return? Have you asked Katy? Have you talked to Katy at all? Could you not have Jim [Martin], on his trips to the Park, telephone and find out when Bob is expected? I am hoping very much that when he does return you will see him without delay, and lay before him all my letters including this one, so that he may understand my feelings and act as he thinks best—same thing I had hoped would be done two or three weeks ago. Please indulge me in this, darling, and let me know if Bob, within the choice of his own best judgment, feels he can handle things—and even after that give me reports as to how he feels about it. I think of nothing more to write.

Love,
DALTON TRUMBO – #7551

[20] On the night Trumbo left Los Angeles for Washington and sentencing, he took Mrs. Trumbo to dinner at the Players' Restaurant and allowed his imagination to wander freely on weird possibilities for the future: the fear that some other act of his could be interpreted as illegal and be blown up into a criminal case against him to be prosecuted upon his release from prison. The whole matter was so far-fetched that Mrs. Trumbo had dismissed it, but Trumbo, idle, defenseless and depressed, began to dwell upon all sorts of mythical legal traps being laid for him.

12. To Cleo Trumbo

Federal Correctional Institute
Ashland, Kentucky
July 11, 1950

Hello, sweetheart!

The shoes arrived yesterday, and what a godsend to my weary feet, weighted down, till now, in army shoes. The last two pairs of glasses arrived this morning (to the consternation of the man whose job it is to turn them over to me, his calculations now crediting me with the wildly extravagant number of four pair) and my eyes at last are at peace. The Los Angeles *Times* and the [*Hollywood*] *Reporter* arrive regularly; and now, if only you should appear on Saturday my cup indeed would be running over.

However, I doubt you shall be here, for when your last letter came, my writing privileges for the week had been expended. I therefore wrote, on forms provided for such matters, a request that a straight wire be sent you, urging you to come. That was last Friday evening, and it is now Tuesday evening, and I have received no reply to my request, so have no way of knowing, nor, indeed, no way of finding out whether the wire was sent. So now I shall wait until Saturday to find out. If it turns out you did not come, what do you think of making the trip in a week or two? I will make inquiries about the most suitable means of travel, and by availing yourself of Sue's experience, [21] you should be able to work up a very nice schedule. I am told that the visiting room here is very nice, and that Saturday visitors may return for Sunday visits also. I don't want you to exhaust yourself on this project, but you might find a trip agreeable, and the plane here might be interesting.

I recover slowly from a hacking cold (the inevitable result of living among so many men), but have not yet got down to any writing. Privacy is impossible to achieve for the present, and I hesitate to undertake any serious work until I can get it. Truth to tell, I am also quite tired at the end of a day's work, and seem content to shower, shave and settle with a book until lights out. Have re-read *A Passage to India* and am now deep in *The Forsyte Saga,* some volumes of which I have never read.

I wish you would copy the following note and send a copy on to Hugo, George and Bob: "In view of the success of moon and spaceship pictures, would this not be an excellent time to attempt to revive interest in *Flight to Portabella.*" Something might really come of it if they got together and began really to figure angles.

. . . . As for the magazines stacking up on you, do with them what you will, only save *British Labor Monthly, International Labor Review,* and *Public Affairs* for me.

[21] Mrs. John Howard Lawson.

In the letter [from] Chris I learned that the Martins' heir has arrived. How proud they must be, and how curiously Melinda must look upon the whole affair. Give Adele my love, and let me know what the young man has been named.

Sue will bring you back word of my home here (if you don't send me daft with joy and surprise by arriving yourself!). I am well, time passes, and I think of all of you constantly. Please kiss Melissa for me as many times as she will permit, write the kids that I send them the greetings of one summer camper to another, and, for yourself, have a happy birthday and a hug from

DALTON TRUMBO — #7551

13. To Cleo Trumbo

Federal Correctional Institute
Ashland, Kentucky
July 12, 1950

Sweetest:

What a fine day this one has been! Two letters—one from you and one from Hugo—a true jackpot! Today I was called to the Parole Officer's headquarters, where it was explained to me, with some apologies, that the wire I referred to in yesterday's letter, which I had asked be sent you on Friday last, had, unfortunately not been sent at all; but that they would be glad to send it today. Knowing you could not possibly come with Sue on such short notice, I told them to forget about the whole matter. My feeling now is that such a trip would be rather a major undertaking with you, and that, since you won't be able to come frequently, perhaps the end of summer would be a better break in the monotony for me. However, if you wish to come tonight, pray do, and my delight will be boundless. Whenever you decide to come, Sue, as an old veteran among prison visitors, will be able to give you full instructions as to the best way to travel. There is one exception to the above: if any complications arise re: Bob, E[arl] F[elton], etc,—you should fly at once. I rather think, however, that Bob will divine the intention of my instructions and clear the matter up quickly, in which event, you will let me know by letter in general terms whether it goes well or not. But, with the solidarity exception noted above (in which event you would come at once) come when you wish and when it will be least tiring for you. I do hope you are enjoying life somewhat, and not working yourself to death.

Hugo's letter was extravagant in its praise of your speech—praise which, incidentally, he said was shared by everyone there. How I should like to have seen and heard you! Hugo's letter also told most amusingly of his and Jean's visit to Chris and Mike. About friends' correspondence: I think at last I have got to the bottom of the mystery. It appears that I shall be permitted to correspond with Hugo, Bob Roberts and Bill Pomerance; but only after all three have been checked to ascertain whether or not they are ex-cons or potential plotters of crimes. Their names should be cleared for me in about two weeks. In the meanwhile, since Hugo's letter came through O.K., I assume they may write to me, but that I may not write to them until clearance. Please tell all three of them, therefore, to write. I ought to get a letter a week out of them. Tell Bob he is on the list, not as a business man or producer, but as a friend. Forget what I told you about cancelling *Hollywood Reporter* and *Masses & Mainstream*. But if you already have cancelled them, forget the whole thing.

I am feeling better and better, and do hope to get down to some serious work soon—I think the clearing up of the Bob business will do more for me than anything else. Perhaps I have blown it up too much, but one has much time for thinking here, and ogres are easily summoned up from the imagination in such circumstances. Incidentally, how is the balance holding up? Well enough, I presume. And you? And Nikola? And Chris? And Melissa? And the Martins? And the Butlers? And everybody? . . . Much love, my dear. I swell with pride whenever I think of you, which is all the time. Such swelling!

DALTON TRUMBO – #7551

14. To Cleo Trumbo

Federal Correctional Institute
Ashland, Kentucky
July 13, 1950

My darling—my beautiful—and my absolutely wonderful!

I do hope I haven't thrown you into a funk, and if I did I'm terribly sorry, and shall absolutely not do it again. The truth is I've had a cold ever since I entered here; and this, combined with physical work to which I was unused, left me in a state of staggering exhaustion every night. Thus my mind went melancholy, and I did nothing but brood over that situation, imagining plots, conspiracies, and heaven knows what. But today the cold was still better, I worked steadily and hard all day, and still felt good when I returned from work to mail call. Then your letter telling me of the settlement figure,[22] and that you had seen Bob. What relief! What joy! By all means pay the money, and good riddance. You have handled it brilliantly, and if I had never loved you before (which I did a little) I would be completely infatuated with you now. It will take two or three days for me to get the powers of attorney notarized, but it shall be done, and sent to you probably next Monday or Tuesday.

The letters, as you can see, are coming through; glasses and shoes are here, and papers, etc. are starting and all should begin dribbling through in another week or two. Changes of address always take time. I received the photographs today, and as a result of having such handsome children and such a talented wife, I am considered a man of distinction by my dormitory mates. I think you can send photographs whenever you wish, so as they are made, send 'em on by all means.

I know you are handling things superbly, and considering the rapidly increasing population of our domicile, under sometimes painful conditions. Do *not* worry about Frazier Park mail schedules; write when you can, and now that I have some idea of the time schedules and the censorship time here, I shall make out fine. Also, get rest, get sleep. It's nice to be busy, but exhaustion is never pleasant. Also—what about your operation? Are you still O.K.?

Tell Melissa it stormed here today. First the clouds came—clouds so dark and angry they hid the sun. The sun, I think, was frightened by the clouds. Then the clouds grew angry with each other. They had a fierce quarrel up there in the sky. They shouted and roared at each other, and the sound was as loud as thunder. In fact, it *was* thunder. Then the angry clouds clashed together in a furious battle. And then one of the clouds was badly hurt. At least, I *think* he was, for he began to cry, and his tears fell very fast against the earth, and some of them even fell on me, getting me quite wet. And my friends here stood about, pointing to the dark sky, and crying, "Look! It's raining!" Tell Melissa also that I love her. Send the same message to tent-leader Chris, and to horse-woman Nikola, and to their glorious mother!

DALTON TRUMBO – #7551

[22] Mrs. Trumbo, working with Rex Cole and Bob Roberts, had found the discrepancy in the 1947 taxes and had informed Trumbo that $2,176 in additional taxes would be due within ninety days.

15. To Cleo Trumbo

Federal Correctional Institute
Ashland, Kentucky
July 17, 1950

Well, darling, Happy Birthday! You see I remember the date, but I can't for the life of me remember the year. Is it 33 or 34? Anyhow, you're much younger than that. Since receiving news that those matters are cleared up, I have been the happiest little convict you were ever married to. The cold has subsided, the work goes well, I am alert in the evenings, time passes, and I am what one would call adjusted. I am getting down to work—not serious work, for I presently see no opportunity for that under the conditions prevailing here—but originals. I hope to have several, and then take my own luxurious ease when I get out. Besides, I calculate that with the slap from the treasury, the exchequer will just about stand in need of replenishment nine months hence. You acted very wisely on the stove (I'll tell Denels off when I get out!) and as for the [*New York*] *Times*—I wouldn't give $380 to edit it, much less read it!

. . . As for the Sam Spiegel matter, you might ask Hugo to copy the following paragraph and hand it on to George:

The deal I made, and which I was told was signed with Spiegel was this: Sixty days from signing he was to pay $4,500. That date expired June 6 or 7, and the entire sum fell due at that time. As extra insurance, it was stipulated that the picture could not be released until my claim was paid. This by no means indicates that Spiegel can wait *until* release date to pay. That clause was simple added protection. The money is due now, and is collectable by (1) attachment against Spiegel . . . (2) attachment of ———————
—— Films (3) attachment of the film (4) demand for payment of the note. Katz can and should scare the life out of them. I have no intention of permitting Spiegel to use my money from June 6 to possibly November. I therefore insist that he be charged 8% interest from June 6 until the money is paid, and that he also pay all legal costs since he is much more likely to respond to immediate pressure than to extended moral persuasion.

The quotes from Nikola and Chris's letters are wonderful. They are really growing up, aren't they? Tell Melissa I dreamed she awakened me last night in the middle of the night. So I spanked her and sent her to bed. When I woke in the morning, I spanked her again. But instead of crying, she just laughed at me. I was so surprised that I turned on her very angrily and gave her four boxes of candy, a cake, three new kittens, a doll bigger than Joe,[23] and eleven kisses. I didn't make it an even dozen kisses for fear of spoiling her.

Just think—next Thursday will be six weeks of my time gone—six

---

[23] Jim and Adele Martin's new baby.

170

weeks sooner that I shall see all of you. What a reunion it will be! Tell everyone hello, give me a report on Joe, send my love to mother, and count me always your most devoted admirer—

DALTON TRUMBO – #7551

16. To Cleo Trumbo

Federal Correctional Institute
Ashland, Kentucky
July 19, 1950

Sweetheart:

The end of the day, and I am feeling tired; not in a bad way, but deliciously so, in the way that makes time pass swiftly. I've bathed, shaved, read your letter and the newspaper, and now, twilight outside, am sitting in bed, cross-legged and wearing only shorts, writing you. The evening is warm and humid, after a heavy rain last night. I received a letter from Bob Kenny saying that sometime between July 15 and July 31 they are appealing to Judge Pine for a cut in my sentence to bring it down to Eddie's [Dmytryk] and Herbert's [Biberman]. (Herbert must have been furious to get so light a term!) Then in August, when Adrian [Scott] goes before Judge Curran, they will appeal for a cut in Jack's [Lawson] sentence. Have you heard anything of these matters?

I think the idea of the book you and Jean [Butler] have projected is an excellent one, and there's no reason why the two of you couldn't do it successfully. Shoot and shoot and shoot—that, I should think, is the secret of illustrating such a job.[24] And by shooting ten times what you need or can possibly use, you may run across shots —will, in fact—which will influence Jean's text, and even expand it, or suggest new subjects for it. Go to it, baby, and earn a little dough while the old man is building his time.

Add[itional] prison jargon: "I appeared before Judge Wills and *pulled* ten years." "It's a lot easier to *build* your time when you're busy." "I got her almost built—sixty-two more days." The day before you leave, they fit you with civilian clothes. It's the day you "dress out." "You're getting *short*" means your sentence is almost finished. You are then a "short-timer." "Only two ways to get out of here—either *pull* your time or die and leave it." Anyone in authority, whether the guard, the department head, the chaplain, the warden or the whole parole board, is "the man," and always,

[24] Mrs. Trumbo is a professional photographer. Apparently the collaboration never developed.

and under all circumstances, so referred to. Thus: "I went up to see the *man* today" (whereas, he went up in truth to see a seven-man parole board). To be placed in solitary or punitive confinement is to go to "the hole."

By the way, the next time you see Bob Roberts, or care to write him, I wish you'd ask him what kind of picture he wants to make with Julie [Garfield] after *He Ran All the Way*—specifically: Western—comedy—crime—love melodrama—or what? By letting me know as soon as possible the general type he's after, I might be able to do some thinking here and save him a lot of time.

I heard that Eddie and Herbert went to Texarkana, and Cole to Danbury, but I've heard nothing about the others. Have you? The news of the campaign and the film [for the Ten] [25] is all to the good. Tell Melissa that I now have four pair of glasses, and that when I put them all on at once I can see far, far away—so far, in fact, that I am looking right at her and seeing everything she does right now, even while you are reading this to her. Say hello to all the Martins, the Butlers, the Trumbos, and especially to your sweet self.

Much love,
DALTON TRUMBO – #7551

17. To Cleo Trumbo

Federal Correctional Institute
Ashland, Kentucky
August 1, 1950

Well, darling—some business (parole business) news.

I have received a letter from Marty Popper [26] relating to his appearance before Judge Pine [27] asking for reduction of sentence. Marty pointed out the inequality of six month and twelve month sentences. Writes Marty: "Hitz,[28] while formally opposing the motion, stated his agreement with the proposition that the variance in sentences were unfair to those who had been sentenced for one year. He also agreed that this situation was unfortunate as far as the attitude of the people towards the courts is concerned. He said it might well be

[25] See Section 3, footnote 35, p. 142.
[26] Another of Trumbo's lawyers.
[27] Judge David A. Pine of the United States Court of Appeals for the District of Columbia Circuit had presided over Trumbo's appeal of the contempt charges.
[28] William Hitz, Assistant United States Attorney, and chief prosecutor during the appeal.

the kind of matter that should be considered by the parole board." Of this statement by the prosecuting attorney, Marty says: "Hitz's concessions and his statement about the parole are very valuable in my opinion. A transcript has been ordered and will be annexed to each parole application." After the hearing, Marty had a talk with Judge Pine, who "went so far as to say that if the Parole Board asked for an observation he would certainly not oppose the application. As to whether he would take an affirmative position, he was undecided at this time, but did request me to send him my views on the subject. I shall, of course, do that." So much for the prospects which, if not wildly hopeful, are not as black as one might have anticipated.

We are eligible for parole October 8. The board will meet here and in Washington in early or mid-October, and if the most favorable and speedy action were taken, we could not hope for release before November 1–15. In relation to this, Mr. Whitlock, our local Parole Officer, is sending you some papers to fill out. I have written Ben Margolis, asking him to help you in this task, and I suggest you do nothing without consulting him. Among the things I must secure are (1) a Parole Advisor, and (2) a Parole Employer. For advisor I have suggested to Ben Rev. [Stephen] Fritchman or Dr. Linus Pauling . . .[29] As to Parole Employer, I have written Ben as follows:

"It has been suggested by Mr. Whitlock, our Parole Officer here, that operation of the Lazy T Ranch might be sufficient employment, coupled with a financial ability to sustain myself and family during the parole period. I do not know whether the Los Angeles Federal Parole Office is cognizant of the disadvantage of full-time employment in the ordinary sense of the term to the earning power of a free-lance writer. I have a verbal contract with Lee Sabinson to do a play upon my release, which I am sure Lee would put into writing. I am committed under my contract with J. B. Lippincott to do my next two books for them.[30] I think also that Hugo Butler would employ me as a literary consultant and research worker. I suggest these if they are necessary to fortify the ranch operation. I am informing Cleo of the contents of this paragraph, so that you may discuss the problem directly with her and arrive at a solution satisfactory

[29] Mrs. Trumbo undertook arduous paper work in anticipation of parole. She secured Dr. Linus Pauling as Parole Advisor and compiled letters attesting to the parole applicant's character from Bert Allenberg, Martin Gang, Bob Roberts, Arthur Landau, John Huston, Sam Zimbalist, Lee Sabinson, Sally Deutsch, Bob Coryell, Nathan Adelson, Elsie McKeogh and Garson Kanin.

[30] When Cleo Trumbo wrote him, Bertram Lippincott argued that J. B. Lippincott Company had only an option on Trumbo's next two novels, a point which could not be interpreted as employment. Moreover, Lippincott, who had published both *Johnny Got His Gun* and *The Remarkable Andrew*, refused to write a character reference.

to the L.A. Parole Officer. Incidentally, Cleo, under her writing non de plume, has certain sums payable to her in 1951."

There! Now you know as much about it as I do, and I leave everything in your sweet and competent hands. Ask Ben [Margolis] to show you my letter to him, which goes out today, and you will have the full picture. Space denies me the pleasure of properly telling you how delighted I was, and am, with your visit. Kisses to all, and special love this time to Nikola.

DALTON TRUMBO – #7551

18. To Cleo Trumbo

Federal Correctional Institute
Ashland, Kentucky
August 9, 1950

Well, darling, another letter!

Things are so dry at the FCI that I'm ashamed to put pen to paper. There is absolutely no news. Today it rained. Yesterday it didn't. My cold persists. I rest. I work. I eat. Time passes more rapidly than it really should. I am not even too badly bored. But there is simply no news.

. . . .

How about buying at least 5 lbs. of black pepper (whole) and putting it away, well sealed with cellophane? I do love pepper! How about buying a calf from Snedden (Jim could do it) to eat up some of that hay this winter, and eventually to butcher? Do you spray my closet with DDT regularly? Did you put your fur coats in storage? If not, do you keep them well sprayed? They'll be worth much more this winter than last. Do the foregoing remarks indicate to you even in a small way how short I am of news, and how trivial my mind is this evening? Hollow as a gourd with three stunted seeds rattling around in it. Do not be alarmed by this babble. I am not depressed. I am merely exasperated in a kind of loud, energetic way. . . . I am gradually getting all my magazines now, and read them voraciously and vacuously. I am writing badly—forcing both the writing and the ideas. Perhaps I am in a slump. Hurray! . . .

I do hope your cold (which I probably gave you) is not too bad by now. If it is, go to bed at once and stay there. Are children driving you nuts? Well, you'll be able to settle down in two or three more weeks. Please keep me informed on Nikola's amorous adventures. Ask Chris where that song is. Tell Mitzi I just called her stubby-toes. Write Elsie [Riner] to do nothing that will ever send her to jail—she's too old to take it. Accept, dear lady, my love.

DALTON TRUMBO – #7551

19. To Cleo Trumbo

Federal Correctional Institute
Ashland, Kentucky
August 13, 1950

Darling—

At last I have got down to work. As you probably gathered, it has been quite a problem. After my first impressions of conditions here, I concluded that the want of privacy would prevent serious work, and that I must therefore do strictly movie stuff and trivialities. However, I tried the trivialities, and not only were they extremely difficult to do, but, upon reading them, I found they were also extremely bad. Followed a period of inactivity and brooding. Then I concluded that precisely because of the conditions and interruptions, a serious work was the only project that could possibly engross my attention so completely that I wouldn't notice either the conditions or the interruptions. Accordingly, I started the war novel (no publicity!). Miracle upon miracle! It absorbs me completely, and neither wind nor rain nor the hounds of hades can distract me from it. I have been working since last Friday night (today is Tuesday), and I have never had time pass so swiftly, which is a great boon here. I move now in a constant glow—you know the mood when it touches me—and inside I am full of exultant smiles. I re-write and re-write—as carefully as when I do verse—and chapter one is now finished, and it is the best prose I have ever written. I am now in chapter two, and glory to Him in the highest, I am a happy man! The project will make my time fly—and if I am refused parole, I shall have a finished novel to hand you when you pick this poor depraved convict up on the front steps. . . .

For your sweet children and your sweet self, the exultant devotion of a man who is busily engaged in an honorable trade—at last!

DALTON TRUMBO – #7551

20. To Cleo Trumbo

Federal Correctional Institute
Ashland, Kentucky
August 15, 1950

Darling girl—

Don't worry about this parole business. There is enough time for you to get it done without killing yourself. And do not worry. The decisions on parole advisor, employer and the character letters will be made by you, and they will be good decisions. I accept them sight unseen, and you must not drive yourself to distraction over them. What suggestions I have made are *only* suggestions. Often circumstances will prevent you from carrying them out, and other times they may not be very good suggestions, since my information is necessarily limited here. Go ahead, then: make your decisions on the ground according to each individual situation, and do not rush yourself sick. I have such confidence in your superlative good sense that I don't even worry about the parole business. Confront me, therefore, with any fait accompli you wish, and I'll not only accept it, but I'll also know it is the best one. So you have complete freedom.

As to Rex Cole, he would be an excellent advisor, if the fact that he is my business manager (as they know here) does not disqualify him. I must say, parenthetically, that I consider some of the wives [of the Ten] have behaved greedily in their purely personal rushes for the best names. If the Ten had been confronted with this task, they would have met, discussed all names mutually, assigned them fairly, and then gone out after them. Your colleagues, taking care of themselves in full knowledge of your isolated situation and your many responsibilities, do not earn my respect.

Enough of this parole business, about which I will not even think any more. . . . I note, with some amusement, that after all my years of windy talk about buying beef by the half or quarter, you have quietly gone out and done it. In fact, my sweet, you are doing so well on all fronts that I see little practical use for myself when I return, except, perhaps, as a household pet.

How was our Nikola, and how many hearts has she wrecked? Was it a festival you attended, or simply a regular weekend? With the summer almost over, I can foresee for you a much relaxed and more restful autumn. I do hope you are getting enough sleep, and that the pressure for town trips will shortly diminish.

As for me, time absolutely rushes by. Every spare moment is spent on the novel; lights always go out too early; the morning whistle always blows too late. There simply are not enough hours a day for my purposes. I am writing very slowly, over and over again, but what I get is extremely close to a final draft. In six days I have done

3,850 words, which means better than 4,000 a week. Not bad. And I think awfully good.

You know what I was thinking last night? I was thinking of the night a weary, frightened, tearful girl climbed into my car and let me drive away with her. I was thinking of the truly remarkable person she has turned into. And I came to the conclusion that the night in question was the luckiest one in my life. Much love to you, sweet.

DALTON TRUMBO — #7551

21. To Cleo Trumbo

Federal Correctional Institute
Ashland, Kentucky
September 8, 1950

My dear:

I presume by this time you are settling down to a more regular life—children in school, Butlers gone, and a little more time to read and rest. The summer probably has been hectic, but on the other hand it probably also passed faster than it would have had you been alone. As for me, today marks the completion of the third month: almost one-third of the time gone. In retrospect it doesn't seem so long. The first part was made interesting by the problem of adjustment, and the second has been more than filled by the book. The pages stack up, and whether good or bad, they give a purpose and a sense of accomplishment to the life here. The thing that always happens when I am working occurs here, too: I am putting on weight. In my clothes I weigh 161 lbs. as against 157 when I entered. I am therefore beginning cautiously to cut down on my food. Our weather here has turned chill. The touch of autumn is in the air, and here and there a venturesome tree has begun to turn yellow. Thus the weather helps give one a sense of time's passing. We should know what action has been taken by the parole board by the end of this month. Even if the decision is favorable, the date is generally deferred somewhat beyond the eligibility date. I suggest that the less advance publicity we give a favorable decision, the less chance there will be for indignant citizens to pass resolutions before we get out which might delay or negate entirely the actions of the board or cause it to reverse itself. And, of course, if the decision is unfavorable, we just take it in stride. We haven't won a round yet, so there really is no valid reason to be surprised if we lose this one too. I think your list of parole people and character letters is absolutely first-rate. It was very nice of Linus Pauling to agree so quickly.[31] I hope you find time to drop him a note of thanks. When I get out I shall write them all. The money arrived and has been placed in my account here. In fact everything is fine, and there is shockingly little to write about. I hope these letters aren't hopelessly dull, but one has to struggle to fill pages. We don't after all, do many new things in this hotel. . . .

I believe I have a boy who is going to be a year older this month. Convey to him my fatherly felicitations. Also I think an elderly aunt [Elsie Riner] celebrates another notch in her gun barrel. Tell her I think of her. And of Nikola and Mitzi. And, of course, always of you.

Love—
DALTON TRUMBO – #7551

22. To Christopher Trumbo

Federal Correctional Institute
Ashland, Kentucky
September 17, 1950

For Christopher Trumbo—Ten Years Old

> About ten years ago today
> (Or rather, in the night)
> Your mother turned to me to say
> A thing that gave me fright.
>
> She whispered with surpassing joy,
> "My darling husband dear,
> We're going to have a little boy—
> In fact, he's almost here!"
>
> I leaped at once onto the floor,
> Fell flat upon my face,
> Jumped up and ran against a door,
> Fell down again—same place.
>
> I scrambled into suit and hat,
> Fell down the stairs, slid through the hall,
> Did handsprings like an acrobat
> To where the car stood in its stall.

---

[31] To act as parole advisor.

I packed your mother into it
And started through the night,
To-whoop, to-whee, to-lickety-split,
To whiddle-de-wham, what a sight!

Then half-way to the hospital
The engine's feeble pop
Brought mother and me and unborn you
To an absolute dead stop.

Oh dear, Oh me, Oh double-alas
And mercy, cried my heart,
The car has just run out of gas,
And having stopped, won't start!

I raced away to a Standard sign
For a bucket full of gas,
Filled up the tank with an old hose line,
Which I threw away on the grass.

Then off again with the speed of light
(The tires and mother whining)
Like a startled baboon through the dark of night,
My eyes all wild and shining.

We got to the place in a mile-long slide,
And seven minutes later
You arrived with a mouth as wide
As a full-grown alligator.

Your mother looked at me, and I
Looked grimly back at her.
"What'll we name it?" I said with a sigh,
And she said, "Christopher."

And that's how it happened, my little son,
My grim and glare and starey,
My gloom and glum and fearsome one,
My beautiful and scarey!

Happy Birthday from Daddy

DALTON TRUMBO — #7551

23. To Nikola Trumbo

Federal Correctional Institute
Ashland, Kentucky
September 19, 1950

My dear sweet Nikola:

What a pleasure it was to receive a letter from you, and what wonderful news you gave me of your stay in camp! I knew you were very good at a number of things, but I never knew you were *that* good at so very many things. In addition to all that, your handwriting has improved remarkably, and your selection of words is excellent. Altogether, you write a very grown-up letter. Sometimes it surprises me to think that in a few months I shall have a twelve-year-older for a daughter. Mother tells me that in addition to growing taller you are also turning prettier. Is this so? Now, now—tell the truth!

How do you like school this year? I wish you would write me what studies you are taking aside from Ancient History. That, incidentally, was one of my favorite courses when I was your age. Also, I don't quite see why wanting Tar Baby should keep you from getting a musical instrument. In fact, I think you *should* get one. Have you found any new friend to replace Peggy Hart? I do hope so. Tell Chris there is a rumor going around the jail here that Peter the Hermit thinks he is a fine boy. I think so too, but I make it a point never to tell him, so don't let him know. And tell Mitzi that I admire her drawings very much and hope she keeps on sending them. Tell her that for her birthday, I shall send her a little verse, just as I sent Chris for his.

Now here is a message that I wish you would give to Cleo about my parole possibilities. The applications of twenty-six men were sent in directly to Washington, among them mine. Four have already received favorable answers. The rest may hear anytime between tomorrow and the middle of November. Men often receive notice of parole several weeks in advance of their release date. More often than not, the date of release is set from several days to several weeks after the date of eligibility. In other words, although my eligibility date is October 9, the actual date might be some time later. This is entirely at the discretion of the parole board. Out of every three men eligible who apply for parole, only one is successful. I do *not* believe that, if given parole, I will know very far in advance. I think the policy with Thomas and May—cases which, like my own, involve considerable publicity—was to notify them very shortly before their day of release, only a day or two. This tends to diminish controversy and publicity. I think, if I get it, mine will be handled in the same way. Therefore time might be so short that I could not notify Cleo in advance, and hence she would not be able

179

to come. In that event, I would fly home as quickly and quietly as possible. If I can control it, I want no one there to know of my arrival. No publicity, no newspaper interviews either here or there. Thus, I do not expect to hear before about October 10, unless the decision is against me, in which event I might hear any day. Give mother an enormous kiss for me, add one for Chris, one for Mitzi, and a killer-diller for yourself. Write again—

Much love,
Daddy—DALTON TRUMBO – #7551

24. To Christopher Trumbo

Federal Correctional Institute
Ashland, Kentucky
September 23, 1950

My dear Chris:

What a pleasant surprise I had yesterday—a letter from you, a letter from Nikola, and a letter from Cleo—all at once! It gave me quite a problem. "To whom," I asked, "shall I address my answer?" At first it seemed that it should be to Nikola, since she had written before, and I had answered, and now she had replied. Then again, I considered the fact that I had just written a birthday verse to Chris. But then again, I said to myself, that was especially for his birthday, and cannot be considered a regular letter at all, since I am also going to send birthday verses to Mitzi and Nikola when their turns come. Therefore, I finally said, Chris has written me his first letter, and I must make my answer to him. So this is your letter.

I am surprised to know that you are playing football. I had always thought of you as more of a baseball player. Center is a very responsible position, but doesn't it get a bit rough with eleven men walking up and down your backbone? Or do you make them do it on tiptoe? You told me in your letter that you had 18 questions on Pan America, but you forgot to tell me the most important part, which is—how many did you get right? I am also surprised that you are able to predict five days before your birthday exactly what you are going to receive for your birthday. How do you *know* it will be a bike with gearshift? I told Cleo especially that I thought one model airplane and a comic book would be quite enough for you. How dare she go against my explicit suggestions like that? Here is some information I would like from you in your next letter: How tall are you now? How much do you weigh? What subjects are you taking in school? How is Nicky Kaufman, and are you and he still best friends? What work are you doing at home? Be sure and write me all this, because it is the only way I have of keeping in touch, and you write such very good letters that I need more of them!

Tell Nikola that her letter was lovely. I am very pleased to hear that she is giving Thunder some exercise. I assume that we had someone pare his hooves and shoe him. She also tells me she is riding Buddy some. Tell her I do hope she is very careful about this, because he could be dangerous for her if he ever got away from her. She tells me she is learning to play poker. Write and let me know if she is any good at cards. You know, she is a terribly pretty girl and just about the sweetest daughter I can think of, although I never let her know such opinions. So be sure she doesn't find out that I said it. Tell her to be sure and write me again when she has time. She's a fine correspondent.

As for little Mitzi—tell her she's so sweet that the minute I get home I'm going to eat her up—just as if she were candy. How is Cleo? You know if your father didn't have such excellent taste, he might have married some other girl—and *then* look who you'd have for a mother! You should be very grateful to me for picking Cleo. Give her a kiss for me. No—give her two. No, three! And one for Nikola and Mitzi; and lots of love for yourself!

Daddy—DALTON TRUMBO – #7551

25. To Melissa and Cleo Trumbo

Federal Correctional Institute
Ashland, Kentucky
September 27, 1950

Dear Mitzi:

The queen of the fairies (she lives right here in Kentucky) visited me this morning. She was riding a golden coach drawn by twenty-two white mice. She told me that I have a little daughter who is soon going to be five whole years old. She told me I ought to do something about so important a birthday. So I decided to write this jingle for you:

For Mitzi Trumbo (Who is five)

When a little girl is one
She doesn't have a bit of fun;
Just eats and sleeps and rolls and turns,
And burps a bit—and never learns.

When a little girl is two

She starts to walk and talk to you;
She learns to use her potty chair
And pull the ribbon from her hair.

When a little girl is three
She entertains her dolls at tea;
She learns to hop and skip and jump,
And now and then she gets a bump.

When a little girl is four
She has a passion to explore
And do each thing in her own way,
And help her mother every day.

But when a little girl is five
It's really fun to be alive!
She never has a pain or ache—
Just cherry tarts and angel cake!

And so I send to a five-year-old,
Whose name is Mitzi T.
A heartful of love and a bag of gold
And a birthday verse to her from me.

When the birthday is over, be sure and write me what presents you received. Don't eat too much cake—just five pieces. And you absolutely must not eat more than ten boxes of candy. Love and Happy Birthday!—DADDY

Hello, sweetheart! This spurt of birthdays is taxing my poetical powers. I think now, however, I have it under control. Your description of the ranch with autumn coming on is most tantalizing. We have it here, too—three-blanket nights, the trees beginning to turn, and fog slipping in each night from the Ohio. Everything here goes nicely, and very comfortably. No word of parole—perhaps no word even until November—and more likely than perhaps, refusal then—and then the time it takes for reconsideration. So hope only moderately, and then you will be only moderately disappointed or immoderately happy.

I am delighted with the book club news.[32] By all means go ahead with consent on the verse.[33] Ask them to send a copy of the book and poems here to me, directly from the New York office, when

[32] The Liberty Book Club had announced its intention to bring out a new edition of *Johnny Got His Gun*.

[33] The same book club considered including several of Trumbo's poems in an anthology but later abandoned the idea when such an edition proved too costly.

they're out. Incidentally, I wish you would tell me what they called the long poem. Sam Sillen said they were going to change it, but I never discovered to what.[34]

I think the pig business is great, and with all that feed I should think at least a couple of calves would also be in order. I received a letter from Bob [Roberts] in which he expressed great admiration for your business ability and voiced the suspicion you secretly enjoyed taking over. Did you order the car? What model? Color? Is there any possibility of getting it? When? Canned goods stock okay? Eating regularly? Love me?

I received delightfully pleasant letters from Catherine and Elizabeth. I shall answer Catherine next week and Elizabeth the next. Please explain to them the problems involved in writing them, so they'll not consider me tardy or unappreciative. Give mother my love, and tell her I shall have to forego a birthday cake this year. No can get it. Spank Chris, kiss Nikola, and keep for yourself an oversupply of love.

DALTON TRUMBO – #7551

26. Extract of a letter to Cleo Trumbo

Federal Correctional Institute
Ashland, Kentucky
October 11, 1950

I have also received some secondhand news of other people's children. I understand A————'s boy has had feelings of hostility against his father for several years, and that it now blazes so fiercely as to constitute a serious problem. His daughter cannot get over the fantasy that her father has numbers tattooed on his arm, and is in a concentration camp. Additionally they have been harassed by other school children, so that they are both in quite bad shape. Thus the mother takes them to see A———— whenever she can, hoping that will help them get over the trouble. I also understand that B————'s boy this fall at school changed his name, and will not permit himself to be called by his father's name. When I consider what appears to be the keen mental health of our kids under the same circumstances, I am inclined to think that our—or mainly your—policy toward them has paid off far better than that of the psychiatrists and moralizers.

[34] "Confessional."

27. To Cleo Trumbo

Federal Correctional Institute
Ashland, Kentucky
October 20, 1950

Darling:

Your letter sounded rather depressed, and I sympathize with you so much. I know from experience how irritating it is to make that trip—even alone!—and find that some idiot has forgotten what he promised. I have just sent, via a letter to Bob, a message to Charley that should curl his hair a little. Such rudeness is really intolerable.[35]

I am not at all worried about the eventual collectability of the Spiegel account, for he can't release his picture without paying. The time, of course, is important. So let me know every development as it occurs, and I shall make arrangements to transfer funds from elsewhere before you run short.

Now, a briefing on the parole situation. As I told you, our papers theoretically were sent directly to Washington, and we waived appearance before the parole board. We were told we would hear [the results] before the parole board sat here in Ashland. However we did not hear, and the parole board sat here Wednesday, Thursday and Friday of this week. I was called before it—a perfectly perfunctory, pleasant five-minute interview, in which nothing of any consequence at all was discussed. Naturally I have no clue and no opinion of chances. However word should be coming back from Washington in about three weeks, so approximately November 10th. If we are among the first to hear, I should know by that date. If not, then I most certainly should hear between November 10 and November 24. In any event, there is nothing to do but wait. And if the answer is negative, even so, over half of the sentence will have been served, and certainly the last half will be easier both for you and me than the first. So things aren't so bad any way one looks at them.

Your accounts of the children are always sharp, observant and wholly delightful. They seem to be developing well, and I am, of course, very eager to look them over. Do you find the ranch satisfactory for this period, or do you wish you had moved into town? Do you miss the Butlers badly? Are you working too hard? Getting enough rest? Let me know about these matters, for they are important.

Have you heard anything more from the Book Club on *Johnny*? Or about the poems? Do you have any idea what the book sells for, or what royalty it will pay per copy? Do not go to the slightest

---

[35] Charles Katz had neglected to keep a Los Angeles appointment with Mrs. Trumbo.

trouble for this information. It isn't important enough. Just tell me if you have it at hand.

Very little more for the moment, dear. Feeling fine. Loving all of you—

DALTON TRUMBO – #7551

28. Extract of a letter to Cleo Trumbo

Federal Correctional Institute
Ashland, Kentucky
October 24, 1950

I certainly wish I were home now to teach the children how to play those instruments correctly. Perhaps they don't know it, but at one time I directed the New York Symphony Orchestra. When I return, therefore, I shall arrange the Trumbo Symphony. Nikola will play the flute, Chris the trumpet, and Melissa the clarinet. I myself shall play piano, first and second fiddle, trap drums, base drums, French horn, tuba and bassoon. I shall also direct and take tickets at the box office. The money from admissions will all go to me, but think what fun the children will have being punished for sour notes! While I grab bank notes.

29. To Cleo Trumbo

Federal Correctional Institute
Ashland, Kentucky
November 13, 1950

Darling:

I do hope (if you have not read it in the newspapers already) that you will not be too disappointed to learn that my application for parole was returned to me today, refused, and dated, significantly, November 8, 1950. It is my opinion that we had perhaps a better than even chance up until about November 5th, when tension suddenly increased all over the world. The elections on November 7th sealed the issue, perhaps irrevocably. I am writing the attorneys at once regarding the problem of a petition for reconsideration, which will shortly go into the works. However it now appears that a flat policy of no parole for political prisoners has been inaugurated. The latter statement is, of course, merely my personal opinion.

Please think back to the time when I left. At that time we had no hope at all for parole. We did not even know that it existed as a legal possibility. So we faced a separation of ten months without flinching. Now we face a separation of only four months and twenty-five days which is, on the whole, not too bad. I keep thinking of the men in Korea, separated for much longer periods from families they love just as much, and facing, also, death. The whole world today is filled with misery and unhappiness; and our portion of it is somewhat less, rather than more, than the average. We have each other, in a kind of love and trust that makes me shout with inner pride. We have the children, healthy and happy of mind. Beside these marvels the present situation is really nothing.

I laughed aloud over your description of the collision with Mr. Burns (whom I do not remember), and the stout assistance you received from the children. Nikola wrote me a charming letter with an excellent picture of a horse, and Melissa sent me some absolutely beautiful drawings, for which I wish you would thank her for me. Don't tell me how loudly Chris plays the trumpet—I know, because I heard him the other night. It was just about eight-thirty, and the blast of sound almost shook the dormitory. Ask him to play more softly, please.

The past two weeks, having been tolerably suspenseful, have found me doing no other work but my job. However, I must now go back to writing, which I intend to start tomorrow. Whether it shall be the novel or no I have not yet decided. The novel was easy for the first four chapters, but after that, as you recall, it was my intention to make it as much history as fiction, and the vast amount of research I had piled up is almost essential to a continuation. So perhaps I shall do something else.

I think of nothing more, dear. Do not feel too badly, and the time will pass more quickly than we think. I share your wish for the world to settle down. You mentioned in your November 7th letter you were going to tell me "something about what's happening here at home (unusual)." Was it Adele's illness about which you were going to tell me, or did you forget, or was the "(unusual)" irony? I suspect the latter. Much much love to you all.

DALTON TRUMBO − #7551

30. To Cleo Trumbo

Federal Correctional Institute
Ashland, Kentucky
November 15, 1950

Dear Cleo:

From your Sunday letter—if I know my girl—you are flat on your back by now with a cold, and feeling pretty miserable. Also, you have received my last letter, and that hasn't lightened your spirits. However, doll, don't be any bluer than you absolutely have to be.

In considering our rejection of parole, I have come to certain conclusions. I was thinking of asking you to report them to Katz. But on second thought, I doubt that such a course of action would do much good. Therefore I suggest that you save this letter, and turn it over to Herbert [Biberman] [36] (write me when you have done so) —either personally, or by mail, as you wish. Here are my opinions.

(1) It was *possible* for us to have got parole.

(2) It was *not* accomplished because of *total* legal inactivity in the east, aggravated by a flat conviction on Martin Popper's [37] part that parole was hopeless. When people have no hope, they are paralyzed.

(3) The parole board was dealt with timidly and legalistically, as if it functioned in a vacuum. There could be no greater error than this. Other men, represented by counsel, are not so naive. And they generally make parole.

(4) It is now *possible,* with proper action, to get a favorable answer to [an appeal for] reconsideration.

(5) I have written Ben Margolis, outlining to him how such action might be undertaken.

(6) In order for any action to be undertaken, we should receive a visit from one of our attorneys. Marty has been asked to come to see us in Ashland. Whether he will—or will even answer a letter within a decent period—is quite open to question.

(7) I feel that our case in regard to parole has been shockingly neglected—not by the wives, not by friends, but by attorneys who have not even made a thorough study of the means by which parole is obtained. And perhaps, also, by others.

(8) I know that these people are very busy. I understand that. I, too, at one time, was very busy. I wish I were so again. Being very busy is much better than being in jail and not busy at all. Herbert will know what I mean.

---

[36] Herbert Biberman, having served his shorter six-month term, was now devoting himself on a full-time basis to defense of the still-imprisoned.

[37] Trumbo later wrote: "My references to various of our defense attorneys during this period were often sharp and unfair. Jail does not improve a man's temper, and completely distorts his view of affairs in the outside world."

(9) This case is important. Parole is important. Although we are out of sight, we still exist, and we should like to hear from these busy people about *every step* they are taking for reconsideration. The precedent has now been set of no parole for political prisoners. Even if we are not important any more, the precedent *is*.

(10) May [38] and Thomas [J. Parnell] both made parole upon reconsideration. Some twenty gangsters in the movie extortion cases made parole. And they all did it by having representation in Washington.

I think Herbert will appreciate all of this. So don't feel sad, sweetheart, just feel mad. Get well. Kiss all your charming children. Don't, however, give them all your love—save a small portion for—

DALTON TRUMBO—#7551

31. To Cleo Trumbo

Federal Correctional Institute
Ashland, Kentucky
November 23, 1950

Well, darling!

Your fine letter arrived this afternoon—Thanksgiving—and made me feel warm and terribly pleased with you all. I have quite got over parole—which is to say that the two month's suspense of waiting for a decision has been relieved, and the steady routine of life here has been picked up again quite smoothly. In one way the suspense provided a variation from monotony, and broke the period very nicely. I am still digesting an excellent turkey dinner, of which I ate so much that I passed up supper except for a bowl of coffee. I took a long nap in the afternoon, to celebrate the festal day. There was an air of good will—almost of contentment—in the dining room, and we were permitted to smoke over our coffee, which made us all feel very worldly. I am now back at a little writing after a long lapse; I cherish my dormitory bed with a fiercely possessive sense, and sit crosslegged on it for long periods of time, to the mystification of my colleagues, some of whom are, I am sure, convinced that I was a tailor on the outside.

On the question of birthday and Christmas: I am not absolutely sure of the Christmas rules, but I am sure that no birthday gifts are permitted. The rules for Christmas have not yet been posted, and, since most of the inmates here are from this general geographic area,

[38] Ex-Congressman Andrew May, convicted on charges of defense bribes, was also serving his sentence at Ashland.

may not be drafted until too late for such a case as mine. I have therefore inquired about last Christmas, and it appears that one four-pound package (exclusive of wrappings, which is to say, net) is permitted to each inmate. The package should probably be mailed ten days to two weeks before Christmas, and should not contain perishables. I suggest, therefore, a stop at Rose Marie de Paris near the Beverly-Wilshire (or some comparable shop), where two pounds of chocolates, one pound of chocolate-covered almonds and one pound of toasted almonds and/or hazelnuts, wrapped as one package and mailed direct from the shop to save you trouble, will make a very welcome addition to our Christmas larder. Actually, and oddly, I have no craving for any particular kind of food. The menus here are perfectly adequate, and I eat so moderately that such a feast as today's dinner was too much.

As to parole, I have already sent to the board my formal letter for reconsideration. For Herbert's information, a letter was sent to Marty [Popper] well over two weeks ago, and a most urgent one was sent ten days ago. He has not deigned a reply to either one. I find this sickening and incomprehensible. For Herbert's information also, the first note I have seen in the press about parole occurs in *Weekly Variety* of November 22, and to my mind, is so calculatedly inaccurate as to indicate a certain nervousness on the part of those who might wish to justify a non-parole policy. For the information of attorneys in the civil suits, *The New York Times* of November 12 carries a Brady story about *Emergency Marriage* made by Columbia with Larry Parks, in which I am given screen credit for the original story. It is, of course, a remake of *The Doctor's Husband*. Aside from the legal aspects, why not keep an eye out for it and let the children have what probably will be their last chance to see their father's name on the screen? It's probably no good, but they have always been a forgiving audience where I am concerned. Don't know about the Book Club; perhaps they have called it off. Tell the children I enclose, as a gift to them, the gobble from my Thanksgiving turkey.

Much, much love—
DALTON TRUMBO — #7551

32. To Cleo Trumbo

Federal Correctional Institute
Ashland, Kentucky
November 26, 1950

Hello, darling!

We are, at the moment, in the midst of the biggest snowstorm seen in these parts since 1917. Remember the Philadelphia blizzard, which was the biggest one since 1888? We seem to attract unusual weather, for you've been having it on the coast, too. Here we have had fine, dry snow for two days and nights. It is slowly coming to a stop now, but traffic is wildly tied up, and going to the dining hall one sees drifts four feet deep. The snow was accompanied by a stiff wind, which left some places bare of snow, and others in carved mounds, like dunes on the desert. Ordinarily snow isn't much of a problem in this country but this is turning out to be an exceptional year.

I am, at the moment, freshly bathed, shampooed, shaved, powdered, and ready to go to bed, glad for a working day coming up in the morning. My boss, who has been absent on a combination vacation-sick leave, has returned, and I was most pleased to see him, for he is in every way a decent and first-rate man. I would like him and enjoy being with him under any circumstances, inside of prison or free.

The time of year goes slowly for me now, with the holiday season so close upon us. I begin to understand Earl's [Felton] old dislike of Christmas. Remember how ostentatiously he used to leave town during the holidays when he was single, in order to avoid seeing the happiness of others? I'm so glad you had lunch with him. . . . Give my best to him whenever you see him.

I have written another letter to Ben [Margolis], considering his answer to my first one quite satisfactory. I have asked him to have one copy made for you, and one for Herbert, so make sure that you get yours. The one point I tried to make was immediacy, immediacy, immediacy. I hope I got it across to him, although anything written in a letter can generally be interpreted to suit the reader's purpose. However, action now is the key.

About Christmas packages, my instructions to you were correct with one exception: on December 1 we shall each be given a Christmas permit. I shall mail this permit to you, and that will clear matters.

I shall now go to sleep—the cleanest convict in America. I shower kisses upon our lovely children, and reserve a great reservoir of love to you, to be doled out day by day until I am with you again.

Goodnight!
DALTON TRUMBO—#7551

33. Extract of a letter to Cleo Trumbo

Federal Correctional Institute
Ashland, Kentucky
December 3, 1950

I think your idea of getting the children onto Sherlock Holmes is absolutely brilliant, and approve it a hundred percent, as lately I seem to approve so many things you do.

Our snow here, which was amazingly deep, has thawed with a speed equally amazing, and the last two days have been warm, with a rain today that has killed what remained of the snow. Looking at those drifts, I was reminded of the ranch, and am moved to wonder if the chicken wire has been put up around the trees. As I remember last year the rabbits were especially fond of those little evergreen trees or bushes—the ones near the canyon side of the back yard— and barked them thoroughly before they were wired. I covered the stripped places with that black tree paint, which seemed to do the job. I suggest that those trees be protected if they are not already, and that any barked places be immediately painted. Hah! Do you not find me helpful?

I'm so sorry my premonition that you were in for a siege was correct. Please tell me that you are now better. Did Adele give you any help? I'm sure the kids were wonderful—they always seem to be able to rise to an emergency. I wonder if they know that Sherlock Holmes was once a student of mine in a little class I taught in detecting. I had two students in that class who turned out very well— Holmes and J. Edgar Hoover. Holmes was the bright student. I had the pleasure of overseeing him and Dr. Watson in one of their early cases—the Case of the Cornish Horror. I'll tell them more about it when I get home.

34. To Cleo Trumbo

Federal Correctional Institute
Ashland, Kentucky
December 16, 1950

Hello, darling—

I have just a little time before the mail goes out, so this letter may at any point be halted. Have just come back from our Saturday night movie—Dick Powell in *Wagon's West,* and after this is done shall finish Budd Schulberg's *The Disenchanted.* He grows steadily more expert technically but has less of a solution for his characters, his readers or himself than ten years ago. Interestingly enough, Thomas Mann, Harlow Shapley, Linus Pauling and Robert Morse Lovett

asked him to join them in heading up a parole group, but at last
word they had heard nothing from him. He has, hitherto, been very
good about the case. The group of four are beginning to receive good
response to the letters which went out over their signatures, and
shortly will make their appeal to the board. As to the material in
Ben's hands you ask whether or not I want, I think not because I
don't believe I would be permitted to receive it.

Have heard this week from you, Hugo, Bob, Catherine and Elizabeth, so correspondence has been hot and heavy. . . . Elizabeth seems
wonderfully busy, and Catherine appears already to be bored with
her new job and considering side ventures into television. Herbert C.
Lewis, Hugo writes, committed suicide, which is sad, but more
than to have been expected. Glad you saw the lad [Earl Felton]—
or talked to him—and that he appears to be recovering from the
lusty blows fate has dealt him. . . . I am, with you, following the
president's [Harry S. Truman] personal correspondence with fascinated interest. . . . I think I also share your general view of world
events and their immediate future, although the points of view one
hears here are, of necessity, the results of restricted living.

I received the package of goodies, and nibble at them sparingly.
The choice was excellent, and the product is delicious although, I
fear, not conducive to trim body line. Tell the kids it's a great relief
at last to have a box of num-nums that I don't have to hide behind
the books in my study. I hide them elsewhere.

Call came. Have to close. Send all children to bed at once without
their dinners. Hello to Jim, Adele—and Melinda. Love to you!

DALTON TRUMBO — #7551

35. To Cleo Trumbo

Federal Correctional Institute
Ashland, Kentucky
December 20, 1950

Darling:

Please write Martin [Gang],[39] thank him for his letter, and tell
him I have addressed certain inquiries to the other attorneys which
will have to be answered before I can give him a decision. Then send
this letter on to Charley [Katz], asking him to return it to you
together with a collective opinion in a form sufficiently succinct for
you to communicate it to me.

[39] Martin Gang had written Mrs. Trumbo on December 11 asking permission to press forward with Trumbo's civil case against Metro.

I have always felt that the whole strength of my case, if there be strength, lies in the fact that I specifically refused to permit a morality clause in my contract, and that the main weakness of the other cases lies in the fact that they did not so refuse. The reason I consulted with Martin at the outset was my disagreement with Ben's [Margolis] theory that there existed no essential difference between my case and the others, and that they all would have to be tried on the same premise. I, on the contrary, have felt that my refusal to accept a morality clause placed me in a better position at law than those who did not refuse. It was precisely in order to obtain this advantage over standard contracts that I insisted on exclusion of the clause.[40]

My feeling that the morality clause is the most dangerous insertion ever made in an employment contract must have some basis in reality, and it is that reality which has always impelled me to believe that there is a very considerable difference between my case and the others—a difference which calls for different legal tactics. I have always preferred a trial on issues of legal fact only, if such were possible, excluding all testimony concerning my personal conduct since there exists in my contract no punitive powers contingent upon such conduct. I have always favored immediate action in my case, and have felt that delay serves me badly. I have, however, consistently deferred to the general judgment lest pursuance of my own case should harm the cases of others. The question is, does that situation still hold? If Martin should go ahead as he proposes, granting agreement to the conditions stated below, is it not true that a victory in my case could not but help the others, and that a defeat

[40] Trumbo's lack of a morality clause did indeed present a ticklish problem for Metro. Lester Cole, also under MGM contract, had the conventional morality clause. The studio could not fire two men for the same reason, in one instance invoking the morality clause when, in the other, no such clause existed. Hence the studio simply suspended both Cole and Trumbo for unnamed reasons. Several of the Ten had been without contracts and hence had no possibility of claims. In the remaining cases, the studios simply invoked the conventional morality clauses as the basis for breaking contracts and terminating the holders' careers.

Trumbo's suit, in spite of his obvious advantages, became the governing menace which compromised the defense of his colleagues. The lawyers could not contend that one case shoud be won because of the absence of the clause and the others should be won because the clause was invalid. Trumbo's suit was therefore stalled and Lester Cole's successfully presented first. Several others received favorable jury decisions (later reversed by higher courts), and Trumbo's unique case never went to trial. Ultimately, after the several years of litigation already so evident in these letters, the claimants and the studios began to bargain, and the studios collectively settled approximately $250,000. Those who had been under contract shared in proportion to their winnings with those who held no contracts at the time of the blacklist. While Trumbo's settlement amounted to $75,000, it totalled a mere $28,000 after sharings and legal fees.

would do them no harm? Based upon the above, I should like to know Bob's [Kenny], Ben's and Charley's reaction to Martin's letter, and to this one, if the following agreements were made.

1. That the case be tried as a straight legal contract issue in relation to which there are no questions of fact calling for testimony from me.

2. That if, however, in the course of the case I should have to take the witness stand, Martin agrees immediately to accept as co-counsel any or all of the other attorneys as I direct.

3. That if any question should arise bearing in any way upon my associations or beliefs, Martin agrees to rely completely upon the joint judgment of Bob, Ben and Charley in relation to such questions, although they need not formally be called in as co-counsel.

4. That Martin, even though there be no formal association of counsel, agrees at all times to keep Bob, Ben and Charley informed of the case as it progresses, and to make available to them, as friendly counsel, any information they may request.

5. That during the course of my case no concession of any kind will be made by plaintiff which might tend to give the impression that he or his counsel recognize any validity in the industry-wide morality clause.

6. That Bob, Ben and Charley get together with Martin, and that between them they agree upon a fair percentage fee in the event we win, since I am heavily indebted to the first for my criminal defense and obligated to Martin for his preparatory work in the civil case. A clarification of the fees is essential.

7. It is perhaps obvious that I, after some discussions here, favor the course Martin proposes. But for all the reasons we all know, I do not wish to act impetuously. Therefore I wish Bob, Ben and Charley, after consultation among themselves concerning this letter, to give you their candid opinion of the project, particularly as it relates to the others.

8. That if it is decided to go ahead, all of the above conditions being acceptable to all parties, Martin will first write Cleo the answers to a set of questions about the case which I shall write to her and the answers to which she will transmit to me.

There! Let that be an end to business. This is the last letter you will receive from me before Christmas. I hope you will be able to give Frank Butler my very fondest wishes for the holidays, and my injunction for his quick recovery. I presume Ted and Elsie [Riner] will be up over the weekend as usual. Remember me to them, and let me know if they're not looking a *lot* older. Everything here is tip-top (parole reconsideration rejected December 14, but delayed in transit to us, so it arrives as a gift—we'll reapply, naturally) and our spirits are high. To Nikola, Chris and Melissa, deep snows, warm fires, sweet candy, many gifts, and Merry Christmas. To their lovely mother, all of that and all of my love to boot!

DALTON TRUMBO—#7551

36. To Cleo Trumbo

Federal Correctional Institute
Ashland, Kentucky
December 27, 1950

My dear—

Christmas is over, a three-day holiday that passed not at all disagreeably. The Yuletide custom of stuffing oneself extends even to prisons, and I'm sure I gained two pounds. We had two motion pictures, one Saturday night and one Christmas afternoon, music at dinner from the inmate orchestra, candy, nuts, cookies and cigarettes from the warden, and general hilarity. We decorated our bars with alternate strips of white and red tissue paper, and then stood back and clapped our hands joyously, and cried to each other—"See? Candy bars!" Christmas morning, by calculating the time difference, I could establish just about the time the children were getting up, when they were opening their gifts, and when they were sitting down to breakfast.

And now we must get down to more practical matters: namely, that I am getting, as we call it, "short"—which is to say that in 102 days I shall be restored to the hectic life of the outside world. It strikes me that the occasion calls for us to have a brief vacation, alone and together, for the first time in a good many years. I am to be released Sunday night at midnight, April 8th. Sue [Lawson] will drive down from New York for Jack. I therefore suggest that you make arrangements to meet Sue in Ashland on that evening. Then you will pick us up at midnight, and we'll drive at once to Huntington, West Virginia, and all spend the night there in a hotel, for which reservations should be made. Next morning Sue and Jack will drive on to New York, while you and I shall have reservations on the first train for the same city. Then a slow, luxurious ride for the next 16 hours. In New York I want to make arrangements for an agent and a nom de plume, which provides an excellent excuse for staying there for a week at Lee's [Sabinson] place. We should have three nights in the theatre—*South Pacific, Guys and Dolls,* and a play—in addition to an evening with the Sabinsons, one with the Pomerances, one with Hy and Rita [Kraft], and one with Jack and

Sue. That kills the week, a perfect orgy of entertainment, fine eating and discreet drinking. When you leave home, make arrangements for the childrens' care for at least two weeks. Then, when we finish our week in New York, we can take the train if we wish still more vacation, or fly direct. It's not too early to think about it, for you'll need at least one new spring outfit, possibly a suit, and a dinner dress brought up to date, and that takes time. In a word—and always of course, if you find it an agreeable idea—let's splurge. And make our plans always with the possibility in mind of some unexpected emergency cancellation. What do you think of the idea?

I received pre-Christmas letters from Catherine, Elizabeth, Bob, Hugo, and you, so I am privy to all plans for the holiday, and all the news about the various participants. I'm re-reading *War and Peace,* and learning at last what a real novel really is, in contradistinction to the one-dimensional sketches and tours de force which currently pass as novels. There's a big difference, and I am O so eager to put my theories into practice when I get out. Tell the children we decorated our tree here with bells, tinsel, dangles and spangles. Some of the dangles were extremely pretty, and sharp enough to cut a man's head off.

Much love—
DALTON TRUMBO—#7551

37. To Cleo Trumbo

Federal Correctional Institute
Ashland, Kentucky
January 1, 1951

Well, sweetheart, happy new year!

This, in case you've mislaid a year or two, is the year I get *out* of jail rather than the year I go in. It is also the beginning of the second half century, and a great one it will be. Your husband, having resided in this place for 208 days, now has only 97 to go. I am, as we say, "getting short." The disease of shorttimeitis develops its own peculiar symptoms—nervous rash, inflammation of the taste buds, and general debility. The traditional cure for the ailment, given by men who have served more time more times than I, is simple: "Take it easy, play it cool, drink lots of water and walk slow." So that is what I am doing.

Your description of Christmas sounded fine. Catherine also told me of theirs, and I expect to hear about it also from Elizabeth. I do want you to tell Nikola how very much I appreciated her sweet and *extremely* well written letter. But four lipsticks—! Really! She can't have grown *that* much, can she? Please have her let me know at once how tall she is, and how red her lips have to be. They always seemed quite nice looking to me. Tell Chris I'm delighted he won't have to loot my desk any more, now that he has equipment of his own. And tell Melissa to stop doing whatever she *is* doing this very minute, or it's off to bed with a sound spanking and no dinner. And if she's already had dinner, then she must give it back at once!

I'm settling down to another period of writing. The approach of parole date in October seemed to throw me off the novel. Once parole fever subsided I tried originals. But I can't do them in here. I think the reason is that basically I hate them, and in order to do them at all must plunge in, hypnotize myself completely, concentrate exclusively on the story, and emerge five or six days later with the thing completed. Here I cannot do that, and the result is that working an hour or two a night, my dislike of the story gets the better of me and I am simply too nauseated to finish it. But the novel, which I do *not* dislike, provides enough interest to sustain the time intervals between writing.

More and more I realize that when I emerge from this place I must at last make the choice of whether I want to live at the rate of $25,000 a year as we always have, or whether I want truly to become a writer. I think it would be better for all of us if the latter course were taken, although it would entail certain sacrifices, including (unless we won a whopping law suit) the ranch. It seems pretty clear that with the kids growing into high school age as they are, we can't live at the ranch more than a year longer anyhow. Selling it, we could live practically anywhere in the world we wished for a year or two or three, during which I could accomplish the rather difficult but pleasurable task of shifting literary gears. But, with everything so unpredictable these days, exactly the opposite might work out. I am getting quite resigned here to surrendering myself amiably to events.

Much love—
DALTON TRUMBO – #7551

38. To Cleo Trumbo

*Federal Correctional Institute
Ashland, Kentucky
January 14, 1951*

Hello, sweetheart!

It's Sunday evening, been raining drearily all day. I've just finished a chapter in the book, and now, fresh and relaxed, I write to you. I'm glad you're for the New York trip—it'll be fun and a good vacation for us both. I believe Sue is going to drive here from New York, visit Jack, store her car here, and go on to the coast and stay there until she returns to pick him up on his release date. I am told that a train passes through Ashland at 1:15 a.m. going to Washington. It is called "The Sportsman" (C and O) and is made up in Detroit. I think it has a through car to New York. You can have Rex buy a bedroom on it there, come here with Sue, pick me up at midnight of April 8th, and in an hour and fifteen minutes later we could board the train at the Ashland station and be on our way. Fun, fun, fun!

There are several things I want to get done in New York. First, I know the editor of Simon and Schuster, which is a go-getting firm. I want him to read what I have ready of the novel, and then I want to have a serious talk with him about my literary future. On his reactions to the material and his estimate of my prospects, a good deal will depend. Then, through him, I want to find a new agent, one who recognizes the need of a nom de plume, and who will market short stories and originals on such a basis. Then I want to make an investigation of television, via Bill [Pomerance] and others; and finally, I want to have a serious discussion about the theatre with Lee. The play I had in view is completely dated and valueless because of the change in conditions. All in all, quite a program, and one which should give me a pretty good perspective about the future.

About the ranch—for my part, I have no wish to sell it unless it became a matter of absolute necessity. Under certain circumstances continuing to live there might continue to be practical and even desirable. Even if we moved away I should like to keep it if it were practical and possible to do so. But it *does* cost more to live there than it should, and I'm of the opinion that by a little work and an absolute minimum of investment (and reshaping Jim's [Martin] work) it could—and, with the cost of food now and in the future, *should*—be made to produce beef, pork, poultry, butter, milk, eggs and vegetables for two families. There, alone, would be an enormous saving. We've run it long enough as a luxury; what it needs now is not a caretaker but a hired man. However, this is all words and dreams, pay it no more heed than it deserves.

I am simply stunned at the reports on Nikola's growth—I'm sure you exaggerate. Delighted to hear that Frank [Butler] [41] has recovered again, and hope very much he takes it easy for a good long while. Bob [Roberts] is coming east sometime in February, and may find it possible to visit me, provided I can get permission for him to be received here. With the work on my novel, the weight has picked up—160 lbs.—but I can control it so well I'm not worried. By the time I step out of here with my wife on my arm, I'll be slim as a sylph. Love to Nikola, Chris, Melissa—to you—and to the world in general. It needs a little. Write Lee again and tell him you've got to have the suitcase.

DALTON TRUMBO – #7551

39. To Cleo Trumbo

Federal Correctional Institute
Ashland, Kentucky
January 30, 1951

Hello, darling!

Tempus continues to fugit at a satisfying pace. I came into this place to the strains of "Mona Lisa," and it appears I shall leave it to the nauseatingly repetitious melody of "The Tennessee Waltz." Weren't the dance hits of ten years ago pleasanter than now, or am I merely growing older? It scarcely seems credible I could be *that* much older, for some of these songs strike me as downright gruesome, and one hears them constantly over the dormitory radio. I shudder to think what the effect of the "Prisoners' Song" must have been in penitentiaries all over the country when *it* came out. I think the three things I want most when I get out of here sixty-eight days hence are (1) a good drink, (2) a rare steak and (3) a symphony.

Today I reached page 100 of the novel. I am now sure that I shall come out with at least 150, which, in terms of my fat pages, will be at least half a book, and the second half will go much faster, not only because it *is* the second half, but because it will be written under better working conditions. I miss talking specific parts over with you as they come to mind, and miss also your reactions to parts already written.

Bob [Roberts] is coming east in February, and will visit me if I can get permission. I applied for it several days ago, but no reply, so I am applying again tonight. We shall see. I can survive quite nicely without visits of any kind, but the eternal suspense waiting a decision

[41] The elder Butler had again suffered a heart attack.

is sometimes annoying, and must be doubly so to Bob, who has a schedule to draw up and deserves some answer.

How did Nikola's birthday turn out? Fine, I'm sure. How those little monkeys must have grown in my absence. I'll scarcely know them. Speak well of me to them and convey from time to time my affection.

It's late, Doll, and news is scarce. I really send this only to let you all know I think of you. Forgive its dullness.

Much, much love—
DALTON TRUMBO – #7551

40. To Cleo Trumbo

Federal Correctional Institute
Ashland, Kentucky
March 9, 1951

Sweetheart—

Your heart-rending account of your vigil over the baby chickens, and its denouement when Jim returned home stirred all my sympathies. A bad, bad day! And our Mitzi—how is she now? Feeling better? Tell her I expect her to drink lots of milk, so she'll be a fat little fish when I return. And how lucky the other charmers are they haven't caught the flu. I've been reading about it, and apparently it's pretty bad everywhere. I do hope *you* don't get it about the time you start to pick up your poor convict husband. That, tomorrow morning, will be exactly twenty-nine days hence. And regardless of what Sue says, I am *not* fat. I *was,* perhaps a little, but not now. When I hit 163 I went on a rigid diet, and am now exactly 156 with my clothes on! You'll be proud of me, and I'll look so wan my friends will weep and beg to buy our dinners. No word from Lee Sabinson yet, I presume. He's a horrible correspondent, but this is really unusual. In any event, if you *do* hear from him, insist on the Algonquin for our sentimental reasons, and he won't be too offended—or perhaps he just plain doesn't want us. People have been known to change under the pressure of time and expediency, and perhaps I'm a dangerous character now. We shall see.

I feel as you must sometimes when nothing has happened all day or week, and you face a blank page of paper. There simply isn't anything to write. I feel wonderful—a rest such as I've never had in my life before and hope never to have again. To keep busy I've been checking and cleaning out the storeroom files—a job that hasn't been completely done since 1947, so I'm going to leave at least that department in a better condition than I found it.

About *Born Yesterday*—I do like the play and am really very anxious to see that girl [Judy Holliday]. She must really be good, for you are not a raver. On March 17th we're going to see *All About Eve* here, which I'm looking forward to with a good deal of anticipation. Haven't been writing much, for several good reasons, but reading a bit. Sleeping a lot. Dreaming a lot. Not eating a lot.

Grab those kids, darling, and give everyone of them a hug and a kiss from me. I shall reserve your portion for personal delivery.

Much love,
DALTON TRUMBO – #7551

41. To Cleo Trumbo

Federal Correctional Institute
Ashland, Kentucky
March 11, 1951

My darling—

Two days hence will be our thirteenth wedding anniversary. I have been lying here on my bunk thinking about it. The thirteen years seem so short a time because it has been so happy a time for me. All that is any good in my life has grown out of it. I think back on each year of it with pride. I think our children take pride in it, too, and will take more pride as they grow older. Being married to you has made these months in prison tolerable, and when I have thought of you, which is very often, happy. We shall have many more years together, under cloudier skies or sunnier, but our love for each other will make its own climate—the climate of springtime which surrounds me tonight as I think of you. Many happy returns!

DALTON TRUMBO – #7551

42. To Cleo Trumbo

Federal Correctional Institute
Ashland, Kentucky
March 15, 1951

Darling—!

All goes well, smoothly, slowly, dully, in contrast to you who are by now probably in the midst of a thousand and one petty details which always precede departures. While I think of it, and while you

202

are already half-daft with lists, you might bring along my cigarette
case, lighter and gold holder. Not only would I like the luxurious
feel of them to reassure myself I am indeed out of here, but I need
the holder, and I want to stop off at Dunhill's in New York to have
the lighter repaired. I think you will find them in the leather cigar
humidor on my desk. Also, since I shall probably have many appointments in New York and shall have to be bright and prompt and
cheery all the while, please bring an adequate supply of getting-up
and going-to-sleep medicine.

About the magazines—allow all to lapse that you think we don't
need. You are quite right in asserting their content to be repetitious.

The pictures arrived, and have been greatly admired by all including me. I can see where you have had trouble with your lighting
equipment, but still they're good. How nice that living room looks.
And how much nicer with a fire on the hearth, and us all in front
of it.

. . . .

I've been reading a lot lately, having nothing better to do—and
what, really, could be better? This week Joyce's *Portrait of the Artist
as a Young Man,* James's *Portrait of a Lady,* Hardy's *Jude the Obscure* and Hawthorne's *The Scarlet Letter.* Last week Fitzgerald's
The Last Tycoon, The Great Gatsby, and his collected short stories,
along with Mizener's biography of him. Next week—? Ah, but there
won't be many more next weeks. We count time by so many more
Friday moppings, so many more laundry changes, so many more
bed changes.

The weather here, after a few brief and glorious days of spring,
has turned gray and chill—snow for the last three days which doesn't
stick to the ground, and perilously icy in the morning. One walks
stiff-legged, hunched over and very slowly. How is it with you? The
snow should help the rye—or did he get it in before this last one?
And the baby chickens—do they prosper? And your own three lovely
chicks—do they? And you—do you feel good?

I'm rather glad you're coming by train. No need to hurry, though,
for I shall be here twenty-four more days. Did Emily's father escape
the recent blizzard which chills the air of Hollywood? [42] I do
hope so.

Much, much love—
DALTON TRUMBO – #7551

[42] Hugo Butler had five daughters: Susan, Mary, Emily, Deborah, and
Rebecca. Since Trumbo was justifiably fearful that Butler was under attack
by the revitalized HUAC, he preferred not to mention his friend's name
directly.

43. To Cleo Trumbo

Federal Correctional Institute
Ashland, Kentucky
March 21, 1951

My darling—

Today is the first day of spring. After three days of soggy rain, the new season was ushered in with a driving storm. I am not an enthusiast for Kentucky's weather. Although Daniel Boone discovered this "dark and bloody ground," it is one of history's most notable examples of intelligence that he was not looking for it, and did not stop in it, but pushed wisely ahead. As I, too, shall do in good time.

Tomorrow morning I shall awaken to seventeen days, four more laundry changes, two more bed changes. How pleasant it seems. I am doing no work at all since this morning a replacement was given me on the job, and I do nothing but watch him work and give him instructions. I am now re-reading Dostoevsky's *The Brothers Karamazov*. Unlike most of the classics I've reviewed here, this one does not at all stand up to my previous estimate of it. While it is still a fine book, it is so loaded with mysticism and neuroticism that it falls far below the level of, for example, Tolstoy. I am, however, finding an increased admiration for Henry James, whom I previously rated as petty, prolix, and sterile. Chit-chat, chit-chat, chit-chat—! Enough of literary babble.

I have just read that Stanley Kramer has finally signed with Columbia—a $25,000,000 deal for six pictures per year for five years. And, best of all, that his new company has included deals for four writers, one of whom is Emily's father. I think it's simply wonderful, and hope you tell the lad [Butler] so when you see him. Now if only Tim's father [Ian Hunter] would get lined up, life would seem very good for our friends.

I think you could well have rather a large garden plot plowed up— and one portion of it that square touching at its corner the water tank. Remember how luxuriantly things grew there before, and how easy it was to get water to them? After the plowing's done, Jim should manure the plowed spaces thoroughly.

Tell that sweet Nikola that I received her Easter card and admired it very much. She's a fine girl, that one, and I'm eager to see how she's grown. Also Butch, the Horror-Boy, and my little fish.

See you sooner than you think now, darling. Much love—

DALTON TRUMBO – #7551

44. To Cleo Trumbo

Federal Correctional Institute
Ashland, Kentucky
March 29, 1951

Darling—

I presume this is the last letter I shall be writing you, for if you leave Wednesday, a weekend letter wouldn't reach you in any event. However, it would be awfully nice to hear from you once more after you've received this, for next week will be a long one, I fear.

Sue—as you may or may not know, depending on the rate of correspondence between the two of you—is driving from New York, and will drive Jack back there. I believe she plans to arrive around two or three o'clock Sunday afternoon. You arrive, as I understand it, at twelve noon. Sue is coming out to the prison for a Sunday afternoon visit with Jack. If you have no other way of making a rendezvous with her, you might make it there by coming to see me. In any event, you've arranged so much for yourself these past ten months that I'm sure you'll be able to arrange this last appointment without further suggestions from me. I understand our train arrives in Ashland shortly after midnight, but that it lies in the yards until after two a.m. This means that we shall probably have a couple of hours here in Ashland to wait on the train. Question: can we board the train and do the waiting in our stateroom? Another question: does the train really lie in the yards that long? The answers to the above you can get from the station in Ashland when you arrive. Based upon such answers, we can decide whether we prefer to wait in Ashland, or climb into Sue's car and drive with them to Huntington, W. Va. (about twenty miles), eat there with them and catch our train from Huntington. All of which we can decide when you arrive Sunday afternoon with the proper information.

Today I "dressed out"—which is to say I tried on all the clothes I entered with. They fit! Now they are being pressed. My shoes were given me. I wore them proudly for an hour or so. After so many months they felt strange. Finally I took them off and sought the grateful comfort of my worn old weejuns which have served me here so faithfully.

I am, of course, wild to see you, wild to get to New York and our friends, wild to get back to California and the kids, wild to get back to work and gather the wherewithal to pay back those who have been so accommodating, so generous, so generally wonderful during the last four years.

Until then, my sweet, kiss the children, and come quickly!

All my love,
DALTON TRUMBO—#7551

P.S.   Did I tell you to thank Nikola for her sweet Easter card? If I didn't please tell her. D.T.

P.P.S.   Your reference to attorney for a friend so obscure I make nothing of it at all. If somebody seriously wants an attorney, though, I've a plethora of 'em. Let me know. D.T.

5.
"This Damned Argosy"

Once Trumbo had paid his "debt to society" and had been sufficiently "corrected" at Ashland, he resolved to free himself and his
family from the economic burden of the Lazy T Ranch and from
the oppressive atmosphere of Hollywood, where the American Legion
and the MPA had vigorously taken up the work begun by HUAC.
Trumbo settled upon Mexico City, as did many other blacklistees,
as a haven free from fear and pressure where he could live handsomely at little cost, thus allowing a large portion of time for serious
writing. He could not have been more mistaken; for in the period
of self-imposed exile the writer found himself isolated, barely able
to exist financially, and beset with some of the most imposing difficulties of his blacklisted career.

His energies were devoted primarily to a task he loathed: the
writing of originals which were marketed under other men's names
for a substantial share of the profits. Powerless to exert his seasoned
know-how in manipulating sales, Trumbo watched good scripts and
stories sell for meager prices or not at all; moreover, he frequently
found it impossible to collect moneys actually due him. These handicaps of distance coupled with the hardships of simply being a blacklistee—and one having no small amount of trouble with the U.S.
Federal Bureau of Internal Revenue at that—proved insurmount-
able, and Trumbo ultimately resolved to return to the center of action
or, as he has phrased it, "to get closer to the teat."

1. To Frank and Maury King

Lazy T Ranch
Frazier Park, California
May 28, 1951

Dear Frank and Maury:

I have waded through most of the books, and found a certain
amount of value.[1] I have now reverted to my old night hours, and
am deep in the project. I think it is making considerable sense and
that we shall soon have something to look at.

I am also badly broke, and could use $500.00 most handily. I am
aware that you have already paid a generous advance, and are under
no obligation at all to pay any attention to the problem. However, if

[1] The King Brothers had sent Trumbo four scripts in need of doctoring jobs.

you could see your way clear to draw a check in that amount to Beth Fincher, against the sum due upon delivery of the script, it would be of incomparable assistance to me, and would eliminate the need of my having to go into town and go through the humiliation of borrowing it.

Please drop me a note, even if it is only to say no, so that I can square myself off as quickly as possible.[2]

Incidentally, I think an attorney is going to be here this coming week-end, so if you were by any chance planning to drop in, it would be best to delay it.

Regards,
DOC

2. To Elsie McKeogh

Lazy T Ranch
Frazier Park, California
May 28, 1951

Dear Elsie:

A thousand pardons for my tardiness. Cleo and I went straight from jail to New York planning on a pleasant two weeks there. However I came down with flu, and shipped out for home by air after only four days, having failed to see most of the people I'd wanted to, including you. I spent five weeks here in bed, and only now am really stirring.

By all means let Peter Cotes have the play.[3] I will sign any contract you negotiate.

[2] The note read: "I am happy to take care of this."

[3] Peter Cotes, a London producer, presented *The Biggest Thief in Town* in a small-scale production in the summer of 1951. After a successful limited run, Cotes moved the production to the West End where it opened to good reviews at the Duchess Theatre on August 14, 1951, and played until January 19, 1952, when J. Edward Bromberg, who played the starring role of a small town undertaker, died of a heart attack. Efforts to re-cast and reopen the play were frustrated by the illness and death of George VI on February 6.

More and more requests for permission to do *Thief* were made. Besides the successful English production, the play was performed in the Netherlands, Rome, South Africa, and at three theatres in Canada: Straw Hat Players, Inc., in Toronto, the Canadian Repertory Theatre in Ottawa, and the Crest Theatre in Toronto. American theatres—the Old Log in Minneapolis, the Showcase Theatre in Evanston, Illinois, and the Bucks County Playhouse in New Hope, Pennsylvania—also performed the comedy. As a result of this attention to a Broadway flop, Trumbo wrote Mrs. McKeogh on December 16, 1951, ". . . go ahead and sign anything your dear heart wishes, for clearly we have a freak on our hands and must grab everything that develops from it. Found money, even in small chunks, is terribly sweet."

I'm wondering how the Liberty Book Club sale of *Johnny* went, and when they pay. Also I wish you might ask them to send me five copies of their edition and charge them against my royalty account, since I haven't even seen it.

I have about twenty-five more letters to write before I can address myself to the more serious enterprise of earning a living, so this will of necessity be brief. I feel fine, and appreciate very much the splendid letter you sent to the Parole Board. I hope it doesn't place your loyalty in question! Prison wasn't so bad as I had expected, nor, may I add, is freedom exactly as uncomplicated as I had imagined it to be.

Best,
DALTON

3. To Al Herd, Los Angeles realtor

Lazy T Ranch
Frazier Park, California
June 12, 1951

My dear Mr. Herd:

I am planning to put the Lazy T Ranch in Lockwood Valley, Ventura County, up for sale, and at the suggestion of my business manager, Mr. Rex Cole of the Equitable Investment Company in Hollywood, I approach you before discussing the proposition with any other realtor.

The ranch is located in Ventura County in the midst of the Coast Mountains, looking, from an altitude of 5,000 feet, across the valley to Mount Pinos four miles distant, which, at almost 9,000 feet, is the highest point in the coast range. It is thirty miles as the crow flies, from the coast. It is reached by a blacktop county road which turns to the left (or to the west) off the Ridge Route two miles north of Gorman. It is 19 miles from the Ridge Route, 12 miles from the nearest village, post office and telephone at Frazier Park, in Kern County.

The property consists of 320 acres, 200 of which are cleared and under cultivation. It is fully fenced, and reached by 7/10 mile of private blacktop road on the property which connects it with the county road. Outbuildings consist of three barns, a garage, a second garage plus caretaker's quarters, a power house and smoke house, all reached by electric lines designed to carry the heaviest possible loads. Water is supplied from a well sunk beside our own year-round stream, and is connected with an 18,000 gallon water tank kept automatically full by a 3-hp electric pump. The place has two gasoline pumps with submerged 550-gallon tanks, a 1400-gallon butane tank, an auxiliary 5000-watt Kohler electric plant operating from either gasoline or butane in case of power failure, a new water pressure system with adequate water outlets throughout the grounds, three cesspools, etc.

The owner's house is all on one level, tile roofed, insulated with rock wool, stucco construction, containing five bedrooms, two baths and lavatory. Kitchen equipped with automatic dishwasher and electric garbage disposal. The living room, 33 x 18, is paneled full length in Duali (Philippine swamp mahogany), with ceiling of Oregon pine, parquet floors of oak and elm and a marble fireplace. Lounge is paved with red Tennessee marble, has fireplace and adjoining bar. Master bedroom has fireplace, and completely mirrored dressing room with matching cedar-lined closets. House is heated by modern forced air furnace which serves as air conditioner during the summers. All rooms in house plus front and rear terraces and caretaker's quarters are connected by a 12-station inter-house telephone system. The house has five fireplaces in all.

Front terrace looks down on private artificial 3-acre lake fed by property's own stream and amply stocked with rainbow trout. Lake and house are separated by seven Ponderosa pines, some over 100 feet tall. Ranch is bounded on two sides by forest preserve; surrounding country abounds in dove, quail, deer, a few bear and cats. Ducks drop down on lake in autumn.

Property is not presently in commercial production, although it is two miles from home ranch of one of the largest cattle outfits in this part of the country, and close to a number of profitable turkey ranches, this being considered the finest turkey country in Southern California.

The place would not be an investment for one who expected an immediate income from it. It would be suitable only for someone of considerable means who wished a luxury place for year-round or summer living in great seclusion; or someone of high income who wished to develop it into a property of great capital value out of funds presently being absorbed by income taxes.

I am prepared to supply you with a complete set of photographs, both inside and out, and, because of the distance from the city, to agree to a fee commensurate with your necessarily greater efforts. I am not prepared to give an exclusive at this time, but on the other hand I have approached no other agent.

This is not a forced sale. I am disposing of the place only because my oldest child is at an age where she will, in another year, need to attend high school in the city, since we do not wish to send her to private school. I am not therefore disposed to sell the place at a sacrifice, nor in a hurry unless, of course, my price is met. I would consider it essential for you to look over the property personally before you decided to list it.

If you are interested in handling such a place, kindly notify Mr. Cole. He is authorized to arrange the terms of your representation with you. He and I are at present considering what price should be asked, and what minimum price we will accept.

I shall appreciate hearing from you.

Yours very truly,
DALTON TRUMBO

4. To a novelist and friend

Lazy T Ranch
Frazier Park, California
June 15, 1951

Dear Nelson Algren:

I am writing this letter in the off-chance that you might be interested in an occasional piece of dirty money. I'll outline the possibilities as briefly as possible:

I have always been rather good at knowing what this town will buy in the way of original stories. After the blacklist, during the years of 1948–49, in order to support my family and a rather costly number of aged dependents, as well as to provide cash for legal fees and a year's enforced vacation, I wrote five original stories for the screen. Two of them sold for $40,000 each; one for $35,000; one for $11,000 and one didn't sell at all. In each instance I used the name of some friend who was at least somewhat known in the motion picture industry, which is to say, the story was by the friend and I had no connection with it whatever. In each instance the man who provided the name took one-third of the price and I took two-thirds.

Since I have been released from jail I find that most of the friends who accommodated me have either left town or are themselves blacklisted or are under some kind of cloud—the variety of clouds in Hollywood is enormous. Likewise my agent has been forced out.[4] I hasten to add that none of the misfortunes befalling these people had anything to do with their black market connections with me, for the whole thing was quite secret.

In considering how to resume operations again, it has occurred to me that you might find such an arrangement acceptable. The procedure would be very simple. I would write a story which I considered saleable and mail it to you. You would send it on to your

[4] George Willner.

agent in Hollywood as yours. If it sold, you would transfer to me my end of the cash made out in my wife's maiden name. You would report the whole sum as received in terms of your income tax, and deduct therefrom the sum remitted to my wife, either as payment for her literary services, or as your outright purchase from her of a literary property. My wife, in our own income tax, would report the money as received from you, and all the legalities would be satisfied. The reports are, of course, confidential, and could be even less specific than I have suggested, provided that the money is honestly accounted for.

I am obliged to warn you in advance that an original story, designed for sale on the local market, involves a combination of prose and construction and sentimentality and vulgarity that appalls even me, who am used to it, and would appall you even more. The only thing which makes it possible for a self-respecting writer to engage in such an enterprise is that the story is never published, and is read only by Hollywood. A good rule, which I have always observed in the sale of such material, is never to permit oneself to be inveigled into taking a job to develop the material for the screen, because such stories are not really designed to *make* motion pictures; they are only designed to *sell* to them.

Also, in contrast to the $126,000 worth of stories I sold under this method in 1948 and 1949, the present prices are on the downward side and purchases are fewer. Hence, while in those two years I sold four out of five, the percentage of hits would be likely to diminish, and the income from those which did sell would likely be less. Even under present conditions, however, I think we could reasonably expect a gross income of $50,000 per year.

When I get ideas for such stories they write very quickly, never more than two weeks. Since I started a book in jail, it is my idea that some such arrangement would permit me a good ten months a year to work on serious stuff without money troubles. It has occurred to me that your end of the loot—if such a percentage were satisfactory —would perhaps do the same for you.

I need not add that secrecy is the first element of success in such a scheme. If I sent you a story, you could be assured that no one would have read it. You, I am sure, would wish to be equally discreet on your end.

If you have any moral compunctions about such a procedure in relation to motion pictures, please forget them. Hollywood is a vast whorehouse, and any scheme by which tolerably honest men can abstract money from it for their own purposes is more than praiseworthy. If, however, you have compunctions in terms of your own personal convictions about such matters, then of course I shall forget about the matter entirely and with complete understanding.

In any event, I'd like to hear your reactions to this suggested bit of thievery.[5] And regardless of them, I add my good wishes to this tedious message.

DALTON TRUMBO

5. To Hugo Butler

Lazy T Ranch
Frazier Park, California
June 25, 1951

Dear lad:

I must say that I've never been so discouraged about a community as I have been from the descriptions sent by you and Jean.[6] We're thinking of sending you CARE packages to supplement your diet of fish and bread. Really, neither of you writes about anything but fish and bread and beer. The limitations of the place stand out in stark relief by reason of those things you don't write about. Fish and bread and beer and beach. Jean gave us an enchanting picture of the beach, but when the grammar was pared away, what was it? A long, desolate roll of the sea upon sand, with six figures standing out against the shore. Alone. A few gulls, perhaps, but they weren't mentioned. Just this vast stretch of loneliness which you monopolize. I can see you returning from this grandeur in the evenings to lobster and bread and beer. I can see you rising in the mornings, scraping dried kelp from the stoop as you set bravely out for the wasteland once more. And the conversations with the accountant. And an occasional fiesta when some large turtle dies and is beached. Really!

You need have no fear that the delights you mention will bring the Lardners—or anyone else, for that matter. Frances is determined to stay in Southern California so that she can pick up some work, and the Indian [7] forsooth has no choice. They have taken another house in town. As for us, I am engaged in buying a new car and turning loose of the Mercury. When this is accomplished and the new car broken in, we are going to come down with a load of lamb, beef and tartar sauce and see for ourselves how you are making out. How about medicines—cortisone, Benzedrine, sulphas, penicillin? And God in Heaven, man—how many sleeping pills will you need to wear out

---

[5] Novelist Algren, who had always strongly supported the Ten and whose feelings about abstracting money from the blacklisters coincided perfectly with Trumbo's, cheerfully agreed. However, Trumbo's life changed so swiftly thereafter that he was never able to put the plan into operation.

[6] The Butlers were living in Ensenada, Baja California, Mexico.

[7] A nickname for Ring Lardner, Jr.

the long summer ahead? Just ask and we'll bring it. I know just how you must feel.

It is our plan to spend a day and a night, then leave the kids and fly to Mexico City, look it and Cuernevaca over, come back about three days later, reclaim our kids, commiserate briefly with you, and depart north.

If we sell this place as soon as we hope to, our plans for the future are by no means definite. If the cost of living is really appreciably cheaper down there, we would be strongly tempted to move down. But not to your fishy little community. To Mexico City, where a man can walk outside his front door and see the blessed sight of another man. Where there are lights, music, gaiety, and no more fish than anything else. Now since you and an accountant live practically in each other's laps, if you were a good fellow you would get some practical information, both for yourself and for me. For example, the answers to the following questions:

1. Is it true that as an immigrante one has to pay only Mexican income taxes? 2. Is it true that such taxes, in their highest bracket, run only eight pecent? 3. Is it true that to become an immigrante, one must undertake to do some work, in movies or so forth, which will be of benefit to the country? 4. Is it true that if one comes into the country with $40,000 in cash, one becomes a capitalisto, and therefore finds it much easier to assume the immigrante status? 5. How long does one have to live in the country before one can become an immigrante? 6. How much does it cost to send a child to an American school? 7. On the Mexican income tax business, does being an immigrante mean that one pays the Mexican tax only on income derived from Mexico? 8. If one goes down, succeeds in becoming an immigrante, and thereupon proceeds to earn money by sales of literary material in the United States, does he have to pay an American income tax on such money? 9. If he does, could not this be solved by setting up a Mexican corporation, putting oneself in the employ of which corporation, transferring to it title to all one's literary work, then sell the said work in the U.S., have the money paid to the Mexican Corporation, receive it in one's own turn from the corporation (or a reasonable portion thereof), and thereby absolutely come under the Mexican tax laws? Maltz tells me he pays $147.00 per month for an enormous house and grounds and pool—much larger than his family needs—furnished, of course; and that he pays 80 pesos a week, which is above the average, for two servants. Is this kind of thing true? If so, then are you not taking a screwing at $90 a month rent and a fish diet and shoveling all that kelp off the step each morning?

Now these are the important things, lad. You must forget the dreariness of your situation, and look to ways out of it. Speak to that accountant—accountants are the most important people in the world

—and quit gorging on bread and beer. If you learn a very great deal from the accountant, you won't *have* to fight kelps from here on out. There are better ways of life, lad, and you who are on the spot, must look into them. I think you owe this much research to me, but if you think differently, then I know goddam well you owe it to yourself. And your family! God, man—have their little bellies begun to swell yet? We thought we saw a suspicion of it in the pictures, but Cleo told me not to mention it, so don't reply to the inquiry.

Now here, in brief, is my point of view. I'm not married to this country—although the next session of the Grand Jury may make the tie closer than I wish. I doubt the foregoing, it's only a witticism. I'm perfectly willing to go anywhere that I can live not, let us say, in peace, but certainly in luxury. If I could spend the next five or ten years in Mexico City or its environs and earn say forty or fifty thousand a year, which isn't at all improbable, and pay Mexican income taxes, and stash enormous sums of cash away—hell, I'd go for it instantly. And here is my thought, purely for speculation:

1. I, too, have a fronteronomi, and an absolute beauty. You have a name. Jean, in fiction, at least, and just possibly in movies too, still has her own. Good. Three names. We all know this racket. We are in business!

2. We establish headquarters near to each other in some aristocratic section of Mexico City or its suburbs. Either separate quarters or a real palazzo shared together.

3. We became immigrantes, either by finding employment, or by reason that we are capitalistos. I should expect to come down with something more than what I'm told is the $40,000 capitalisto classification. In any event we become immigrantes. Now if that puts us under Mexican tax laws, fine. We are made men and women. If it doesn't—that is, if we should still have to pay American taxes on American earnings—then we set up a corporation, with a Mexican national as partner. And we write for that corporation, and money paid to us out of the U.S. is paid to that corporation. And by Guadalupe, *then* we pay only those lovely Mexican taxes. And we live on ten thousand dollars a year cash, and we put away thirty thousand dollars a year each in the bank at that lovely six percent, and by Joseph and Mary, we have three or four hundred thousand dollars apiece in ten years, and we laugh and laugh and laugh. We have all of our bread flown to Mexico City from Ensenada, and we don't have to eat fish unless we really want to.

Now please find out about these things. Stop driving yourself wild on that lonely stretch of sea and sand and discuss practical matters with señor el accounte. Pesos above poy! Richness and luxury. Money in the bank. Those are the things to look forward to. You're not stuck there forever, lad. And your friends are coming in five or six weeks with adequate supplies. All will be well.

Hasta luego or some such thing. O Pioneer, my gender endings are bad but I still have my wits about me. Gather yours and between lobsters jot down a little of the realistic. Wish you could be with us this summer—the fish in the lake are all about ten inches long, and so fresh that the little devils are still snapping when they hit the skillet. Bread's lousy. Better times are coming for us if you'll only get your mind off your troubles. We all send you felicitaciones y misereres y fraternitados y commisereres! [8]

TRUMBO

6. To Hugo Butler

Lazy T Ranch
Frazier Park, California
July 16, 1951

Lad:

Merely because I'm tied up and can't answer your letter immediately is no reason for you to break off the correspondence entirely

I appreciated very much the financial information given us. I am, however, somewhat troubled by its very exhaustiveness. If you went about getting it only after my letter of inquiry, you are a hopelessly foolish fellow. If, on the other hand, you had it all along, you are an extremely bad friend for not having passed it on sooner.

Preceding your letter was one from Jean, in which the monomania which currently afflicts your household reached new heights. It was the tangiest letter we have ever received. Literal quotes: Calico bass. Live bait boat. Hugo is getting to be a great fish cook (Ed. Note. I should *hope* so!). Navy packing box fished out of the surf. Fishing nets. Corks. Shells. Sand dollars. Marine flora and fauna. The catch is great. A little breezy this month.

The letter ended with an ominous threat of bouillabaisse should we be so unwary as to drop in. Altogether, it was probably the saltiest piece of literature since Conrad.

I spent an evening in town with John Wexley,[9] full of happy chatter about mordito or some such custom of which he approves. He is

---

[8] Trumbo is obviously making no attempt at correct Spanish usage and spelling.

[9] John Wexley, a successful playwright (*The Last Mile, They Shall Not Die*) and O. Henry Memorial Award winner in the short story, is a blacklisted writer whose screenplays include *City for Conquest, Hangmen Also Die, Cornered, The Long Night, The Amazing Dr. Clitterhouse, Angels with Dirty Faces* and *Confessions of a Nazi Spy*. During the blacklist he wrote several films and published *The Judgment of Julius and Ethel Rosenberg*.

going to sell his house, turn east and rent his farm, and then return to the south again, perhaps permanently. He had a number of snapshots, some of you, in many instances with your hand on some rather good-looking woman. Cleo said I should not write about this in a letter Jean was bound to read. I said what the hell, she can't leave him with four kids, he's got her hopelessly trapped and probably impregnated by now anyhow. Furthermore, I said it's good she learns these things from a friend rather than from some gossipy nobody whose only motive would be to cause trouble. Anyhow, you looked terribly smug.

We have made certain inquiries about the east. Not so good. To buy a place which would sustain itself one would have to lay out about a hundred Gs. Bill Pomerance has looked around, and reports that all the 25 to 40 G places are burdens—which is to say, perhaps as expensive as ours. Ring's mother has 360 acres in Connecticut and they've never carried themselves. Suburban living is as expensive or more so than L.A. living. So I think we shall not turn east in the unlikely event we find some fool with more money than agricultural knowledge to take this place off our hands.

More likely south. If, after our exploratory trip down there, we should really find it possible to live on ten thousand a year in such a style that I could get out of the goddam kitchen and back to the typewriter, I am quite certain we would jump at it. I like the sound of Cuernevaca better than most others. Apparently it's a little cheaper than Mexico City, and with the new highway one could have its advantages (that is, the city's) whenever one wished. The English homos who are said to infest the place wouldn't bother me greatly. I would, of course, like to think that you and Jean were living there too. Just what are your plans, if any?

We shall probably be down sometime between the first of August and its middle. Hunter will accompany us on some preposterous pretext that he has story discussions of enormous importance to engage in with you. We shall give you due warning. We shall bring saffron for Jean, although as far as I'm concerned she can take the goddam fish stew she plans to use it in and do something other with it than feed it to me.

We have bought a new car. A Packard. Ridiculous. $3,500. It is recommended by Consumers Union above all others. Very pleasant to have sound machinery under my harassed stern once more. I tell myself it was all I could do. I had to get rid of the two Mercurys, for they were falling apart again. To trade *two* cars in on a sensibly priced car would have reduced the trade-in value some thirty-five percent. So I went for a biggie out of self-protection, and as a piece of economic shrewdness. Or so I tell myself. Damned lie. Nice car though.

Some interest abroad in the ranch. It would be our accursed luck to decide to sell it in the midst of the greatest drought since the passage of the Volstead Act. Creek's dry. I lie to the suckers in a way that would qualify me for the state department. We're asking $59,500, and will take a minimum to ourselves after commission of $54,000. I have a hunch we shall take less. What we shall do with this heap of goods we have here I don't know. We haven't room for the stuff as it is. Place vastly overfurnished. Furniture prices catastrophically low. Probably store the stuff. From nothing would I derive quite so much satisfaction as getting rid of everything except a few books and a set of clean drawers.

My limited view of the economy of Hollywood indicates it's not too good. Employment extremely low, and many deserving hacks starving. I find enough to do, but don't enjoy doing it, and stall a great deal of the time. I remember how I started stalling and ate my way through the Beverly Hills house pillar by pillar. I have the ugly feeling I am now eating my way through this one tile by tile. I don't seem to worry much, which is worrisome in itself. I just slunge about and bipper at people, and dream of the time I'll be shet of everything. There is some talk of a settlement by studios. Deadline tomorrow, I think? I doubt if it'll go through, but there's always an outside chance. Would be nice. Settlement for all, I mean, not just for me.

We have heard, via someone who lives next door to Catherine, my sister, and who has been looking at Frank's [Butler] town house with a view to buying same, that Frank has been ordered to stay permanently at the beach, the ranch being out for him. We have no verification. Another circuitous piece of information comes from Alice H[unter] through Jack Shearer (is Jack his first name?). Anyhow he says that he was talking to Frank, and Frank said he didn't know where you were, but that if he *did* know he would turn you in. I don't know why I tell you this, aside from a perfectly human willingness to stir up bad blood. I am irritated at Frank anyhow. They visited here (just before dinnertime, natch) several weeks ago. I fed them, sent them home loaded with trout and a picture of you (that offensive one in which you sit with a glass, a cigarette and your feet on one of my red leather chairs). Next week we got an invite to dinner there. Rejected by nice polite note because had no one to care for kids. Week or so later (the day Jean and Ethel said goodbye to each other over phone) we dropped in. They had a pair of desiccated Bel-Air vomits with them. Frank asked if we wanted drinks. We said yes, Scotch and sodas. Frank said to me to come to bar with him to fix them. But the Scotch bottle (pinch-bottle) had only a driblet in it—not enough for one, much less two. Frank said would we take a bourbon. I said yes. But illuminated on the shelf were two more pinch bottles. He saw me look. He said the stuff was quite expensive, and he was sure we'd enjoy bourbon as much. So bourbon we got.

First time he's been outright rude to me, and we haven't dropped by since, nor they here. Enough gossip.

John Sanford has written a book. It was rejected by thirty-four publishers. He printed it himself. I have just finished it, and in many ways it's a fine book. A really admirable one. I shall write him about it. It's called *A Man without Shoes*. Beautifully got up at ten bucks a a copy. But shocking commentary on American publishers, for it's a top-notch job, and absolutely superlative when compared with best of current output.

Nothing more to write. Tell me your plans if any. Tell me how you all are. What's happened to the bread situation down there? No word of bread in last two letters. Bread here's no better than it has to be. Bread there may fluctuate. Season and weather has a lot to do with the mix and the rise. Don't worry if there's a temporary falling off in quality.

I am impatient for something to happen to us, good, bad, or indifferent. I want to move somewhere. Once the decision is made, I grow overpoweringly impatient with the process of putting it into effect. I think we might live handsomely and grow rich in Mexico. Don't you?

Give our love to all your fisherfolk.

TRUMBO

7. To John Sanford

Lazy T Ranch
Frazier Park, California
July 17, 1951

Dear John:

Paul gave me a copy of your book (Paul Jarrico,[10] I mean). I started to read it Saturday night, and stayed up all night and didn't go to bed until I'd finished it. Sunday afternoon Cleo and I brought the kids to town for a show. I telephoned you twice but you weren't home. That is, if you are the John Sanford at State 4-1255 I telephoned you. Now I am writing. If you are *not* the John Sanford at State 4-1255 then you also are not the John Sanford at 4912 White Oak Avenue in Encino. So just in case you are neither of those John Sanfords (who are the same John Sanford), and wanting this letter to reach the John Sanford who wrote *A Man without Shoes,* I am sending it to the Plantia Press.

[10] Paul Jarrico's pre-blacklist credits included *Song of Russia, Tom, Dick and Harry* and many others. Since the blacklist he has worked anonymously in almost every country in Europe. He resides in London.

What do you say about a book you've liked? The letters I've received which go all out I've always disbelieved. Nothing, I say, can be *that* good. Of course I love such letters even if I don't quite swallow them (or didn't when I was getting them) —but since writers are a self-doubting tribe, they've never seemed quite as good as those which approached the problem of praise with restraint.

Well. I read the book. I think it's a fine novel, which is as much as you can ask of any novel, and more than you ever get these days. I think it may even be a great novel. When people say: the proletarian novel is dead, this proves they lie. The proletarian novel died of bad writing. And for you it never died at all and by God you've proved it.

It is so clean. It is so blunt. In parts it is so beautiful. It shows such tremendous growth on your part, and such fine command over yourself and the material. I read the chapter in which the boy comes home and discusses the fight at school with his father. I meant to say I read this chapter aloud to Cleo and all three children and they howled with delight. Children are very important critics. You do what no one dares do these days, and in such a simple, charming, self-evident manner that the reader simply cannot question it: namely, that a rich man is a thief. You say lots of other things too, all of them good, all of them true, and none of them ducking any question at any time. The delineation of the younger Danny from beginning to end is wonderful—his cheating, his pathetic failures, the things we've all done or thought of doing, yet the things which are never portrayed as part of a decent man, of a hero if you please. And much more, much, much more.

I think I have some idea of what you went through with it. I was in jail ten months and missed parole once, finally got out upon expiration of the term. You must have been in jail with this for five years, and Paul [Trivers] tells me you missed parole thirty-four times, and finally had to buy your way out. What a disgrace, what a vomitous comment on American publishers, what a terrifying thing to all writers that you had to publish it yourself.

Well, that was the thing to do. It had to be published.

I have not too much liked your earlier books, although I recognized remarkable things in them, remarkable portions, that is. Perhaps I was crazy, or perhaps you have taken a great leap forward, perhaps quantity has changed to quality. In any event, for this book and for my money, you can piss on any author who has been published in this country in the last five years (how stupid that arbitrary figure of five years really is!)—and if, in the process, you spatter your boots a little, send them to me and I'll clean them for you.

Affectionate regards to Maggie.

DALTON TRUMBO

8. To Hugo Butler

Lazy T Ranch
Frazier Park, California
August 6, 1951

Dear lad et brood:

If all goes well with us—as it seldom does—we shall set forth for your community on Friday, August 17th; either that or the following day. We propose to arrive on the same day we start, God willing as He rarely is. We shall come equipped with sleeping bags and saffron. Two of the former, one of the latter. From little rumors which seep through the salty curtain behind which you live, we are convinced that it might not be unwise for Cleo and me to seek out a hotel, for we hear that your quarters, while specious (unintentional slip—spacious is the word I meant) enough for the seven of you, might be somewhat strained for all twelve of what will then be us. I know it's the custom of the country to sleep en masse, but I think we should not too quickly plunge into local ways. We'll enjoy them more if we sort of ootch in, so to speak.

You appear to harbor some justifiable impatience with me, in terms of what I propose to do in the immediate future. I share your feelings. Here, then, are our present conclusions and our present situation:

Were everything else in the world equal, which it is not, I should still be tired of drudging my life away for forty thousand a year, coming out at the end no better than even, and up to my stern in dishwater the whole time. I therefore face the possible sale of the ranch, not with regret, but with the most tremulous yearnings. I want, and must have before I die, the opportunity to learn whether or not I can become a successful writer in my own terms. That is primary with me.

Very well. Investigation shows that there is practically nowhere in the U.S. where we can live much more cheaply than at present, unless we are willing to take a five room bungalow and live in dishwater clear up to the nose line. This being impractical, as well as self-defeating, since I cannot write and decently share household work at the same time, plus see my kids, I should be as bad off as at present, only on a more miserable scale.

Hence—I am determined that Mexico is the answer. If the ranch were sold tomorrow, I should be down the next day, without even a preliminary survey. As it is, we are going to make the survey. But a prejudiced one, for I am determined to like the place. I think Cleo is too. Therefore, unless there should occur a miracle the like of which never happens to me, we shall, sooner or later, be residents of Mexico.

There is a certain amount of interest in the ranch, and it is possible that we might make a sale any day. On the other hand, it is possible that we might not make a sale for a year. This latter prospect terrifies me, for I dread another year of slavery here, during which I shall have to buck this black market, earn more than a man should, and end up with nothing to show for it.

I am therefore trying to evolve some plan by which we might move down in September for good, battening down the ranch against a sale, cutting expenses, etc. I do not mean cutting expenses in our new home. The whole object, so far as I am concerned, is escape from domestic servitude, and I wish to live well there. But I mean cutting down various expenses here. I think the amount of money saved in living might well compensate for the expense of keeping someone about the ranch, etc.

The problem of such an immediate move is, of course, money, of which presently I have none, but possibly may shortly. However remote it now appears, I still cherish the hope of a move this year—1951.

Now as to what I should prefer in living down there. I really don't give a damn—although I should prefer that place in which one could live most regally for least. I don't particularly care about the composition of the other English speaking inhabitants; I probably shall dislike them as greatly as those I see here, and see as little of them.

But I would consider it most desirable for your family and mine to live in the same town and within a reasonable distance of each other. There are many reasons. Children. The fact that our wives do not hate each other (an advantage not to be underestimated). The fact that you are one of the few people I can bear to see every day, whom I *like* to see every day. The fact that we can mutually spur each other on to work. The fact that, in movie and originals, two minds often strike sparks, provided both are hard enough, as I think is the case. The fact that we could provide for each other and broods a sort of mutual aid society in time of need or other harassments. And other reasons.

Economically, when I am shet of this place, I should be healthy. Paying off government and all else, I should come off with a net thirty thousand, and still possess cars and all household equipment. Presently I am, of course, broken; but have 5Gs coming in this week, which will just stand things off.

From my observations here, there is no reason why you and I cannot make an absolute minimum of 15Gs apiece each year directly out of Hollywood—with plenty of time left over for serious work. This is all I should want, and I daresay the same goes for you. I can't imagine a better life . . . In any event, we shall talk of this exhaustively when I see you, and lay practical plans. But if you wonder about my determination, or if your own future plans are predicated in any degree upon what I do, as mine preferably would be in relation to you—be assured that I am single-minded about this matter, and Cleo is too.

Thief has opened in London. As perhaps you know, they open plays there either in a tiny 2 or 300 seat theatre, or in the provinces. By opening in London in a tiny theatre they got the advantage of London reviews, and have a pretty good idea whether or not to take the play on into the West End for a run. Point being, the London press reviews as exhaustively as if the play had opened cold in a big house—which they never do. Result: lesser investment and clearer idea of whether to go ahead or not.

Carefully selected quotations about *Thief*: "Brilliant and ghastly comedy . . . The dialogue is packed with satirical and explosive wit at the expense of the medical, the legal and the clerical professions" —*News Chronicle*. "Brutally funny farce . . . an essentially American entertainment, not at all the kind that is usually exported . . . an interesting exotic"—London *Times*. "Admittedly a grim sort of gaiety, but it is redeemed from unpleasantness by the author's sprightly gift for ghoulish jokes and the almost endearing villainy of Hartley Power's undertaker"—*Daily Mail*. "The author, Dalton Trumbo, had not a grain of reverence in his make-up, and when last night he let his macabre sense of humor loose among such sacred subjects as death and religion, I felt a Puritan ancestor or two stirring uneasily in my subconscious. But I laughed . . . I laughed when the corpse proved not to be so dead as was thought, and at the readiness of various interested people to use any means short of murder to make him die in earnest. I dare say I should not have laughed, but the fact remains that I did"—*Daily Telegraph and Morning Post*. "What might have been bad taste is excellently avoided by the strong drawing of the characters and their matter-of-fact, materialistic, money-making philosophy. The play, indeed, turns out highly amusing and entertaining. The religious-minded apothecary earnestly praying to 'the Lord' to hurry up and take the resuscitated old man is satirical comedy at its richest. But there is a good deal more than entertainment here. It is a subtle criticism of our old friend, the 'American way of life,' with its professions of admirable sentiments so conveniently subordinated to the almighty dollar"—*The Stage*. "Should prove a hit at this pocket-size theatre. But it is doubtful whether the theme would be acceptable if it were transformed for a normal, commercial West End run . . . rich in humor as well as satire"—London correspondent, *Variety*.

There was additionally an enormous rave in the *Daily Worker*, and two bad reviews. One in the *Kensington Post* which ended, "In fairness one must say that the funeral jokes amused the rest of the audience far more than they amused me." The other in the *Daily Herald* damned it but admitted "rich laughs."

There appears to be doubt whether the play can pass censorship for a commercial run, but they're trying. Natch I've quoted only the best of the individual reviews, but if we'd had such quotes in New York we'd have stayed there for two years. I am now encouraged to believe that the next play I do—provided I escape censorship by staying out of the cadaver department—can be put on in London direct under my own name, by-passing New York altogether. Which I should like. Play is also running in Australia. I give you this extended account only because you are an investor. Too bad you fellas didn't hold the New York show open thirteen days longer. You would then have an economic as well as a cheering interest in what tiny royalties now drift my way.

. . . . *National Guardian* wants me to do a weekly column for a tiny stipend, and I may take them up. Be a good place to get rid of my grouches, and also would love to pierce a few enemies. Have proposed column filled with malice, personal spite and rancor. We shall see . . . Want to know how lousy it is in this country? Read following beer quotations, per case: Blue Ribbon, National Premium, Schlitz, Van Merritt's, Budweiser, Blatz—$4.60. Ballantine, $4.92. Carta Blanca, $7.10. Urquell Pilsner, $9.89. Heineken, $8.75. Guinness Stout, $8.95. Bass Ale, $9.50. Ran into good bread at Farmer's Market. Probably only temporary.

Now don't be sullen about slight delay in answering—write me at once, so I can hear from you before we set out on this damned argosy.

Selah!
D.T.

9. To Nelson Algren

Lazy T Ranch
Frazier Park, California
August 8, 1951

Dear Nelson:

What you suggest seems perfectly feasible. Of course your New York agent will have to read this crap, and her opinion (or his opinion—mine's a female there) may fall disastrously. But in times like these it's anything to swindle the infidel.

After all my big-mouthed bragging, I haven't even begun a story yet. In order to feed my spawn I grabbed off a black market job, which supported me just so long as it lasted, and then I grabbed another, and now all I think about is how to make a dame, who murders two husbands in cold blood for their money and who is a nymph and a drunk to boot, sympathetic to the half-wits out front. However, when I finish this one I'm swearing off long enough to make a dash for freedom in the form of our previously discussed plan. Only one, and I'm free of these leeches for a long time.

Story market's going to be fine this fall and winter, due to the insane economics of this business. When the box office is down and people are staying away by the millions, pictures necessarily have shorter runs, and so the studios must make more of them than when business is good. That means more stories needed. All studios have announced the largest schedule in years. It's kind of like trying to drink your way out of the Pacific. I remember in 1933 the studios were going full blast and only five people went to movies that year. The studios rolled up a net loss of 55-million, and the writers all got fat. I think those times, praise Allah, are coming back.

Yours in Christ,
DALTON TRUMBO

10. To Gordon Kahn

Lazy T Ranch
Frazier Park, California
August 8, 1951

To the Great Kahn—Greetings! [11]

I who also used to be a Great Kahn but am now a lowly sheik, scarce able to dip mutton into broth for the howling of infidel dogs and the imprecations of wine-bibbers and pork-eaters, address you upon an urgent matter.

My mate and I are going to be in your community sometime between the 19th and the 25th of August. We want to inquire about living costs, schools, rent, mordito, immigrantes and the Virgin of Guadalupe. We are told that you possess more practical information on this subject than any other living person.

Gather, therefore, what information you can, together with all helpful household hints, and hold it against our arrival. We shall be there only briefly, this being in the nature of a preliminary swoop rather than a final roosting. But we are fascinated with cost, cost,

---

[11] A newspaperman turned prolific screen writer, Gordon Kahn succeeded Trumbo as editor of *The Screen Writer* and was one of the original nineteen persons called to the Hollywood hearings which produced the Ten. After blacklist he moved to Mexico and later to New Hampshire. He wrote regularly for *Holiday,* the *Atlantic,* and other magazines under a pseudonym until his death in 1962.

cost. I want again to live like a prince, and here, alas, it's ass and elbows in dishwater seven days out of every week.

Allah preserve you!

TRUMBO

11. To Herbert Biberman

Lazy T Ranch
Frazier Park, California
[c. August 12, 1951]
Monday

Dear Herbert:

The enclosed paper (since I endorsed it at the bank, I have, as you see, defaced it) is probably the best thing that has happened to me in a long while; and I am curiously grateful for what befell me as a result of it. When it turned out to be not quite good, two things happened very quickly: (a) I perforce cancelled my Mexico City trip, and (b) the government attached my bank account to recover a promised (but skipped) payment. I came home with eleven cents in my pocket to face some very healthy realities, as follows:

When a man is in such a position that the accidental miscarriage of so miserable a sum can throw him into immediate penury, he has no one but himself to blame and had damned well better take the most energetic measures to get financially well. I should, in the first place, never have taken this assignment, for the simple reason that I knew it would consume a minimum of two months of intensive work and probably longer. I now, somewhat belatedly, realize that I can't afford to do it.

I sired these kids of mine, and I've got to support them, and even the noblest intention to write a screenplay with social content cannot excuse me for not having at present the money to buy their badly needed clothes for the new school term. That is a primary obligation, and, in accepting the assignment for reasons which were perfectly decent, I made it secondary. That was wrong. Since the problem is exclusively mine, I am the only one I know of who can solve it, and the first step to solution is clear.

I am, from today on and for some time in the future, not interested in pamphlets, speeches or progressive motion pictures. I have got to earn money—a considerable sum of it—very quickly. I cannot and will not hypothecate two or three months, or even a month, for any project that doesn't contain the possibility of an immediate and substantial sum. Once I have earned the money, once I have sold the ranch, once I am in a position where the slightest mishap no longer places me in peril, I shall again function as I should like to. But this is well in the future.

I'm absolutely certain, with the large number of progressive writers available, there must be several who have had an opportunity to work in the past year, and who therefore are financially able to undertake the task which I relinquish.

Did I say I was grateful? You betcha! And also furious with myself. Because if this hadn't happened, I wouldn't have understood the seriousness of my situation, and would have been stuck with a job that might well have been my economic ruin. Hence, dear fellow, I pass the torch back. Catch it and find someone who will hold it high while your deservedly harassed friend wrestles with the government and the groceryman!

In the Name of Him we Adore,
DALTON

12. To C. C. Pearson of the California Bank

Lazy T Ranch
Frazier Park, California
September 7, 1951

My dear Mr. Pearson:

I have received a letter explaining your refusal to honor a perfectly good check signed by Mr. Herbert Biberman. Your lapse has caused both Mr. Biberman and me a good deal of trouble. I am, however, not entirely displeased to discover that bankers—who require the most rigid perfection from all others—are themselves guilty of occasional imperfections.

As a long-time depositor I would have more admiration for the manners of your institution if, in your letter to me, you had accorded to Mr. Biberman the normal courtesy title of "Mister"; and my confidence in the future accuracy of your records would have been vastly increased had you spelled his name correctly.

Yours, etc.
DALTON TRUMBO

13. To Hy and Rheata Kraft

Mexico City
May 4, 1952

Dear Hy and Rheat:

And Jill too—how are you all? Last night we participated in the housewarming of the new [Ian] Hunter menage, and thought how nice it would have been had you been there too. Cleo and I like Mexico very much,[12] and shall probably remain here another eighteen months, after which we propose to come east and settle down somewhere near New York City. Nikola is going out with boys—she heavily prefers Mexican boys, too, which pleases us—and has turned soft and feminine and very large. Which is to say she is only an inch under Cleo and shows no sign of halting. Size 9 shoes, for example! But she is handsomely proportioned, and appears to find her size no disadvantage at all. Chris and Mike Butler, inseparable and delightful, are thriving; and Mitzi proceeds with her usual intensity. All in all, we are happy.

As you knew, we sold the ranch. Got enough cash to pay up income tax, etc., and took the rest in a trust deed. The settlement from Metro was about $19,000 after attorneys but before taxes, and we have been living on it. I have been working since arriving here on a script of the Jean Field story, which we hope shall do some good. Having thus earned no dough, I am beginning to get a little short; and if it is convenient—and *only* if it is—we might soon be in a position to use that 5Cs. However I know better than most that to appear to be making money is no actual proof of having it, and if you find it difficult, I'm sure you understand that I understand.

Write us when you get time, and tell us about *Top Banana* and Rheat's work, and whether or not that damned star hasn't yet had a cold, permitting Jill to go on and knock them over. Our *Thief* couldn't survive Joe's death, and closed; [13] but productions are readying in Holland, Denmark, France, Sweden, Italy and South Africa, so it still may bring in some more. If I could only get a passport, I'd go to England and do another with Peter Cotes, but that is straight dreaming, so the hell with it.[14]

Our love to all of you, and to those of our friends whom you see.

As always,
TOS *(somewhat battered)* [15]

[12] The Trumbos moved to Mexico in November 1951.

[13] Joseph Edward Bromberg, the star of Peter Cotes' London production of *Thief*.

[14] Trumbo had been denied a passport to travel to England to see the production of *The Biggest Thief in Town*. Thus began a six-year controversy with the passport office culminating in the letters to Frances G. Knight, July 1 and 10, 1958, Section 8, #8 and 9, pp. 429-436.

[15] After the HUAC hearings, Kraft referred to Trumbo with ironic affection as TOS: Tower of Strength.

14. To Hy and Rheata Kraft

Mexico City
May 31, 1952

Dear Hy and Rheat:

The dough arrived in plenty of time, and there were celebrations everywhere. My situation is not desperate, but for a six-week period, until certain sums came in, it was extremely bad. This tides me over the hump of the first of the month, and all is well, for which many thanks. I still have the trust deed on the ranch, which I don't want to discount for cash unless there is a real urgency; and the furniture, equipment, etc., as well as our cars. So, while I am not flush, I can still look forward to a period during which starvation will not be an immediate threat.

I have the feeling that I shall be able to make some money down here, and if present plans materialize, I am sure I shall. It is my dream to remain another year, and then return and raise as much hell as then is possible and as I then am capable of. I am downright mad, and don't think the battle is lost by a long shot. However, from the comparative safety of this lovely city, it is easy to write such sentiments to people who are in the midst of the filth. But I think the world looks kind of bright, old boy, I really do.

. . . . Cleo and ours appear to thrive. Never having lived in a foreign city, I find this experience interesting, stimulating and restful; and, as I indicated in my other letter, Cleo loves it. She takes Spanish lessons thrice weekly, and is way ahead of me. I, however, work; and I insist my tongue is English; and that as long as I can indicate hunger and express thanks for its satisfaction, I am sufficiently fluent to get by here. It is, however, an attitude that is generally frowned upon by my compatriots. They feel a positive obligation to learn the language which, I presume, is justified. However I'm so old!

Dear old boy, don't be discouraged. There are more good people in the world than bad, and history moves with decency, and the sorry story of betrayal and disorder is no new one. Try to get that ulcer smoothed over, and save a little dough, and the Lord who loves us all more than He is prone to indicate, will take care of the rest. We think of you and Rheat and Jill very often, and with all the old affection, and we look forward to the time when we shall see you. One day, before you and I die, we will sit back and talk of the past five years as old soldiers discuss most lovingly those phases of the battle which were the toughest.

To all of you our thanks and our love.

DALTON

P.S. The elephant went to the jungle stream for a drink. He thrust his trunk into the water up to the mouth level, and an alligator swam

231

up and snapped it clean off. The elephant gazed reproachfully at the alligator and said, in a heavily nasal tone, "Very funny."

P.P.S.   Vince Hallinan (presently in custody) has five or six boys. He is profane, and so are the youngsters. The smallest, Butch, aged five, was a couple of months ago on the street in downtown San Francisco with his nurse, when an eager matron stopped and cooed: "*Where* did you get those big brown eyes?" Quoth Butch: "*Where* did you get that big fat ass?"

15. To Elsie McKeogh

Mexico City
June 3, 1952

Dear Elsie:

. . . .

About a play for Cotes. Some day I wish to do one, and I told him I would, but I did not tell him when. I am at present on the verge of making a chunk of dough, in the course of which I shall be able, I think and hope, to take advantage of the new 18-month tax exemption law. I am absolutely beady-eyed with greed, and cannot be distracted from it at the moment. I want to make a lot of money, and, with this as security for Cleo and the kids, come back to the United States as fast as the Lord will let me, and raise enough hell about what is going on there to really *deserve* to go to jail the next time.

I do, however, get awfully good ideas now and again for serious stories, short and long; but I am convinced they couldn't be marketed at present under my name, and this somehow diminishes one's enthusiasm. However I make careful notes of them—hah!

I feel better than I ever did in my life, and so do Cleo and the kids. Nikola, at thirteen, wears a size 9 shoe. There must be considerable height somewhere on Cleo's side of the family. I have lost so many pairs of reading glasses while out on the street that I now have a pair of pince-nez (how do you spell it?) tied around my neck with a fine black cord and a little silver slide. Headwaiters stiffen with alarm at the sight of me. The whole effect is one of rakish respectability which Cleo likes and which, of course, pleases me immensely.

What a nice long letter I've written you!

As always,
DALTON

16. To Sidney S. Neblett, Department of Internal Revenue, Motion Picture Division

Mexico Ctiy
September 7, 1952

Dear Mr. Neblett:

The first portion of this letter is an explanation of my failure until now to reply to your letter of August 6th, 1952.[16] In Mexico City the houses have no mail boxes, the postman simply dropping the mail onto the sidewalk inside the front gate. From time to time, apparently to make his work easier, he inserts letters inside the paper wrappings of magazines, or even inside the magazines themselves. Thus it has happened several times that we have not discovered letters until weeks and even months later, depending upon how thoroughly we read our magazines, of which we receive a great number.

Yesterday I received a form notification from the U.S. Record Service . . . informing me that "my name appeared recently concerning official publication of a legal notice affecting your property." This produced an immediate search through old magazines on my part, and brought to light your August letter. I do hope you will take this circumstance into consideration in evaluating the disposition of my case: for certainly I have a considerable property interest at stake in this matter, and would instantly have answered your letter had not this accident intervened.

I came with my family to Mexico on November 14, 1951. Liking Mexico City and feeling there were certain opportunities here, I resolved to make it my permanent residence. On December 1, 1951, I leased for one year the house at Montes Auvernia 315, Lomas de Chapultepec, Mexico, D.F., where I presently reside. For some five months thereafter Mr. J. S. Rex Cole of the Equitable Investment Corporation in Hollywood continued to handle my affairs in Los Angeles. I assumed—although I had no especial right to assume—that he had informed you of my change of residence and my present address in Mexico City.

Now, with that explanation, to the problem of the trust deed and your lien against it. Naturally I hope very much that you will be able to extend me a little more time on it. The initial expenses of settling down here were heavier than I anticipated; I had six months of ill health during which I earned no money; and Mrs. Trumbo herself enters a hospital ten days hence for surgery. The trust deed on the ranch, in which we hold an equity of $20,000, is our only

[16] On August 6, 1952, letters signed Sidney S. Neblett, Division Chief of Motion Picture and Radio Taxation Division, informed Trumbo that he owed $7,556.72 in 1951 income tax plus interest at $1.25 per day and that if the account were not paid within thirty days, the trust deed held on the Lazy T Ranch would be seized and sold to the highest bidder.

property of any consequence; and it would involve an almost tragic loss to us if it were sold for the approximately $7,500 representing the Federal Government's claim against it.

My present situation is this: I have just received word from the British Government that an income tax refund on royalties earned by a play of mine in London, in the sum of 551 pounds, has been approved and is on its way to me. Of this sum I pledge you $1,000 within thirty days of the date of this letter, the thirty days being requested to allow for transatlantic mail and the problem of immediately cashing here a check drawn in a foreign country.

In addition to the above, I have ten thousand dollars owing me for work recently done, coming in in installments of $2,500 each between now and January 1, 1953. Out of this sum I pledge you the balance of my tax obligation; and if I do not make such payment, I waive all my rights in the matter of the trust deed.

Thus, if you can see your way clear to grant me leniency, I shall be able to pay off the entire sum between now and the beginning of the year.

I realize the problems which confront your office in the discharge of difficult and complex duties; that it is your obligation to collect rather than to temporize, and that the taxpayer is, in the long run, responsible for his troubles. But, in view of the high liquid value of the security against which you have a lien, I most respectfully ask that you consider that the forced sale of the trust deed at this time would probably cause me to lose twice as much money as the sum I owe the government.

My record, over a period of fifteen or twenty years, shows tens of thousands of dollars paid in income tax. The record also shows, I regret to admit, a consistent lateness in paying. But in the end I have always paid; have never protested a tax or penalty; have never engaged in any practice of avoidance; and have never, even when matters appeared blackest for me, approached your office with any offer of compromise payment. I have paid, and I have paid without protest, in full. That record, while not the best, surely is one which indicates consistently good intentions and a consistent ability to carry them out.

I therefore beg your leniency for the next three and a half months, under the conditions stipulated above, and promise that I shall, as in the past, faithfully fulfill the obligations herein set for myself.[17] If some crisis arises—or if you find yourself unable to consider my request—I should appreciate some telegraphic word of your intentions, so that I may have as much time as possible to try to salvage

[17] On September 17, 1952, the Internal Revenue office agreed to defer recommendation for seizure and sale of the trust deed, provided Trumbo met payments as outlined in this letter.

something from the wreckage. I shall be happy to pay the cost of such messages.

Sincerely,
DALTON TRUMBO

17. To Hy Kraft

Mexico City
October 27, 1952

Dear Hy:

I am at the moment so concerned and harassed and generally—although I think only temporarily—bitched-up that this letter is going to skip all the amenities because they would of necessity sound forced and hollow.

I need $500, right away and desperately. The first of the month arrives Saturday, and I haven't even rent money, nor has anyone else.

I am owed $5,000 by my boys in Hollywood, payable before the first of the year, and have every reason to believe it will be paid me, together with possibly a little more. Thus I *think*—although it would be dishonest to say I can guarantee—that I should be able to repay you within sixty days. A cable would be immensely appreciated.

Nothing more. Love to you all.

Apologetically,
TOS

18. To Sidney S. Neblett

Mexico City
November 17, 1952

Dear Mr. Neblett:

I have not received the 551 pounds from England referred to in my letter of September 7, 1952, which formed the basis of my promise of an initial $1,000 payment.[18] This money is due and forthcoming. When I wrote you, I had received notification that the

[18] On November 4, Neblett wrote Trumbo that the first payment of $1,000 had not been met, as promised, on October 7, 1952, and that if October and November payments (totaling $3,500) were not received by the Internal Revenue office by November 22, 1952, recommendation for seizure and sale of the trust deed would commence immediately.

British Government had approved the tax refund. I did not know that thereafter there would have to be an exchange of affidavits of non-residence in England during the past three years, as well as other documents which have passed between me and them for several weeks. Once these preliminaries were accomplished, the second problem was the conversion of pounds into dollars at the official rate of $2.80 rather than $2.51. This is now under way. It is being handled on this end by Banco Internacional, and in England by their correspondent bank, Barclay's. The process involves the deposit of the British draft in pounds to the account of an American firm in England, and then, by this device, the transmission to me of the sum in dollars at the official rate of $2.80. The moment this comes in I shall forward it.

Although I know that I am in no position to quibble about words, I do believe there is a slight misunderstanding between us as about schedule of payments. In your letter of November 4, 1952, you write: "In the referred to letter you requested permission to make a payment of $1,000 on October 7, and the balance of tax and interest at the rate of $2,500 per month and the total amount to be paid in full by January 1, 1953."

This is not exactly what I said in my letter. I indisputably did promise the first $1,000 on a specific date, explanation of which comprises the first paragraph of this letter. But I didn't promise payments of $2,500 per month thereafter. I wrote: "I have ten thousand dollars coming to me for work recently done, coming in in installments of $2,500 each between now and January 1, 1953. Out of this sum I pledge you the balance of my tax obligation."

The reason I did not promise specific sums on specific dates was that I did not have control over the time the payments would be made to me, and hence could not give exact promises to you. The money is owing me, and by a financially responsible concern, before January 1, 1953. I have every reason to believe I shall collect it, although technicalities have thus far withheld settlement. I do not want to bring legal action to collect, because this would throw the thing into the courts, and although I eventually would get relief, the money would do no good in terms of avoiding the great loss which would be imposed on me by reason of forced sale of the trust deed. I know I am going to get this money, and it is more than sufficient to lift my entire debt to you.

Since your first letter I have received, as income, some $1,600. I have had to use this for living costs, and for medical expenses attendant upon the illness of my wife, who at present is living through intravenous feeding at a cost for plasma, amino acids and drugs alone, of $30.00 per day. I say this not to make an appeal for sympathy, but to point out that I have not needlessly or foolishly been spending money which rightfully belongs to the Federal government.

In view of the above facts and prospects—and in further view of the fact of the security you hold and my long previous record of payment—I respectfully request you to defer recommendation of seizure and sale of my trust deed.[19] This account will most surely be paid before the first of the year.

Sincerely,
DALTON TRUMBO

19. To Harry E. Day, Internal Revenue Agent

Mexico City
March 29, 1953

Dear Mr. Day:

Your letter to me dated in Los Angles March 17 was somewhat delayed in delivery because of my negligence in failing to inform your office of a recent change in address: Elba 21, Apartment 9, Colonia Cuauhtemoc, Mexico, D.F. My telephone number is 36-33-66.[20]

On April 1, 1953, a check is being mailed me from Los Angeles in the sum of $2,000.00 This will go, upon its receipt by me, directly to you. However it may not arrive here until April 3. There are two problems involved in this. (1) Our banks in Mexico close on April 1, Wednesday, and remain closed for the remainder of the week out of respect for Holy Week, which involves a closing of all government offices. Hence I shall not be able to present my check to the bank until a week from tomorrow. (2) You require a cashier's check. In order for me to draw an international cashier's check on the check received from the United States, I shall have to wait at least seven or eight days until the worth of my check is certified in Los Angeles. Sometimes this can be done by telegram, and I shall try to have it so done in this instance, but the possibility of the delay I mention still remains. Once the check I receive is validated as good, I can purchase the cashier's check and it will take no longer than two days thereafter for it to be in your hands.

In addition to this, a story which is my property was sold last

[19] The deed in question was one which was still owed Trumbo by the purchasers of the ranch.

[20] Day said the balance of $2,902.47 must be in the hands of the Bureau of Internal Revenue on or before April 1, 1953.

month in Hollywood under the name of a friend. My friend died before he received payment. Payment was accordingly made to his estate. I shall, within the next ten days, receive my portion of the proceeds of the sale from the estate. This sum alone will several times over care for my obligation to the government.

Finally, I have in storage in Los Angeles, in two warehouses . . . furniture, paintings, first editions, silver, china and other items worth considerably in excess of $15,000. I give you this information so that, if you need additional protection for the short time it will take me to gather this money together, you are now in a position of placing a lien on the above items.

I have tried to calculate my dates carefully and conscientiously in this matter; the money will be in my hands on the date I owe it to you—or most of it, that is—but everything comes at one time, and the time for verification and transfer of funds is absolutely essential to me unless I am to lose everything I have.

I ask you to recall that on January 1, 1953, I paid $2,000 on this account, and on February 1, 1953 another $2,800; and that I certainly shall clean the balance up within the time I state. Otherwise it would have been foolish to pay $4,800 on a trust deed that would be sold out from under me in any event. It is upon this basis that I ask this further small extension. I am trying very hard, the security is good, and I have every intention of fulfilling my obligation to you and thus retaining the security for myself. Otherwise I shall lose approximately $17,000.

I thank you and your office for the courtesies you have extended to me in the past. I hope very much you will see fit to grant me this further extension because of the reasons I have stated.

Very truly yours,
DALTON TRUMBO

20. To Professor Y———, University———

Mexico City
March 30, 1953

My dear Prof. Y———:

I have just received your letter of March 26th, addressed to Dr. John Abbott.[21] I must therefore introduce myself to you at once: my name is Dalton Trumbo. I am a novelist, playwright and screen writer. Fuller information may be found about me in *Who's Who* or

---

[21] Prof. Y——— had found correspondence indicating that Dr. John Abbott (Trumbo) and Y——— were working on a scenario together.

Twentieth Century Authors. I have been, since 1945, a friend of your brother, Y——. I am also "Dr. John Abbott," that being the name under which Y—— and I corresponded, for reasons which shall later be explained in their relation to certain literary projects.

I last wrote to Y—— on March 16, and since then have discovered the incredible fact that he no longer lives. Thus I was prepared for the sad burden of your letter. Y—— was our friend, and both my wife and I were profoundly moved when we learned of his death. However, you do not know me, and at this point in a communication which will be very long it would be indelicate of me to speak of my emotions or to offer my condolences. I shall, with your permission, reserve them for my conclusion, and begin with an apology for writing at a time when you have sustained a great personal loss. I hope when you have finished reading me you will be able to forgive and to understand why I feel compelled to write so fully.

What follows, therefore, beneath the asterisks, is a simple recital of facts, written, of necessity, in self-interest. Because I am so deeply aware of, and embarrassed by, that self-interest, I shall refrain from the vulgarity of giving my immediate account an emotional overtone. It is a difficult task to which I am addressing myself, and I beg your indulgence of it.

* * *

In June of 1945 a party of six or seven war correspondents embarked from San Francisco by air upon a three-month tour of Pacific battle areas. Among the correspondents were Y—— and I. He was by far the youngest of our group, certainly no more than twenty-two. His background had given him a method of speech and a pattern of polite conduct which differed from others. These qualities, combined with his very considerable intellectual capacities and his youth, were seized upon by certain of our party as an excuse to make small jokes at his expense. Because I admire intelligence and understand how painfully youth can suffer even from inconsequential affronts, I came to his defense, and together we made common cause which resulted in a more comfortable situation. It was this circumstance, he later told me, which made him like me.

Our friendship continued from that time forward until our last meeting in January of 1953. At first, I should say, it partook somewhat of the nature of a father and son relationship. As it developed through the years it became a friendship between equals. He discussed his personal problems with me, enjoyed the companionship of my family and friends. He told me of his deceased father's work with ————; of his mother's early sponsorship of the paintings of ————; of his one-time relative-in-law, ————; of his work with the journalist known, I believe, as ————, to whom he later introduced me and my wife in Hollywood; of his activity during the November campaign with the Eisenhower forces under Governor Dewey; of his intention to write an official biography of the governor. I mention these matters only to establish that the relationship between us actually existed.

To return to the Pacific expedition: after our party had visited such places as Guam, Saipan, Tinian, Iwo Jima, Manila, Okinawa and other areas, it was flown back to San Francisco, where transportion had been arranged for it to continue on to New York. However, at my invitation, Y——— separated himself from the group and came with me to our house in Beverly Hills, where he was our guest for two weeks before going on to New York.

We corresponded for a short time thereafter; but the birth of our youngest child in October distracted me, and I did not write him until after Christmas. On Christmas of that year I received from him a French edition of *Madame Bovary*. It carried an inscription, of which the following is a photostat:

> Y———
> to one who appreciates
> such things
> Dalton Trumbo
> Christmas 1945
> (are you dead?)

Our correspondence continued spasmodically thereafter. I received a letter from him while he was in India, and later a short-snorter bill from the same country. In 1949 a play of mine tried out in New Haven before starting out on the road. Y——— saw it, and recalled that I had told him the plot while we were overseas, and sent a note to me at the theatre. By the time I received it, however, the company had gone on to Boston, so I did not see him.

I must digress here to explain that in the autumn of 1947 I was summoned before the House Committee on Un-American Activities and asked to state whether I was or ever had been a member of the Communist Party. I refused to answer the question and was thereupon indicted for contempt of Congress. Immediately thereafter my contract with Metro-Goldwyn-Mayer was abrogated and I was banished from the motion picture industry. In the spring of 1948 I was tried in Washington, D.C., convicted and sentenced to $1,000 fine and a year in prison. I remained free on bail during the process of appeal, and it was during this period, in 1949, that my play appeared in New Haven and finally in New York. In June of 1950, appeal being lost, I surrendered to Federal authorities and was imprisoned in the Federal Correctional Institute at Ashland, Kentucky. I was released on April 9, 1951.

In the summer of 1951 Y——— visited Los Angeles, and wrote me at our ranch in Ventura County, California, the Beverly Hills house having been sold. I saw him a number of times during this period.

He was at that time an editor for _____, and he suggested to me that I do a novel for them, for which he would arrange publication under a pseudonym. We discussed it at several luncheons, one of which, I recall, was at Romanoff's in Beverly Hills, and attended by a friend of Y____'s—a blond young man, an engineer, I believe —whose name I do not recall.

During this same period Y____ also came to the ranch, which is some 85 miles north of Hollywood, twice for week-ends and once for a day. He had undertaken a motion picture assignment, his first, for _____ and was, as all newcomers are, amazed by and infuriated with the process of getting a decent script on paper. He was also interested in selling his biography of _____, of which he had given me an inscribed copy, to motion pictures. We had a number of conferences about the book, discussing how it could be offered to the studios in the most dramatic treatment form. During one of his visits to the ranch Y____ met Mr. Paul Trivers, a house guest. Their mutual interest as graduates of Yale College provided the background for an acquaintanceship which has a later bearing upon the subject I must deal with.

In the course of our converastions during the summer of 1951, Y____ asked me how I managed to support the ranch, my family of five, my mother and my mother-in-law, when it was impossible for me to work in pictures and likewise impossible for anything bearing my name to sell to films, magazines or as a book. I told him the only way I would earn a living was, first, to write either an original story or a screenplay for films; second, to solicit the aid of someone whose name was acceptable to the motion picture industry; third, for this person to place his name on the story and submit it to the studios through his agent; after which the profits were divided two-thirds to me and one-third to the person who permitted the use of his name, with a top limit of ten thousand dollars going to the person whose name was used. I explained that the essence of such an operation was secrecy, so that no one, neither agent, friend nor relative, should know the identity of the true author of the story.

Y____ then volunteered to permit me to put his name to any story or screenplay I might write, without in any way participating in the profits of a possible sale. I told him I could not, in conscience, agree to such an arrangement, since the name attached to a story had cash value which should be paid for; since the process involved a risk to the person lending his name, which risk ought in some degree to be compensated for; and since publicity often attended the sale of a motion picture story, with the consequent assumption on the part of friends and family that the author had suddenly become rich. Y____ finally agreed to the validity of these arguments. Indeed, once I had pointed them out and he saw their justice, he was pleased. He told me that, although he had a sufficient income, he never, at the end of the year, had quite as much as he had thought or as had seemed desirable.

I do not mean that money was a principal consideration in his decision to do what he did, for money would never have influenced him toward a course he considered wrong. The main reason was our friendship. He did not agree with my political affiliations in any way that I ever discovered but he was morally opposed to blacklisting and to the sending to jail of people for refusal to state political affiliations or convictions. Moreover, he detested the men who control the motion picture industry, and the thought of participating in a plan to frustrate what he considered their unethical behavior delighted him. If one could sum up all of his reasons for doing what he did in a single word, I should say the word is gallantry.

We then discussed our future mode of operation, the basis of which was complete secrecy. I told him that I preferred to write in straight screenplay form, but that the submission of a technically correct screenplay by one who had had no previous experience in fiction or films might arouse doubts among Hollywood purchasers. However, his brief experience with _____ might provide sufficient reason, and I suggested that he inform his agent well in advance that he was going into the original story and screenplay market, and that, as a result of his _____ experience, he was disposed to try the screenplay form first. Thus the agent would not be surprised. It was, of course, understood that neither the agent nor anyone else would have knowledge of my connection with the story. The plot, or idea-content, of the story was never discussed between Y_____ and me, since I had not yet decided what I would write.

When Y_____ returned east, he departed with the following understanding: that I would write an original or screenplay as soon as possible and send it to him with his name affixed to it, and that he would submit it to his agent as his own; that we would divide the profits of any subsequent sale two-thirds to me and one-third to him, his top earnings to be ten thousand dollars; and that we would repeat the process at future periods.

Shortly thereafter, in September of 1951, the financial burden of the ranch proved too heavy for me to bear. My wife and I sold the property and moved our family to Hollywood for a period of weeks while waiting for the escrow papers to be completed. This delayed the writing of anything, and I wrote Y_____ in New Haven explaining that I had sold the ranch and hence had written nothing. I also asked him the name of his Hollywood agent, to determine for myself whether he was of the first rank; and asked whether or not he, Y_____., was a member of the Screen Writers' Guild.

In reply, I received his letter dated New Haven, October 24, 1951, answering my questions. The "series of catastrophes" to which he refers in the second paragraph have to do with the _____ assignment during the preceding summer. The letter, in photostat, follows:

New Haven, Connecticut
October 24, 1951

Dear Dalton:

I am delighted to hear that the ranch is sold. Beautiful though it may happen to have been it was certainly an albatross around your neck, which is good to have gotten rid of.

And now as to other matters. I have Mr. Beck of William Morris as my agent. As far as screen plays are concerned, they expect anything from me—child genius department—so don't worry about the style. As far as the Screen Writers' Guild is concerned I am not a member as I had a series of catastrophes last summer which didn't make it necessary, but I think this is rather an advantage in the present situation in that it will make it less suspect. If you have any feelings on the subject, it is easy enough for me to become a member however.

With very best regards to Cleo and yourself.

Regards,
Y____

I replied to this letter, telling him I didn't know Mr. Beck, but that the William Morris agency by which he was employed was one of the largest and best, and that hence I thought our story would get excellent representation. I told him that it was not necessary for him to join the Screen Writers' Guild and probably even undesirable for him to do so for the present; and that I was moving my family to Mexico.

On November 14, 1951, my wife and I crossed the border with our family, and on December 1, 1951, moved into a house I had leased at Montes Auvernia 315, Lomas de Chapultepec [Mexico, D.F.], telephone 20–39–05. Y____ telephoned us a number of times there. The winter passed getting settled in a strange city, with a consequent rash of small illnesses, and it was not until spring, as I recall, that I wrote Y____ again, telling him of our general welfare and declaring my intention to get to work very soon on our story. To this he replied on May 10, 1952, as indicated in the following photostat:

New York
10 May 52

Dear Dalton;

Delighted to get your letter and learn that everything is well with you and the family.

I still have Mr. Beck of William Morris sitting on the edge of his chair in a sweat of expectancy awaiting the "Y____ Masterpiece." Therefore, the sooner the better as far as I am concerned.

You shall be able to reach me here at almost any time as I am in the process of hacking two books after just having been given advances for them in England. Thus my movements are confined to the narrow path between typewriter and bed.

Best to Cleo and yourself,

Yours ever,

Y____

I replied to this, stating that I was being held from our project by a rush job, but hoped to get started soon. I also suggested that in the future correspondence between us dealing with our project, we should couch our language in deceptive terms in case inquisitive border officials ever looked into the mail, as I have been told they sometimes do. I suggested, therefore, that he address me, either by letter or telephone, as "Dr. John Abbott" at the Montes Auvernia house. I suggested that the story be referred to as prescription or patient, and that our communications generally be conducted in pseudo-medical terms. And finally I suggested that he destroy, as he received them, all letters from me dealing with the subject. My object in this, of course, was to protect Y____ from any unpleasant publicity, since I myself am beyond hurt.

During the summer I had an illness, and as autumn started my wife began a more serious one, with the result that I had little time to correspond or write. This silence on my part was interrupted on September 8, 1952, by a letter from Y____. Whereas in all our previous correspondence he had addressed me as "Dear Dalton," in this one, for the first time, our medical nomenclature began to be used, and he started it "Dear Doc." The letter, in photostat, follows:

New York
September 8, 52

Dear Doc:

How are things with you? It seems an age since I heard from you.

Is there any chance of your coming to the United States in the near future, if so let me know what your plans are?

Sincerely,

Y____

To this I replied that I was at last at work and that the prescription would be forthcoming soon. I told him that, after all our care to prepare the agent for a screenplay, this one worked out better in narrative or treatment form, and suggested that if Mr. Beck had been expecting a screenplay, it might be wise to inform him in advance that he had changed his mind and decided upon narrative form after all. In a previous telephone conversation Y____ had suggested that before submitting the story we meet, possibly in Los Angeles. I suggested that he might come to Mexico City as our guest. In reply to my letter, I received the following undated letter from him. It was written after September 8, 1952, and before October 4, 1952. In it I am referred to as "Dear John" (Dr. John Abbott), and the medical terminology becomes more frequent. The Morris agency becomes "Dr. Morriss." And the "climate" for "recuperation" refers to Mexico City as a place for rendezvous. A photostat of the letter follows:

Dear John;

Just a line to say that I am all set for the treatment, Dr. Morriss having been told what to expect. For recuperation, however, there might be climates more salubrious than the one you suggest, but this is a mere detail.

Let me know if there is anything further to be done.

Yours,
Y_____

On October 4, 1952, I completed the story entitled _____. It was 95 pages long in typescript. I typed it myself on my own machine as I always do, and corrected it by typewriter or in my own hand. I sent the original and first carbon copy to Y_____, retaining the second carbon for myself. In the same envelope with the manuscript went a letter. The following is a photostatic carbon of the 3 page communication:

Dear Y_____:

Enclosed herewith you will find an original and one carbon of the story _____ which you sent to me and which I agreed to work upon.

The other project which you suggested I do in screenplay form, I found impractical to do. Therefore I dropped it. This, as you will quickly note, is done as an original story rather than a screenplay.

All of these stories, as you know so well, are sheer gambles. They may sell and they may not sell. I've seen some of the best go begging, and some of the worst snapped up. In any event, I know the kind of material submitted in Hollywood well enough to assure you that, whether this sells or not, it cannot possibly do you any harm. It is better written than ninety-nine out of a hundred submitted there by the hacks, and hence cannot in any way be disadvantageous to you. I would not send it on if it were. At the same time I do not pretend that it is any masterpiece. It has certain advantages and certain disadvantages. It could sell for $30,000 and it could sell for only $5,000, and there is always the very good chance it won't sell at all. It will probably sell, if it does, in the first three weeks after your agent submits it. On the other hand, I've known some of them to sell two years later, but they're usually dead dogs in a month.

I would write my agent as follows:

1. Tell him the reason you abandoned the screenplay—it just didn't work out. You may do the screenplay later when it becomes clearer to you.

2. Tell him you believe, from your own experience, in a flood coverage of the market. Hence you would like to have an initial submission of 100 mimeographed copies (for which you will pay if the story does

not sell—and we will). Tell him you would like it to go not only to all the studios, to which it will go anyhow as a matter of routine, but to every comedy director in the business, to every comedy writer in the business, and to every comic in the business, as well as to all independent producers, and to individual producers at studios even though their studio has received a story department submission copy. (I consider this mass coverage extremely important—saturate the market *in one day*—and hope that out of all this scatter-shooting you find a pigeon. So emphasize this.) Tell him it would be good (provided he felt confidence in the story) if all the submissions were preceded by a telegram from the agent, announcing this as a story that is something special, and urging immediate attention and quick reading.

3. Tell him, finally, that you have several other ideas on the fire, and that if he likes this one, you'll be glad to submit another very quickly— or as quickly as he feels it advisable for this one to be followed up with a second and/or a third.

Now about the price: you should indicate, without saying so, that you hope for a very large price. Frankly, it's terribly speculative. This might go big, and it might go small. After three weeks, take five hundred dollars and run like a thief. The point is not to lose a sale because of demanding a price too high for the market and the demand—and on the other hand not to let your agent think so cheaply of you that he will grab the first offer that comes along without trying a little heisting on the boys to get it up. If two studios show interest, then you're in clover.

4. I would also indicate to the agent that a friend of yours showed the script to George Abbott, and that Abbott indicated an interest in doing it as a play. This merely for sugar, if you feel it worthwhile. It'll give the agent a nice little talking point, and the thing is kind of George Abbottish anyhow.

Now about division of the spoils: I propose, as in all my previous deals in which I have re-worked somebody's manuscript, the following parcels:

(a) Up to $10,000—split fifty-fifty, each paying his share of the agent's fee.

(b) Up to $30,000—33⅓% to you, 66⅔% to me, each paying his share of the agent's fee.

(c) Above $30,000—$10,000 to you and the rest to me, each paying his share of the agent's fee.

Now: Keep one copy for yourself, and get the other off instantly, airmail and registered. Ask them to wire you upon receiving it, so you'll know it got through safely.

And as for information concerning the results: they should have it mimeographed by the end of the current week, and should have it distributed the following Monday. Kind of check on them regarding this, to be sure just when it is submitted, and in how many copies.

Two to three weeks thereafter should tell the tale. Try to get the best price, but don't lose a sale because of a rejected offer—for another may not come.

If it sells—wire me, Dr. Abbott, as follows: "EVELYN WILL RECOVER. DOCTOR RECOMMENDS 18 DAY VACATION." The figure 18 (or 10 or 20 or whatever) will represent the sum which the studio is paying for the story.

If it sells, and after I have received your wire telling the price, I will send you a letter telling you exactly how to remit my share down here in the least conspicuous fashion.

Incidentally—and again, if it sells—the agent will deduct his commission there and send on the net sum to you. For the sake of avoiding delay, ask him to send the net to you in the form of a cashier's check.

If there are no results in a month, I'll have the other story you sent me back in your hands, all ready to go. Frankly the handicap to this one is for a broad comedian, and there are very few in Hollywood. This may (a) pull the price down, or (b) result in no sale. On the other hand, this kind of stuff goes like hell at the box office, and it might sell big. Hope and Crosby could play it. Martin and Lewis could play it. Even Abbott and Costello could conceivably play it. Donald O'Connor certainly could play it. Ditto Eddie Bracken. And there are a number of others, quite aside from the fact that it could easily be altered so that a less broad comedian could take over. Be sure that a producer named Leonard Goldstein at 20th Century Fox gets a personal copy. He's a very important man these days, and did a lot of stuff similar to this at Universal-International. Be sure also that directors Frank Tashlin and Norman Taurog get personal copies. All of the actors I mentioned above should get personal copies. Red Skelton also should get one. So should producer Paul Jones. And Claud Binyon. And Preston Sturges. And Joe Mankiewicz and Charley Bracket. And there are many others, but you might mention these.

That, I think, is all. I hope this may be the beginning of a profitable relationship, but don't be downcast if nothing at all happens. And, incidentally, wire me when you get this. Service sometimes is uncertain down here.

Best of everything to you, old boy.

> Selah!
> ABBOTT

P.S. In submitting this, be sure to give your agent a set of telephone numbers and addresses where you may be reached at all hours of the day or night, weekends included. You may, if you're lucky, have to make some quick decisions.

There are two passages in the foregoing letter which require comment and explanation:

First, the financial terms are changed. In our verbal agreement the money from a sale was to be divided two-thirds to me and one-third to him, with a ten thousand dollar limitation upon his share of any given story. In this letter, however, I set forth that if the story sells for ten thousand dollars or less, Y——'s share shall be increased; namely, from one-third to one-half. I did this because it seemed to me that if the story sold cheaply, Y—— would not receive as much as he deserved. It was a revision upward from our talks, voluntary on my part. I repeated the other terms merely to be sure he remembered them before he embarked on his part of the project.

Second, in paragraph one . . . of the foregoing letter, and again in paragraph [nine] . . ., the distinct impression is given that our project involved my working over or re-writing some story Y——— had previously given me. This is not the case. Writers do not permit stories to get out of their hands without retaining a carbon copy in case of loss of the manuscript; and no copy of a story in any way similar to ——————— will be found among Y———'s effects, nor any notes pertaining to such an idea. Y——— had no idea of the content, plot or subject matter of ——————— until he received the completed story from me. I wrote the story in its entirety, without consulting him about its content or telling him what it would be. Y——— was perfectly satisfied to have it that way. He had had no experience in fiction or films, and I had had a good deal: he trusted me to the point that he knew I would not give him anything that would discredit his name or reputation. The indications that Y——— *did* have a story which I re-worked were deliberately placed in the letter by me as a protection for him if any other person ran across the letter. It was a measure of the caution we exercised. It could not in any [way] protect me, for I am beyond protection; it could only protect Y———, and this I was most concerned to do.

In the foregoing letter I had also asked Y——— to write me when he received the manuscript and its accompanying letter. The photostat which follows is his wire acknowledging receipt of them:

DR. JOHN ABBOTT
PRESCRIPTION ARRIVED ABSOLUTELY MAGNIFICENT ARRANGED IMMEDIATELY TO HAVE IT FILLED BEST REGARDS

After receipt by me of the foregoing wire, there was a period of silence. On October 25th, 1952, I wrote him asking what reactions he had received from the agent and suggesting certain procedures to speed matters up. Receiving no answer, I wrote him again on November 1, 1952. Feeling that Y——— might not be in New York, I sent two copies of the letter—one to New Haven and one to New York. Following is a photostat of my carbon copy of the letter:

Nov. 1

Dear Y———:

I wrote you last Monday, air mail, special delivery, at the Park Avenue address, but have received no answer. Perhaps you are in New Haven, or somewhere else, so I try again, addressing the same letter both to NH and NY.

I wanted to know the date of submission to the studios, the reaction of your agent, and whether you had received any reports. There are several expedient reasons why this information in my hands would be

valuable to both of us. However, there is another and over-riding consideration which makes my knowledge of the facts important:

The love story which you suggested we do in screenplay form is almost ready, and I think it is as good as you hoped it would be. It should
be ready by November 15. There is a dead selling period from approximately December 15 to January 5th, because of the holidays. I think a
little advance consultation with your agent would be in order. But first,
to know whether it would be wise in terms of the spacing, I should
know exactly when your first was submitted. Then, if correspondence
makes it seem feasible, arrangements should be made for submission of
the second to the studios, in mimeographed form, by no later than
November 25th. All of which would require keen co-ordination and a
little planning, and all of which depends greatly also on the date of
submission of the first, your agent's reaction to it, and what news comes
of or from prospective purchasers, if any.

I am putting "Please Forward" on each of these letters, or rather on
the original and its carbon, and sending them air mail special delivery.
Please wire me whether you received the first letter, and when and if
you receive this one.

Don't be afraid to correspond. My caution is not based on any kind
of experience, or any evidence that my mail is disturbed.

Regards,
DOC

Here again in the foregoing letter, in the third paragraph, reference
is made to "the love story which you suggested we do in screenplay
form." This was merely to inform him that I had started a love story,
and that it would be in screenplay form. As in the preceding example, he knew nothing about the story.

In reply to my letter, I received a telephone call from Y_____. Mr.
Beck of the William Morris agency had held the story for days without reading it; had finally read it and rejected it with a curt note in
which he said he found it completely unbelievable, could not handle
it for motion pictures and was sending it back. Y_____ said he had
given, or was about to give, the story to Mr. Sam Jaffe, a Hollywood
agent who was then, I believe, visiting in New York. Y_____ professed his own pleasure in the story and his contempt for Mr. Beck's
judgment.

About the 24th or 25th of November Y_____ telephoned again. I
was not at home, but Mrs. Trumbo, who was recuperating from a
siege in the hospital, received the call. Y_____ reported to her that
Mr. Jaffe had been enthusiastic about the story but believed it would
not sell to motion pictures. He suggested that, with a few changes,
it could be sold to *Redbook* as a serial. Y_____ said he was going
to Hollywood shortly after Thanksgiving and would take the story
with him and see what could be done there.

Either one or two days after this, I telephoned Y_____ for a fuller report. He told me substantially what he had told Mrs. Trumbo, adding that he had a friend in Hollywood, Miss Lenore Coffee, a very successful screen playwright, and that he was going to take the story to her. I said I thought this an excellent idea. He said that while in Hollywood he would be staying at 636 South Plymouth Boulevard, and that I could reach him by telephone during the days at Hollywood 9-3674.

The above conversations occurred around Thanksgiving. On December first, our lease having expired, I moved my family temporarily to an apartment a Elba 9, Apartment F, Colonia Cuauhtemoc, telephone 14–94–38. I notified Y―― of this change of address at his 636 South Plymouth Boulevard address.

Sometime between mid-December and Christmas I received a telephone call from him in which he said that Miss Coffee had liked the story and had sent it, together with her recommendation, to Miss Mary Baker. Miss Baker, incidentally, is the story editor of the agency of which the previously-mentioned Sam Jaffe is head. We thereafter referred to Mary Baker as "the practitioner." Miss Baker, Y―― said, was enthusiastic about the writing of the story but felt certain reservations about it as a film. She thought that after a few changes, which she was still thinking about, and which Y―― had not yet discussed with her, the story could be made more acceptable for pictures. Y―― said he would telephone me when he knew what the changes involved.

On December 30, as I recall, Y―― called me from Palm Springs. I was not in, and he left word that he would call at a certain later hour. The following day, not having heard from him and our apartment telephone being forbidden to send long distance calls, I went to the central telephone office and called him at the Racquet Club. . . .

Parenthetically, the reason I try to give dates for these telephone calls, and accurately to relate their contents, is that international telephone calls are automatically recorded. Hence, knowing the approximate date of calls, one can, with a sufficient reason, verify everything that was said by both parties.

In the December 31 telephone conversation, Y―― listed to me the changes which Miss Baker thought advisable, and I made notes of them. (1) She believed the story should start with a presentation of Joe, rather than with the undersecretary of war. (2) She thought a clearer emotional reason should be given for the undersecretary's urgent desire to adopt the child which starts the action of the story. (3) She believed that the physical means by which the mistaken wedding between Joe and the undersecretary was brought about were unbelievable and perhaps offensive. I told Y―― I would start on the changes at once.

I immediately wrote the changes, which affected only the first 17 of the story's 95 pages, and mailed them, together with a letter, to Y——'s Plymouth Boulevard address. The following photostat of my letter which accompanied the changes does not bear a date, but I believe it to have been written approximately the 4th or 5th of January, 1953.

Dear Y——:

Here are the re-writes—one original, and one carbon.

In them I have tried to overcome three objections:

    (1) It now starts with Joe.

    (2) A tiny bit of different emphasis is placed on the child.

    (3) The marriage business is corrected as to:

        (a) Its brutality of movement and bad taste.

        (b) The credibility of such a screw-up is a little helped.

With these concessions to your excellent practitioner, I do very much hope she will get it out *at once*.

I think at least thirty copies should be mimeographed, for which we shall pay.

Sometimes stories are not as limited as agents think. I think we should *assume* no limitations. It should, on the contrary, be as widely distributed as possible. Skelton might like it. O'Connor. Lewis and Martin. And a dozen others.

Also I call to someone's attention that Cary Grant appeared quite successfully in *I Was a Male War Bride*—a farce quite as broad as this, and which certainly might have been considered primarily for O'Connor or Skelton. But no—someone with imagination read it, and it turned out to be a Cary Grant and a smash at that. Therefore—insist as best you can that we not damn our yarn in advance—that other people's imaginations be permitted to play upon the *idea it contains*—from which might easily develop a most unexpected sale.

I suggest that you yourself superintend the putting together of these first 17 pages, comprising both new and original pages—for a secretary will almost be sure to screw it up. I mother 'em at that stage, because typos are important.

Now, dear fellow, please blast ahead for *immediate*—urgently immediate—submission. Immediately upon mimeographing! And, despite what we think of its limitations, let's get it around!

Salud to you. Please, on the very day it is finally submitted, *write* to me (not telephone: expensive—not telegraph: non-informative)—but write a pleasant letter letting me know the instant of submission, and the quantity submitted.

Felicitations
JOHN

Address (for the next week at least)
Elba 9-F
Col. Cuauhtemoc, Mexico, D.F.

Meanwhile, because Mexican import duties on my car were falling due and I could not afford to pay them, I drove the car out of the country, crossing the border at Matamoros on January 10, 1953, storing the car in Brownsville, Texas, on the same day. I flew from Brownsville to Los Angeles on January 11, 1953. I spent January 11 and 12 at the home of Mr. Paul Trivers. On January 13, I checked in at the Plaza Hotel on Vine Street in Hollywood.

I telephoned Y_____ at the Hollywood number, and was informed that he could be reached at the _____ on Sunset Boulevard. I telephoned him there and we had our first meeting either that or the following day. I might add that I, of course, registered properly at the hotel; but that whenever I left a message for Y_____ at the _____, it simply stated that Dr. Abbott had called, and when Y_____ called me at the hotel he never asked for me by name, but for room 507. When he visited me he came directly to the hotel room, by-passing the desk. Thus he always dealt with Dr. Abbott and never with Dalton Trumbo.

Generally we met in my hotel room. He was there, I should say, at least ten times; sometimes for dinner, which we ate in the room or in a rear booth of the hotel coffee shop; sometimes for pre-dinner cocktails; and sometimes during the day for breakfast or conferences. He insisted on taking me out to dinner several times, and when we did so I required that it be to some obscure restaurant where there would be no danger of someone recognizing me and identifying Y_____ with me. Y_____ selected for these dinners a small Chinese restaurant about three blocks from the hotel. We were in telephonic conversation every day and sometimes two or three times a day. He always called me John. Once he brought a friend to the hotel room for an hour or so, a _____ whose family, he told me, owned the Washington _____. He told me in advance he would introduce me to Mr. _____ as Dr. Abbott. Once, amused and irritated with the situation, he apologized for calling me John instead of Dalton when we were alone. He said, however, that experience had taught him to accustom his tongue and mind absolutely to subterfuge when subterfuge was being employed, since private lapses invariably resulted in public ones. In this way we protected our "prescription."

Returning now to the project which had brought us together in Hollywood. The dates will all be "about," for I do not remember them exactly. We saw each other first about January 13. Y_____ told me he had submitted the changes in the script to Miss Baker; that he had since been unable to see her and learn her reactions to them or her plans for the story; and that in the last day or two, when he telephoned the agency he had been told that Miss Baker was ill and would call him upon her recovery.

I suggested to him that Miss Baker probably didn't like the changes, or hadn't bothered to read them, and that we should take the story away from her and find an agent who could devote more time to it. Accordingly Y—— wired the agency that he wanted the story and would pick it up himself. This he did about January 14 or 15. We then were confronted with the problem of finding a new agent. I asked him who his New York agent was. He said, as I recall, George Bye. I suggested that he get in touch with Mr. Bye and discover the name of the Hollywood agent who handled Bye's film business. This he did, and was informed that Mr. Bye's Hollywood representative was Mr. Jules Goldstone.

At this point we took Mr. Trivers into our confidence. Mr. Trivers had experience as a story editor and knows stories and agents and studio relationships very well. Mr. Trivers said he thought Mr. Goldstone would be a good man for the story. Y—— likewise thought that Mr. Goldstone would be eager to give good service to a Bye client, because he had learned from Mr. Bye that the latter was displeased with his association with Mr. Goldstone and was thinking of discontinuing it, which possibility was alarming to Mr. Goldstone and hence should make him doubly obliging. It was agreed that Y—— would telephone Mr. Goldstone, make an appointment and take him the story.

This was done about January 15 or 16. Mr. Goldstone took the story, as I recall, to read over the weekend. About January 19 Y—— saw Mr. Goldstone again at his office. Mr. Goldstone thought the story was excellently written, but doubted that it would sell to motion pictures. This reaction being one to which Y—— and I by now were quite accustomed, we had agreed upon a tactic to answer it. Y—— told Mr. Goldstone that, since the latter thought the story well-written, he, Y——, felt its submission to studios, even though it did not sell, could not be harmful to its author's Hollywood reputation. Mr. Goldstone stated that, on the contrary, such a story . . . would do the author good. Y—— then said that he did not expect a sale; he hoped merely to receive, through this story, a decent introduction to Hollywood story departments, so that his name, when he made future submissions to them, would be favorably known. Y—— then offered to pay the cost of mimeographing fifty copies of the manuscript if Mr. Goldstone would submit the story to the studios. Mr. Goldstone agreed and the deal was consummated.

In the course of this conference, Mr. Goldstone said he didn't like the title, ————. Y—— and I thereupon went through the script and found, on page 28 of the original manuscript, the word ————. Therefore, when Y—— took the manuscript to the mimeographer, he changed the title to ————. Y—— supervised proofing and binding of the copies. About January 22 he received fifty mimeographed copies for which he paid $100. He turned thirty copies over to Mr. Goldstone for studio distribution and kept twenty which he intended to distribute himself. Among the persons he gave a copy to was Red Skelton's sister. Mr. Goldstone agreed to distribute the story to the studios, and, I believe, did so on January 23, 1953.

On January 26, 1953, Y—— and I saw each other at my hotel for the last time. Our project was launched, after many vicissitudes, and we were buoyant. He told me that, if the story sold, he preferred not to transmit my share in the form of a cashier's check made out in my wife's name, as had been previously suggested, but through a trustee arrangement about which he would talk to his banker in New York. I agreed.

I outlined two stories to him which I proposed to do next: one, the love story which I had already started, and the second a comedy. I told him I was going through the plot of each for him, so that he could begin to talk about them, and thus lend credibility when they appeared as fully developed screenplays. He liked the love story, which was somewhat mystical, and brought me a copy of *Peter Ibbetson* which he thought might give some ideas along the line I was thinking. He was eager for the next story to be finished. He hoped it would be ready in a month. I told him I thought that was too fast, but perhaps in two. He said that as soon as the next story was ready, he proposed to return to the coast with it. I told him I thought that unnecessary, now that the agency arrangement was set, but he said he preferred doing it in that way. I told him the next story would be in screenplay form, and he said he would so notify Mr. Goldstone.

He had had many luncheons with Mr. Robert Sisk, a motion picture producer for whom I had in the past done many films. Mr. Sisk is now in television, and he suggested to Y—— that Y—— try a TV series. Y—— suggested to me that we work together on it; but I told him that distance and my own inexperience with TV precluded the possibility.

He appeared to be in the best of spirits, and certainly gave no signs of ill-health. At one time during my stay there he had expressed a certain, but perfectly natural, degree of depression, but it passed. He said he was tired of what he called "the Princess Pignatelli set," and that he believed in very little; that he was, in fact, a complete cynic. Shortly thereafter he brought a copy of my novel *Johnny Got His Gun* for me to inscribe. I wrote in it my belief that he would ultimately fulfill himself completely. He telephoned me the next morning to thank me for it. He said: "I hope I can live up to it." These were the terms upon which we parted on January 26.

Early in the afternoon of January 27, 1953, I flew to San Diego, took a cab for the border, and boarded a plane for Mexico City, arriving there at 4:30 in the morning of January 28. About February 3, I wrote a note to Y—— at Park Avenue, giving him, as I had agreed to do, my new address, my wife having moved during my visit to Los Angeles. The address given in the note was our present one: Elba 21, Apartment 9, Colonia Cuauhtemoc, telephone 36–33–66. I thought nothing of the fact that I received no reply. He might have stayed over in Los Angeles; it was too early to have anything to report on the story; and he preferred the telephone to writing anyhow.

On Sunday, March 15, 1953, a friend brought to the apartment a number of old Hollywood trade papers. He knew that I, as an exile from the motion picture industry, was always avid for information about it. In going through them I found in the issue of Thursday, February 26, of the *Hollywood Reporter*, the following item: "20TH BUYS '_____.' " The body of the story read: "_____, an original Korean war story by Y_____, has been bought by 20th-Fox. No assignments have been made."

On March 16, 1953, I wrote a registered letter to Y_____. I didn't get it mailed until the morning of March 17. The following is a photostat of my carbon of that letter:

March 16, 1953

Dear Y_____:

Four or five days after I got back from our Hollywood rendezvous I dropped you the note I had promised with our new address and telephone. (You'll be amused to know that when I stepped off the plane here at four-thirty in the morning, I had to telephone a friend to get my own address!) Anyhow, the note may have miscarried, as sometimes happens with mail here, so at the tail end of this one you'll find the information in full. It's a pleasant apartment and the children seem happy. Cleo likes it very much so nothing is left to be desired.

I've been busy and out of touch, and since my subscription to Hollywood trades long ago expired, the news always reaches me late. Thus when a friend brought over some back issues of the *Hollywood Reporter* for my greedy consumption, I was pleasantly bowled over to read in the February 26 issue that our macabre little number variously called _____ or _____ had sold to Fox.

I suspect the reason I didn't hear the news from you is either because you didn't get the address note, or else you are waiting for the check just to be sure, and then propose, in your usual expensive fashion, to telephone instead of writing. However, the secret is out, and I am absolutely delighted. The only thing the *Reporter* didn't mention was the price. How much, old boy, I beg of you, how much?

I'd like to have seen the face of one Beck at William Morris when he opened the same trade paper and discovered that a story he had refused even to submit, which he had held unread for so long, was perfectly saleable all along. And the same, I may add, goes for Mary Baker and Sam Jaffe. What a struggle to break through the barriers of stupidity —and how little they really know about stories anyhow. I'm glad for Jules, even if he didn't think it would sell. At least he got behind it and sent it out, which isn't brilliant work, but at least it's competent. He actually is a pretty good agent and a nice person, so I'd stick with him from now on for our Hollywood stuff. I think I saw you last on January 26—which makes it exactly one month to the day of sale. A month isn't at all bad, for I've seen some of them take a year.

About the transfer of funds, you mentioned that if we sold you wanted to transfer through some trustee arrangement. That's perfectly fine with me, although I am of the opinion that an international cashier's check made out to Cleo in her maiden name would be quite as inconspicuous. However, do it in any fashion you think best. I have $2,800 due the Department of Internal Revenue on April 2, and they're threatening to execute their lien on my ranch trust deed unless I kick through—which would mean a tremendous loss to me—so the sooner you can get the money down here the better. It generally takes from three weeks to a month for a studio to pay off, but with an agent pressuring them they sometimes speed it up. Anyhow, if, without embarrassment, you can indicate to Jules that you'd like the pay-off quickly, it might help.

One thing more: the hundred dollars you paid out for mimeographing. Be sure to take it into account when you reckon the final division. We should share its expense in proportion to our sharing of the winnings, which is to say that if the yarn sold for ten thousand or less, we absorb the mimeographing cost fifty-fifty; but if (as I hope and pray!) it sold for more than ten, then you should charge me with two-thirds of the mimeographing cost and yourself with only a third. As for our over thirty thousand arrangement, I gravely doubt that we shall have to take it into account on this one, although there is always a hopeful chance.

About the next prescription: I decided on the way back to do the comedy rather than the love story. It'll be in screenplay form; for now that the big hurdle is accomplished and your name is established there, no one will think it odd that you should decide to try a script instead of narrative. Also, unlike the saga of Joe and his miserable marriage to Madame the Undersec, which probably could only have been done in narrative form, this one actually requires a full screenplay to get the best out of it. It should be done in another month, and will go forward to you at once. I think it's very funny, and will be much easier to sell than _____.

I think of nothing more, except that you really have no idea what a relief the sale is to us here. It's been so long and so terribly difficult, and even if the story didn't sell for too much, it'll get me out from under the pressure. Cleo sends her love, to which I add my own. Tell me—have you started the Dewey book yet? There's a job I don't envy you. However, plow through it and wait for happier times.

Salud!
JOHN (DOC)

New address: Dr. John Abbott, Elba 21, Apartment 9, Colonia Cuauhtemoc, Mexico, D.F. Telephone: 36-33-66

Shortly after sending the foregoing letter I was at the house of a friend of mine who subscribes to *The News*, an English language newspaper published in Mexico City. Because this newspaper publishes Miss Louella Parsons' Hollywood column, I began to go through her back columns to see if she had mentioned the sale. In the March 14th issue of the paper I found the following items in Miss Parsons' column: "I am sorry if my item about ———— gave the impression that Y————, a fine young man, is still alive. He did write the story, but he died about a month ago."

This was my first intimation of what had happened. I searched all over issues of the newspaper for the previous item to which the correction I had read so obviously referred. However, I found nothing. Miss Parsons' column here is frequently truncated for space, and old items often appear in later issues. I next went to the Benjamin Franklin Library and searched through back files of *The New York Times*. There, in the issue of February 1, 1953, I found and copied Y————'s obituary.

It was only on March 27, 1953, that *The News* carried Miss Parsons' original story about the sale. It recounted the sale of ———— to 20th Century-Fox as a role for Tommy Noonan and Marilyn Monroe, contained a brief plot-outline of the story, and stated that Y———— was going to write the script.

Thus, when I received your letter, I knew what had happened. In the interim between learning of Y————'s death and receiving your letter I was greatly perplexed about what I should do to state my interests and protect them. I thought of giving the information contained in this letter to my New York agent, Mrs. Elsie McKeogh, and having her take it at once to George Bye who, in turn, would communicate it to Y————'s next of kin. I thought of turning it over to my lawyer for handling through Y————'s family lawyer. Both processes I rejected as distasteful. The arrangement between Y———— and me was confidential. We had gone to considerable pains to keep it so. He wished it so and so did I. I did not wish to violate that confidence after his death by revealing it to outsiders.

From the obituary I had copied down the name of your mother. I made inquiries in New York, without stating my reason for making them, and discovered that I could reach her only by writing her in care of Mr. ————, trust officer at the City Bank Farmers Trust Company, 22 William Street, New York. If I had not heard from you, I presume that ultimately I should have had to write to her, although I did not wish to. So I simply delayed, hoping that I would receive a response from some member of his family to the last letter I had written to Y————. It was your response which now enables me to write directly to you.

There are at least two questions which would be right and natural for you to ask, and I think I ought to answer them in advance. First: why was there no written agreement between us? And second: how can you be sure I am telling the truth?

In answer to the first, let me say that the whole arrangement was a matter of mutual confidence and trust. Y————, having placed his whole reputation at stake in case of discovery, would have rightfully been insulted had I asked for a written agreement on financial terms. We were interested that each of us should understand the terms, but the thought of legal protection in the event either of us should reneg on them simply did not enter our minds. An example of this trust: when I voluntarily changed the terms in Y——'s favor, allocating to him one-half instead of the previous one-third should the sale come to ten thousand dollars or less, I placed him in a position where he actually could earn more money for himself by selling the story for ten thousand dollars than he could by selling it for twelve or fourteen thousand dollars. He was in complete charge of the selling. Thus he could have received an offer of fourteen thousand dollars (which would have given me approximately nine thousand dollars to his forty-six hundred dollars), refused it and sold it instead for ten thousand dollars (which would have given us five thousand each). The thought that he would actually do so was inconceivable to me. This was the measure of our trust and the reason why, in an arrangement which was so completely confidential, we did not even consider making a legal written record of our rights. Neither of us could, of course, have anticipated what actually happened.

In answer to the second question of whether or not I here write the truth, I suggest at the outset that if it is not the truth, it is an extraordinarily imaginative and well-documented lie. In simple fact, if they do not contain the truth, these pages constitute most damaging evidence of attempted fraud, or extortion, or both. My own position in perpetrating such a fraud would be extremely perilous, since I am not in public favor and have, unjustly as I conceive it but nevertheless actually, served time in a Federal prison. But these reasons are merely philosophical or speculative. There are, I think, better ways of testing my veracity:

1. The knowledge of Y——, all of which can be checked, which I have demonstrated as extending over a period of years, plus the specific and minute knowledge I have of every step in the conception, writing and sale of the story in question.

2. I have outlined herein at considerable length communications Y—— had about the story with such persons as Mr. Beck, Miss Coffee, Mr. Jaffe, Miss Baker, and Mr. Goldstone. I have seen none of these people for several years. They are all living, can call to mind everything they said to Y—— about the story, and their statements can be checked against those attributed to them in this letter.

3. The photostatic evidence included in this communication.

4. The letters from "Doc" which you tell me you found among Y——'s effects. These will confirm what I have related herein, as well as afford scientific tests relating to my typewriter.

5. The international telephone calls, the recorded contents of which can be checked against what I have here written.

6. The switchboard records of the Hollywood Plaza and the _____, which will reveal how many times he called my hotel, and I his.

7. Mr. _____, who spent two hours in my hotel room with _____ and me, can identify me or my picture (I have pictures of Y_____ and me together), as the man to whom he was introduced by Y_____ as Dr. Abbott.

8. Mr. Paul Trivers, with whom Y_____ and I discussed the project, will attest to what I have said, insofar as it dealt with him.

9. You will find among Y_____'s effects the copy of *Johnny Got His Gun* inscribed by me to him and dated in Hollywood during the period I was there. In his library you will also find a copy of my first novel, *Eclipse*, published in England, and inscribed to Y_____. The hero of this novel is named "John Abbott." In 1938 I did an extremely successful film called *A Man to Remember*, produced by Robert Sisk at RKO. I christened the hero of that film "Dr. John Abbott."

10. But the best proof is the original typescript itself. Y_____ has the original copy and first carbon; I have the second carbon. The whole manuscript was typed by me, in Mexico, on an IBM electric I have owned for years. I brought it to Mexico with me when I came and it has never been out of the country. A comparison of either Y_____'s original or first carbon with my second carbon will scientifically establish the whole job was done here. On both Y_____'s original and first carbon you will also find here and there, small typographical corrections in my hand. In order for you to establish this to your satisfaction, I am including with this letter, the following:

A. A photostat of my carbon of the title page of the original story, the first copy and first carbon of which were sent to Y_____.

B. A photostat of my carbon of page 28 of the original manuscript, in which occur the words _____ _____ from which the second title was taken. The photostat also contains erasures and other errors which are identical in Y_____'s copy.

C. A photostat of my carbon of page 31 of the original manuscript, which contains corrections typed in without carbon.

D. My own carbon (no photostat) of page 59 of the original manuscript, which contains typed-in, non-carbon corrections on my typewriter for comparison with letters from me to Y_____ now in your possession. The page also contains written correction in my own hand. I am sending you the original of my carbon of this page, retaining a photostat for myself, so that you will have everything necessary for scientific tests in your possession.

. . . .

I presume that the legal niceties demand—although I consider it unnecessary and should prefer it otherwise—that at this point, the evidence being submitted, I make request for moneys due me from the sale of _____, such moneys to be allocated as outlined in the photostat of my carbon of my letter to Y_____ dated October 4, 1952, minus deductions for mimeographing costs as set forth in the photostat of my carbon of the last letter I sent him. This request I therefore make, apologizing simultaneously for the legal necessity of doing so.

I should like to mention also that in my last letter to Y_____, at the top of page two, I told him of the extremely urgent matter that hangs over my head in relation to the Department of Internal Revenue. I shall add to it only that the sum of my equity in the ranch trust deed is $20,000; that it is the only asset remaining to me and my family after the debacle of the past five years; that the Federal Government has a lien against it in the exact sum of $2,902.47 payable April 2, 1953; that I fear, in view of the age of the obligation and extensions previously granted, I can secure a delay of no more than a week or ten days before the lien is executed and the deed offered at public auction; that I have no money to bid in on the sale, and therefore stand a loss possibly as great as seventeen thousand and certainly no less than ten thousand. I shall not belabor the obvious point of how greatly I need my share of the proceeds from _____.

This concludes the factual account of Y_____ and me, our friendship, and the literary arrangement we had. It is so long because it is a surprising sequence of events, designed never to be known, and must give rise to many pertinent questions in your mind which only a complete account of everything can answer.

* * *

What moved me most in your letter was the line: "It is tragic that something Y_____ had always hoped for should have happened after his death."

I thought about that line for hours before writing this letter. I thought seriously of misrepresenting the truth, of stating flatly or at least implying that Y_____ had some part in the conception and writing of the story. But to do this I would have been obliged to lie in a letter the very nature of which requires the entire truth. The misstatement would not have been born out by our correspondence, not by the unequal division of the profits we had agreed upon. Moreover, in explaining a complicated series of circumstances, one single mistruth, no matter how courteously intended, can, upon close analysis of the whole, invalidate all that is true. Therefore I resolved that to you, at least, I must state the thing fully and precisely as it happened.

The above considerations, however, need not hold if it becomes necessary that your mother, by reason of her position as next of kin

and presumably heiress to Y——'s estate, be told of my claim against
the story. I am sure that you, being now in possession of the facts,
understand that they reflect in no way upon Y——'s talent, his ability or his honor. But a mother's pride in the last accomplishment of
her son might be cruelly wounded by the information I have given
you. This no one would wish to happen. Therefore I suggest that if,
in order to effect a transfer of funds, it becomes necessary for your
mother to be informed, some better method be devised than revealing to her the full contents of this letter.

It might be that you could communicate what you consider to be
the essentials to her, withholding such information as you think it
best for her not to know, without ever showing her this letter. Or
it might be possible that I could help. Based on your request and
wishes, for example, I could write another letter to you, a letter
which is presumably the first. Written to you, it would be intended
for your mother's eyes. In it I will write whatever you wish me
to write; and will willingly state that Y——'s and mine was a
full collaboration in any way you wish it said. I will include in it
only such information as you wish included. Then this letter,
with its fuller documentation and interpretation, would never be
seen by anyone, and the possible hurt to your mother would be
diminished.[22]

Please let me say in relation to the above paragraph, that there
was never any question in my mind about the brilliant future that
lay ahead of Y——. You know the qualities of his mind better than
I, and they were extraordinary. He thought with precision, and he
was spectacularly well-informed. He had not really decided, once and
for all, in which particular field of literature he wished to specialize.
With a little more experience in the actual practice of writing—experience which he was acquiring very rapidly—he would have been
immensely successful in any field he selected. If he had finally decided to become a screen writer, the two or three stories of mine to
which he would have put his name would have served merely to
introduce him to the studios. Writing for film, more than any other
kind of writing, is *learned* from the *inside*, which is to say that it is
learned *after* one has entered the studios, rather than before. The
sale of the stories would therefore have helped him only in securing
that inside position a little sooner than otherwise. Thereafter he
would have learned quickly and gone ahead brilliantly on his own.
If he had wished to make motion pictures a career, he would have

[22] Prof. Y—— felt that the "collaboration" explanation would be best
for his mother's sake and agreed to explain the situation to her. Trumbo
merely wrote her (see letter below) a kind tribute to Y——'s memory with
an almost incidental mention of their collaboration. Payment of Trumbo's
share of the sale was made promptly and willingly.

been richly able to do so without ever having known me or heard my name.

In writing this letter to you, I do not feel that I have in any way dishonored Y____'s memory. On the contrary, I have revealed to you that his last professional act was a profoundly generous and noble one. To help a friend and fellow-writer who had been rendered mute by circumstances, he placed his name, his reputation and his career in jeopardy. If the facts of my authorship of the story had ever been disclosed he would have been blacklisted throughout the motion picture industry. Ever since my unhappy profession first was practiced, writers have been at loggerheads with constituted authority, and efforts to suppress them or starve them out are as old as the history of government itself. There are many examples in past literature of one writer lending his name in order that another, temporarily out of favor, might continue to write. This is what Y____. did. He did not consider it dishonorable, nor did I: it was, on the contrary, an act involving the essence of honor, and the moral courage it required in these troubled times is very considerable

There is little more I can say, save this: it is never easy to reconcile oneself to the death of a young man; but when the young man is as brilliant, as sensitive and as kindly as your brother was, with a future that promised so very much, not only to himself but to a world whose cultural values are fast slipping away, the sense of injustice becomes almost overwhelming. I, who do not know you, who have caused you pain by writing this letter, should perhaps refrain from adding to it my deepest sympathy to you and your family. But I cannot refrain. I am grieved for myself. I shall never forget him

Most sincerely,
DALTON TRUMBO

21. To Mrs. Y____, mother of Y____

Mexico City
April 5, 1953

My dear Mrs. Y____:

I have had the pleasure of hearing from your son, Prof Y____ and have received permission from him to write to you directly, which I hasten to do. I want to tell you about Y____, and my relationship with him, and of my wife's sorrow and my own that he is no longer living.

As Prof. Y____ has no doubt told you, I am a writer named

Dalton Trumbo and also the mysterious Dr. John Abbott with whom Y_____ has been in correspondence for the past eight or nine months. It has been my privilege, since 1945, to be Y_____'s friend. It came about in the following manner:

In June of 1945 a party of six or seven war correspondents embarked from San Francisco by air on a three-month tour of Pacific battle areas. Among the correspondents were Y_____ and I. He was by far the youngest of our group, certainly no more than twenty-two. His background had given him a method of speech and a pattern of polite conduct which differed from others. These qualities, combined with his very considerable intellectual capacities and his youth, were seized upon by certain of our party as an excuse to make small jokes at his expense. Because I admire intelligence and understand how painfully youth can suffer even from inconsequential affronts, I came to his defense, and together we made common cause which resulted in a more comfortable situation. It was this circumstance, he later told me, which made him like me.

Y_____ had great self-respect, and the determination of any intelligent man not to die needlessly. Nevertheless, at every point in our tour he was in the midst of the heaviest action, when he need not have been. He had a deep sense of his obligation as a correspondent. The government had gone to considerable expense to send him abroad, and he rightly felt that in accepting the invitation he had pledged himself to see action where it existed, rather than to learn about it in ward-room comfort or rear area press relations headquarters. He experienced every kind of fire, from flak over Japan and bombs on Okinawa to artillery and small arms in Borneo, and always was ready for more.

In the early stages of our tour we visited Oahu, Guam, Saipan, Tinian, Iwo Jima, and Manila. From Manila _____ and Y_____ and I went on to Okinawa. There, in late June, Y_____ and I, in separate planes, flew with a bombing mission of 60 B-25s over the Japanese island of Kyushu, the target city being Kagoshima. AA fire was radar-directed and heavy. We lost one B-25 and six Navy Corsairs who were flying escort. On the same day, _____ flying as observer over Formosa, was shot down in a B-24, with all hands lost.

Our group reassembled in Manila and flew to Tawi Tawi in the Sulu Sea, where we joined a fleet of some three hundred vessels gathering for the last amphibious invasion of the war—the Australian Seventh Division's assault of July 1 upon the oil port city of Balikpapan in Dutch East Borneo. Y_____ and I and a third correspondent, now dead,[23] went ashore in a landing boat between the first and second waves. I should add here that others of our group, including

[23] Herbert Clyde Lewis.

the two who had been most unpleasant at the outset, remained aboard ship during the entire campaign, preferring official briefs from Australian public relations officers to first-hand experience.

Two hours after the first assault and some six hundred yards inland, Y⎯⎯ and I, from a trench outside the Governor's Palace, saw a hilltop we believed would give us a better view of what was going on, and decided to climb it. The third correspondent joined us; our accompanying captain refused to on the perfectly legitimate ground that it was a needless risk, justifiable for a correspondent but not for an escort. He had a child at home and his decision, as an American press relations officer in an Australian theater, was a correct one.

Y⎯⎯ and I and the third correspondent started out alone. Midway up the hill, which was without adequate cover, the third correspondent halted and suggested that we go back to the trench. There was a certain amount of shooting going on around us, and Y⎯⎯ and I considered the spot where we had stopped ill-suited for forensics. We therefore opposed return and suggested that the safest spot would be the top of the hill itself. Y⎯⎯ has since quoted back to me, with considerable amusement, one of the arguments I used to persuade our reluctant colleague. I pointed out that neither the third man nor I were in any danger, since no Japanese would waste a bullet on short men when so magnificent a target as Y⎯⎯ was with us to draw fire.

When we reached the top of the hill we found an abandoned radar-directed AA gun that had been knocked out by naval fire, and no sign of a human being. Perhaps fifteen minutes later a grim-looking Australian major charged up the other side of the hill at the head of an assault group, all bayonets heroically set. His pleasure in capturing the feature for king and country was somewhat diminished by the presence of three American correspondents already in firm possession. To break the tension we asked him and his men if they knew where we might buy a good glass of cold beer. The major thought it unfunny, but his men laughed, and dubbed the hill "Mount Pilsner" on the spot. I am told that in the division's history of the campaign, the hill, which by map was Hill 78, is still called by the name they gave it.

Late that night, having dined on K-rations, Y⎯⎯ and I rolled up in our ponchos under a bush and courted sleep. It was raining steadily, and surprisingly cold for the tropics. We were wet and miserable, and Y⎯⎯, with his usual fastidiousness, had worn his own oxfords instead of G.I. shoes. As a result his feet were quite painful to him. As a further handicap to slumber, we were in an area which both sides were infiltrating. The night was lively with the sound of machine-gun and small artillery fire.

After what seemed an interminable period, I fell asleep. Perhaps an hour later someone nudged me violently. I was awakened to see

Y—— kneeling over me. The artillery fire was still going on, and we had almost to shout in order to be heard by each other. "What's wrong?" I demanded. His whole face was laughing. "You were snoring," he said gently. "I was afraid you'd draw fire." I was obliged to smother my sense of outrage and laugh with him. He had paid me back for my quip on the hillside. There was no more sleep for the rest of the night.

The next morning, after boiling tea from a five-gallon can, Y—— and I, the third American correspondent, and two Australian correspondents, joined up with a patrol composed of the 7th Platoon, I Company, 2/10 Battalion of the Seventh Division. We crossed the mountains which intervened between the point of invasion and the city of Balikpapan, entered the city and penetrated half-way down its main waterfront street before cross-fire obliged us to return. The two Australian correspondents were killed. Y—— was thus with the first patrol to enter the city. It required three more days for the occupying forces to fight their way to the point where he had been, and two more before the city was secured.

On the fourth day of the campaign, the outcome being beyond doubt, our group decided to return to Tawi Tawi. The only way we could go was by an Australian mail courier, a small Catalina flying boat. It was a nasty day with a fairly heavy sea, and two Catalinas had already cracked up trying to get off the water. The third one, on which we were going, was the last available for courier duty.

The plane was held in position by a line thrown from the LCI, and we went to it singly, in a small boat, standing erect and pulling hand over hand along the line. Then, on the rise of the wave, a scrambling leap onto the nose of the Catalina, from which point its crew dragged us aboard. There were eleven of us. For the takeoff we were all jammed into the tiny navigator's cabin to give more weight for the nose against the hammering waves that had smashed our two predecessors. Once off we retired to the main cabin.

Somewhere off Japanese-occupied Celebes, the alarm signifying air attack went off in the cabin. The alarm on the Catalina is a horn that emits sharp bursts of sound not unlike the bawling of a calf: an insistent, loud, terrifying sound to those who have not heard it before. It could only mean that a Zero had risen from Celebes and was attacking. The gunners rushed from the forward cabin to the two rear blisters and tore the covers from their weapons. We in the cabin put on our helmets and lay down wherever we were.

Our two gunners opened fire. The plane began to lose altitude rapidly, the only possible way for a slow-moving Catalina to escape a Zero being to get so close to the water that the Zero, in making its pass, will crack up. We who were in the cabin could do nothing: we could not see outside; we could not fight; we could not take shelter; we could not run; we could only lie quietly, realizing that our chances for life had all but run out, and wondering why we had ever permitted ourselves to be placed in such a position.

I was on the top bunk. I looked down. Y——— was lying full length on the floor between two other men, his helmet on. He looked up at me, and although his face was, I daresay, as pale as my own, he smiled. Then he said: "Goodbye, Trumbo."

I cannot quite describe my emotions at that moment. Perhaps I thought of my own son, then only four; perhaps I thought of my father, long dead; certainly I felt that a son not my son had chosen me from among that company as the one he wished to say goodbye to; and that a father not his father had responded. The fact, as it later turned out, that there was no Zero within a hundred miles and no danger, that the whole incident was a ludicrous mistake of nerves on the part of the crew, in no way diminishes my memory of that moment, nor the surge of love I felt for your son.

When our party returned to San Francisco, Y——— and I separated from it and flew to Los Angeles, where he remained with us for two weeks at our home in Beverly Hills. Mrs. Trumbo, seven months pregnant, was not too sparkling company for a young man, and our two children pestered him interminably. They appeared to regard him as some rare and wonderful curiosity, not only for his height in contrast to their father's lack of it, but also because of his speech. Through their mother they are fourth-generation native-born Californians, and I am a Coloradoan. As flat-accented, wild little westerners, they thought Y——— was speaking to me in a foreign tongue. They would stare at him with rapt interest while he talked, and then demand to know what he had said. He answered their bewildered "Whats?" with far more indulgence than any young man is obliged to grant. Still and all, I think he enjoyed the visit as much as I know we did.

We have managed to correspond intermittently ever since that visit. Y——— went to India, and later published his first book; I went before the House Committee on Un-American Activities and later served my first term in the penitentiary. In the summer of 1951 we saw a great deal of each other, both at our ranch and in Hollywood. I was at that time, as I am now, blacklisted by motion pictures, publishers and magazines. Y——— was indignant at what had happened to me, not because he agreed in any way I ever discovered with my political views, but because he was morally opposed to sending people to jail for opinion, and outraged that the slow starvation, via the blacklist, should be visited upon men after they presumably have paid for their misdeeds. It was typical of his generous nature that he offered to collaborate with me for motion pictures, and to put his name alone to the product of our mutual endeavors. It was typical of my need that I accepted. One afternoon at the ranch, threshing story ideas out together, we turned up the comic situation that later resulted in _____.

In the course of exchanging manuscripts and ideas by mail, as is necessary in any collaboration, I devised for Y____'s protection the idea that I should become Dr. John Abbott, and that our story in future be referred to in pseudo-medical terms. He had a brilliant career ahead of him, and I wanted him fully protected from any disclosure of our collaboration. Disclosure could not have harmed me, for I am beyond harm; but it could have ruined Y____, since I am considered by persons with whose judgment I am bound to disagree to be so contaminating that mere association with me is sufficient to incur the penalty of professional death. It is a measure of Y____'s gallantry that he placed himself in such jeopardy in order that a friend might continue to earn a living at his profession.

We finished our work on _____ in October, but the incredible stupidity of agents who refused to submit it obliged us both to go to Hollywood, where I met him in mid-January. For ten days we worked closely together finding a proper agent and making certain the story would at least be seen by the studios. On January 26th, our work being completed, I saw him last. We had drinks and dinner in my hotel room. We were extremely pleased with ourselves and with the world. Y____ recited limericks; I told him stories about Hollywood and its extraordinary mores. We parted expecting to see each other very soon. Y____ was returning in two days to New York. I left the next afternoon for Mexico City. It was almost two months later that I learned of his death.

Because with a person like Y____ it is almost intolerable to think what he might have been had he lived, I have chosen in this letter to write about what he was. I have lost members of my own family. I well know what chill comfort a letter of sympathy can be, and so I have not written you one. Rather I have tried to make Y____ live again for you in certain moments of his life you could not otherwise have shared, hoping thereby to give you some of the deep pleasure that I shall always have in remembering him.

During our last visits, in a moment of temporary depression common to young men who are both sensitive and intelligent beyond their years, Y____ told me that he thought he believed in nothing; that he felt himself a complete cynic. It was, of course, not true. A day or two later when he brought a copy of my novel *Johnny Got His Gun* for me to inscribe, I wrote in it what I really felt about him and his future. He telephoned me the next day to thank me. He said: "I hope I can live up to it." I should have told him then, and now have only you to tell, that he already had.

Most sincerely,
DALTON TRUMBO

22. To Harry E. Day, Internal Revenue Agent

Mexico City
April 7, 1953

Dear Mr. Day:

In accordance with the promise contained in my letter to you of March 29, 1953, I enclose herewith a cashier's check made out to the Director of Internal Revenue in the sum of $2,915.00, covering in full the delinquent 1951 Federal Income Tax of Cleo and Dalton Trumbo.

On April 1, 1953, as your letter informed me, the total due, with interest and lien charges, was $2,902.47. Because I am a poor computer of interest, and wished to make certain of full payment, I have drawn the check for a sum that is $12.53 in excess of the above sum, to cover the additional seven days' interest. If this is in excess of what I actually owe, you can, at your convenience, refund the overage.

Permit me to express my thanks to you and to Mr. Neblett for the cooperation you have shown in permitting me to redeem an asset of considerable value which otherwise I should have lost.

Very truly,
DALTON TRUMBO

23. To Hy Kraft

Mexico City
April 6, 1953

Dear old boy:

How can TOS explain all of this? He cannot, at least in terms of excusing himself. But your line "I never treated you this way when you had dough" is so true and so funny that I must at least make an attempt.

To start in: I was a fool for coming down here. The line of supply to my living source is so tenuous that when I do work the people who owe me for it mistake my absence for my death, and simply do not pay without the strongest kind of pressure being exerted. I went flat about June. Then I wrote an original screenplay and sold it for $10,000. But the bastards didn't pay. I had to make two trips to enforce collection, and still have not got it all. Then Cleo got sick. She went from bad to worse, into a complete malnutritional breakdown. It took daily quantities of amino acids, vitamins, blood plasma and finally whole blood even to get her in condition for the hospital. Then the stern business, which ordinarily is not bad, but which in

268

this instance disclosed four ulcers. All cut out, all fine. But she had the spinal, and it went wrong, as it does in one of perhaps 2,000 cases. Six and one-half days of the most terrible headache medicine knows. Then abrupt cessation, and a thin and wan girl was finally dismissed.

Four days later we vacated our house—too expensive—and moved into an apartment. Then the government slapped an extra 1950-51 assessment of $7,500 against me. With it went a lien on my $20,000 trust deed against the ranch, and a promise they'd seize and sell the lien if I didn't pay by the end of December, 1952. I sold some stuff and gave them a G for thirty days extension. Thirty days later I flew to L.A. and got a note out of the guys who owed me the 10 Gs (for $3,000) which I cashed with Seniel Ostrow,[24] thus permitting me to bring the balance down further—with a further 60 day extension.

As the 60 days approached an end, I hadn't pot nor window, and stood to lose the whole deed. Here occurred a curious thing. In the autumn I'd written another original, and sent it out under the name of a young man who's never been heard of in Hollywood. He submitted it. Meanwhile, unbeknown to me, he died. Two months after his death the story, in which I'd given up all hope, sold for $7,500. My problem—how to get my share before the government moved. By the most extraordinary sequence of correspondence, I managed to get $3,000 just in time to raise the lien. So the ranch is saved (that is, the trust deed is)—and things look better.

Now in the midst of all this, I had daily hope of writing you and sending a small part of the owings. As this prospect diminished, I grew ashamed of the fact of my silence, and out of this shame the silence persisted. And then it seemed that each day, each hour almost, some new emergency was upon me. Letters stacked up. I said—"In three more days I'll have time to sit down and spend a day or two on back correspondence." And they never came. And so, and so, and so.

Even now it is hump like hell trying to find fifty bucks; but up until the first of last month, it was even worse. I begin to learn (and appreciate) what others have gone through. I always did admire the way you handled adversity, but I never actually realized (how can one without doing it?) the series of acute internal crises and belly-gripings that accompany the task. Anyhow, there is my confession, full and complete. I truly am sorry—and if I'm ever lucky enough to assemble enough dough in one pile to haul my stern (and those of my family, all of which are growing into larger sterns) back to the U.S.A. I think I'll have things licked.

. . . .

Cleo is feeling fairly well. She hasn't much energy, needs lots of

---

[24] Ostrow was the president of the Sealy Mattress Company.

sleep, and is still shockingly thin. We stuff her with cream and other disgusting things. I think she needs the California altitude and climate to stage a full recovery, but she actually is better now than she has been in a year. Nikola is taller than Cleo and, damn it all, goes out with boys. At this cursed American school they apparently start love as they discard diapers, and I find it a burden, a bore and a worry. However there's nothing but to let her do it, for this is Rome, and we must all wear togas. I will, however, be damned glad to get her back to L.A. or somewhere. Chris is extremely handsome, terribly strong, and tootles a trumpet in the high school band. He parades with others every Saturday at the football games, clad in immaculate white trousers and a red jacket. He blows very hard on his trumpet and practices it with maddening devotion. I forgot to say that Nikola is also very pretty—although at present in a kind of blowsy, over-fleshed way, for she has got fat. It's girl fat from eating too much, and vanity will ultimately whittle down both her appetite and her arse. Then she will be quite a thing. As it is, when I watch her slunge around with the vacuous eyes of adolescence and the body of Shirley Booth in *Come Back, Little Sheba*—I blow my cork, old boy. I blow high, and little good it does me. Mitzi, to complete the report, is dazzling both physically and intellectually. And I am in perfect shape. Turning gray as a goat, but I think it's not age (only 47) but the shorts that does it.

Now! I have done it. I have given you a full report. You said if I did you'd write. I shall therefore expect a reply from you within ten months, since my own record does not qualify me for prompter service.

Please give Rheat all of our love, and ask Jill for us how many times she has fallen in love lately. We do think of all of you very often, and look forward some day to seeing you under fairer skies, which, I feel, may not be too far in the future.

Always,
TOS

24. To the King Brothers

Mexico City
April 10, 1953

Dear Frank and Maury:

I enclose herewith *The Boy and the Bull*.[25] It consists now, as you

[25] This is the first mention of a story, written by Trumbo, which was produced by the King Brothers under the title of *The Brave One*. In 1956 the credited author, Robert Rich, was awarded a writing Oscar by the Academy

can see, of 133 pages instead of the former 172 pages. However, within these 133 pages there are many further cuts, which bring the whole down to 121 pages.

In doing this I have ruthlessly cut all extraneous material and scenes, and kept rigidly to the simple story of the boy and the bull. In my first letter accompanying the script, I told you that two relationships could be lifted entirely: (1) the love story between Manuel and Julietta (which is here cut completely); and (2) the development of Don Alejandro Videgaray's dissolute but sympathetic character through the American girl Jean and other scenes (most of this has now been cut). I feel we lose absolutely nothing. On the contrary, we gain in simplicity, directness, and hence in dramatic forcefulness. You now have a script which I think you should be able to budget almost exactly.

About Maury's suggestion, based on the French picture he saw, that a dream sequence be inserted—I don't like the idea. This picture is very simple, and deals with very real things, and will best be done if it is done in simple realism. I suspect the French picture was somewhat less realistic than this one, and a sequence which might therefore go well in it, might hurt ours. Also, our boy cannot have a dream glorifying bullfighters, because bullfighters are a menace to the bull he loves. He cannot have a dream imagining himself as a bullfighter, because then he would become the murderer of his pet. In no place in the picture does he manifest the slightest desire to be a matador; rather, he spends his time trying to devise ways to save his bull *from* the matador.

Likewise, I would suggest that we refrain from trying to find scenes to *add* to this picture, unless they are essential or extremely unusual. The addition of a scene, simply for its own sake, often weakens the dramatic line of a story, and therefore its punch to the audience. Of course if we can think of a scene that is brilliant, has never been done before, and will add to our story, we should do it at all costs.

Now about money: you know how I hate to talk about it, but I must. I got the two hundred dollars, and it was a life saver, and it is gone. That, of course, is not because I am extravagant, but because it was all spent before it arrived. You said to me when I saw you last in Los Angeles that I should budget my income. This, of course, is perfectly correct. I live very cheaply, but it is impossible to budget income without the income. If one earns money and then cannot get it, one runs so far behind that by the time one does get it, budgeting is out of the question.

---

of Motion Picture Arts and Sciences. Of course, no Robert Rich appeared. The entire episode pointed up the ludicrous nature of the blacklist and is referred to extensively in subsequent correspondence.

There is another factor that I feel I must explain to you in justification of my needing money at the present time. When one is owed money and cannot get it, one's obligations go on just the same, and they must be paid. Thus I have had to sell things in order to keep living. In November I had to sell my Packard—a perfectly good car that would have lasted for years. Because I couldn't collect what was owing me, I had to wholesale it for $1,060. I took at least a seven hundred dollar loss that I should not have had to take had I in my possession the money I had already earned. And again: when I had to come north in order to raise the money to save the trust deed temporarily—I finally managed to collect $3,000 (and you were damned nice in doing what you did in order for me to get it)—but the point is, it cost me $500 to make the trip and collect the $3,000 I had already earned. By these two deals I felt compelled to make, I had to throw in, as a complete loss, $1,200 of the $10,000 the *Boy and Bull* brought me. In a word, when a man can least afford it he has to take the greatest losses. Additionally I have had to sell other things to keep alive—probably my whole loss for not being able to collect the 10 Gs coming to me amounts to two thousand dollars. Under these circumstances a man simply cannot budget, as you suggest I do. He can only sit to one side, and watch his last assets draining away. He has worked, he has earned money, but he does not have it, and hence he is stripped of everything he owns. This is a terrible thing to happen to a man, and I now simply do not know what I am going to do about the ranch trust deed.

I haven't wanted to worry you about this. I haven't written much about it. You didn't mention it on the telephone the other day, and I didn't want to embarrass you by bringing it up. The money was due April 2, 1953. That was the sixty days they gave me to pay the $2,900 when I was last in Los Angeles. I set that date because—although you did not guarantee it—you said you were morally certain that my remaining $2,000 would be forthcoming by that time, the whole thing depending upon your production deal on either one of two pictures. I wrote the government frantically, telling them I had 2 Gs due which I expected daily (this because Maury had assured me the German deal was set)—and asked them for fifteen more days. I have not heard from them, but I think it is probably granted. Otherwise they would have had to notify me of seizure and sale. This is the tenth. They must have the money by the fifteenth. And what am I to do?

You see, if they execute the lien and sell, I shall not only lose everything I have in the deed: I shall lose the $1,000 I paid them in December (and in order to get that $1,000 I had to sell a car at a $700 wholesale loss, for a total cost of $1,700). In addition I shall lose the $2,000 I paid them in January (and in order to get the $2,000 I had to sell jewelry, cameras, etc. down here at about an

$800 loss under their real U.S. value—for a total of $2,800). And I shall also lose the $2,900 I paid them out of the note you have (which $3,000 cost me $500 in travelling expenses to get, for a cost of $3,500). And I shall have nothing. And yet I have worked decently and honestly and long for the very purpose of getting the money to save myself. It seems so hideously wrong that I should have taken the losses already taken, and that I should have to take this further $17,000 loss, when I have done nothing to deserve it—when I have delivered everything I said I would. It is, really, enough to make a man think of cashing in on his insurance by a well-placed bullet, rather than to see his family, through no fault of his own, steadily descend into bankruptcy. They'd be better off.

Also I know that recently you have been able to pay another writer—a writer who has not done nearly as much as I in your service—who has never turned over to you an original screenplay, and who has never re-written for you without cost as a part of his original bargain. Yet he gets the money—and I am, of course, glad he did—while I, because I have not got mine, am being ruined.

Now this letter is not a reproach, because I know that you are decent men and I value our relationship. It is not written in anger, for anger will do no good. It is actually written to beg you—to supplicate you to pay me the $1,800 if you possibly can, and before the fifteenth so I can save my trust deed. And to please write me, telling me what the situation is, and what future there is, if any, for me with your organization. If you really want me—that's the point; and perhaps you don't, in which event kindness would dictate that I be told so. Because this worry, this loss, this dread of tomorrow, this slow stripping away of everything one has simply because one can not get the money already due—it is too much for a human being to bear.[26]

Please—in God's name, write me quickly and tell me.

Regards,
DOC

---

[26] Trumbo, throughout this letter, is using one of his favorite literary devices: hyperbole. He needed money badly; without intending to lie, he was forced to exaggerate his circumstances in order to achieve the desired effect—and results.

25. To Ring Lardner, Jr.

Dear Ring:

The book [27] has arrived and a preliminary report will go forward
to you in about a week. I am going to violate your injunction in a
small way and ask Cleo to read it too. The reason for this I shall
try to make clear.

Recently Albert [Maltz] finished a re-write of his book and sent
it to us. I read it and found two or three major things I didn't like.
Cleo read it and found two or three other major things that she didn't
like. I was so chagrined at having overlooked her points (with which
I at once agreed) that I went back to the book and read it most
thoroughly again, taking many notes. The result was that in addition
to what I originally did not like and what she originally did not like,
we found several other major points that we together didn't like.
Conversation each night over drink developed these points and added
to them. Cumulatively they took on a much uglier significance than
any two or three of them separately could reveal. The result was that
our combined efforts found absolutely nothing in the book, aside
from a couple of minor speeches, that we did like. Thus, when we
finally confronted him, we presented a united front of such bristling
and implacable hostility that, in combination with others who had
found still other faults in the book, we were able to overwhelm him
completely. He has now retired for a re-write and will not be heard
from for another year. Having gone out of our way for Albert, we
certainly wish to do no less for you.

There are several ways and approaches for critical help such as
you desire:

1. Discover the main weakness in the book (every book has one);
then go back over the book page by page, line by line, making exhaustive notes which will support your judgment and emphasize the
weakness. Then give the weakness an ideological significance. Go
back over the book a second time with ideology in mind. This will
more than double your notes. Assemble the whole. It is at this point
of assembly of total evidence that your passions become inflamed.
The involvement of passion in the process is extremely important.
Without passion, which is to say anger, you are likely to present the
author with your findings in a humble and apologetic fashion. He
can mistake your obvious reluctance to go at him hammer and tongs
for lack of confidence. This is fatal. With passion you can approach
him in cold hatred, reject his every defense, accuse him, by implication, of a good many things he hadn't ever thought of or wished for,
and defeat him utterly. This method results in a complete re-write.

[27] Lardner's newly completed satiric novel, *The Ecstasy of Owen Muir.*

2. Instead of concentrating on the main weakness in the book as a whole, search for the main weakness in every character and in every scene (these also exist in every book). This more comprehensive approach takes a good deal more time and is reserved, therefore, for one to whom one owes a great deal in terms of help and advice. By the time all of the line and word quotes to establish all the weaknesses are assembled you have a document almost as long as the book itself. The nice thing about method two is that when you finally confront the author you don't need to be passionately involved yourself. The evidence itself is so voluminous and so absolutely damning that it need not be fortified with venom. One pities rather than hates. One speaks gently, softly, as if in the presence of the dead. One terminates the conversation as quickly as possible, leaves the evidence on the coffee table, and slips out of the house. Method two has a further advantage over method one in that the author does not re-write; he throws the whole thing away. Quite often his folly is so clear to him that he goes out and seeks honest work and never writes again.

3. This involves a study of the author as exhaustive as that of the book. It can only be successfully done if you know and love the author and are privy to many of his secrets. Naturally one reads the book, but one reads it always with the character of the author in mind. A written report is not necessary. Assemble the evidence in your mind, seek the author out (preferably when there are several other people discussing the book with him) and ask him: "Tell me in a sentence what the theme of the book is—what you were really trying to say." This opening has the advantage of revealing to the author at once his foolishness in having used 250 pages to say what obviously could have been said in less than one. He is taken aback, but he will try at least once to rise to the challenge. In the course of this he will invariably hesitate. At this moment the critic intervenes, and tells the author what he really *has* said. What he really has said relates to what he really is. The assumption is that he is as ignorant of one as of the other. Thus the weakness of the book becomes his personal character weakness. The weakness of each character illustrates still another facet of his own depravity. The method must be employed on several levels—political, ethical, sexual and economic. The instant he seeks to defend himself on any score, the critic dredges up from his memory some folly or vice or worse in the author's life which is clearly reflected in the matter at hand. Everything goes in method three. Nothing is unfair. The object really is not to change the book but to change the man himself. He must therefore be stripped to the buff and forced to see his deformities for what they are. He has no defense at all. Method three has the following advantage over methods one and two: whereas method one merely sends the author off to work for another year without

committing the critic in any way to the final product, and whereas method two destroys the book completely but leaves the author a clear alternative, method three destroys both the book and the man. It produces a real qualitative change, and this is criticism on the highest level.

Because Cleo and I are so fond of you we feel a deeper obligation to this book than we have ever felt before to such a project. Therefore we are going into it thoroughly; and instead of applying only one method of criticism, we shall apply all three. We think the result will give you a pretty rounded picture.

. . . .

D.T.

26. To Ring Lardner, Jr.

Mexico City
June 25, 1953

Lardner:

In 1942 or '43 or whenever it was we were working on something you had dreamed up called *The Fishermen of Beaudrais,* I was not only an older and therefore more experienced man than you; I was also a better drinker, drove a more powerful car, owned a bigger house and drew a larger salary.

During this period I explained to you at some length that the proper way to make a dash on a typed script is (—) rather than (-). Now, glancing over your most recent fable, I observe that you still persist in the incorrect (-) instead of the proper (—).

Pigheadedness is an ugly thing no matter where encountered.

Yours,
TRUMBO

27. Rough draft of a letter to Michael Wilson

Mexico City
November 15, 1953

Dear old boy: [28]

I have at hand what purports to be a letter from you dated November 5th. In it you make boozy statements to the effect that I told you during your gaudy visit to our parts that I was returning to the United States during the summer that has just passed. In fact and in truth, I told you—and asked you to convey to other friends—the specific information that we should not return until immediately after January 1 of 1954. I went into great detail on this matter, explaining all reasons therefore.

I now see that, for all the effect it had, I might as well have been whispering to an empty gin bottle. I do not blame you too much, however, for your badly confused impression of what I thought was clear English. I should have waited until I caught you sober to convey information of such importance. However you were only here a few weeks, and I was neither wily enough nor persistent enough to catch you without strong waters in your hand. Now that you have the truth of the matter, I trust you will dispel all the misinformation you have so obviously been dispensing.

Speaking of your devotion to the blood of Christ in its holiest and most sacramental sense, I sneaked off the other night to that place where we had such elegant revels together and was beset with solicitous questions about "El Borracho" as they simperingly refer to you. Rosalia is the same, and asks to be especially remembered to you. Paquita, the one with the enormous wen, made the most lusty

[28] Michael Wilson, one of Trumbo's most admired friends, has, in spite of the blacklist, achieved a solid list of credits. Four months after being summoned before HUAC in 1951, *A Place in the Sun,* his pre-blacklist screenplay adaptation of *An American Tragedy,* received an Oscar. The following year his screenplay *Five Fingers,* was produced and nominated for an Academy Award. Two years later another of his old scripts, *Friendly Persuasion,* was produced and released without any screen credits. When it appeared Wilson was likely to win another Oscar, the Academy ruled that blacklisted writers were ineligible for awards; ironically, it was the same year (1956) that Robert Rich won the award for the best original story. *Friendly Persuasion* went on to win the Cannes Film Festival Award. Wilson, like Trumbo, continued practicing his craft in the black market. He wrote the final draft of *The Bridge on the River Kwai* for Sam Spiegel and David Lean, as well as the first draft of *Lawrence of Arabia.* Although the British Writers Guild Award for Best Dramatic Screenplay of 1962 was presented to him and Robert Bolt for the latter film, his name did not appear on the screen. His most successful recent film is *Planet of the Apes.* Wilson was a captain (later major) in the Marine Corps during World War II, on active duty in the Pacific Theatre of Operations.

and complimentary comments upon your physique. She suggests, however, in view of certain matters that have lately been brought to her attention by complaining customers and the department of health, that you avail yourself immediately of the services of a good clap doctor. I don't know what she means and I felt it indelicate to inquire more specifically. You know how modest she is anyhow. So I simply pass the hint on for what it is worth.

As for our condition, we are living out an old truism: "The first time you see Mexico you are struck by the horrible poverty: within a year you discover it's infectious." I am as broke as a bankrupt's bastard. I am by now an old customer of the Monte de Piedad (Mount of Pity), so called because it is the government pawnshop and charges only 36% interest per year. We have at the moment reposing in the vaults of this benign institution a diamond ring, two gold cigarette lighters, a gold cigarette case, my watch, a Leica camera, as well as certain objects of the Butlers' I hocked for them in a moment of need. The appraisers down there regard me as a thief, but apparently one who knows how to stay out of trouble, hence they respect me.

Precisely how we are going to get back I don't know, but we keep up our brave intention to try. Indeed, we have no other course, for I cannot make it here. Three months ago I wrote and submitted to the general market an absolutely sure-fire shooting script. Normally it would have brought a quick 20 Gs. It has just sold (or so I am told, the papers theoretically being in the works) for $2,500 down, $7,500 in six months, $10,000 deferred and to be taken out of recoupment of the negative cost, and $10,000 against five percent of the producers' share of the profits. Holy Christ! And this was what one might call a successful enterprise!

. . . .

My general plans are this: return in January, rent some large, gloomy, drafty, run-down old house, get my furniture out of storage, and try to devote half my time to earning a living and the other half to serious work. I am not too sure of pictures any more, and therefore am trying, through a front, to open up the magazine market, in which I used to be an occasional dabbler. (Incidentally, that nauseating deal I mentioned a paragraph ago is all minus 20% that goes to the front! Madre de Dios!)

Poetry? Who the hell has time for poetry? I have one that is in the works which has a nice jumpy start that I like:

> The week-end dies with the sunset gun
> And a hundred thousand green convertible Cads
> Turn right on the carbon-monoxide trail
> Toward the chemical shrine of the plastic grail
> Where the pulse flickers high in a neon flower

As night filters down
    through the steel-cut lace
        of an arabesque ivory tower.

And one about Mortimer Adler, who told *Time* magazine he always got A's in school and never took off his clothes in the daytime, which poses the question "Whatever became of Mortimer Adler?" and tries to end with:

Did he pay off his debts?
Did he just run down?
Did he take off his clothes in the sun?
Or did God bend low on a desperate day
To award him a last and permanent A?
Is that why he seems to have been away?
Nobody knows
Nobody knows
Nobody knows at all
    Just what
    ever became
    of
    Mortimer Adler.

Then sometimes I get terribly upset about the pixies—especially the literary ones—and have delusions that they are on the verge of taking over completely. And I try to mimic them:

Now is a time to taste delicious fears
To analyze perception's agony
And gaze on murdered purity's sweet corpse
Let's sing of prisms, cubes and shivered shards
Of mysteries and signs and artichokes
The whole embroidered with derivatory jokes
And graven carefully upon our secret sand
In words that none but us will understand

Come now we arm in arm to purple evening
Into this weird and somber loveliness
Under this rotting phosphorescent star
Where perfume hisses from the dead quince tree
Here to lament with all our neutered kin
God's really unforgivable sin
Which laid out Eve upon the morning lawn
For Adam to inform upon

<pre>
                        Thus
                     we dance
                   the may-pole
                 tree, mad as poets
               only be, two by two and
             three by three, writing verses
           daintily, triolets of mystery and
         couplet of a history that poor blind
       Homer never knew—that doltish, cloddish
               Homer never knew
     And if by chance one of our number starts to shout
             We simply turn upon his eyes
                        and
                        peck
                        them
                        out
</pre>

And then there is this:

> To do justice to the stature of a political person,
> One must judge him not only by what he has achieved
> but also by what he aimed to achieve.

> He who wants to master destiny,
> To point new paths for his epoch to pursue,
> Who feels he has a task and avocation to fulfill
> And sets out to kindle his spiritual flame in others,
> Challenges a world of incomprehension,
>   Of rejection
>   Of hostility.

> For the only thing
> That makes sense in life
> Is struggle.

This last is a direct quote from a letter written by Ernst Thaelmann in 1944 and smuggled out of prison shortly before they murdered him. I think it astonishing how well it breaks down into poetry.

I consider that your question about poetry has now been answered. Nothing completed, nothing really satisfactory.

Please write at once and tell me what you mean by that's [Hollywood] where the money is. Do you have any visible evidence of this? Are some of us actually sneaking a crumb now and again? Or is the whole thing just another hysterical rumor? In any event, tell me about it fully, tell me over and over again about all that money because Lennie [29] likes to hear such talk. Lennie *needs* money.

On the other hand, maybe you'd better not write at all. I'm an older man than you, have greater responsibilities, and my time on

[29] Trumbo is referring to himself as Lennie, the well-known character of John Steinbeck's novel, *Of Mice and Men*.

this earth grows short. Already it has cost me a great deal of effort and half a pound of typewriter ribbon to answer the silly inquiries contained in your last communication. If you answered this letter, you would consider me discourteous if I did not once more reciprocate, and I simply haven't got the strength to do it. So forget about it. No reason to start something we can't stop. I wish you hadn't written in the first place. People ought to stop interfering with each other and writing all those letters.

Please give our regards to Zelma [Mrs. Wilson] .... Within sixty days, God willing and the winds favorable, our ragged caravan will arrive, nervous, hungry and beady-eyed with greed. If our fortunes have not improved by that time somebody will simply have to move over.

Fretfully,
D.T.

P.S. Paquita sends her best to [Paul] Jarrico. She makes merry quips about his health, and hopes he's getting well. Also you, you sonofabitch, still owe me fifteen pesos.

28. To Sam Sillen

Mexico City
December 5, 1953

Dear Sam:

The book [30] due perhaps to the irregularity of local mails, arrived four days after your letter. I sat down and read it at once. I concluded I could do a good review of it; however, as I made false start after false start, I realized that it was going to be much more difficult than I had thought. Then, going back over the book several more times, I began to doubt it would be possible for me to do a review that would do the book justice. Late last night, after many false starts and being hung up for over a week on it, I came to the conclusion that I ought not to do it. I was going to wire you this morning (Saturday), but I realized that probably the wire wouldn't reach you until Monday anyhow, due to week-end office hours, and that a special delivery letter would be just as fast and much cheaper.

I think that portion of the book—over half—which analyzes the content of cold-war pictures is absolutely brilliant, and very long overdue. I agree completely with the theoretical basis of the book, and with its conclusions. These conclusions, however, do not carry

[30] John Howard Lawson's *Film in the Battle of Ideas.*

conviction to me, nor do they logically urge me to action to carry them out, mainly because I feel that the book lacks the real evidence to support its conclusions.

It would take me pages to put my reasons for the above paragraph into comprehensible English; and it would require certain reference material on motion pictures which I do not have at hand, due to my accursed residence here without books of practically any kind. But let me summarize as briefly as possible what I object to in the book— or what I think I *would* object to if I had the material at hand to support my conclusions:

It is indicated that about 1945–47 a *change* in the *content* of motion pictures was essential. The change in content that ensued is magnificently dissected and proved. But nowhere is there a clear statement of what the change was *from*—what *previous* content was objected to and had to be destroyed to advance the present cold-war content.

It is stated—and I agree—that films should not be abandoned, that the fight for employment of progressives is one with the fight for progressive content. But this statement, however true, exists in a vacuum if it is not shown what small concessions in content *were* obtained when progressives *did* have the employment that they now are urged to fight for. If you do not show what they *did* accomplish when they had the chance—if, indeed, you imply that they accomplished practically nothing, as is implied here—then you lend credence to the theory that no accomplishment is possible.

I think the inevitable result of ignoring the fierce and sometimes successful struggles in the motion picture industry for trade union organization, for industry-wide anti-fascist political action, and for concessions in the content of film itself which occurred from 1933 to 1945—in which concessions *were* wrested from the medium, although naturally its function as a class spokesman was not shaken— in which progress *was* made—if all this is ignored, if it is actually derogated—then regardless of the theoretical soundness of an injunction to fight for content and employment—regardless of statements that it can and ought to be done—still there will be immobilization and inactivity, because there is no evidence that it ever *was* done, or that it is actually possible.

The total effect of the book, in this respect, seems to me to engender this response to its argument: then why fight? Why help the bourgeoise perfect its own instrument? What hope is there of wresting even the slightest concession in this period, when apparently all of our efforts during a much more favorable period came to nothing?

In spite of mistakes, which were many, and defeats, which were great—I cannot get over the idea that the Committee [HUAC] attacked Hollywood for a *reason*. I think it had three reasons: (1) to destroy trade unions; (b) to paralyze anti-fascist political action; and (c) to remove progressive content from films. There *must* have been *some* progressive content, *some* results of progressive action in Hollywood, or Jack would not write (page 27): "There was to be no more talk of human aspirations and national social objectives." What *was* this talk of "human aspirations and national social objectives?" We must know what it was, we must see what limited successes were achieved, in order to feel that even minor concessions are possible in the future. I think the content of films was *better* in 1943 than it is in 1953. I think that anti-fascist films *were* being made in 1943 (not perfect, not profound, but still anti-fascist) and that anti-communist films are being made in 1953. Yet this is not gone into. If it is not gone into, then I'm afraid negative results will be obtained today in any fight for even the slightest progressive content in films.

This is my main fear concerning the book. I'm afraid it is a deep one, and does not permit me to review the book as constructively as it ought to be reviewed. It is deep because I'm afraid the purpose of the book—to bring about action based on sound theoretical knowledge—is negative by lack of the material I cite above to show that it is possible.

There are minor things which I also might question. For example, the implication on page 94 that TV has nothing, or very little, to do with falling box-office receipts; and the corollary implication that sex and sadism are more likely responsible.

I haven't read the Geoffrey Wagner piece cited in support of the implication that TV can't be held accountable for the film box-office drop, but I do know this: there are 25,700,000 TV sets in the United States today. They were purchased at an average cost of $250 each, for a total capital investment on the part mainly of the lower middle class and workers of $6.5 billions. The $6.5 billions came directly out of the entertainment budget of the American family. At fifty cents per theatre ticket, it means that the American public paid out the equivalent of 13 billion movie tickets for their TV sets. Add to this the cost of operation, the cost of repairs, and the rising cost of living which daily requires more money for necessities and less for entertainment, and I think the drain from film to TV is immensely increased. One show alone costs its sponsor $25,000,000 per year, and the sponsor believes he is getting his money's worth because he believes he is getting an audience. At this very moment 40% of all motion picture directors, 50% of assistant directors, 40% of technicians, and 33% of writers are working for TV. Additionally, TV in color is coming in this year, and the industry anticipates that all black and white sets will be replaced by color within four years—at a further immense investment on the part of the formerly movie-going public. Somehow all of this *must* have its repercussions on the motion picture box office.

Now one might say that the rise in TV audience is due, not to the invention of TV, not to the expenditure of $6.5 billions in sets, but because the quality of pictures has declined so greatly that the film industry has forced its audience to go elsewhere. Indeed almost this is said in the next paragraph on page 95: "It remains to be seen whether sex and sadism can be made more alluring in three dimensions than in two."

But in regard to this, we have to remember that in a period of enormously declining motion picture box-office receipts, there have been certain pictures that have been immense hits; pictures that for the most part really surpass the success of the great hits of the most prosperous years of Hollywood. And these, by and large, are precisely those pictures which *are* composed of "sex and sadism." And they are selling it in two dimensions, also. Namely: *Quo Vadis, Salome, David and Bethsheba, Samson and Delilah, The Greatest Show on Earth, Gentlemen Prefer Blondes, Come Back, Little Sheba, From Here to Eternity.* I do not believe that there is any other two-year period in motion pictures which contained so many really smashing box-office successes. And, from all appearances, certain pictures will be just as successful in the new wide-screen process, as for example *The Robe* and *How to Marry a Millionaire.*

In a word, we can't have our cake and eat it too. We cannot, on the one hand, assert that people abandon films for TV in revolt against content such as sex and sadism, while on the other hand the figures seem to show that in a period of declining box-office, the only films which can woo people by the millions from TV back to pictures are precisely those pictures which specialize in sex and sadism—in bad content.

I think other conclusions could be drawn, some of them perhaps even alarming and calling for the most energetic action. I think their discussion would deeply involve the matter of esthetics, of *taste.* I think it very important for us to consider to what degree the public revolts against current content, and to what degree it accepts it, and is conditioned by it. Taste as a part of the superstructure, or as a direct result of it. But I don't think we should blink off the success of rotten films, nor ignore the fact that 25 million television sets might even diminish the audience for good films.

Anyhow, you see how complicated it is? And how impossible it is for me, without movie research material here, to deal with the book justly? I think much work is going to have to be done on this problem, that it is one of the most complex cultural problems we face, that it has always been so, and that Jack's book is a remarkable addition to our literature on it and a step ahead.

But I simply cannot review it. . . . Our affectionate regards go to you and yours and all our friends.

DALTON

29. To Betty Parsons Ragsdale of *McCall's* Magazine

Mexico City
December 14, 1953

Dear Miss Ragsdale:

We were out of the city when your letter arrived, and have returned only today to discover that you are going to take "The Child-Beater." [31] I cannot tell you how pleased I am, nor how grateful for what seems to me a very substantial price.

In relation to the story, there are two small word changes I should like to make, if you will be so kind as to do them for me. On page 13, very near the bottom, there occurs the phrase, "They all ran true to form . . ." I should prefer to cut the *true,* so that it reads, "They all ran to form . . ." Again on page 17, second paragraph, occurs a phrase, "but with that particular frown . . ." I should like to change it to, "but with that particular expression."

About myself, there is very little of interest. I was born in California in 1916, and educated there. I have been married twice. My second marriage, which proceeds most happily, has produced three children—a boy and two girls—ranging in age from seven to fourteen years. I have written a number of things in my spare time, and this is the first that has been accepted. My husband is engaged in selling. We have lived in Mexico for something over a year, but shall return to the United States in January or February of the new year. Whether we then shall live in Los Angeles or in Chicago depends upon my husband's work.

The Demaine in my signature to the story is a family name on my maternal side. The C. F. is obvious. I have the feeling I should prefer what readers I may have to think of C. F. Demaine as a man, for I am thoroughly persuaded that for a while longer at least it is still

---

[31] The black market was so well established among popular magazines by 1953 that Trumbo would not risk his name for submission. He wrote "The Child Beater," signing C. F. Demaine and had Mrs. Trumbo sign the cover letter with her maiden name—Cleo Fincher. On December 9, 1953, Miss Fincher was notified that *McCall's* had enthusiastically bought the story for $850.00. When the fiction editor wanted to know something about Cleo Fincher, Trumbo improvised the fabricated biography that concludes the letter. As to the line, "My husband is engaged in selling," Trumbo says, "a truer line was never written."

a man's world. And until I am much more successful than I presently feel I shall be, I don't wish anyone but my family and a close friend or two to know that I am writing.

Once again let me tell you how very happy your letter has made me.[32]

Sincerely,
CLEO FINCHER

30. To Mr. and Mrs. Hugo Butler and Mr. and Mrs. George Pepper

La Canada, California
[c. February, 1954]

Dear Butlers and Peppers: [33]

Because I so hate to write letters, this will constitute, in original and carbon, my definitive report to both of you. Then, in addition, I enclose a specific letter to George and another to Hugo about specific matters—the personal touch, so to speak.

We started out well and happy on a certain morning, driven by Señor Camargo, who made sheep's eyes at the señorita. I saw to it that no physical contact was had by either party, although there was a certain amount of leering on both sides. We arrived for the first night in Victoria, and, about four the next afternoon, in Matamoros, where we checked into the San Antonio Hotel, Camargo departing immediately for his return trip.

I then went to Auto Servicio Cuesta to look into the matter of the

[32] Other inventions had to follow: On December 18 literary representatives Mavis McIntosh and Elizabeth McKee asked to handle Miss Fincher's work. Trumbo replied on December 22, 1953. "I am most pleased that Mrs. Ragsdale considers my work worthy of representation by your office, and shall be equally pleased to send you whatever I may do in the future. I am at present finishing another short story which probably shan't be ready until after the holidays." The literary agents wanted autobiographical sketches, more stories, and permission to sell "The Child Beater" to television. On May 19, 1955 Cleo Fincher received a check for $360.00 from Lewisler Television Productions and still another plea for more fiction.

[33] George and Jeanette Pepper became close friends of the Trumbos in Mexico. Mr. Pepper's diversified career has included concert violin training, motion picture production, and political activities. Before leaving Hollywood he was Executive Secretary of the Hollywood Democratic Committee, successfully managed several California political campaigns and became a high ranking official for the Independent Citizens' Committee for the Arts, Sciences and Professions. He produced four films anonymously in Mexico—among them Robinson Crusoe and Torrero—before his death in 1969.

trailer. It was stored in an open shed. The seals were all broken. In fact both rear doors were broken also, although the hinges had been cheaply welded back on again. A long and somewhat anguished talk with Señor Cuesta revealed that the trailer had been inefficiently stashed away on the truck; that it had overturned somewhere along the road while inside the truck; that both doors had been torn off by the impact; that the truck driver had stopped and repacked it, meanwhile slyly having the door hinges welded on again to distract attention from the damage. The repacking was brilliant in its perversity—all light and crushable items being expertly stowed away at the bottom; all heavy ones on top of them. I repacked the trailer on the spot, at cost of God knows what labor and profanity. The only things missing were two vases—the Chupicuaro abstract duck and the Chupicuaro vase that George had given me. They had been packed inside a jacket on top of the load, and apparently had been broken in the crack-up, so the driver shrewdly discarded them altogether.

There ensued a discussion with the kids who were extremely anxious to get across the border that night, since it appeared improbable we would be able to get the jeep out of storage in Brownsville on a Sunday. So, with a flash of inspiration, I realized that the jeep could easily enter Matamoros on a perfectly legal basis. I promptly telephoned, and had it sent to the hotel. Then I hooked it onto the trailer, and, it now being dark, we sailed away to the border.

Bringing the jeep across was a mistake. Mexican custom officials professed the darkest suspicion. They demanded papers on the car, and in vain did I explain to them that it had been in storage for a year. They professed to believe, on the contrary, that I had been illegally using it in Mexico during the entire period. There ensued a long argument, during which I engaged some six or eight different persons in my fluent conversational Spanish. They demanded papers; I countered with storage receipt. They threatened jail and nationalization of car; I countered with yelps for the American consul. Finally I got hold of a man who understood decent Spanish, and this part of the situation was cleared up.

But something more ominous had been brewing. There had been fights all day long all along the border, braceros trying to get across and Mexican officials trying to prevent them, with Gringos on the American side beckoning to them over the heads of their own government. This made for a feeling of nastiness which, aggravated by a particularly hot day, and their original suspicion of me *re* the jeep, caused them to set upon the contents of the trailer with loud whoops of vindictive joy. Every blessed thing was unloaded and carefully pawed through.

There was one violent argument about a label "silver foxes." The man knew what silver meant, and he went on a skillful hunt for the plata. When I protested that the label referred to "un animal, color de plata," not only did they increase their search for the silver, but they scurried about trying to find the extra animal I was trying to sneak through.

At this point somebody came upon the replica of the Mayan head I purchased at the Museum of Anthropology. They had previously, to my relief, passed all the genuine items over. But this was too much! Here, indeed, was a national treasure! Perhaps from the museum itself. When I confirmed that it was indeed from the museum the shit was in the fan for fair. All the cosas were unpacked before my horrified eyes. We went through the whole blessed pack, down to the last fragment, with loud yells of "son autenticos" and "son falsas." Or something like that. In any event, everything was snatched, including some of Nikola's fake Teotihuacáns, and a couple of rag dolls. They almost seized the porcelain figures of the nativity, but doubtless because of their sacred nature, they finally spared them.

These unpleasantries completed, my whole boodle was kept, and I given a receipt for it, together with an appointment for Monday with the Aduana. Then, amidst savage shrieks, they threw everything together again and heaped it into the trailer in such a fashion that the doors wouldn't close. I tied them together, and crept across the border at about midnight.

On the American side we caused almost as much consternation as we had on the Mexican. We had an efficient new official, serving his first year, and neither he nor his more experienced associates had ever seen quite such a passel of stuff come across under such peculiar circumstances. I was therefore obliged to unload the entire mess, and reload it—all myself, no porters at that time of night. I tell you, friends, I was tuckered. Also it was 2:30 a.m. After all had been settled, and the trailer repacked, one of the customs officials, who, after all, was still a human being, called me aside and, warning me not to say anything to anybody about it, said that right across the road was a city police car that had been staked out waiting for me to take to the road. Once I did this, it was the intention of the copper to arrest me on a charge of having no plates.

Oh worry, worry. I thanked the fellow, and inquired where the police station was. It turned out to be just in back of the customs office. I jumped into the jeep and moved across the government parking lot, stopping in front of the police headquarters. This finesse brought the pursuing officer up in surprise, and he hung in the background, grinding his teeth and pretending not to be there at all. I went to the gent in charge of coppers and told him my situation *re* the license plates. He was properly sympathetic, and told me to get to a motel, and that if I was picked up on the way, he would stand in back of me. However I could not drive the car on Sunday, nor, indeed, until I got plates on Monday, the drive to the motel excepted. I thanked him and went back to the jeep.

I stepped on the starter. Nothing happened. The battery was out. It was three o'clock in the morning, and I just collapsed over the wheel and began to sob. The children consoled me. I bucked up, went back to the gent in charge of coppers, and asked if there was a wrecking truck that could haul me away to a motel. He averred there was, called one on the spot, and even told him which motel was most likely to have a vacancy, this being a big tourist day in Brownsville, although God knows why. Front end was thereupon hoisted into the air, and away he went. The motel had no vacancies. I started to sob again. At this point the copper in the car who had originally been laying for us drove up. He had just received instructions to pick up two kids, dog, cat and old man, together with bags, and drive them in his car until proper accommodations were found for them. So in we piled, bag, baggage, kids and beasties. The wrecking car moved off toward a garage with the car. The copper, a little sullen at thus being obliged to chauffeur one whom he had been sure was destined to become his victim, drove to four courts before we found refuge. He was heartily glad to be rid of us. And we were heartily glad to place arses to sheets. End part one.

Part two. The next (Sunday) afternoon I cross the border to get in touch, somewhat tardily, with Señor Palacios. Take wrong bridge, and earn undying hostility of officials there, who sternly warn me to take other bridge hereafter. Antigringo feeling still strong. Talk to Palacios. He is very very sorry. Couldn't have done anything in first place, now finds it doubly impossible, since to interfere would make the customs people think bad of him. Curse you and your squeamishness, Sr. Palacios! Also, there is no possibility of influencing the Aduana, for he is a new man, a former judge, and "the most honest man in Mexico." Imagine! My heart burst on the spot. I returned to Brownsville, my shaggy head bowed with distress, and fell into a restless, nervous slumber.

Next morning to license department for a $3.00 drive-through permit on car. Then excelsior, and on to Matamoros, where I am now widely known and making fresh enemies by the hour. I discuss with the Aduana, who even looks honest. Then I discuss with his expert, who likewise has been convinced by the Mayan head that some looter is at work. I am regretfully informed that they will hold the stuff for thirty days. If within that time I do not secure a permit from the Secretary of Education, they will be seized and sold. I counter with the idea that, since I live in Mexico City, I send them back there. It is agreed upon. Bravo, bravo!

Immediately the air clears. I am given a room in the customs house, and my dear ones are brought to me. I am provided with paper and materials and assistance. I pack each with loving care, shedding a tear over this one and that one before tucking it away. Then the man with metal tape appears, cinches them. Then we are off to the express office, a whole convoy of us, and they are returned, seven packets, each insured for 1,000 pesos. Then back to the Aduana, who merely looks at the express receipt, thanks me, returns it without even making a note of the transaction, and, after liberal tipping to all concerned except the Aduana, I am off again for Brownsville and its ceaseless round of pleasure.

Tuesday morning, the children munching hamburgers and Hershey bars as they have been steadily doing ever since striking the auld sod, we take off. First day, 504 miles to Sanderson, Texas. Second day 545 miles straight through Texas and New Mexico to Globe, Arizona. Third day, 510 miles to Altadena, and the blessed arms of my mate, who is snuffling from a cold.

There a motel for daughter, son, father, dog, and cat. Dog for first time shits on floor, costing ten bucks upon vacating the joint. Son and daughter steadily eating hamburgers and Hershey bars. Tootsie Rolls coming in a strong third. I sniffing bourbon and hunting for houses, of which there are none. Those we can afford are too small, and those that are large enough we can't afford. I spend three days each in various sectors, begging like a runaway slave. No good.

Then we stumble upon this place, which was originally an old Spanish fort, used as a redoubt in the early wars against the Coast Indians. It is very high on a hill, and very deep in a forest, and for years had been forgotten. We took it for two hundred bucks a month, six months and an option for six. Four bedrooms, four baths, study, loggia with TV, dining room, living room, breakfast room, kitchen, maid's room and bath, immense laundry, vast barbecue outside in one of two walled gardens, has nine holes just like a shithouse.

We borrow a fast $1,200 to get our furniture out of hock, and pay for moving expenses. Turns out that our gates are too low—we have gates here, with lights, and a quarter mile driveway—for the trucks to pass through. Already we have one truck from one warehouse with three men, another truck from another warehouse with two men. Being unable to get within gunshot of the house, they each telephone their masters, and two small trucks manned by two more men are dispatched. Altogether seven men and four trucks are now involved, neighborhood is in an uproar, and guards are being posted all along the route to forestall an attack from the old fort. Total cost, over four hundred bucks for one day's misery. But we are in.

Well, yes and no. Some stuff isn't yet unpacked. Some may never be. We have too many books, too much silver, too much of everything; God, why am I such a packrat? We see, when the Johnston-Fidelity stuff is unloaded, that we have paid dearly for some old Butler crap. Justice has come its full turn, for Butler stuff is now in *our* garage, and *our* cars are outside.

Yes, we have two cars. Second, a three-month-old Nash hard top sport Rambler, very sleek, very racy, with a tire on the back and six little cylinders in front that draw about twenty miles to the gallon. Poor devil who had it had paid in $1,000, saw he couldn't make it, and turned it over to us in return for nothing—we just keep up payments. Run five thousand miles, it gives thrills by reason of the fact that one's arse is so close to the ground in it. Everybody turns around and looks at the five of us, I can tell you, when we're out in our Rambler.

Made a speech, going to make two more, going to write a pamphlet. People here all seem in good shape. A few starving, many just getting by, some doing well. Many writers have completely changed profession. The Lees have just opened a ladies' apparel shop in the valley. Adrian [Scott] has gone to work for Norvell Crutcher's toy factory, which now grosses half a million a year. Rinaldo is still selling paper, and apparently making a go of it. There was a revue at the Embassy the first week we were here—a musical called *State of the Nation*—which I thought excellent. Fred [Saidy] had done some of the lyrics. The place was perhaps two hundred short of capacity, so, since it seats over eighteen hundred, it was a hell of a crowd, and very encouraging. I would say offhand that people here have less dread of the future than some of our friends in Mexico, and are able to act much more freely.

I went to work five days after I arrived, have finished the job, am taking on another today, and also am experimenting in TV. Have an agent. Think I can make a pretty good living, probably 25 and 40 Gs per anum (or how do you spell it?). I think we can live practically as cheaply here as there. Meat is higher, of course, but it all has flavor, and the lamb isn't goat. Coffee terrible. Many paper products and drugs much cheaper. Clothes cheaper and shoes. Liquor terribly high. We now drink bourbon and water. We save by buying by the quart rather than the fifth; we also save by taking a case at a time at 10% discount, which considerably lowers it. But still it is naturally much more. Example of one thing that is considerably cheaper: our rent there, 1,200; tuition, 450; transportation, 100; books, about 20 per month. Here our rent is two hundred dollars (not bucks)—and the rest, including bus transportation and books, is all free. This is a substantial saving. Also, we no longer lay out that $80 a month storage. Of course we have no help, and shall have to buy washing machine and dryer, and hire a woman two days a week at $10 per day or thereabouts. Our house has stove, icebox, and TV. Our total expenses will probably be up about 20%, but then our income will increase by more than that. *Thief* has been optioned for an off-Broadway production, which, if it goes through, will have Zero Mostel as the undertaker, Rex Ingraham (excellent idea!) as the doctor, and Will Geer as the druggist. Also a possibility of a reprint of *Johnny*, the plates of which I own. And other possibilities.

Cleo still has not got over her cold, and, her experience with doctors not having given her too great a degree of confidence in their judgment, has concluded to cure herself by sleep and food and liquor in appropriate quantities. Chris at the moment is at home with a general gland infection. Mitzi wishes she were in Mexico. She hit her head at school and the kids laughed, and she was hurt and opined that her friends in Mexico were not nearly so fiendish, especially Mary. Chris, I think, is still lonely, but will get going quickly. Nikola is gloriously adjusted, announces that already she is in with the best gang at school. She has some new clothes, and sweaters that stick out in front with those two handsome things, and is peeling off a little weight. Her hair is cut short also, which is a blessing and adds to her attractiveness. I am back on cigarettes in limited quantities. Weakness of will? Perhaps. Actually, my appetite increased so enormously, and my weight shot up so steadily—ten pounds!—that my clothes wouldn't fit, so I went back on the weed almost as a matter of economic necessity, and the weight is now dropping again. I also passed an insurance physical exam with flying colors. I trust that [Dr.] Jake gives me a good send-off down there when the inquiry concerning me arrives from the insurance company.

Interruption: the quack has just departed, after a discussion about Chris. Symptoms, recurrent fever, accompanied by sore throat, headaches, swelling of glands in neck, armpits, and groin. Tentative diagnosis, to be confirmed tomorow by a blood count: mononucleosis. If so, the only cure he knows is about six weeks bed rest. I give you all these symptoms with the idea in mind that someone will ask Jake if such signs indicate some mysterious Mexican disease that local quacks are not equipped to recognize or diagnose.

Salt of the Earth [34] opens March 15 in New York City. I haven't seen it. [Paul] Trivers, who is fairly tough, however, tells me that despite a few minor technical flaws, it is a magnificent film. He says he was so carried along by the sheer honesty of the story and the remarkable performance of the actors that he felt his emotions constantly threatening to choke him up. They have been having a series of previews in New York before large groups. All of the reports that have come back are absolutely stunning. It was shown to labor leaders, then ministers, then lawyers, then professional people. All agreed to its right to be released, regardless of the various ideological differences they may or may not have had with its content. Even Morris Ernst spoke in behalf of its right to be seen. Thus the campaign of preparation has been very careful, and may pay off in allies if there is strong pressure against its being released.

One great advantage they had in shooting it: the women they show

[34] An independent film with social and proletarian subject matter prepared and made by a number of Hollywood blacklistees. Michael Wilson wrote the screenplay. Herbert Biberman directed and Paul Jarrico produced.

on the picket line are actually the women who were on the line; the
women they show in jail are women who *were* in jail under the
precise conditions of the screen story itself. The result is, or so I am
told, a kind of honesty that has never before appeared in American
films. Mike left last night for New York and the opening. There will
be opposition, but there will also be support, and one way or another
the film will be shown, which is all to the good for everybody. I
think you will be seeing Ben [Margolis] down there if he's not there
already.

Three or four days later: (been working)—Forget about Chris. It
is a virus. The Pasadena School System, to which La Canada belongs,
is fine about this kind of thing; if a student is to be out two weeks or
longer, they send a teacher for free every day to the house. Chris
takes a dim view of such solicitude.

About the picture [*Salt of the Earth*], it opened last night. It was
well policed and there was no trouble of any kind. They had a pre-
miere at upped prices. House filled. (I think between 400 and 500
seats.) Then they went right on with a second show at the regular
dollar-twenty. Line a block long and turnaways. They called after
the reviews came out. The report was meager, and they were very
naturally exhilarated. They said Crowther in the *Times* gave it a
"magnificent" review; the *News* was "good"; the *Herald Tribune*
was "long," said the film was a fraud, but that everyone should see
it (to be sure of such idiocy, I presume). Anyhow, they have done
it, and good, bad, or indifferent I bow to them. Mike will be back
soon. We are going to see a private showing of it this Thursday, the
first such one here.

Work thing looks better and better.

There! I have done it for one of the few times in my life. Hereafter my notes shall be curt and to the point. But let no one raise his
voice to say that Trumbo didn't write a detailed account of his adventures in gringoland. We're glad to be here; we miss those we left
behind; and we find our thoughts recurring to the idea of a Mexican
vacation!

Salud!

D.T.

P.S. I suggest that the story of the cosas—which could, I realize,
afford much hilarity—not to be told to anyone, it being solely for the
ears of Butlers and Peppers. For I really do not intend so easily to be
cheated of my prey . . . DT

31. Extract of a letter to Albert Maltz

La Canada, California
March 10, 1954

I have sampled the waters here briefly, and have reason to believe I shall be able to earn a living. In fact, I have already made an
encouraging start in that direction—the first earned money to come
into the treasury in some time. People here seem generally well, and
in good condition. Friend Joe [McCarthy] has suffered some severe
setbacks lately, and the democrats are fighting in fair form. Many of
our old friends have given up writing entirely, and turned to other
lines of work. None is getting rich, some are actually suffering, but
by and large an adjustment is being made. I noted, with keen interest, Phil Dunne's picture in the paper the other day, accepting an
award for some biblical film he wrote.[35]

32. To Elsie McKeogh

La Canada, California
March 15, 1954

Dear Elsie:

About this mysterious publisher in England: [36] I would, of course,
be glad to make changes which have pertinence. *Johnny* is kind of
its period, and I should be interested in what the suggestions are that
would bring it "up to date." I think, if published there, it ought to
have a brief preface explaining the period, etc.

About another novel from me: I am, and have been steadily,
sweating away on a rather long novel, dealing with the San Francisco
Peace Conference and the last phase of the Pacific War. I am obliged
to do this between spurts of money work, but it progresses. I haven't
yet any opinion about it, except that its subject matter will probably
not be popular in the United States, provided the United States a
year hence continues in the same direction it presently is headed.
(There are, incidentally, I think, certain signs that the direction
won't pay off, with the consequent possibility of a reversal.)

[35] Philip Dunne, a distinguished and prolific screen writer, is the son of the
late humorist Peter Finley Dunne. As a consistent opponent of the blacklist
he testified for the defense in Trumbo's contempt trial. Albert Maltz had
written a first draft screenplay of *The Robe* before being blacklisted; Dunne
was called upon to write the final draft. Because of various agreements the
Screen Writers' Guild had made with the Producers' Association, Maltz's
name did not appear on the screen.

[36] Mrs. McKeogh wrote Trumbo on March 8 that an unnamed English publisher was interested in bringing out a revised version of *Johnny Got His Gun.*

As to your pleasant question about me "working on anything in your line"—I must confess that I have, for the first time, been unfaithful to you. You recall that some years ago we discussed the possibility of a pseudonym, and you felt that in view of your years of friendship with editors you could not in conscience sell such a story without telling them of my connection with it. This attitude I respected, as we have both respected each other's points of view, and discarded the idea entirely. The truth is, of course, that I simply do not believe any top notch, commercial magazine will purchase anything from me, under mine or any other name, if they know of my authorship. Hence the agent must become—if such it be—a party to the conspiracy.

Late in the autumn, while still in Mexico, a short story idea struck me. Not having hit the market since 1937 or thereabouts, I was curious as to whether I still could, given an equal chance with anyone else. I wrote the story—seventeen pages—and sent it direct to a magazine under another and non-existent name, combined with the most elaborate, although entirely legal, apparatus through which I could cash a check and pay taxes on it. It would amuse you to see the naive letters that went to that magazine, the timidity, the reasons for using another name (reasons of the author of the story, that is, who wasn't of course me) and the general squid-like cloud that surrounded the whole business.

The story sold for $850, which I duly collected and cashed, singing praises to heaven. The editor of the magazine then went to an agent in New York and told them about this promising new writer, and the agent wrote suggesting representation, and another simple-minded letter went forward accepting the offer. There the matter stands. There is an agent; there is a name; there are connections. Of course neither agent, editor nor anyone else knows how directly the whole business is connected with me. And perhaps this is best, because at least an outlet has been hacked through the curtain—what is it, iron, bamboo, red-white-and-blue or a simple slick paper curtain?

But dammit, I've been with you longer than I have with Cleo. I have wandered away from you in open lust, and I feel sinridden and guilty. I therefore have the compulsion to confess before you catch me in that other agent's apartment, purse wide open. On the other hand, men are notoriously creatures of appetite, and if they don't find what they want in the home nest the swine are just naturally bound to wander.

The point of this is that I shall, if necessary, continue the deceit. But it would be much simpler and pleasanter if I let this new-born fictitious child of my infidelity vanish completely. Then I could create a new one, legitimatize it with a fake identity—not fake, really —and turn it over to you.

In a word, what if Cleo should write a story; what if she should send it to you using one of her family names and saying that she was taking a pseudonym for personal reasons. The story would then be signed by "John Doe"—although the real person would be Cleo—that is, the person who wrote and submitted it to you. Would you then feel compelled to reveal that Cleo was Mrs-You-Know-Who to an editor? Your checks could be made out to Cleo under her family name, and she would have an account here in that name, the income would be included in our joint income tax return, and all the world would be bright with dawn!

Cleo has come to the conclusion that she has a flair for short stories, and especially for novelettes of from 12,000 to 40,000 words in length.[37] She has sold some original stories to motion pictures, and has about decided that it is more work to write a novelette than a movie original; that there presently is a wider market for novelettes than for movie originals; and that a published novelette would stand as good a chance as an original of selling to movies, presenting the advantage of a double sale possibility for each one rather than a single sale, as in movies; and that, by doing it in this way, she would build up through copyright a literary estate, which it is impossible for her to do now, since she sells her stuff under the name of real writers to movies, pays them one-third of what is paid for the whole story, and surrenders all rights in perpetuity, or even for longer.

Now mind you, this comes from an honest penitent who has told all and who wishes to enmesh no one in his web of conspiracy. But on the other hand . . . well . . .

Best of Everything,
DALTON

33. To Robin, Asa and Dasha Bond

La Canada California
[c. March,1954]

Dear Robin, sweet Asa, beautiful Dasha—

It was such a wonderful surprise to hear from you and to receive that consoling little volume.[38]

In these times of apparent error, when mortal mind in its most malignant form seeks to confuse our material senses as to the true

[37] This is, of course, myth which Trumbo knew Mrs. McKeogh would recognize.
[38] The Bonds were Mexican residents who apparently sent Trumbo an annotated book of religious devotions in jest.

nature of Him who always stands willing to open His ears and heart to the truly penitential supplicant, it is a deep spiritual comfort to know that one has friends (even in a country prone 'neath the rump of the Whore of Rome) who think of one, and buy books for one, and read them for one, and then send them on to one all marked for one, the kernel sweetly separated from the husk.

However, until one does find a more adequate response, may one suggest that you purchase another volume—or better still three more volumes!—and then shove them up your asses, collectively or respectively, cooperatively or privately, violently or gently, with or without unguents, as God wills?

I.H.S.V.
TRUMBO

P.S.   The glory of my declining years is well, excepting a drizzly nose; she has an Italian haircut, very sluttish and appealing; she hungers and thirsts for righteousness, beefsteak and bourbon in reverse order. Her spawn continue trailing around after us and will, I daresay, keep it up until they run across a stronger scent.

P.P.S.   Could some member of your ménage à trois sneak away from prayers sometime in the next week or two for long enough to take the enclosure over to Elba 21-3? [39] It is not hot, being sent in this fashion merely to confound the curious and bewilder the infidel.

---

[39] Reference to black market work to be delivered to George Pepper in Mexico.

6.
"Work at Midnight in Thick Fog among Strangers"

Trumbo returned from Mexico an angry man with two dominant aims: to get into the black market and cultivate it, and to break the blacklist rather than let the blacklist break him and his colleagues. While the first of these objectives absorbed most of his energies during the years 1955 to 1957, he found the climate for a thriving black market greatly improved: the monolithic and monopolistic nature of the motion picture industry was fragmented by the growing success of small independent producing agencies and Hollywood right-wing groups such as the Motion Picture Alliance for the Preservation of American Ideals were shattered by their own successes. The House Committee on Un-American Activities, although it maintained a permanent investigator in the film capital, could find no more victims. The number of studio employees actually blacklisted—reported by Adrian Scott in a 1955 article for *The Hollywood Review* to be 214: 106 writers, 36 actors, and 11 directors—remained relatively static.

Early in 1955 Trumbo put out a few discreet feelers for under-the-desk work. Soon producers of low budget pictures who were used to paying roughly $3,000 per script realized that they could hire a writer formerly valued at $75,000 for their humble price; hence, while black market writers had to accept their greatly diminished value, they were simultaneously forcing many of their legitimate white market brothers out of jobs. In his first eighteen months back in the United States, Trumbo wrote a total of twelve low grade, low budget pictures. One of his strongest selling points was the fact that he guaranteed his work, rewriting without additional pay until the producer was satisfied.

So great was Trumbo's popularity with the independent studios that he soon had more work than he could handle and began to act as a clearing house or general agent for other blacklistees, again guaranteeing his own rewrite should the producer prove dissatisfied with his colleague's work. If, he reasoned, the black market could really thrive, then the blacklist itself would appear ridiculous; its purpose—to starve out leftists until they yielded to the committee—would be nullified.

1. To Hugo Butler

Los Angeles, California
[*c. January 1955*]

Dear lad:

I shall try to sketch the situation as it exists here and let you draw your own conclusions, since I am presently unable to draw very definite ones for myself.

Last year was a good year, but carried with it such imposing expenses as two moving jobs, the acquisition of two cars, a house, etc., with all the consequent economic waste, that I ended it in a state of optimistic collapse.

Taking for myself the slogan "Fifty-five is jump and jive," I decided that the time had come when I must speculate in order to get off the dreary necessity of working for mere wages. Accordingly I wrote one original screenplay, and ninety pages of a second. I stopped on page 90 of the second, because by that time the first one was launched and on the market, and I suffered psychological paralysis.

I did not take into account the new state of the market, which is that it exists, but that it is an entirely different one from that in which I had previously dealt. Whereas in the old days one dealt almost exclusively with six major studios, one now deals with them and, additionally, thirty or forty independents, each of which is quite able to pay major studio prices. The result is that a sale takes a great deal longer than I had ever previously tolerated.

For example, original screenplay #1 has now been out five weeks. It has received one rejection from a major studio (Fox—it is not hot at Fox)—yet even there one director has decided in favor of it, so Fox is not entirely out. It is described as "in the process' at other studios. There have been six inquiries as to price, and the agents have apparently given no answer, waiting for a better situation. Some big people are interested, and some little ones, and beyond that I do not know, because I have certain difficulty in contacting my front, who is new at this sort of thing, and timid. The basic soundness of the property in any market indicates to me that the property will undoubtedly sell—but when, I have no idea. And I must, of course, mother it.

Now having lived on borrowed money (from that splendid fellow from whom I purchased this house) during the two-month period of speculative writing, I concluded that I wasn't in any position to turn down cash business if it came in. The situation simply was that I did not wish to borrow further, therefore I had to discount all possibilities of speculative sale if I was to play it safe. I hoped very much not to have to take jobs, because it was precisely the jobs I was trying to avoid.

However, the dilatory progress of screenplay #1 obliged me, as a matter of caution, to take whatever came along. My year of urinating on strange bushes around the town, my careful depositing of spoor wherever it seemed likely to be smelled, produced a sudden flood—to be precise, three jobs. One screenplay is due April 15. One is due May 15. One is due May 24. Thus I am set up as far as operating expenses are concerned clear into the summer, or even into the early autumn. And my speculation is still alive. But I am hopelessly tied down until June—and although I am and was aware of my obligation to you, I simply didn't see how at the moment I can do otherwise and survive. I do hope you and George [Pepper] will find it possible to forgive me, and to understand the plight of one who insists upon living well and therefore must earn accordingly.

I want very much to do your job,[1] not only for the dough, not only for the accommodation it might be to you, but also because of the splendid free vacation it offers, and the chance of revisiting that most beautiful of cities. I have reason to hope I shall be able to make it (in a state of collapse) by mid-June. But the question is—can you wait? And if not, would you wish me to do it here, where I could actually get at it any time by stealing from other people their time? I have talked to C———— and he is both amenable and pleased.

To continue with other matters that presently hold me here. I ran across a producer of complete—almost child-like—honor with a very respectable production record in back of him, and many years of experience in the business. His was one of the three jobs I took on. After talking to him and learning of his problems, I decided to make a gamble. I told him I had 90 pages of an original screenplay; that if he would guarantee to find an acceptable front for nothing I would let him read it. He agreed. He read. He cared for deeply. He made a deal. He is to have the script for ninety days after it is completed. It will be completed in four or five more days. During the ninety days he will, as any other independent operator must, go out for stars and money. If he succeeds—and I genuinely think he will—he will pay me fifty Gs over a period of time extending from the end of the 90 day period to the day principal photography begins, plus 10% of the producer's share of the profits. I shall naturally continue on the project through every re-write, and shall have the power of decision, so my percentage will have a reasonable chance of protection in terms of not letting the screenplay get screwed up. If, at the end of the ninety days, he has got nowhere, and if in my opinion there is no reasonable prospect of his getting anywhere, and if he does not lay down a substantial sum of cash, I shall again own the script, and may

[1] Butler had requested Trumbo's collaboration on a black market project in Mexico.

put it on the market under the front name he has secured. This kind of a kick involves a certain speculation, but if it goes through—and it is a good enough project that I think it may in these days of absolutely horrible writing—I shall get all the cash, with nothing paid to agent or front, plus a splendid participation. Naturally I must guide this one very carefully.

A few facts about the story and script market as it looks from here. It is good. Of course I always come in on the tail end, generally following four complete drafts by writers whose names would surprise you, all drafts desperately bad. It is really an eye-opener, and guarantees, for anyone who can rescue one of these dreadful wrecks, a continuing market in the future.

Second: the spectaculars are apparently going to pass. Fox, for example, has taken a terrible beating with them recently. *Desiree* cost $4 million. The studio will be happy if it gets back its advertising and print costs, plus one-half of its production cost. This, of course, is extremely bad. The trend is fairly general. This I consider to be a hopeful sign for fellows like us. Nobody can sell one of these epics as an original, and nobody in the black market can get a crack at the screenplay for them.[2] Hence their imminent departures from the scene as a general product will be very good, in that it will return the emphasis to story, and thus help all writers, including ourselves. I think it is also interesting that for two years now the Oscar winning picture has been in conventional screen and black and white. You know how I hate color anyhow.

A third recent thing I've noticed is that there is a consistently greater chance for guys like us to get pieces. Two of the three jobs I took involved pieces, plus day of photography deferments, plus cash. I never went for pieces, but I am finally won to your view, and shall insist on them in future, and, apparently, generally be able to get them.

Other gossip: the industry is making money, but a perilous percentage of it comes from the foreign market. For example, *The Barefoot Contessa*, which went out at $900,000 plus enormous deferments for everybody except [Ava] Gardner, who had to be bought for cash from Metro, will just barely get its production cost out of the U.S. But it will bring in $300,000 from *Italy* alone! Germany is, of course, still terrific.

Also the slow, but still perceptible, improvement in the political climate has resulted in more and more producers having the courage to look in on the black market. A competent man can now make a living, although he must be good, he absolutely must deliver if he is to keep a client for a second and a third, and it takes about a year

[2] Ironically, it was with the spectaculars *Spartacus* and *Exodus* that Trumbo made his "come back" under his own name.

to establish oneself with sufficient clients to insure a base annual living. I, goddam it, am going to have to hire a secretary, simply because this sudden rush doesn't permit me the luxury of typing them myself as I have always liked to.

I must add another reason, to be perfectly honest, which makes me at this moment hesitate to come to Mexico (although if the other immediate and urgent reasons didn't exist, I would find a way of solving this particular one)—and that is that I should be ashamed to see Gordon [Kahn] without having made him a more substantial payment. It would look like a vacation trip on our parts, and I shouldn't be able to explain it to him, and I would feel quite bad about it, because he has behaved absolutely nobly during this period of not hearing from me and receiving nothing, while I've been speculating. Actually, he was one of the reasons I *did* speculate— I've simply got to come through for him pretty soon, because he needs it.

I write in such detail, so that you will have a clear picture of the many things that presently perplex me. I think I'm on the verge of complete independence for at least a couple of years, and the chance is so precious that I simply have to nurture and protect it. I haven't, of course, touched the play,[3] except for voluminous notes which improve it vastly over my bare recital of it to you. It shall be reserved for the period when independence sets in—if it does.

That is about all. . . . Cleo is well, and hates housework with an intensity that is almost holy. I am deep in negotiations for the purchase of the small house at the end of our drive.[4] It would give us possession of the road, and the house is new and excellently built. I am buying it in Cleo's name. She will then equip it as a studio. . . . She will start out to go after family business—a venture in which her name will be of some value in getting customers. Certainly she is able to do a much more sensitive job of it than most family and child photographers. She will set up her car also as a deductible thing, both as to capital investment and as to expense—and then we can have a woman work in the house from noon to eight, and Cleo will be free to do her own work. I am very hopeful we can do it soon, for it is shameful to have her so tied down to the damning monotony of housework, of which she now does absolutely all except the ironing.

Nikola wants to join the Sobell Committee, which will shortly open a very important campaign. We tell her she'll be marked for

[3] Trumbo had begun work on a second play, *Morgana*, intended for Broadway production with Joe Manchester. Lengthy Trumbo-Manchester correspondence concerning the play appeared in the New York *Herald Tribune* October 1, 1961.

[4] Trumbo had, by this time, purchased the home in Los Angeles in which he and his family lived until the fall of 1964.

life, not as her father's daughter, but on her own as an adult, and she says she wants to be, and we are very proud, and will let her develop as she wishes. She actually has—even if she *is* our own, don't people always say?—an extraordinary social feeling, sympathy and indignation. She is in constant wrangles at school over labor unions, socialism, Quemoy, Formosa, the local Fourteen, and whatever else occurs to her to throw at her teachers. First they entrapped her in false arguments, but she has learned fast, and now, as nearly as I can figure it, they are quite wary of her. She has kept my profession a secret (until it came out recently), choosing, apparently, to accumulate infamy strictly on her own talent for it.

Chris opened our local Red Cross parade, standing in the lead auto and proudly tooting his bugle, I mean trumpet. He aroused all of Figueroa Street, and says he played very badly. He is now taking, in addition to trumpet lessons, French horn (which the school lent him so he could learn) and practices with hideous intensity. He has just about decided he wants to be a professional musician. Whether this will last we have no idea. We don't want him to make a moral commitment from which, with a change of mind, he will hesitate to withdraw; yet we feel that such a career would be satisfying if he went on with it, and that if he later determined on something else, the cultural advantage of loving music would still represent a net gain. His present determination, thank God, is to take a liberal arts course in college, keeping up his music, and then to go to a conservatory. It's an ambitious program—but at least it *is* a program, and that is something our children thus far have lacked. We shall see.

Mitzi appears to be exactly as she was at the age of one, two, three, four, five, six, seven and eight, and I dare say she will be for all of her life: demanding, stubborn, argumentative, shrill, incredibly careless with possessions, profligate with acquisitions, and tolerably bright. [Paul] Trivers tells me a curse has been laid upon me, in that I have in her a daughter who remarkably inherits or imitates all of my worst features. I remain aloof from such speculation, and fight back at her with everything I've got.

There! A full report. I wish it were more specific. But, as its detail indicates, it cannot be. At least you now know as much as I do.

I salute you and the other male of your family, bestow an avuncular kiss upon your spouse and female dependents, and solicit information about them all.

Selah!

D. T.

P.S.   The fact that I have creditors in your part of the world would indicate the greatest discretion with respect to the deals herein outlined and the finances involved with them: I shouldn't like the golden gleam in my eye to be translated into cash in hand by those to whom I am obliged.

2. Extract of a letter to Ring Lardner, Jr.

Los Angeles, California
February 18, 1955

I am as startled as the next man to learn that your first novel isn't going to make you rich. Best not to whine about it, though. If you find the climate unfavorable, why not assume a different identity and take ship for England? I'm sure you could get away with it. You passed for fifteen years as a screen writer.

3. To Norman Cousins of the *Saturday Review of Literature*

Los Angeles, California
February 18, 1955

Dear Mr. Cousins:

I enclose herewith a letter I hope you will be able to publish. Because I am unhappily aware that in the game of letters-to-the editor a few excisions can sometimes make the communicant appear to be an uncommon fool, I request that no alterations be made without my consent, save corrections of spelling or grammar for which I'm always grateful.

If cuts are needed, I don't particularly cherish the first paragraph. If you wish I can perhaps remove some of the heat from the final paragraph. I do think what I have written needs badly to be read. I shall not scream clichés at you, but the stark fact of a calculated literary blacklist becomes increasingly clear. It is not—as the extreme right has moaned for years—that books are reviewed unfavorably; it is that they are not reviewed at all. It is silence—utter, devastating silence—that kills both the writer and his work. Literary historians in a more civilized future will not accord to those editors who have yielded with such remarkable unanimity to the distempers of our time the one accolade which justifies their existence: honor.

If you can't accept it for the regular letters column, I have it in mind to publish it at my own expense. Could your advertising department calculate the space it might consume as a paid insertion and let me know the cost?

Very truly,
DALTON TRUMBO

4. To the Editor of the *Saturday Review of Literature*

Los Angeles, California
February 18, 1955

I have published three novels in the United States, all of which were favorably noted in *The Saturday Review*. I am now preparing a fourth, and therefore have a natural interest in the magazine's reviewing policy.

In January of this year Ring Lardner, Jr. published a novel called *The Ecstasy of Owen Muir*. I should have thought a first novel by the son of a distinguished American humorist might have warranted a review on the basis of literary curiosity alone, as in the recent case of Damon Runyon, Jr. To this date, however, I have seen no mention of the book in *The Saturday Review* or any other major publication.

Of course, there are books so dismal that silence is kindlier than comment. But *The Ecstasy of Owen Muir* had been previously published in England, and there received wide and enthusiastic critical acceptance. *The Daily Telegram* called it "provocative, witty and fiercely sincere." *The Sunday Times* noted that "the wit is constant," and called it "remarkable for its sardonic intelligence." So the profound American silence cannot be laid to kindliness.

Can it be that our principal publications refuse to review books with which they are not in agreement? No: *The Saturday Review* itself, as it properly should, has considered the literary output of ex-Nazis, German generals, revisionist historians, a reformed prostitute and, lately, such a novel as *Fragebogen*—and has indicated agreement with none of them.

Can it be that Lardner's name is unmentionable because he had the bad luck to invoke the First Amendment as protection against Congressional inquiry into writers and their work, and served a term in jail for this bull-headed misconception of Constitutional privilege? No: for if the name of every writer who has done penance in the lock-up were stricken from the record, we should all be even greater fools than we are.

Or, by a process of elimination, can it be that *The Saturday Review*, whose passionate devotion to free inquiry and free discussion is acknowledged everywhere, has, in common with the most vulgar gossip-sheet, a sonofabitch list comprised of writers who believe that such freedoms are even more desirable and somewhat less prevalent in these United States than *The Saturday Review* proclaims them to be? And, if so, does the Index include this communication and its author?

DALTON TRUMBO

5. To Louis Goldblatt of ILWU

Los Angeles, California
March 14, 1955

Dear Lou:

There are in my community between three and four hundred blacklisted former directors, actors, writers and artists who have lately turned themselves, without excessive wails of self-pity, into salesmen, day-laborers, clerks, accountants and piece-workers. Despite the change they remain what they always were—decent human beings quite as capable of passions, loyalties, resentments and hopes as a regularly employed trade union official.

As one of them, I have been pondering tonight how many thousands of words I have written in the past fourteen years in defense of Harry Bridges and the ILWU; how many speeches I have made in their behalf; how many meetings I have chaired for them; how many times I have thrown my house open to solicit funds for them; how many times I was cited by the House Committee on Un-American Activities for my work in the various Bridges cases; how many hundreds of dollars (I would say "thousands" but for the fact the sum doesn't quite reach the two thousand mark) my wife and I have contributed out of pocket to Bridges and his union.

I have spared myself the task of calculating how many speeches, meetings and dollars have issued from Harry Bridges and the ILWU in defense of my several hundred colleagues when their own moment of struggle arrived.

I do not regret any of it, and neither, I think, do the many others in my profession who fought loyally in Bridges' behalf. But I would be less than honest with you if I did not now inform you that I am saddened and angered by the insensate arrogance you have displayed toward me in the last seven or eight months—an arrogance which it is only logical to assume must characterize you and your union in its dealings with all persons whom you seek to exploit, and whom you believe to have no means of protecting themselves against your profoundly contemptuous and anti-labor attitudes.

Sometime in 1954 during the month of June—my dates here will be merely approximate, because I had no idea that in dealing with you I should ever have to refer to records—you approached me in Hollywood, gave me a mass of material and asked me to do a pamphlet for Bridges and the ILWU. You outlined to me several general theories upon which the ILWU might act in the forthcoming case, although none of them had yet been finally decided upon. I agreed to do the job and gave you a completion date. The project was important enough for you to telephone me when the date was passed. I truthfully informed you I had been delayed by a sequence of minor surgical treatments. In August a first draft job was completed and mailed to you.

In a covering letter I explained to you that I was keeping the source material for reference in the re-write. I explained that there were probably errors in my work, since it dealt with matters unfamiliar to me, and that you might well want considerable changes. I stated my willingness to make such changes once you had decided upon them. Shortly thereafter I received a letter from Mr. Glazier stating that the project had been received, that you were out of town, and that you would communicate with me upon your return.

It is ironic that at this point I should feel the necessity of interrupting my narrative and explaining to you, a trade union official of many years' experience, the economics of a writer's life. Clearly, however, I must do so.

I have been a professional writer for twenty years. That is the way I earn my living. My wife and I feed and house and clothe ourselves and our three children out of money derived from the sale of my writings. I have a place in which I work for which I pay rent. I have money tied up in an electric typewriter which wears out infinitesimally with every word it hammers out. I have capital invested in a desk for the typewriter, and in a chair to sit on. I pay for the heat and light in my workroom. In order to have something to write on, I purchase paper and carbon paper and envelopes, and when I mail a project I purchase the stamps for its transmission. I also pay for and consume pencils, erasers, ink and other articles in the course of writing, whether I write for nothing or for money. All of this I finance out of my earnings.

When a writer agrees to do a job for a trade union, he agrees to cease writing for money, and for a period of two or three weeks to work for nothing. During this period of charitable endeavor he finances himself out of accumulated savings, or by borrowing against future income. He does not just stay even with his living costs, he goes behind. When he is blacklisted the problem of course becomes much more complex.

I know this comes as a surprise to you, since you are regularly employed and paid, and have been for a long while. You would, however, understand the economics of the thing instantly if I asked you to go off salary for two or three weeks and, out of sheer loyalty to like-thinking people in trouble, spend the time assisting Hollywood's blacklisted artists. Until that unlikely moment, and your most improbable acquiescence, you will have to take the economic facts herein given on faith. You will also have to take it on faith that when a writer undertakes a job for a trade union, he does so in the fatuous belief that his work will be read within a reasonable time, that the working rules of his own union will not be too seriously violated, and that he will receive in the course of the transaction at least the simple courtesy still accorded him by the most reactionary members of the publishing monopoly.

In your case, however, approximately four months elapsed without any word concerning the project beyond the cursory acknowledgment of its arrival. On December 13, 1954, I therefore felt obliged to inquire about it. That I did so in sharp terms, I freely admit, but apparently they were not sharp enough. I told you that your long silence was contemptuous. I admitted the possibility my work may have turned out unsatisfactorily for your purposes, but insisted on my right to be so informed. And finally I clearly advised you of my membership in the Authors' League of America, and of its working rules agreed to by all publishers in the United States, governing submission, reading and return of material submitted. These rules, incidentally, have even greater force in the case of material written on assignment than of speculatively submitted manuscripts. I advised you that the manuscript was my property, and I requested that you return it to me.

On December 29, 1954, I received the only written communication I have had from you since we discussed the project the previous June. You seized upon a point I had made about my work not being acknowledged—it *had* been, by Mr. Glazier—and made it the whole burden of your letter. You had been busy, you had been out of the city, you had enjoyed a vacation, etc., etc. Your point was made in a paragraph I shall always cherish:

"We hope that the officers here are aware of the mistakes made in many trade union circles to derogate contributions made by writers and other intellectuals to the progressive fight. We try not to be guilty of this offense, and pride ourselves on the fact that there is a strong feeling of friendship among the people in our office and our staff toward all those who pitch in to help the good fight. *If you feel that proper acknowledgment of your contribution was not made then I want to apologize.*"

By implying mere wounded vanity on my part and offering formal apology, you cannily omitted any reference to the most practical part of my letter: that you stood in violation of my trade union rules, that the manuscript you had been holding for so long a time was my legal property, and that I had demanded its return.

I have dealt in my life, both on a trade union basis and a personal one, with too many employers not to recognize in your omission the cunning spoor of the professional labor relations expert, eager to place the matter on a personal basis and loftily reluctant to acknowledge or even to discuss any trade union connotation. I recognized it and I was appalled by it.

But this simple, barefoot anti-trade union solution to the annoyance was not enough for you. You have managed to do something beyond that, something that no publisher has dared to do in my entire professional life and does not presently dare to do, even in my unblessed state of blacklist. You have held my property for between seven and eight months, *and you have not to this day informed me whether or not anyone has even read it!*

This is unforgivable and inexcusable. It goes even beyond the diseased anti-intellectualism so characteristic of professional trade union bureaucrats. It penetrates to the very heart of human relationships, to the natural decency one human being should feel for another, to the minimal courtesy that all self-respecting men demand of their fellows in simple recognition of the fact that they live, that they work, that they are not animals.

The sadness of the whole episode lies in the fact that I am constantly approached for such charitable work, that my time for it is limited by the economic requirements of my life, and that I might well have devoted my time and energy and money to another project involving more sensitive people, and one much more likely of fruition.

For, incredible though it may seem to you and your fellow officials, there are in these United States other men and organizations fully as virtuous as Harry Bridges and the ILWU and in as great or even greater jeopardy. Thus I am left to regret that my efforts— whether good or bad, whether skillful or inept, all this now being entirely beside the point—were wasted on sectarian men who deny to others the respect they have so long and rightfully demanded for themselves.

For myself, I am no longer interested in the virtues or defects of this pamphlet, nor in any future project of any kind with which you or your organization may seek to involve me. I am now interested only in the rules of my trade union and in the protection of my property rights. You are hereby placed on notice, for the second time, that you stand in violation of the working code of the Authors' League of America. You are further notified that this letter constitutes a formal demand upon you and the ILWU for the return of my manuscript on or before midnight of March 23, 1955, or, failing its return, adequate compensation for the work I have done on it, payable on the same date.

If you fail to comply with this demand, I shall, on March 24 take the following steps:

First, I shall do what your rules require any loyal member of your own trade union to do: I shall notify my brother and sister writers that you, having had knowledge of them since December 13, 1954, stand in willful violation of the working code and rules of the Authors' League. I shall inform them of the methods by which you engineer such violations initially and evade them thereafter, and warn them to protect themselves with legal documents in all future dealings with the ILWU or its officials.

Second, I shall send my grievance, together with all pertinent material relating to it, to the executive council of the Authors' League of America, with instructions to their legal staff to take immediate action against you. Since you are not signatory to the code agreement, they will not bother to go after you on fair practices charges. They will simply haul you into court and force you to pay for my property or return it to me.

When you read this I suggest that you not raise your voice in righteous horror to exclaim, "Trumbo has gone sour!" I'm exactly as I always was, neither sourer nor sweeter. Before you set about the task of casting the mote from my eye you had best make certain you do not perceive it through a beam in your own. I think you may find it invigorating to lift your eyes for a moment from your martyred navels and behold a very large country which contains other men, other organizations, other trade unions whose rights are quite as sacred as your own. I am, furthermore, utterly convinced that your political health will be improved by the simple lesson in trade union decency I will surely teach you if you do not meet my demands on or before the exact date given above.

Sincerely
DALTON TRUMBO

6. To Hugo Butler

Los Angeles, California
[*c. June, 1955*]

Dear lad:

Hearing your voice made me decide to write after all, although in a briefer form than originally intended. Let's face it: the probabilities are that I shan't see you during your Ensenada stay. If we did meet, I should want to come there and stay over a night, and drink and gossip and enjoy myself and return the next day. But looking matters squarely in the face, I can't be at all sure I'll have the time. It's impractical for you to come here for the same length of time, because you'd be overwhelmed with other obligations and people to see. And a mid-way meeting would simply be for a meal, which we can eat just as well and much more cheaply apart. So I have decided to write my letter. You may know all that is in it from previous knowledge. But it contains my ideas—as objectively as it is possible for a partisan to write—about how things look here, there, and everywhere.

It seems to me that barring some insanity like a new Korean War, which daily grows less probable, the world is undergoing a fundamental change. I think the change is moving under the surface much more rapidly than it is on the surface. I think peace has been accepted as the only possible solution; that the result of peace will necessarily be more trade between peoples; and that out of this may come a longer period of comparative stability than we presently suspect. Prediction is impossible, and prophets are all fools; yet from everything I see and hear and read, what I have written in this paragraph appears, from the objective evidence, to be much more likely than anything else. The forces for peace are powerful and growing, even in the United States.

The first great break, of course, was the Geneva Conference at which the Indochinese question was solved, the war stopped, and China recognized as a world power. It was followed by the really great triumph of the Bandoeng Conference in Indonesia, and after that by the Austrian Peace Treaty, foreshadowing an approach to the German problem. Then came the Yugoslav-Russian rapprochement; then the acceptance of the Four Power meeting of heads of state; then the tenth anniversary celebration of the founding of the United Nations in San Francisco, with the Four Power meeting presently in prospect, which probably won't accomplish great practical decisions, but which will make negotiation once more acceptable: it's the first such meeting in ten years—since Potsdam! Additionally, and of tremendous importance to the whole world including the United States, is the recent visit of Nehru to Moscow and the Eastern European countries; the agreement on principles reached in Moscow between India and the U.S.S.R.; and the forthcoming return visit to India of Bulganin. It would seem to put all of Asia except Thailand, South Korea and the Philippines in the peace camp—and what a miserable three exceptions they are! Each of these incidents, all of which have occurred within the last year and with dramatic speed, is in itself a diplomatic sensation, and each makes for peace. Despite the elections in England, Bevan's hand was greatly strengthened in the Labour Party; it was a Tory Prime Minister who has just told Chiang Kai-shek that British commerce in the China Sea will hereafter be protected from Nationalist attack originating in Formosa by British men-of-war. They're going to have their trade with China and the hell with it—and our own industrialists will soon be clamoring for their share of it. The fall of Scelba in Italy is extremely interesting as was the previous election of Gronchi to the presidency; Gronchi being very friendly with Nenni. The turmoil throughout Africa and the growing divisions in the Muslim world likewise point to an end of colonialism, which is always a boost for peace. It seems to me to be just everywhere.

Almost equally striking things have been happening in the United States—they are striking because here the hysteria had gone furthest, and here it had found its strongest citadel. When McCarthy was censured by the Senate he mustered 22 votes against censure. When, last week, he offered a resolution that would oblige the President to put on the agenda of the Big Four Conference the question of liberating the "satellite states" of Eastern Europe, he tried frantically to withdraw the motion when he saw it would be smashed; but they brought it to the floor, and he got only 4 votes—77 to 4! He is openly cartooned throughout the press as a deflated ogre, and ridicule is heaped upon him. Of course the -ism he represents isn't dead; but he personally is. Dead and disgraced.

Here in California a state loyalty oath was required of property-holders in order for them to claim certain exemptions. Who went to court to fight it?—Paul G. Hoffman's daughter. She got a favorable decision in Superior Court, and the state has appealed, and so it will go to the top. Three churches are also contesting the same thing in a separate suit, which shows chances of victory. Two especially obnoxious bills came up in the legislature this year; bills which would, in effect, oblige half a million professional persons licensed to practice by the state to take the oath. There was a tremendous outcry against them on very broad levels, and both were defeated resoundingly. A third didn't even get out of committee. A Federal jury in the east has just acquitted a man charged with perjury for swearing under oath that he hadn't known Harry Gold was a Soviet spy. The government brought Gold in as a witness to prove the man was lying; the jury acquitted the man, indicating that it believed Gold was the man who lied. This is a most extraordinary thing for a jury to do in these times—to repudiate the veracity of the man whose evidence was so important in killing the Rosenbergs. It shows a change even among juries. The Lattimore case is dead. The Federal Judge twice threw out the two principal accusations, condemned the government for its assertions, twice was sustained by the Circuit Court—and now all charges are dismissed. If the case had begun five years earlier, Lattimore, innocent as he is, would nonetheless have still been in prison.

In Denver six or seven people were recently convicted of Smith Act violations. The attorneys were all court-appointed, most of them Republicans, all of them corporation lawyers. Their leader was a past president of the Colorado Bar Association, past Republican National Committeeman, and a past National Chairman. He came to California and conferred with—Ben [Margolis]! He told Ben that what impressed him even more than the outrageousness of the government's case was the personal quality of the defendants. The court-appointed attorneys stated that the government's case was one of no evidence—and they rested the defense on this plea, without calling a single witness. It was an extraordinary and different tactic; and although they lost, they are hell bent on appeal. Said the leading attorney: the trouble is that the government is trying to make a conspiracy out of a mass movement.

Here in Los Angeles the Court of Appeals has just turned down the California Smith Act people, citing as a praiseworthy piece of legislation the old Alien and Sedition Acts! Result: a member of the Board of Governors of the California Bar who was Warren's campaign manager is going to associate himself with the defense in its appeal to the Supreme Court. In San Francisco, Telford Taylor, who is rapidly becoming one of the most influential members of the American bar, is defending Harry Bridges. In San Francisco also, the perjury conviction of Hugh Bryson (who received maximum sentence) is in itself a victory, in that the man was acquitted of membership, but convicted of affiliation. It seems that such a curious and significant jury decision will force a reversal somewhere along the line on the vagary of "affiliation" and the fact that the man has been acquitted of membership. So even defeats have their significant and extremely hopeful sides.

In an eastern Federal Circuit including the state of Pennsylvania, the Circuit Court of Appeals sat en banc on a Smith Act appeal, giving a 7 to 2 verdict against the defendants. But the dissenting two, in an opinion written by Judge Hastie, came through with a magnificent document—something that is absolutely new in Smith Act cases—and were for setting the defendants instantly free. This, too, is something new. Even better is the majority opinion of the Supreme Court written by Chief Justice Warren in the Emspak, Quinn and Bart cases. Here the defendants having relied on the First "supplemented by the Fifth," had been indicted and convicted and having lost their Circuit Court appeal, suddenly were sustained by a majority of the Supreme Court. Their problem was curiously like the Ten's: they were tried because they evaded clear invocation of the Fifth. They refused to answer questions, and they refused to admit they were refusing to answer. They insisted that the committee had no right to inquire into their associations and beliefs. They stood on the First, and threw the Fifth in, as if in afterthought: so that the government in its prosecution contended that they were deliberately vague about the Fifth in order "to obtain the benefit of the privilege without incurring the popular opprobrium which often attaches to its exercise." Said Warren, in reply to this: "If it is true, as the government contends, that petitioner feared the stigma that might result from a forthright claim of his constitutional right not to testify," then bare mention of the Fifth was enough to obtain its protection. "No ritualistic formula is necessary to invoke the privilege," said the Court; and *then* it said: "The power to investigate, broad as it may be, is also subject to recognized limitations. It cannot be used to inquire into private affairs . . . Nor does it extend to an area in which Congress is forbidden to legislate. Similarly the power to investigate must not be confused with any of the powers of law enforcement . . . Still further limitations . . . are found in the specific individual guarantees of the Bill of Rights."

There are many more exciting things said in the three decisions, and the nugget of them is that the Court used, in some instances and almost word for word, the arguments submitted by counsel for the Ten. Different times tell the different story. Scribner, counsel for the three men, declared in a public address here that nothing said in the decision had not "been said before more forcefully and more eloquently by the Hollywood Ten." In a word, even *we* are beginning to get a little vindication, for the Court here indicated a great interest in the First Amendment, which it is hoped will develop in the Lamont and O'Connor cases (in which it and it alone was invoked) into direct confrontation. We may win yet!

Even the passport situation offers possibility of change. Somewhere in the East a leader of a party called the Independent Socialist Party was denied a passport. He brought suit in Federal Court after his appeal to the passport bureau failed. Federal court said the bureau was sole judge, its hearings the final word. On appeal, the Appellate Court majority held that this was nonsense; that the right to travel was a fundamental right; that the passport bureau was not the final arbiter in the matter, and ordered the lower court to accept this man's case. A small victory, but in a vital area, and promising greater ones.

The confessions of Matusow and three other government informers has had a really deep public effect; as have also the publication recently of a small flood of books by eminent persons, damning the encroachment on civil liberties: Barth's *Government by Investigation*; Telford Taylor's *Grand Inquest*; Chenery's *Freedom of the Press*; Gillmore's *Fear The Accuser;* Harold Taylor's *On Education and Freedom*; Pritchett's *Civil Liberties and the Vinson Court*; Dean Griswold of Yale's *The Fifth Amendment Today*. Additionally the Ruben book on atomic spies and the Wexley book on the Rosenberg-Sobell case contain such shocking and authenticated material that they cannot fail to break through into areas where hitherto no doubts were entertained. Robert Hutchins, with $15 million from Ford for his Fund for the Republic, is making speeches everywhere, planning a radio program which will use the names of blacklisted people, publishing a book soon on the blacklist in entertainment.[5] I spent several hours with the investigators here—and while the book may not be what one would wish, it appears there is no doubt it will

[5] The text in two paperbacks (Vol. 1, Movies: Vol. 2 Radio, Television) was finally written by John Cogley in 1956 and titled *Report on Blacklisting*. Cogley himself was then blacklisted.

attack the blacklist with considerable vigor. Even Dore [Schary] [6] recently made a speech against blacklisting!

The black market reflects this, in certain qualified ways. A friendly person has recently acquired ownership of a studio in England, and is offering from $20,000 to $40,000 for acceptable scripts that may be filmed there. If you know nothing about this, write Ring [Lardner, Jr.] and he will give you all the details. Another group has recently formed in the east, and signed Arthur Miller to do a film: $15,000 down plus 10% of the net. His name to be on. This is a real break-through. They have also approached me—I have, in fact, a script I haven't had time to read yet—on the same basis, although I'm doubtful about the name part. I have on the boards three assign-ments which I cannot do. They should pay from $4,500 for the worst to $10,000 for the best. I am having a hell of a time trying to find a way to sub-contract them, because really capable writers are so scarce: Mike [Wilson] can't take any work, or rather, doesn't want to at present. I hesitate to sub-contract unless I'm sure of my man because I took a powerful screwing that way on a louse of a script, and had to make good on it myself. But if you were here these things would be available, and you could handle them. Also, if my or-ganizational plans go through I shall retire entirely from the market. This means that I shall try to snag any assignments that come my way for others. Recently I was offered $1,250 a script plus 10% of the producer's 40% ownership of a forthcoming 26-week TV series. I turned it over to somebody else, although they didn't get the per-centage offered to me. One large advertising agency is reputed to have received orders from Ford Corporation to buy stories where they're good, and damn the blacklist. Several are working and making a living in TV. Others beside me are working in films.

But—

I did six scripts last year and only earned $18,000. Two of them were $3,000 jobs done in collaboration with Mike,[7] wherein we split

[6] Dore Schary, former M-G-M producer and executive, appeared before the Screen Writers' Guild and requested acquiescence in the blacklisting of the Hollywood Ten in 1947.

[7] The Trumbo-Wilson collaborations, of which there were about six, were low paying, low grade pictures. Since neither of them could afford the time, they worked in this fashion: Wilson, whose pseudonym for phone and contact purposes was Franklin, was the constructionist, and Theodore Flexman (Trumbo) was the dialoguist and script writer. Since the two men lived some distance apart in the Los Angeles area, Wilson would construct the characters, situations, and plot outlines scene by scene in the course of a single day. At night he would send the day's work special delivery to Trumbo. Upon receipt of the material the following morning, Trumbo would script it and at night, send it back to Wilson. By working in this manner the two writers were able to turn out a completed script in seven to ten days. Frequently Trumbo would write a section without the vaguest idea of what the characters would be

the 3 Gs. Now that is a hell of a lot of work. And I guaranteed satisfaction (and gave it) on every script. When I say a hell of a lot of work, I don't mean it arrogantly. It just happens to be true that my physical constitution enables me to work at high speed for long periods, and most can't do it.. Therefore they don't make as much. I started from scratch, without any contacts and operated on the theory that every satisfied customer was a future customer for steady work at rising rates. I think this was a correct assumption, and that if I wanted to be a slave it can and will pay off. The blackmarket is like the old one on a much lower scale: that is, you enter it virgin and new and unknown (I haven't had a screen credit for ten years —styles change—writers fade). Therefore I decided I had to prove myself as a newcomer. This is generally true, I think. Starting prices hence are low and then you force them up, just as in the regular market. So one entering fresh would start a little lower until his contacts were all made. It is a hard struggle.

So tough, in fact, that I am starting this bloody corporation,[8] which, if it goes, will provide me with relief: if it doesn't, perhaps I shall not have to work so hard on the black market in future years as I have in the past eighteen months, but still I shall have to work much harder than I like to think of. I now have some pieces and some deferments and more work than I can handle; but the situation is far from satisfactory from my point of view, certainly no cinch, and certainly nothing to look forward to as a life's work. I *think* the corporation will work, because I have some beautiful ideas for it, and will, of course, work for it in a way I would never be able to work for mere wages, piece or no piece. This one will slice everything right down the middle, and I, with half the stock and half the directors, am in a position to veto any damned thing I don't like. I dream and dream of it . . . but we shall see. I understand the hazards and no longer count unhatched chicks.

Why do I write in such detail? Of course because I'd love to see you all back here. I miss you, old boy, and wish you were near. But since things go well economically where you are, I cannot paint a paradise here, although I would do everything in my power to make

---

doing or what would transpire in the story on the next day. Trumbo never saw the films prepared in this way; indeed he rarely learned the final titles attached to the pictures or inquired about whose name appeared on the credits. One of these Wilson-Trumbo collaborations, however—a story of Brazilian prostitutes along the Amazon River—was voted by a group of Harvard students as the worst picture of the year. Amusingly, that judgment was passed in the same year that Trumbo (alias Robert Rich) won his Oscar for *The Brave One* and Wilson was denied nomination for an Oscar for *Friendly Persuasion.*

[8] It was Trumbo's idea to establish a business corporation whereby he could act as agent for blacklisted writers and actually secure undercover work for them. No such corporation materialized.

it so from the point of view of cooperation on contacts. I will say one thing only without equivocation: I *know* that intellectually life is much more stimulating here than in Mexico, more stimulating for an American than it can possibly be in any other country, because here is where the decisions that affect everything are being fought out. I am certain it is better for the individual and for the children in this one aspect.

But I am well aware that there is an economic problem for us all, and that five children necessitate one servant (which we cannot yet afford here ourselves), and that costs are very high, and that a livelihood is precarious (although I'm certain that your abilities would make you ultimately successful here). I think I suffered a net loss economically by going to Mexico; and I speculate that if your energies had been expended here as faithfully as they have been there, you would find that you had lost economically also.

But the past is past and the present is what has to be considered. I think right now the black market is beginning to grow, and that eventually—barring a Korean War or some such disaster—it will break wide open, and that, viewed from the long haul, now is an excellent time to get into it and build. I think the time will come when names again appear on the screen. When, I don't know; or what group will be first; or how it may come about but it *is* now within the realm of possibility. This I hadn't ever expected to believe.

Basically, you see, I am arguing both sides. I *do* wish you were here. I don't say this in the political sense. First, I wouldn't want you here if you should have to go through some agonizing legal or- deal. Second, although I *do* think that politically and intellectually it is better for a man and his family to be in this country at the present time—still I know of no one who has appointed me your political and intellectual keeper. Nor do I know of anyone who has the right to take over that function. And therefore I believe that end of it is supremely your business, have always so maintained, and will continue to.

Then why do I write so? Well, one reason is that I don't think I have ever seen the situation here clearly enough to write with any degree of conviction about how things are turning. I would have written before, or later, depending on how things seemed. I think they are just about as I have presented them. And so you are my friend, and I write you and confide my opinions in you. I would not write similarly to anyone else, because I don't have the feelings about anyone else I hold for you. Basically every man has himself and his family, and every family has its peculiar needs and problems, and no one outside that family can make arbitrary decisions about what is best for it, and no one should try to do so, and I do not try to do so.

Then, to repeat: why do I write? I write selfishly, lad. You are my dear friend, and I wish we and our families were near to each other. It's as simple as that. Am I forgiven? Please write.

DALTON

7. To Miss Rodell of the Elsie McKeogh Agency

Los Angeles, California
October 30, 1955

Dear Miss Rodell: [9]

Hanging on my study wall is a framed letter from Elsie McKeogh announcing the sale of my first novel. It is dated December 12, 1934. During the twenty-one years that have ensued she has been my friend, my advisor and my most trusted representative. Although I have lately done very little serious writing, I still hope to do so in the future, and with Elsie gone I have the curious and angry feeling that if she cannot handle it then I want no one to handle it, no one at all.

She treated me with courtesy and consideration during a period when I starved for recognition; and when later I became successful in motion pictures I insisted for a number of years that she participate equally with my Hollywood agent in commissions on my earnings. She often referred to this as "unearned money" but it wasn't and couldn't have been. Much later, when my film career was at an end, I was in Mexico with my family—all of whom knew and admired her—and I ran short of funds and wrote her, and she succored me instantly.

On matters of religion and politics we differed perhaps as greatly as two people can, yet we never sought to influence each other and never had an argument and took pains never to wound each other's feelings. After I was blacklisted I suggested that she handle my work under a pseudonym, keeping my true identity secret from publishers. She declined on ethical grounds, and I understand completely. She always stood ready to represent me under my own name, no matter how dangerous or compromising association with me might be, but she could not enter into deceit with others. While I was in prison and unsuccessfully seeking parole, it was Elsie who wrote the parole board a beautiful letter urging them to release a man with whom—although she didn't say so in the letter—she stood in direct ideological opposition.

Now our relationship is at an end, and I have the painful pleasure

[9] Successor to the Elsie McKeogh agency informed Trumbo of the death of his good friend and literary agent of twenty years.

of paying my small tribute of respect and love to her memory. She often said that she thought I would like her mother, and that she thought her mother might like me. We never met. If her mother still lives, I shall be grateful for her name and address. If she does not live, perhaps you will pass this letter on to the person Elsie loved most.

Sincerely,
DALTON TRUMBO

8. To Alice and Ian Hunter

Los Angeles, California
December 28, 1955

Dear Alice and Ian:

I am at the end of a day's work and a little beat, yet so buoyed up by the extravagance of today's expression of friendship from you that I have repaired to my study to reply at once, lest lethargy come on as the surprise wears off and I never write at all. I have beside me a sufficient supply of Scotch—two cases incoming for Christmas! —so the typos will increase as the garrulity of alcohol asserts itself.

It's so damned nice to hear that affairs go well, that the days of the cave are behind you, that you are living once more with the furniture I remember with such pleasure. You people had a tougher one to beat than most, and that you have done so is testimony to something or other that my tendency to homilies and prosody warns me against defining. We are absolutely delighted, and well understand the relief you must feel after those incredible days in Mexico, when all of us snapped at each other because we could not lay hand on enemies to blame our plight on.

The proud and pleased word you pass on about Timmy, while no surprise, is also pleasant to hear. Cleo and I have always thought of him as perhaps the brightest kid we ever ran into. Disagreeable at times he was, and probably still is. By disagreeable, I don't mean just normally so: a little more than normal at the time. And you should, as I daresay you do, thank Jesus for it. It was his way of making a little room among people whom he basically, and perhaps not unnaturally, considered idiots. The occasional offense he may give your friends by innocently clouting them with old family china will be more than compensated for—to you if not to them—by your future pride in what he does. I remember with many elderly chuckles the day on Montes Auvernia when I asked him quite civilly to leave the room after a pleasant conversation and he said "Make me!" and before the offensive little angel could draw a breath I was on him and whooshed him out of the room and into the yard with such speed that his little feet were on the grass before the first shriek burst from his lungs. When it came it was a beaut, and I recall with some satisfaction my own agility which brought me, via the kitchen, to a leisurely descent of the house staircase about the time he was sobbing his outrage into his mother's lap. My appearance, in such a state of composure and so far from the scene of the crime, did not, I am sure, raise any doubt of his veracity in Alice's mind, but at the very least it gave me such a good circumstantial case that I escaped all reproach. If this talent is already showing itself, in God's name feed it, feed it, feed it. And to hell with baseball. If he likes baseball he can buy his own team when the time comes, but not by playing on it. We also remember his deep and affectionate sweetness and the slow, calculating innocent smile with which he would test the ground of one's susceptibilities. If, with all this, he can write too—! Tell him the old cocker who whooshed him sends a wary greeting and such love as he is presently able to divert from himself.

For reports of our own:

Nikola is dark and beautiful and does not do too well at school, although she is still somewhat above average. She plans to go to Antioch next year, and we are willing, although we think her dislike of concentrated study will cause her to flunk out. We do not care, so long as it doesn't bother her, which I think it shan't. She continues to have a deep, almost brooding interest in all kinds of people, and spends agonized hours trying to figure them out. She is so far left that she terrifies me and occasionally reprimands me for backward habits. The extent of her direction exceeds her practical knowledge, but I daresay that will be cured in time. She is a pushover for anybody's sympathy, and is thoroughly taken advantage of even by adults, from time to time, and is outraged if we tell her so. She is getting expensive: every time I drive with her the car veers almost uncontrollably to the right each time we pass Bullocks. She has no particular career in view, and is serenely undisturbed by such aimlessness at 17 (an anniversary which will occur next month). She appears to like us, although I think it her secret opinion that we are somewhat over-rated by outsiders. At the moment she is having a very sweet going-steady affair with a young Negro two years her senior. He stands 9 inches taller than her 5 feet 5, and has what she calls a "head scholarship" to San Jose State, to which he returns next month to complete his last two years. His sweater, which she wears, is almost knee length on her, and contains innumerable stripes on the rolled-up sleeves as well as side decorations involving football, baseball, track and basketball in immoderate doses. He intends at the moment to be a physicist. They escape a lot of the trouble attendant upon young mixed couples by her neat and apparently quite believable device of blandly identifying herself as a Negro. He seems to like me, but that may be sheer guile and expediency. Nikola calls me "Daddy" when there is an object in view, "Father" when she is sore, "Pop" when I am under the anaesthesia of the fruit of the grape and therefore in a mood to make jokes, and "the Old Man" to her friends over the telephone. I think she often wonders how someone she considers faintly ridiculous could exercise over her the rather large powers of fatherhood.

Christopher has suffered—or, as we see it, profited from—a complete change in character during these last seven or eight years. From the most fearsome-tempered kid I remember, with physical power to match it and a heart that was clearly in his murderous work, he has changed into an extraordinarily gentle and considerate boy. When he first moved into Highland Park, which is a neighborhood not noted for the reticence of its younger citizens, he engaged in four tolerably bloody fights the first week, and has had none since. The reason, as he asserted and we later confirmed by cautious inquiry, being that he won each fight. Having thus achieved peace, he selected one friend. The friend comes of a Jewish family that is now raising its third generation in this community. Chris's social life therefore revolves about the local Jewish community. He belongs to something approximately called The Young Jewish Social League (or something with that meaning) and thus far has not gone to a dance outside the synagogue grounds or had a date outside the membership of the group. His tastes run toward music; and I have a hunch he aspires to be a cantor. He has kept up his trumpet with touching devotion, and for the past year has been taking lessons from an L.A. symphony guy who is extremely good. The teacher in his reports to us is torn between warnings that all musicians starve to death and assurances that Chris shows genuine promise. Chris has determined that the trumpet shall be his life work. He plays in the band, in the orchestra, and in the laundry room downstairs for hours on end. Our doting ears find his tone pleasant and his assiduity appalling. He is always home when he promises to be, cheerfully does all work required of him (although he will forget if not given occasional reminders), rarely loses his temper, doesn't want to smoke, scorns liquor (doubtless from the horrors of parental example), gets steady A's at school, and intends to go to Harvard. He finds his parents, by comparison with others, rather more satisfactory than the general run, and tells us so. He calls me "Pop" and both he and Nikola still call Cleo by her first name. To our eyes he is not unattractive. Our surmise is borne out by the rather large number of telephone calls he receives from girls. He appears not to be shy of them, but on the other hand he rarely takes time from his extremely active cultural life to go out with them. I don't understand him, but I like him exceedingly, and hope all will turn out well.

Mitzi is, as usual, assertive, talkative, enchanting, calculating, stubborn, selfish, impolite, demanding, sensitive and wonderfully bright. She calls me "Daddy" and Cleo "Mommy." She regards Cleo as someone to love her and work for her; me as someone to play with in lighter moments. She genuinely thinks I'm an amusing codger, and is always at me, not, God forbid, to engage in her childish sports, but to make up jokes. She is taking piano lessons, regards herself as approaching the concert phase of her career, and improvises horribly on such themes as the Dance of the Elves or A Visit to Tommy's House. Her emotional life is so exhausting that she can gain or lose pounds over a day's unhappiness (or the reverse), and we are fond of her. I daresay the latter's a common trait that we share with dogs and mice, and hence unworthy of further comment.

Cleo is Cleo, only perhaps a little more so. She has fleshed out, and observes her brood with smiling eyes, seeing much to praise in them and little to condemn. Her health is really excellent, and we are looking forward now to a foreseeable future when she will need to spend less time on housework and more on the photography which she loves. We bought a small adjoining house for her, and she has made the kitchen into a darkroom, hence for the first time in two or three years has adequate facilities for her work. There has been, so far as I can see, no perceptible change in her character or her appearance, both of which are well enough known to you to require no description from me. She tolerates me with apparent ease, and bestows upon me more affection than Pepe gets. You will be startled to hear that she calls me "Trumbo" on most occasions. When I have cleaned my own bathtub she calls me "Trumbo darling," and when she is put out with me she calls me "Darling!"

As for me, I have celebrated this month with proper solemnity, my mid-century. The children make happy remarks about what their fatuous minds conceive to be my increasing decrepitude, and make leering book on how much longer I shall survive. I drink quite a bit and smoke a lot, and I cannot imagine that my other activities have a place in this report.

. . . .

Here is a side-issue that promises me some amusement in the next months. There was mailed to me on December 9 (my birthday) via the Dramatists' Guild, a book by a man named Virgil Geddes. The book contained four plays, the title being *From the Life of George Emery Blum.* The book was self-published in 1934. The four plays comprised a cycle dealing with two undertakers, one of whom unluckily was named Bert (the name of my undertaker in *The Biggest Thief in Town*). One incident involved a corpse that came to life, such being discovered by formation of a soap bubble at his lips during the course of soap-and-water washing. Guy (deceased) wasn't rich, but at least he was a fee, so undertaker shoved cotton down his throat and made certain of the job. Thereafter suffered pangs of conscience that couldn't be allayed by positive word of attendant doctor that stiff was actually dead (although doctor *did* have a certain professional interest in supporting his own first diagnosis). Undertaker in another play invents a life-saving machine, and moons endlessly over indisputably deceased persons, trying to atone for original tinge of selfishness. A final play makes him a member of the state senate. Anyhow, the volume is dedicated thus (in handwriting, of course)—

> For The Biggest Thief in Town,
> Dalton Trumbo, this extra copy with
> my compliments. One is seldom so
> honored.
> —Virgil Geddes

Poor Trumbo steams. Goddam it, he can't even think up his own flops! Not having heard of Virgil Geddes, gets information. Fellow is a fifty-eight-year-old poet, critic and playwright, who had a vogue in the early days of depression. Was considered a lefty. Was with WPA. Wrote and produced plays in his own outfit called Brookfield Players, Brookfield, Connecticut. Plays were apparently of the kind that caused self-supporting playwrights, soiling their hands in the dirty commercial theatre of the period, to feel vaguely guilty about this great talent that sternly resisted all temptation and wrote strictly for Brookfield. Fellow apparently had promise, despised money, also despised those who prostituted their lesser talents for dough, and ended without either the talent he promised or the dough he scorned. Hence a bitter, bitter boy.

Thinking cautiously how to respond to this assault of 58-year Virgil Geddes upon my honor, I take a piece of my most expensive note paper, carefully type the following message:

December 18, 1955

Dear Mr. Geddes:

Mr. Trumbo received your birthday remembrance and was touched by your thoughtfulness.

At the moment he is deep in play revisions, but the new year will find him somewhat freer.

He promises to read your poems very soon, and to let you know what he thinks of them.

> Cordially,
> Sonja Rabb (in cramped
> for dt   imitation of how
> Sonja Rabb would
> write)

Mind you, the fellow did mail it on my birthday, and he has written poetry, and I am sure he has published it, although he was calling my attention to his stinking plays. I intend to write him, on a regular piece of paper, shortly after New Year's, the following message:

Dear Mr. Geddos: (note intentional misspelling)

One of the nice things about growing older is the chance one occasionally gets to write honest words of praise to a newcomer.

I've read your poems, and they impress me a good deal. One or two are absolutely stunning, and all of them are first rate.

It's all right and perhaps even necessary to publish a first volume oneself. However most of the printers engaged in that kind of thing are thieves, and the problem of distribution is a scandal.

When your next batch is ready, why don't you send them on to me? I'm not exactly in favor at the moment, but I still have friends, and it's quite possible I might be able to arrange something with an established publishing house. You wouldn't get rich, but neither would you be money out of pocket, and the audience for the worth-while things you have to say would unquestionably be larger.

> Best wishes,
> Dalton Trumbo (in my own
> cultured hand)

I think this second note will bring so sensitive and stupid a fellow out of his corner with a howl. He almost has to write me that he sent plays not poems; that I couldn't have read the poems I claim to have; that I am therefore the hypocrite and liar that my ugly kind always are with my false and lying compliments and promises. (Or else he will be seized with the thought he *might* have mistakenly sent me his poems after all, and correct it with another copy of his atrocious plays, which would lead to other possibilities.) If he sends a letter such as I hope for in the unparenthesized portion of the above, I shall have Miss Rabb write him roughly as follows:

That she opens my mail and has come across his enraged letter. That she is terribly embarrassed, because when she received the volume she assumed it was a birthday gift, since it was postmarked on my anniversary. That she looked at the cover and assumed it was poetry, without verifying her assumption, and told me so. That I am a man who receives hundreds of things from young writers to read, and never reads them, and am far too nice to say so, and that therefore I invariably [write] glowing reports of things I don't even know exist. And will he —since I am a man of short temper and might well take reprisals against her if I discovered her error—forgive her error and forget it: or at the very least, write her at some other address than Trumbo's house (my sister's address) so that she can know whether or not he agrees to keep her mistake from her employer's knowledge.

If he goes for this, the fun begins. For if he agrees and forgives her and wishes to let the whole unfortunate matter drop, I shall write him more requests for poetry, and threaten to visit him on a forthcoming visit to NY, and assert the world needs such young poets, etc., etc., until he will lash out once more. And so on.

At any rate, it's fantasy I thought might amuse you, the first note of which has been sent, and the second of which surely will be.[10] Thereafter, if God is as kind as I have reason to think him, this fool will be delivered into my hands—and those of friends, too—and will think twice before again he falls into that child's habit of considering every thought that crosses his mind unique and original and never before conceived of by lesser or later persons.

I am now quite tired, as are you too. Write me. I bid you all an even more prosperous new year, and send you our good love.

TRUMBO

9. To a Mrs. Williams, a leader in the Highland Park Campfire Girls

Los Angeles, California
February 23, 1956

Dear Mrs. Williams:

I have been informed that some person unknown to me in the Campfire Girls organization has received a letter from me demanding that my name be "cleared up"; and that as a result of this letter a meeting is to be held to determine whether or not I am a fit person to continue as sponsor for the chapter of which my daughter, Mitzi, is a member.

I wish you to know that at no time in my life have I written such a letter to any person or organization, for I have never considered my name to be dirty. If such a letter from me is in existence, it is a

[10] Although he received a furious letter from Geddes threatening suit, Trumbo did not send the second note at the time. The matter was apparently forgotten until August 17 of 1961 when Trumbo wrote:

Dear Mr. Geddes:

Mr. Trumbo asks me to write concerning the poems you so throughtfully sent him on his birthday in 1955. He begs forgiveness for his six-year lag in giving you his opinion of them. Actually he has been quite busy, out of the country a good deal of the time, and only now has caught up on reading the many manuscripts he receives.

He finds your verse "youthful, and even naive in part, but filled with a passion that makes naivete the utterly delightful quality it really is."

He feels you have a bright and promising future, and sends his best wishes along with the apology for his long silence.

Cordially,
MARY CARR
for dt

forgery. If no such letter exists, then the person or persons claiming to have received it are guilty of a shocking violation of the truth. In either of the above events, the responsible person is ethically and morally unfit to be placed in a position of authority over young and impressionable children, lest the children themselves learn to forge and to lie.

The trouble apparently stems from certain circumstances in the life of my husband.[11] For many years he was a writer in motion pictures. During this time he was extremely active in the affairs of his trade union, the Screen Writers' Guild, of which he was a director, and founding editor of the Guild's magazine. He also wrote a pamphlet defending the union leader, Mr. Harry Bridges. (It is interesting here to note that the United States Supreme Court last year agreed with what my husband wrote of the Bridges case fourteen years ago, and has dismissed all charges against Bridges and his union.)

During his Hollywood career, my husband was also active in the affairs of the Democratic Party. He worked closely with John B. Elliot, Rollin McNitt, and Mike Fanning, later postmaster. During the 1944 presidential campaign he was national chairman of Writers for Roosevelt. In 1946 he was active in the campaign of Attorney-General Robert W. Kenny, Democratic candidate for Governor of California against Mr. Warren. In 1945 he was called to the United Nations Organization Conference in San Francisco to assist Secretary of State Stettinius in preparation of his public speeches, and received the thanks of the Secretary and an autographed photograph.

In 1947, however, a Republican Congress was in control of the House, and my husband and nine other Hollywood persons were called before the House Un-American Activities Committee and asked the question: "Are you now or have you ever been a member of the Communist Party?" My husband stood on the First Amendment and denied the Committee's right to inquire into any area relating to personal or political or religious belief. He thereby deliberately invited a court test of a basic constitutional issue. He was indicted for contempt of Congress, tried, convicted, and after a long legal struggle, sent to a Federal Correctional Institution for a term of ten months.

In the course of this long court battle my husband and his co-defendants received support and commendation and friendly counsel from such outstanding persons as Albert Einstein, Nobel Prize winner Linus Pauling, Nobel Prize winner Thomas Mann, Pulitzer Prize winner Arthur Miller, pianist Artur Rubinstein, pianist Arthur Schnabel, Norman Mailer, Dorothy Parker, twenty-two professors

---

[11] Although this letter is from Mrs. Trumbo, there is little doubt as to its authorship.

from the Yale University Law School, and numerous other distinguished citizens. It was not a simple issue: it was a political issue of great importance, and a very considerable body of persons supported my husband's position, and still support it, and are confident that the Supreme Court will within the very near future establish that my husband was right in his approach to the problem, and that the courts of that period were wrong.

My husband was sent to a Federal Correctional Institution—not a Federal Penitentiary: he was convicted not of a felony, but of a simple misdemeanor; he suffered no loss of voting or any other civil rights as a result of the ordeal, and his crime was of such a minor nature that he is not required by any law even to register as a former convict. The chairman of the committee which succeeded in sending him to prison—Congressman J. Parnell Thomas of New Jersey—was later discovered defrauding the government of money, was tried, convicted of a felony, and sentenced to two years in a Federal Penitentiary. This was the quality of the man who destroyed my husband's career, and these are the facts of the only crime ever charged against my husband.

There is, however, much more to a human life than one single act. A life is the sum total of many years, and since his family is to be judged by what he—rightly or wrongly—did at a certain time, I am sure those who do the judging would wish to know the rest of the story, beyond that single act. Therefore, I add the following information for consideration:

My husband's novel, *Johnny Got His Gun,* was acclaimed by every publication in the United States, and won the National Booksellers' Award for that year. He has written for such magazines as *Liberty, The Saturday Evening Post, McCall's* Magazine, and many others. During his Hollywood career he wrote more than twenty-five films.

Not one of his films ever corrupted the mind of a child, for he refused throughout his career, to write anything dealing with gangsters, murder, adultery, rape, or physical violence. An annual convention of Juvenile Court Judges publicly commended his work in films for its constructive effect upon American youth. His film, *Our Vines Have Tender Grapes,* starring Margaret O'Brien and Edward G. Robinson, was awarded a silver medal by *Parents'* Magazine as the most wholesome entertainment of the year for the whole family. During the war the Chaplain-General of the United States Navy asked him to supervise a group of training films for the Navy, the object being to bring high moral values emphasizing home life to young men widely separated by war from their families and subject to many temptations. The Chaplain-General explained in his letter that he wanted my husband, because he, above all other writers in motion pictures, had emphasized home values and decency in all his films.

Two of his films—*A Guy Named Joe* and *Thirty Seconds over Tokyo*—were commended by the government for their "magnificent patriotism," and have just been re-released after twelve years as M-G-M Masterpieces. They played at the Park Theatre only a week ago, and I am certain that no one who saw them would fear to have her children see them also. In the midst of the war Winston Churchill cabled President Roosevelt to be sure and see *The Remarkable Andrew,* written by my husband from his own novel, since Churchill said the film was a morale-lifter. The proceeds from the English publication of *The Remarkable Andrew* were contributed by my husband in their entirety to the Lord Mayor's Fund for the Relief of Bombed-Out Children of London. During the war he also contributed tens of thousands of dollars to the Red Cross and the USO.

Being over military age, he went to the Pacific as a War Correspondent in 1945, and accompanied the armed forces in air raids over Japan, as well as in the last amphibian invasion of the war in Balikpapen, Borneo. During the period he was in jail, our eldest daughter won the American Legion's school award for good citizenship. For over seventeen years he has been a loyal husband and a devoted father to our three children. If such a man is "disloyal," or if his family is to be punished in 1956 for a legal tussle in which he engaged nine years earlier in 1947—then I, a third generation native Californian, have sadly mistaken the meaning of America and the quality of decency which I have always felt sustained it.

I have never concealed any of the essential facts of my marriage from my neighbors, and I have never solicited for myself any position in any organization in this community. When I have been called upon to help, I have gladly helped, seeking no reward but that of doing my best for such children as came temporarily under my care.

During all of last year I drove the Bluebirds to and from their meetings, and threw my home open to them whenever it was desired. When I was asked to become a sponsor of the Campfire Girls group of which my own daughter is a member, I naturally accepted. I do not think I have corrupted the minds of these children, nor ever failed in my obligation to care for their safety while they were with me. Some of the children have been overnight guests in our home, as Mitzi has been in theirs. I believe the best evidence of my character as a mother might come from the lips of those children who have been in my care, and from their mothers, who are in a position to know whether or not their children were harmed by contact with me.

It is therefore shocking and painful to me that I should be the object of secret letters and the subject of confidential meetings. I have read very carefully the literature of the Bluebirds and the Campfire Girls, and I find there a high devotion to honor and fair play and truthfulness. But I can find no evidence of honor or fair play or truthfulness in the secret charges that are now secretly being considered. And I am bound to ask myself this question: can an organization which tolerates forged letters and secret charges be trusted to instill in the minds and hearts of young children the virtues which it violates itself? My position therefore has to be this: I have sought no preferment. I have been asked to serve. I have served. Now that anonymous persons appear who wish to banish me from any contact with an organization of which my daughter is a member—how can I permit such a thing to happen without the strongest protest against its cruelty, and against those who stoop to such methods?

In conclusion, permit me to say this: if a letter has been sent over my name, it is a forgery. Forgery is a crime in the state of California. If the letter has been sent through the mail, then a Federal crime has been committed. If the letter is simply a story that has been invented, then the invention of the lie itself is a crime, punishable by law. No matter how it is viewed, a felony has been committed here, and I am bound to investigate the felony as fully as possible, and to determine what criminal complaints can be filed against the perpetrator. My husband was convicted and sentenced for a mere misdemeanor. Am I now to be humiliated and tried and sentenced on the evidence of persons who are themselves guilty of felonies? My husband has paid for his misdemeanor years ago: am I not, in all honor justified in asking that the forger in our midst—or, if there is no letter, then the bearer of false evidence—likewise be punished, rather than I, who have done nothing but give my services when they were requested? Are we all so free of blame that we can drag down another on the basis of such evidence? And does not the Golden Rule, which I have accepted all my life as a supreme law of human conduct, apply to the Campfire Girls, to me, to my children, as it should apply to all persons everywhere?

Cordially,
CLEO TRUMBO
(MRS. DALTON TRUMBO)

10. To Mrs. Eleanor Barr Wheeler, Principal, Annandale Elementary School

Los Angeles, California
May 18, 1956

My dear Mrs. Wheeler:

It appears that a small storm has arisen in this community concerning me and my family. The storm has centered in the Annandale Parent-Teacher Association. I am informed that within that organization there has been held a series of small meetings devoted to a discussion of Mrs. Trumbo's character, and of mine. I have been informed that at those meetings there was circulated the record of the House Committee on Un-American Activities in which my name is mentioned.

Since on the one hand you are the head of the school, and on the other the leading teacher member of the PTA, and therefore a person of considerable influence and moral authority within the school and within the community, it appears to me that you are the person to whom I should first address myself. I am saddened to report to you that the activities I have described above are now producing their intended fruit in the clearly visible psychic destruction of a ten-year-old child for whose mental and physical welfare during school hours you bear legal responsibility.

What most astonishes Mrs. Trumbo and me about the affair is this: that not one of the persons who take such extraordinary interest in us and in our affairs has come to our home to discuss at first hand the problems which so deeply trouble them. My wife has been tried and condemned in absentia—which I am sure you do not consider an American custom—by persons who have not had the moral courage to confront her with whatever defects in her character they find displeasing and dangerous to the community.

And what most disappoints us is that you, a professional woman of great intelligence and understanding, whose life has been dedicated to the welfare of children—you who above all other persons were in a position of moral authority—did not once warn us of the shocking torment which a coterie of grown persons was preparing to inflict upon our daughter Mitzi.

Mrs. Trumbo and I moved with our family into this community in the autumn of 1954, having purchased our new home at 6231 Annan Trail from Mr. and Mrs. Lionel Sternberger. We are both American citizens. My family came to Virginia some thirty-six years before the American Revolution and fought in that revolution for the independence of the United States, to which I have heard you pay heartfelt tribute. My wife is a third-generation native-born Californian, her paternal grandfather having given to California the land upon which one of its first institutions of higher learning was established. We have thus, so to speak, inherited the belief that we can live where we choose so long as we violate no right of our neighbors. I do not by this mean to imply that we feel we have a greater right than the newest arrival from the most remote country: we simply believe we have an equal right with all others.

During the school year of 1955–56 Mrs. Trumbo attended the meetings of the Annandale PTA. Various officials of that organization requested her to perform various services for it. Let it be clearly marked that at no time did she seek or solicit or especially desire any kind of personal advancement or position within the organization.

However a seat on the board fell vacant, and she was asked to fill it, and, after being confirmed by the board, she did so.

At the end of the 1954–55 term Mrs. K., the new president, asked Mrs. Trumbo what position she desired on the 1955–56 board and in the councils of the PTA. Mrs. Trumbo replied that before she could accept any regular office in the organization—the first having been, she felt, temporary—she thought it her duty to communicate to Mrs. K. certain facts about her husband's background. She then told Mrs. K. that I was a novelist and screenwriter who in 1947 was called to Washington by the Committee on Un-American Activities under the chairmanship of Rep. J. Parnell Thomas (who shortly thereafter was convicted of defrauding the government of money and sentenced to two years in prison). She informed Mrs. K. that when I was asked whether I was a Communist and whether I was a member of the Screen Writers' Guild, I declined, on the grounds of the First Amendment, to answer either question, and was subsequently sentenced to a year in prison for the misdemeanor—not the felony—of Contempt of Congress.

My wife told Mrs. K. she wished her to know these facts out of consideration for her new position in the PTA. Mrs. K. could appoint her or not, as she wished, and my wife would serve or retire, as seemed best for the PTA. My wife stated further she did not wish it to appear that she had sought to keep secret something which later might be revealed and thereby subject Mrs. K. to possible attacks for an unwise appointment.

Can you think of a more honorable course for my wife to have followed, taking into consideration as she did Mrs. K.'s personal position in the community and the general welfare of the PTA as an organization? And do you not think that when the time arrived for my wife's character to come under such searching scrutiny, it would have been pleasant if one person—just one person in what I am informed is a moral Christian community—had come forward to reciprocate her forthrightness? That, as you may know, did not happen.

Mrs. K. was the only person in the community with whom my wife discussed the matter. When the 1955–56 term began my wife was not assigned to any position or function, and she was content. Then came those circumstances arising out of our daughter's affiliation first with the Bluebirds and this year with the Campfire Girls. During the first year my wife drove the children to and from meetings when she was requested to do so, and the requests were so frequent as to be regular. She threw her home open to the children whenever it was desired. And she sought no position or advancement within the organization.

When the small Bluebirds became mature Campfire Girls, Mrs. Trumbo was asked if she would act as assistant leader of the group.

She agreed to do so. Thereafter occurred a series of secret discussions —secret, that is, from my wife, who was the person they discussed. She was then informed that she had written a letter to the Campfire Girls headquarters demanding that her name be "cleared." She had never written a letter of any kind to that organization, hence if, as it was asserted, such a letter existed, it was a criminal forgery. If no letter existed at all, then those who circulated reports that it did were departing somewhat from the accepted standards of truth. This, I beg to remind you, among persons in an organization dedicated to those high principles of honor which it asserts to be its mode of life.

My wife received vague reports of certain of these meetings, and when a specific one was called to pass judgment upon her character, she wrote a letter explaining her position in the matter. One of the persons attending this meeting was, I believe, a clergyman. The group considered the facts and informed the headquarters office that it was the "unanimous decision" that Mrs. Trumbo be "fully accepted." It continued that "expressions were made of her high leadership qualities and contributions to community affairs."

Thus the only group which examined both sides of the affair found my wife to be a person of character. The verdict, however, was not to stand. A second letter was written declaring the meeting invalid "due to an error in notification." Is it possible that since then you are unaware of what has happened within the inter-locked organizations of the PTA and the Campfire Girls?

The charter for the youngsters was withheld. My wife was verbally informed she would receive a letter clarifying her situation. No such letter arrived. She has apparently been dismissed although she has not yet received the courtesy of official notification. It appears that the Campfire Girls conduct hearings under a double set of rules: if the defendant knows of the meeting and is able to present her side and is found to be "fully accepted," the meeting is "not legally constituted"; but if she is tried in secret and without her knowledge and found to be wicked, all the legalities have been strictly observed.

Since then other things have happened which command our interest and may shortly command yours. My older daughter is a member of Liberal Religious Youth, a national organization sponsored by the Unitarian and Universalist churches of the United States. Being a Christian organization and hence functioning under the concept of the brotherhood of man, the LRY does not practice segregation. The Los Angeles-Pasadena group have held some of their meetings at our house, attended by boys and girls both Negro and white.

The Communist issue, emanating from the Annandale PTA, has been picked up and expanded into a kind of holy crusade which bases itself on the fact, to quote one person directly, that "the Trumbos are Communists so they have niggers in their house." An uncommon number of rocks, buckets of filth and carcasses of dead animals have found their way at night into our pool. On one occasion a garden sofa was discovered at the bottom of the pool. Threats have been relayed to our older children, through friendly sources, that "black ink will be poured into the pool to match the color of the niggers who swim in it." There are reports of a petition being circulated to force us to move from the community, although how this will be accomplished I have no idea. And, of course, there have been intimations of physical violence to come.[12]

We have not reported these incidents to the police nor will we, short of actual physical assault. We should not like to bring trouble to youngsters who really have no idea what they are doing. They are not delinquents. They are doing what they believe they *ought* to do. They are simply behaving as they have been taught in the schools and homes of this community that a patriotic American *ought* to behave. To them what they do is an expression of civic virtue.

They have taken their values from adults who consider it right and honorable to meet in secret and pass judgment upon a neighbor without permitting any kind of defense. Such persons have entirely surrendered the function of independent judgment. They no longer think rationally; they merely react to the stimulus of a label. The intellectual acts of violence committed against my wife in the Annandale PTA find their clear and perfect reflection in the physical hoodlumism committed or threatened against her home.

The most curious factor of the whole situation is that in much more troubled times we have encountered this intellectual and physical violence in no other community. During the period of the Washington hearings and my subsequent trial, which were attended by wide publicity, we lived on our ranch in Ventura County, and our two older children attended school in Lebec, California. And there the school officials and the PTA moved swiftly to surround the children with love and security and neighborly affection. Immediately before I left for prison our older daughter was awarded the American Legion Citizenship Award by the local post. It was a small community, with only one church and that one without a regular pastor, but it was deeply civilized and thoroughly American.

Later our three children attended the American School in Mexico City for two years. The school is sponsored by the American Embassy, the Ambassador invariably delivering the graduation address. It is attended by the children of embassy personnel as well as others of the American colony and of the Mexican community. The children were not discriminated against in any way. My wife participated freely in the affairs of the school. She received at all times those

---

[12] This was the year in which Trumbo, returning home from a dinner party with Mrs. Trumbo, was assaulted by three youths in his own front yard. He received numerous cuts, a black eye, and two fractured ribs. Dreading the publicity he knew would ensue from a complaint to the police, he made none.

courtesies which come naturally to those who are so intent on the conduct of their own lives they have neither the time nor the desire to interfere with the lives of their neighbors.

Nor do our two older children report any difficulties in Franklin High School, where our daughter is graduating this spring and our son, who brings home straight-A cards, has just received a composite score of 98 in his Iowa tests. They love Franklin. Only here in this small and pleasant community have we found in our family a child who doesn't love her school. She loves her teachers, and she reveres you as the source of all authority and virtue. But the school itself has become to her a misery and a wound.

The reason was made quite clear to my wife when she appeared at school several days ago to assist Mitzi in a rehearsal of the Camp-fire Girls for a PTA meeting. There she encountered some ten or eleven women all of whom had worked with her last year in PTA affairs, one of whom was Mrs. K. to whom that fatal information was so honorably conveyed, and another of whom was a woman my wife last saw when she had been asked to attend a shower in her home and bring a gift for her expected child. With a single exception, none of the women present knew my wife or spoke to her.

I don't mean to present this as a tragedy because actually it holds considerable amusement. Adult persons were obliged to go through the elaborate pretense that a person who clearly stood before them in the room actually wasn't there at all. Yet obviously they knew she was there, for not one of them tried to walk through her nor did anyone stumble over her. This, of course, is reversion to the primitive rites of the tabu. I have studied it at first hand among certain tribes in Mexico, and while I was in the Solomon Islands during the war for a brief period I saw it functioning among the Melanesians who stand less than a century from cannibalism.

If the ladies of Annandale find it reassuring to deny the evidence of their physical senses, no one can object, least of all my wife who seeks no position among them and entertains no desire to change the social customs they find meaningful to their lives. Nor would she wish to change you, Mrs. Wheeler, who suffered also on that day from this curious form of myopia.

Since my wife has put forward no policies in the PTA, urged no course of action upon its members, interfered in the private life of no person in the community, persecuted no child, engaged in no gossip and committed no crime of any kind in her life, it becomes clear that you consider her unfit not for anything evil she has done but merely because she is my wife, and I am a man who served a term in prison some five years ago for a misdemeanor committed nine years ago.

The fact that I have paid whatever penalty the law requires, and have lost no civil rights, and am presumed by law to be a rehabilitated member of society carries no weight in your judgment upon my wife. Perhaps if she had violated her marriage oath by divorcing me she might become acceptable to the ladies of your organization. But since she has clung to the sanctity of those vows you have punished her. The innocent are guilty because they are related to the guilty.

We now discover that the taint is hereditary also; that it has been passed down to our daughter; that a child of ten has been punished and continues to be punished for something she never did and doesn't even understand. Her teachers at Annandale have always told us that she is a pleasant child, as clean and polite and obedient and studious as any other of her age. We have scientific evidence that the quality of her mind is high. She loves all forms of reading and writing and music and art, and there is almost nothing in the world of things or ideas that doesn't attract her immediate and compelling interest.

At the beginning of the 1955–56 school term we entrusted to your care a happy, healthy, comparatively well-adjusted and demonstrably intelligent child who loved school, adored her teachers and enjoyed the friendship of her small circle of contemporaries. Eight months later you have returned to us a spiritually devastated human being who begs us not to send her to school.

What has happened is clear, and you who are highly trained in this field should have known from the outset that it would happen. The children—all of them lovely youngsters and completely blameless—have put into effect against her the tabu they have learned in their homes. And this, as the direct result of meetings within a PTA dedicated "to promote the welfare of children and youth" and "to secure for every child the highest advantage in physical, mental, social and spiritual education," and which firmly declares itself "nonsectarian and non-partisan."

The Campfire Girls as a group seek to develop the mother-daughter relationship in all its constructive aspects. Yet Mitzi finds that the Campfire Girls seek to destroy and to deny, and at their meetings, actually to forbid her relationship with her own mother. Efforts have been made to cause the members of the group to disband and then to form a new group without Mitzi as a member. The group is permitted to meet at the homes of all mothers except Mitzi's mother. Certain children in the group are forbidden to accept rides in any car driven by Mitzi's mother. Most of the girls, as individuals rather than as members of the group, are forbidden to enter Mitzi's house, and Mitzi is not permitted to enter theirs. This, Mrs. Wheeler, represents the spiritual values of the Campfire Girls.

Mitzi, who started out the school year with many friends, has found herself in the past three months the object of the scorn and ridicule and hatred of those whom she liked most. Small childish conspiracies are directed against her—patterned in secret after the conspiracies of the parents—and she is quietly and incessantly persecuted and boycotted and shunned as long as the schoolday lasts. Her one remaining friend is called "traitor" by the other children because it was discovered she still associated with Mitzi. Considering the pressure of group psychology among children, I do not see how this child can long continue the friendship without suffering on her own account the same cruelties presently inflicted upon Mitzi.

This slow murder of the mind and heart and spirit of a young child is the proud outcome of those patriotic meetings among a few parents in Annandale School under the sponsorship of the PTA and the Bluebirds. It is a living test of the high principles of both organizations—principles noble in word, ignoble and savage in application. The principles are what they say: Mitzi is what they do.

There remain only two or three children in the group whose attitude toward her is not expressive of hate, and one of them whose attitude remains the purest is from the Optimist Home across the street. He has no parents. His mind has not been poisoned.

Mitzi now asks us: "Will so-and-so like me in the *sixth* grade?" She says: "Can't I go to another school?" She tells us: "So-and-so is my friend, and yesterday she said such-and-such. What did I do?" That is her incessant question: *"What did I do?"* What would you, with all your experience, care to tell her she has done? Well, we are going to have to answer the question. We shall be obliged to tell her that she has done nothing; that she is being punished by organized authority, with the school functioning at its very heart, for something which not she but her father did. And when she asks: "But why am I punished for what someone else did?"—what would you answer to that, Mrs. Wheeler? Open your heart to that question, for one day your conscience may demand an answer.

I should like for you to see the lines of nervous exhaustion on our daughter's face when she returns from school each day; I should like you to watch how decently and bravely she tries to suppress her bewilderment at her first encounter with barbarism parading as American virtue. Barbarism which began at your school among adult persons. If the tiny spark there so secretly ignites flares ultimately into some act of physical violence, you will then see the other and even uglier face of the psychic violence which has been perpetrated in your school.

What do the parents of the victims do under such circumstances? For one thing, when the pressures build too high, we keep Mitzi home for a few days to allow the atmosphere with which she is here surrounded to repair somewhat the damage incurred in the atmosphere of schoolroom and playground. Then we send her back to school until the sickness again becomes manifest. She is thus deprived of her right to uninterrupted education, but at least she has a certain respite from the ethical poison which at Annandale has become a principal part of that education. We now entertain the hope that she may be in condition to return to school on Monday after missing practically all of this week. But we can never be certain how long she will be permitted to remain.

There are, of course, other alternatives. We shall naturally secure competent treatment to rid her of the scars already inflicted. We may seek to transfer her to Eagle Rock before the current term is completed, in which event we shall of course give a full explanation to the proper authorities. But Eagle Rock has this disadvantage: once she is happily established there another Annandale child may enter, and through its parents the same storm once more may be raised to undo all the good which the change has accomplished. We dare not risk two such psychic shocks. We may therefore employ private tutors, or, as seems more likely, send her to a private school which has as its objective the encouragement of honor, of friendship and of learning rather than their destruction.

But before we take such action there are other things we shall, as parents and citizens and taxpayers, feel obliged to do. We must try to make certain that what has happened to our child is never in this community visited upon another child. For a child is of great importance to the world, and its welfare is a matter of primary concern to all humane persons.

We shall therefore lay the whole matter before the Superintendent of Schools, and before each individual member of the Board of Education, and before the Board as a group. In the matter of the PTA we shall send a full report to every person in this community who occupies a position of leadership, and to every district officer, and to every state officer, and to every national officer. We shall follow the same procedure in relation to the Campfire Girls. We shall present in writing the full details of what has happened at Annandale to every religious leader in Highland Park, to the Executive Board of the Los Angeles Chapter of the American Civil Liberties Union, and to the Ministerial Association of Los Angeles.

If it then seems advisable we shall employ competent counsel to seek a court test of the responsibilities of the school and of school organizations for the mental health of the children entrusted to them. For it is within these school organizations that Mitzi has suffered an assault. That the assault has been upon her personality and that the injury she has sustained is psychic makes it no less real than if, in a physical sense, the men and women of the PTA and the officials of the Campfire Girls had incited their children to trample her senseless on the blacktop and thereby disable her for classroom attendance.

However before we do anything—and I'm sure you agree we must do something, and very quickly—it seems altogether proper for me to make a suggestion to you. Why don't you and three or four of those whom you know to be most active in the secret hearings that have produced the results herein described constitute yourselves a committee to visit the home of the persons who have been the object of your interest, and there obtain at first hand that knowledge about us you have hitherto sought at second hand and in secret?

We should like two or three days notice, for we propose to have with us when you come an attorney and a clergyman. We shall be happy to show you through our house and to take you through our own and our children's rooms so that you may judge for yourselves whether we maintain a proper physical establishment with adequate space and air and bathroom facilities. We want you to examine the kitchen to discover whether our children receive adequate nourishment under sanitary conditions. We should like to show you the recreational facilities including the pool which last year was filled with Mitzi's splashing friends, from which this year they are banned by edict of Annandale PTA. We will show you the children's medical and educational records, including a few modest awards, if they will assist you in determining what sort of parents we are.

We want you to look at the paintings on our walls to judge whether or not they are likely to corrupt young minds. We will be pleased to have you go through several scores of musical records so that you may judge the kind of music we have sought to make them love, and we should like to hear from you if you consider any of it evil. We want you to go through the children's personal bookshelves to discover for yourselves what literary and cultural forces are shaping their lives and their minds.

Then we can repair to my library, which is always open to them and which they are learning to use with some skill, and you may inspect two thousand more volumes, and examine them carefully to discover any ideas which you may consider to be dangerous. We want those persons who have met so constantly and talked so much and know so little about us now to have an opportunity to know everything and anything. They may, if they wish, examine our wardrobes and our checkbooks and our personal letter files.

We shall give you a list of personal references with whom you may check your findings, and a list of local merchants with whom we maintain accounts so that you may find from them whether or not we meet our obligations promptly and in good spirit. We shall be pleased to give you a list of all the publications to which we subscribe, and lend you copies of them for your personal and private scrutiny.

Then we shall sit down, you and your invited committee and my wife and I and our two friends, the lawyer and the clergyman, and we shall talk as long as you wish. Although I will not permit you to question the children, Mrs. Trumbo and I will be happy [to learn] from your own lips—and from faces at last made visible—precisely what it is that disturbs you so deeply. We shall gladly tell you our hopes for our children and for our country and for the world.

Such a committee should have been formed at the inception of the matter. I urge you in all sincerity to form it now. This letter constitutes our invitation and our assurance that you will be received with courtesy.[13] I await your early reply.

Cordially,
DALTON TRUMBO

11. To Nikola Trumbo

Los Angeles, California
[c. June, 1956]

Dear Nikola:

I have been doing a lot of thinking about myself these past days, and some of the conclusions I have come to about myself I have not much liked.

First: I swear far too much, and in front of you and the two children, at that. I learned my general "goddams" at my grandfather's knee, for he was a rough and ready man from another era—a frontier era. They are not so bad, although I use them far too frequently.

The sexual profanity I use is much worse. This I picked up during eight years in the bakery, and have somehow clung stubbornly to it, even to the point of defending it. I have decided that it is indefensible in my home for me to use it, and I propose to cut it out. In front of you, of Chris, of Mitzi and of Cleo.

I intend also to cut out a good deal of the lesser profanity, also. You will help me if you call my attention to it when I slip. I

---

[13] Trumbo gave this letter to Robert Kenny—former key lawyer for the Ten, Attorney General of California, and unsuccessful candidate for governor against Earl Warren—who in turn took the letter, unofficially, to a member of the school board. As a result, a school nurse, sympathetic to Mitzi's problem, visited the Trumbo home and recommended that Mitzi be withdrawn for the remainder of the school term. Because of her scholastic record she was passed without formally completing the year. That fall she transferred to Eagle Rock Grade School and continued on at Eagle Rock High, where she graduated with the English award, social science award, Rotary Club award, and a high scholastic average. Melissa attended Reed College for two years and the University of California at Berkeley. She has also studied art and participated in the family photographic enterprise, Art Forms, Unlimited. During the filming of *The Fixer,* she accompanied her parents to Budapest, Hungary, where she served as her father's secretary. She was married November 14, 1969, to Bruce Post Campbell, producer of the film version of *Johnny Got His Gun* which will be released in 1971.

shouldn't much like you to call my attention to it insolently, or leeringly, or triumphantly—but rather as one would help a friend. I authorize you to do this, and I promise you no sharp reply will ever be given by me to such correction.

Second: I drink. I have drunk for years. Luckily, I am not an habitual, which means that when genuinely interested, I can get into my work, and forget drinking altogether for months at a time. However there are evenings when I am bored or tired that I do drink around the house.

The point is this: that even one drink affects a person's actions. Several affect them considerably. Certainly when a person has had two or three, he is not in proper mental condition to lay down the law to a son or daughter. Often he becomes repetitive; often he does not clearly catch the child's answer or correctly interpret it; and often he gets too angry too fast.

Therefore—I pledge myself not to correct you on any *major* problem when I have been drinking. I think I may be permitted to say "Take your foot off the table," or "You used 'ain't' incorrectly in that sentence." But under no circumstances should I lecture while drinking, not even on those minor topics. And any major criticism I ought to reserve for such times as I am least likely to be unfair or harsh. I therefore authorize you—and again to do it on a friendly rather than any other kind of basis—to quietly point out to me whenever I get too fierce, or too talkative *to you,* that I have promised not to do it.

Third: I will try not to drag things too far out of the past in discussing some present problem. And I will always always do my very best to understand your side of any discussion—but first you must learn to present it to me. If we can keep resentment and anger down on both our parts, we shall, I think, find that we can discuss our opposite opinions on many matters, and become pretty good friends in the course of it.

I will also appreciate [knowing] if there are other things I do that annoy you. My job around the house is not to annoy people, but to get along with them. I am not perfect, and sometimes I am tired or worried and get angry—and these factors cannot be controlled altogether in any person who is not a saint. Everybody loses his temper from time to time. But the annoying things I do I can and will stop, if you will do me the very real favor of telling me what they are. Chris once took this course, and I have never since annoyed him on the score he complained about.

And any other problem or thing that bothers you about me may be discussed. And any problem you may have that can be appropriately discussed by me will find me a ready listener. And if you ever want to know something about the nature and temperament of the male animal—I am as good an authority as any. And if I can help on school work, I will. And on anything.

Please start in now and help—

THE OLD MAN

12. Extract of a letter to Bill Pomerance

Los Angeles California
August 11, 1956

As you know by now, yours and Edwina's delightful offer of hospitality for Nikola was snapped up in one gulp, and she arrives Tuesday, probably before this letter.[14] She will fly across with Bob Roberts, and since he doesn't know exactly on what day he will leave, her stay in New York will be indefinite, but only a matter of days at the longest. We're spending too much dough on her, but Cleo and I have just been turned down the second time on passports,[15] and when Nikola got hers we suddenly had the yearning to see Europe, if not through our eyes, then at least through hers. We want her to stay a year, six months with the Roberts' in London, and the last six months on student tours through Europe.

13. To Christopher Trumbo

Los Angeles, California
September 1, 1956

My dear son:

When a young man leaves the house of his parents for the first time it is altogether proper that his father impart to him certain basic truths by which the son can guide his actions, solve his difficulties, enrich his mind and increase the scope of his activities.[16] I append, therefore, a few homilies for your consideration:

Stealing: Never steal more than you actually need, for the possession of surplus money leads to extravagance, foppish attire, frivolous thought and other vices which ought, especially among the young, to be discouraged.

[14] Nikola, now a high school graduate, was en route to Europe for a year.
[15] See Section 8, #8 and 9, pp. 429-436.
[16] Christopher and Mitzi were visiting the Butlers and other old friends in Mexico City.

Borrowing: Give not security, for such is the lowest form of borrowing. In this context, it can be accomplished only in the circle of your dearest friends, the circle itself diminishing by one with each transaction, since if your friend refuses to lend he is no longer your friend, while if he yields to your importunities you can no longer afford to be his. It follows that not only are there fewer opportunities to borrow than to steal, but that borrowing is also immensely more difficult, requiring as it does the most artful admixture of wit, intuition and intelligence. Contrary to the rule for stealing, prudence commands the borrower to think not only of present but of future needs, from which we derive the formulation: either borrow not, or over-borrow.

Lying: The art of lying is the art of the practical. It ought never be indulged for the pure pleasure of the thing, since over-usage dulls the instrument, corrodes the character and despoils the spirit. The important thing about a lie is not that it be interesting, fanciful, graceful or even pleasant, but that it be believed. Curb, therefore, your imagination. Let the lie be delivered full-face, eye to eye, and without scratching of the scalp. Let it be blunt and forthright and so simple that you can repeat it in detail and under oath ten years hence. But let it, for all its simplicity, contain one fantastical element of creative ingenuity—one and no more—designed to capture the attention of the listener and to convince him that, since no one would dare to invent the improbability you have inserted, its mere existence places the stamp of truth upon everything you have said. If you cannot tell a believable lie, cling then to truth which is always our surest succor in time of need, and manfully accept the consequences.

Girls: Girls are what boys want, young men get, and old men think about. I have long intended to counsel with you on this matter as a father should, and will delay it no longer.

The most agonizing problem for a young man of your age upon encountering a girl who suits his taste in this: If I ask her for a date will she accept me?—or will she reject me? One shivers with joy at the prospect of acceptance: one trembles with shame and mortification at the mere thought of rejection. The following mode of conduct, being an infallible guide for determining in advance whether your request for a date will be granted, can save much heartburn and embarrassment:

Let us assume you are at a dancing party, and a girl strikes your fancy, and you ask her to dance, and she accepts, and you dance. Be not too uplifed by this, for your case is really very little advanced. Although she dances with you, she also dances with others, while the date you wish to make with her involves, I trust, your own company alone.

Therefore, at some moment during the dance when the music is soft and languorous, draw your lips close to her left ear and whisper

—distinctly but not so loudly that others can overhear—a sequence of lewd and obscene words. Do not weave them into a sentence, and if inadvertently you do, in no circumstances allow the sentence to conclude with a question mark. Far better the short, simple, sturdy words in artful arrangement, and nothing more.

If she draws back slightly and regards you with a look of wild surmise, say nothing. Compose your mouth into a gentle leer and lower your left eyelid slowly until the eyeball is entirely covered. Then, just as slowly, open the eye. Arch the neck slightly, and, showing plenty of white in both eyes, gaze at her with admiration.

If she turns from you and runs across the floor to her mother's arms, chattering away and pointing at you, put her down for a prude, and turn your eyes otherwise, content in your knowledge that if you had asked her for a date she would most likely have refused. If, however, she smiles and resumes the dance, you have the strongest assurance that a call on the morrow will neither be misunderstood nor ungraciously received.

In this fashion, working your way slowly through the group, you will by the end of the evening have discovered those who favor your cause and those who do not, without once having made an advance or lain yourself open to rejection. The number who turn away from you may be considerable, but in them you have lost nothing. If, however, among all that company of girls, just one continues to dance with you—oh my boy, my boy!

Your mother and I send our blessings. Cherish us in your heart and honor us by your conduct.

I am, sir,

Your father,
DALTON TRUMBO

14. To Nikola Trumbo

Los Angeles, California
September 3, 1956

My dear daughter:

Since the day you left the house of your parents for the first time, I have spent long hours running through character points your mother and I may have overlooked in your upbringing. As you know, I am conscientious about such matters and have drilled you in them till I thought I should faint from exhaustion. We have, I believe, covered the general probities with great energy, and you should by now be well honed on them. There is, however, a rather larger point, the epitome of all points that have gone before, about which I have thus far felt diffident. I address myself in these pages to correcting the oversight.

I refer to character itself: not character points, but the whole character which is the rounded, final sum of those points. Let's get our meanings straight at the outset. Character may loosely be defined as something James G. Blaine didn't have very much of. Or, conversely, character is what the world knows about you. The character of a man is determined by what he does: of a woman by what she doesn't.

This is an extremely powerful thought, and I want you to dwell on it almost every day. Talent for the ringing negative can by no means be a negative trait in itself, nor emanate from a negative character. On the contrary, every homiletic addressed to the subject has emphasized that to say "no," and mean it, and make it stick, is one of the most difficult tasks in this world. For this reason parents of a girl baby are always greatly cheered if "no" is the first word to escape her infant lips. If it isn't, you may be certain they'll see it's the second.

I think I have indicated the trend of my thoughts sufficiently for you to perceive the subject at hand. I have a certain knowledge of the world, and of my own sex, and your journey to alien lands compels me at last to share it with you. Hear me out, then, while I tell you of men, men of all colors and dimensions and temperatures, men as various as the sands of the sea are many, yet each one of them as like unto the other as new-coined dimes in that most urgent aspect of their lives which, if they have any brains (and I fear they have), deals, my dear, with you.

We shall move through the list in orderly fashion:

The British: Throughout a long and unruly history the British have propagated not because it was nice but because it was necessary. The lower classes have been driven to it to keep warm. The upper classes have engaged in it for reasons of patriotism, since each upper class family owes to the empire one parliamentarian, one administrator for the fuzzy-wuzzies, one headmaster and one clergyman.

In the course of delivering the male quota a good many girls have happened in England. The British, in most things so similar to the Chinese, enacted legislation protecting girl babies somewhat earlier than their eastern counterparts. Daughters are now accepted almost everywhere among them as perplexing evidence of providential deviation. They are educated as quickly as possible, usually in the sewing room and by nanny. Thereafter they are swiftly buffed at St. Swithin's-on-Tynesdale, and got rid of early and green like any other perishable.

The boys are quite another kettle. They are rushed off at a tender age to father's school. Father's school, like father, is old and dank and cheap. There, behind brick walls and between floggings, they eat boiled roots, shiver before open fires, read Scriptures in converted cisterns, sleep on boards in drafty halls, morosely defecate in clanking chamber-pots, and yield themselves under duress to cold showers to reduce the amatory instinct which appears in them to flourish most highly during this improbable ordeal. Such training has made them great horse-lovers.

Although they are permitted a brief recuperation at Oxford or Cambridge, the shock of father's school remains with them all their lives. They issue forth at last in such an advanced state of debilitation that forever afterward, and all over the world, they may be found huddled together in clubs where the only sound louder than a stunned whisper is the quiet, rhythmic, contemplative licking of old wounds.

It's improbable any of them will present more than a sporting hazard to a healthy American girl like yourself. But occasionally one of them, mistaking you for a horse, may leap at you. In such unlikely event, the tactic is this: turn on him, smile invitingly, and open wide receptive arms. The next sound you'll hear will be retreating footsteps.

As for the lower class boys, I trust that your own discretion and that of our friends will cause you to give them a wide and vacant berth. They are fearless, resourceful and very treacherous. They can sometimes be bought off with a nice plate of skittles, but not often.

The French: Frenchmen are all about five feet six and they wear black suits. Cabinet members also wear black hats. Since cabinets change with great rapidity and the French are in all things thrifty, over thirty percent of male Parisians now wear black hats.

Most Frenchmen, due to a large consumption of leeks, are attractive and lively as crickets. Their reputation for suavity and elegance of approach is a mystery to everyone, especially Angles and Saxons. A Frenchman announces he is in love with you by rubbing up against you in some public place. You will be standing there admiring the horse chestnut trees, and you will notice that someone seems to be rubbing you. On turning around, you will discover standing there a little fellow who means business. Walk away from him at once. Don't speak to him, and don't summon a gendarme or you'll be whisked off straightaway for soliciting. Walk and keep walking.

The reason for this tactic will soon be clear to you. You have written us, and I have read with some alarm, that you are studying the French tongue. Perhaps you will respect a father's wishes and cater to his fears by learning French after your visit rather than before. I urge this course upon you because his language is the Frenchman's deadliest weapon, and by acquiring any knowledge of it at all you surrender your surest shield.

That little fellow who is following you isn't dangerous in any fashion Americans can understand as danger. He'll never lay a violent hand on you, yet he belongs to the only race on earth that has consistently talked itself into pleasant situations. This curious ability to transmute linguistics into love makes him the most cunning of sexual adversaries.

Read carefully the letters of Madames de Motteville, de Sévigné and de Montespan along with the memoirs of Madames de Maintenon, de Pompadour and du Barry, and you will discover that sex in French is no more than a carnal period between interminable conversations. An affair with a Frenchman thus degenerates into mere prolixity; the penalty is lifelong logorrhea. I beseech you, therefore, walk away from the little fellow, or, taking to heart the course of wise Ulysses, stuff up your ears with wax.

The Spanish: Two years' residence in Mexico leaves you perhaps better equipped than I to deal with this proud and passionate race.

The Italians: Because the Italian boot, protruding into the Mediterranean Sea, has for centuries caused British commerce to sail around it instead of through it, the Italians have been greatly disparaged throughout the English-speaking world. Believe nothing you hear about the Italians. Their young men are far and away the most attractive and the most dangerous in all Europe, and perhaps in all the world.

The French custom of talking oneself into bed is unknown to them. Understanding the essence of such matters, they preen their bodies rather than their minds. But let this not deceive you that they are stupid. They are, on the contrary, wise as serpents, pertinacious as panthers, and strong as the Scythian bear. Their strength comes from carrying things away. Everywhere you go in Italy you will be impressed by the large numbers of young men carrying things away.

I think it may be best to pass up Italy entirely. If you must go, arrive by air, drive straightway to Vatican City, look at the paintings, and come directly away. Purchase while there a small vial of holy water for a purpose later to be described. Your safety under Papal jurisdiction gives me no concern, for I am persuaded you can outrun anything on this earth that wears skirts.

The Swiss: The Swiss, along with the Dutch, prove the fallacy of Madame de Staël's faith in chocolate as an aphrodisiac. Swiss males do not captivate the imagination, nor will you captivate theirs. They accept life heavily, engage in no gallantries, and carry cloth briefcases. Their daily life achieves its most stimulating climax at one-thirty every afternoon, when great herds of them may be found all over Switzerland assembled in cafes as they linger over pints of bad wine, tot up lunch-checks, and enter them into pocket budget-books. In this they differ somewhat from the Dutch, who memorize the check to the last pfennig and record it secretly just before retiring at night. Both the Swiss and the Dutch spend far too much time glutting the world with commonplace cheeses. Eat a fondue at the Cafe Bristol in Zurich and you've had everything Switzerland offers except the scenery.

As a result of all this amatory lethargy you can travel the length and breadth of Switzerland, unescorted and wearing shorts, with only cows to take note of your passage. There are, in the higher Alps, a few men whose heads will swivel at your approach, but the compliment is slight. They are either ski instructors or Tyrolean fairies casing other game. The only interesting thing that can happen in a Swiss bedroom is suffocation by feather mattress.

Nordics: (Germans, Swedes, Norwegians, Danes, Balts, most Finns and certain Poles). The young men of this group, while not homogeneous, share certain general characteristcs which it would be wise to take into account. In disposition they are what the Italians are presumed to be but aren't: erratic as a flight of fleas, unstable in their emotions, and hugely gassed-up with poetic abstractions. They [gorge] at table, begin to swell at the half-way marker, and, like bears, retire immediately to assuage their torpor.

The Nordic suffers from long brooding spells during which he regards womankind as the only pollution upon earth's pure and northern breast. The passage of such moods brings him forth smirking and capering like an expectant goat. In this phase he will lie, leer, fawn, flatter, plead and often wound himself or you. From this he may immediately, and without warning of any kind, pass to apocalyptic rage, roaring out his anguish to heathen gods, invoking catastrophe unto annihilation upon his enemies. A moment later, like as not, you will discover this appalling fellow writhing at your feet, dissolved in his own tears and half-destroyed by penitential chills. All of this can happen in the course of a single evening. It makes for liveliness and no security at all.

The enigma of Nordic passion is not wrapped in so thick a mystery as people think: unlike the French, who understand women, or the Italians, who love them, the Nordics merely prefer them. Since no man can tolerate being denied a casual preference, it follows the Nordic is always dangerous. Stay away from him entirely. If he can't be avoided, the following rules apply:

If he speaks amorously, ask him whether he likes meadow larks broiled or roasted. Meadow larks are the only creatures he really loves and can wax passionate about. He will launch into so savage a denunciation of the French—who amuse themselves by intercepting east-bound larks and serving them in a rich sauce—that you'll be snugly abed in your hotel before he even misses you.

If he becomes passionate—giggle. He'll fall at once to weeping, and all you need supply him for the rest of the evening is a handkerchief.

If he turns violent, reach into your handbag, withdraw the pearl-handled .45 I gave you, and shoot him through the heart.

Russians: (*Great, Little, White, Red, etc.*) The lines to Muscovy are somewhat clogged with oratory these days, and I am of two minds about the matter. Having in the past crawled out onto some rather thin limbs for those boys, not to mention the twigs, I am grown wary of all saws and especially of old ones. Discount the yarn invented by some frustrated Nebraska libertine that the natives are so timid they daren't invite foreigners into their homes. It's my feeling you can gain entry to any apartment in Moscow, and I hope you won't. Re-read *The Brothers Karamazov* and you will be reminded that love among the Russians is rigorous, exhausting and fraught with hellish perils. That such as survive spawn heroes is not very remarkable. The book, of course, deals with the Russian of old. A refresher course in tractors and soil bacteria should prepare you for the new.

Abortion is free in the Soviet Union, so if somewhere along the line you have lost a fall, time your eastern visit to coincide with your needs. On the other hand, never go after anything simply because it is a bargain. In the initial stages of Russian romance say "nyet." In the clinch accuse him of hooliganism. If that doesn't make him blanch, force and violence may be resorted to. Make sure, however, that you're the last one to stop slugging.

Should honorable marriage be proposed, ponder the immaculate boulevards of Moscow and discover who keeps them so. Check with the Ministry of Culture about my royalties, so strangely delayed these many years; and if, upon some midnight street, you should encounter the sheeted ghost of Stalin, hurl the holy water full in his face and with it your father's curse.

Moroccans, Algerians, Turks, Riffs, Berbers and kindred folk: Forget them entirely. You can't make the weight.

Pakistani: Avoid mandragora, asoka, spirit of ambergris, myrtle, lecithin, phosphorus, philtron, hippomanes, vervain, telephilon, myrrh, orris, Pizz a Ugurdu, vorez, Provinea, endive seed, basil, oil of peppermint, root of the sea holly and bark of the yohimbé. Drink nothing but sealed, imported spirits, and check every hour with the American Consulate or the local offices of Thomas Cook and Sons.

Indians: The same means should not be used for differing ends. Passive resistance, however effective in political conflict, is likely to be misunderstood in the war between the sexes. Fight.

Kurds, Afghanastani, Kashmiri, Nepalese, Inner and Outer Mongolians, Tibetans and such-like: These people live deep in the mare's milk cum yak-butter belt, where women are scarce. Travel light and move fast. They are excellent shots, and they also roll rocks down on you. Beware of the Yeti, who is not the fiction he pretends to be.

Chinese: The Chinese male is not very hirsute, and his body lacks the rich bouquet to which we of the free world are accustomed. No matter what you are told, and likely as not he'll be the first to tell it to you, the Chinese male is exactly like all other men in every important detail. Dalliance with him can no longer be classified as anthropological research.

Americans: Any American traveling abroad is to be shunned. The formidable difficulties of getting a passport necessarily imply that anything so hard to come by entitles its owner to all manner of felonious delights. By the time he has it in his pocket it has assumed the aspect of some higher form of hunting license. Armed with it he is possessed of immense confidence and an almost divine immunity to threat.

There is, however, one thing Yankees have never had much stomach for—cold steel. Purchase a good stiletto—approximately the length we used to practice with—and insert it just left of center between the fourth and fifth ribs. With any luck at all you should sever the large aorta. Don't be impelled by thrift to withdraw the blade or you'll be badly spattered. Leave it where it was intended to be and buy another.

The hour has turned surprisingly late, and I can think of nothing more for the present. Your mother, who is still in somewhat delicate tooth, sends you her love, to which I add my tenderest blessings. Walk straight the path on which we have set you and none of us shall have anything to fear. Exercise regularly.

I am, as always,

Your loving father,
DALTON TRUMBO

15. To Dorothy and Seniel Ostrow

Los Angeles, California
September 9, 1956

Dear Dorothy and Seniel:

The next voice you hear is that of one you thought no doubt had died or fled the country. He has done neither, but has merely kept himself at home over a steaming typewriter, trying in the only way he knew to dig out of some rather formidable difficulties.

I dropped you a note when I arrived from Mexico shortly over two years ago. I pulled into town with a wife, three children, a dog, a cat, one mortgaged Jeep, and $400 in my pocket. I had no assets except that cursed trusted deed, which then and for two years thereafter was in litigation with the Department of the Interior, since we had, during our occupancy, inadvertently built on ground we thought was ours but which was in actuality, part of a national forest. Thereafter the problem was to exchange land that was legitimately ours and contiguous to the national forest for the land of theirs which we had appropriated. It was finally squared off about six weeks ago.

There were other problems. I had lost all of my life insurance during that disastrous Mexican holiday. I lived on borrowed money for the last nine months of the visit. I couldn't even get my furniture out of storage because of a $1,200 storage bill I couldn't pay. I sat down in a motel in Pasadena with the dog, cat and one child, while Cleo and the two girls moved in with my sister. I had kept my electric typewriter, and by the second day of residence, I was operating it as fast as the Lord gave me the strength to do.

Most of my black market connections had dissolved during my absence, and it was like trying to find work at midnight in a thick fog among strangers. Also, with no credits for the past ten years, it was wondered whether I still had whatever touch they had thought me to have in the past. Hence I started at the bottom, like any newcomer, for as little as $1,000 a script. In the first 18 months I wrote 12 scripts—which normally would take between 4 and 6 years to do. The necessity of keeping the money grinding in made it impossible for me to take as much as a month off and gamble on an original which might sell for enough to give me gambling room.

Six months later I bought a house for $200 down and $200 a month—the same sum I was paying to rent one. It was an expensive house built in a lower middle class area, and Lional Sternberger, a restaurateur, the owner, was eager in that particular year to take a capital loss on it. He took the government-disputed trust deed as security, and we had shelter, which now has mounted into a certain kind of security. Unluckily, the house had a swimming pool, and the problem of owing everybody on earth and yet possessing (or seeming to) such an extravagant luxury made me somewhat timid. Also, I am overly timid and evasive when I owe money and can't see just how I'm going to pay it back.

Anyhow, I ducked practically everybody and began my long stint of hitting the typewriter. I first accumulated again sufficient insurance to give my family some kind of protection in the event of my death. Then I started in on the list of creditors. I myself was owed some $26,000 in personal loans, but all who had borrowed from me had themselves been ruined in the political earthquake which had smashed me along with them, and there was nothing to be had there. I started monthly payments to creditors, taking as first those who were themselves in trouble and needed the money as badly as I. I have, by now, paid off some $6,000 of these, as I termed them, desperation-creditors; and now am turning to three other accounts which I felt were better equipped to withstand delay. Among them, thank God, is yours. I enclose a check for $50, which I shall now be able to repeat every month until the money you so very graciously lent me is paid off in full.

This letter, then, is an apology which I hope you will be generous enough to accept. I have been rude and discourteous to almost everybody, because I was seized with a kind of desperation, and knew the only solution lay in privacy and very long and arduous spells of uninterrupted work. I never went anywhere, except to some political function when it appeared necessary or desirable for me to show up. Aside from that, I've been a monk—a surly and ungrateful one, perhaps, on the surface, but not really so at all.

I am enclosing under separate cover a copy of a recent pamphlet I did on the California Fourteen; [17] and also a first edition of *Johnny* which I ran across by luck. The first edition is rather scarce, and I thought you might like to have it. It is the copy used in the Norwegian translation.

With all good wishes to you,

Most sincerely,
DALTON

16. To Herbert Biberman

Los Angeles, California
September 22, 1956

Dear Herbert:

When a long time ago you telephoned me about my debt to Seniel Ostrow—a call which came while I was at dinner and necessitated a conserable explanation to the children who were naturally listening—I wrote you a letter about the matter and then decided not to mail it. Your recent warning that "Seniel Ostrow will be there," while no doubt well intentioned, convinces me that I ought to have sent the letter. This thing has really gone far enough.

I am not a fugitive from Seniel or from you: neither am I a thief, swindler, deadbeat or panhandler. I have the notion that personal debts are personal matters and I will not now or in the future appear in houses where they have been the subject of such conversations as you have indicated to me. If I ever appointed you mediator between Seniel and me I withdraw the appointment and beg you not to trouble yourself further about the matter.

[17] *The Devil in the Book,* a pamphlet written in defense of the fourteen leaders of the California Communist Party convicted under the Smith Act. All convictions were reversed by the Supreme Court.

Neither am I much interested in lawsuits such as the one in which you are presently engaged, although I wish you nothing but victory in the matter. I should have thought, in the course of your discussion of my financial peculiarities with Seniel, that you might have explained that I am a little weak-minded in money matters, and therefore ought to be left to my own devices, most of which are fairly honorable.

You might have adduced this from your recollection of previous experiences you have had with me relating to money and to property. In 1946 I demanded a new contract from MGM, and, to enforce my demand, took a seven month suspension at the rate of $3,000 a week. I considered that sum, slightly in excess of $75,000, well lost, since it produced what I felt necessary for my economic security in a rapidly darkening political situation: namely, a new contract.

That contract ran for five straight years without options. It had no morality clause. I held in my possession: (1) the contract as submitted by MGM *with* a morality clause; (2) the contract as finally signed *without* a morality clause; (3) stenographic notes of every conversation between MGM and my attorney, initialed by both parties, stipulating that my reason for eliminating the morality clause lay in the fact that I feared a political investigation and did not wish my contract to contain any clause permitting cancellation for what I said during that investigation; (4) personal correspondence between me and MGM reiterating these arguments.

That contract was negotiated while all others of the Ten were signing contracts of an opposite nature. It was achieved without the political or legal advice of any group or committee. It was the first contract of its kind in the history of the motion picture industry. It cost me a large sum of money and I valued it highly. Without harming anyone or competing with anyone, it insured the future of my family. It was a piece of property, precisely as a mortgage or a bank account or a trust fund or an inheritance is a piece of property. It was property earned by me, negotiated by me, and owned by me. It was worth, in all, $780,000.

Contrary to the most enlightened political and legal beliefs of that period, I felt that time ran against rather than for the Hollywood Ten, and I proceeded energetically to press my claim against MGM, securing the earliest possible trial date for enforcement of my contract. How that date was cancelled so that another contract suit could take precedence over mine, how by a vote of nine to one, as I recall, my attorney was discharged and my contract suit placed at the disposal of committee decision, and how affairs were managed so that all contract suits but mine had their day in court—these matters you know about perhaps better than I, for you were very active in them.

It seems, therefore, that you might have said to Seniel: "This man is broke because his property was taken over by a committee and subordinated to the requirement of property belonging to his colleagues, and all of it was subsequently lost to him. A man so quixotic as to permit such disposition of what clearly belongs to him may be equally quixotic about what clearly does not. Suffer for a little while his stupidities, and all will turn out well."

I do not mean this letter unkindly, Herbert, but even in the closest and most affectionate relationships there are areas of pride and privacy which cannot be encroached upon without somewhat damaging the sensibilites of those whom you seek to help.[18]

As ever,
DALTON

17. To Mrs. Michael Wilson

Los Angeles, California
October 6, 1956

Dear Zelma:

I've received an unsigned letter written improbably enough on the stationery of the Galle Face Hotel in Colombo, Ceylon.[19] My only clue to the identity of its author consists of references to "Zelma" such as "oh, my aching b---s," "what a superby proportioned p---e of a-s," "have found nothing here to equal h-r" [20] and such like.

I have gallantly assumed my correspondent to be Franklin[21] and shall write this letter as if it were. If I'm mistaken, it can only mean you've found a friend whose enthusiasm somewhat exceeds his sense of discretion and who has, I take it, fled to the Orient to reflect and cool off. If such be the case, destroy what I've written here and rely on my honor to keep your secret. If that unnerves you, consider that I don't know many people anyhow, and certainly nobody who amounts to a d--n or doesn't already suspect.

Anyhow, this Celanese seems upset about something and keeps calling me a loggerhead. He writes: "That story is dated, you loggerhead, and they've passed three options on it already, and you aren't obliged to do anything you don't want to do, you loggerhead."

[18] Biberman replied that every time he gave Trumbo Ostrow's regards, Trumbo interpreted it as interfering on the loan business.

[19] The Wilsons had moved to Paris. *The Bridge on the River Kwai* was being filmed in Ceylon, and Wilson was working with David Lean during its shooting.

[20] The deletions are Trumbo's.

[21] As has been mentioned, Mike Wilson used the name Franklin and Trumbo used Theodore Flexman for their black market collaborations.

What chills me about those words, aside from the personal abuse, is a suble shift of terms that begins to creep into Franklin's view of the situation. What formerly was "us" tends to become "you," and what once was "our" problem slurs gently off to "yours."

I recall only too clearly that certain day he emplaned for New York, a greedy, gray-black Irishman, hot-eyed after money; and I can't erase from my mind the memory of that cruel smile on his lips when at last he returned with a pair of festered scalps dangling from his belt. I further recollect how proudly aloof I stood from the whole affair, having little faith in, and less taste for, the dramatization of political homiletics.

Will you therefore be good enough to inform our dreamy hero that all he writes may be true, but that his victims can't for the life of them see how it's possible for their three thousand dollars to become out-dated. They proceed enthusiastically to make plans and arrange conferences, and a guy named Alpaca is shortly going to be in Paris knocking on Franklin's door, and if Franklin isn't home the guy is coming to California to knock on mine and I never did want this d----d job, and I don't propose to let Franklin sneak off to Ceylon or any other g-d d----d Shangri-la and brag about how well-mated he is and leave his cuckoo's egg steaming in my nest, and if he thinks for one minute he's going to get off without doing at least half the job when and if the Alpaca comes up with the dough, then by J---s C----t we'll see who's a loggerhead, we will indeed.

It's a very thin choice between the Alpaca and the Eagle [22] (don't let Rebecca West get hold of that title or she'll write twelve hundred pages underneath it), and I'm the one who knows because about eight years ago I was loggerhead enough to do a job for the Eagle and am still owed $2,500 for it. That Eagle is constipated and hasn't s--t on schedule or in full since 1932 when Cantinflas caught him with his fist in the wrong place and administered on the spot an enema that reduced the Eagle's waistline a full seventeen inches. He has ever since been an Eagle that only f-r-s.

Cecil Blount DeMille's *The Ten Commandments* was previewed this week for a company of two hundred and sixty-three archangels in a temple of strawberry meringue especially built for the occasion on the Paramount back lot. Y. Frank Freeman led vespers with a reading from the letter of "a Protestant church leader" to the effect that "The first century had its Apostle Paul, the thirteenth century had St. Francis, the sixteenth had Martin Luther and the twentieth has Cecil B. DeMille."

After heaping portions of the Sacred Host had been served up in a rich sauce with seconds for everybody, de Mille himself, clad in the rosette of the Order of the Holy Sepulchre, appeared among

[22] The Eagle was Trumbo's nickname for Sam Spiegel, for whom Wilson was at that time working on *The Bridge on the River Kwai.*

them on a Technicolor screen to explain his affection for the Almighty. The picture was then revealed.

Mr. James Powers, reviewer for *The Hollywood Reporter*, having pondered all night over the warm entrails of a virgin peafowl, arrived next morning at the seat of judgment with tidings that the film represents "the summit of screen achievement." "If there were but one print of this Paramount picture," wrote Mr. Powers, "the place of its showing would be the focus of a world pilgrimage." In order adequately to describe what he had found to be "a new human experience," Mr. Powers was obliged to wallow in adjectives I had always thought protected by copyright of Howard Fast: "exciting, thrilling, extraordinary, great, lofty, crowning, magnificent, breathtaking, monumental, unique, sublime." He concluded with the eerie information that "the screenplay . . . is based on incredible historical background and advice."

Local Notes: The Beldon Katlemans (El Rancho Vegas) are miles apart. She's moved back to NY, says she will no longer live in Las Vegas. Beldon heads east next week to try and change her mind . . . Those in the know are sure Aly Kahn weds Paris model Bettina after obtaining a Swiss divorce from Hayworth . . . Esther Williams claims that Cuban trip is a vacation—but there's a plantation owner there who wants to sink his sugar in her indie pix.

The American working class hurrah is fine, and has asked to be remembered to you and Franklin. It holds the womb of the future in its hands and from out here in the bleachers the placental substance appears to hold something that looks very like a 1957 Oldsmobile. The more heavily oppressed of the toiling masses are going to have to settle for Chevrolets. Those in the forefront of the struggle who comprise the cadres of the most advanced sections of the working class will smartly lead the vanguard on reconditioned Schwinns.

Having always wanted a pen pal in the free world, I promise to let you know how it is in here if you can abandon your debaucheries long enough to fill me in on how things look from out there. Give my best to Franklin, if, indeed, it was he who wrote; imagine the impress of my lips against your cheek; and assure the two pixies of my continuing adoration. Don't be content merely to look at the appearance of things: look into their innerness, their essence, their sameness and their difference, their separateness and their interconnection, their ertia and their inertia. That's what does it.

Faithfully,
THEODORE FLEXMAN

18. Extracts of a letter to Hugo Butler

Los Angeles, California
October 12, 1956

· ·

I think about you quite a bit in terms of the suffocation of your talent—I speak of you now as a director—that goes on down there [Mexico City]. It is my conviction that you, having a year or two's backlog financially, could go to England and in that time establish yourself as a director of the first rank. The film business now is so completely international that the ability to travel is almost essential. For example M[ike] W[ilson] was overwhelmed with offers in Paris, turned them down, and accepted one from that sweaty man from whom you tried to get my money (not the former business manager), and the last I heard from him he was in Ceylon. Everyone else who goes over seems to get work also. You could start as a writer and graduate to the thing you like best, and in five years would be at the absolute top.

· ·

Nikola appears to be enjoying her stay in London. There is in prospect a three week bus trip through India which I hope she takes. She'll begin her student tours after the first of the year. Mitzi is settling down nicely and happily in her new school, and misses Mary [Butler] constantly. I now go to football games to watch my son down there risking his very stern for good old Franklin High. We are the smallest school in the league, yet consider that we have already beaten Glendale and San Pedro, and you can see how good we are. I stand while the school song is sung at the conclusion of each game, and watch Chris out there on the turf with the team, standing reverently facing the stands, helmet off for the hymn, and bless my old soul if I don't for a moment think that there are things one can believe in with all one's heart. Although, when the hymn is over and I've returned to the house and sit with my first drink, I can't for the life of me think what they may be.

Cleo is within two weeks of completing her course at Sawyer's Business School. Her typing is now well above 60 words a minute, and her dictation will easily be a hundred. She's going to become my full time secretary, and will in her own turn hire a full time housekeeper, and there are tax advantages to be had in addition to the fact that I need relieving of much drudgery that doesn't seem necessary for the job of writing.

Our best love to Jean and the quintet.

D.T.

19. To Nikola Trumbo

Los Angeles, California
November 30, 1956

Dear Nikola:

Don't judge my affection for you by the brevity of this letter. I'm back from New York, deep in the play [*Morgana*], the musical [*Orpheus*] and two movies. I arise at five a.m. and toddle off to sleep at eleven, and life is filled every minute between with whining producers who seem to think they should get their copy when I say they will, and the nagging demands of my own conscience to keep on my personal projects.

Ian [Hunter] spoke wonderingly of your beauty, and the Pomerances with great pleasure of your stay there with them. I enclose a check to cover a few of your forthcoming expenses. Travel wherever you will and as much as you will. This is a basic part of your education—a looking around at the world, a journey of discovery, a little time to rest before the great lunge ahead into education and life. We want you to make the most of it, because no one knows how soon the opportunity will arise again. In a way you travel for all of us, and all of us will learn from you what we presently can't learn first-hand for ourselves.

. . . .

Much love to you, darling. We miss you greatly, and shall miss you even more on Christmas. However, we'll have you back soon. But I warn you, the first moment you get that dark and lonely look in your eyes—off you'll go again! To Ecuador or Cambodia or wherever else there are sights and sounds and smells to put the light back in them.

Be cute.

DADDY

7.
"The Steamy Cesspool"

Trumbo's first objective—to get into the black market, cultivate it and achieve success and security within its secretive and artificial framework—had been accomplished; hence it yielded to a second objective to which the screen writer now devoted his time and energy: the ultimate destruction of the blacklist for Hollywood writers. Trumbo did not know at this point how the death blow would—or indeed if it could—be struck. As he clearly explains in the first letter of the section, he would neither yield to the committee nor turn informer. Sure as he was of his purpose during 1957, he was searching for the part he could play, for the method by which that hated institution could be toppled.

Then, as *The Brave One* controversy "bubbled merrily" and Hollywood sought in vain to locate the mysterious screen writer and Oscar winner, Robert Rich, Trumbo saw his first clue to the fitting and important role he would ultimately assume; for, as he wrote Murray Kempton in the striking letter of March 5, 1957, "It has done a lot of good. People are laughing again . . ."

1. To Guy Endore

Los Angeles, California
December 30, 1956

Dear Guy: [1]

I have had several days to ponder our discussion of the Saturday before Christmas. Although I have not yet had the opportunity to talk it over with others, I have second thoughts of my own, and a strong impression I didn't make myself clear as to my real opinions on the matter.

The reasons (for which I hereby apologize) that I may have left behind me areas of misunderstanding, are these:

First: I had thought the discussion would center around the

---

[1] Trumbo noted on this letter: "Written to Guy Endore. House in which we met belonged to Ben Maddow, who was present, and to whom the letter refers occasionally. D.T." Endore, a writer, is probably best known for his historical novel, *King of Paris*. Before being blacklisted, he was a screen writer.

previously proposed Hungarian statement, and hence was quite unprepared for a consideration of clearances.

Second: I have long been aware (and have often been told of it by Cleo) that I tend to swift partisan judgments bordering on intolerance. Lately I've sought to correct this defect of character by trying to be more respectful and understanding of other persons' points of view. My nature being extreme in all things, I often carry correction to such lengths that my own point of view becomes totally obscured. This I believe happened in greater or lesser degree that Saturday morning.

Third: I was caught in the climax of a three-day bout with virus diarrhea (as I mentioned at the time); and this infection, as I'm sure you know, leaves its host rather wraithlike and removed from affairs. He is much more attentive to inner turmoil than to the outer light.

It was this feeling of not having stated my position with clarity that caused me, some two hours after my departure, to telephone both you and our host to clarify a single point: that in favoring clearance for those who want it, I do not favor informing.

Let's see if I can correctly summarize what occurred: I stated at the outset that I had no interest in taking action of any kind to reinstate myself. I also stated my anger at the lost careers and the unused talents of this community, as well as my grief that certain persons have been hastened to their graves by what has happened.[2]

I stated I felt ways must be found as quickly as possible to get people back to their jobs; that I felt the problem should be widely and openly discussed; that all possible areas should be investigated; that all kinds of thinking should be devoted to it. I stated I thought such a search for ways was necessary, not only because it was desirable but also because I had the feeling that in certain areas of blacklisted people there was a trend toward getting back at any cost, and that people affected by such feelings should very quickly be presented with the possibility of honorable alternatives.

I disputed the idea that the committee has any rights in the area it has entered, as well as the statement that informing under compulsion has somehow been incorporated by judicial decree into law. We agreed between us that informing was an act of capitulation. It was stated that informing had now only ritualistic significance, and I'm afraid I agreed. It was stated that the damage inflicted by informers today is far less than it was several years ago, "since nobody can any longer be hurt and all are known"—and I (probably wrongly) agreed.

And then, entirely on my own, I went much further: "thinking out loud," as I believe I explained it, I summarized arguments *for*

[2] Samuel Ornitz, one of the Ten, died of cancer in 1956.

informing. The fact that I telephoned back to express my opposition to informing would indicate that I was only summarizing and developing such argument rather than approving them. However, I could easily have left the impression I was advocating them as well. If so, the fault is mine and not yours, and I shall use a part of this letter to correct the impression at greater length than was possible in my telephone calls.

There's one other impression I feel I should correct, or at least explain. I stated flatly that I was able to make a living under the blacklist (although by working three times as hard) and that I have been a happier man since the blacklist than before it. Therefore, I continued, let us eliminate moral principles as a reason why I refuse to take measures to reinstate myself

I said this because I did not wish to appear pompous, or patronizing, or platitudinous, or morally superior to decent and talented men who *were* looking for means to return. I *am* a happier man, perhaps because I am a wiser man than I was ten years ago. At least I *hope* that a decade has brought forth some small improvement of my mind.

After I told you it was self-interest and not principle that led me to prefer my present situation to a return-to-work based on capitulation, I thought about it and realized that I hadn't told the whole truth.

Of course I should like to have the million dollars in salary Cleo and I have lost (blacklisted for exactly half of our married life). Of course I should like to have back our house in Beverly Hills, and the ranch we built with so much love and money, and the cars and life insurance and a lot of other impedimenta that were very pleasant. Of course I should like to have back the year in which jail separated me from Cleo and our children. (Ten percent of the blacklisted half of our married life.) I wonder at your restraint in not shouting "hypocrite!" as I uttered the words.

If, liking money as I do, and missing it as I do, still I will take no measures to reinstate myself, is it then true that I refuse because I am actually so much better off now than then? No. Then why? With averted eyes and a shamed face for my momentary deception, I confess that it is also with me a matter of principle.

With that final correction, I want to think about certain other things that were discussed:

A prominent and liberal producer (whose motives I do not at all doubt) was quoted as saying to one of us: "Look, you people are simply stubborn and foolish. Regardless of what you think of the Committee, it is here. Regardless of what you think of informing, it has become a part of the law. The Committee and its requirements are a part of our time; they are the law; they are the country; they are the flag. That's the way it is, and those who refuse to recognize this no longer arouse sympathy: they only isolate themselves and prevent their voices from being heard." [3]

The more I think of that the more I disagree with it, and the more puzzled I become about the workings of the mind that produced it.

First: I know and can read the First Amendment as well as anyone else. I know it is the basic law of this country. I know that if it goes all will go. I know that it prohibits this kind of inquisition, just as the Fourteenth and Fifteenth prohibit certain discriminations against the Negro people. That these amendments are violated is sad; but it is no logical basis for asserting they have been negated or no longer exist.

Second: the Supreme Court has never to my knowledge held the First Amendment per se invalid. In my own case I did not specifically invoke the First or any other amendment, and the Supreme Court did not rule. However Frankfurter went out of his way to state that refusal to hear the appeal of the Ten could not be interpreted as approval of the lower court's decision that they must go to jail. Nor has the Supreme Court ever ruled that a person is obliged by law to inform at the command of this committee. (The immunity provisions, I believe, have never been tested before the Court in relation to the committee.)

On the contrary, the Warren decision has carefully and specifically outlined the exact method by which persons can *refuse* to inform. It is almost as if the Court had decided to provide citizens with a textbook on how to *avoid* turning informer. The result: no man can be compelled either by law or by this committee to inform. Conclusion: those who become informers are motivated not by legal necessity but by personal choice.

Third: even though the Court has told us how we may avoid becoming informers, it has refused thus far to protect us from private or popular odium or exclusion resulting from the invocation of the constitutional privilege. Indeed, if the Court came out tomorrow with a flat ruling that invocation of the First Amendment *without* the Fifth was sufficient to stymie the committee's inquiries, the situation would not be greatly changed. Exclusion would follow in any event.

Thus the Court has presented us with a dilemma that lies at the heart of all philosophies and religions, the dilemma best symbolized

[3] In order for a blacklistee to be reinstated, it will be remembered, he had to meet the following committee requirements: appear before them, tell the truth about his political affiliations and give the names of other communists, past communists or near communists; make a public appearance for the American Legion or the Motion Picture Alliance for the Preservation of American Ideals; and write a magazine article attacking communism. This last requirement was suspended by 1956.

in the Faustian legend: yield up your principles and you shall be rich; cling to them you shall be (not, in our cases, impoverished, totally unable to work, not hungry, but——) less prosperous than you presently are.

That's the problem: choice. Not compulsion: choice. Committee or no committee, law or no law, capitalism or no capitalism, movies or no movies, it is the constant necessity to choose that dogs every action of our lives every minute of our existences. It is one reason why we became writers rather than grain speculators or loan-sharks. And I'm afraid we're never going to get away from it until we die.

Fourth: who is it, then, who compels us to inform? It is not the Court, which instructs how not to. It is not the law, for there is no such law. It is not the committee, for hundreds of persons have defied it and gone unpunished by authority. The committee does not come to us even now and ask us to change our minds and give them names and reinstate ourselves. Who is it that asks us to do this? Who is it that denies us work until we seek out the committee and abase ourselves before it?

Since it is neither the Court nor the law nor the committee, the man who compels informing can only be the employer himself. He is the one who urges us to inform, and he is the one who withholds work from us until we do. He is, in fact, that same liberal producer who was quoted at our Saturday discussion.

Nobody compelled that man to be a producer in a business that enforces the blacklist; he occupies his position because he wanted it and prefers it to any other. Whether he is powerful or weak in the industry, whether he makes policy or merely enforces it, whether he is miserable or happy about employment practices, whether his feelings are liberal or nakedly reactionary—none of this makes any difference in terms of what he actually is and what he actually does. He is an employer, a blacklister and a solicitor of informers. It is he, and not the committee, who applies the only lash that really stings— economic reprisal: he is the enforcer who gives the committee its only strength and all its victories.

Now mind you from what I have heard of him he is a nice man, and I think consultation with him as to tactics of clearance might be helpful. But when he says that the committee's requirements to inform are a part of our time, that they are the law and the country and "the flag," I think I have spotted the core of what he *really* said.

Disliking the nasty business of blacklisting but nonetheless practicing it every day of his life, he places upon his country and his flag the blame for moral atrocities that otherwise would be charged directly to himself. And thus, since informing has nothing to do with the law and the country and the flag, and since the necessities of his life as he sees them oblige him to enforce what the committee can never compel, and since without his enforcement the committee would have no power at all—what he actually said is that *he* is the law and the country and the flag.

I say one can't carry any water at all in such a bucket; that he deceives himself completely as to the nature of his country and his flag; that the people of this country are far cleaner and wiser than he thinks; that the flag which represents them is therefore a flag of honor; and that informing and blacklisting—the very antitheses of honor—are not represented in that flag and ought not to seek concealment behind it.

Now just as I've never been confronted with the idea of informing as a debatable subject, similarly I've never felt impelled to sit down and analyze my feelings toward my country, as that producer now forces me to do. I presume America is a different thing to each American. To L. B. Mayer it's a meal ticket and a fast dollar; to our own Bob Meltzer, killed during the invasion of France, it was a cause to die for; and between the two there are probably a hundred variants. It seems to me that my particular attitude toward my country carries just as much validity as our producer's and does it somewhat greater honor.

This country means to me the place where my mother's and father's people have lived and worked and died for over two hundred years. (In Mexico, where people could say the same thing of their ancestors for ten thousand years, I lost whatever pride of antiquity I may have felt about this matter.) Having come here, as practically everybody else did, to earn more money and live more freely than was possible in the countries of their birth, they left a very large heritage to their children: the country itself.

It means to me the country in which my slave-holding maternal great-grandfather, raiding into Ohio with General Morgan, was killed by a bullet that could have been fired by my abolitionist paternal great-grandfather.

It's the country in which my grandfather built one of the first log cabins in his county. In that cabin my mother learned her beginning letters out of mail-order catalogues and month-old periodicals. There my grandfather was twice elected sheriff (as Populist and Bryan Democrat) and there he kept his jail open all winter long for the shelter of vagrants and tramps.

It's a country in which I have always felt very close to the frontier, although not of it. Through my grandfather I met his friends, Chief Ouray and (as she was known) the great Squaw Chipeta. As a boy I delivered newspapers which recorded the final sortie of the Ute braves as they stormed out of their reservation only sixty miles from our town, burning and shooting along the brief route of their last warpath. There are less than two thousand of them today and they are very peaceful: but in my lifetime, in my country and very near to my home real bullets and real blood announced their final defeat.

From the moment of my birth I was surrounded with the atmosphere of dissent. My grandmother, burning with hateful memories of the Yankee Invasion, dissented from the Union until she died. My grandfather joined with the dissent of the Populists, and then with the dissent of Bryan, and finally with the constantly dissenting La Follette.

During World War I my father became secretary of a private and secret but officially inspired group of snoopers after German treason. When he discovered its real purpose he resigned his office and his membership, thereby arousing the permanent enmity of community leaders. Concluding that George Creel's atrocity propaganda was false and unworthy, he thereafter refused to display the Red Cross symbol in our front window. Approving of the Red Cross and supporting it, he felt display of its symbol would aid propaganda he considered bad; and so we lived throughout the rest of the war in a suspiciously unlabeled house amidst a sea of labeled ones.

My mother belonged to the Congregational Church, one of the most independent sects in the country. When her congregation was torn apart by doctrinal dispute, she joined, and I thereafter attended the services of, a despised sect who called themselves Christian Scientists. Many were the wrong-headed but victorious battles waged by my parents against the school board to prevent my vaccination and to make certain no health officer and no follower of "materia medica" laid hands on me.

The Christian Scientists during my youth observed a bylaw which forbade their members to reveal their religious affiliation to the census-taker or to any other public or private agency, although they were ardently public in acknowledgment of their faith. This prohibition was based on the Biblical injunction that "Thou shalt not number the people"; and whatever its spiritual value, it certainly served the mundane end of keeping the names and numbers of an unpopular minority, then in constant conflict with the law, off the public records. I believe that to this day the governing body of the church will not reveal the number of its members.

Neither my mother nor my father ever spoke of socialism, but both had powerful leanings toward independence. About the time my father changed from Republican to Democrat, and my mother changed from Democrat to Republican, they were both struck with the idea that their political affiliation was no one's business; and thereafter and for the rest of their lives they wrote "decline to state" on their registration forms. My first registration as a voter similarly declined to state.

So when, some years later, the committee sought to "number the people," . . . [I again] "decline[d] to state." It was a sense of personal rights built into my bones and diffused through my blood at so early an age that acquiescence would not have been merely wrong, it would have been freakish and unnatural.

And now, thinking back to our producer and his concept of country and flag, I am more than ever bewildered. I wonder if he has really seen this country, if he has really seen these American people, if he has really seen that flag. If he has, and his conclusions are honest, he has seen something I never imagined and don't believe exists.

I've delivered newspapers, peddled vegetables, clerked in stores, waited on tables, washed automobiles, picked fruit, hosed down infected cadavers, shoveled sugar beets, iced refrigerator cars, laid rails with a section gang, reported for newspapers, served an eight-year hitch on the nine-hour night shift of a large industrial plant.

In that plant there were no communists, no socialists, no trade unionists, and hence no trade union. But there was an informer. ("This man smoked, that man slept, this man jiggered the time-clock, that man dumped a rack of pies, give-me-a-raise boss.") After we discovered him not one of his six hundred fellow workers spoke to him again except for the necessities of work. For five and a half years (to us), and all of his life (to him; he died on the job) that lonely man who told on us and polluted our lives tasted the flavor of our hate.

I've looked at many American faces: I've seen them as flak burst around them nine thousand feet over Japan; in a slit trench on Okinawa watching the night sky to see where the next bomb would fall; in an assault boat as they moved toward a beach that tossed more violently than the surf through which they rode.

I've counseled with a paroled prostitute on how she might escape the clutches of a policeman who had caught her and was stealing half her earnings and sending his friends to her with courtesy cards that entitled them to take her without pay. I've also counseled with Tom Finletter on how the Secretary of State might better explain his policies to a perplexed people. I've talked with General MacArthur in Manila and dismissed as fantasy his warning that an atomic bomb might be developed (just twenty-two days before it was dropped). I've been asked by Louis B. Mayer why I had no religion, and by a ranking member of the State Department how I could bring myself to work with "all those Hollywood Jews."

I've seen American faces in a Congregational Church in New Hampshire, to which a colleague and I traveled with a bodyguard of students. I've seen their faces in a miners' union hall in Duluth on a night when the wind off the lake blew the snow so killingly and so deep that cars couldn't be used and everybody walked to the meeting. I've seen their faces in the banquet room of a New York hotel when the American Booksellers' Association gave me a National Book Award; and I've seen them again in a jury box as each of them twice said "Guilty as charged," while one of them wept as she said it.

I've been stripped by Americans and paraded naked with them and before them and obediently bent over on command to present my anus for contraband clearance. I've lived with and trusted and been trusted by car thieves and abortionists and moonshiners and embezzlers and burglars and Jehovah's Witnesses and Quakers. I've watched their stunned faces as they entered prison, and seen in their eyes that look of curiously apprehensive joy as they said goodbye and hoisted their bedrolls and trudged toward the rotunda and freedom.

I've stood on a gray day in the Fifth Marine Division Cemetery on Iwo Jima, and looked off at the graves of 2,198 Americans, and copied in my notebook the tributes left to them by other Marines who felt somehow they still lived because those men had died:

> Reach down, dear Lord, for this Marine who gave his all that we might live. May he Rest in Peace. R. W. Dillon.

> P. Pittser. A good boy. Sea Bee—Denver, U.S.A. Missed by all.

> In memory of my Uncle, John Basilone.

> Private A. Danton—1945——God bless you. Your buddy, Al Provitola.

> E. M. Rolla. In memory of My Brother.

> Zeke—May God keep you—your childhood buddy.

In the center of all those graves a slim white pole on a concrete pedestal flew the American flag. And I swear it was not the flag of informers. And if I could take a census of all the American faces I have seen and of all the dead whose graves I have looked on—if I could ask them one simple question: "Would you like a man who told on his friend?"—there would not be one among them who would answer "Yes."

And this is only natural, since we are taught from earliest childhood to bear no tales and to shun the person who does. The lesson is absorbed with our first dim apprehensions of our families, our friends, our countries and our world. The idea of a mother reading her children a fairy tale about the good informer—even if one had ever been written—staggers our imagination.

From this early beginning, from this anxious and even urgent indoctrination against informing, the child moves in his developing years through growing vistas of history, literature, philosophy, theology, art, logic; and everywhere—and by the most powerful and beautiful minds our race has produced, from Hammurabi to Einstein—the idea is strengthened, enlarged, and re-emphasized. Great poems, great plays, great books, great prayers in all languages and countries proclaim universal detestation of him who betrays his friend.

In each historical crisis the informer has always sprung up as a bondservant of tyranny. Gibbon devotes pages to denunciation of "that reptilian tribe" as they corrupted Roman society and prepared the way for absolutism. The Reformation swarmed with them. Puritan New England, as it sank into despotism, gave them free rein. Every American slaveholder solicited informers among his slaves, and found them, and rewarded them (for the mark of the informer is always his reward). They fed like lice upon the prostrate body of the French Revolution, and Napoleon freely acknowledged his indebtedness to them and to Fouché. As the Russian Revolution succumbed to dictatorship the informer throve because he was necessary to the suppression of human liberty. China was governed by informers until she rose up and threw them out, and the Hungarian people wrought their most horrible revenge upon the informer and his master, the secret police.

The more I think on it the more it appears to me that the curse upon the informer which characterizes all religious and all philosophies lies at the very heart of the social compact: that without it there can be no decent relationship anywhere for anybody: that informing as a crime is worse than murder or rape, since the murderer and the rapist harm only specific victims while the informer poisons and destroys the spiritual life of whole peoples.

The informer himself is best proof of the odium that attends his trade. A murderer will confess to murder, a rapist to rape, but no informer will ever admit to informing. It is too horrible to confess. It is, indeed, so ghastly that if he is to live with it at all he must transform it into a virtue, and at that point the flag goes marching by.

Can it be that all this loathing and self-loathing is the result of Communist propaganda? Aristotle would have thought it unlikely. I once heard you make a brilliant observation at the Unitarian Church: you said that men could not hope to achieve peace until they rid themselves of the idea that peace is a Communist plot. Just so, they will not cleanse this country of informers until they apprehend that honor is not a Communist invention.

I remember on that Saturday morning a hypothetical question was asked, relating to what I would do if called to testify against you in an automobile accident trial. I said I would truthfully testify if summoned and sworn. And then, as I recall, some corollary was struck between testifying and informing. But that, of course, is logically impossible. Every automobile accident represents a social injury about which the truth must be told. Otherwise, society can't function. Under such circumstances, I must testify against you or against my own son; and I must, of course, be very careful not to accept a reward for my testimony.

Just so, if a man joins the Communist Party and finds treason, espionage and violence afoot, he has no choice but to report everything, including names, to the authorities, exactly as he would report a murder. He doesn't do it to get a job or to make some money or to clear himself: he does it to fulfill a legal and moral duty. He is not an informer; he is a good citizen and a patriot.

But show me the man who informs on friends who have harmed no one, and who thereafter earns money he could not have earned before, and I will show you not a decent citizen, not a patriot, but a miserable scoundrel who will, if new pressures arise and the price is right, betray not just his friends but his country itself. I do not know of one Hollywood informer who acted except under duress and for money; such men are to be watched; I cannot imagine they are *not* watched, and very closely at that, by the various security agencies of the national government.

The idea was stated that informing at this late date has no more than ritualistic signifiance, and I wrongly agreed. Rituals celebrate significant ideas or events. Indeed, the ritual often becomes more meaningful than the idea or act it symbolically recreates. If informing were a small ritual, the committee would place little emphasis upon it. Since the committee places it in a position of first importance, I'm obliged to give it that position also. The committee does not view it as a ritual; it views it as an act—an act of such urgent importance that if men refuse to perform it altogether the committee must cease to function.

I also left an impression of agreement with the thesis that informing no longer harms those who have often been informed upon. But viewing myself as an active candidate for such mention, I am obliged to reverse myself completely. Let us assume that I had been in a position to inform on you at the time you were negotiating with the Book-of-the-Month Club for distribution of your novel. Let us assume that I had chosen that moment to appear before the committee and give them your name in return for clearance of mine. Would you not have been harmed? You would have, indeed. You might well have lost most of what you have earned.

There are others who wish to publish novels and produce and write and direct and act in plays, and the time rapidly approaches— as, for you, it has actually arrived—when they will be able to do so. I am one of them. And I swear that he who informs on me, privately or publicly, adds to the cumulative burden I already carry, and postpones or possibly destroys my chance to break through. He destroys my work, he ravages my wife, he steals from my children, and he does it, like a thief in the night, for nothing more important than money.

The fact was mentioned that we were isolated. I agreed, for in a sense, we are: but in another sense we are not at all. I have saved, and someday will show to you, packets of mail from all over the country which I received—and which our children often saw despite our care, for many of them were postcards—in which the most incredible things were said: letters rotten with anti-Semitism ("where are all your jew friends now?" referring not to my friends but to Hollywood as a whole) and with anti-Negro sentiments ("Go back to Russia, you nigger-loving ————!") and with the wildest physical threats. One which I particularly cherish is decorated with a smear of the sender's faeces.

Well—from them I am isolated and have been from my birth. But from the hundred and seventy million Americans who hate informers I am not isolated, in the sense that I have not committed the one crime they all abominate. If I did commit that crime, my isolation would be complete and intolerable.

We are, it is true, temporarily excluded from a small industry which employs 30,000 certified patriots. But Hollywood isn't the country and it isn't the flag and it isn't the world and it doesn't occupy the summit of human culture: and who among us can honestly complain of intellectual malnutrition for not having talked this week to Jack L. Warner?

As for our voices not being heard—they *are* heard. Our host lives in a pleasant house; there are two cars in his garage; his wife is well dressed, and his two beautiful daughters glow with health. I am persuaded he earns his living as a writer; and although his name may not yet be heard, surely his thoughts have found an audience, and his ideas and his hopes and his aspirations. He is heard indeed, and he speaks with a tremendous voice in a medium no Negro writer has ever been able to use. His talent is great and therefore his message is good. Although the voice that speaks hasn't yet been identified, it will be, and I hope soon, and I will give him my hand and my help for what they're worth to hasten that day.

As for you, scores of thousands of persons in thirteen different countries read your book and therefore hear your voice. You speak more loudly than ever before in your life and to a larger audience. With it has come economic security, and an assured income for a decent period in the future. You are on a best-seller list; you are distributed by one of the largest book clubs; you are reviewed by the most respectable and most popular organs in the country; you address luncheon clubs; you are admired by innumerable thousands whose faces you will never see: you have, in short, been suddenly confronted with fame.

Only one medium is denied to your book, and I cannot imagine it will be long denied, and if it be, the value is there and it is yours and they will come to you one day and pay dearly for it. At this moment I am signing BBC contracts for a one-shot television production of *Thief*, and I am negotiating for sale of the movie rights in England where it will be produced under my own name. You could do the same thing tomorrow in England or France, and earn more money by far than from an outright sale here.

They want to grade us like quarters of beef. They want us to present our rumps and receive thereon, in purple ink, a seal which reads "Accredited Writer." But it wasn't a government stamp that made you a novelist and a screenwriter; it wasn't a government stamp that made Ben a poet and a novelist and a screenwriter; it was in each instance the man himself sweating out in solitude long hours and days and years of drudgery. That is what makes a writer, and not these silly seals of accreditation. Nor will absence of the seal make any of us poorer writers, nor keep our work much longer off the screen.

Month in and year out the courts slowly hack away at peripheral issues, and at each hack they approach more closely to the central one. Wide areas within the motion picture industry itself are restive under the restraint of the blacklist, and want means of destroying it. The theatre has the committee entirely licked, and is a free medium. The blacklist grows less and less powerful in the publishing world. As the hate magazines run out of names they run out of value also.

For the first time in years voting opposition to the committee's indictments appears in Congress. The last visit of the committee to these parts was a distaster, in that it turned up no new informers; without them it dies, as a vulture starves without carrion. For the first time the committee itself is being investigated—and by the leaders of our conservative Los Angeles Bar Association. There is not one even vaguely liberal publication in the country (*Harper's, Atlantic, Saturday Review,* etc.) which supports the committee.

Newspaper opposition increases, and coverage decreases. Thousands of church members have joined in new opposition to the blacklist and the committee, and scores of church counsels and church leaders come out more forthrightly against it. The legal reviews and the university presses are almost solidly against it. The committee is going down and the celluloid curtain is slowly going up, and what could not have been said ten years ago can now be said with certainty: in a foreseeable future the blacklist is going to collapse.

In the meanwhile, I want people to go back to work, just as many of them as possible and just as quickly as possible. I think new methods are developing, and that open discussion will reveal approaches as yet unthought of. I think we need resiliency and tolerance as we think through to these new methods. I think individual approaches will vary as greatly as the individuals themselves, and that this will be good.

I think each man and woman has the right of free choice, with two exceptions: none should consider a path that makes it impossible for his fellows to take another; and of course no one has the right to consider informing as a possible solution, for then all others will fear to speak openly and honestly before him, and the purpose of discussion will be destroyed.

Within these bounds I cheerfully offer my friendship to such as manage the course; I will rejoice that their talents once more are openly used; and I will to the best of my ability defend them from any kind of attack or aspersion.

For myself, believing that every political party has a right to exist, and that every American has the right to belong to a party of his choice, regardless of whether that party be right or wrong or popular or hated—these being my convictions, I shall re-enter motion pictures when it becomes possible for Communists to re-enter them. In holding back until that happy time I assume no position of moral superiority over others who, while refusing to inform, enter by doors I do not choose for myself.

I have been noticing lately that I sneak small naps in the afternoon. It's just a little more difficult to summon the energy to write this letter than it was five years ago. Wine goes to my head more quickly than it used to. I walk forward instead of running, and although there is much life in me, much has also gone. To sum up, I evaluate, I calculate my course more thoughtfully.

There are certain men of my time who have waged great battles and now look out upon the world from hilltops or from peaks where the horizon must be immensely wider and more revealing. But I, who have only skirmished, stand on a ridge, lower than I had hoped for and yet perhaps higher than I deserve. The horizons I had thought to see will probably be denied.

I still hope (if I conserve energy and absorb the meaning of my experiences) that I shall be able to ascend one of the middle hills— a little hill, but still a hill and not a ridge. Be that as it will be, even from my ridge I look back on two decades through which good friends stood together, moved forward a little, dreamed that the world could be better and tried to make it so, tasted the joy of small victories, wounded each other, made mistakes, suffered much injury, and stood silent in the chamber of liars.

For all of this I am grateful: that much I have: that much cannot be taken from me. Barcelona fell, and you were not there, and I was not there, and perhaps if we had been the city would have stood and the world been changed and better. But we were here, and here together we remain, and our city won't fall, and if it should, better that we lie buried in its ruins than found absent a second time.

Salud!
DALTON TRUMBO

2. To Nikola Trumbo

Los Angeles, California
January 10, 1957

Dear Nikola:

I may not write frequently, but, as I think you'll agree, my communications are rarely sparse. I've a number of things on my mind, and I'll bring them up in order:

Don't worry about money. I receive a check on the 15th, and we will send to you in Paris a minimum of $300 and a maximum of $500. We do not anticipate that this will be the end of it, either, for you'll need more, and will receive it.

First: Now that you are traveling alone, do not hesitate frankly to be what you are: i.e., a tourist. There is nothing disgraceful about it, and there are many nice Americans who share your state. Pay your money and climb on a tourist bus and take in the sights of Paris. Climb on a number of buses and take in the sights a number of times. Make friends with your fellow rubbernecks. You are not, after all, a Parisienne, and it would be inverse snobbery to pretend you are. So resign yourself in every city you visit, and look and listen and be guided. You can, later and on your own, make such independent investigations as you wish. But you need to get an idea of the general (through guided trips) before you can appreciate the particular.

Second: In Paris there *must* be ways and means of going on tours to other countries in the company of other persons. Please look into it. Don't select a tour that involves the smart watering places and the luxury hotels, for on such a tour you will learn little, and the quality of your fellow-travelers will be low. Find a tour that keeps economy in mind, and there you will find yourself among tourists who are more seriously interested in what they're seeking, as well as an itinerary that will bring you somewhat closer to the people whose countries you visit.

Third: Regardless of homesickness, do not limit yourself in time. We will furnish the money if you will give the time. Put out of your mind the delightful thought of homecoming, and think of immediate pleasures just ahead. I learned this trick in jail, and all convicts know it well. You don't permit yourself to think of your release date, for that is too exciting and too distant. Rather you think forward to next Sunday, when there is no work; or to Labor Day, and then Thanksgiving, and then Christmas. Thus time becomes much shorter because it is segmented. This is a good trick to learn in any event, and you might as well try it now.

Fourth: Life being short and uncertain, you must face the possibility that this could be your only opportunity to see Europe. See it well and thoroughly. Do not hesitate to linger a little. Here are some of the places I should be very disappointed if you didn't visit:

1. France: Paris, of course. I think you might skip the Riviera if need be, and I know of no other specific French cities that it would be necessary to see. But I do think it is *essential* that you take a guided tour of the château country. You will see not only the great monuments of feudal and Renaissance and imperial France, but you will also see that other and enormously important face of France which is her farms and her villages.

2. Spain as you wish: and your idea of going to Barcelona for your birthday is charming.

3. Something of Switzerland, as you wish.

4. Italy: you *must* visit Venice, Florence, Rome and Naples. Anything less would be a crime.

5. I should very much like you to see Athens, to stand on the Acropolis and offer, on behalf of your father, a suitable sacrifice to Zeus, who was a very wise god: not Apollo, whose judgment was invariably bad, and not Athene, who was a conniver, and not Dionysus (strongly disposed as I am in his favor)—but to the wise and urbane Zeus himself.

6. Going out of Italy can you not take a train over the Brenner Pass and visit Vienna? No matter what route you take, you *must* see Vienna. (The American Ambassador there was my room-mate and fraternity brother, and he is reprehensible enough to get you out of any scrape you might get into.) [4]

7. You should see Berlin, for history is in the making there.

8. Despite your previous aversion to Poland, I think a trip to Warsaw essential. Something wonderful may be going on there, and you should see it. You should visit the ruins of the Warsaw Ghetto and think on what happened there. I can give you letters of introduction to persons who would be happy to see that you meet some Poles and talk to them directly. Please consider this.

9. I think you ought to visit Stockholm, Oslo, and Copenhagen. Stockholm because it is the seat of a unique kind of government, and because it has evolved a pattern of adolescent sexual relations that shock and fascinate all Europe. Oslo because (or *is* it Oslo?) there is a public fountain there that's a sculptural wonder I've always wanted to see. Check on this fountain (it's in a park)—and if it isn't in Oslo it's in Copenhagen. And even aside from the fountain (wherever it is), I'd like you to visit Denmark because *Johnny* was a sensational best-seller there just before the war. Such people interest me.

---

[4] Llewellyn E. Thompson, Jr., a classmate at the University of Colorado whom Trumbo had last worked with in ghosting the Stettinius speech at the United Nations Conference on International Organization in San Francisco in 1945; later Ambassador to the U.S.S.R., presently Ambassador-at-large with the State Department.

10. The Low Countries—as you wish. I have always wanted to see that charming statue of the pissing boy which is, I believe, in Brussels.

11. There is one more place I'd like you to see, although it may be impossible: Egypt. I have always wanted to see the city of Alexandria, to look at the Pyramids and the Sphinx, to see Luxor, and to visit the ruins of the great temple to Diana which was destroyed by a madman. Please inquire from time to time about the advisability of making such a trip (in company, of course, with others).

That concludes what I consider to be the essentials of a decent itinerary for one who may never have a second chance. Please think about it, inquire about tours, forget about the time it takes and stop worrying what it will cost. We'll need to know the cost, of course, somewhat in advance, but that shouldn't be too difficult. Consider, and let us have your thoughts.

You mentioned in one of your last letters that you are getting all "straightened out." This is nonsense, because you were never twisted up. You were merely unhappy, and your horizons had closed down on you and penned you in. Insofar as we are concerned, you travel not to straighten yourself out, but to learn happiness through learning of other people, other countries, other points of view.

The first child, as we observe it from our lofty parental peak, always has a fierce time of it. The parents are fighting through to a new understanding; they are pioneering (as one day you will see) into a new area of life; they have this extraordinary first child, and they want to do everything right (thus very frequently doing much that is wrong), and so a mutual torment occurs. Parents watch a first child more jealously, wtih greater anguish and concern than they do their succeeding children. The first child, on the other hand, reacts to this lack of experiences on the part of parents with certain protective devices necessary, I daresay, to the situation. Indeed, I sometimes think that a first child is regarded with so very much affection (and with such timidity) by its parents that the love itself must often seem to the child a reversal of love.

Anyhow it's a common experience, suffered equally by all first children and by all new parents. In breaking through to a balanced relationship they inflict much pain on each other, have many misunderstandings, and arrive at many unthought-for conclusions. You have taught us as much as we have taught you; and Chris and Mitzi have better parents for the efforts you expended in instructing us about the nature of a growing child.

The important thing for both parent and child is that each, at a certain point, should conclude what is right and what is wrong with himself; and that, before the child becomes entirely an adult, all the troubles should be solved and forgotten. We think this is happening. We think you are going to be a happy girl and a happy woman, and this will make us happy, and that, in its turn, should make you happy. And so it will and must go.

You have, in common with every child who ever grew up, made minor mistakes—I repeat, *minor*: but are you also aware that regardless of those small concerns we may have felt from time to time about your development (and all parents feel such concern), you have given us so much more happiness than discontent—in a ratio of, roughly, a million to one—that we shall never be able to reward you adequately for having entered our lives.

We wanted you, took measures to have you, got you—and are forever the winners. One of the problems about these long distance telephone calls is that Cleo weeps when they're completed. Her first chick is away, pecking at sights and sounds and sensations that are so distant Cleo may never experience them—and she misses that chick. And so she weeps a little: happily, to be sure, but nonetheless there is salt in the tears.

The story that we "sent you away" to evade _____[5] is, of course, the nonsense you labeled it. You, better than anyone else, know how the whole idea occurred: a suggestion from Bob [Roberts] over a dinner table which had occurred to no one until that moment, impetuously accepted and instantly carried through. True, we *did* want you to escape the deadly limitations of Highland Park; we *did* want you to have a broader view of the world and of your own future; we *did* want you to see how sterile this squalid little community is in terms of the great wide world, and how sterile (even though good-hearted and loyal) were the intellects and futures of some of your friends. That was our concern: not _____.

As for marriage, we did and do very much want to turn you out as an educated young woman before you take upon yourself the crushing burdens of marriage, home and children. This we have fought for; this we consider essential (not for us, but for you) if you are to be what we are determined you shall be: i.e., a *happy* person.

We are so very, very pleased to hear that you are going to finish your college education before you undertake marriage. You state it positively. Are we correct in taking it as your pledged word? If so, we are immensely pleased and relieved.

Both _____'s love for you and yours for him must be firmer and wiser and more enduring than the love between most young people, because the challenge to your love and the problems arising out of it will be greater. He must *not* love you because you are white; you must *not* love him because he is a Negro; he must

[5] The unnamed person here was a college student Nikola had been dating seriously.

not feel he is marrying upward; you must *not* feel you are marrying downward; he must *not* plan a life for you based mainly on Negro social relationships; you must *not* plan a life for him based mainly on white social relationships: and above and beyond all else, neither of you must feel that your marriage makes any kind of a racial point, or serves as a guidepost for final solution of the racial problem, or demonstrates the virtue of any particular social point of view.

Love is the thing: people must marry whom they love and no one else. Love is the only criterion, and a marriage of love must, of necessity, look forward (through learning and patience and change and much trouble) to a relationship that is *permanent*.

There! I have preached my heart out to you. Do you mind? Please write us what you think of the itinerary, and what you think of the world, and what you think of yourself, and what you think of various things mentioned at such length in this letter.

We shall have fine times and fine lives, and we all love you very much and miss you greatly.

DADDY

3. To Michael Wilson

Los Angeles, California
January 11, 1957

Dear old boy:

As perhaps you have heard, we've a chick in Paris. If you and Zelma have the time and heart for such an enterprise, I'd like you to take her one evening to dinner at the finest restaurant in Paris, and order for her the finest meal that it is possible for two such continental sophisticates to conceive. If I, God damn it, can't eat such a meal, at least Nikola can act as my second, reporting back to me belch by belch.

This will cost dough, and I shall play host to the three of you (provided you shed a tear for me over dessert). If you will tell me the size of the bite, a check or some kind of international money order will be in the mail next morning. If, on the other hand, you roll in the stuff and are offended by my suggestion, I shall promise to do the same for your pixies when they come back to visit the strange land of their birth, if I am, improbably, still alive. I think the odds favor my purse in the latter event, so you'd best send me the check. Besides, I'll be damned if I want you running around the oyster houses telling how I begged food for my daughter. So just send me the bill and the hell with you.

Zelma's comments on the play [*Morgana*] were received today; they in addition to your own, are both helpful and encouraging. Idiotic though the do-it-yourself critic's kit may have seemed, it has opened my eyes considerably. I am re-writing as soon as I can get to it, and will leap ahead through Acts II and III, which may be done by summer if the moon holds in its present position and there isn't too much dew in the mornings.

I am thinking of issuing a personal blast against the blacklist, addressed primarily to the *New Statesman* in England. Do you think a slightly altered blast would be accepted by *Le Monde*? Please think on this and investigate and let me know. The thing won't be ready for a couple of months anyhow, so don't sober up for it right now: later will do.

At the request of your wife's sister's husband I send you herewith a copy of a communication privately addressed by me to a famous American novelist. On my own initiative—so that you may know under what instructions she travels—I include a copy of Trumbo's Rules of Order for Young Girls Traveling Abroad, as compiled and sent to Nikola. If either of *you* has a problem, let me know by return post, and I'll gladly solve it in ten single-spaced pages.

D.T.

4. To William Faulkner

Los Angeles, California
January 24, 1957

Dear Mr. Faulkner:

In the autumn of 1947, after a series of hearings by the House Committee on Un-American Activities, a blacklist was established in the American motion picture industry. During the nine years that have ensued over three hundred writers, directors, actors, musicians, artists, and technicians have been driven from their profession and denied passports that would enable them to work in other countries.

Those who remain in motion pictures work under the surveillance of private pressure groups, a permanent Hollywood representative of the Committee, and a system of clearances which certify them to be patriotic American artists. The blacklist, once thought to be a temporary reflection of troubled times, has become institutionalized. Motion pictures, policed and censored by Federal authority, have become official art.

Will you, as an American writer whose work has been transferred to the screen—perhaps by some of those same persons in whose behalf I make this request—send me a statement condemning the Hollywood blacklist? And will you permit me to release your statement to the press as I see fit in still another effort to destroy this hateful business before it overwhelms us altogether? [6]

Sincerely,
DALTON TRUMBO

5. To President Dwight D. Eisenhower

Los Angeles, California
January 24, 1957

Dear Mr. President:

It has been suggested to me that I write a series of articles for certain (non-Communist and anti-Communist) publications in Britain and France, explaining how hundreds of American artists have been driven from their professions and deprived of their civil rights by the legislative, judicial and executive branches of the Federal government. It is hoped that such information will be of value to European intellectuals who wish to preserve in their own countries a tradition of cultural independence that in America has been suppressed.

I have the belief that injustices often occur simply because they are not known to persons in authority. Before consenting to write such a series as has been suggested, it seemed to me that I had the obligation first to apprise you of certain facts concerning the blacklist as it functions in the American motion picture industry.

The motion picture blacklist begins when the artist is summoned to appear before the House Committee on Un-American Activities. There, contrary to the First Amendment's clear intention, he is commanded to reveal his political thoughts, affiliations and associates.

If he refuses to answer he is cited for Contempt of Congress, indicted, arrested, tried in a Federal district court, convicted, fined and sent to a Federal prison. If he invokes his constitutional privileges in proper form he escapes criminal prosecution, but is very often publicly branded a liar, a subversive, and a traitor by the Committee or its counsel.

Whether he escapes indictment or not, he is instantly discharged from his employment in motion pictures and informed that he will not be re-employed until he appears before the Committee and yields

---

[6] The same letter was sent to A. B. Guthrie, Ernest Hemingway, William Saroyan, John Steinbeck, Thornton Wilder, and Tennessee Williams. Trumbo did not receive a single reply.

to its demands. The Committee maintains at taxpayers' expense, a permanent investigator in Hollywood who advises motion picture executives on whom they may employ and whom they may not.

If the blacklisted artist holds an employment contract with a motion picture producing firm, he may bring suit in Federal court to enforce its terms. In all suits thus far adjudicated, juries have found in favor of the blacklisted petitioner and against the blacklisting film company—and each jury verdict has been reversed by higher courts.

Having been blacklisted by the legislative arm of the government and denied relief by its judicial arm, the artist next turns to the executive for a passport which will permit him to engage in his profession abroad. Denial by the Department of State completes the chain of Federal authority, and with it the destruction of the artist's career.

I have been told by producers of motion pictures that they did not want the blacklist and do not want it now; that they maintain it only because they fear the influence of the Committee that instigated it.

You, Mr. President, have greater influence upon your countrymen than any living person. If you find what I have written here to be the truth, one public word from you will permit the motion picture industry to turn its back upon a practice that is hateful to the whole world.

Respectfully,
DALTON TRUMBO

6. To Mr. Gerald D. Morgan, Special Counsel to the President

Los Angeles, California
February 12, 1957

Dear Mr. Morgan:

Thank you for your letter of February 5 in response to my communication to the President of January 24.

As indicated in my letter, the blacklist in the American motion picture industry is enforced by all three branches of the Government of the United States. The expansion of American motion picture production throughout Europe has carried the blacklist with it, and writers abroad are now alarmed lest the American policy of suppression be imposed, by sheer weight of financial power, upon countries where such practices are abhorrent.

I have been asked to discuss this matter in very respectable publications in Britain and France, and I consider it my duty to do so. I felt, however, that I was first obliged to make the essential facts known to the head of my own Government, in the hope that relief might be obtained.

This I have done, and you have informed me the President can make no comment. My moral obligation being thus fulfilled, I shall proceed in good conscience to warn the intellectuals and artists of Western Europe to resist with all their strength that policy of inquisition, imprisonment, blacklist, and denial of passport which in America has destroyed hundreds of artists and intimidates all of them.

Sincerely,
DALTON TRUMBO

7. To Nikola Trumbo

Los Angeles, California
[c. February, 1957]

Dear Nikky:

I could cheerfully have boiled you in oil when I received your cheerful little cable. But time has cooled my temper, and you wouldn't look at all well boiled in oil, so I've abandoned the project.

You see we've been pecking steadily at you to get going on the investigation of tours, the reason being that we wanted in advance to have an idea of the cost, and be prepared to meet it when the time came. I'm really quite disappointed you were obliged because of time limitations to abandon the triple tour idea, which would have been a lovely thing for you. If you had only let us know thirty days in advance, we could have budgeted the two thousand for it without any trouble. (Don't tell me those tours aren't planned by their sponsors well in advance, or I'll steam again!)

Anyhow, I send herewith a cashier's check for $300 for your immediate use. The $700 will be forthcoming on the date you requested it (or before). I haven't your letter at hand so I don't know the precise date, but it was, I believe, April 20. Then, as you suggest, we'll send whatever additional sum you need to Mike [Wilson] in Paris. I *do* very much hope you'll be able to make at least two of the three tours you originally planned. In fact in your letter, you say that you're going to do just that; and then in the next paragraph you reverse your field, and state that you're canceling reservations already made for the two. You then propose plan three, which would bring you home sooner.

I honestly have no objections to plan three, and you, my fine sprout, are not going to push me into the position of asking you to stay away from home when you want to come back. But the point is, the wanting to come back seemed rather spontaneous, after other plans to remain longer had seemed to you to have fallen through. The thing is entirely up to you to do as you wish; but I would like you to grab as much as you can while you have the chance. So please think it over, huh? Figure out how much more you'd need for the two-tour job, and let us know, and we'll arrange the money. But in advance, my sweet; in advance! Ahead of time. Give this poor old man a chance to grab the stuff off in advance, and I promise you I'll grab it. Why not occupy some of your waiting time in London seeing Dublin and perhaps Scotland? Or are you planning a quick return to Paris? Anyhow, it's up to you.

Let me see what news I can dredge up. Mitzi received a fat envelope from you this morning, but it is being held for her return from school. She is growing up rapidly, and can't talk so much with her new braces (hurrah!), which of course infuriates her. Chris is a member of AZA, which is the junior branch of B'nai Brith. He was challenged because he wasn't a Jew; but he found a Jewish boy belonging who was a practicing Methodist, so with this evidence he and his sponsors bowled over all opposition. Last night Kathy, David Angel and, I'm told, about six hundred other kids, attended a meeting in the Hollywood High School auditorium which was addressed by Gerald L. K. Smith, a notorious anti-Semite. The kids gave him a horrible time, and Chris returned home in a state approaching shock: he simply had not believed that men like Smith existed, and that the filth they utter could ever have been taken seriously. It's given the lad to think. He has resolved, for private reasons I don't understand, to be nice to Mitzi; and she is stunned and delighted to bask in the sunlight of his young manhood's glory and approval.

Lester Cole, as perhaps you know, has divorced and remarried. Poor Sam Ornitz, after three weeks in a coma, died, and so the first of the Ten has left us. He was a man of immense dignity, sincerity and learning, who has had a bad time of it. Luckily, he left life insurance, so Sadie is not too badly off economically.

As you know, Mike's *Friendly Persuasion* won the Writers' Guild Award, and was nominated for the Academy. The Academy, faced with a certain win by him, cancelled his nomination with a new rule making ineligible for prizes all who had appeared unsatisfactorily before the committee. It was an absurdity, but a great victory against the blacklist. To complicate matters further, *The Brave One* was nominated for the best story, and won. Meanwhile, K[ing] B[rother]s are being sued for plagiarism on *The Brave One*, and it may come to court, and if it does they're going to reveal my connection, and I'll go to court and defend the suit, Oscar in one hand and some convenient amendment in the other. And then there will be a lot of that nasty stuff hit the fan, and I'm not too much concerned. It may, as a matter of fact, be still another blow against the blacklist.

I have completed the sixth draft of the first act of *Morgana.* It is vastly improved over the one you saw, and I am now content with it, freezing it, and going to the second. I have also finished the first act of *Orpheus,* the two-act musical I'm doing with Yip [Harburg], and I'm absolutely enchanted with the songs, the music, and, of course, what I've done with it myself. The second act will be finished in a couple of days. Then I shall go back to *Morgana* (between about four movie assignments which are current), and try to finish it by mid-summer.

As you have perhaps guessed, I'm trying, at fifty-one, to make a shift in my writing career: namely, the theatre. It requires time and learning, but I think it's possible I may break through. If I do, it means no blacklist, lots of money, and my name attached publicly to good work. Yip hopes to get *Orpheus* on in the late fall, and I hope to do the same with *Morgana.*

If these plans don't work (toward the theatre, I mean) I'll simply develop new projects until I do make the break-through. Then we'll leave movies for the cowbirds and move to New York. With luck, we should be able to do it next year.

Now this brings me to another thing—now don't bridle, it's just a timid little suggestion!—to wit: my name is not dirty in the theatre. Hence, those who were born to wear it until they change it by marriage to a new one would find no discrimination against them if they entered some phase of theatrical work. And of course if you, for example, should enter such work, and I became successful, my name and friends would be a great help to you to get started in such line as you chose. In fact my friends would be of value to you even if I didn't make the breakthrough for myself.

What I'm getting at is this: I think (or rather I know) there is in New York City a very fine school called The National Academy of the Theatre, or the National Theatrical Institute, or some such. Anyhow, it's very old, well-established, and altogether excellent. It has turned out many distinguished workers in the theatre. I am under the impression that it offers two year and four year courses. That, instead of the regular college liberal arts education, it would specialize in all aspects of the theatre: history of the theatre, history of plays, the writing of plays, direction of them, production of them, costume designing, set designing—the works. With, I assume, the right to specialize within the broad framework of the courses in that particular area of the theatre that interests you. I've always thought you could make an actress, but I know your tastes have never run to it, and they're what counts. But you do hate such things as math (a taste in which my own coincides) which you would take at a regular college; and you do love art, stage decoration, scene designing and the such—or at least I've always assumed you might, since you have a flair for creating with your hands, that is to say, a flair for art. Or you might want to direct. Or even write—who knows?

Anyhow, think about it as one possibility for your education. It strikes me as something that would be fascinating—and to be doing it in New York, where you're absolutely surrounded by theatre—well, it's an idea. Let me know whether you'd like me to inquire about it and send you a catalogue.

I think of nothing more. Cleo, as usual, hung up the phone last time we talked to you, and wept. That girl misses her chick, make no mistake of it.

How shall I greet you when you return? A bow? A handshake? A diffident kiss on the cheek? Or with the loud whoop of a parent who confuses the returning adult with a child?

Very much love to you from us all!

DADDY

P.S. I'm *so* glad you like Mike and Zelma so well. Don't let Zelma put any of that female chauvinism of hers in your mind. She's a lovely girl, but a little nuts on woman's rights. You may tell her I said so, if you wish. She thinks that Rosa Bonheur is a better painter than Picasso, and you just let her go right on thinking it, even if it's crap. Aside from these curious feminine delusions, she's as solid as they come, and much prettier.

8. To E. Y. Harburg

Los Angeles, California
March 3, 1957

Dear Yip:

I felt so very sorry for you Sunday night when you called, for I could feel the pain in your voice. And you should feel no pain about it at all. Your call was as honest and kind as you yourself are, and I appreciated it very much.[7]

What, after all, has happened? You gave me a chance to work with an expert in a field I knew nothing about. You probably overrated my versatility, but that is in itself a judgment of kindness. You were

---

[7] Harburg telephoned Trumbo that the submitted draft of *Orpheus* was too political in nature. The project was postponed. Trumbo later dropped out and was replaced by Henry Myers. While the music and lyrics remained intact, the central figure was changed from Orpheus to Lysistrata and the musical, *The Happiest Girl in the World,* proved unsuccessful.

not afraid of my name or of associating with me. I had the pleasure of studying your songs, memorizing them, and trying to figure out how on earth you handle them so superbly. Then I had two weeks of immersion in it, when I thought of nothing else, and enjoyed myself thoroughly. All of those things are on the plus side of life, and I'm glad they happened.

You didn't ask me to rush into a script; you only asked for an outline, which you hoped would enable you to steer me away from inacceptable material in advance. It was I who wanted to go into script, and did. And I have not lost, even though no word of it will see the light; for I have done it, and enjoyed it, and that in itself is a profit.

I do hope, however, that this unsuccessful experiment has not convinced you that you must re-write the lyrics. Perhaps in my letter of explanation I laid too much emphasis upon what I considered to be their political content. In that I was wrong, for I feel absolutely certain one day they'll be sung, and, with the help of a different kind of writer than I, will not sound, in the context of a show, one-tenth as political as I have made them sound. So please think a long while before you destroy one word of your own work simply because my work didn't capture your meaning.

I'm sending under this same cover two scenes of Act II. I had done, together with a brief plot outline of the rest, in the hope that perhaps a plot point or two might be useful to you in some later version. In the field of the theatre, as in every other thing I have tried in my life, I'm a very slow learner. It will come painfully, but one day, if I persist, I'm persuaded it will come. But it can only come through having my mistakes pointed out as gently and as honestly as you have done in this case.

The Brave One controversy bubbles merrily, and I am well covered, and rather enjoying it. They're such preposterous asses that when their temple is profaned their wails ring sweetly in my ears. I gave an interview today to Murray Kempton which you may have read before this letter reaches you. He's a nice person. And so are you and Eddie, to whom this letter goes with much love from Cleo and me.

Viva!
DALTON

9. To Murray Kempton

Los Angeles, California
March 5, 1957

Dear Murray Kempton:

I am so extremely sorry I didn't catch your name at the beginning of our telephone conversation instead of the end, for I'd have warmed up much sooner and perhaps given you more to go on. I know your work well, and was especially moved by your piece on the Wellman children. I was alerted for *Part of Our Time,* and received probably the first local copy.

Being classified a ruin before I have finished the course troubled me somewhat; but my wounds were soothed, if such is possible, by the quality of prose that inflicted them. I'd rather be stilettoed than rasped to death, and you handle the sharper instrument with disconcerting skill.[8]

Sometime when we see each other, as I hope we shall, I'll explain certain accounts which I think were given you inaccurately. By that I don't mean the sources were dishonest, but that memory itself marvelously parallels necessity. At least I've found mine does, and as I grow older my sense of personal uniqueness diminishes steadily.

Another objection might reasonably stem from the contempt you feel for those who write motion pictures. Such contempt, of course, isn't uncommon among intellectuals. Indeed, it's often seemed to me that Hollywood is as necessary to the intellectuals as the nigrah to his cracker neighbors. We're going down, boys, but look at *him.*

Having spent long hours, at their request, with such disparate characters as Sinclair Lewis, Theodore Dreiser, Scott Fitzgerald and John McNulty (how fortunate for my story they're all dead!), attempting to explain a writing technique they wanted very much to learn, I can assure you consistent performance of the job requires a high order of skill. The four men I mention didn't fail because their intellects were too lofty, nor because they were too pure of heart, nor because they held the medium in contempt. Successful in other fields of writing, they failed as screenwriters because they had no talent for that particular and difficult form.

All of this is by way of getting around to a second instance in which I think your informants served you badly. I worked in motion pictures from 1936 to 1947. During the eleven-year period I had a hand in over twenty-five films. The first three or four years I count my apprenticeship, for I am a slow and stubborn learner. Your research man credited me with five obscure pictures written in 1938

---

[8] This letter, constituting Trumbo's refutation of Kempton's *Part of Our Time,* was the beginning of a lively correspondence between the screen writer and the New York *Post* staff writer.

and 1939 as "a *representative* list" of the films by which my merit was to be judged. *Life* magazine did the same thing.

To speak of credits and money is a dull business, but your Hollywood chapter mentions both to the disparagement of blacklisted persons. I speak here only of myself, for that's a subject I know a great deal about. I assume that others could make similar complaints on their own behalf. In 1947, when the hearings were held, I held a straight five-year contract at the highest salary ever paid to that date for writing services alone on a long term basis.

The contract had other interesting features. It was the second in Hollywood history to have no morals clause, the first having been signed by me three years previously. The studio had no option clauses and no power of suspension. There was no limit to the amount of time I could spend writing each script, although I had the option to switch the deal from the weekly salary to a stipulated flat sum for any script whenever, in my judgment, it seemed profitable for me to do so. I was guaranteed choice of assignments, and could read and reject stories indefinitely at full salary. I had the right to take such vacations as I chose for as long as I chose at the end of each assignment, the contract being extended by the length of my vacation period, but the studio having no reciprocal rights to impose vacations upon me. I could work wherever I chose, in California or out of it, and the terms under which the studio could summon me for consultation were carefully stipulated.

I can only add that the proprietors of M-G-M were never deceived about my political affiliations, and that so long as I worked there I informed each producer of those affiliations before I accepted an assignment from him. There were no objections. The point is this: without sighing for past glories (to which I wouldn't return if I could), how does one account for such a contract on the basis of my representative work as given in *Part of Our Time?*

It would, of course, be ridiculous to deny that one is "not very attractive," or "not especially appetizing." But one can, perhaps, cavil at the idea that his "habits were Hollywood's" if he had spent most of his Hollywood years in quiet family life a hundred miles away from the city and twenty miles from a telephone. Or again, one might prefer to read that his prose had descended from a style that won a National Book Award to "the muddier depths of a Nash-Kelvinator ad," if only to understand how precipitous and extreme the decline actually was. And one could even turn a little angry to read that the practice of his profession, so necessary if a growing family is to be sustained, had turned into a "pathetic effort to cling" to what he formerly had.

There are, of course, other books which touch upon the subject. Paul Blanshard in *The Right to Read* states that *Johnny Got His Gun* was "produced during the period of the Hitler-Stalin pact." The book was finished six months before the pact in a period when the Communist Party was actively hostile to pacifist tendencies. If my beliefs were as powerful as my hopes that the Blanshard book will go into a second edition, I'd ask for a correction and probably get it, as I'm sure I'd get a correction of fact, as opposed to opinion, from you. I wouldn't, of course, ask Toledano to retract his statement in *Seeds of Treason* that Alger Hiss brought me to the San Francisco Conference, for he wouldn't do it. Nor would there be great point in asking Alistair Cooke to reconsider his judgment, in *A Generation on Trial,* that the committee and its victims were similarly "squalid and rowdy."

The truth is that little by little one grows accustomed to the public picture of oneself. Each newspaper and every book adds something to the portrait. New features emerge from the shadows, the imperfections stand out ever more sharply, the general ugliness acquires perspective and dimension. And there is nothing one can do to stop it except that which one would not do. So one averts his face while the mould cools and the materials harden to their last, irrevocable shape.

One comprehends also that the contemporary records which have fashioned that visage will become source material for future history; that some person yet unborn—perhaps one's own grandchild— searching through dusty library shelves for the minutia of the past's truth, will discover a face looking up at him: the unappetizing and unattractive face of a squalid mediocrity with no streak of goodness in him, having preferred to waste his life with treason and muddy prose for the advancement of wicked causes. It will be my face he sees.

When my children say to me: why does this man call you a traitor, why does that one give a false setting to your book, why does another say your worst work typifies your whole, why does the reporter call you disloyal and the judge confirm you criminal?—I answer, "The man lies." I know, of course, that he really doesn't; that no man can be called a liar for writing what he believes to be the truth. I use the word because it comforts my children and is instantly understood.

What I don't explain to them—but shall later—is that these men and other men and I, caught up in the furies and complexities of an ugly time and searching for the truth of them, have turned cruel and frightened and immensely wicked. We seek so passionately that we strike down all who seem to stand between us and the answer, or even those who assert a different answer. We have been touched with the madness of moral infallibility, and we know it, and we must put the blame from us, so I put it on you, and you on me, and all of us upon everyone else. The vision in the mirror has struck us blind. Some of us, revolving upon our private center and firing steadily, will withstand the fury, and some will fall. The victors will shine forth as heroes—perhaps; the fallen will be forever execrated as villains—possibly.

For myself, I've long since concluded that very few of us are conscious liars, that none of us acts except upon a principle he calls good, and that many of us are closer together than we think. In the meanwhile, I look forward and backward. I shouldn't like to go through the last fifteen years again; but having got through them I have the most curious feeling they were inevitable. Each month and year has been an experience quite outside of ordinary experience. Having acquired the experience, one would not, of course, wish to move backward in time simply to avoid the principal thing one has gained.

Under the pleasant goad of three children who will require educations, I labor hard but not too uncomfortably in such scraggly vineyards as come to my attention, and accumulate paradoxes only a farceur could imagine. I warn my clients the fee for a second job will be twice that of the first. By emphasizing the hellish peril of having me in their houses, I compel them to drive thirty miles to my back door. I invent assumed names which, spoken to their secretaries, bring them leaping to the telephone like startled hares. I permit them one conference at the beginning of a script and bid them come well prepared. A second conference is granted upon completion, but between conferences not a word nor a page. For the good of their souls I surround myself with legally phony bank accounts, mysterious rituals, and awesome oaths.

Only the boundless courage of cupidity enables them to survive such an ordeal. Once they emerge from it, clutching a script as good or as bad as their taste, I crown them with the accolade Great and Dauntless Enemy of the Blacklist. They stagger off in a glow of moral grandeur, better, sounder-sleeping men for my ministrations.

When good luck with the first job impels them to return for a second at double fee, the game turns a little grimmer, and I can feel in their eyes the soft, phosphorescent lights of resentment when my back is turned. The third time around it's fireworks. Charges of "I kept you alive when you were starving!" Countercharges of "You came to me a pigmy, and now you tower above your kind!" Some of them remain for the diploma course; others stride angrily off to disaster. I feel no rancor toward the lost, for by that time replacements are confidently moving up the ladder.

The advent of Robert Rich has, of course, been a godsend. I'll tell you about it and others some day. It has kept me happily absorbed in tossing dead cats and false leads into the steamy cesspool that now lies exposed for all to see. It has done a lot of good. People are laughing again, and all the solemn asses of the Academy (who broke the story) have taken shelter behind something strongly resembling the fifth: refusal to talk "on advice of counsel." Your own article was a delight, and I'm indebted to you for the very pleasant way you dealt with me. I don't give much of a damn whether the blacklist ever ends, but it's bad, and others do care, and with good cause, so I try to keep an oar in.

In the meanwhile, I work on a play. If I'm as competent as I think I am, it or a second or a third will ultimately deliver me to New York and a different and very difficult medium. If I'm not competent, it'll be an excellent joke. There is nothing funnier than misjudgment of one's own self. The point, of course, is to see it.

Cordially,

DALTON TRUMBO

Postscript: I'd not reveal so much of myself to you if I didn't admire your work. Even so, and knowing it's not necessary, innate canniness compels me to risk offending you by the addition of that accursed word "personal," which is always a stain upon friendliness.

10. To the King Brothers

Los Angeles, California
April 19, 1957

Dear Frank and Maury and Hymie—and dear *dear* Mama King—!

Some time ago I wrote you an angry letter. I wish I had never written it. Yet in a way I'm glad I did write it, for the result of it was that we agreed never again to mention past points of difference between us. And neither of us ever shall.

However, that letter, like all angry letters, was one-sided. I remembered everything I felt you had done *to* me, and I forgot everything you felt you had done *for* me. This is a common failing of angry men, and I displayed in my letter a full share of it.

I forgot that just before I went to jail you gave me an advance on a script; and that immediately thereafter the court decision went against me; and that I went to jail without writing the script I had agreed to write; and that you did not ask for your money back for non-performance as you had a right to do; and that when I got out of jail the commitment still stood with you, so I stepped out of jail into a job.

I also forgot that when I recently sold you a script the terms were $7,000 plus $3,000 when the script went into production—but that you paid me the whole sum, and that the script has not gone into production until this day. It was an extra $3,000 which you knew I needed, and which you were not obliged to give me, and which you did give me.

These are the things men forget when they're angry—but they really can't be forgotten forever. I apologize for having temporarily forgotten them.

I have worked with the biggest men in this business (at least, that was their billing). I have had contracts with them sixty and seventy pages long, arranged by the shrewdest agents and the shrewdest lawyers. Not one of those big men was capable of telling the truth, and not one of those contracts was worth the paper it was written on.

The other side of the coin is this: I have worked for you for ten years on the basis of a handshake here and a letter there. And I say to you, a handshake with the King Brothers has more honor behind it, more integrity, and more value than any legal document sworn under oath by any producer or production firm in the motion picture industry.

This blacklist is going to collapse because it is rotten, immoral and illegal. I am one day going to be working openly in the motion picture industry. When that day comes, I swear to you I will never sign a term contract with any major studio. I will, proudly and by preference, do at least one picture a year for King Brothers, and I will try to make it the best picture that I have it in me to do.

You and I have never finished college, and therefore we are low-brows; you and I have come up the hard way, and therefore we are roughnecks who have no right to be in this high-minded business. Yet I look forward with relish to the time when we shall prove to the industry and to the world that we know more about making motion pictures than the whole gang of publicly known and convicted liars, rapists, tax-evaders and dope addicts who presently control this business and are busily engaged in destroying it and themselves.

With deep affection,
OLD DOC ABBOTT

11. To Alvah Bessie

Los Angeles, California
[c. June 18, 1957]

Dear Alvah:

. . . .

Now as to the work situation breaking in the near future let me try to give you the real low-down as I see it.[9] Very few people are

[9] Bessie, one of the Ten, wrote Trumbo on June 18, 1957 about the possibilities of getting back to screen writing. Bessie was stage manager of the Hungry i nightclub in San Francisco.

making their entire living out of the writing of motion picture scripts. Mike Wilson, the year before he left for France, earned $6,000 from motion picture writing. That gives you an idea.

I have been able to earn a living which over three years ran from 16 to 18 to approximately $40,000 for the respective years. I did this because I am able to write continuously on two or three projects at the same time; because I write very swiftly; because I have a hell of a lot of physical energy; and because I have, in the course of writing some sixty screenplays, almost learned by heart a certain mechanical proficiency which is still desirable. To this day I occasionally accept a job for as little as $3,500 for a script. I consider a $10,000 script a boon and a windfall. Not only that but in order to earn what I do earn I have felt compelled to make a policy of absolutely guaranteeing my work. Thus I may rewrite a script three or four times. Certainly it is not worth it for the one job and the one fee involved; but the man comes back if he gets this kind of service, and thus I am assured of a continuing income. Many people in the black market won't do this. They demand the conditions and hope for the money that we had when there was no blacklist. It just doesn't exist and a man has to face up to it on its own grounds.

A few people are making money out of television but I do not know anything about that medium. I have once or twice recommended other persons for jobs that were offered to me that I felt I did not wish to take; and each time it has turned out unfortunately for me. That is to say, the producer was disappointed with the work that he got and was also disappointed with the attitude of the writer which was now-that-I-have-my-money-take-the-script-that-I-give-you-and-the-hell-with-you. The result was that in each of those instances I felt obliged to redo the script to the producer's satisfaction. In the black market a recommendation very often means what amounts to a guarantee of the recommendee's work.

If you could work as rapidly as I, and if your experience in motion pictures were as extensive as mine, still I would not and could not honestly advise you yet to come down and undertake to earn your living from the writing of motion pictures because it takes at least six months to get involved in the black market—to get your feelers out—to get your clientele established. Therefore, miserable as your present work is, it is less miserable than that which you would encounter down here for the time being. I do think this blacklist is going to blow up in their faces within six to eight months. And then a horrible thing is going to happen: those who were most successful in the old days will be the first to be called back. And so it will filter down in the renewal of the free market until those least successful return to work. I don't see any other way for it to happen. And I feel when this does occur so many bitter feelings will be engendered that I am not at all certain I wish to have any part of the whole mess.

Anyhow there is my report of . . . how it looks from here and from my point of view. I think you'll be back here and I think you'll be writing scripts but I think that it's going to take a little more time than either you or I hope. . . .

God bless and salud!
DALTON

12. To Bill Dobbschutz of the Noll Auto Company

Los Angeles, California
October 24, 1957

Dear Mr. Dobbschutz:

Early in July I brought my 1955 Packard Four Hundred to Noll Auto, and delivered it personally to you. I gave you a written list of the things I found wrong with it which I wanted repaired. In addition, you told me of other things wrong (particularly the transmission, torsion bar and stabilizer), and it was agreed that they also be repaired. In addition to all things specifically discussed or noted, I told you I wanted to have anything else you found wrong attended to. I told you I wanted the car put in first class shape, and I did not limit you as to the cost. I did not, as a matter of fact, even ask you what it *might* cost. I was content in the knowledge that I had placed my car in the hands of a long-established, ethically-operated business concern, whose services would be expensive but whose work would be worth the expense.

You kept the car for over six weeks. I telephoned several times inquiring about progress, for I'd had no idea I should be deprived of transportation for so long a time. Each time the problem of completing the job lay either in the fact that you were unable to secure Packard parts, or that you were so rushed in the shop that it was impossible to finish my work sooner. Each time you promised to telephone me when the job was done. You never did telephone; and when, toward the end of the six-week period, I began to express a reasonable desire to get the car on the road again, it was I who had to telephone you—and several times, at that—before I succeeded in getting delivery. I received the car on September 3, and, without testing it or even going over the bill with you, paid $583.56 on the spot.

After having paid the bill, I examined the car. I noted five minor examples of careless workmanship or bad organization that caused me some misgivings. They were: (1) I was charged for a full tank of gasoline, but received only slightly more than half a tank; (2) I had paid to have a new motor installed in the right door window, but upon delivery the window did not function; (3) when I turned the car over to you the interior lights worked perfectly when the door was opened and closed but by the time you were through with it $583.56 later the lights didn't work at all; (4) I was charged for a wash job, but the car you returned to me was spattered on the right side, and the windows were heavily coated with dust; (5) since the engine was missing, I looked under the hood and found one spark plug disconnected.

I frankly could not understand any first-rate business organization returning a car to its owner, after a costly repair job, with such slip-shod inspection. However none of the problems was very important, so I mentioned only the window and the lights to you. I did, how-ever, begin to fear that an organization which is not equipped to handle small matters is rarely efficient in large ones. And so it turned out to be. I telephoned you the next day, informing you of major de-fects which had not been repaired. I told you that I absolutely had to use the car around town for a few days, but that I wanted it on the record that the things I complained of had not occurred through such use, but had been reported to you before any but test use.

I want here to pause to point out one of the most annoying things you had failed to correct. When I first brought the car in I had listed that it boiled, and that the heat gauge did not register such over-heating. I told you to find out what caused it to boil and repair the cause and to check the heat gauge so that it would properly register the engine's temperature. I naturally assumed this had been done. Here are the defects I informed you of over the telephone:

1. It still overheated, it still boiled, and it still didn't register on the gauge.

2. In its overheated condition, the brakes would not work prop-erly. One would step on them hard; the car would come to a stop; at the moment of stopping it would seem as though the brakes had sud-denly slipped, and the car would lunge forward six to eight inches before coming to a final stop.

3. Hot or cold, the motor died at every slow-down and at every corner. This occurred (along with the brakes) while I was trying to make a New York plane, and I very nearly missed it. It also was in-credibly dangerous to have it happen on the freeway.

4. The shifting to second and high was jerky.

5. The motor was uneven and made considerable noise when idling.

I should like at this point to make it clear that during all of the period I held the car, it was never driven more than an hour at a time, and never at high speed. I used it very cautiously. A few days later the steering apparatus froze up completely, and I gave up. I telephoned for you to pick up the car, and with it I sent a full list of the defects you had tried to repair, which I had paid you to repair, and which were not repaired. The list, that is, which is enumerated above, plus the newly developed steering apparatus freeze-up. That, incidentally, you discovered was due to a leak. Did no one check the fluid in that apparatus when you turned the car over to me? Was there no way to detect such a leak? Is this the way an order to return a car in "first class condition" is filled?

Anyhow, the car came back on September 14. The right window functioned this time, and the inside lights. A radiator cap of a different kind, apparently, than that which I had, was put on the radiator. I think the carburetor was speeded up somewhat to stop the stalling (but if so, not enough). The bill was $23.54—*and not one of the major faults was corrected.* The car still boiled. The brakes still worked as previously described. The motor still died in traffic at inopportune and even dangerous times. The motor still growled ominously. For two or three days the jerkiness in shifting seemed cured; then it returned abruptly with all its old jumpiness.

I telephoned you again, getting it on the record. Shortly thereafter my wife drove the car in, and, with another list at hand, you went to work on it again. This time the bill was $14.50 more, all of it devoted to the radiator, presumably to cure the over-heating. (In theory, of course, this had been done twice before—except, apparently, no one in the garage had then, nor has to this day, any idea of what it is that causes a car to over-heat.)

I telephoned you once more, and you professed surprise and suggested I bring the car in soon. I said that I wanted to bring it in at some time when you would have the manpower and time to handle the job in a few days, since I had purchased the car in order to drive it. We agreed that should be done. But I haven't yet heard from you as to when you may be able to handle it.

The last repair job was finished on September 21. The last telephone call referred to above was made to you some two days later. In it I told you that you had cured the motor-stalling (after two trips in), but that *not one other God-blessed thing, including the boiling, had been changed or improved in any way.*

I knew that it would be foolish to bring it in for the fourth time unless I took the time to do exactly what I am doing now—write you a detailed letter and demand satisfaction. But I am a busy man. I've been to New York twice since September 21, and it is, at best, an intolerable burden to have to spend so much of one's own time and effort trying to get another man to do the work he has honestly contracted to do. I knew it would be worse than a waste of time to send the car in with another list. Lists do no good. They are not heeded. Therefore I had to wait until today, when at last I have the time to attend to the matter.

However—in the intervening thirty days, the car has been very little used. It is not used at all when I am out of the city. Its general use is a matter of ten blocks. Three times it has been driven to Beverly Hills and return. We have not taken it on any extended drive out of the city (with one exception) because we were afraid to. That exception occurred because we wished to give it some kind of test (I am satisfied that no one in your organization has ever road-tested it; if you had, the faults would have been as clear to you as they are to me, and to return it with those faults uncorrected would have been shameful). The car was driven to Gorman, at the top of the Ridge Route, and return. This is a total distance of about 120 miles.

Its performance was disgraceful. The drive was at moderate speed. The car labored along, most of the time in second gear, and even then sluggishly. It had no power at all in high. When we reached the top of the Ridge we stopped at a service station. The heat gauge (which you checked and repaired) registered normal. The car blew its radiator cap at the attendant's touch, and gushed a full three minutes before water could be slowly dribbled in while the motor was carefully kept running. You had turned over to me, after billing me a total of $621.60, what is unquestionably the most inefficient machine I've ever driven.

About ten days ago I drove it to Beverly Hills. I here want to emphasize the fact that you have worked on the over-heating upon three occasions within a period of a month; but that our faith in your work was so slight *that we never took this car out of the drive, no matter how short the distance we wished to travel, without first filling it with water*. At the end of the twenty-minute drive, although your repaired heat gauge recorded normal, I stopped at a service station— and again the eruption of boiling water occurred. You will note inside the hood-cover that the insulation has been boiled off by these two eruptions. I drove the car very slowly home. As I arrived, a slight knock sounded from the motor. The next morning the battery was dead. When the car finally started, the motor knock was extremely loud. I took the keys from the car and it has been sitting there for the past week, awaiting the time when I could get around to trying to settle the matter with you.

Now here is a list of the things on this car I want repaired. I suggest that you read them very carefully, and keep them, and before you turn the car back, check them to see that they have been taken care of:

1. The transmission (or perhaps something else: I'm no mechanic)—the car has a vibration period of considerable intensity around 35 mph whether accelerating or decelerating. A similar vibration period occurs between 60 and 65 mph, both accelerating and decelerating. There may be other periods at higher speeds but we've never felt we could drive the car that fast because of its abominable mechanical condition.

2. It is jumpy and erratic on gear-changing. In normal traffic, on a level paved street, it will move from second to third at 30 mph; or again the change will not occur until 40 mph; or, upon occasions, we have found it grumbling along in second at 50 mph. We have a way of releasing the gas and kicking it in again which will effect the transfer to third when it is not accomplished automatically.

3. It grinds in low; it has no acceleration at all in high; and of course all these difficulties are greatly increased when it is over-heated. We have no way of knowing when it over-heats because you have been unable to make the heat gauge register heat.

4. A quick stop, and the brakes react like a Mack truck. They also react when the car is heating up, as previously described.

5. I positively think the car rode better, stabilized better, when we first brought it to you than it does now, after we have spent a considerable sum on torsion bar, stabilizer, etc.

6. The engine labors irregularly.

7. On some occasions, when the car is started in the morning, it shoots clouds of blue smoke from both exhausts; other times it shoots no smoke at all.

8. Moving very slowly in reverse, one can hear a hydraulic hiss or moan or howl, or whatever the sound is. Doubtless something else that was overlooked in putting it into "first class" condition.

Now these items noted above are only those that *I* have noticed. All of them, according to your invoices, have been repaired. There may be other defects which cause the defects I note above, but it is not my job to find them out, it is your job. I have no knowledge of automobiles. I can only tell you, from my point of view as driver, the symptoms. I can't diagnose the cause for you, and I should not be asked to do so. I say this because you have a tendency to under-rate what I say to you. When I told you by telephone the second time about the boiling, you said you couldn't understand it, and asked me if I noticed a radiator leak. I hadn't, but you who had had the car for weeks, certainly should have noticed one if it existed. When I told you how the steering mechanism howled when the wheel was turned, you assured me they all howled but when I said it had frozen to immobility in the midst of a howl, you admitted that I might possibly be right, that some little thing might be wrong with a car that had frozen completely.

I have talked to you, over the past three months, a number of times, for I have two problems: *one,* getting the car out of the garage in any reasonable time after it's in, as well as, *two,* getting the car to run after I *have* got it out. Each time, explaining the inumerable delays, you have blamed them on too much work in the shop, or an inability to get parts. Upon one occasion I mildly suggested to you that I was in over $600 on the job, that I had not yet received what I paid for, and that in terms of your over-crowded repair shop, I felt that the size of my bill should give me some kind of precedence and I think you agreed with me.

I want to take a second look at this unavailability of Packard parts. Packard, as I understand it, is a going corporation, still in business, and has certain trade obligations to provide parts for automobiles that are less than three years off its assembly lines. Yet it appears to be failing in this obligation. Example: one delay in returning the car was explained to me by the fact that you were unable to get a proper radiator cap out of Packard. A second example: when I first brought the car in in July I ordered all dented chromium replaced. When you turned the car back to me in September, you had taken the bottom body strip of chromium off the right side but had not replaced it with new stripping. You explained that the strip was on order, but had not yet been received. You assured me that I would be notified when the order was filled by Packard. I have not, of course, been informed at all, and probably never will be. I merely point out to you that this strip has been on order for almost four months; and that if it is not forthcoming within the next week, I am going to address myself directly to the president of Studebaker-Packard to find out if they truly are this far behind on their orders, or if they have discontinued providing parts for recent models. If that gentleman gives me no satisfaction, then I shall appeal to those various agencies which protect the car buyer for a reasonable length of time on parts service. I think we shall be able to break this particular logjam.

One final thing: when you take this car in to repair what was originally wrong with it, and to repair the inefficient repairs you have thus far made on it, *I want somebody to road test it.* I *know* you have driven it at least a few blocks, because I was with you and a mechanic drove it once with my wife in it. In relation to your drive, and your mechanic's, your mechanic noted that each time one brakes the car, the loose front seats jump forward two inches, hurling everyone in the seat roughly forward. The mechanic said something should be done about it; it was a simple job. I am not complaining specifically about this, because it was not on my lists. But how could anybody have road-tested this car and not discovered the front seat lurching forward? And why would not any efficient organization, having noticed it, repair it? It's your job to find out what's wrong with the car and repair it, not mine. I point out the seat problem because it actually is so very small and so very little trouble. If you are unable to recognize and repair such an obvious and simple fault, how shall you ever be able to do the larger jobs?

You well may ask: "Why does this man afflict me with such a long rambling, repetitive letter?" And I must answer: "Because, Mr. Dobbschutz, I want to attract your *interest.*" I have not yet, after three trips, almost two months in the garage, and $621.60 in money, really found a way to get you *interested* in this job. And I know if your interest can be aroused, then you will repair my car as you agreed to. But I must have your *interest!*

I am not an avaricious man. I am not a man who objects to paying top price for top service: indeed, I prefer to. Nor, considering the time I allowed you on the original job, am I an unreasonable or impatient man. In all of our telephone conversations, and through all the loss of time and money your incapacity has cost me, I have not once spoken to you rudely, angrily, or even discourteously. That, perhaps, was a mistake; if so, it's a mistake I prefer to make.

But I must beg you to consider that neither am I a man who can or will subsidize you or the Noll Auto Company. When pressed by adverse circumstances, as your unsatisfactory work has pressed me these past four months, I am quite capable of demanding honest service for the honest dollars I have paid. I am capable not only of demanding it, but, if necessary, of compelling you to render it. I hope I shall not need to compel you, for I think all such matters are capable of amicable settlement. I am sorry your establishment has more work, as you tell me, than it can efficiently handle; I am sorry that Studebaker-Packard violates all its trade agreements and refuses to sell parts for cars it has manufactured; but that is your problem, and the Noll Auto Company's problem, and I refuse to pay the cost of it. I promise you—and you will be ill-advised to doubt me—that if you push me far enough, I shall cease *asking* you to repair my car, I shall *compel* you either to do so or to refund those moneys you have taken from me under the pretense of repairing it.

I have a carbon copy of every list of repairs I sent you. I have invoices totaling $621.60—of which, unfortunately, I have paid in cash $538.56—carefully put away. I shall, of course, retain a copy of this letter. If you yourself do not arrange for a satisfactory disposition of the matter, then I shall send copies of all pertinent material together with a covering letter, to the president of Noll Auto Company. If I do not get satisfaction from him—as I am confident I shall—then I shall turn the matter over to my lawyer, and, no matter what it costs me, take measures that will protect both myself and other well-intentioned persons from such treatment in the future. In connection with this, I urge you to read a recent issue of *Time* Magazine, which deals with irresponsible, incapable or dishonest repairmen as a national problem which costs trusting citizens hundreds of millions a year. As a matter of fact, I shall send you this article under separate cover, with a personal note, if for no other reason than to make it legitimately a part of the court record in the event you choose to deal with me in the future as you have in the past.

Now here is what I want: I want this car repaired, as you agreed to repair it almost four months ago. I want a stipulated time limit for its repair. And I do not want to be charged twice for the repair. In other words, those repairs I have already paid for I will not pay for a second time: I simply want them made, and quickly. In other words, I want no more than any other customer, and no more than you should have given me in the first place.

I am sending this letter to you by registered mail, return signature requested. I shall expect to receive a telephone call from you relating to the matters herein brought to your attention before six p.m. of Monday, October 28. My telephone numbers are CLinton 5-4047 or CLinton 4-1719. If I do not hear from you regarding your intentions, I shall proceed at once to protect my interests by other means.

Yours very truly,
DALTON TRUMBO

13. To Branch Manager of Bank of America, La Canada Branch

Los Angeles, California
November 23, 1957

My dear sir:

Attached to this letter please find notice of a $20 overdraft against the account of Cleo and/or Dalton Trumbo, together with your customary $1.50 charge for such service. Permit me to suggest that you would have been a wiser man and a better banker had you paid the check instead of returning it and charged me under the category of "Paid against insufficient funds.". . .

In passing, I may add this isn't the first time I have received similar intimations of your disesteem. I am a writer, and a bad mathematician, and a poor bookkeeper, and I may upon occasion be briefly and minutely overdrawn. But most of the expense to which I have been put by your idiotic charges, and most of the embarrassment I have suffered by returned checks, have been the result of your own inefficiency, rather than mine.

Example: I have deposited checks drawn against the Sunset and Clark Branch of the Bank of America in my account in the La Canada Branch, and drawn against the deposit, and had my checks returned because my deposit had not been cleared between your branches. No telephone call was made to the Sunset and Clark Branch—which is, after all, the same bank—to see whether my deposit was backed by sufficient funds in that bank. (It always was, for the signature to the Sunset and Clark Branch checks was the Paul Kohner Agency, which is one of the wealthiest talent agencies in Hollywood.) Nor was any call made to me. The checks I'd drawn were simply returned. You have grown so enormously as a system of banks that you are no longer one bank. You don't trust your own accounts and apparently you have no way of verifying them. You don't just shoot first and think later: you shoot and never think at all.

Example: Upon a certain Friday afternoon I was so stupid as to deposit by mail a check drawn on the Sunset and Clark Branch in the sum of $2,700 in your La Canada Branch for my account. On the following Tuesday a businessman telephoned me that he was holding my returned check for $80 odd. I told him to run it through again, since I had made a substantial deposit. He differed with me. He had just talked with your branch, and had been informed my account did not have sufficient funds to redeem my check.

I telephoned your bookkeeper. True enough, my account held less than $80.00 and there was no record of any $2,700 deposit. I told her of my Friday mail deposit which certainly should have arrived in La Canada in Monday's (the previous day's) mail. She bestirred herself. She reported back that the check had, indeed, arrived the preceding (Monday) morning before the opening of the bank. I then asked why the check hadn't been posted to my account, and why, some thirty hours later, you were giving out information over the telephone that was not only hundreds of dollars wrong, but thousands. She then tried to explain to me a new and dazzling system of posting checks by which you penalize depositors by delays of up to two days in placing his own funds at his disposal.

I then asked the young lady to telephone the aggrieved businessman to whom she had given her misinformation. I requested this small favor so that the gentleman in question would cease thinking me a liar so he would understand that it was the bank that had erred and not I. She promised effusively to do so. At five o'clock that afternoon I telephoned the businessman. She had not called him. She clearly had no intention of doing so. You will briskly advertise a man's small accounting errors to all his associates, and charge him for it to boot, but you will not make the slightest effort to rectify your own by the same route.

Example: During the spring a thousand-dollar deposit in my account was erroneously entered twice by your teller in my bank book. My wife quite naturally entered both deposits in our check book. About six weeks later we were rewarded with a blizzard of returned checks, to each of which an appropriate charge was attached. Again I got on the telephone, and again I ran down the error, and again it lay at your door. One ten-cent telephone call, one decent little business courtesy, would have stopped the whole sequence at the outset. But you don't do business that way. The only recognition of error I got out of you was a series of charges against my account which placed me in the happy—from your point of view—position of standing the bill for a typical banker's blunder.

I am not a rich man, and I am not a bookkeeper, but neither am I a pauper or a hot-check artist. I have a $26,000 equity in a house which you yourself approved for a $10,000 loan. I carry $60,000 of insurance on my own life, and $34,000 more on the lives of my family, plus two family health policies. I own four insured automobiles, a great deal of furniture and household and office equipment, a large library, certain valuable copyrights, blocked sums of money in various foreign countries, and other real estate. My income is all earned personal income, and most of it, although not all of it, has been deposited in your branch. My present deposit book accounts only for the past twenty-three months. I find that I have deposited in that period some $76,630.46, for a rough average of $3,330 per month. It's not a large account nor a large income, but I am informed by your extensive advertisements that you are eager to accommodate such small accounts as mine. What the ads don't say is that you are inefficient, unaccommodating, as inclined toward error as you are toward delay, and eager at all times to destroy the good names of your depositors.

I have selected my new bank very carefully. I have gone over these figures and examples with them in order to make certain I shall not be subjected at their hands to the same stupidity I have encountered at yours. They assure me that they handle such matters with intelligence, good faith, efficiency and reasonable celerity. I ask for nothing more.

I shall allow a week for present checks to clear, and then close my account. I have an escrow pending with you. Cancel it and return whatever funds remain in it to my account. I recently ordered two new checkbooks printed up. Cancel the order. If I am too late for cancellation I shall, as usual, pay the bill and leave them with you as my last gift to the Bank of America.

Very truly,
DALTON TRUMBO

14. To Aubrey Finn

Los Angeles, California
December 8, 1957

Dear Aubrey: [10]

I'm dictating this letter into my machine, and Cleo is transcribing it, so forgive its wandering and badly organized nature.

. . . .

[10] Trumbo's lawyer.

Now here's another thing that has gradually dawned on me: the blacklist is breaking so very fast that we may wake up one of these fine mornings and discover it isn't here at all. One example: Ned Young and Hal Smith recently wrote an original screenplay [11] It was submitted by Ingo Preminger with, I believe, a pseudonym for Ned, but no secret at all was made of its origin. When Ingo peddles a property like this he now very wisely tells people the truth, and if they object, he says "What about _____?" That seems to do it. Anyhow the script sold for, I believe, $45,000 down and $30,000 on the day of production, plus a small piece. Stanley Kramer bought it, and the sale is probably one of the most open that thus far has occurred. He appears not to give a damn. The "he" in that sentence being Kramer.

. . . .

Then I began to think about _____ [title of film], which I believe, with a little luck, can be a world-wide winner. It will probably be released six to eight months from now. It is our hope to get it in production in January or early February in England. I am writing the picture under two invented pseudonyms. What the King Brothers plan to do about screenplay credits at the time of release I do not know. However I have a little plan for them which I think I can put over, but about which they, nor anyone else, has any present knowledge. Here it is:

_____ is a comedy, and has many exploitable angles on its own. However there is one exploitable angle that could be added to it that no one as yet has thought of. I am going to persuade them if humanly possible to keep the pseudonyms on the picture throughout the period of cutting and advance publicity and also throughout that period when the picture is trade-viewed for the press and so forth. However on the night the picture opens, there will be a switch. The credit will read: screenplay by Robert Rich.

The Robert Rich incident is well known throughout Italy, France, England, and the United States. It is one of the truly comic names in recent motion picture history. The incident is remembered, particularly in entertainment circles and in the international press as a whole, as an entirely delightful one. I believe the reappearance of Robert Rich on a second King Brothers picture will be worth just about a million dollars worth of publicity. I think the King Brothers are too shrewd not to see that fact when it is properly presented to them.

The first Robert Rich incident caught them unprepared. This one will find them loaded to the guns in advance, and waiting for it. I will devote a good deal of energy to press releases which we will have

[11] The film, *The Defiant Ones,* won an Academy Award for 1958. Young's pseudonym was Nathan Douglas.

prepared in advance, to interviews with the various King Brothers, and to other aspects which can be exploited by good copy: jokes, gags, and so forth. Of course it will be made perfectly clear that the King Brothers met Robert Rich in Spain a second time, and at this time, instead of an original story, he had a complete shooting script which so enchanted them that they bought it on the spot. It also happened to be based on a book they owned, which was a bit of a coincidence.

We will drag the gag out as long as we can, with TV and radio interviews and all the press exploitation we can get. I think that I can persuade them to feature the author in their ads as the mysterious winner of last year's Academy Award. I think I can get them to have Saul Bass draw up a sketch of the Oscar itself covering its eyes with its two hands. Or in some other kind of secretive, or furtive pose. The prospects are absolutely inexhaustible. The King Brothers, from their own experience, know it cannot harm them. To do it again would be so outrageous that I think they personally would captivate the imagination of the press. The whole thing would probably culminate in the identification by them of me (in some ingenious fashion) as Robert Rich. Thereupon I would claim the Oscar from the Academy, and if they didn't come through with it, bring suit against them. The whole idea being to stir up as much stench as possible, and to laugh this fucking blacklist out of existence. I think it can be done.

Thinking along these lines, it has occurred to me that the name Robert Rich itself has enormous value. One of the threats that I shall use—if it comes to threats, which I think it won't—is that if the King Brothers don't care to use the built-in money and publicity value of the name Robert Rich, then I shall. I think they'll see the possibility that I bloody well can; and I think they will choose to reap the reward themselves, rather that let some other producer have it.

Carrying this idea further, and keeping in mind the fact that I don't give a damn whether my true name is ever on the screen again, I think that I shall ultimately appropriate the name Robert Rich for myself for all work that I do for motion pictures when the blacklist is over. It is, after all, the best publicized writer's name in the world motion picture industry; and since I made it, I should reap such benefits as may accrue from it.[12]

. . . .

Regards,

DALTON

[12] In 1970—thirteen years later—Robert Rich Productions, Inc. was incorporated in the State of California as the prodution vehicle for *Johnny Got His Gun.*

15. Extract of a letter to Hugo Butler

Los Angeles, California
December 15, 1957

I am fifty-two years old, and I have three children who shall soon require expensive education.[13] I have perhaps ten years of peak work capacity remaining to me. During these ten years, in addition to educating the children, I must somehow accumulate enough reserve capital to provide for Cleo and me in old age. Otherwise I shall become a public charge. I am absolutely alone in the world. All of my relatives, instead of giving me money or willing me money, have cost me money. There is no one to provide for me except me, and there never has been. About six months ago I decided to face up to these facts, and to set myself a schedule of work which would absolutely guarantee me the freedom I need to do that work which I hope and think will solve my final problems.

At the time B———— was in town, and since that time as well as before it, I have been simultaneously engaged in the following projects:

1. A screenplay for a major studio, where I am represented by another writer. When that writer needs copy, I must give it to him, or he will lose the job. Furthermore, that writer has no prestige and cannot argue as I would be able to do were I doing the job openly; hence there is much waste copy, much re-writing, much annoyance. The first draft of this script, begun in August, was finished yesterday, which is why I now am able to take time to write this letter.

2. An original screenplay for B—— H———————— [a well-known actress], of which I now have 54 pages.

3. An original screenplay for ————— [producer] (and possibly [John] Huston) of which I have 43 pages done.

4. A final draft of a screenplay for the KBs, in which I presently stand at page 71.

5. An original story for G———— K———————— [a well-known actor] which, at 60 pages, is almost two-thirds done.

6. A screenplay, based on a book, for United Artists. This I am *pretending* to them is started, but actually it isn't.

7. A dialogue re-write on a science fiction yarn, which will be finished Monday or Tuesday.

8. Your project, which I must get to after the first of the year.[14]

In order to fulfill this schedule I must move from one to the other,

---

[13] Trumbo wrote this letter—incidentally giving a vivid picture of the scope of his black market activities—explaining why he was forced to break a luncheon date with a friend of Hugo Butler's, who was also financial backer for a Butler production.

[14] Butler's colleague offered to put up $70,000 as producer. Butler was to direct and Trumbo to write the script. The film was to feature Butler's four daughters. At the time of this letter Trumbo had already received $4,000.

and then on to the fourth, giving out sections of copy on each at a rate which will satisfy each purchaser. At no time since August has there been a week in which I have not been obliged to do some work on at least three different projects. Crises, as you may imagine, are frequent; deadlines occur unexpectedly, and when they occur I must meet them, *and I do meet them,* just as I met yours and will meet it again.

In order to keep this madhouse going, I awaken each morning between 3 and 5 a.m., although rarely as late as five. I work steadily until about one. Then I take a half-hour nap. Work steadily until 7 or 7:30 p.m. After that I take three stiff belts of whiskey to uncoil on, eat dinner, and go to bed. This schedule is absolutely unfailing, Saturdays and Sundays included. I was never a social person, but I am much less so now than formerly. I dread going out because it means drinking and lowered vitality for tomorrow. We do, however, go out perhaps once a month. Certain people are angry with me for turning down simple dinner invitations on the plea of work. It is getting to be assumed that either I am (a) getting snobbish, or (b) crazed for money. I cannot help these impressions, and I don't give a damn about them. I am doing not what is pleasing to me to do, but what I must and am determined to do.

8.

"Better Times a-Comin', I Think"

The following group of letters tracing the events of 1958 clearly indicate how the once highly secretive black market had become institutionalized and how it existed as an accepted Hollywood fact. Writers had adjusted to it, and many did not desire a change in the status quo: they were not rich, but they were making a comfortable living; they were growing older and had little drive for the competition of the open market; and they were relieved of responsibility by their very anonymity. Trumbo could not agree with this indifference; he had developed a consuming monomania: a fanatic hatred of the blacklist. Moreover he feared that the general recognition and acceptance of the market might prevent any moves to crush the blacklist.

The letters chronicle a gradual shift from Trumbo's pessimistic view that, in eleven years of blacklisting, there had been no single victory and was no real hope, through his belief that only a qualified victory would be possible, to his final positive awareness that the blacklist would eventually crumble. It is interesting that two years before the fact, in his May 21, 1958, letter to Alvah Bessie, Trumbo outlines precisely how the blacklist will dissolve.

Meanwhile, Trumbo, who devoted much of his time to securing work for his fellow blacklistees, found himself "in the jam pot" or as he also phrased it, "This poor damned rat was driven crazy by all the cheese so suddenly available." With some financial ease came the ability to devote more time to his private life, travels, health, and his college-age children with whom, as young adults, he established a remarkable rapport and sense of trust.

1. Extract of a letter to Albert Maltz

Los Angeles, California
January 21, 1958

Work here gets easier and easier, and work sources tend steadily to flow from higher echelons than formerly. I try to steer work which I must turn down to others, and sometimes succeed. However, every adventurer in the black market tends to demand either Maltz, Wilson, or Trumbo. It's difficult to explain to them that others, too, are quite capable. If you care to take on another assignment, please let me know: they pant for you. In the event a major independent buys

413

Howard Fast's *Spartacus* [sic], would you care to do it? I have tentatively agreed to do it, in the event of purchase, at some vague time in the future but I'm not tied to it, and may not be able to take it on. I think it could make a hell of a film: it would also have a vast budget, big stars, and a piece would make some dough. As I say, I've got my claws in it, but I may be obliged to disgorge it, and they'd be just as happy, or happier for all I know, to have you.

2. To Michael Wilson

Los Angeles, California
March 30, 1958

Dear old boy:

Your letter was a joy. Hearing your voice and that of your mate was also a joy, though somewhat qualified by the sum it cost. I am, actually, kind of swamped at this moment, and in no mood to write a letter to anyone. However I do think you should have certain clippings, herewith enclosed, relating to *Kwai*,[1] while they're still fresh and amusing. All in all, the writing [Academy] Awards were gloriously screwed for a second time running, and a great glow of health runs through the community. Scheuer's editorial[2] in the [Los Angeles] *Times* (he has succeeded Schallert as film editor) is really a major statement coming at exactly the right moment from probably the most powerful right-wing newspaper in the country. Weinstock's column, although a bit screwed up, lines up the *Times'* less conservative subsidiary in the same corner. This truly gives people to think. Bill Stout [KNXT-TV] did a program on blacklisting the night before the awards presentation; and CBS Studio One did a bit on the [Robert] Rich episode two days before the presentation. I've been quietly active in stimulating the whole thing; representatives of the press work with me in complete confidence, and protect me and which is more, they desire the material to be directed to the same end as I. As occurred last year, the entire industry publicity machine worked overtime trying to smother, and failed: this was infuriating and frustrating because they couldn't for the lives of them put their finger on the source of all this heresy and squash it. All in all, the results have been excellent.

[1] Trumbo refers to *The Bridge on the River Kwai*. Although Pierre Boulle, who had written the original novel, was given screen credit, it was widely believed that the screenplay was written by Michael Wilson and Carl Foreman.

[2] Philip K. Scheuer in the Los Angeles *Times*, March 27, 1958, commented on the confusion surrounding Academy Awards in recent years and concluded that possibly the best American films were being written by blacklisted screen writers.

A cursory report on local conditions anent film writing by those who shouldn't be doing it. They are, in greater and greater numbers. Even the hottest of them. I have far more than I can handle or should have taken on. The people [3] who have been talking with you about doing *King of Paris* for them are in up to their necks: they are also seriously considering, and actually working on the idea of springing me and my name upon the public, like Pallas Athene from the brow of Zeus, as a fait accompli—the man has written a script and we've made it, and that's that. They've even hired a special publicity man to go into this precise project, and have discussed it with Wasserman [4] who did not reject the idea. Perhaps it will go, perhaps not.

Anyhow, things go well. I do far more work than I should; have been doing a little over $26,000 per year for the past two years, and should double or even triple it this year on the basis of work done and not yet paying off. However, that isn't important. I want to work less, rather than more, and I haven't solved the problem yet, but hope to—and *that,* goddam it, isn't very important. I give you the information and figures only so that you may evaluate matters here in terms of your evaluation of them there.

In all other directions, I am extremely po'd. After eleven years of investigation, blacklist, jail, pamphleteering, platform rhetoric, TV debates and interviews, I lift my shaggy old head above the horizon, and I behold—nothing. Only a bunch of blacklisted artists doing work they shouldn't do because they're prevented or forbidden from doing work they should. Everybody else seems to be fat and happy. The politicos, the great generals of theory and field marshals of strategy, all appear to be in good shape. Their case, speaking broadly, has been won in the courts. They can theorize and orate to their heart's content, and be fairly certain that their rights to do what they wish to do are protected by the courts. The dishonorably discharged soldiers have won, and now they are getting honorable discharges. The court has upheld the lawyers in the contention that certain conduct on their part does not entitle the state bar associations to deny them the right to practice. The power of the committee has, by and large, been curtailed to an almost crippling extent.

I look about me and I see lawyers practicing law, as they always have. I see doctors practicing medicine. I see fired politicos working at regular jobs for the first time in years, and earning more money than ever before, and kind of liking it. By and large, I see people doing the thing they're equipped and trained to do quite openly and in a state of normal prosperity. Casting my eyes to those lofty politi-

---

[3] "The people" refers to Kirk Douglas' Bryna Productions, Inc.

[4] Lou Wasserman, Kirk Douglas' personal manager, was also president of Music Corporation of America. As head of the largest talent agency in the world, Wasserman held such power that the project would have been immediately dropped had his reaction been negative.

cal altitudes where the popes of the left devise theory for lesser men, I find even there a certain freedom and happiness: they're theorizing and analyzing without the slightest legal interference that I can see, hurling anathema at each other, along with the most ferocious names, discussing mistakes in shrill, vindictive tones and blaming them on somebody else—in a word, they are busily disgracing themselves and revealing for all to see the mediocrity of their minds and the squalor of their ethics.

The only persons to whom no real change has occurred in this time of adventurous change are the intellectuals, and specifically the writers and artists of Hollywood, who in my book have always been the most generous in their sacrifices and the most ethical in their conduct. They too, like the politicos and the doctors and the lawyers and the dishonorably discharged soldiers and many other groups, have had their day in court. Unlike the others, they have never, in eleven years, won even a qualified victory. Absolute victory is impossible for anyone in this world, but qualified victory is and has been proved possible. For everyone, that is, but the Hollywood contingent.

Under the guidance, not to say absolute dominance, of a legal theory that somehow just doesn't work they have spent scores of thousands of dollars for a sequence of absolute and unqualified disasters. Here are some, but not all of the cases involving Hollywood writers: People versus Lawson, People versus Trumbo, Cole versus studios, Scott versus studios, Lardner versus studios, Jarrico versus Hughes, Wilson versus Loew's—ten years of litigation, ten years of expense, ten years of blacklist, and not a single victory, not even a minor legal concession in any defeat, nothing but total, consistent, absolute loss.

The result is that while, as I said and say again, other groups have established their rights and now are peacefully and even prosperously using them—we have established no rights at all. Worse than that, we have no support: neither local nor national, neither in the courts nor in the press, nor among those very groups and persons whose fights we have supported and paid for with our careers. I think there *are* people in the community who rather cherish us; decent people with progressive views and quite comfortable incomes who dearly love to have a martyr or two about the place. It pleases them to point at us and say, "Look! He could have had everything that I've got, but he gave it all up for a principle. What a man!" This pleasures them somewhat: but my experience in favoring Joe Welch over Ben [Margolis] and company [5] informs me that these well-padded and

---

[5] Trumbo writes: "Ten thousand angels could not have saved the Ten, nor could ten thousand lawyers have persuaded the higher courts to allow jury verdicts to stand which awarded large cash judgments in their favor. The 'well-padded and successful progressives' was not intended to include Ben Margolis and his associates but rather certain others in the liberal community against whom, at that moment, I felt quite hostile. My friendship with Ben

successful progressives can get quite nasty if you show the slightest inclination to stop being a martyr, to seek ways of laying aside the mantle of sainthood. That they don't like. That they will oppose, and with surprising viciousness. They are much more concerned with *your* ethical purity than they have ever been with their own. I have a hunch they'd even like more litigation, so that their pet martyrs, by continued profitless activity, may for the rest of their lives stand as witnesses in their stead to the indomitability of the human spirit.

Now as I say, old boy, I am sore as a water buffalo, and I'd like to discuss it with someone. Word travels so fast here that I am unwilling to reveal my thinking verbally: it would be bound to seep out with all the customary distortions. I would like to discuss it by letter with *you*. I'd like to tell you of development after development that enrages me, and see if you yourself have had similar feelings. I can't believe you'd suspect I would consider capitulation to brother Walters [6] and his goons, but just for safety's sake, I'll add that I'm not. But nothing is happening now, and nothing, so far as I see it, can happen that will give the kind of victory we were after: so I'd like to tell you things that have happened here, and discuss future moves. If okay—let me know. If not—so be it.

We are all delighted with that routine of Switzerland, Cannes, Monte Carlo, and a pinch of Lollobrigida with lunch! We're pleased with *Kwai* (even though we haven't seen it yet); we're pleased with the profitable activities that lie ahead of you. But I, goddam it, am greatly displeased with a bunch of sonsofbitches around these parts, and would love to see what you think.

Love,

D. T.

3. To Ring Lardner, Jr., and Ian Hunter

Los Angeles, California
April 13, 1958

Dear Ring and Ian:

Last night a guy named G———— called me from Mexico City. He represents down there (they *want* foreign production now, and are laying out the red carpet for all kinds of politically soiled arti-

---

Margolis has survived large and petty differences of opinion for over 25 years. It was, indeed, through the good offices of Ben Margolis and Simon Lazarus (producer of *Salt of the Earth*) that I was finally able to finance the production of *Johnny Got His Gun* as a film."

[6] Congressman Walters, Chairman of HUAC.

sans)—anyhow, he represents Hugo [Butler] and Albert [Maltz] among others. He had a comedy, laid in Mexico: payment, $20,000 and 5% of the picture. I'm six months ahead, so it was not entirely generosity that impelled me to suggest you two. To his credit, he said he had already thought of you, and would get in touch at once. Did he?

A_____ can buy Shaw's *The Showing Up (or Down) of Blanco Ponset*—or, some such outlandish title. Before he buys he wants to be sure someone capable of imitating Shaw can be had to write it. He asked B_____ to contact me. B_____ did so tonight. I can't do it, suggested you two. B_____ thought it was a hell of an idea (in fact, he sounded as if it were a better idea than that of getting *me*, which I thought ungracious), and said he'd convey it to A_____ with enthusiasm. This play, incidentally, I am told is *not* subject to restriction that at least seventy-five percent of Shaw's dialogue be used in the film.

There you are. Affairs are booming. A program for six small films, $200,000 budget, $10,000 per script came my way. I think I placed three of them, declining them for myself. Need dough but can't do. Always need dough.

Everybody here is at work, how profitably I don't know, but at work. Black market prices are leaping, and the market is expanding as smart film lawyers, handling star clients with full production programs, realize that both quality and economy can be achieved in the black market, and accordingly recommended to their starry clients that they go *entirely* into the black market. One rather large outfit has done so. They're blacklisting white market guys, getting better work at cheaper prices—but the black market writers who work for them are getting far sweeter deals than they're accustomed to. Some of these jobs naturally require a certain geographical centralism, others don't. If you bastards would let me know your schedules, tastes, needs (or, if not needs, then desires) I might be able to do you some good, unless, as I hope and think, you yourselves are doing so well you can't handle more. Anyhow God Bless you, your wives, your children, and all with whom you come in contact. I love that word contact. . . . Tell yourselves I'm devoted to you. Better times a-comin', I think.

D. T.

4. To Dr. Frederick C. Copeland, Director of Admissions, Williams College, Williamstown, Massachusetts

Los Angeles, California
April 19, 1958

My dear Dr. Copeland:

I am writing you about my son, Christopher Trumbo, who has applied for admission to Williams College in the autumn term of the current year. I am impelled to address you in his behalf because of some rather startling insights into the hazards of college admission gained during a recent visit to New York.

While there I encountered a number of friends who were seeking admission for their children to some of the better eastern colleges. To the last individual they were in a state of advanced hysteria lest their children not be favored over others on the day of acceptance or rejection. One person, himself an alumnus of the college to which he sought admission for his son felt it wise not only to make a substantial contribution to the college's endowment, but to join its fund-raising committee as well. In another instance I discovered a group engaged in a circuit of living-room meetings, during which they pooled experiences and sources of academic and other influence with an eye to getting each of their collective brood into at least one of a large number of selected institutions. One group-action had applied to sixteen schools.

I returned to Los Angeles feeling our western son stood small chance of attending a good eastern school, as he wishes to and should. My name is of no value on fund-raising committees and my purse lacks amplitude. I have not a single acquaintance in the eastern academic community who has ever laid eyes on my son. I presume I could mount some sort of campaign to persuade you that my candidate possesses more merits than actually he does—but I cannot believe it would influence you nor fail to diminish him.

On the other hand, the high standard of interest in their childrens' welfare set by those who put forth the efforts I have described may well convict a parent who does nothing at all for his child of indifference. In view of the complexities, I've decided to steer a middle course which consists in giving you herewith a father's opinion of his son, together with such verifiable records as may support it. Since the gesture itself indicates my disagreement with the idea that parents know less about their children than anyone else, it follows that I place some value on my judgment, although I quite understand it must be discounted by that degree of natural and even desirable subjectivity which you are better able to detect in it than I.

Christopher is a fourth generation native-born Californian. Although his great-great-grandfather gave to the state of California

420

lands on which one of its earliest educational institutions still stands, the reasons why he and his parents believe his college education should be pursued in a socially and historically different part of the country are obvious. Equally obvious are the reasons why we wish him to attend a school of the first rank.

He has applied for admission only to three colleges: Columbia, Harvard and Williams. They were selected for their similarly high standards and their disparate natures. Our son has a predetermined choice; we have another. His choice will prevail if acceptance permits him to choose.[1] Although he is eligible for a scholarship to almost any college in California, and will reject certain automatic scholarships, we have the means to maintain him in any college of his choice so long as his work is acceptable and his desire to attend endures. Hence, no scholarship is here applied for.

Christopher was born on September 25, 1940, in Hollywood, California. He first attended Hollywood Progressive School, a private institution. For several years thereafter he was educated in a small country school at Lebec, California, where four teachers instructed students from the first to the eighth grades. For two years thereafter he attended the embassy-sponsored American School in Mexico City, where he received bilingual instruction. He graduates this spring from Franklin High School in Los Angeles.

We are aware that Los Angeles high schools do not set the highest standards for their students. Franklin High School, in our view, falls somewhat below the general standards of the area. It is situated in an area which ranks second in the city in juvenile delinquency, and its curriculum is weighted on behalf of the student who, after graduation, will be unable to continue his education. It devotes a very large portion of its facilities to crafts and trades, shops, manual arts, cooking, sewing, secretarial and beauty shop training, and the like. Christopher was unable, for example, to study French because there were not enough interested students to justify the establishment of such a course. I am aware that high scholastic standing in such a school must be discounted by the standards of the school and the community, and, in this instance, discounted to my son's disadvantage.

His activities in the school have been mainly devoted to music and athletics. He won his letter in "B" football in both his junior and senior years, the "B" teams and league differing from the varsity by reason of their lighter weight. He has been a member of the Key Club, a campus service organization somewhat similar to Kiwanis, and of the Spanish Club. He plays the trumpet and the french horn,

[1] Christopher, who had preferred Williams from the first, was accepted by both Williams and Columbia. A Williams alumnus took him to lunch and urged acceptance of Williams "because there are very few Jews there and Columbia is full of them." Christopher reversed himself and chose Columbia.

having served for six semesters each in the orchestra and the band. He has been vice-president and president of the band.

During the spring state-wide Bank of America scholarship contests he won the gold cup in liberal arts, in which category he now represents his school in elimination contests being conducted in some 2,500 California high schools. He holds school certificates of merit in English and Spanish. He has been a member for five semesters, and treasurer, vice-president and president of the Athenians, the school's honorary scholastic society. He is a life member of the California Scholarship Society. He is a life member of the California Scholarship Federation. His present high school grade average is third in a class of 249 students.

. . . .

His home background has been liberal and agnostic. He has always had access to our library of several thousand books, and has roamed freely through it. He has had the same father and mother all of his life, and he gets along well with an older and a younger sister. He has driven his own car without accident since he was sixteen. He is careful to the point of conservatism in his expenditure of money.

Tobacco and liquor are always available in our household, but he has not yet chosen to use them. His rejection thus far is based on physiological rather than moral reasons. He appears to have solved the emotional problems of adolescence, if not triumphantly, at least well. Music has always been his means of discharging emotional tensions. No school or governmental agency has ever complained to us of his conduct. He responds readily to requests, but resents any command that isn't based on reasons he can comprehend.

I think his dearest wish for a career lies in music. However he believes he took it up too late in his life and doubts that he can be successful as a musician in terms of what he considers success to be, which is excellence. He has profound respect for knowledge and a searching attitude toward it. He feels that with a sound education in the humanities he will discover that professional activity to which he is best suited. He suspects it may lie in writing or in education.

There is nothing more I can say of him, but I felt I had to say at least this. I am grateful and apologetic for the time it has cost you in the reading of it.

Sincerely,
DALTON TRUMBO

5. To Alvah Bessie

Los Angeles, California
May 21, 1958

Dear old boy:

For eleven years I have been trudging up and down the country from one banquet to another, being "honored" by left wing organizations and causes as a representative of those defeated heroes, the Hollywood blacklistees. The point of all these appearances has not been to break the blacklist, but to attract persons and money to the sponsoring cause. Hollywood blacklistees have adorned other causes long enough. They, like every other organization or group in the country, must from this point forward look strictly to their own best interests, and to nobody else's. Interconnection be damned.

Hollywood blacklistees have suffered sixteen straight defeats in the courts. They can expect no legal relief. As of this day they have fewer civil rights than the editor of the *People's World*, or, for that matter, even than officials of the Communist party. In the eyes of this community, and in the minds of all forward looking persons throughout the country, the Hollywood blacklist is an old, not a new issue; it is small rather than large; it is an accepted institutional procedure, worthy of an occasional sigh, a periodic word of regret, and no more. Times have brought new and more important issues, and we have been forgotten save when we are needed to advance somebody else's cause. If you today had to choose between hearing DT talk on the blacklist or Linus Pauling talk on peace and the H-Bomb, where would you go? Obviously.

The public fight against the blacklist has failed just as the legal struggle has ended. Such inroads on the blacklist as have been made thus far have not come through organizations or mass meetings or honoring banquets or petitions; they have occurred through the stubborn efforts of a very few individuals who have conducted a small guerrilla warfare strictly on their own, and whose activities have produced valuable publicity in the popular press rather than just in the left press. It will be a continuance of these individual efforts that finally breaks the blacklist, and not the work of any organization nor the result of any "fight."

To explain the blacklist in San Francisco to a group of people who already disapprove of it, and to attack the Academy and others before such people, might provide them with half an hour's entertainment, but otherwise it would be a complete waste of time. First, because there is no way such an audience can act against the blacklist. Talk that fails to produce action is worthless. Second, because it would not hit the general press. Publicity against the blacklist that appears only in the left press, while, I presume, of a certain value, misses entirely the audience that must be appealed to or impressed by newsworthy events and performances. Since my appearance in San Francisco can contribute nothing toward breaking the blacklist, and since breaking it is my purpose and my *only* present purpose, declination is obvious.

There is a further reason I think we must begin to understand. Artists in a mass medium such as motion pictures live public lives, and (as we may have learned) depend on public approval for their very existence. More than any other group of people in the United States, Hollywood artists are dependent upon their public relations. I don't say this should be true, I merely say it is. A restoration of good public relations for Hollywood blacklistees is the sine qua non of breaking the blacklist, like it or not. It is not good public relations for me to appear at an event sponsored openly or covertly by the *People's World.* If it *were* good public relations, you would have no trouble getting Frank Sinatra instead of DT—and probably would have approached him first, as would be only wise and natural.

This has no relation to my opinion of the *People's World* or anything else; it has relation only to the cold-blooded needs of the most thoroughly trounced bunch of people in America. They have been "honored" to fill other purses than their own long enough. If it is good that the blacklist be broken, then it is good to pursue the attack to that end, not on the basis of the way things should be, but as they are. As a final thought I might add that the pusuit of absolute victory on any single issue is folly. It cannot be had. The problem, after eleven years of seeking the absolute, is how to find qualified victory, and how much must be yielded to achieve it. Qualified victory over the blacklist will mean qualified defeat for the blacklisters. If their present absolute victory can thus be changed, I shall be satisfied. How about you? Let me know.

God bless!
DALTON

6. To Charles Humbolt

Los Angeles, California
May 12, 1958

Dear Charley: [8]

The piece on not snitching is no go.[9] I'm terribly sorry, but that's the way it must be. In relation to Hollywood and the blacklist, this simply is not the proper time for it to come out.

[8] Humbolt, now deceased, was editor of *Masses & Mainstream.*
[9] Humbolt wanted Trumbo's permission to publish the December 30, 1956, letter to Guy Endore. Section 7, #1, pp. 363-376.

I don't know whether you realize that of all the groups who have fought through this period, the Hollywood blacklistees are the *only* ones who have never had even a qualified victory before the courts. They have, on the contrary, had sixteen straight defeats. There is no legal recourse left open to them, and they number over two hundred careers.

The defeat of Wilson vs. Loew's [10] has made a qualitative change in the air around town, and compels a completely new approach to the blacklist. One approach *not* needed and wrong is to hark back to the past—and informing is an issue of the past. The committee is presently making it comparatively easy for people to return to their jobs *without* informing. All they have to do is privately answer the main question. A few have done so. More may. Any article such as mine, indicating that informing is the main present evil, would serve to encourage the new route-to-work so temptingly offered by the committee. Since, says Joe Blacklistee, the main moral wrong is informing, why should I not return by truthfully answering one question and not informing on anyone? I do hope you see the problem involved.

The letter at this time will hurt rather than help the blacklistees —and the blacklist is my one and *only* present interest. Do you realize that after ten years of litigation and expense and loss of career, the Hollywood blacklistees still have fewer civil rights than an open official of the Communist Party? They won: we didn't. Now we have to think of new ways to break through, or the committee will control the decline of the blacklist precisely as it set down the conditions for its rise.

All the best,
DALTON

7. To Edward Lewis

Los Angeles, California
May 31, 1958

Dear Eddie: [11]

I've no intention of seeking to influence our friend and what he

[10] The suit, filed by Michael Wilson, actress Anne Revere, actress Gale Sondergaard (wife of the Hollywood Ten's Herbert Biberman), writer Guy Endore and nineteen others, charged that they had been blacklisted and asked $52,000,000 for losses and damages inflicted upon them. The plaintiffs lost their case in the district court, Court of Appeals, and Supreme Court.

[11] Edward Lewis was executive vice-president of Bryna Productions, the organization that made *Spartacus* for Universal Pictures. Trumbo was signed as screen writer for this six million dollar epic—perhaps his biggest project since being blacklisted.

says to the man he meets Monday in Washington. I do, however, want to apprise him of certain facts he may not be aware of.[12]

Of the original 19 witnesses who were called before the first committee hearings in 1947, there were some who were not Communists, and some who had never been Communists. It is also my recollection of these hearings that when they became nasty and most violative of individual rights, Mr. N[ixon] absented himself from them, and it was generally taken as evidence of his disesteem for the chairman's methods.

As for the present day, eleven years later, I doubt that there are five members of the Communist Party left in all of Hollywood. Most blacklistees have been out of the party for years. Some of them have become conservatives, some have become democrats, and some have maintained a generally socialist point of view. But to the last man they cannot in conscience admit the right of any legislative committee to judge their loyalty. Beyond this, they view a forced confession of former guilt or stupidity as no different in principle from the public confessions that have characterized Russian justice, or the brainwashing that is charged to the Chinese. For this reason, and this reason only, scores of them have kept silent and suffered the consequences.

I do think there are very *very* strong arguments against the blacklist in terms of the industry's present need and its international relations—and I have taken the liberty of setting down a few notes, in a style which I hope is cool enough and detached enough that they might be left in the possession of Mr. N[ixon] without compromising the person who turned them over to him. I do hope he [the "friend"] can at least see them before he takes off.

Best,
SAM [13]

---

[12] "Our friend" was Kirk Douglas, head of Bryna Productions. He had arranged to meet then Vice-President Richard M. Nixon, who had been a member of the HUAC committee which subpoenaed the Hollywood Ten, in his offices at the Capitol. Douglas hoped, first, to get a statement from Nixon condemning the blacklist or failing that to get a statement supporting a producer's right to employ whoever he wished should that producer publicly break the blacklist. (Douglas was already contemplating openly announcing Trumbo's authorship of the *Spartacus* screenplay.) Nixon refused a statement, pointing out that the blacklist was an industry problem which the industry itself should consider without governmental interference. Trumbo has observed, "It is interesting that from the beginning of my association with Eddie and Kirk to the present day, neither of them once asked what my political affiliations were or are."

[13] Sam Jackson was Trumbo's favorite pseudonym during the *Spartacus* project.

The Effect in Other Nations

England.

A number of blacklisted Hollywood persons migrated to London, where British motion picture unions intervened in their behalf for the procurement of residential status and work permits. Prominent members of the British film industry cooperated in finding jobs for them, and openly expressed sympathy for them. Inherent in such sympathy was a thinly veiled anti-American attitude which the existence of an American blacklist permitted them to disseminate. Certain specific cases have been widely publicized:

1. Carl Foreman. Foreman was blacklisted five or six years ago after having written such films as *The Champion* and *High Noon.* He moved to London, where he worked steadily under various pseudonyms in the British film industry. His true identity and the reasons for his residence in England were known and widely commented on. He worked directly with leading British film personalities. His connection with *Bridge on the River Kwai,* one of the most successful American-produced films in recent years, has been the subject of much comment in the British press. As lately as May 15 of this year it occasioned an article in *The Reporter,* an American magazine published in New York City.

2. Donald Ogden Stewart. One of the most prominent of American screen writers, Stewart also took up residence in London after being blacklisted. Like Foreman, he has won wide acceptance in film and theatrical circles there. He has worked openly with the British industry, although the problem of American release compelled him to use pseudonyms. He presently has a successful play running in the West End under his own name. The British press has not failed to point out that he is a man who cannot use his name in his native America.

There are numerous other blacklisted Americans working in British films, theatre and television; wherever an American motion picture personality goes in London he is subject to politely satirical remarks about his blacklisting homeland. . . .

France.

1. Jules Dassin. A blacklisted director, Dassin took up residence in Paris. There, under his own name, he directed an immensely successful film entitled *Rififi.* In addition to making everyone associated with it rich, the film won numerous European prizes, as have subsequent Dassin productions. He has become an ornament to the world of the French cinema, and his films are regarded as representative not of American but of French art and culture.

Rififi enjoyed great success even in the United States, with Dassin's name prominently on the screen. American producers who saw the film were made uncomfortably aware of a talent which produced both profits and honors for the French film industry, yet which could not be used in the American. The Dassin case is regularly cited in French intellectual circles as a criticism of American democracy.

2. Michael Wilson. Wilson is the blacklisted author of the Academy winning film, *A Place in the Sun*, and of the more recent *Friendly Persuasion*. Having been blacklisted in the early fifties, his name was removed from the latter film. Meanwhile, he had taken up residence in Paris. When *Friendly Persuasion* was honored at the Cannes festival, Wilson's authorship of the film and his lack of credit for it drew scathing and overtly anti-American notices from the French press. At a formal ball in Paris honoring festival winners, Wilson was given a place in the central box, where he was deliberately seated beside Europe's most widely publicized actress.

The enormous success of *Bridge on the River Kwai*, and the gossip in international film circles that its script was written by two blacklisted Americans (Foreman and Wilson) burst into the open during the 1958 Academy award season. For a full week the American blacklist was front page news in metropolitan newspapers throughout Europe, as well as in America, where the film editor of *The Los Angeles Times* took occasion to devote a good deal of space to the matter. Wilson made no comment to the press in Paris, and is understood to have foiled a scheme by friendly French journalists to reveal the truth of the matter. . . .[14]

Italy.

The most important film producers in Italy are now availing themselves of blacklisted American writing talent. This is perfectly open, and occasions a good deal of cynical comment in Italian intellectual circles. It was commonly known throughout the Italian industry that *Summertime*, an English production filmed in Venice which won numerous European prizes, was written by Donald Ogden Stewart, although other names appeared on it.

Latin-America.

Blacklisted American talent has now become integrated into the Mexican film industry. Many Mexican films are financed by the government itself, and officials are perfectly aware of the past histories of those Americans whom they employ. Two Mexican films involving blacklisted American talent have won high honors for Mexico in various European film festivals. Mexican film circles openly deride the United States for its blacklist of film personalities, and the derision fortifies Mexican nationalism at the expense of Mexican-American friendship.

[14] Michael Wilson's most recent film was *Planet of the Apes* written under his own name. The film was enormously successful.

One of the most successful American films ever released in Latin America was *The Brave One*, which dealt with a Mexican boy and a fighting bull. In Mexico City the crowds on its first day were so great that the pressure of people waiting for the theatre to open broke down the glass doors [leading into] the lobby. In Caracas the film broke all existing records, with the exception of one film starring Cantinflas several years ago. It was exuberantly praised by critics throughout South America as a warm and friendly portrayal of Mexican life.

Yet its reception was clouded by the world-wide publicity given to the fact that when the Academy voted an award to its author, one Robert Rich, no one could be found to claim the honor. Press speculation that the missing Robert Rich was in fact a blacklisted writer led reporters in Los Angeles, New York, Mexico City, London and Paris to a series of inquiring interviews with blacklisted persons resident in each city, and their interviews received world coverage.

The unfortunate part of the blacklist is that it arouses adverse feelings in every country among the very persons who have direct access to the press and public opinion, persons who because of their profession actually create public opinion. Thus a correspondent for *Excelsior* in Mexico City, mocking what he called American "cultural values" wrote that the vulgar content of most American films, in contrast to that of *The Brave One*, should be attributed to the fact that in Hollywood ". . . the talent of writing a political oath is more demanded than a talent of writing thoughtful films." The Paris edition of the New York *Herald Tribune* reprinted an editorial which originally appeared in the Louisville *Courier-Journal*. . . .[15] This kind of press is always bad.

The Motion Picture Academy.

During the 1957 award ceremonies, the Academy was ridiculed throughout the world because Michael Wilson's name was removed from *Friendly Persuasion*, and because the unknown Robert Rich would not come forward to accept his award for *The Brave One*. In 1958 scandal again gathered about the award given to Pierre Bouille for the screenplay of *Bridge on the River Kwai*, since it was internationally accepted that Foreman and Wilson had actually written the script. The reaction in Paris, where M. Bouille is highly regarded, was particularly unfortunate. There is no assurance that similar disasters will not attend future Academy presentations.

Academy night is probably the most widely publicized cultural event in the world. It is also uniquely American. A situation that brings it into disrepute year after year is greatly damaging to American prestige. The blacklist, which other nations use as an excuse for anti-American propaganda, is not good for the Academy, nor for

[15] Trumbo attached copies of the reference articles to his notes.

the troubled American motion picture industry, nor for our government, which detractors of America invariably blame for it.

The existence of the blacklist also jeopardizes the possibility of holding an international film festival in this country. In addition to the fact that there is a certain reticence on the part of European artists to compete for honors in a country where all artists are not permitted an equal chance to compete, there is the further possibility that winning films may turn up with no visible authors, and that this will increasingly publicize the blacklist, thus destroying every advantage the festival could have brought to the country, and opening the American film industry to further caustic comment from abroad.

The American Motion Picture Industry.

The industry has for three long years been in a state of economic crisis. Its public relations throughout the world are a matter of first importance to it. Hollywood cannot exist without its world market. The films which it sends out to the world are, or ought to be, ambassadors of American good will toward the world. Yet its own blacklisting casts doubt upon its good intentions. Its necessary dealings with European producers and studios are greatly complicated by the blacklist. It is constantly plagued abroad by the embarrassing question of whether American democracy is for all or just for some. On the other hand, it is engaged in a bitter struggle with the film industries of other nations for a fair share of the world market. Under such circumstances it is unforutnate that many of the most successful foreign films presently competing with it for that market are now written or directed by blacklisted persons whose talents may not be used by the American industry that first discovered and developed them.

8. To Miss Frances G. Knight, Director, Passport Office, Department of State, Washington, D.C.

Los Angeles, California
July 1, 1958

PT/LS-130-Trumbo, Dalton and Cleo
My dear Miss Knight:

This letter relates to those complete and properly executed applications filed by Mrs. Trumbo and me in Los Angeles on June 29, 1956; and to a series of wrongful, capricious, and calculated actions by which, for a period of seven years, the Department of State has contrived to deprive us of passports.

These wrongful acts, seven in number, consist in communications from the following persons: (1) H. H. Bolds, September 18, 1951; (2) Willis H. Young, October 26, 1951; (3) Miss Frances G. Knight, July 31, 1956; (4) Willis H. Young, October 8, 1956; (5) Miss Frances G. Knight, January 11, 1957; (6) Miss Frances G. Knight, February 15, 1957; (7) Edward J. Hickey, June 13, 1958.

The wrongfulness of the first two acts consisted in flat refusal to issue passports; of the last five in their repeated assertions that the Department of State is empowered to withhold passports until an affidavit concerning beliefs and associations is filed. To make the matter worse, these wrongful acts continued despite the fact that on four different occasions I assured you our beliefs and associations did not come within your purview, that our applications were complete and legally executed, and four times called on you to adhere to the law by issuing passports forthwith.

The Department's persistence in wrongdoing has gravely impaired Mrs. Trumbo's liberty and my own; it has hindered us in the pursuit of our careers and the development of our talents, inflicted upon us irreparable financial loss, damaged our reputations, and caused us to suffer great mental anguish. It is not possible for the Department of State wholly to escape the consequences of such wrongful acts directed against the lawful activity of citizens.

On September 24, 1951, in a letter to Mrs. Ruth Shipley relating to an application then current, I informed her that issuance of a passport was "essential to the welfare of myself and my family. The present political climate in this country has made it impossible for me to earn a living at my profession. This climate, however, does not prevail in England nor in those countries on the continent through which I wish to travel . . . my passport applications are made for business reasons essential to my continued existence as a writer. I am not undertaking a speaking tour. I have not been invited, nor is it my purpose, to attend any congress, conference or assembly of any kind."

To this civilized appeal the Passport Office replied in the dull, brute tones of a garrison state: ". . . your proposed travel abroad would be contrary to the interests of the United States. In the circumstances, a passport is not being issued to you." No explanation was given, no law cited, no recourse admitted. One must go to Hitler or Stalin, to Franco, Trujillo or Batista to match such insolence. If you doubt the correctness of my position at that time, I refer you to Supreme Court decision in the case of Kent-Briehl, June 16, 1958, wherein the Court declares that, *"Travel abroad, like travel within the country, may be necessary for a livelihood. It may be as close to the heart of the individual as what he eats, or wears, or reads."*

As to my current application of June 29, 1956, on July 21st of the same year you wrongfully demanded that we file affidavits relating to our beliefs and associations. On August 28, 1956, I pointed out the illegality of your request in the following words: "The affidavit solicited from us relates to our past or present political affiliations or sympathies. Not wishing to lend ourselves to a violation of the First Amendment to the Constitution, or of the many state and federal statues which derive from constitutional affirmations of freedom of association, action and thought . . . we have refrained from executing the affidavits you request." Despite this clear invocation of basic law, you persisted in your wrongful demands.

I urge you now to consider the foregoing paragraph in the new light of the Court's decision: *"To repeat, we deal here with a constitutional right of the citizen, a right which we must assume Congress will be faithful to respect. We would be faced with important constitutional questions were we to hold that Congress . . . had given the Secretary authority to withhold passports to citizens because of their beliefs and associations. Congress has made no such provision in explicit terms; and absent one, the Secretary may not employ that standard to restrict the citizens' right of free movement."*

In the same letter I pointed out to you that, "The citizen of a dictatorship cherishes his passport above all other possessions, not because he can travel under its protection, but because, having it in his pocket, he can get out—he can escape. Its denial, of course, similarly means that he cannot escape, that he is confined. While I trust the State Department does not wish to invest American passports with this spurious value, the tenor of your regulations and of your letter clearly indicates that the Department itself places the right to depart from this country very high on its list of desirable privileges."

Compare the paragraph above with the words of the Court: *"In part, of course, the issuance of the passport carries some implication of intention to extend the bearer diplomatic protection. . . . But that function of the passport is subordinate. Its crucial function today is control over exit. And, as we have seen, the right to exit is a personal right included within the word 'liberty' as used in the Fifth Amendment."*

I similarly reminded you of "the natural right of all persons to travel upon the earth to which they were born." The Court states the matter in this fashion: *"Chafee, Three Human Rights in the Constitution . . . shows how deeply engrained in our history this freedom of movement is. Freedom of movement across frontiers in either direction, and inside frontiers as well, was a part of our heritage."* I also informed you that we desired passports "in order to satisfy our cultural and spiritual needs as we have every legal and natural right to do." Contrast those words with the Court's observation that, *"Freedom of movement has large social values . . . where activities or enjoyment, natural and often necessary to the well-being of an American citizen, such as travel, are involved, we will construe narrowly all delate powers that curtail or dilute them."*

In another vein, I informed you that, "We have no desire to escape whatever it is in this country the Department of State believes American citizens fear so greatly and find so oppressive that they will endure the ignominy of test oaths for mere exit rights. This, perhaps, is because we have conducted our lives in such a manner that no agency of government can ever bring charges against us which would make escape either desirable or necessary. We wish merely to travel and return . . ." I suggest there is a similarity here to the Court's view of its appellants: *"They are being denied their freedom of movement solely because of their refusal to be subjected to inquiry into their beliefs and associations. They do not seek to escape the law nor to violate it."*

I also pointed out to you that, "I am sure that . . . the Department misunderstands the temper of its applicants, the nature of our society, and the scope of its own powers," and gave you the strongest assurance that "the impediments you seek to place in our path are contrary to law . . ." The Court speaks of this matter in the following language: *We, therefore, hesitate to impute to Congress, when in 1952 it made a passport necessary for foreign travel and left its issuance to the discretion of the Secretary of State, a purpose to give him unbridled discretion, or withhold a passport from a citizen for any substantive reason he may choose. . . . Since we start with an exercise by an American citizen of an activity included in constitutional protection, we will not readily infer that Congress gave the Secretary of State unbridled discretion to grant or withhold it."*

On January 21, 1957, I addressed to you a request for due process in these words: "If you consider Mrs. Trumbo and me such resolute and dangerous persons that our presence abroad will unsettle the Government of the United States, you must let us know immediately and in detail what information has led you to so erroneous a conclusion. In this way the affair can be settled in short order. If you have no such information, or are disinclined to submit it to us, I'm sure you agree that our passports must be sent to us without further delay." You then sought to avoid due process by attempting to cancel our applications. The wrongfulness of this act may be judged by the Court's opion: *"The right to travel is a part of the 'liberty' of which the citizen cannot be deprived without the due process of law of the Fifth Amendment."*

Even as lately as May 21, 1958, I still sought to dissuade you from wrongful conduct, explaining that "recent Federal Court Decisions indicate your office has used illegal means to withhold passports, and that pending cases indicate there is a substantial issue of law involving such restrictions as you still seek to impose upon the right of citizens to travel." On June 13, 1958—three days before the Supreme Court's decision—your office, assuming once again the voice of Caesar, repeated its demand for that dreary oath about beliefs and associations. Be good enough now to read in full the Court's denial of the Secretary of State's presumed power *"to curtail in his discretion the free movement of citizens in order to satisfy himself about their beliefs or associations."*

The point of the matter is this: for seven long years, through two complicated passport applications, I have correctly explained the law to the Department of State and the Passport Office, and besought them as best I knew how to obey it. My failure at persuasion is sad enough; but your failure to comprehend what was so clearly elucidated is even more grievous. It's not uncommon for a citzen to be commanded to obey the law—but what can one make of a Secretary of State and a Director of the Passport Office who must be commanded to cease breaking it? Was the Secretary, despite the reasoned constitutional protests of his victims, ignorant of the law? Did you not pass my letters on for his illumination? Or did he hold himself above the law, like any other criminal, and willfully set out to break it?

What dread thing happens to men and women, once they have attained to great or petty official power, that causes them to lust like weasels after the liberty of their fellows? What is the citizen to do when caught in the cunning web of their incessant usurpations? And what are children to think of a Constitution which is loathed and covertly ravished by hordes of civil servants whose powers— whose livelihoods, even—derive solely from a pledge to preserve and protect it? I haven't the answers, and I doubt you have them either; yet they are worth thinking on, since both of us are caught up in the evil of a time that makes them cogent, and both of us, in one degree or another, are its victims.

For years Mrs. Trumbo and I have been shamelessly chivvied and immobilized by your wrongful acts. A week has passed since the Supreme Court's decision, yet still we have received no favorable word from you concerning our applications of June 29, 1956. A proper regard for citizens' rights should now impel you to be as swift in correcting your misdeeds as you were slow in recognizing them. Perhaps you desire new photographs of us. This would seem reasonable, since applicants do age remarkably availing themselves of your service. The enclosed photographs accurately reflect our present condition. Contrast them with what they are intended to replace, and ponder the ravages of time and hope deferred.

You, Miss Knight, are a paid public official whose function is to serve citizens rather than snoop on them. You must no longer trouble yourself about our thoughts and beliefs and associations, for they are private. They do not concern you at all, and you must not ask us about them any more. As a citizen-taxpayer deeply concerned with the moral health of public servants, I cannot too strongly urge both you and the Secretary to resist with all your might that tendency to morbid curiosity which has enfeebled your administrations. Remember always that the people have set up your offices and established your rates of pay not to have passports withheld, but for the far better purpose of having them issued. It is to this principal function—the issuance of passports—that I now direct your attention.

As you no doubt know, there is a considerable group of American artists who have been deprived by various government agencies of their right to professional employment. They have been suppressed, or—as Mr. Dulles sometimes puts it when referring to other countries —they have been purged. They may not act, dance, sing, play or compose music, direct, or write in the media of motion pictures and television. I am one of these purgees.

There are, however, certain countries of Western Europe in which all persons are guaranteed freedom of speech and thought and association. Their governments are not permitted to purge the arts. Their concept of freedom and private enterprise has been so highly developed that they actually protect by law a man's right openly to engage in any profession for which he is qualified. I have been invited by an important European film producer to write a motion picture in one of these countries. I have accepted this offer.

Based, therefore, on my letters to you of August 28, 1956, January 21, 1957, and May 21, 1958; my telegram of September 30, 1956; the Constitution of the United States; Article XIII of the Universal Declaration of Human Rights, to which this country is signator; and the decision of the United States Supreme Court of June 16, 1958, I demand that you send our passports immediately.

Very truly yours,
DALTON TRUMBO

9. To Miss Frances G. Knight, Director, Passport Office, Department of State, Washington, D.C.

Los Angeles, California
July 10, 1958

PT/LS-130-Trumbo, Dalton
Dear Miss Knight:

As you perhaps know, we have followed the advice contained in your letter of July 2nd, and filled out the new application forms. My passport arrived today. I still think I may have had one coming under the application of June 29, 1956—but what kind of litigious swine would I be to deny the last word to a lady?

I saw your photograph the other Sunday in "This Week," and felt a twinge of guilt at having risked unpleasantness to such a pleasant-looking person. If such occurred, I apologize. Our correspondence, now at an end, has had no effect on the issue at hand, and was probably a waste of time. Nonetheless, it has always seemed to me that direct communication between official and citizen is better—and from my point of view, much cheaper—than lawyer-directed communication. Neither of us initiated the problem that arose between us, and neither of us, unfortunately, was able to terminate it. But we tried.

The curious thing about this whole ugly business of compulsory revelation lies in the fact that most people actually *prefer* to be open and forthright about their beliefs and affiliations. To believe in something that can't be expressed is an absurdity, and they know it. There was, for example, a period in my life (and in my wife's, though from matrimonial rather than political considerations) when I was a member of the Communist party.[16] I made no secret of it at all. Whenever political discussions arose whether among friends, adversaries or mere chance acquaintances, I never failed to state that I spoke as a Communist; and before I was approached to write a motion picture I invariably informed the producer of my political affiliations in advance of acceptance. Yet when a Committee of the Congress, in clear violation of the First Amendment, sought to compel a revelation I had always cheerfully volunteered, I refused the answer and paid the legal penalty which refusal entailed.

Just so, after we had resigned from the Communist Party, for reasons which seem to us sufficient and final, neither Mrs. Trumbo nor I felt the slightest reticence about revealing our changed opinions. Yet if I were summoned tomorrow before an agency of state or federal power and ordered to testify concerning either my former or present opinions and affiliations, I should again refuse, despite the

[16] Trumbo wrote: "I joined the Communist party in 1943 and left it in 1948 on the ground that I should in future be far too busy to attend its meetings, which were, in any event, dull beyond description and about as revolutionary in purpose as Wednesday evening testimonial services in the Christian Science Church.

"Although when I returned from Mexico in 1954 I was convinced that there was no discernible future for the CPUSA, I was so outraged at the Smith Act trial and convictions of 14 California Communist officials that I immediately applied for re-admission and was accepted some two months later. The Smith Act trials were so sinister, the madness off McCarthyism so corrosive, the cowardice of the CIA liberals so loathsome, that I wanted—I *deeply* wanted—to associate myself as closely as possible with their victims. It was in this spirit that I wrote *The Devil in the Book*. When the California convictions were reversed and the defendants set free, I left the party once more, as privately—as opposed to publicly—as I had joined it."

fact that my compliance would restore me to a hundred-thousand-dollar annual income in the motion picture industry.

I think there are sound philosophical, historical, legal, and moral precedents for such a position. But even if there weren't, many people would still resist compulsory revelation out of an almost primitive conviction that a man's religion, his politics, and his marriage are nobody's business. Pure cussedness, if you will: yet a cussedness that has served the country well in bleak moments of its history.

I write to you in this fashion for three reasons: first, the requirement for compulsory revelation, which creates rather than dispels secrecy, no longer stands between us; second, because I haven't the slightest objection to anybody on earth knowing anything that interests him about my political life; and third, because I feel that both citizens and officials should explain themselves to each other, and, to their ultimate mutual advantage, understand each other. It's the only way I know of to live in a democratic republic.

Mrs. Trumbo and I thank you for our passports. We shall not dishonor them.

Cordially,
DALTON TRUMBO

10. To Edward Lewis

Los Angeles, California
July 24, 1958

Dear Eddie:

. . . .
Now the schedule looks to me about like this: I finish *Spartacus* by August 1. Then I go on to complete *The Brave Cowboy*.[17] Then, or in between, there will be considerable rewrites on *Spartacus*. Then, *Cowboy* finished, I must deliver *Contagious Game*,[18] as I understand it, by about October 15. That is crowding it terribly, but I am committed, and I will do it. *Contagious Game* will be for any price you decide on.

But after these three are completed, we simply must have an arrangement which relieves both of us of the painful embarrassment of working with each other in an artistic relationship while at the same time being compelled to deal with each other as businessmen.

I am all for some kind of an arrangement if it can be made. One

[17] This film, an adaptation of Edward Albee's novel *The Brave Cowboy*, was released under the title, *Lonely Are the Brave*.
[18] This script was abandoned.

that is advantageous to both of us, but mainly one which is tangible and understood. It's much worse to dream of $10,000 and get only $5,000 than it is to make the original deal for $5,000. So many aspects of one's life depend on knowing what to expect in advance. I am willing, however, to gamble with anybody. As a matter of fact, I have gambled. Two months ago I turned down (or rather, steered elsewhere) $20,000 plus 5%. Last month ———————— ———————— offered me $50,000 and 5% plus a European trip for Cleo and me, and I rejected it. A year ago I did a script for $10,000. Last autumn I speculated with a man, and did a job for $1,500 down against the gamble. A deal, based on the script [*Montezuma*], has now been signed which will give me $93,500 plus six and a quarter percent. That's the way it goes. I allocated the $93,500 over the next three years in three equal payments, in order to have a minimal secured period.

Anyhow, I wanted to give a picture of the situation as it presently is, and my feelings about it, and the practical plans and choices with which I am confronted. I do know—and I beg you to believe it—that not one word set down here is a reflection in any way upon you. I am, frankly, most grateful to you. You have been fairer and more generous than anyone I've worked with. But where that old devil money comes in, there also arrives irritation, and ultimately hostility, based on misunderstandings which are bound to arise when people carry things in their heads, or hesitate to inquire, or feel obliged to proclaim their own worth. You know how it is when you have to face somebody like the U-I man, and barter for *yourself*. It is undignified, embarrassing, and impossible. The attorney should represent me to your attorney in affairs involving us. Then all we'll have to think about is the pleasure of making good films.

Incidentally, I simply cannot give you that copy today. It will be one or two days more. Please don't think that it in any way affects our August first date for the final. It does not. I pledge my life on it. This segmented business of turning in copy kills me anyhow, because of my work method, which is unitary rather than partial. But tomorrow, or possibly the next day, this segment. August first the balance without fail.

Believe me, Eddie, I apologize a thousand times for this letter. Will you forgive it?

SAM

11. To Edward Lewis

Los Angeles, California
July 24, 1958

Dear Eddie:

I cannot go to sleep tonight without dropping you this note. I am so very heartily sorry for the mental state into which I let myself drop, and this morning's letter which resulted.

Let me tell you this: you *have* demonstrated more interest and acted more energetically and successfully in raising my income than anyone I have encountered since the blacklist began. You have done it voluntarily, and in a way that often surprised and delighted me. The $93,000 deal I was gross enough to mention was a fluke and a gamble, not an established market value on my services. Aside from that, *no* one has even offered to try to get me $75,000 and a piece—whether we succeed or not. I am not certain that anyone else would try to, or pay me that sum if I demanded it. You have produced a qualitative change in my life, and I shall try to make it as profitable for you and your outfit as you have made it for me.[19]

Upon sober analysis, what happened is this: in the last six months I've received numerous offers, and rejected them. For so many years I've been compelled to accept *every* offer that somehow I got disturbed about turning down comparatively good ones. In addition to that dreary recital I gave you this morning, I've turned down _____ __ _ _____ at sixty and a piece, and today (!) I turned down the new _____ _____ novel at fifty. And somehow these sums, so long remembered from a dim past, alarmed and disturbed me. It seemed that I was behaving unnaturally, and so I began to torment myself about those actually better ones I have with you—and, I presume, I got greedy. And I was tired and irritable. And god *damn* it, what a perversion to turn down assignments!

In the course of it I forgot your position entirely, and the difficulties which will arise for you in negotiations until the credits are there. I recalled and remembered them instantly when you related them to me. But my intense self-interest had caused me to forget them entirely.

Now look: if I had any brains at all I would understand that under present circumstances and those in the near future, it is impossible to get the same price for every script. Later, I'm sure, we can—but when we're established. I'll be *glad* to do *Contagious Game* for *$25,000*. Make your arrangements at once based on that sum. And if we only get fifty for *Spartacus*—I'll be *glad* to get that,

---

[19] From the beginning of the *Spartacus* script to its end some eighteen months later, Edward Lewis worked steadily, and without prodding from Trumbo, to increase the sum which U-I would pay him for his extended labors.

too. I understand entirely how you couldn't act otherwise in that matter—and the fifty will be a blessing, and the seventy-five, if it works out that way, will be a holy and delightful miracle.

Forget all I said: don't trouble yourself about me any more. I had to come to a decision, and I've come to it, and I'm glad of it: you and I are married [20] until you want a divorce. Later on, if we decide to, we can stabilize prices, etc., but now, practically and realistically, it's impossible. Besides, I'm doing fine. It was just a little tattletale greed showing. No mistrust. Just the ragged little fringe of larceny that comes when a man find's he's in the jam-pot, and feels it simply can't last. So will you forgive me, and not worry yourself about it any more? This poor damned rat was driven crazy by all the cheese so suddenly available.

We'll make this thing go, Eddie. And we'll enjoy it, too. I am most grateful to you. Now, by way of recompense, I want the quality of my work to make you grateful to me. And then, nothing but love, gratitude, money, success, increment earned and unearned, glamour, six-hundred dollar whores and a torrent of good pictures. And it couldn't have happened unless you'd had the guts to put across an altogether extraordinary proposition, and the generosity to deal with me more fairly than anyone ever has before.

Put this away somewhere. Then, the next time I begin to imagine I'm abused, show it to me. I mean that.

> *Affectionately,*
> *Hungry, dazzled, greedy old*
> SAM

12. Extract of a letter to Edward Lewis

> *Los Angeles, California*
> *August 6, 1958*

The following may or may not interest you, but it could have some bearing on certain thoughts that have occurred in your organization: therefore I felt you should know.

Because they could not, or would not, produce Robert Rich as chief defense witness in a plagiarism suit brought against them by the Nassours, the King Brothers were compelled to settle out of court for something like $35 thousand and a piece. This naturally infuriated them.

They are now confronted with a second suit alleging plagiarism by

[20] The marriage resulted in *Spartacus, The Last Sunset, Lonely Are the Brave, The Fixer,* and *The Horsemen,* all produced by Lewis and written by Trumbo.

the author of *The Brave One,* filed by the widow of a writer named D_____. I haven't seen the complaint, but they say it's stacked with lies, and is clearly another shakedown.

Added to the fact they don't relish shakedowns is the circumstance that the distributors of the film (RKO) have thriftily decided to hold back from the KBs certain moneys presently due, on the grounds that they're defendants too, and must cover themselves.

The result is that the KBs are in a rage. They are determined to defend the suit in court, and I have agreed to testify as the author of the original story and screenplay of the contested material. To catch this elusive fellow R. Rich on a witness stand will attract a certain amount of public attention.

Realizing this the KBs have decided to jump in advance. It appears to be their present intention, about two weeks hence, to issue a public statement, accompanied by page ads in both trade papers, in which they will assert that the blacklist is a stench, and announce their intention henceforth to hire any writer they please and use his name on the screen. . . .[21]

13. To Dean of Admissions, University of Colorado, Boulder, Colorado

Los Angeles, California
August 11, 1958

My dear Dean:

This letter more properly should be addressed to the gentleman with whom I spoke over long distance last Friday afternoon concerning my desire that our daughter, Nikola Trumbo, attend the University of Colorado this autumn. In accordance with his instructions we have urgently requested the proper persons at Los Angeles City College immediately to forward to your office the Dean's form and our daughter's official transcript. I enclose herewith her application for admission separately, other material to be sent directly from L.A.C.C.

I note on page 11 of your brochure entitled "Admission Policies and Transfers" a paragraph relating to transfers which states that "if your college transcript does not give complete information about your high school record, or if your college grades are marginal, an official high school transcript is also required."

Los Angeles City College informs us that it has Nikola's high school record in its possession, but that after one year's attendance

[21] The release was tabled until January of 1959.

the record becomes property of the institution and may not be sent to any other institution. Franklin High School in Los Angeles, from which she was graduated in the spring of 1956, is completely shuttered; and the Board of Education official in charge of such matters doubts an official high school record can be made up in time to be in your hands on August 15th.

In rummaging among the children's records I have come across a "Transcript of High School Record" which I enclose herewith in the hope it's the official one required. If it is not, will you kindly wire me collect at once so that I may renew my assaults upon the Board of Education? I observe the transcript contains no mention of the Iowa Tests, which Nikola took only once during her high school career—during the spring semester of her senior year in 1956. I enclose a copy of the test which she brought home from school. I realize it is not official, but I hope it may add to the fullness of the record we are so hastily assembling.

The high school record, as you observe, is not brilliant. We were compelled to change residence three times during our daughter's high school term, and the shifts were quite unsettling for her. Her eighth and ninth grades were spent in the embassy-sponsored American School in Mexico City, a bi-lingual institution. She now speaks Spanish fluently, but the abrupt change from American to Mexican educational standards and requirements combined with the initial language problem to lower her average somewhat.

Upon our return to the United States she attended La Canada High School in the suburb of the same name, and Franklin High School in Los Angeles, from which she was graduated. During the first semester of her junior year (1954–55), a sequence of severe strep throat infections, culminating in a tonsillectomy, compelled her absence for almost half the total semester days, with a consequent drop in grades. Although she was graduated in the upper two-thirds of her class, thus fulfilling one of your freshman entrance requirements, it seems clear to us that her average would have been much higher had she not labored under the disadvantages above enumerated.

Since she was graduated at seventeen, we decided to interrupt her formal education for a year abroad. She spent most of her time with friends in London and Paris, spaced with intervals of travel that took her to most parts of the continent. She returned to us with a much acuter apprehension of the world and its people, and a genuinely urgent desire for education. She enrolled at once in Los Angeles City College.

Her grades there are not marginal, as the transcript will show when it arrives. She has enrolled in 24 semester units, passed 14 units with A, 10 with B, and earned 112 grade points. In order to renew and refresh a somewhat uneasy relationship with algebra (previously taken in the ninth grade in Mexico), she enrolled for the subject again at L.A.C.C. in the summer session presently ending. She hopes—a bit nervously—for a C in the course. I append herewith (knowing they're not official, but purely because of the time problem and the dreadful possibilty of a slip-up) her Student Grade Reports from L.A.C.C with the official transcript, upon its arrival, will verify.

As for her family background, it's quite unremarkable. Her mother is a third generation native born California who has had only one husband, and her father is a native of Colorado who has had only one wife. Her brother is enrolled as a freshman in Columbia College this autumn, and her younger sister still attends high school. It seems likely there will be enough money to see her through C.U. if she is admitted and if she maintains an acceptable grade standard.

For myself, I've always remembered Boulder with affection and nostalgia, and this is as good a reason as I know for wishing to see my daughter enrolled there. I spent my freshman year as freshman in the old rust-brick Delta Tau Delta house just off the campus in 1924–25, and had my heart set on a degree in journalism. A disease (clearly more malignant in those days than now) called money-trouble not only prevented my return as a sophomore, but also my acquisition of a degree in anything anywhere. Since then I've written short stories, plays, motion pictures, a novel that picked up a National Book Award, and enough pamphlets, protests and other objectionable material to get myself into a modest amount of trouble. Until I removed to Mexico in 1951 I was listed in *Who's Who*; and someone tells me I'm still in the humbler *Who's Who in the West*. The horizons, alas, diminish; but there's the record.

Please wire me collect if any problem arises in this last-minute rush, or if any document is dangerously delayed—and accept in advance my thanks for your consideration of this matter, and for your courtesy.[22]

Cordially,
DALTON TRUMBO

[22] Nikola was enrolled at the University of Colorado in the fall of 1958; she graduated from the same institution in the spring of 1962.

14. To Christopher Trumbo

Los Angeles, California
November 8, 1958

My dear son:

I have at hand your most recent letter addressed, I believe, both to your mother and to me. That portion which I assume was designed to capture my attention has. I refer to your addled account of an exchange between you and Mike [Butler] relative to mensal checks from home. You may be sure I shall give it much thought.

You also inform us you haven't made holiday travel reservations because you haven't the money to pay for them. Artful fellow! Do you truly think me so stupid as to send the fare directly to you, who'd only squander it in high living and end up stranded on Christmas Eve begging poor-man's pudding in some snow-swept Bowery breadline?

The procedure is this: go at once to an airline office and make round-trip reservations (not de luxe, not a milk-run either). Do it immediately, for the seasonal rush is already at hand. Notify me of the airline, flight number, date and hour of arrival, and within twenty-four hours a check made over to the airline will be delivered into your greedy fist. Take it to the seller and the deal is consummated without laying you open to temptation.

I am sending you two books I think appropriate for a young man spending five-sevenths of his time in the monkish precincts of John Jay Hall. The first is *Education of a Poker Player,* by Henry O. Yardley. Read it in secret, hide it whenever you leave quarters, and you'll be rewarded with many unfair but legal advantages over friend and enemy alike, not to mention that occasional acquaintance who has everything including money.

The second book I think you should share with your young companions. It is *Sex Without Guilt,* by a man who will take his place in history as the greatest humanitarian since Mahatma Gandhi— Albert Ellis, Ph.D. This good man has written what might be called a manual for masturbators. That is to say, in one slim volume he has clarified the basic theory of the thing, and then, in simple layman's language, got right down to rules and techniques. This in itself is a grand accomplishment; but what most compels my admiration is the zest, the sheer enthusiasm which Dr. Ellis has brought to his subject. The result (mailed in plain wrapper under separate cover) is one of those fortuitous events in which the right man collides with the right idea at precisely the right time. It makes a very big bang indeed.

It is Dr. Ellis' idea to spring masturbation from the bedroom's crepusculine gloom, where for endless generations it has lain a saprogenic curse on millions of little lechers, and turn it loose in the parlor where it rightfully belongs. This chap doesn't find anything wrong with it at all: indoors or out, he ranks it right up there with ping-pong, gin rummy and "Maverick" as a time-honored, health-giving, red-blooded patriotic pastime.

What Ellis wants to do—and by gad he does it, too!—is remove that gnawing sense of guilt so characteristic of the act, the awful tension of it, the leering, searing, sneering fear of it. (Oh Phalloform, dread Phallio— / Let never me deride / My onanistic, irresistic, post-pubescent bride!) Once all that unhealthy brooding is dissolved, nothing remains of a former vice but unadulterated fun. And that's what Ellis is after. He doesn't want American youth to go about guilt-twitching like a pack of inbred Chihuahuas for nothing more serious than a raging appetite for fescenninity. He doesn't want those golden hours of childhood festered over with concern about the imminent putrefaction of genitalia. He wants young people not to give a damn! He wants them to relax. He wants, in short, a world of *happy* masturbators.

This whole new approach—this fresh wind blowing under the sheets, so to speak—this large-hearted appeal for cheerful self-pollution, invokes perhaps a deeper response in my heart than in most. For I (sneaky, timorous, incontinent little beast with my Paphian obsessions) was never wholesomely at home with my penile problem, nor ever found real happiness in working it out—all because of that maggoty, mountainous pustule of needless guilt that throbbed like an abscess in my young boy's heart.

On warm summer nights while exuberant girl-hunting contemporaries scampered in and out of the brush beneath high western stars, I, dedicated fool, lay swooning in my bed with no companion save the lewd and smirking demons of my bottomless guilt. Cowering there in seminal darkness, liquescent with self-loathing, attentive only to the stealthy rise and Krafty-Ebbing of my dark scrotumnal blood, fearful as a lechwe yet firmer of purpose than any rutting buffalo, I celebrated the rites of Shuah's son with sullen resignation. Poor little chap on a summer's night, morosely masturbating . . . !

There *were* lads in Grand Junction, Colorado (most of whom became civil servants or evangelistic clergymen) who strode the sunlit streets of that never-to-be-forgotten town like fierce young gods, lean and supple, tall and strong, pace brisk, shoulders well thrust back, frank of face, forthright of smile, clear of eye, innocent of heart, clean of mind. But I was not one of them.

Oh no, not I. Not your poor father.

When *I* appeared in public, toad-blinking against the unwonted and revelatory blaze of day, I conveyed the immediate impression of ambulant filth—of obscenity, so to speak, in transit. I lurched through those years like some demented crab, shoulders at a goatish hunch, eyes a-scum with fantasies of defloration, my acneous skin (hot with crimson shames) exuding from every greasy pore that sour effluvia which marks imagined love. My sweaty nippers—ah, cursed, cursed paws!—I carried thrust to the very bottom of my trouser pockets, in which humid and forbidden depths they secretly envaginated that marvelous little pendant I knew must drop from its frazzled moorings the instant I withdrew my helping hands.

I turned thin and pale; my odor changed from sour to stercoraceous; reflexes vanished altogether; palpitations of the heart set in, accompanied by giddy spells and sudden faints. My left eye developed so fearsome a tic that its aftermath may be seen to this day in the crapulous squint with which you are perhaps far too familiar. My blood ceased to coagulate: for eleven months I went about completely swathed in bandages. Satyriasis, ever latent in my yielding genes, turned chronic and then acute: treatment consisted in the rapid alteration of ice packs with cauldrons of scalding water. I was placed on a diet of loblolly laced with seaweed extract.

It was this revolting dish even more than my rampageous libido that brought my nervous system to a state of utter dissolution. I would start up briskly at the slightest sound and begin to canter counterclockwise, and in ever widening circles, crepitating all the while like a Percheron at close trot (*you* know that horrid sound—thup-thup-thup-*thurp*-thup), and nickering suspiciously. I became so unhinged that the mere sight of a girl reduced me to mucilaginous pulp, identifiable as human only by a pair of inflamed eyes and a faint squinking sound that seemed to proceed from the hepatized heart of the mess. Ah, sweet suppurating soul of Satan, I thought I never *would* get adjusted!

Even now, more than three decades later (and I, as you know, a tower of moral strength, a civic leader, a respected—nay, beloved—community figure), even now when I forget a friend's name, or mislay my spectacles, or pause in mid-sentence idiocy (my thought having died twixt concept and delivery)—even now such lapses set a clammy chill upon my heart, while purulent memories of my secret shame incarnadine the sallow of these aging cheeks.

It's then, while panic tightens my sagging throat, that I whisper to myself: "It's true after all. It *does* make you crazy. It *does* cause the brain to soften. Why, oh why did I like it so much? Why didn't I stop while I was still ahead of the game? Was it only one time too many that caused this rush of premature senility? Or a dozen times? Or a thousand? Ah well—little good to know it now: the harm's done, the jig's up, you're thoroughly raddled, better you'd been born with handless stumps."

An instant later I blessedly recall the name, I find the spectacles, I complete the sentence—and the salacious ghoul of my sickened fantasies retreats once more into the shadows, not banished to be sure, but held off at least for a few more days or hours. I ask you, dear boy—if the mere memory of past guilt has such power to swoon my adult mind, can you imagine the effect upon a naturally depraved constitution of what then was *present* guilt?

I recall a certain chill winter night on which my father took me to one of those Calvinist fertility rites disguised as a father-and-son banquet. I was in no real shape to mingle with respectable society, being then at the dismal nadir of my lechery and much given to involuntary belching, squirching, belly-rumbling, wind-breaking, nasal pearl-diving and the like. The banquet consisted of dead fish, stale bread, soft-boiled potatoes and leather-bottomed pie.

Master of the revels was an acrid old goat named Horace T. McGuinness who kept a doxy, engaged in brutish orgies, and reserved his public hours for denunciation of everything dear to a little boy's heart. This excrementitious old fornicator was greatly venerated in our town, and much in demand for such festivities as that which I describe.

He buttoned his protruberant vest on discs of decayed egg yolk and brayed like Balaam's ass voiding hot barbed-wire. His nostrils extruded threads of ductile mucus which streamed downward in gay opalescent loops to a scraggle of brush which concealed practically all of that moist, pink, vulviform cave of the winds that served him as a mouth. When speaking—and he always spoke—he displayed the carious ruin of what in his youth had been a gaggle of strong yellow teeth. With every phrase he emitted dense clouds of sewer gas, while his harsher consonants shot forth such poisonous showers of spittle that full-grown bull blowflies fell stunned to the tablecloth the instant they flew in range.

The old debauchee opened his discourse with a series of blasphemous demands that the Almighty agree with his ghastly notions and make our young minds (his whole talk was addressed to us youthlets, never to pa) receptive to the bilge he proposed to pump into them. Then he got down to the meat of the program which, to no one's surprise, was girls. When you go out with a young lady, he slavered, you go out with your own sister. As you treat her, so will your sister be treated. It followed that you must not think of it in relation to her, you must not suggest it to her, and certainly you must not do it to her. If you did, you were a blackguard, a degenerate, a runnion, a cullion, and a diddle-cove.

To this day I don't know why that crazed old rake's clapper-claw affected me as it did. I was a menace only to myself. For all the harm I was able to do girls, or they me, their whole concupiscible tribe had just as well been my sisters. On the other hand, it seemed plain to me that if one day I did burst upon the world as the hymeneal Genghis Khan of my dreams, I'd be in for an extremely incestuous time of it.

Several winters later, when my headmaster at McTeague's Chicago

Academy for Distraught Boys, enraged by the nocturnal racket of my solitary revels, clapped hands on me and dragged my quaking hulk to a lupanar much favored by the faculty, I stood spellbound and terrified as the grisettes paraded for my selection. The vile, incestuous objurgations of old Reek-mouth still fevered my brain. These girls were my sisters—the tall one over there, and the tiny one with the dazzling blue curls, and that charming creature with the wise clitorial wink (the first I'd seen to that time)—all of them sisters! How could I even *think* of—

Piteously I tried to explain the tabu that held me apart from this naked herd of mooing female relatives. Headmaster (he was a good-hearted man but quick with his right) cuffed me about for something under an hour. Toward the end of the beating I was enabled to see the thing from headmaster's point of view rather than that of old Stench-tooth. I began to regard the lovely denizens of that establishment with rising interest. My heart grew light. My temples ceased to throb. My eyes began to glitter brilliantly. I found myself laughing, as Columbus must have laughed when first he spied the shimmered green of Hispaniola.

Ah-ha, my darlings—no sisters ye nor brother I, blessed be the sapient gods! (Descend, Murgatoyd!) Flee for your lives, thou still unravished brides of quietness—thou foster children of slow time! (Down, slavering monster!) Weep, ye Sabine maidens—cringe, ye moaning seraphim! (*Abajo*, little Sir M!) That which ye greatly feared has come upon you! The stuprator is at hand! *Estoy aqui! Me voici! Adsum!*

I learned, so to speak, the hard way. (Ah, Chicago, Chicago— stud-barn of the western world!) Not once in those three wild aphrodisiacal weeks did headmaster or I set foot outside that house of ecstasy. We ordered the telephone disconnected, and had our meals sent in piping hot from the Pump Room. I, who had barely matriculated, qualified for graduate work in three fiery days. When finally we returned to the vertical world (headmaster, being without tenure, lost his appointment at the Academy, while I, poor lad, was sent down for simple venery) I was a new boy: snake-lean, rock-hard and ferociously determined that earth herself should reel beneath the measured thunder of my copulations. That, however, is a different story to be reserved for later times and nicer problems. Returning now to that atrocious hugger-mugger which set me thus to dreaming:—

Having deranged our building psyches with this sister business, old Pus-head passed on to the subject of procreation—or, more precisely, non-procreation. In unbelievable detail he shambled through the story of Judah, son of Jacob, son of Abraham (nee Abram), son of Terah, son of Nahor, son of Serug, son of Reu, son of Peleg, son of Eber, son of Salah, son of Axpharaxed, son of Enoch, son of Jared, son of Mahalalcel, son of Cainan, son of Enos, son of Seth, who was born to Adam and Eve in their autumnal years.

Now to the story. Judah had three sons improbably named Er, Onan and Chezib. Er caroused so heroically that "the Lord slew him," making of his wife Tamar a widow. Judah thereupon commanded his second son, this Onan chap, to marry his brother's relict and have children by her. Onan yielded to the first command and moved in with the girl (note how that sister theme creeps in again?), but he flatly refused stud service, devising instead an escape route that ensured his memory and made his name practically a household word to this day. He spilled his seed out onto the ground. (Hence onanism, onanistic, and the like, for you know what.)

By closing my mind and abandoning all sanity I can still hear that demented old reprobate howling his bill of particulars against poor Onan, shaking his fist at us all the while and sweating like a diseased stoat. "He wasted his seed! Oh monstrous, shameful, nameless act— he spilled it right out into the ground! *All* of it! Yes sir, every last drabble of it! And this *displeased* the Lord. and the Lord *slew* him!" This ringing period he concluded with a gust of spittle so noxious that a waitress, caught in its mere fallout, sank fainting to the floor beneath a tray of priceless cut-glass fingerbowls.

Without even a sideglance at his gasping victim, old Spruetongue rushed on to a warning against the most dangerous period of a boy's day, which he leeringly defined as those last ten minutes before the coming of blessed sleep. This period, he rasped, was Onan's hour, that dread time of temptation which separated the men from boys. He commanded us, on pain of Onan's fate, as we loved God, loathed sin, and cherished our immortal souls, thenceforth to sleep with our hands outside the covers "until, in the unpolluted glory of young manhood, that chaste girl of your dreams appears on the transept of God's heaven to give you, through holy matrimony, that love which no man deserves and all desire." Whereupon we were ordered to rise en masse, lift high our swearing arms ("All the perfumes of Arabia will not sweeten *this* little hand!") and take the pledge.

Well. You can imagine how I felt, poor shuddering pertinacious masturbating little dolt! My young companions, their faces shining with devotion, rose like eager chipmunks to recite that preposterous oath as solemnly as if it were a Te Deum. I felt compelled to join them, my skin flushing beet-red beneath a field of yellow pimples then riotously in bloom from the base of my throat to the farthest border of my scaly scalp. Seated once more, I vomited softly into a cannister of caramels my father took with him wherever he went. As for father—from that time forward a murk, a dark estrangement rose between us. How could I, degraded sperm-wasting voluptuary that I was, ever again look squarely into the calm serenity of his grave

449

sperm-thrifty eyes? I couldn't and never did. For us, that moment was the end.

When I went to bed that night the thermometer shivered at twenty-three degrees below zero. I slept alone in public, so to speak, on an open porch with only a dismal flap of canvas to separate my quarters from those glacial winter winds that howled for three straight months each year on the other side of it. Shuddering like a greyhound bitch in heat, I burrowed beneath mounded covers. My congealing breath formed a beard of frost on the quilt beneath my chin. My pale hands, like twin sacrificial lambs, lay freezing outside the covers. It made no sense at all to me, yet I'd been gulled into taking their peccant oath, and now in my own dim-witted fashion I proposed to keep it. It was the witching hour.

While I lay there pondering Onan's fate, nerves twitching, gona-ducts aflame, ten chilly digits convulsively plucking at my counter-pane, I tried to divert my tumescent thoughts from their obsession. I thought on heroes and their heroism: on Perseus, Jason, Odysseus, Achilles—and it was on Achilles that I paused, evaluating again that dip in the Styx with only his left heel exposed. It occurred to me that the tragedy of his death stemmed directly from the triviality of the wound that brought him low.

At this point my incomparable flair for nastiness took charge. What would have happened, I asked myself, if Thetis had held the little tyke by his tippet instead of his heel? Since everyone under-stands there's utterly no point in living once your tassel's been shot off, all tears and sympathy would have been focused on that gory dopple, reducing his subsequent death to mere blessed anti-climax. The whole point of the yarn, it seemed to me, would have been changed, and for the better. Thus musing, I fell asleep. The next morning I was rushed off whooping to the hospital, brought low with quick pneumonia and seven frostbit claws. So much then, for keep-ing pledges.

There are still other stories I could tell you—tales of those cory-bantic pears that would inflame your bowels and thin your heart's young blood. They would, however, be merely cumulative: if my point isn't made by now it never will be. Yet the more I think on it the more positive I become that you will never truly be able to com-prehend in all its horror that interminably sustained convulsion which was your father's youth. It's only reasonable that this should be so, since you've had so many advantages that were denied to me. To name but three of them—a private room, a masturbating father, and Albert Ellis, Ph.D.

Neither, I think, will you ever be able to understand that flood of savage joy which filled my heart on first reading Sex Without Guilt. I felt, with Keats, like "some watcher of the night skies. When a new planet swims into his ken." Having passed through such flaming pubic hells as would altogether carbonize a weaker lad, can anyone hope to imagine the wild surmise that stunned my soul on discovering that I'd been right all along? That all my Brobdingnagian juvenile debaucheries had been as innocent as so many taffy-pulls? That I was, in truth, an example and a martyr for all who'd gone before me and for endless millions still to come?

For that's what it amounts to, son. I carried the ball for all of us, and carried it farther than anyone had a right to expect. I was the Prometheus of my secret tribe—a penile virtuoso, a gonadic prodigy, a spermatiferous thunderbolt; in fine, a masturbator's masturbator. In that sad hour when you lay me away, remember with awe what I did, and carve those words in ageless granite above my resting place, that your sons and your sons sons may not forget the blood of champions coursing through their veins.

I am still, as you may suspect, somewhat distraught from reliving for your instruction the calamitous tale of my youth. That it's been painful I can't deny, but what is pain compared to the immeasurable satisfaction of being a proper dad to you? I am also, perhaps, still too deeply under the literary and erotic spell of *Lolita,* which I've read four straight times in four straight days. If you don't know the book, you must get it at once. This chap Nabokov, like Dr. Ellis, is a way-shower, one of those spirits who understands that everything under the sun has its time and place and joy in an ordered world.

His description of a two-year Saturnalia between an aging pervert and a twelve-year-old female (a "nymphet," as Nabokov so charmingly describes young girls in the immediate stages of pre- and post-pubescence) is something to make your mouth water. Now that *Lolita* has brought nymphetophilia into the world of fashion and made it, thank God, as respectable as ornithology, I'm willing to place it on record that my own sexual taste in young girls runs strongly to larvines, beside whom your average nymphet seems gross and dissolute. A larvine begins to glow at five-and-a-half and generally is quite hagged out before her eighth birthday. Perhaps it's the very brevity of her flower that so attracts me. The man fortunate enough to catch one of these delightful creatures at the very peak of larvineal bloom —provided, of course, no one catches *him*—will be rewarded indescribably.

A pair of them approach even as I pen these words. They live two houses down. I spy on them night and day with a 40-power Stankmeyer-Zeitz. They're on the point of passing my study door en route to Sunday School. One of them's already in the third grade. Soon she'll be too old. Closer and closer they come. My excitement mounts like the fires of Krakatoa.

Now (squish-squish-squish) they draw even with the door. Glowing grandeur of tiny milk-fleshed thigh. Liquescent breath of gay vulvaginous pearl. (Psst! Speak to the nice old man. Come into my parlor. Ice cream? Candy? Morphine? Exciting photographs?) They continue down the drive. Patter of footsteps fainting with my heart. Nubescent rumplets winkling wild their nappled wonder. Scent of loinwine sighing, crying, dying on soft amber-tawny singing little legs. Oh my God—

Goodbye, boy!
DAD

15. To Nikola Trumbo

Los Angeles, California
December 3, 1958

Dear Nikola:

For Christ's sweet sake, child, stop filling your financial letters with protestations of sorrow, regret, horror and self-recrimination. You make me feel like Scrooge holding some young slavey in fear with a whip. I didn't complain about your bills: I told you to continue to call on us when you need assistance, "and with no feelings of guilt."

I do, however, wish to voice a complaint about the last-minute quality of your appeals. You should be able to figure out in advance what your bills and needs will be, and then let me know in advance. Your last letter was an emergency: we received the request by mail in the morning, and the same request by wire in the afternoon. You must remember that the mails are not instantaneous: they take *time* —and on both ends. So calculate when a letter will reach us, and then think a week ahead instead of two days ahead. Second example: this morning (December 3rd) I hear for the first time that your plane reservation expires day after tomorrow. You could have told me this two weeks ago, saving yourself worry, me some 30 cents in extra postage, plus a night trip to catch the last mail delivery. Don't wait until the last minute—give me a chance to address an envelope, and fast planes a chance to reach Boulder. That's all.

College costs money, and young people cost money, and you cost money, and this is not a moral matter, it is a fact of life. I was aware of it on the night you were conceived, and have steeled myself for it ever since, and feel nothing but pleasure in fulfilling a responsibility which is mine, not yours. So ay-lay off the ap-cray, stop beating your maidenly breast in sorrow for needing what you need. Ask and it shall be given unto you. But G----*! $--#*$--! $*---!!! Ask in *time!*

Now I've examied your expenses very carefully (you may be sure). I see nothing in them that could turn a parent's heart from you. I have been to college in that same town, and I know that many un-anticipated purchases must be made when first you settle in. I know far better than you the cost of operating that Packard. It was I who sent you off in it, and therefore it is I who am responsible for every bill you accumulate in its behalf. I quite understand that one's dimensions change, and that clothes must be altered in relation to them. I do *not* wish you to exist throughout a week-end on "one dried out hamburger." I applaud your determination to eat during this abstemious period, and your ingenuity in managing to do so.

Now about the tires: if they *can* be re-capped, I should like you to have it done one by one, as the need arises. I do not wish to purchase new tires at this time for that car, because (don't sob)! it is my present intention to get rid of that car upon your return, and supply you for next year with one in better condition.[23] Hence new tires would not give *us* their full value—they'd be for the next sucker.

Now here is one tiny area in which you are not thinking well or logically. You have just told me (and I understand) how many repairs that car requires. You and I both know that the need for repairs arises from using the car. Therefore we can assume, in relation to this particular car that use equals repair costs. You have also told me that your tires are so thin they're dangerous, can be used in certain circumstances, cannot or should not be used under others. Hence, tires are a critical problem. Another assumption: bad tires become worse tires through use.

And then you write: "If there are no objections, I think I'll leave my car with Sharie. *There's no sense in leaving it here when someone can use it.*"

There is *great* sense in storing your car at Ardourel's for three weeks instead of having it, through three weeks' use, subjected to further wear and tear which will result in increasing repairs; and subjecting already tricky tires to three weeks' more use, which will only hasten the time when I shall have to lay out more money for them. If you are truly interested in this money problem, you will save me a substantial sum by giving that car a rest (thereby diminishing wear and tear and tire consumption for 21 full days), rather than seeking to find some way in which my expenses will be increased by seeing to it that 21 extra days' wear are charged to me. Do you see? I love Sharie madly, and I want her to have 63 automobiles—but any bookkeeper who checks the accounts on that car will tell you that each time it moves a mile it takes a dime from my pocket. And any insurance man will tell you that if Sharie has an accident in which she is in no way at fault, another $50.00 automatically is abstracted from my wallet.

Now I know if you'd really thought this out, you'd have come to a

[23] Trumbo's actual plan, which materialized at Christmas of that year, was to give Nikola a new car of her own.

different conclusion. Just as, by thinking your needs out somewhat in advance, you'd give me sufficient time to fill them. I would *rather* pay a storage bill at Ardourel's than have your car lent out for the holiday season. However, if you have committed yourself in any way from which it would be embarrassing for you to retreat—by all means give the car to Sharie. But if you can explain to her that on writing home for permission to lend it, you made the unpleasant discovery that your father was a miserly old bastard with a hatred of all co-eds and a heart of flint—and that he told you plainly he'd cut you off without a farthing if you lent that precious piece of junk to *anyone*—then I'd prefer you did so. But if it will even slightly embarrass you, the hell with it. Give her the car instantly, and we'll forget it. Except that (for your own future purse) I trust you'll remember that regardless of fuel, any piece of machinery diminishes in value and increases in cost to its owner every minute it operates. Selah!

. . . .

Finally: (and these two things I really want you to do)— (1) make me co-signator with you on your bank account. Tell the bank, and they'll send the proper form for my signature. This doesn't mean that both of us will have to sign every check. It means that I can sign also, and withdraw funds from the account if I wish (in case, for example, of your death). I will not, of course, ever draw a check, but my signature will make me equally responsible with you for the good economic health of your account; and it will permit me to step in with assistance directly to the bank in case you get the account screwed-up, or make mistakes in calculating that you have on deposit more than you actually have. (2) Get to the airport a good hour ahead of departure, and take out the largest possible amount of insurance on yourself for the round trip home. (It costs the same for a round trip as for one way—about $7.50 for about $125,000 worth of insurance.) Make Cleo your beneficiary, and *mail the policy to her from their airport.* (No good going down with it in your pocket—it burns.) This is a good habit to get into, and now is the time to start it.

There, dear child, I'm finished. I'm cheerful, and this is a cheerful letter, and there's no reason in God's green-blooming world why you shouldn't be cheerful on receiving it. You well know by what a long-winded s.o.b. you were sired, and so, when you present problems, you must expect the old gasbag to comment on them.

I can't tell you how impatiently Cleo and I await December 19 (if it turns out to be that day—there's a strike), nor how fervently we hope you'll enjoy the holiday at home with us, nor how much we ourselves shall enjoy it.

> *I love you dearly,*
> *first-born—!*
> DADDY

P.S. One small word about grades: I know your capacity for learning (better than you do), and I also know your delicious capacity for
pleasure (of which I heartily approve!).

My feeling is that study-wise you've goofed a bit. There's nothing
wrong with goofing studies in favor of fun. Pleasure and fun must be
balanced exquisitely, else there's no possible life for any of us.

By the time you receive this letter, you will have about 12 days—
288 hours—to make up for all your happy, necessary, and beneficial
goofments. I beg you to spend those 12 days—those few 288 hours
—without pleasure: to spend them only with study. Balancing the
pleasure (which we want you to have in abundance), this is not a
bad or supervisorial thing to suggest.

Attend, during these last 12 days, the advice of your tutors. (We
understand you *do* have them, you said you did, how much do they,
or he, cost?) Cram (a bad method but the only one now left open to
you) *ahead* of all tests. Do it. You *can*. The only excuse would be
that consciously or unconsciously you do not *wish* to do it.

I don't suggest this in my own behalf, or in Cleo's, or for anyone
else in this whole world except you. My cunning estimates of your
letters informs me (perhaps wrongly) that you are due for two failures at least. These can be avoided if you to avoid them. If you prove
all my cunning wrong, I shall be delighted (it's not a happy trait nor
an admirable one anyhow, this cunningness).

If the ultimate record proves me right, I—and we—shall love you
not one whit less. But if you *do* fail in enough courses to make you
inadmissible to the university next semester, it will be on *you* that
the final grief descends.

The reason for this is clear: we love you. We cannot love you more
if you win the Nobel Prize. We could not love you less if you were
miserably executed tomorrow morning for the most depraved murder.

But you, who have never learned to love *yourself* (and who *must*
ultimately learn to do so), will be utterly grief-stricken, self-condemn-
ing and miserable if you should, by sheer oversight, flunk out. Since
such a failure would mean real grief for you—deep, serious, self-
cursing grief—I urge you with all the love and hope I have to buckle
down these last twelve days, and do what you truly want to do—stay
in that school, learn what it has to give, enjoy to the fullest all the
pleasures it has to offer (because pleasure is a terribly important part
of life)—and prove to yourself (not to us, who already know) that
you are able to do it.

Now if all of this postscript is based on a fallacy—if the facts are
that you are *not* in any scholastic difficulties, if you are *not* going to
fail in any one or two courses, if you are *not* at this moment in any
jeopardy of being denied re-admission for the next-semester—then
please forgive this whole later effusion. Charge it up to the fact that

an aging man (who is also your father) loves you so much that he idiotically anticipates the worst for you in his great gulping desire that only the best may happen to you.

After all, when you see a beloved object—a flower, a painting, a sunset—your concern is always that it shall not fade. To be concerned that it shall not fade requires a consideration of the fact that it may, that it could. This consideration is the first fact of love. Please understand it.

Again—our deepest and dearest love, without any regard to your acceptance or rejection of the thousand dubious things I have feebly, and perhaps erroneously, put in this letter.

16. To William Hunt, the Franklin Hotel, Rochester, Minnesota

Los Angeles, California
December 9, 1958

Dear Mr. Hunt:

Your note of October 14, thanking Mrs. Trumbo and me for our patronage of the Franklin Hotel, contained reference to a pot.[24] I apologize for the tardiness of this reply. The truth is, our ordeal in Rochester took considerable wind from our sails, and we have, so to speak, been recuperating ever since. Nonetheless, I want you to know your pot has been much on my mind.

Perhaps we can throw light on the matter by recreating the circumstances surrounding our visit. We arrived, as you will recall, on the night of October 2, 1958, a quiet, inoffensive, middle-aged couple filled with hope that the Mayo Clinic could somewhat ease the inevitable dolor of our autumnal years. We were assigned bedroom-living room 782 (the very floor from which your pot disappeared), at the rate of thirty-eight smackers per diem.

Immediately on being installed we ordered a pair of double scotches with soda. We are people of settled ways and somewhat crotchety about our wants. We like hot coffee straight off in the morning, and cold whisky at the sunset gun's first boom. While waiting for drinks we fell to browsing through the institutional literature with which our quarters were awash. Each piece of it, even to those brief little screeds that kept popping up in bath and closets, was breezily signed by "Mr. F," whom we assumed to be Mr. Franklin himself.

[24] Hunt had written that, shortly before their departure, the Trumbos had been served coffee in their room in a new Stanley thermos pot which the management had since been unable to locate.

Mr. F wanted us to visit the Franklin Coffee House, the unique Hemisphere Room, the stately Elizabethan Room, the Cloud Room, the pharmacy, the tobacconist, the barber shop. Mr. F felt we should spend some money in the distinctive arcade stores. Mr. F urged us not to miss the starlit penthouse bagnio. Mr. F besought us not to steal the ball-point pens. Mr. F expatiated on the traditions of Mr. F; on the quality of Mr. F's eggs; on the celerity of Mr. F's service; on the splendor of Mr. F's taste; on the privilege that was ours of living in Mr. F's hotel.

After thirty or forty pages of such brain-washing, Mr. F became (to us, at least) much more than merely human. He assumed the aspect of an actual physical presence in those rooms—a brooding, wheedling, hectoring spirit that leered at us through argus eyes from every nook and corner. It was not until three days later, when we read the inscription beneath that painting of him which dominates the Elizabethan Room as Stalin's copper statue dwarfs the Volga, that we realized he was dead. We couldn't believe it. We never shall.

By the time our whiskies arrived we were startled to discover that we'd spent forty-five lyrical minutes with Mr. F's memoranda, and built up a raging thirst to boot. Pondering that forty-five-minute trip from bar to seventh floor, I realized at once that if our drinks were to be spaced at such stately intervals we ran the risk of sitting down to dinner cold sober. I therefore pressed a large sum of money on the bellboy and bade him bring us four more doubles as quickly as house rules permitted. They arrived fifteen minutes after we had consumed the first round. We fell on them with cries of pleasure. Dinner followed, warm and dry and not Lucullan. Thus our first night of revelry with Mr. F drew to an end.

On our bedside table lay an order pad and breakfast menu, together with a note from Mr. F instructing us to write thereon our choice of foods and the hour we desired them served, turn the pad over to room service and all would be arranged. We did so, drooling over the menu's rhapsodical asides. I had already wheeled our dining table into the hallway. I stepped outside, placed our order in a conspicuous position atop the table, and forthwith telephoned room service, informing them of the table's location and alerting them to the breakfast order thereon. I explained I had written on the order that we desired service at 7:30 a.m. As a further direct instruction, I added that we wished to be awakened simultaneously with the arrival of our victuals. We fell asleep, comforted by the knowledge that Mr. F was watching over us.

We awakened of our own accord at 10 a.m. No breakfast. No morning call. No nothing. Two clinic appointments missed. All subsequent appointments necessarily to be rescheduled. I mention such trivia not because we spent that morning half-hysterical with hunger and frustration, but rather for the clue it may give us to your missing

pot. Who filched my orders? Some fan or forger seeking my auto-
graph? Does it not strike you as significant that my breakfast order
vanished on the same floor at almost exactly the same spot from which
your pot disappeared. It gives a man pause, don't you think? Makes
him reach for the old thinking-cap.

I spent the rest of that wasted day rescheduling appointments and
meditating on the best way to get along with Mr. F. As would only
be natural, the problem of whisky supply seemed the first obstacle
to be surmounted. It occurred to me that if I bypassed the bar by
switching our custom to a liquor store, delivery of our drinks might
be expedited somewhat. On returning to the hotel that evening I carried a fifth of Scotch and three quarts of club soda. I telephoned the
bellboy at once for ice, calling out cheerfully to my wife that our
drought had been broken. Twenty-eight parched and weary minutes
of our lives seeped down the drain of mortality. I telephoned a second time. Right, sir! Cheerio! Up in a jiffy! Twelve minutes later two
smiling lads appeared bearing two buckets of ice. I gave them a fan-
tastic tip. They were so pleased that they smoothed both our counter-
panes, cleared up three pounds of Mr. F's tracts, combed my mous-
tache, and kissed me full on the lips. When the door closed behind
them, my wife and I felt at once to boozing against that glutinous
hour when once again we should match our digestions with the incomparable imagination of your chef.

Just before retiring we held a tense conference about morning services. As I have explained to you, coffee immediately on rising is a
necessity for both of us. We knew the hotel was so infested with pot-
thieves and autograph-snatchers that we didn't stand a chance with
Mr. F's order pad. We decided to give up breakfast altogether and
concentrate on coffee-cum-wake-up. I thereupon telephoned room service with the request that we be awakened at 7:30 a.m. with two
pots of coffee.

But no. We weren't going to get off *that* easily. Not with Mr. F. It
turned out that two cadres of help were involved, and after a certain hour there was absolutely no communication between them. The
young lady to whom I was speaking had no way to transmit my
coffee request to room service. Nor did anyone else in the establishment. It would therefore be necessary for me to arrange with the desk
for a 7:30 call. Then, upon being awakened, I myself should have to
tackle room service for the coffee. I begged the young woman to leave
a note, to send a telegram, to go to any lengths to break down that
barrier which separated her from room service, and us from coffee.
Impossible. There were rules, there were departments, there was an
organization, there was Mr. F, and what I desired was altogether out
of the question.

I fell into an exhausted slumber, twitched nervously all night long,
dreamed about Mr. F, and was awakened promptly at 7:30 by the

desk. Instantly I asked for room service. A-ha, my hearty! Not so fast there! We have a convention of roistering proctologists. There's a run on coffee. Take it easy. We'll call you back in five minutes. We lay back and waited. My wife sobbed quietly. My own nerves were jangling like that carillon atop the Plummer Building. Five minutes stuttered into past time. No call. I seized the phone and tried again. Coffee, in God's name! Two pots! Quickly! Thirty-two minutes later a cute little thing arrived with one pot of coffee. Not two; one. I flung her my wife's emerald brooch as honorarium, and wrenched the pot from her lifeless hands. Our nerves were now so ravaged that my mate and I passed the pot back and forth between us, drinking it straight from the lip, wasting not one precious drop.

I began to give the coffee situation serious thought. In two frenzied capacious days I had tossed perhaps a hundred and fifty dollars into Mr. F's capacious lap, and we had not yet been able to wangle a single cup of coffee when we wanted it. Between clinical probings, proddings, insertions and withdrawals, I devised a plan which went into effect the instant I hit the streets. From a drugstore I purchased two cans of Sterno, a pair of plastic cups, and a child's toy coffee pot. At Piggly-Wiggly I latched onto a pound of instant coffee. From your own institution I filched a teaspoon. Burdened with all this loot I sneaked up into old 782.

That night, on the terrazzo window-ledge of our living room, I set my Sterno can into a complicated device consisting of two wire ash-tray holders, the whole thing topped by coffee pot rampant. After a few words of prayer I padded off to the bedroom. When our wake-up call came through the next a.m.—the third morning of our stay with Mr. F—I leapt from bed like a young cheetah, loped barefoot into the living room, filled my pot with hot water, lighted the Sterno, and stood back expectantly. Hot coffee. And at the Franklin. A thing the gods themselves could not arrange.

Neither, it turned out, could I. Or not yet, at least. My toy pot was a piece of shoddy. The seam at the base of its spout burst asunder to send sputtering drops of water into the Sterno can below. The fire yellowed out, burped plaintively once or twice, and then gave up the ghost. My wife screamed. I sank to the floor in a stupor. And the morning and the evening were the third day.

Just before vespers that night I crept outside to a five-and-dime. From its ample stocks I selected a small, stout aluminum pot, well designed and perfectly balanced. It cost me sixty-five cents. Back in 782, I rearranged my heating rig to accommodate its greater weight and surface. Directly on receiving our call next morning, I tiptoed into the living room, filled my aluminum pot, fired up the Sterno can, and waited tensely to see what would happen.

It worked! I bellowed joyously for my wife. She scampered into the room in her nightdress, clutching a pair of plastic cups to her breasts. My aluminum pot—ah, blessed, blessed little pot!—began cheerfully to simmer. Gay designs of steam limned fantasies against the windowpane. With trembling fingers we pinched portions of instant coffee into our cups (somebody had filched back the spoon I'd filched the day before), and filled them to the brim with scalding water. We stayed beside that small terrazzo hearth for almost an hour, marveling at the triumph of ingenuity over organization, hugging each other, and laughing, and crying, and toasting Mr. F in good hot Java.

From that day forward our charts at the clinic showed dramatic improvement: diminishing blood pressure, near-normal respiration, happy urinalyses, and the like. It's true we suffered a set-back the next day, but it was only temporary. Wishing to lunch in our diggings, I telephoned room service and received that particular dining room which carries a savage warning that no service will be rendered after 2 p.m. I asked for the menu to be read off. No menu, gloated the young lady: we could have ham, or we could have eggs, or we could have a sandwich. But no menu. Absolutely no menu. Luncheon service closed at two.

I checked my watch. It was not yet two. Since I, like your staff, am possessed of a certain animal cunning, and can always recognize a contest when it's offered, I telephoned the desk to check on time. It was four minutes until two. Instantly I called back room service, and—between gales of maniacal laughter—told them Mr. F's clock held them in error, and demanded an immediate run-through of the menu.

The young lady said wait a minute. There ensued a long pause. I could hear sullen whispers at the other end of the line, punctuated by soft, ferocious expletives. A customer was demanding his rights. What to do, what to do? Presently a second female picked up the phone. Without explanation or apology she read off the menu in high, tigerish tones. I made our selections. Forty-five minutes later we received approximately what we had ordered. I think they brought it up by rope, hand over hand. It smelled of sulphur.

Although I had beat them soundly in this round, I foresaw that if I lost the next my wife and I could easily starve to death. Evasive action was indicated. With all the guile of pack-rats we set about preparing ourselves for a state of siege. Each time thereafter that we sneaked through your lobby toward our quarters, we carried concealed on our persons or pouched in our cheeks a bottle of wine, a tin of biscuits, a foil of cheese, a tube of pâté, a brace of grouse. These we stashed away in the most improbable crannies we could find. In three days we were practically self-sufficient. The help observed our preparations with sullen hostility. Our spirits soared like twin eagles.

During all these tribulations I made no complaint to the management. I'm aware that one of Mr. F's chat-sheets begs all lodgers to favor the front office with instant reports of bad service, but I'm also aware of what happens to those incautious souls who fall into that trap; the entire staff, headed by president Watson Jr., lines up outside the kitchen corridor and spits into their food as it trundles by.

Another reason why I held stoically to silence lay in my deep, perhaps my mystical, conviction that such an unexampled run of bad luck had to be partly my fault, a feeling that somehow I really hadn't proved myself to Mr. F. Eager to be accepted as a member of the team, I began heavily to patronize every tourist-trap Mr. F's effusions recommended. I chartered a permanent table in the unique Hemisphere Room. I lechered in the starlit penthouse bagnio. I shopped leisurely in the distinctive arcade stores. I decked myself with stylish haberdashery, and purchased so many paste jewels that my wife began to glitter like a bawd. I stepped up the board-and-room account to a dizzy ninety bucks per day. I took to pelting the staff with money. I shed dimes and quarters and half-wheels like a slot machine. I floated through the mezzanine on a high green cloud of dollar bills. No managerial posterior passed within range of my osculant lips without salutation. I wanted to be liked.

Such prodigality made a natural dent in my poke. I wired to Los Angeles to send a check payable directly to Mr. F. This, I felt, would not only bolster my sagging account, it would prove my loyalty as well. When I made timid inquiry concerning the check's arrival, I received the austere information that although it had indeed come through, management would be obliged to verify it by telegraph if I could wait that long, or by phone if I required scratch on the double. I told the gentleman to verify at my expense in any way he chose, and slunk off like a wounded gnu. It was only a certified check for a thousand dollars drawn on the largest bank in the western hemisphere, but to Mr. F it was just another piece of cozenage by some rascal of a tenant trying to improve his miserable way of life. Fawn though fain I would, naught could avail me.

There came, as we knew and prayed it must, that day of jubilation which marked the end of our term with Mr. F. We had acquired a number of books we wished to send to Los Angeles by post rather than fly them with us at extra rates. Three days before I had seen a young lady with the same problem almost stoned to death in the lobby by a herd of outraged flunkies. How, they bellowed between missiles, could *they* be expected to know what the postage charge might be? To make certain that I didn't become the principal in such a Donnybrook, I instructed the cashier by telephone to withhold $10 of the $400-odd balance still remaining from my certified yard, and to keep it as a deposit against postage for books which we'd turn over to the bellboys for shipment. For some curious reason she let me get by with it.

It's only six minutes to the airport, as you know. Not being fond of airport benches (nor in any condition for them, either) we waited as long as safely we could before making a break for it. We thought ten minutes would nicely accommodate the routine of checking out. At what we judged to be the proper moment, I telephoned the bell captain to come for our six bags. My wife and I then descended to the lobby. While I approached the cashier's desk, she continued to the street to hold for us one of three cabs that waited there.

While the cashier fussed through her archives for my bill, I requested a 4-cent stamp for a local letter I wished to mail. She shook her head grimly. She didn't sell stamps. She instructed me to trudge across the lobby and euchre-up to the stamp machine. I protested I was catching a plane and didn't have time. She said she was sorry, she just couldn't go around selling 4-cent stamps like that. I pointed out that I already had a $10 postage deposit on record. She said yes, that was for books, not 4-cent stamps. If I would just cross the lobby to the right, and put my money in the stamp machine—

My right hand leapt like a cobra for her pulsing throat. It established contact. It held tight as an innkeeper's purse. I counted slowly up to twelve. She began to gasp. Her cheeks turned chalky. Her soft brown eyes stared up at me in mute appeal. I thought of going on to thirteen, but didn't. Instead, with a mysterious smile, I released her. Flinging me not only the stamp but my $400 refund as well, she rose like a pheasant for the guests' storage vault. I was, so to speak, sprung.

But not quite. My wife ran in from the street: our bags were still in transit, and all three cabs had been usurped. She returned to her post while I launched a general search. I grabbed an elevator for the seventh floor and sneaked up on 782, hoping to surprise the bellhops in a bit of baggage-frisking. Both cells were empty. Worse than that, they were already being swabbed down for the next victim.

Back down the elevator and so to the street. No bags. No cabs. My helpmate, keening at the curb, had gnawed her nails down to the second knuckle. I ran back to the lobby entrance. As I started to pass into the hotel, two bag-laden bellboys thundered through the doors. A less nimble chap than I would have been trampled to death. It had taken this panting pair exactly fourteen minutes to move those bags from 782 to curb. I endowed them both on the spot unto the third generation. A cab roared up. Bags flew through the air like basketballs. My wife and I were flung into the back seat. The cab aimed like a projectile for the airport.

We scrambled into an Ozark C-47 at a dead run. Bang went the door. Up lurched the plane. The stewardess was drunk. She told us she'd been on one hell of a party, and you only live once. She sat behind us all the way to Minneapolis, loudly ridiculing a dignified old gentleman who sat across the aisle. There followed—for twenty-six bucks—a night of horror at the Clark in Minneapolis. Next morning —forty minutes for coffee. I thought you'd like to know your competitors are quite as loyal as you to the national Innkeeper's Oath not to kill the poor bastards, just worry them to death.

At the Minneapolis Airport a burglar in the uniform of Western Air Lines informed us that family rates (full fare for husband, half for wife), in effect Monday through Friday, didn't *really* go into effect until Monday at noon. Since we were departing Monday at 9 a.m., we could either be had on the spot or wait five hours for the afternoon milk-run. I ponied up $50 or $60 more in addition to the round trip fare for two I'd already paid for. We took off like a pair of molting partridges. Champagne Flight, it's called. The champagne is yellow bile bearing the label of a California pharmaceutical laboratory.

Which brings us back to your note of October 14, 1958, in which you express the hope that we were comfortable during our stay with you. Such hope is altogether misbegotten. We were not comfortable with you at all. Not since my confinement in a federal reformatory (for a harmless tort which is none of your business) have I undergone such a rigorous course in character-building. The reformatory, however, was free, while your ministrations set me back a hundred fish each day.

Yet even now I wish to voice no complaint. Expensive though it may have seemed by any humane standard, I packed away exactly $25,000 worth of experience in ten days flat—and what is even more important, I escaped alive. This latter circumstance may not seem as remarkable to you as it actually is. During our visit I bribed the county clerk to let me poke through his vault of secret vital statistics. I discovered to my horror that Rochester, Minnesota, has the highest transient death rate in the western world. How many of them turned up their toes in Mr. F's establishment I've no way of knowing, but I'll wager you've got your fair share of pelts stacked away in the attic.

If you have followed me thus far, I think we've now arrived at a position to zero in on that missing pot. You inform me we had coffee in our room on that wild morning of departure, and I dimly recall some such miracle; you say it was served by a young lady, and this too could be correct; and in a "new Stanley thermos pot," which may or may not be true. So far so good. Your reasoning is speculative, but why not? Life's a crap game anyhow.

You then ask me whether I placed the pot in the hall, at which point, you theorize, "someone may have picked it up." A likely story. People at the Franklin don't pick up empty coffee pots, they lust for full ones. Who on earth do you think would have picked that pot up? And why would they pick it up? If they did pick it up, why didn't they put it down again? Pick it up, indeed. Let's pull ourselves together, Mr. Hunt. We'll have to do much better than this. We're not *thinking.*

In my opinion you are guilty of fundamental error in your whole approach to this mystery. Instead of concentrating on your pot, you've become obsessed with the idea of this ghostly "someone" who "may have picked it up." Even if this were true, I say—in heaven's name, why not? There's nothing wrong in picking up a pot. Everybody does it one time or another. The tortuous act consists in walking away before you put it down again. This you are very careful not to charge against our phantom "someone." You merely infer it. You hint at it. And you don't even trouble to veil your suspicions.

Doesn't this whole affair—this sly substitution of innuendo for proof—come dreadfully close to character assassination? And isn't it kind of silly to start that sort of thing before we have the foggiest notion whose character it is we're going to assassinate?

I really feel that if we're ever going to fight our way out of this maze (which I fear you've only complicated), you must dispel all fantasies of pot thieves and the like, and fasten your eye everlastingly on the ball which is, of course, your pot. You describe the vanished article as "a new Stanley thermos pot." If you were reporting the loss of an automobile, would you describe it merely as "a new Stanley Steamer?" Of course not. You'd get right down to brass tacks. You'd really describe the thing, wouldn't you? Of course, you would.

For example, you describe the pot as "new." How new—brand, or almost? Were there any dents, marks, scars or scratches on it? Was it made of gold, silver, steel or common pot-metal? Did it have a bright, shiny chrome finish? Was the lid of that certain hinged type which, unless carefully lifted in advance of pouring, bursts open with a soft *thlook,* overshoots your coffee cup and gushes half its contents into your lap? Instead of being simply a "Stanley thermos pot" was it not, in fact, a "Stanley 'It Will Not Break' Thermos Pot" made in New Britain, Connecticut, U.S.A., by Landers, Frary & Clark? Did it bear on its base the serial number 6-54? If so, perhaps I can help you, since such a pot sits this very moment in our strong box at the First Western Bank in Pasadena, California.

Now the pot which First Western (assets over a billion) holds may or may not be the pot to which you refer in your note of October 14, 1958. One thing is certain: your description of whatever pot you have in mind couldn't prove your ownership of *my* pot to your own wife. But granting that it is, or was, your pot—how shall we account for its presence at this moment amongst my household treasures? Did it walk there all by itself? Of course not. Did I bribe some disloyal bellhop to despoil you of it and send it to me? Much too complicated. Did I myself steal it? One look at my honest face gives any man his answer. Then how on earth . . .?

Do the clouds begin to lift? Does a shaft of sunlight penetrate the cerebral hemispheres? Does a little bell begin to ring up there? Exactly! There was no theft at all. You and I traded pots, Mr. Hunt. I took your Stanley thermos pot which is utterly useless to your guests, and left for my successor in 782 a stout aluminum pot that well may save his life, together with a can and a half of Sterno and half a pound of Maxwell House instant coffee. This will be laid up to my account in heaven as an act of charity. As for Mr. F—well, God help him, he's crossed that bridge already.

The books I left behind for you to mail have arrived in good order. They bore postal charges of $1.94. Deducting that sum, plus the 4-cent stamp I charmed out of your cashier, from the $10 postage deposit I trustingly left in your care, it appears that $8.02 of my money has stuck to your palm. I'm troubled that you haven't been as concerned these two long months for my $8.02 as for your miserable (and probably imaginary) pot. I suggest, therefore, that you climb on top of the situation at once.

I am, Mr. Hunt,

Ever your servant
DALTON TRUMBO [25]

17. To Frank King

Los Angeles, California
1958

Dear Frank:

A good many months ago, in settling a dispute between us, we agreed that neither of us would ever again mention the past. But you *did* mention the past in our Saturday conversation in a way that might affect the future—and so I feel that I must mention it too.

You said that after the blacklist was over, and I was in a position to claim for my work its fair market price, I should remember that it was you who became the first to buy my services and work and make advances during the days of the blacklist. This is true. I do remember it, and always will.

But, since the past has been brought up between us again, there is another aspect of it that you yourself must remember. I sold my work to you at very low prices, and from it you produced two films which, as you have told me, not only saved your company from closing its doors, but also returned such large profits that it has, in effect, become self-supporting and self-financing from its own earned capital.

So each of us has something to remember and be grateful to the

---

[25] This letter was never sent.

other for. Carrying this same idea over into the forthcoming white market days—and it is your idea—does it not mean that my remembered gratitude will command me to give you the very finest work of which I, a successful writer, am capable? And that your remembered gratitude likewise commands you to pay me the very highest price a prosperous corporation can afford?

Anyhow, that would seem to be the logic of it. It just shows how right we were in agreeing to bury the past. We presently live, however, neither in the past nor the future. Concluding that since you, a good business man, employ a lawyer, certainly I, a bad business man by your own words, should also get legal assistance (especially in view of the fact I have no agent), I have discussed ＿＿ ＿ ＿＿ with Aubrey Finn, and he will shortly write you what his client, Miss Beth Fincher, thinks would be a fair deal for writing the screenplay.

God bless us all . . .

DOC

9.
"Guerrilla Warfare"

By 1959 Trumbo believed he had waited long enough. If he was going to fight for the destruction of the detested blacklist, he recognized the necessity of establishing an appealing and novel public image. After all, he reasoned, it would be impossible to get public sympathy for $100,000 a year men who were now earning somewhere around $10,000; he knew, also, that most intellectuals and writers considered screen writers to be hacks and would offer little support; he was aware that the whole case of the Hollywood Ten was remote and probably forgotten; and finally, he realized that no one was interested in victims, in angry martyrs, or in public weeping. Therefore, prompted by the amusing Robert Rich scandal, Trumbo resolved to play the scamp who snipes at the tender parts of upright Hollywood institutions and has a good deal of fun doing it. He appeared on numerous television shows, offered press statements, wrote articles attacking the blacklist and the Academy of Motion Picture Arts and Sciences, refused to deny or confirm authorship of any film thereby getting credit for much that was not his, and extolling the black market—all in the image of fun-loving scallywag. He made himself and his colleagues out to be victors over the blacklist: the black market was working; everyone was in on it; why not admit the fact and bring it out in the open?

Many people resented Trumbo's outspokenness, maintaining that he was seeking attention only for himself. Others feared his talk would cause the committee to investigate the black market itself by going after the producers who had hired blacklistees. But Trumbo, prophetically, felt that the result would be a different one. He waited for a break. Meanwhile he was hard at work on the Bryna production of *Spartacus,* a major spectacular, to be released by Universal. In time the six leading actors found out who their writer was, and that was as good as a public announcement. Sam Jackson became the joke of Hollywood. There was no time for flare-ups—for disputes with the Motion Picture Academy, for revitalized attacks by the American Legion, or for personal attacks against Trumbo's political beliefs—that would impede what now seemed inevitable: that a blacklisted writer, without compromise or capitulation before the committee, was going to see his name appear on the American screen.

1. To Albert Maltz

Los Angeles, California
January 9, 1959

Dear Albert:

I am giving you a résumé of what goes on here, and then striking off a copy of the letter to send to Mike [Wilson] in Paris, together with specifics pertaining to him. Thus I'll save a little time.

The sequence of events leading to the present situation is this:

Since September rumors have floated through the town concerning the identity of Nathan Douglas (Ned) [1] Stanley Kramer [2] had taken to the air in some university TV program, announcing that as far as he was concerned there was no blacklist, had been none for the last five years, and that he had and would continue to employ persons who had been subpoenaed by the Committee. There was no press storm, not a word.

About 2 weeks before Xmas Hal and Ned were approached at a luncheon by George Seaton [3] and Valentine Davies, representing the Academy. They recognized the possibility of [The] *Defiant* [Ones] being nominated for the Academy, wished to avoid a third scandal in as many years,[4] said they were going to try to get the Academy rule rescinded,[5] and asked Hal and Ned to help them by giving a friendly interview (non-political) to Tom Pryor of *The NY Times,* which would reveal Ned's true identity, and permit them then to go to work within the Academy to get the rule abolished.

Ned, Hal and I held a conference. I contended that, this being the season for honors and silver plate, Hal and Ned should wait until they had picked up a number of other awards before considering breaking anything. I felt it was the Academy's problem, not theirs; and that they should save all their fire for a fight if one developed, rather than wasting a single inch of newspaper space when they did not need it. They agreed. They gave no interview.

On December 31 they won the New York Film Critics' Award.

[1] Nedrick Young and Hal Wallace, screen writers of *The Defiant Ones.*

[2] Producer and director of such successful films as *The Men, The Champion,* and *Death of a Salesman.*

[3] Seaton, a Paramount producer, had been president of the Motion Picture Academy in 1957. At the time this letter was written both he and Davies were active members of the Academy Board.

[4] In 1956 Robert Rich won an award for *The Brave One,* but no Robert Rich could be found; in the same year Michael Wilson was denied an award for *Friendly Persuasion* by the Academy ruling. In 1957 Michael Wilson and Carl Foreman were widely rumored to have written *The Bridge on the River Kwai.*

[5] At the time of the 1956 awards, the Academy ruled (section F, article VIII of the Academy by-laws) that no person who had refused to give evidence before the Congressional committee was eligible for an Academy award. The rule was rescinded on January 12, 1959.

This compelled Tom Pryor to threaten that he would break the story with or without them. Since it was now better *with* them, they gave him an interview. This was given on the afternoon of New Year's Eve, and was printed in the *New York Times* New Year's morning.

Meanwhile, I'd had Bill Stout alerted.[6] The instant Pryor forced their hand, I tipped Bill. Result: Bill's New Year's Eve program had both Hal and Ned on, breaking the news locally in a most dignified and advantageous way. There was nothing else to do. Bill Stout is far and away the most influential commentator in this area, and for forty-five mintes after the show his board was clogged with calls— all for, only one (Dick Macauley) [7] against!

For 3 days the industy greeted this with a silence which convinced me (and still does) that we have the best chance of our lives. I shall not go into an analysis of the situation, because it changes swiftly, and each issue must be met the *minute* it arises. I only ask you to trust me, and to believe that I think I'm acting in the best interests of all. If not, small harm will have been done: if so, much good will result.

. . . .

In the meanwhile I had lunch with Lou Irwin, radio news announcer for KPOL, and TV news commentator for KABC-TV, Channel 7. Last night (January 8), he did the first half of a two-part series on the blacklist, and what he hails as its end. Such a forthright anti-blacklist thing has never been done on the air. Pasternak, of course, is the theme—the American Pasternaks, and the right of a writer to be judged by his work instead of his private opinions.

Tonight Irwin completes the series. (I read both shows in advance and made suggestions.) Tonight, in relation to *The Defiant Ones,* Hal and Ned in particular, and all blacklisted personnel in general, he will broadcast anti-blacklist statements from Ed Hartmann, president of the [Screen Writers'] Guild; Max Youngstein, vice-president of United Artists; Frank King of the King Brothers; Ambassador Hill, our envoy to Mexico City; and John Nettleman, information officer for the Department of State in Washington, D.C. Theme of all statements: the work, not the private life of the writer. Even George Stevens, president of the Academy, will cautiously echo the sentiment.

Opposed will be . . . the following from Ward Bond, President of the Motion Picture Alliance for the Preservation of American Ideals: "They're all working now, all these fifth amendment communists, and I don't think that anything I say about it will make much difference. There's no point at issue. We've just lost the fight and it's as simple as that. I think the fight might be resumed some

---

[6] News commentator for Los Angeles station KNXT-TV.

[7] Macauley, it will be remembered, was one of the friendly witnesses at the 1947 HUAC hearings. He died in 1970.

day in the future. I don't know. It's going to take a tremendous change in public opinion, and I don't see how it's going to come about with the courts acting the way they have."

Meanwhile, Seaton has confronted Y. Frank F[reeman] with the flat statement that the Academy rule is silly, embarrassing, and untenable, and that he intends to introduce at the Board a motion to rescind it. Freeman wasn't nearly as hostile as usual. Muttered something about changing times. Asked if Ned Young would talk to him, and the answer is that Ned will some time next week. Yesterday the Film Daily Poll awarded a plaque to Ned and Hal for best screenplay—poll of 2,000 critics. Jewish award came through also.

Next on program: about Wednesday of next week (Jan. 14), with full consent of the King Brothers, Bill Stout is going to produce the real Robert Rich, alive and before the cameras.[8] The story will be told without rancor, without attacks on anyone, with good humor, *and with no digs at the Academy or its leaders.* (This, I think, is the tone for everyone who has anything to say from the blacklistees' side—restraint, cooperation with pleasant professional relations, etc., etc. Nobody's a martyr, nobody's mad, history hurt everybody, all made mistakes, and la-de-da-da-do.) The reason I make a point of this is that there can never be an *official* end to the blacklist—this is as close as we presently shall come. Therefore we must *pretend* this is the end (which it damned near is), and pose not as angry martyrs, as the persecuted, but as good *winners.* In this guise we assume our victory at last, and carry no grudges forward into the future.

Now at the end of the Stout program, which probably will be ballyhooed for two or three days in advance, Bill will announce, as a matter of mere news interest, that the K[ing] B[rother]s have called a press conference for eleven o'clock the following day (probably Jan. 15).

The press conference will be held. The King Brothers will announce that they, for one, are through with the blacklist once and for all. From now on they're going to do openly what everybody else in the business is doing secretly: they are going to hire the best writers they can get, regardless of what the writers may or may not have been or thought. They're going to be tough on this, and they'll be loaded with ammunition.

They will then announce that, upon the completion of the writers' current schedule of assignments, they have made the following deals with the following persons:

1. A deal with Albert Maltz to develop an original screenplay entitled *Gift from Guilty Men.* It will be the story of those Southern convicts who offered themselves as human guinea pigs in the early fight against pellagra; and of the Austro-Hungarian immigrant, Dr.

---

[8] Rich was, of course, Trumbo. Apparently the before mentioned intention to break this news in August of 1958 was abandoned.

Joseph Goldberger, to whom they entrusted their lives during the experiments.

2. A deal with Michael Wilson to write a screenplay, based on his own original story entitled *A Sound of Bells.* The story is set against the background of Paris during the first delirious days of the liberation. It tells the story of an American soldier and a young French street girl who has been deceived into collaboration with the Nazis.

3. A deal with Dalton Trumbo to develop a screenplay from his own original story entitled *King of the Golden Isles.* The background is Cuba during the civil war of 1917. The story concerns an American diplomatic attaché and his four young daughters.

There they are: *Gift from Guilty Men,* Maltz; *A Sound of Bells,* Wilson; *King of the Golden Isles,* Trumbo. Remember them. Each may expatiate to the press as much about his own theme and story as he wishes—the KBs here will not go one word beyond the story theme sketched in above.

If the press calls at your door, your employment *must* be confirmed, because the KBs are going out on a long limb for what is, with them, a matter of principle. And because they know how treacherous press relations are, they must have some guarantee in hand that you and I *will* confirm.

Hence—to *Mike Wilson*: Please cable the KBs (cable address KINGPROD, L.A., U.S.A., approximately (or the same affirmation in better words): EXTREMELY PLEASED TO BE DOING A SOUND OF BELLS WITH YOUR ORGANIZATION, AND HAPPIER STILL TO BE ACCEPTED AGAIN AS A WRITER IN MY OWN COUNTRY, MICHAEL WILSON.

Hence—to *Albert,* who is closer and can cable more profusely, something like this: IF OUR PICTURE IS AS WORTHY AS THE WORK OF DR. GOLDBERGER AND HIS CONVICTS IN THEIR FIGHT AGAINST PELLAGRA, I CAN IMAGINE NO GREATER SATISFACTION. SINCE 1947 THE FILMS I HAVE WRITTEN UNDER PSEUDONYMS HAVE GROSSED MORE MONEY FOR FILM STUDIOS THAN THOSE WRITTEN UNDER MY NAME BEFORE THE BLACKLIST WAS INSTITUTED. THE ONLY CHANGE NOW WILL BE AN END TO A RATHER ABSURD SITUATION IN WHICH THE PRODUCT OF MY PEN IS USED, WHILE MY NAME IS NOT. WITH ALL GOOD WISHES, ALBERT MALTZ.

As for me, I shall be at hand somewhere, hence no cable. These cables should be sent by the fastest carrier—and at once!

I think I've made plain to Albert by telephone (and I hope by now also to Mike), that we are actually under no obligation to do *any* film for the KBs, and certainly not these quick inventions (although all three of them somehow sound very good to me!). Nonetheless I have assured the KBs that I feel myself under a moral obligation to do at least *one* film for them as soon as I am able—which may be in about 18 months. Albert has also expressed himself to me that if, after his schedule which he estimates at 2 years, is completed, he and the KBs can find a mutually satisfactory project, he will also do one. I'd like Mike to consider this seriously, too. There is really no reason why these guys have to do this at all—it may be of the greatest monetary and morale value to some 200 blacklisted personnel—and I think we owe them consideration, courtesy, respect, and, if possible, that which they value most highly from us, and which we are or will be very capable of doing—good work. But this is for the future. To get back to the present:

The cables must be sent; we must hold firm to our public recognition of these commitments; we must attack no one; we must view this victory (which we assume it to be) in good spirit, without jumping producers, Academy, Guild, or anyone else. Because, in a curious sense, our former enemies are now compelled to make efforts that coincide with our own. *But by all means we must not make liars or fools of the KBs, nor fail in any way to sustain them through the public relations dept.*

Forgive this intolerable length: I had not time, as the man says, to make it shorter. We have a great chance to do something, team! Each man in his hole and hup-hup-hup!

God bless!
DT

2. To Michael Wilson and Albert Maltz

Los Angeles, California
January 12, 1959

Dear Mike and Albert:

. . . .

Tonight at 8:30 the Academy Board meets in its first effort to rescind the rule. This is extremely secret, because if Seaton (who works like a dog for rescission because he must) and his group fail, they hope to force the issue through a second time with better luck. All very complicated. Sounds like they have a faction going.

Carl Sandburg, who is celebrating some kind of anniversary year all over the country, is flying here next week (secretly, insofar as the present is concerned) to deliver a red hot TV show damning the blacklist.

Later comes the R[obert] R[ich] exposure (good-naturedly if the Academy rescinds, viciously if it doesn't)—followed by the triple employment announcement of the KBs (God and Mike willing). If the Academy rescinds, we shall celebrate all this as a good-natured victory dance, with the winners generous. If the Academy does not —then they will catch more hell on radio, TV and the press than anyone could have imagined even eighteen months ago. And we'll eventually win anyhow, and force a later rescission from the Academy.

There is a curious current of excitement all through the town, as if this were the night or week before Waterloo. The [Screen Writers'] Guild is lining up for the blacklisted. People feel a decision is afoot, and they begin to move, either as they always secretly wished to, or as opportunism directs. The old and bearded guerrillas move out of the woods and onto the plains, and they are greeted by all who have lived cozily during the war with the cry, "Hail! Welcome! We want to help you!"

Tomorrow's dispatch will arrive in God's time.

Salud!
DT

3. To Bill Stout of KNXT-TV

Los Angeles, California
January 16, 1959

Dear Bill:

There's one problem about this business that troubles me deeply. Lew Irwin [9] in three TV reports, has done a magnificent and boldly editorial job on *The Defiant Ones*, the blacklist, and the Academy. I know he is going to be hurt and shocked, and perhaps damaged somewhat with his superiors, when you break the [Robert Rich] story tonight. There are so few who have been willing to go out on limbs on this issue that I shrink from the idea of letting any of them down.

With your permission, I should like to see him this afternoon, put him under oath of secrecy, tell him what you and I have done together, that you have had the story for two years, and that I was honor bound to see that you and you alone wound the story up. Then I would like to arrange something for his program, which goes on fifteen minutes after yours leaves the air.

What I have in mind is a forthright, amusing and incisive interview between him and Frank King. If Irwin wanted a brief statement from me, I'd be willing to make it on film, or any other way.

[9] Irwin was a commentator for KPOL and KABC-TV.

Thus, if you broke the Rich story, Irwin could come on some fifteen minutes later and say, "As I predicted two days ago, the true identity of Robert Rich has at last been revealed. Late this evening, D.T. informed me that he . . ." etc. *Then* he could direct his emphasis to Frank King. You would have Rich, he would have King, and I would have done my best to cooperate with all who have been helpful.

If you agree, my personal and ethical problem would be immensely simplified if you left Frank out of it, aside from the confrontation and confirmation which occurred yesterday afternoon between you and him.

If you do not agree, I shall, of course, do whatever you wish, for you're the guy who has done more for blacklisted people than any writer or commentator in the country. But even in this area, I should like to protect Frank, first because he needs it, and second, because I *like* him very much.

As to our interview, I'll do absolutely what you wish. Without pretending to know your business nearly as well as you do, I suggest that the following questions might be pertinent:

1. Do you regard this as the end of the blacklist?
2. From now on do you plan to use your own name on scripts?
3. Do you still maintain your position of political privacy (or whatever) ?
4. Now that you're returning to films, would you be willing to work on a picture with men like Adolphe Menjou and Ward Bond, who led the crusade which supported blacklisting?
5. Do you plan to ask the Academy for the Oscar?
6. If they give you the Oscar, what will you do with it?

If you think questions 5 and 6 are of any value, I'd like to end my part of the show with them. I'm sorry to be such an old maid about the thing; but at this point the blacklisters need as much help as the blacklisted in finishing the dirty business off. Seaton and his friends, who represent probably the largest and most influential group within the industry, are now apparently determined to wash the thing up and end it—not only in the Academy, but in the Guilds, and finally, among the producers themselves. Therefore, in pretending to be the victor in a ten year fight, I must be more cunning than Satan, more generous than Jesus. I'm not well fitted for the role, so I fret about it.

The best,
DALTON TRUMBO

4. To George Seaton

Los Angeles, California
January 20, 1959

Dear George:

I enclose a copy of the Stevens statement in the bulldog of last night's [Los Angeles] *Times*.[10] Happily for all concerned, and due to your astonishing talent for mediation, it was killed in the morning edition. I'm glad I followed your advice, for Stevens' statement and my reply were set for the tag of the Stout show. He held two endings, and kept a phone open for me for possible cancellation.

I wonder if it wouldn't be helpful if you explained to Stevens that my breaking of the story had nothing whatever to do with the Academy? To that end you have permission to show him all or any part of my recent correspondence, including the present letter, if you think it wise.

As for the award, that should be no issue between us. It would be absurd for me to "claim" it, and I will not do so. I have documents establishing authorship, and Stevens or any representative of the Academy may request and examine them. The [Screen Writers'] Guild will be of no assistance, since my membership lapsed long ago. I have no quarrel with the Guild, but it simply wasn't possible for me to work and abide by its code and by-laws. I chose to be a former member rather than a dishonest one.

It seems to me it will be rather difficult for the Academy to withhold the award and still maintain its dignity. If, however, they do decide to withhold it, I shall cooperate with them so that the least harm possible be done to everyone concerned. I cannot, of course, hold silent for any attack upon my personal or professional integrity. My objective, as you know, is much more important than the physical possession of an award which can never be dissociated from my person anyhow.

I think Stevens should also be told that I deliberately broke the story on the worst night of the week for news so it could die over the week-end; and that far from casting any aspersion on the Academy, I have repeatedly declared it an innocent party to the *Rich* affair, and privately restrained the press from acts which would embarrass it.

He should also be made to understand that I am no longer in a position where men can throw mud at me with impunity—particularly men toward whom I feel no ill will and whom I have never injured in any way. The working press are on my side, not only the

---

[10] After the identity of Robert Rich broke on January 16, 1959, George Stevens, president of the Academy, issued a statement to the Los Angeles *Times* attacking Trumbo's former deception. Seaton, acting as mediator, persuaded Stevens to withdraw the statement before it achieved wide circulation. Trumbo then withheld proposed counter-attacks.

wire services, but local and New York staffs, and TV commentators as well. The story broke far bigger in Europe than it did here, and you can imagine whose side *they* are on.

The reason has nothing to do with me. It relates to a changing country, the cruel idocy of the blacklist itself, a whole sequence of fortunate accidents, plus one constant element which the Academy and its publicity counsel should always assume to be the fundamental fact of the Academy's existence: the Academy is Hollywood in the public mind, and Hollywood is always fair game. The Academy, being Hollywood's most important institution, presents not only the biggest target but also the most coveted trophy for any maverick hunter who roams the forest.

For the same reason that a Hollywood writer is always a "hack," while the worst novelist is at least a "writer," the Academy is not regarded by the professional world outside Hollywood as a true academy, but as the official representative of a rich and self-seeking industry. Despite the fact that its film library, its theatre, its rich accumuation of film history and technical materials, its research facilities, its open door to colleges and universities—despite the fact that all these services (of which nobody outside the industry has any real knowledge) entitle it to a high among the world's cultural organizations devoted to the cinema, it does not receive such recognition because of that same anti-Hollywood animus which makes us all so susceptible to attack.

It appears to me that the Academy must sooner or later recognize the vulnerability of its position in the public eye, and adopt a public relations point of view which will diminish rather than increase its vulnerability. To this end, it seems to me, it must discourage the misconception that it is merely the public relations arm of the Producers' Association; it must separate itself entirely from any responsibility for, defense of, or attack upon the employment practices and policies of the various motion picture companies; and never risk its institutional prestige by assuming the posture of oppression or pomposity toward any mere individual. For when the Academy attacks an individual, the object of its anger instantly becomes a brave little underdog—and the whole press corps takes out happily after the big-bully institution which has precipitated so unfair a fight. Beyond this, one must always take into consideration the secret hankering of every healthy person to see dignity unhorsed.

This process is automatic and spontaneous. And it is almost always set off by the Academy itself. All that's required is the slightest slip of the tongue or judgment of any Academy official. It shouldn't be so, but it is. And that is the reason why there must be no showdown in the press between George Stevens and me.

I will do all I can to prevent it, but somebody must give me a little help. George Stevens simply *must* abandon such words as "odious" and "deception." He simply *must* restrain his desire to injure me—or, at the very least, he must not injure me to the degree that I am compelled to fight back. The blacklist is being swept away so fast that some spectacular open hirings are at hand, and victory over the blacklist must not appear to the public as a victory over the Academy.

There's another reason why George Stevens—*particularly* George Stevens—should not appear, as unwittingly he does, in concert with blacklisters and vigilantes: it simply doesn't match the consistent theme of his life work as a film director. I wish some day he could hear my friend and his colleague, Curt Bernhart, describe the process of the Nazi blacklist as it struck the German film industry. It was the early success of this and other Nazi blacklists which finally enabled the Gestapo and the SS to seize the throat of Anne Frank. How, then, can the director of *The Diary of Anne Frank*, in the dying hours of the American blacklist, permit his name to symbolize the last rally of a tiny handful of fanatics, all of them immensely inferior to him both intellectually and morally? It will not and cannot be understood, and ought not happen. However sincere his motives (and I know they *are* sincere), I fear that one day he himself will be uncomfortable with the memory of it.

This business of the award is really a very small affair, which is being blown up out of all proportion to its significance by the hesitation, public deliberation, and grumbling attitude of the Academy itself. If it can be solved at a level somewhat above the gutter, it should cause no one any harm. My own suggestion to the Academy would be to accept the situation with a certain amiability, wry if it wishes, but certainly with an awareness of general amusement— and get rid of it as fast as possible. I even have some ideas on the matter, if anyone is interested. Delay and indecision only play into the hands of a press that is mischievously avid for Academy embarrassment.

Why don't you and [Valentine] Davies, whose judgments in this situation I will unhesitatingly accept, move as friends of the industry into the public relations vacuum which clearly has settled over the Academy? A great deal of past difficulty could have been decently avoided if only the lines of communication had been left open. You and Val could constitute yourselves an independent line of communication which would prevent both me and Stevens from precipitating a conflict through ignorance or error.

So long as I am neither spat on nor gratuitously insulted I shall, with your assistance and only if you think it wise, coordinate my every statement and act with Stevens' statements and acts—even if it means finding a decent way to withhold the award altogether. But I cannot function either wisely or intelligently in the dark.

Please tell George Stevens that I shall forget everything he has said thus far, that I have no animus against him, that I want to engage in no fights, that the award is not my fundamental or overwhelming interest, that I am solely interested in breaking the blacklist, that it *will* be broken—and that even there I can see no possible conflict between his interests and mine.

Regards,
DALTON

P.S.   Please apologize for me to Phyllis [Mrs. Seaton] for having broken up her evening with my difficulties; and thank her for so promptly recognizing them as real.   DT

5. To Michael Wilson

Los Angeles, California
February 24, 1959

Dear Mike:

Your lament is fully justified, and I apologize. I got so deeply involved in so many things that I kept postponing a letter to you on the grounds that a few days more would permit me to give a fuller account of what has been going on.

Even now, I'm dictating this letter and my sister is transcribing it for me, so don't expect any very thoughtful organization of what I have in mind. It's just as it comes to me at this moment.

Yours and Albert's cables arrived and were ready for use. As I told you at the time, each of you would have been notified in advance when the news would break. The truth is that publicity developments surrounding *The Defiant Ones* and *The Brave One* turned out to be more important than had been anticipated. Once I saw how very greatly the times have changed, I shelved the King Brothers' idea altogether.[11] It would have been, in a way, anticlimactic; it was not, in any event, big enough to top what had gone before; and it was just faintly illegitimate. The illegitimacy wouldn't have bothered me if the situation had been such that desperate measures needed to be taken to keep the general publicity flow moving and alive. However, the thing continued of its own momentum, and you may be sure that your cable to the King Brothers will never be used.

The situation within the industry, the various guilds and unions, and the Academy, may, I think, accurately be summarized as follows: there is no longer a left, and there is no longer a right, and

[11] The plan outlined in the January 9, 1959, letter to Albert Maltz (#1, pp. 470-474, above).

there is no longer a centralized control of the industry tight enough to enforce the blacklist. This general fragmentation of the industry, and of the political forces within it, has opened the field for straight guerrilla warfare. The movement within the Academy to revoke its rule was originated, led by, and accomplished by the center. The movement within the Screen Writers' Guild to revoke some of its more absurd working rules is similarly led by the center. They are moving of their own volition because they must.

One of the main problems has been to restrain certain die-hard elements of the left from making organizational moves. There was, for example, the idea of placing an ad in the trade papers and in the Los Angeles *Times*. . . . I was able to torpedo it, thank God. I pointed out to them that the slightest appearance of an organized and organizational effort at this moment would frighten off the center forces which are actually doing the job without anybody's assistance. Not only would it frighten them off, but it would give the old right an opportunity to reactivate itself and bring to the forefront issues and arguments twelve years old which have no relation to the present. Similarly, it was proposed that the Guild have an open meeting to which all the blacklisted persons would be invited. And there the blacklisted persons could present their point of view to the Guild. I objected to this on the grounds that it would call forth the right onto the floor of the Guild, and again the argument would be conducted between right and left, while the center would fade away entirely. The point here is that we simply must not permit the arguments and issues of 1947–48 to be repeated in 1959. No greater service to the idiot right could be rendered than to give them the opportunity to revive the argument as it was. Since they cannot handle the argument as it is today, they are completely silent. And they will remain silent unless some fool gives them a platform.

The theory behind what Hal [Smith] and Ned [Young] and I have done in the last six weeks is simply this: there is no way the blacklist can officially be rescinded. How can an industry officially rescind a blacklist which legally it cannot admit the existence of? There *was*, however, the Academy rule. Revocation of the Academy rule was the nearest thing to an official rescission of the blacklist that could or will occur. Therefore we hailed this official revocation by the Academy as an official revocation; we know that the black-list still exists. But the public relations problem was to create throughout the industry an atmosphere which would accept the end of the blacklist as an accomplished fact. In other words, by repeatedly stating that the blacklist is over, we actually convinced large segments of the motion picture industry and the public at large that it was really over. Once this *idea* was accepted by the industry, a great step forward was made toward breaking the blacklist in fact.

It is my very strong feeling that our triumphant bellowings were correct; and that the worst possible tactic now would be for anyone to present himself as a martyr, or to wail, "Oh, the horror of it all!" People hate martyrs, and as if that weren't bad enough, there is the added fact that martyrs simply do not make news. If we were to reach the press we had to make news, and the news value of the present situation does not lie in publicizing a blacklist which was stale news five years ago, but rather in hailing its demise which turned out to be very hot news in the present. To some persons—formerly writers and artists in motion pictures, who changed professions and are still suffering both economically and morally from exclusion from their own profession—our happy chortlings in the press have seemed cruel, untrue, and self-serving. For such persons I have sympathy but very little tolerance. If they cannot understand that what is good for one is good for all, then they've learned nothing in the last twelve years of the blacklist.

Before this thing is over, a number of persons who were not outstandingly successful before the blacklist are going to have to face some bitter truths. The first truth is this: that whereas, prior to 1947, there was a place in the motion picture industry for the writer who earned twelve-fifty a week perhaps twenty weeks a year, there is no place for that writer now. If he is lucky, he will end up in television. If he is not lucky, he will end up peddling Fuller brushes. Consider the Board of Directors of the Screen Writers' Guild at the time of the 1947 blacklist, and consider where they are today. . . . They were basically middle-bracket writers—successful mediocrities—and today I doubt that one of them has had a full credit for the past three years. Most of them are in TV, and those who aren't are simply starving to death. When this accursed blacklist is finally broken, we shall discover the same situation applying to blacklisted writers. Those who just barely got by in the old days will not be able to survive under present conditions. For them, therefore, the breaking of the blacklist will have no significance at all, and they will probably lay the blame for their failures on those persons whose successes made the breakthrough possible.

Any studio in town will pay a writer of your stature from seventy-five thousand to a hundred and twenty-five thousand dollars for a script. But it will not take a ____ ____ or a ____ ____ for ten thousand dollars. They want what they think is the best or nothing. The result will be that only the best blacklisted writers will profit from the end of the blacklist, while the rest will be confronted with a terrible competitive struggle.

About six months ago I had a discussion with Albert Maltz on this very problem. It was his feeling that the proper tactic to break the blacklist would be to sneak in small people obscurely, thereby setting small precedents which would admit the more notorious blacklistees ultimately to come forward. I disagreed altogether. It was my feeling then, and still is, that the blacklist will be broken by the shock troops or will not be broken at all. The shock troops are Wilson, Maltz, and Trumbo. You can put ＿＿＿＿ ＿＿＿＿＿＿ publicly to work tomorrow and nothing will happen. Put Wilson to work tomorrow and the blacklist is over. The reason for this is pretty clear in my mind. (Incidentally, Albert is now in agreement with me.) Wilson, Maltz, and Trumbo are better writers today than they were when the blacklist was promulgated. This is because they deliberately set out to build second careers in the black market. These second careers are now at their peak. By not abandoning their professions, those three writers, accepting the handicaps of the second career, are probably better writers today than they would have been had there been no blacklist. Those who were compelled to abandon their professions, those who took other work to support their families, have probably become poorer writers than they were when the blacklist began. You cannot cease practicing your profession and grow better at it simultaneously. You're bound to retrogress.

This blacklist will not be broken by the triumph of morality over immorality. It will not be broken by the triumph of one organziation over another orangization. It will only be broken by the sheer excellence of the work of two or three blacklisted writers. Call it talent, call it competence, ability, craftsmanship, or what you will— still in all, that is the only practical weapon for the job. I think we have that weapon, and that within the next few months, or the next year, we shall have to use it. Which is to say that each of us individually, acting in coordination with each other, must very soon use the excellence of our work to compel the use of our names, or of established pseudonyms which will be used on other pictures and will become identifiable with us. This seems to me to be the next step.

· ·

Now let me get down to this little union of three called Wilson, Maltz, and Trumbo. I think our minimum objective should be for each to establish a pseudonym which he will then use on all of his films, and for that pseudonym ultimately to be openly identified with the man himself and his real name. The maximum objective would be, of course, to use our own names from the outset. I think very soon we three shall be able to undertake what amounts to a strike, using the weapon of our excellence: no name, no work. Albert agrees with this. He has one or two big ones (I don't know what they are) and he is going to move in that direction. I think you should too.

Now let me give you, in great confidence, a situation which is developing in relation to me. As you may or may not know, I have done the screenplay on *Spartacus*. It's costing six million dollars, and stars Kirk Douglas, Tony Curtis, Laurence Olivier, Peter Ustinov, Charles Laughton, Jean Simmons, Nina Foch, John Gavin, and a bunch of others. For this job I am receiving seventy-five thousand dollars and five per cent of the picture. Eddie Lewis is executive vice-president of Bryna, which is producing the picture with Universal money for Universal release. Eddie Lewis is a thoroughly decent man who feels that the secret will be impossible to keep.

During the first week of shooting, Tony Mann (who shortly thereafter was succeeded as director by Stanley Kubrick) brought Peter Ustinov to my house to discuss various scenes involving Peter and Charles Laughton. I was rather surprised, because actors were not customarily brought in touch with blacklisted authors of the scripts in which they appeared. We spent several pleasant hours, during which Peter drew a cartoon of what he was going to do to Charles (a knife in the back) and later did.

The next development was, of course, that Ustinov told Olivier, and that Olivier then wanted to come over and talk about his part. This was arranged by Eddie [Lewis] and Kirk [Douglas], and last Sunday occurred a repetition of the Ustinov scene beginning at two in the afternoon and ending, somewhat in the cups, about nine-thirty. In addition to this, Lou Wasserman, president of Music Corporation of America and the most powerful single person in the business, knows that I have written the screenplay, and actually has been negotiating for the moneys from UI which ultimately reached me. Others at MCA also knew the secret, if one can call it that. In fact, the only people in town who do not know the identity of the author are the two chief executives at UI.

The picture still has four and a half months to go. It is the focus of a great deal of publicity. It is inconceivable to me that a secret so open at the present time will not be much more open by the time the picture is finished, particularly when two of the people who know the secret have every conceivable motive for revealing it. I think it not at all unlikely that the credit for this picture will fall to me or to my pseudonym like a ripe fig. I doubt that by the time credits are to be determined there will be found one person in Hollywood who will be willing to let his name go on the film. Hence I stand a chance of inheritance by default.

Running parallel to this is another situation, which is equally confidential. Some time ago I wrote a two-hundred-and-sixty page script called *Montezuma*. John Huston is going to direct it. The budget will be in excess of five million dollars. Lou Wasserman is handling this script, and Lou knows that I have written it. John knows that I have written it, and we have had conferences together about it. Kirk Douglas has read it and is ready to make a deal to star in it along with Rock Hudson. Universal badly wants a Douglas-Hudson picture, and this would probably be it. I have already tentatively informed Bryna that I shall probably demand at least my own pseudonym on the script of *Montezuma.* Since I still control the script and every aspect of its final disposition, I think that I will be able to put the pseudonym across—if not my own name. Now the point is that at a certain time perhaps three months from now or five months from now when *Spartacus* is nearing completion, and *Montezuma* is in the first stages of practical preparation, I intend to make a frank power play. Depending upon the circumstances of personal honor and so forth, I am going to go on strike; I'm going to demand my name on both pictures and, if not my name, then the same pseudonym on both which will be identified with me. The tremendous leakage on *Spartacus*, for which I am in no way responsible, will be of great assistance to me. I don't say that I shall be successful in pulling this little coup off, but the chances are considerably better than they ever were before. And this, like a good many other breaks in the black market, may at any moment be determined by sheer accident, or by the unanticipated act of one of the many other persons who know the secret. Anyhow, I am prepared to roll with any punch, and I certainly propose to take the position that it is morally wrong, and downright stupid in terms of public relations, for me to be denied credit on these pictures.

Now again, as these affairs develop, things will be developing with you, and they will be developing with Albert. We should keep in touch with each other, because my knowledge, for example, of what you are going to do or have done can be used as a weapon here for me to do what I wish with it. Similarly with Albert.

This letter is so ungodly long because I've dictated it, some of my judgments in the general situation may be wrong, but I think most of them are right. I'd like very much to hear what you feel, and what you think the possibilities are from your point of view. I promise to be a better correspondent than I have been, and to notify you instantly of anything which may have bearing on our tripartite alliance. But I think the key line is in guerrilla warfare, the almost unscrupulous use of our only weapon (which is our excellence), and highly individual tactics as each man slashes for an opening. I am sending you a few clippings which may help you in evaluating the new situation which I feel exists in this town and in the country generally. Much love to Zelma and her two pixies.

Oh— I almost forgot. De Laurentiis was in touch with me a week ago and wants me to do *Bolivar* based upon a script which he hopes to have ready two months from now. Full of windy plans about moving us all to Europe and so forth. Since it was my impression that you were doing *Bolivar* I want to know whether this encroaches upon your territory. . . . I don't think I'll have time to take de Laurentiis on, but if I do, how does he react to money problems? I mentioned the price on *Spartacus*; for *Montezuma* I'm getting ninety-three thousand and six-and-a-quarter percent. Is de Laurentiis prepared to speak in manly figures, or does he take a more thrifty approach? [12]

Salud!

DT

6. To Dan Lundberg

Los Angeles, California
April 9, 1959

Dear Sam [sic.]:

These are rough, dictated notes, hence they'll be prolix. Kindly forgive, abide with me to the end of them, and perhaps we can discover a way that you can get an interesting show, in the course of which I shall not have to run unnecessary risks.[13]

The changing times, and the more salubrious climate of the present, inform me that we are long past that period in which I need expose myself to public and open red-baiting. Similarly the new times indicate that I attract no unfavorable attention to myself by attacking the Motion Picture Producers' Association. The point of view in relation to Hollywood is simply this: I did not want the blacklist, Hollywood does not want the blacklist, and both of us are therefore its victims. Hence neither of us are heavies.

To the degree that they are legitimate, I do not mind questions about my going to jail. My position is that the Hollywood Ten went to jail on a First Amendment issue which the Supreme Court at that time felt unable to review, but which has since been sustained by later decisions of that Court. The result is, as I see it, that were we to assert the same right today, no conceivable prosecution could result.

I do not wish to be asked whether I was, or now am, a Communist. It is very interesting to me that this question was not propounded to Ned Young by a single reporter in the course of a three-month publicity flurry preceding the Academy revocation of its rule, and Ned's later winning of the Academy award. I was asked the question on Night Beat in New York [14] and I replied then, as I

[12] A de Laurentiis project materialized in the spring of 1963. Mr. and Mrs. Trumbo lived in Rome for one year during the writing of a script titled *The Dark Angel*. The script was not shot.

[13] Dan Lundberg, KPOL, had chosen the subject, "Is the Hollywood Blacklist Being Shelved?" and had invited Trumbo to be his guest for the April 12 show.

[14] On September 19, 1957 Trumbo had been interviewed about blacklisting by John Wingate, Night Beat, Channel 5 TV, New York.

would reply at any time since, that I am perfectly willing to sit down with the TV commentator, or with any newspaper reporter, over a private drink, and answer any question he is genuinely interested in asking about any phase of my political life and affiliations; but that I will not do it in public in order to get a job, or to "clean myself up" from something which was not at all dirty.

I am quite willing to answer any questions relating to the historical effort of any government to suppress, censor, prosecute, exile, blacklist, or kill writers for their beliefs. That holds for Greece and Rome as well as for France and England; it holds for the United States, for the Soviet Union, for the present government of Hungary, and for any other government of whatever political complexion that has sought to suppress the opinion of its writers. This, it seems to me, gives you a rather wide latitude in discovering for your audience not what I am, but what I think of writing, of freedom of opinion, and of any government which suppresses them.

I will not answer any questions concerning my present work, any work that I have done in the past under the conditions of the blacklist. By this, I mean that I will not name pictures, aside from that one which has already been named—*The Brave One*. In relation to *The Brave One*, I think I have some interesting background material relating to plagiarism, and so forth,[15] and the various problems for all writers which that particular picture posed. I will, of course, be willing to say that I have been steadily employed throughout the blacklist (twelve years of it for me), and that I am presently steadily employed, and that my commitments last many months into the future.

While I understand perfectly that the interviewee cannot be in charge of the show, either in relation to its format or its content, nonetheless, having watched your show, it does not strike me as the sort of show Night Beat was. There I was warned in advance that I could expect all manner of ugly surprises. It was a different period, I was willing to take that risk, and I believe I put my point across. But your show, if I am correct, is an information show—that is to say, it presents differing points of view, but it does not present the dramatic spectacle of a kill, intellectually or any other way. I am in a position where I can be badly hurt by an ugly surprise question. There is no reason why I should take such a risk at this time, and I feel that ugly surprises should be barred from our consideration of this show. . . .

[15] There were about six suits totally. When no Robert Rich could be found, it was inevitable that others should try to take advantage of the situation. Also, as Trumbo points out, when you have a story about a Mexican boy with a pet bull, it is bound to bear a resemblance to a number of other human interest stories. Claims were put forth in behalf of Robert Flaherty, Orson Welles, Jesse Lasky, Jr., Willis O'Brien, and Paul Rader.

Under no circumstances do I wish to be asked about any picture which I may or may not currently be writing. For example if the picture's title was "X" and if it had been rumored that I were writing it, I simply could not permit such a question as: "Is the rumor that you are writing 'X' true, or untrue?" I would not wish "X" to be mentioned at all.

In conclusion, please do not think that I am trying to censor your right to conduct your own show in any way that you see fit. Please believe also that I am sure your intentions are the best. On the other hand, in times so pregnant with good possibilities, I simply dare not risk a bad public relations burble. In the course of your professional life, this is simply another Sunday night show. In the course of my own professional life, it could represent a mortal danger to my entire career and to the careers of others in similar situations. I have the right if I wish to risk such danger for myself, but I do not have that right in relation to some thirty or forty others. What I am actually trying to say (and with it I shall conclude) is this: that I do not mind an objective interview, but that for three years I have insisted on going only where I shall not be the victim of a hostile program; granted that I am able to make my point of view comprehensible to an audience (if I can't it's my fault, not yours), I absolutely refuse to enter into any position of public jeopardy; every press story and TV thing I have done in three years has been prearranged in my favor as a condition stated off the record and understood in advance; I give my time to a station, to a program, to an interviewer for nothing—it must return a profit to me or I don't go. I'd be a fool if I did. On the other hand, we are both actors if the show is to be any good, and your demeanor and tone can be as severe as you wish. Your questions can appear to be as severe as the most objective viewer could wish. But there must always be a way for me to get out from under them. And the intent in your mind and heart must not be severe toward me. For if I thought it were, I should not have consented in the first place.

Forgive me for this. It's important to me and to others. I'm sure you understand why I feel that I have to be explicit. In the meanwhile, thank you for thinking of me in relation to this show; be assured that I shall do my poor best to make it no loss for you either.

Cordially,
DALTON TRUMBO

7. Extract of a letter to Edward Lewis

Los Angeles, California
June 3, 1959

I've found it! For several years I have kept a checking account at the United States National Bank on Colorado Avenue in Pasadena, under the name of James and Dorothy Bonham.[16] I used it as a clearing house for all checks made out to me under pseudonyms. A check would reach me payable to John Abbott; I would then forge my pseudonym's signature, endorse the check as James Bonham, and deposit it. When it had cleared, James Bonham would then draw a check payable to Dalton Trumbo's Bank of America account.[17]

I went through this ridiculous routine because I have *never* endorsed any check with my own name, lest the looseness of Hollywood banking clerks would cause it to be known that DT was working for this or that producer.

About fifteen months ago, however, DT took his money out of the Bank of America, and opened a new checking account in his own name with First Western Bank in Pasadena. I made an arrangement with bank officials that on all checks paid me and drawn to one of my pseudonyms, I could endorse them, as I've done most of yours, "Pay to the order of First Western Bank, Pasadena, California, signed Sam Jackson"—and the money would go directly into my account without my Trumbo endorsement ever appearing on it. All of this trouble was taken to protect my clients from any bookkeeping identification with my name.

I then allowed the United States James and Dorothy Bonham account to lie fallow, having no further use for it. But for some reason I can't presently remember, when I received your personal check for $2,500 against the contract we had signed for *The Brave Cowboy,* I ran it through the James and Dorothy Bonham account. This I had completely forgotten, and was actually under the impression that the $2,500 had been paid me in 1957.

When this spring income tax time came along, I realized—or strongly felt—that I did not have a record of my entire 1958 income clear. I secured a postponement on filing, and wrote the only three persons I could think of who might have paid me moneys early in 1958 . . . Each replied that no funds had been paid me by them. And *still* I didn't recall the $2,500. However, under the spur of your queries, I remembered that account, and checked into it.

You are of course right: on January 16, 1958, I deposited in the Bonham account your personal check drawn on the Bank of America in the sum of $2,500, payable to Sam Jackson. I forged Sam's name,

---

[16] The central figure in the novel *Johnny Got His Gun* was named Joe Bonham.

[17] The intricacy involved in the financial and banking affairs of a blacklistee is strikingly disclosed in this letter.

490

endorsed the check as James Bonham, and deposited it in the United States National Bank. I've run off a copy of the bank record, and enclose it. Actually, I'd have been in real income tax trouble hadn't you prodded me into action.

Now that *this* fuck-up is explained, I enclose herewith copies of the receipts I gave to you for all moneys of any kind received during 1958 from you. The receipt for the $2,500 is not among them for the simple reason it was the first sum I'd ever received from you, and we hadn't yet decided on the prudent device of giving receipts. Thereafter, I made out a receipt on the payment of each check, made a copy for my own records, and sent the original on to you.

8. To B. B. Kahane, Vice-President, Columbia Pictures, Inc.

Los Angeles, California
September 29, 1959

My dear Mr. Kahane:

On or about 22 August, 1959, you appeared before the Americanism commission of the American Legion in the city of Minneapolis. As president of the Academy of Motion Picture Arts and Sciences, you discussed a proposed [Legion] resolution directed against the Academy. As vice-president of the Association of Motion Picture Producers, you discussed a proposed resolution directed against the film industry as a whole.[18] As vice-president of Columbia you discussed a proposed resolution against Columbia for its contractural association with Mr. Carl Foreman.[19]

I make no comment on the fact that, although the Academy was excoriated in a subsequent Legion resolution, and not all members of the Association were delivered from adverse comment, your own corporation received commendation rather than reproof.

Nor do I belabor the point that for the first time an official representative of the Association of Motion Picture Producers has confirmed, for all to hear, the existence of a conspiracy to blacklist entered into between the Association and the Legion in 1947, continuing to the present day, and now renewed for the future. Neither shall I presently comment on your statement that your own studio

[18] Both the Motion Picture Academy and the Producers' Association were condemned by the Legion for honoring or employing people whom the Legion considered un-American.

[19] A formerly blacklisted screen writer now working openly under his own name.

has never knowingly sinned by employing persons with whose ideas the Legion is in disagreement, although it is my personal conviction that even here your state of grace can be proved a legal fiction.

What most compels my attention—and ought, I think, to compel yours also—is the weekly *Variety* story of 26 August, 1959, in which it is revealed that you described me to the Americanism Commission [of the American Legion] as "a hard-core Communist" whose alleged associates are unaware that I am doing "undercover work" for Communism. As a result of such statements, the national convention of the Legion passed a resolution which used my name in a way that has damaged my career and laid upon my family a burden which is intolerable.

You have privately been made aware of my reaction to your pleadings before the Legion. A channel has been opened through which your denial or retraction can be transmitted to me. It was my hope that wisdom, as well as that decent regard for the rights of others which governs civilized conduct in a democratic society, would persuade you to avail yourself of the opportunity offered to make amends to a man whom you scarcely know, who has done you no harm, spoken no ill of you, and given you no offense. You have declined that opportunity.

I have no desire to enter into controversy with you, yet I cannot and will not permit you to make of me a public scapegoat for the shameful and probably illegal conduct of your principals. For too many years the social climate of America has been poisoned, and its moral atmosphere corrupted, by just such remarks as you so freely made about me before the Legion. The past willingness of victims to suffer such attacks in silence has served to increase the pernicious influence of delators, and to surround delation itself with an aura of immunity so substantial that any common scoundrel, no matter how depraved, can achieve public absolution and even approval if only he is willing to divert attention from himself by branding someone else a heretic.

You have permitted your remarks to stand for over a month in a situation in which, as you perfectly understand, the damage increases with time. You have shown no disposition to settle the matter in the quiet, gentlemanly fashion I made available to you. I, on my part, have decided that it is just as reprehensible to endure such attacks in silence as it is to make them. Therefore, I intend to put a stop to them altogether.

I expect to receive from you, on or before midnight of 5 October, 1959, a letter which, in all substantial respects, shall read as follows:

Dear Mr. Trumbo:

On 26 August, 1959, the weekly edition of *Variety* carried a story relative to my appearance before the Americanism Commission of the

American Legion in the city of Minneapolis on or about 22 August of this year.

In that story it is stated that I described you to the Americanism Commission as "a hard-core Communist" whose associates are unaware that you are doing "undercover work" for Communism.

Please be advised that I have no knowledge that you are a Communist of any kind, hard-core or otherwise, just as I have no knowledge that you are doing undercover work for Communism or any other ideology.

It follows that, insofar as I have knowledge, there is no patriotic reason to deplore your employment by, or to impugn the integrity of, any motion picture company that chooses to purchase your work or to release films based upon it; nor is there any patriotic reason why films you have written should not be credited to you on the screen.

I tender this letter as a personal and public apology, and authorize you to make such use of it as may seem necessary to repair the injury which I have quite unintentionally inflicted upon you.

(Signed)   B. B. Kahane

If you fail to send me such a letter,[20] I shall undertake energetic public actions to compel you to do so. If a suit at law eventuates, it will be of your choice and on your responsibility, since I myself have done everything possible to avoid it.

Your personal veracity will be central to such a legal action. It will be tested by discovering under oath the truth or falsity of each statement you made to the Americanism Commission of the American Legion. I, too, shall take the stand, as will many other witnesses, both voluntary and involuntary. There, before judge and jury, in the precincts of law and justice rather than the easy forum of self-serving calumniators, it will be decided once and for all which of us is a liar and conspirator.

I am, as you would expect, bringing this matter most urgently to the attention of the Association of Motion Picture Producers, the Academy of Motion Picture Arts and Sciences, the national leadership of the American Legion, the chairman of the Legion's Americanism Commission, and the editors and publishers of the *American*

[20] Kahane and his lawyer prepared and submitted to Trumbo's lawyer, Aubrey Finn, a letter of retraction that was not as comprehensive as Trumbo had demanded. It was rejected and the legal representatives of Kahane and Trumbo proceeded to the task of composing an acceptable letter. Since the Legion protest over *Spartacus* was not harmful, Trumbo dismissed the matter upon departing for Israel to work on Otto Preminger's *Exodus*. Soon after, Kahane died. Trumbo's real motive in confronting Kahane was to ensure that the latter never publicly denounce Trumbo or any other blacklisted person. Hence, when Kahane began drafting letters to placate Trumbo the writer knew he had won the battle.

Legion Magazine, the Minneapolis *Star* and *Tribune,* and weekly
Variety.

Yours truly,
DALTON TRUMBO

9. To Aubrey I. Finn

Los Angeles, California
August 4, 1959

Dear Mr. Finn:

This letter refers to recent conversations you have had with Mr.
Mendel Silberberg relating to the American Legion, a certain motion
picture I have written, and a request that I furnish Mr. Silberberg
with a statement concerning my past and present affiliations, together
with reasons therefore. This naturally diverts my attention to the
power and influence of the American Legion, as I am sure it also
diverts the attention of Mr. Silberberg and his clients.[21]

[21] Trumbo explains this letter in the following way: "Silberberg was the
lawyer for the Motion Picture Producers' Association and for Columbia
Films. There had been advance rumbles about what the Legion would do at
its annual meeting. Kahane had been delegated to represent the Producers'
Association at that annual meeting—to defend them—to deflect as much fire
as he could. Columbia's problem lay in the fact that they were doing business
with Carl Foreman, and the Legion had regularly blasted them for it, even
though Foreman had cleared himself before the committee (he did *not* inform). Universal's problem was that (because of their own mistakes, not
mine) everybody in Hollywood knew that I was writing *Spartacus* which was
to be released in autumn of 1959. Silberberg, as council for the Producers'
Association, advised the heads of Universal to get a letter from me stating
that I was not a communist. The Universal company executives told him
they had tried and failed, and did not believe a second attempt would be any
more successful than the first. It was at this point that Silberberg expressed
to the Universal officials 'an opinion of my politics directly opposite' to that
which Kahane conveyed to the Legion. In short, Silberberg told them flatly
that he didn't believe I was a communist. Kahane's appearance before the
Legion convention and his blast at me followed very shortly thereafter. There
was no way for him to escape from it through public denial, because the
leading newspaper editor in Minneapolis had him stone cold on the quote
about me. The report of these various meetings and so forth was always related to me privately and confidentially by Eddie Lewis.

Finally, late in 1959, it was rumored that the committee was going to come.
Mr. Ed Muhl, production head of Universal, asked Eddie to arrange a tripartite conference between him, Eddie, and me. He wanted to know what I
would do in case the committee did come to Hollywood, and if it subpoenaed
me. I told him that the minute I got a subpoena I would take a full page ad

For some reason the American Legion has been able to convince Hollywood—and Hollywood alone—that it is the largest and the most powerful organization in the country. It simply is not. Consider the following organizations, each of which has certain purposes, certain aspirations, and a certain unity of action which allows it to exercise much more actual power than the Legion: AFL-CIO, 13,-500,000; Parent-Teacher Association, 11,018,156; Boy Scouts, 4,-632,472; Girl Scouts, 3,500,000; Y.M.C.A., 3,342,931; Eastern Star,

---

in *The New York Times* announcing to the committee that in no circumstances would I answer any of their questions about my politics. The ad would urge them to save the fifteen or twenty thousand dollars which such a trip would cost them, since they already had their answer in the mail. The ad would also say that I have never been reticent about discussing politics with anyone, as perhaps their researches had disclosed; that I did not regard my politics as secret, and never had—I regarded them as *private*. Although, of course, Muhl preferred a letter saying 'I certainly am not a communist," he was quite pleased at the idea of such an ad, and hinted that perhaps it should go into a larger number of newspapers throughout the country, and that perhaps Universal would not be averse to taking care of the cost.

But the committee did not come. Even later, as the opening night of *Spartacus* drew near, Muhl still hoped that I could see my way clear to do something. I finally told him, in effect, 'Let us wait and see. One thing I promise you is that I will not let the American Legion or the fanatical right destroy this film. If it seems they are about to, I will act; what I will do I do not know, but I promise I will do something.' But, of course, it turned out that the attacks of these organizations had no effect on the picture at all. Later on I suggested to Muhl that when United Artists brought out *Exodus* they would be in the same boat that Universal was with *Spartacus*, and that if they were really concerned about the presence of my name on both pictures they should unite in their public relations campaigns which involved me rather than operate separately. Later on I was told that Universal did approach United Artists to establish a common front with them in relation to the Trumbo name on *Spartacus* and *Exodus*. United Artists, however, replied that they weren't worried at all, since they already had a letter from me saying that I am not a communist, and that all Universal needed to do was to get a similar letter and the problem would be solved. I was astounded when I heard this and so was Ed Muhl. I told him that all United Artists had to do was to send to Ed Muhl a copy of the letter I had signed and I would then sign a duplicate of that letter for Ed Muhl and for Universal. Of course, the letter didn't come because it never existed. About this time, also, Universal ran a Sindlinger report on me. I forgot what the percentages were but I was told the figures in round numbers. The first question in the report dealt with whether or not the person interviewed recognized my name. I was pleasantly surprised to discover that something over four million did. The next questions were related to whether or not my name would affect their attendance of the picture. My recollection is that half of the people interviewed said it wouldn't make any difference one way or another. Thirty-seven and a half percent said my name on the picture would be reason for them to see the film. The remaining twelve and a half percent said that my name on the picture would cause them to pass the film up altogether."

3,000,000; De Molay 3,000,000; American Farm Bureau Federation, 1,578,107 *families*. Each one of these organizations influences more people, and can, if it wishes, exercise more power than the American Legion. When you pass down to organizations with a million to a million and a half you find others which, because of qualitative selection of membership, can also out-pull the Legion in influence and power.

Beyond this, I wish to address myself to the implication that the American Legion in some way controls, influences, or represents the approximately 17 million veterans presently alive in the United States. The misconception that it does represent that enormous group has been so widely disseminated over so many years that the motion picture industry appears actually and sincerely to believe it. No objective examination of the facts can support such a conclusion.

The 1959 World Almanac catalogues 47 national organizations of veterans, of which the American Legion is but one. Of these 47 organizations, 23 list their membership, and 24 do not. The American Legion, for example, has 2,749,000 members. The remaining 22 which list have 1,968,000 members. When one considers that such a relatively obscure group as the Italian-American War Veterans alone numbers 300,000 men, it becomes apparent that the 24 veterans organizations which do *not* list their membership (among which are such important groups as the Military Order of the Purple Heart, the Catholic War Veterans, the Jewish War Veterans, the National Association of Korean War Veterans, the Military Order of Foreign Wars, etc.) would add at least a million more to the census of organized veterans who are not members of the Legion.

The conclusion is inescapable. The American Legion does not represent 17 million veterans. It does not even represent the majority of *organized* veterans. Neither do all veterans' organizations combined represent more than one-third of the 17 million total of veterans. Two-thirds of American veterans are so indifferent to veterans' organizations that they don't even trouble to join them. How, then, can anyone assume that the overwhelming majority of veterans who belong to no organization will be influenced by a 24 hour scarehead resolution passed by an organization which represents only a minority of that minority which *is* organized?

It is true that the American Legion is the largest group of organized veterans in the country, just as the Teamsters' Union is the largest group of organized labor. But to assert that 1,355,000 teamsters represent or speak for all 16 million Americans organized into unions is dangerously wide of the objective fact. And, since the 16 million organized workers are a stunning minority among the 65 million employed persons in the United States, it would be equally impossible to maintain that the organized minority, or the largest minority of that minority, can be assumed to speak for the over-whelming majority who belong to no union at all. Just so, the Legion.

I wish further to point out the established fact that no social, fraternal, religious, union, or veterans' organization is ever unanimous; that it can never guarantee delivery even of its own membership to any political cause or crusade. The Legion, for example, can't enlist one of its most distinguished members, former President Truman, in its crusade for a Hollywood blacklist. Mr. Truman is against the Hollywood blacklist; he is against the blacklisting activities of the Committee; and he has said so plainly and publicly. In this sense—and it is a very real sense—the Legion cannot even be said to represent and speak for even its own full membership.

That membership, incidentally, is itself in a state of decline, which is another sign of the times and of the organization's fading influence upon the national scene. Since the palmy days of 1948, when the Legion could and did force the withdrawal of *Monsieur Verdoux,* to a 1959 in which exhibitors vie for Chaplin films and film-goers would snarl at anyone who attempted picketing them, the Legion has lost over half a million members—523,060 to be exact. It is losing members not only because of the death rate which, barring another war, will steadily diminish its ranks; but also because its members weary of the organization and simply drop out.

But one can go even further in proving the overrated status of the Legion as an effective influence upon the nation. Not only does the Legion comprise a minority of organized veterans, but the members of its women's organization, the American Legion Auxiliary, comprise a minority of its own wives, mothers and sisters. For whereas there are 2,749,000 veterans in the Legion, they have been able to influence or persuade only 1 million of their wives, mothers, and daughters to join their auxiliary. As for the children of those 2,749,-000—would it not be safe to hazard in these days of early marriage and high fecundity, that they have produced close to 4 million sons? If so, the influence of 2,749,000 Legion fathers upon 4 million Legion sons may be measured by the fact that the organized Sons of the American Legion from coast to coast number exactly six thousand. Is it not time that we placed in its proper perspective the power and influence of an organization that can recruit only one in five of its women and one in 458 of its sons?

As to whether these Legion resolutions have any actual effect or power, aside from bombast and a day's headlines, let us consider the fact that no institution is more sensitive to the demands of real power, of real influence, of real movements among the people, than the various agencies and departments of the Federal Government. Any organization which has power in its own right, and, much more importantly, the power to influence public opinion, is bound to receive the most respectful attention from government officials. Yet no one—I repeat, no one—in the State or Federal Government has even deigned to recognize the existence of certain resolutions passed by the recent California Legion Convention. Consider the following resolutions:

1. Favoring retention of the California State Loyalty Oath. Yet important sections of the oath remain unconstitutional.
2. Opposing the United States Status of Forces Act. The act remains.
3. Demanding that Congress restore the effectiveness of the Smith Act. Yet Congress has not acted, nor even noticed.
4. Objecting to the American National Exhibition in Moscow. The exhibition continues.
5. Protesting the exhibition in Moscow of 34 American artists whom it accused of Communist associations. Not one artist saw his work removed by the State Department.
6. Demanding a change in the citizenship oath. The oath remains, and no one has even replied to the demand.
7. Demanding withdrawal of the United States from the United Nations if Russia "continues its obstruction tactics." There has been no noticeable change in Russian tactics, and no one but a fool would even consider American withdrawal from a world organization in which she holds paramount power.

All of these resolutions were the same in nature, and what has happened, in spite of the American Legion, is quite the opposite. Nixon has visited the Soviet Union. Russian dancers appear tonight in the Hollywood Bowl under the sponsorship of whom? Mrs. Harry Chandler. Khrushchev is to visit the United States; Eisenhower is to visit Russia. The London press ecstasizes; *The New York Times, The Wall Street Journal,* the Los Angeles *Times* and *Mirror-News* applaud. *The Mirror-News* finds the exchange "electrifying," while the *Times'* Dr. Polyzoides writes: "This is the main event on this, the 45th anniversary of World War I, and it may be stated without fear of exaggeration that today's event may prove of equal if not actually greater importance."

As to the resolution condemning the Motion Picture Academy and the Producers Association for employing people whom the Legion disagrees with—it is of the same pattern as the other resolutions referred to above. The various government agencies have answered by doing precisely the opposite of what the Legion resolved for. No angry editorials have assailed the government for conducting its business contrary to the advice of the Legion, and none would appear if the motion picture industry courteously stated that the first right of private enterprise is that which permits a producer to hire whomever he considers the best man for each job.

I have heard much speculation as to the reason for Mr. Eric

Johnston's silence in the face of the resolution in question.[22] I find this not at all mysterious. The Legion resolution places on the public record for the first time what the Producers Association, as a matter of policy, has steadfastly refused to confirm; namely, that a blacklist has been established by the American film industry.

The Legion resolution puts it this way: "WHEREAS, this policy was established in an agreement with the American Legion after a conference with the officials of the motion picture industry of 1947, and was reaffirmed three times thereafter by the industry, . . ." etc.

Obviously Mr. Johnston cannot answer the resolution, since the first and three subsequent meetings were separate conspiracies to violate the law. If he responds that no such meetings or agreements were held, the Legion will impugn his honor. If he admits that they were held, he affirms for the producers what the resolution has already affirmed for the Legion, i.e., that a continuing conspiracy was entered into. If he says we are sorry and shall reestablish the blacklist in those areas where it has broken down, he not only confirms past conspiracies but enters into a new one.

Similarly, I don't see how individual studios can very wisely reply to the Legion that they have not violated the terms of the conspiracy, and are indeed faithfully blacklisting to the present day. Certainly U[nited]-A[rtists] will make no such statement, since it doesn't belong to the producers' organization and has solved its own non-blacklisting policy without damage of any sort, and even with a certain profit. Why others should placate a Legion that has no large power, by confirming a conspiracy, I simply cannot understand.

The last time one of these statements was issued, over $50 million in civil suits resulted. With overwhelming evidence of conspiracy now made public by the Legion, it appears to me that a producer confirmation could start a series of suits on an entirely new basis that could make the first round look like tiddlywinks. Not only would all the conspirators be certain to receive subpoenas, but every person signing such a statement would undoubtedly be compelled to explain under oath his own connection with the black market. Every major studio in the industry has, or has had, provable connections with the black market, and few juries are innocent enough to believe that a studio hands over to an independent producer $100,000 for a writer without coming in time to know the identity of the writer selected.

Let me hasten to add that I have no desire to enter into such a suit. I am sick unto death of seeing my name in the paper, and I

[22] At the time, Johnston was president of the Motion Picture Association of America. It was Johnston who, after vowing that he would never be a party to a blacklist, had emerged from the two-day Waldorf meeting of 1947 with a first clear intimation of a blacklist: to bar from work all people investigated by the committee or "known" to be communists.

loathe participating in the processes of court. However there are those who very well might consider the financial rewards tempting enough to carry a case forward, and there are distinguished counsel of national repute who have professed interest in bringing the blacklist to bay through such means.

The truth is that neither the changed times nor the changed industry any longer supports or justifies the blacklist. I know as many of the essentials of the Waldorf Meeting which established it as some who participated, since I have read long depositions by persons who attended. The Hollywood representatives did not want it then as they do not want it now.[23] Since the day of its inauguration it has been a disgrace to the industry and to the country. If I do not lift my weary voice condemning Soviet attacks upon, and suppression of, the writer Boris Pasternak, it is because some 200 persons have been suppressed by the Hollywood film industry, and I am far more interested in seeking to correct the evils in my own country, where I may ultimately have some effect, than in baying for publicity purposes at a Russian moon I can't affect in any event.

The producers employ blacklisted persons not for charitable reasons, but because they prefer them for specific jobs to other personnel, because their work has a quality which makes them upon occasion not only desirable but necessary. They have all done it at one time or another, they do it now, they will continue to do it so long in the future as competition exists among them; and there is utterly nothing wrong with it.

The systematized blacklist is something unheard of in America until the last twelve years. It is as degrading to the independence and dignity and actual manhood of the producer as it is to the person against whom it is aimed. It is logically and morally indefensible, and presently supported and advocated only by a handful of crackpots, authoritarians and fanatics. It has been proven over a period of years, and in many film projects, not only by the blacklisted writers but by the producers themselves, that the blacklist cannot be sustained and it cannot be enforced. This being the case, it is bound to go.

The problem on both sides—and I myself pledge the utmost restraint and forbearance—is to get rid of the filthy thing quietly, gracefully, and with as little publicity as possible. It must be got rid of not only because it is wrong, not only because it is ridiculously contrary to present national policy, but principally because it has not worked, does not work, will not work, and cannot be tinkered with in any way so as to make it work. It must go as a matter of practical business policy in order that management may regain its essential

[23] Depositions taken from persons at the Waldorf meeting are said to reveal that it was the New York motion picture executives who had demanded and engineered the blacklist.

function of hiring and firing without regard to the opinion of persons who haven't the foggiest notion about the making of motion pictures.

As I say, the crumbling blacklist which no one wants *can* be eliminated altogether if management either ignores irresponsible attacks as the government ignores them, or if it quietly and with dignity asserts its right and responsibility and duty to employ personnel on the basis of skill alone. But sudden capitulation to the Legion will neither solve the problem of the blacklist nor ward off future attacks upon an industry that has already been attacked too often without fighting back.

A denial of knowingly employing blacklisted persons—even technical denial—is impractical for several reasons: (1) it would constitute a flat untruth which the Legion or others may well be eager to expose; (2) it cannot be unanimous, since one major concern doesn't even belong to the Producers Association, and there may be some among those who do belong who will not care to assume the risks inherent in denial; (3) it would constitute a public affirmation, hitherto denied, of the conspiracy of 1947 as revealed by the Legion resolution, and the sequence of conspiracies that followed thereafter. The result could well be a scandal and a sequence of court cases in which the producers themselves could not escape becoming the principal victims.

The sad thing is that this is probably exactly what will happen. It is sad because nothing the Legion can do will arouse them. Nothing the Legion can do, in present, changed times, can have the slightest effect upon the motion picture industry if only the industry knew it. The Legion can now be ignored with impunity, or its attacks can be met with a dignified exception. Two days in the headlines and the whole thing would be over.

As for the information conveyed to me [from Mr. Silberberg] that I am personally the principal target of the Legion campaign, I am not at all disturbed. The Legion is as powerless against me as it is against the producers. The difference lies in the fact that I know it, and the producers are only becoming dimly aware of it. Legion or no Legion, I have enough work contracted for to keep me engaged in my profession for the next three years. If, at the end of that time, I find it impossible to obtain employment in Hollywood, I shall simply move my family to Europe. There, relieved of tax problems which burden me here, I shall net more money writing films to compete in the world market with the American film industry than I have ever earned by writing films *for* that industry.

In the writing of certain black market films which have earned large sums of money for the American film industry and brought certain honors to it, I have not served that industry badly: I have served it well. That I am a decent, law-abiding American is attested by the characters of the producers who have employed me, for they, too, are decent, law-abiding Americans who would certainly not associate themselves with a traitor out of sheer desire for profit.

It is perhaps this sense of my own security and this positive conviction of the Legion's diminishing nuisance value in changing times which cause me to bridle at the thought of writing any statement of past or present political beliefs for the sake of mere employment. But on sober thought, I'm sure there are more compelling reasons.

I was born of a family that has lived in America long enough to feel comfortable in it. Believing as I do that men who daily repeat the wedding vow to their wives open themselves to a natural presumption of adultery, I have never felt a compulsion to chatter about my loyalty, whether to God, country, government, or system.

Neither am I proud to be an American, although I appear to be surrounded by people who loudly are. It has always struck me that a man who takes pride in the geographical accident of his birth must also preen himself on the genetic accident that gave him green eyes instead of blue, or six toes where ordinary men make do with five.

But to be proud of America herself—yes, that I understand and share: proud of her people, proud of all the good in her history (and ashamed of the bad), glad that I was born in her midst, and grateful to parents who selected so fortunate a site for that supremely unimportant event.

From the days when Virginia was a British colony it has come down to me from grandfathers through fathers to son that an American is a free man; that his race, his religion, his politics and his marriage are no one's business but his own. I myself was born in the west, where the sense of human dignity stood so high that no one even thought of asking a stranger where he came from or what his past had been. If he volunteered the information, fair enough. If he did not, then no authority on earth had the power to inquire, much less to compel an answer.

I have believed this, and I have lived by it. The curious and ugly thing about this whole business of compulsory revelation lies in the fact that most people actually prefer to be open and forthright about their beliefs and affiliations. To believe in something that can't be openly expressed is an absurdity, and they know it. At no time in my life have I made any great secret of what my political affiliations were or are. Whenever political discussions arose among friends and associates, I never failed to state the exact political platform from which I spoke. During my last open contract period at MGM (terminated abruptly in 1947) I wrote for three different producers. Since a successful writer-producer relationship is one of close intellectual intimacy, it seemed perfectly natural for me to inform each in advance of my politics.

Yet when a committee of the Congress, in clear violation of all previous concepts of the First Amendment to the Constitution, sought to compel a revelation I had always cheerfully volunteered, I refused the answer, and paid the legal penalty which refusal entailed. During the years that ensued I have occasionally made a fool of myself, as men will under stress, and occasionally I have conducted myself wisely and compassionately; but fool or wise man, I have never been able to convince myself that I can retain any dignity as a man, as an American, if I yield to the committee's demand for compulsory revelation.

How much less, then, could I make the statement under economic compulsion, which is to say for a job, for a credit, for money. Yet that is what I should now be doing if I acquiesced to Mr. Silberberg's request for such a statement: I should be violating principles which have guided my family in this country for over two hundred and forty years, principles which have cost me a year in jail and twelve years of the blacklist—and I should be doing it for money. The largeness of the reward under such circumstances is full measure of the degradation I should feel for myself and leave to my children.

Let's imagine the same situation with different principals and circumstances. If Mr. Silberberg were offered a million-dollar case on condition that he issue a written statement concerning his political affiliations over the past twenty years, plus a denunciation of certain organizations the prospective client disliked to which Mr. Silberberg may once have belonged—I am certain the refusal would be instant and final.

I think there are sound philosophical, historical, legal, and moral precedents for such a position. But even if there were not, many people would still resist such compulsion. Pure cussedness, if you will: yet a brand of cussedness that has served this country well in bleak moments of her history, and could have served other modern countries also had it only been asserted.

In 1949 I wrote a pamphlet called *The Time of the Toad* in what I'm sure was an unsuccessful attempt to explain the hellishly complex problems that confronted the Hollywood Ten when they took the stand before the House Committee on Un-American Activities. One section of it reads as follows:

"The most striking example in recent history of a nation passing through the Time is offered by Germany. In its beginnings in that unfortunate country the Toad was announced by the shrill voice of a mediocre man ranting against Communists and Jews, just as we in America have heard the voice of such a one as Representative John E. Rankin of Mississippi.

"By the spring of 1933, the man Hitler having been in power for two months, substance was given his words by a decree calling for the discharge from civil service of all 'who because of their previous political activity do not offer security that they will exert themselves for the national state without reservation,' as well as those 'who have participated in communist activities . . . even if they no longer belong to the Communist party or its auxiliary or collateral organizations,' and those who have 'opposed the national movement by speech, writing or any other hateful conduct' or have 'insulted its leaders.'

"Thereafter in a welter of oaths, tests, inquisitions and inquests, the German nation surrendered its mind. Those were the days in Germany when respectable citizens did not count it a disgrace to rush like enraptured lemmings before the People's Courts and declare under oath that they were not Communists, they were not Jews, they were not trade unionists, they were not in any degree anything which the government disliked—perfectly aware that such acts of confession assisted the inquisitors in separating sheep from goats and rendered all who would not or could not pass the test liable to the blacklist, the political prison or the crematorium.

"Volumes have since been written telling of the panicked stampede of German intellectuals for Nazi absolution: of doctors and scientists, philosophers and educators, musicians and writers, artists of the theatre and cinema, who abased themselves in an orgy of confession, purged their organizations of all the proscribed, gradually accepted the mythos of the dominant minority, and thereafter clung without shame to positions without dignity."

Ten years later, I would not change one sentence or alter a single word of that statement. Neither would I wish to turn my back on almost 200 blacklisted writers, directors, producers, actors, actresses, musicians, artists and technicians whose innate self-respect will not permit them to offer a political statement which has no relation to their creative abilities in return for a job which ought, in a free society, to be their inherent right rather than an object for political bargaining.

I happen to know that of those 200 persons who still resist compulsory confession, a good many were never in their lives members of the Communist Party. Of the remainder who actually were Communists at one time or another, I should be greatly surprised if 3% remain Communists to the present day.

Why, then, do men and women who haven't belonged to an organization for years still refuse to sign a statement they no longer belong, even though that act alone would reinstate them in their careers? Is it a continuing devotion to the Communist party? No. If devotion remained, they are not the sort of persons who would have departed in the first instance. Has it, in truth, anything at all to do with the Communist party? No. It never did have and it doesn't now.

It has to do with themselves as human beings, with their concept of themselves as free American citizens, with their feeling for the nation itself—the United States of America and its traditions and its Constitution. That is the reason for those long years of refusal, and the only reason for it. The best proof lies in the fact that years after their attachment to the Communist party has ceased, their attachment to the finest of American traditions still continues, and will, I am persuaded, continue for the rest of their lives.

Let us take the case of a most distinguished actress [24] who, at the peak of her career and the flower of her womanhood, declined the question and has not been seen on the screen since. I happen to know that she has not been a Communist for many years, and has, in fact, vigorously opposed the Communist party on various occasions. Yet to this day she refuses to step up, as a good German would, and take the pledge.

Quite aside from the financial loss, consider the changes ten years of life and idleness have produced in the lines of her face, the conformation of her body, the memory of her reputation, and the quality of her relationship to the medium of film. The most terrible thing that can happen to an actress has befallen her: she has become altogether a different woman, a stranger to herself and to her public. What, then, can she possibly have gained to offset so frightful a loss? I should say that she has gained dignity; and if that simple statement isn't immediately understood, it can never be explained.

This is not to assert that she and her scores of colleagues in oblivion have taken, or ever did take, vows of perpetual political secrecy. Socially and informally and quite casually they speak of politics, past, present, and future, because they are interested in the flow of history that surrounds them and [are] eager to understand it. They speak freely of the politics of themselves and others; but most of them, I venture, will continue to think it infinitely degrading to announce publicly and for a job those essentially private relations which can be discussed socially without any qualms at all.

Just so in my own case. I have recently received offers from two publishing houses for a political autobiography and I shall probably write such a book. When it is published my political affiliations and thoughts over three decades will quite naturally be revealed. But *not* under the compulsion of a federal agency, not in order to qualify for a job or a credit or a sum of money, and not to "clear" myself with an American Legion that has been more often in disagreement with our government than I have been, but because I voluntarily choose to write such a book in the hope it may have certain value for my contemporaries and illuminate a tiny area of American history in some future time.

It appears, however, that even if I were minded to give a statement of political affiliation and opinion, not even that enormous departure from principle would entirely clear the matter up, for it is

[24] Anne Revere, who won an Academy award as the best supporting actress with her portrayal of the mother in *National Velvet,* returned to the screen in 1970 in Avco-Embassy's *Macho Callahan.*

suggested that along with the statement I denounce, let us say, the suppression by the Soviet Union of the Hungarian revolt.

Now Hungary was a prickly affair, as both Russia and the United States learned, to their regret. I yet do not understand all that went on during those tragic weeks. I do understand and sympathize with the desire of the Hungarians to throw off foreign domination. I also understand the bloody revenge which the people of Budapest wreaked on the secret police who were the instruments of that suppression. I do not understand the frightful atrocities they simultaneously inflicted upon the Jews of Budapest. Perhaps all of this will be made clear at some later time when Hungary is free.

Nonetheless, I was probably quite as distressed and outraged by the Hungarian affair as were the heads of Hollywood production. Yet did they during that crisis sit down and compose for their respective boards of directors long denunciations of the suppression? Did they protest the arrest and subsequent imprisonment for seven years of the Communist writer Tibor Dery, who was one of the leaders of that revolt? Did they attend or address rallies, head up committees, donate money, and make public statements to relieve the sufferings of the Hungarian people? If even one of them uttered a single word, I have not heard of it. Perhaps they felt such denunciations were not included in their executive duties, just as I feel they are not a part of my function as a writer of scripts.

This business of being required to denounce governments, peoples, and social systems in order to get a job, breaks down into two questions: first, is it right that a man should have to do it; and second, is it wise of him to do it—is it expedient?

The answer to the moral question is negative and comparatively simple. Deeply imbedded in the fabric of English law and American Constitutional traditions is the principle that no man may be denied employment because of his opinions; that no employer has the right to inquire into those opinions, and, as a pre-condition of employment, to require a written statement that the employee's opinions agree in every important detail with those of his prospective employer. The proposition would seem beyond argument.

The wisdom of issuing such denunciations as a condition for open employment is more puzzling. I myself, in younger, freer, more ardent years, spent a good deal of time denouncing Hitler's Germany, Beck's Poland, Horthy's Hungary, Mussolini's Italy, Laval's France, Franco's Spain, Trujillo's Dominican Republic, and Peron's Argentina, for their brutal suppression of peoples. Then a change occurred, and presently I found myself blacklisted and in jail. One reason for that sorry predicament lay in those public denunciations which, in an earlier time, had been considered fulfillment of one's public duty, and flourishing evidence of the democratic spirit in action.

Today, when it is suggested that I denounce an entirely different set of nations and systems, I am somewhat wary of the idea. Having more forcibly than most been reminded of the changes which time can bring about, I ponder on how my present denunciation may be regarded in some different future. How, for example, can I divine what changes may get under way when Eisenhower and Khrushchev come together? How can I be certain that, though I may satisfy him now, my employer's opinions may not change again in the future? Having accepted written agreement with his opinions as a first condition of employment, I should then find myself in the ridiculous position of having to denounce my former denunciation in order to keep the job it originally won for me. And if I should by then have lost the mental agility to comprehend these dizzy reversals, I'd find myself again cast into darkness amidst a new and tumultuous clamor of patriotic execration.

I agree with Mr. Silberberg that compromise is necessary to the settlement of all great issues, and I think I should be willing to go very far with compromise if it promised a real end to the blacklist, not only for me but for all the others. However, the statement which he would like me to write at this time fails, as I see it, on two counts to qualify as compromise: (1) to deliver now a statement one has for twelve years refused on principle to write savors more of surrender (as when virginity is compromised) than of true compromise; and (2) compromise involves reciprocity which I find altogether missing from the current discussions, in that Mr. Silberberg would get specifically from me what he wants for the defense of his producer-clients, while he offers nothing tangible in return for my spiritual clients—the blacklisted personnel of Hollywood.

When he states that in the present situation my personal interests and the interests of his clients entirely coincide, I agree, with this exception: the two interests have *always* coincided. The now-blacklisted artists of Hollywood spelled out the coincidence of interests in great detail twelve years ago, while the producers have become aware of it only lately.

I suggest to you and to Mr. Silberberg (and authorize you to hand him a copy of this letter) that the interests of the Hollywood blacklistees and the producers always *will* coincide, and that when this fact is fully understood on the producers' side we shall be able to meet together and put a civilized end to a situation which presently is far more embarrassing (as distinguished from painful) to producers than to blacklistees.

I am truly sorry that I find myself unable to give Mr. Silberberg the statement he desires, for I should like in every way open to me to put an end to the trouble of his clients. It would take only ten minutes to write the statement, and it would, perhaps, solve for me two decades of economic and professional problems. But it would also destroy my soul. While I'm not greatly interested in the disposition of that soul after death, I find its preservation while yet I live enormously important.

In the meanwhile I wish to assure you and Mr. Silberberg that I shall conduct myself and my utterance most discreetly during the next days, and that I shall do nothing to jeopardize the good standing of his clients in the public eye. I think he undertakes his mission at a most propitious time, for surely international tensions will diminish until after the heads of state have concluded their forthcoming visits. Just so, if the mission fails and the Legion unleashes its little storm, there has not for twelve years been as hopeful a time in which to take protective measures against the flurry.

If the thing should occur, I shall be pleased, through advance consultation, to coordinate any public statements I may be forced to make with those of his principal client—in this instance, that particular producing and distribution company to which I owe my present professional loyalty.

Most sincerely,
DALTON TRUMBO

10. To Carey McWilliams, editor of *The Nation*

Los Angeles, California
October 26, 1959

Dear Carey:

Here are some thoughts I've been having: [25]

1. About two years ago, a young woman ran through a crowded N.Y. street, crying, "Please help me! He's going to kill me!" Her pursuer finally caught her, and killed her, and no one helped at all. In several cities crowds have chanted "Jump!" to crazed persons atop skyscrapers. In Los Angeles the other day an elderly man, gasping and weaving, staggered through a downtown street. Finally he fell to the sidewalk. No one offered him help. An hour later, when picked up by the authorities, he was dead. Diagnosis: heart attack. Two days later a middle-aged woman guided her stalled car to a side-island of the freeway. For five and a half hours she signalled for help. No one helped. From one, or a sequence, of such appalling daily events, I could develop an article on our fear of each other (and hence perhaps our hatred), and the horrible lack of love in our lives.

[25] McWilliams had asked Trumbo for a list of topics to be used in a possible *Nation* series of Trumbo articles.

2. Again: every month or so a troubled parent murders his entire family—wife (or husband), children, everyone—and then commits suicide. From this I should like to take a good look at the American family. How many times in these past twelve years have I been cautioned, "You must think of your family; the home is your first obligation; what of your children?" This fragmentation of a nation into separate dens of animals is the worst kind of moral anarchy, as deadly to our own souls as it is to the nation and the world.

3. Again: based on a proper news item, such as a tragic abortion, a consideration of the absolute idiocy of teaching children all about sex, and then announcing to them that their knowledge may be neither used nor tested for truth until they are properly licensed. The romantic idea of love so carefully nurtured: does one fall in love, or does one learn to love?

4. Again: the constant repetition of oaths vulgarizes not only the oath itself, but the object toward which loyalty or fealty is sworn. Oaths are sacred, necessary, and morally good. For that reason alone they must be kept scarce. Not to mention all the other stupidities of constant oathing.

5. Again: based on the experience of the Korean War, plus our own precious domestic immunity to the violence of war, is there not a very serious doubt that the nation's morale could survive a war which involved any kind of attack upon the homeland?

6. Again: if I had covered the Chessman execution, it was in my mind that the moral point of the piece would be that I had watched a man be killed before my eyes, and had not made one protest, either by word or my physical action, to stop the killers, or to seek at least to dissuade them.

7. Again: the hideous savagery of American prison sentences as contrasted with those of western Europe. What in our national character makes us so ferocious? Lack of faith? Lack of love? Lack of respect for man himself?

8. Again: from experiences I have had right here in Highland Park with the public schools, I am absolutely persuaded that lower middle-class and working-class neighborhoods are serviced by schools —and particularly high schools—which are specifically designed to provide industry with manual labor, just as schools in richer neighborhoods (and most universities) are designed to provide industry with technical and intellectual personnel.

9. Again: there is a local TV show which I'm going to take a look at. It involves jousting with cars, ten cars per joust, and ten jousts per show. A joust is not completed until all but one car has been hopelessly smashed. Thus a hundred are smashed a night. Moral obvious.

10. Again: the national taste in art, literature, cinema, theatre, TV, etc. is not spontaneously self-generated; it is created; it is *made*.

By whom? Basically, by the creators acting as agents for the corporate owners. Thus bad TV, bad films, etc., are not simply bad in themselves; they actively and continuously create a national taste for badness. I think this systematic debasement of taste in cultural areas is real, and can be successful. When bad art creates a national standard of bad taste, then that which is bad will become good, and that which is good will become bad. There is a horror working here.

11. Again: religion, based on Saturday church ads in the Los Angeles papers, and Monday's summary of sermons. What has happened to Christianity, and specifically, to love in the church (as your clipping indicated)?

12. Again: the curious lack of anti-clericalism in American Catholicism. Why is anti-clericalism—which is the leaven of the church throughout the Catholic countries of Europe—so rare and silent here?

13. Once more: the American fear of death. They simply will not discuss the subject. Can a people which fears death so terribly really appreciate the beauty, the joy, and the creativity of life? Does this relate in some way to morale? I had a play spoofing death: it lasted 13 days in New York, and received absolutely savage reviews (which may or may not have been deserved). It went to London, received smash reviews, and played two years. This was six years after London had known death quite intimately in World War II, and had suffered 30,000 civilian casualties in its rubble. Was it this which made them able to laugh about death, and lack of it which made unblitzed New York shudder at the bad taste of such an attempt at laughter?

14. Again: love of country as expressed in honest income tax returns.

15. Once more: how far have we really got away from the idea of women as a sexual possession? In New York State I am told it is illegal, and therefore absolutely impossible, for a married woman to receive artificial insemination without consent of spouse. There is, however, no practical way to prevent her from achieving insemination through adultery, for which she does *not* have to obtain the legal consent of her husband. Just who owns that womb, and what rights go with ownership?

16. Or again: is it not true that Communism, at least as it has existed in the United States, is actually a religion, a secular faith? If so, what immunities should it have? And what would be its corresponding handicaps if granted such immunity? Separation of church and state, etc. Might be amusing, and might even have a certain validity.

17. Again: the acquiescent American. His marvelous and meek acceptance of shoddy workmanship, bad telephone service, involved tax forms, community drives, official pomposity, absurd laws, stop

lights at three in the morning on silent and deserted street corners. There are practically no acts of rebellion. There is no feeling of individual independence; of the right to self-assertion and error. Our only form of rebellion is evasion, which is not rebellion at all, but implicit acceptance.

18. Again: our mania for written contracts; the growing length of contracts, and the moral insanity of them. They are morally insane because their interminable length is based on the assumption that parties are faithless, and that words and clauses can make faithless performance impossible once the contract is signed. A contract is worth no more than the good faith and clear understanding of both parties to it. I think contracts *are* longer; and that they show an increasing lack of faith among us—either that or a sublime faith that dishonest men can be hedged about with clauses that will make them honest.

19. Once more: an attempt to estimate the total number of *all* the blacklisted persons in America: i.e. blacklisted from their basic work. The morality and meaning of it, and its result. Free inquiry's surrender to dogma that may not be questioned without punishment.

20. Again: Titus Oates and Senator McCarthy. The extraordinary parallel between Catholics then, and Communists during the last decade.

21. Once more: the staggering immorality of liberals who advocate civil rights, desegregation, educational reform, better housing, Federal health aid, etc., because their enactment would aid us in our struggle with the Soviet Union. Good is advocated not because it is good, not because it is needful to common decency, but because it is *expedient.* Look into this long enough, and you can see madness.

22. Or again: the State Department and the Communist Party (American) during the years from 1945 to 1957. Each was utterly paralyzed by the Kremlin. Neither could move without the Kremlin moving first, making the ultimate action of each a reaction to that which happened there. Each looked steadily at the Soviet Union, each saw there a thing directly opposite to that which the other saw, and neither saw the thing remotely as it actually was. Their frightening mysticism; their inflammatory propaganda words; their use of the lie to achieve a desired (good) end.

23. Again: I have a thesis which has always amused me, but which is probably too hot to handle. It involved, as its premise, complete acceptance of the Biblical version of the crucifixion, and the Church's interpretation thereof, from which it proves (or tries to) that the Jews, by killing Christ, preserved the principle of monotheism, while most of Christianity, by accepting Christ, has descended into polytheism. Hence, that Cardinal Newman was wrong in contending that there is no via media between Rome and atheism. Rome *is* the via media between atheism and the God of the Jews.

24. Another one: this, for obvious reasons, has troubled me for a long, long while, and I've done much thinking on it. I am not yet entirely clear (as between a principle that must be defended and the right of people to know what a person's basic philosophy is)—but here are some of the problems. In defending the political privacy of a writer, it's always been said that the written work speaks for itself. But does it? Does not the reader have certain rights in the matter. When *I* am the reader, I always try to find out everything I can about the writer, in order to form a final judgment of both the man and his work. I am helped by knowing that Proust was a homosexual; that Chesterton and Waugh were converts to Catholicism; that Dreiser ended a Communist and Howard Fast did not; if a book attacking medical quackery is written by a Christian Scientist, I want to know that fact; if a book attacking Catholicism is written by a renegade priest, I want to know that, too. You perceive the problem. In terms of his religion and politics, is a writer a private person, or is he a public person. Perhaps it depends to some degree on what kind of thing he writes, but there certainly is a public nature to writing and the writer. Just so, the school teacher. One can have no objections to one's child being taught by a Catholic schoolteacher—but one would want to know that fact in relation to what the teacher teaches in order, as a parent, to adjust the balance in what the child learns, if there has been imbalance. Just so a Communist teaching certain subjects, or a Christian Scientist, or many others. It seems to me that a teacher should be able to teach *any* subject, but that in certain subjects the teacher's religion or politics should be known to the parent. It would be marvelously healthful to education if the basis from which a teacher teaches could be known to all without harm to the teacher. Equally writers. Problem: to shape a society in which it is *safe* to let one's beliefs be known. But safety itself can be ignoble under certain conditions. If people will not dare till it's safe to dare, then I fear they will not dare till it's safe to let one's beliefs be known. Morality can be a damned delicate business, but I know if I had my own life to live over again, hindsight tells me I should have risked no more by openly stating my political affiliation than I did by concealing it—and should have had considerably less explaining to do both for the public and for myself. It's something to think about.

25. Again: the Schlesinger Jr. *Vital Center.* I'd like to look at the thing exhaustively in a survey from, say, 1947 to his present piece for the Democrats. I would try to withhold my spleen, although I feel the spleen because I feel there's something terribly wrong in his prospective for America.

In relation to #16: if atheism is the work of Satan, then it *is* a religion!

In relation to #17: the abject acquiescence of the proud independent American is best observed when, in full light of day, a traffic signal gets stuck: cars stack up by the hundred behind the frozen red light before some timorous soul, eyes furtively darting right and left for the law, does at the end of twenty minutes what any intelligent and uncowed man would have done in five—drive through the damned thing.

26. Once more: during the San Francisco Conference in May and June of 1945, I lived at the Fairmont Hotel, unregistered on the blotter, in a room between Harold Stassen and Foster Dulles, and worked on a speech for Stettinius. Some of the problems that went into that speech were blood-chilling. Example: I was given an entire fact outline of the Argentine admission (our reasons for it). I wrote that section, based on the information given me, and discovered that it made no sense. I told them so when I gave them the section. I explained why the facts they'd given me simply could not be true. They agreed, and gave me a new set of facts! I worked most closely with Tom Finletter, Webb Miller, and my old fraternity brother and former roommate, Llewellyn Thompson, although what I have just stated does not relate specifically to them.

27. Or again: I married only once, and have remained married till now. I've sired children now aged 21, 19, and 14. They've had no trouble with the law. Yet for the past fifteen years I have been exhorted and hectored about the proper way to raise a family by an aging bachelor named J. Edgar Hoover. I'm sick of it. Bachelors have no knowledge of married love—having chosen to evade its problems and its responsibilities—and as for adolescent children, old bachelors should be kept by law as far away from them as possible. By what authority does he, or his bachelor associate, Tolson, lecture me on proper family life and the proper raising of children?

28. Again: how does Hoover get time to write so much? I think it can be established that he has been published far more often than either Hemingway or Faulkner. Should he be classified as author or cop? Does he write on his time or mine? If on his own, how does he get any sleep at all? Is the deal fixed—does somebody else really do his writing?

29. Once more, please; the June rash of honorary degrees. This is a real absurdity, and could be nice clean riotous fun.

30. And again: in the same vein as above, the giving of prizes for all kinds of merit; the endless sequences of testimonial dinners generally organized by the guest of honor; the hundreds, perhaps thousands, of awards, plaques, shields, cups bowls, parchments, etc.

I'm going to number the above, so we can refer to them in future correspondence without stating the thesis of each. Maybe they're bad, or, more likely, some are bad and some are good. It would be my idea, if you agree, to use some item from the press pertinent and dramatic, as a springboard for each piece. Thus I shall seem to have drifted into my general point from a specific incident. All this, of course, in addition to your suggestions.

Best,
DALTON

11. To Nikola Trumbo

Los Angeles, California
November 13, 1959

Dear Nikky:

From day to day for the last ten, I've been meaning to answer your two delightful letters, and now your emergency call causes me to take the time for answering I should have taken earlier.

I've been heavily occupied, as usual: Spanish scenes for *Spartacus,* presently being shot there; retakes for it to be shot here in December; completion of the first draft of *Crazy Horse,*[26] and the final draft of *Coin,*[27] plus the innumerable conferences that accompany such idiot enterprises. Then again, I'm undertaking to do a series of pieces for *The Nation,* which Alfred A. Knopf later wishes to publish as a book. The quiz thing apparently touched a raw nerve.[28] I've received letters on it from all over the country. New York University's School of Communications has asked permission to reprint it, and I'm recording it Tuesday for radio broadcast locally.

As for the letter to me which you feared was sarcastic—there wasn't a word of sarcasm in it. I think you mistake sarcasm for irony. It was richly ironical, very funny, and, I'm pleased and proud to say, extremely well-written. I'm not at all surprised you've landed a berth on *The Coloradoan,* for you're developing a style and approach to material that can be very promising. Indeed, we like all your letters, and especially appreciate their frequency in view of the fact that your mud-head brother scarcely writes at all.

The news about your grades—and the consistency of them—is truly marvelous; but what's even better is that you have learned the pleasure of study, the excitement of intellectual stimulation and accomplishment, and the grim but honest truth that nothing can be accomplished without consistent hard work which becomes, in it-

[26] *Sundown at Crazy Horse,* a script written for Eugene Frenke and later sold by United Artists to Universal. It was released under the title, *The Last Sunset.* Kirk Douglas and Rock Hudson starred; Robert Aldridge directed.

[27] *The Other Side of the Coin,* a script for Otto Preminger, which, due to situations in Malaysia and Southeast Asia, has been cancelled.

[28] "Hail, Blithe Spirit!" in *The Nation,* October 24, 1959, an article on the television quiz program scandals.

self, a pleasure. All in all, you're developing splendidly in that winey mountain air, and Cleo and I are very, *very* pleased with you. I don't have to add, keep it up, for I'm convinced you're in the swing and will continue to be without parental nudging.

Now to the emergencies, for which you have asked emergency responses. Cleo and I are writing separately in response to your wail for help. Our opinions and advice may be different in detail or in general, but that's of no account; you'll have our various ideas, and can separate the wheat from chaff on your own.

First let me tell you of my own experience in the same general area while I was a freshman at CU. Rush week was differently governed then than now, I judge; but one rule was fundamental: no approach to pledge a freshman could be made until a certain day stipulated by the Inter-Fraternity Council. I spent a breathless, foolish week being rushed by four or five houses. My mind had been made up from the beginning that I wished to pledge Delt [Delta Tau Delta], although I wasn't sure, as one can never be, that their wishes would coincided with mine.

Among the other fraternities rushing me was Sigma Phi Epsilon. They had just moved into an expensive and newly built house, were therefore considerably in debt, and wished, in consequence, to pledge a very large freshman class out of economic necessity. One night, well before the fatal day of pledging, they cornered me in separate conclave, informed me they had decided I filled their particular bill of specifications, and asked me to become an informal pledge on the spot, the arrangement to be confirmed by actual pledging on the big day. I declined, saying I hadn't quite made up my mind yet.

I pledged Delt, as you know; and on that solemn and portentous night, the Delt pledges were assembled, placed on their honor, informed of the pledging rules of the Inter-Fraternity Council, and asked to speak up if any other fraternity had sought to pledge them before the proper date. I, virtue-infected dolt, stood forth and told on Sig Phi Ep. I hadn't known what the consequences were to me. The matter was taken up by the Council, and Sig Phi Ep received a stern and official warning to be true-blue Greek in future.

Each spring each fraternity house had the privilege of naming two of its freshmen to some sophomore honorary society. The Delts proposed my name and that of another. However, each fraternity had the right of blackball on all proposed members of the honorary. Result, I was blackballed, quite naturally, by Sig Phi Ep and the Delts were obliged to replace me with another. The honorary outfit was unimportant, and I didn't get back to CU for my sophomore year anyhow, but that isn't the point. I had violated a confidence out of what I considered to be my larger moral responsibility to the Inter-Fraternity Council and my own fraternity. Later I realized the whole thing was so trivial—Delta Tau Delta, Sigma Phi Epsilon, and the Inter-Fratternity Council itself—that I had made a moral choice in a matter unworthy of moral choice; that I had actually nourished my own smug sense of virtue at the expense of violating another's confidence on a matter that had no virtue inherent in it, and no importance of any real kind. So I resolved for the future, as a general rule, that it was not my duty to police an organization to which I belonged or owed allegiance. If the organization wanted policing, let it do its own; I would govern my own conduct in accordance with the organization's rules, but if others chose to violate those rules, the organization would have to catch them, not I. I still think it's a pretty fair standard for social conduct.

Now to your problem which I'll try to analyze in order that both of us may think it through. None of this analysis bears moral condemnation of anyone; it should be taken simply as my way of ordering my thoughts and getting at the truth of acts, motives and decisions.

I understand that you live in a duplex owned by Mrs. D_____ _____ who is personally responsible to the university for the conduct maintained inside her establishment—an establishment which provides her with income, profit, a living. One can easily understand that, as a businesswoman, it is her responsibility to see that her business is conducted according to the agreement she made with the university, from which, indirectly, she receives her customers. Legally, and from a point of her own self-interest, I think I may state flatly that the running of her business according to the rules of her business is her responsibility, and hers alone. That should be considered the basis of our analysis.

I further understand the duplex is socially divided into two units: your side, and the other side. And that each unit has a Resident Advisor; and that each Resident Advisor is responsible to a higher authority for the enforcement of rules (Mrs. D_____? Ultimately the university?) And that the girls of each side of the duplex elect a Standards Chairman, whose duty it is to assist in enforcing the rules. I assume the Standards Chairmen work directly under the Resident Advisor in the chain of authority.

Carol H_____ is Resident Advisor for the other side of the house, and, I assume, a student has been elected Standards Chairman there. Mary M_____ is Resident Advisor for your side of the house, and you are the elected Standards Chairman. Is that correct?

Or were you elected Standards Chairman for the whole house— your side as well as theirs? And do you then work under two Resident Advisors—Carol H_____ for their side, and Mary M_____ for yours? You see the first thing I'm trying to clarify is the matter of your jurisdiction. If you are Standards Chairman for both sides, then the events on the other side clearly come under your jurisdiction. But if you are Standards Chairman only for your own side of the house (as certain things you write indicate), then what happens on the other side of the house is clearly the concern of their Standards Chairman, or their Resident Advisor, and not of you.

Now to the question of your responsibility, and of your sense of responsibility. You have always been cursed with a sense of responsibility—a good and noble thing in itself—which has caused, and even invited other people, and very often older people, to impose shamelessly upon you, basing their aggression (for that's what it is) on an appeal to your deep sense of responsibility. Combined with this sense of responsibility, and with a cheerful acceptance of responsibility, you are afflicted with an exquisitely sensitive conscience. You are now feeling some of the pain that can occur when responsibility and conscience collide.

Some time ago you wrote us that you were worried about the girls on the other side, because the Dean of Women had announced at the beginning of the semester that rule violations would cause the whole house to be closed within 24 hours. You and Corrie and Mary, even then, were apparently giving much thought to the situation on the other side, since Carol, Resident Advisor for the other side, wasn't living up to her responsibilities. The point I'm trying to make here relates to your responsibility. It seems to me that your responsibility involves persuasion, warning, and, above all, a good personal example. If, in spite of your exercise of those three functions, the house is closed down—well, there have been greater tragedies; you'll find other shelter, and so will they. But the person who is really responsible is Mrs. D——————— herself. She is making money at the university's discretion, has promised to conduct a proper house, and she, and she alone, bears the responsibility for conducting her business according to the rules of that business. She: not you, not even the Resident Advisor, but Mrs. D——————— herself. You can and should feel responsible to her for your own personal conduct, but under no circumstances should you permit her (or should she seek) to impose upon you a responsibility that is basically hers. This I fear she has done, and I beg you to look back on other instances in your life in which adults, unfairly and lazily, have placed upon you responsibilities which were actually their own, and to remember the pain and disillusionment that usually have accompanied such invasions of your good nature.

Now we come to the weekend of the Trouble. Mr. and Mrs. D——————— were out of town. Resident Advisor for your side was in California. Mrs. D——————— had asked another Resident Advisor to look in on the place during her absence, as well as a member of her own family. As you write, in this situation you "feel a great responsibility to Mrs. D———————." Well and good. More, apparently, than Mrs. D——————— felt, since she was out of town, and had not provided for any other authority to replace her *in residence.*

Now to the situation. Three girls on the other side have been drinking and having boys to their quarters. Morally, I see nothing wrong about this, except that it's against the rules. Certain kinds of college students have always considered it a part of life to violate such rules, and sometimes the violation is wholly innocent and with little motivation beyond sheer exuberant and mindless defiance. I should be distressed if you did it, because I think you have better sense than to risk so much (expulsion) for so little (a boy and a bottle). I would condemn you as stupid and thoughtless to take such a risk, but I couldn't go so far as to condemn you morally for it.

Anyhow, these three girls have been raising merry hell over there, and Mrs. D——————— hasn't been efficient enough in her work to discover it, and Carol H————, their Resident Advisor, has had guilty knowledge of what was going on all along, has done nothing about it, and therefore has become, in fact, an accomplice to it by implicit consent. And at this point, you write, "I got wind of a cocktail party being thrown by these girls." And there the trouble begins.

I am assuming, from this point on, that you are Standards Chairman for both sides of the house. Now you possess this knowledge. I can quickly tell you what I would have done at this point: I'd have said to myself, "If their own Resident Advisor doesn't care, neither do I." I'd have said, "Let the people who set up these rules enforce them." I'd have said (possibly), "If it comes to being responsible for having the house closed down, or those girls expelled, I'll let them close the house down." And I'd have walked away from the whole situation.

But here both your conscience and your sense of responsibility come to the fore. You could not do what I might have done, because you are not me, and have no wish to be. You could not turn your back on the problem as blithely as I could have, and that is probably greatly to your credit. You had been elected to a job, and you could not in good conscience fail to do your duty. This being true of you—and perhaps one of the best things in you—you knew you had to act.

You decided, correctly, I think, to go to another Resident Advisor, since your own was out of the city. Exactly why you did not go to the R.A. Mrs. D——————— had selected to keep an eye on the house, I do not know. Possibly because you didn't know her well enough, and couldn't be sure you could trust her with a confidence. If that is true, then, again quite probably, you went to Polly, an Advisor you knew and trusted. You asked her to "drop rank," by which I assume that you talked to her off the record, under a mutual pledge of confidence. Is that true? If so, then you took every possible measure to protect the three persons whom you were reporting. It seems to me that here you satisfied every requirement that honor can impose upon a responsible person.

It was agreed to by Polly that she would casually drop in on the forbidden cocktail party, lecture the girls, soundly, perhaps frighten them into future compliance, and the whole affair would be forgotten. The solution seems to me to have been excellent, both tactically and diplomatically. Had it been carried through, the culprits would have been corrected but not punished, and all would have been forgotten.

But before the party could begin, Dave D_____ "pulled a raid" and confiscated four bottles. Here I begin to frown. Just who is this Dave D_____, that he can enter young women's bedrooms and confiscate their property? Is he Mrs. D_____'s son, or nephew, or brother, or something? Even so, he has no right to enter your bedroom without your consent, and you have every right to forbid him entrance. I gravely doubt that Mrs. D_____ can delegate to her male relatives a right to enter girls' bedrooms whenever fancy strikes them. That right belongs only to the police (with warrant), to Mrs. D_____ (under the rules of her agreement with the university), or to an accredited representative of the university authorized to make that specific sort of entrance, search, and seizure. I don't believe any parent of a college girl will be pleased to discover that his daughter's privacy can be invaded at will by an absent landlady's male relative, and I strongly object to the idea of him entering your room under any circumstances, regardless of what rules you may be violating, regardless of whether he searches for a bottle, a pot, or a cadaver. But right or wrong, he raided them before the civilized plan devised by you, Corrie and Polly could be put into effect and now "the kids were really in hot water."

Your next sentence reads, "They had no idea who stooled on them." And two or three sentences later you write, "Polly and Dave D_____'s main concern was that nobody find out who informed, but I guess Dave was talking and let it slip that someone from my side had told."

Now aside from the fact that Dave D_____ behaved outrageously, what most puzzles me is how he came to know anything about the proposed party in the first place. Did you tell him as well as Polly? If so, why? What is *his* official connection with the matter? If you told him the names in confidence, then his action shamelessly violated your confidence. If Polly told him in confidence, then Polly also violated her pledged word. Did Dave know of the plan you had worked out with Polly to interrupt the party, and settle the whole matter quietly? If so, he not only behaved like a criminal, he behaved like a fool, and betrayed both of you and Polly into the bargain.

As a result of Dave's talking, the culprits discovered the area from which the information came, and later confronted you with it personally. Why did Dave talk? Why did Polly talk? Why did one or the other of them betray your confidence, and violate their pledged word to you? What sort of people are they? And finally *why* were the girls in "hot water" the instant Dave confiscated the liquor? Because Dave would report it to Mrs. D——————— and Mrs. D——————— would report it to the university authorities to protect herself? If so, then Mrs. D——————, toward whom you feel such responsibility, certainly has not felt the same responsibility toward you. For she has allowed your name (or someone has allowed it) to become known as the complainant in official areas extending clear to the Dean of Women's office. In my view, every one of your superiors has thrown you to the wolves, each doing it in order to shore up his own interests. And this is rotten.

You see, my dear Nikky, the problem of responsibility and conscience is this: they can thrive only in a social climate in which others possess the same qualities in the same degree as you. You did what you felt to be right; in doing it, you acted in confidence so that no one would be hurt. But right down the line your confidence has been violated, and the instant that violation on the part of others occurred, it made you the betrayer of the three girls whom you had sought, under the rules, to correct, but not to harm. You are completely innocent of wanting to get them into trouble (quite the contrary, you were actually trying to keep them out of trouble)—but the instant *you* and your confidence were betrayed, in that instant your act of responsibility and conscience became, quite against your will, an act of betrayal which may result in the expulsion of three girls you only wished to help for the good of all. Witness, then how different the *intent* of an act can be from its *result*. The problem, then, is always to analyze the possible results of a good intent before one acts; and if there is a reasonable possibility that the results may be bad, then the act, if committed, will also have been bad regardless of the intent behind it. In a word, think, think, think, before you act, particularly in matters of responsibility and conscience. For your real responsibility and your real conscience lie with your own generation, and not with Mrs. D——————'s. From my point of view, the expulsion of a child is much more tragic than closing down Mrs. D——————'s business concern.

Now I know you couldn't have thought of all these things, and clearly you didn't, and I love you for the seriousness of purpose and the high intent which led you into the mess. However it turns out, it will not blight your life, but it will, I think, cause you to think, and guide you in future actions of a similar nature. The moral problem you were confronted with is one that has driven philosophers to madness, and I defy anyone precisely to define the right or wrong of the dilemma.

For myself, I long ago made this resolution: I will never accept any position, elective or appointive, which compels me to report the illicit acts of my fellow men to a higher authority. Let authority enforce itself. Let it police itself. But let it not ask me to become an agent or authority against my own kind.

That may be a weak, even a cowardly resolution of the question. But it does solve such puzzles as the one you're working on by eliminating the cause—by refusing to accept authority's responsibility for the minor misdemeanors of others. These things are qualitative, you know of course: I'd report a murderer, but not a shoplifter. Let the shoplifter and the law take care of the shop. It may be mixed and even amoral, but I'm inclined to think it saves one much pain, and may save others more.

What I'd do now? I don't know. If you were wronger or righter, it would be much easier to make suggestions. But the areas of right and wrong here are blurred almost beyond recognition, and I feel you're much more betrayed than betraying.

Perhaps I would resign my Standards Chairman office with a frank explanation of what has happened, or, if the explanation is impossible, with the forthright statement that I no longer wish to be the representative of authority over my fellow students.

When affairs simmer down and you can see your way clear to do so, I would go to those three nasty little cocktail-drinking, boy-entertaining girls, and tell them what is in my heart, and present the problem as you saw it to them, and seek their understanding. Since you did them no wrong until your confidence was betrayed, I don't see why forgiveness from them should be asked for, or why they should think it necessary for them to forgive you, since, insofar as I can see, *you did nothing wrong.* It's understanding of the whole problem, and your perplexing position, that you seek from them, and, quite probably, they from you.

I might announce to Mrs. D———, Polly, the Dean of Women, and all of them, that they have placed me in a position which compromises my honor, and puts me in a completely false light before certain of my fellow students. And I would tell them I am absolutely through talking to them about the matter in any way.

And if the three criminals on the other side of the house are seriously threatened with expulsion, I would go just as high as I could —even to the president of the university—telling the truth of what happened, relating the series of personal betrayals which caused it to happen, and defending the three to the very end.

Cleo will probably have other suggestions. This letter is awkwardly written, because done in haste. It is so long and exhaustive because I felt you wanted it to be so. It's as honest as I can make it, but certainly not as clear or decisive as I'd like to make it. Men have spent lifetimes trying to solve the tangle into which you've stumbled, and even then, by heaven, they haven't arrived at clear decisions. Morality, conscience, responsibility—they tear us apart, they hurt us, they make us hate ourselves and sometimes hurt others. How much better, however, to have them than to be amoral, unconscientious, irresponsible. Suffer with them, child, and find your own answer, and then act upon it. But *think* before you act; analyze; consider; be absolutely sure you're right. And then you probably will be.

The other matter you questioned us about will have to wait for my answer, at least, until tomorrow. I've work to do, damn it, and you've stolen half a day from me. On the other hand, what cheap payment is half a day for the confidence of a daughter!

Much love, my dear,
DADDY

12. To Peter Ustinov

Los Angeles, California
Tuesday [1959]

Dear Stonewall: [29]

In addition to gratitude I enclose for you two dainties.

The first is the scene with the girls. I've combined yours and mine and shot it in to Eddie [Lewis] as what I hope shall be the final version, leaving to him the task of confronting Gracchus [Laughton] with it as a fait accompli. I like Charles [Laughton] (though *he* prefers Shakespeare), but his sighs and grunts and soft reproaches somewhat unhinge me at close quarters. I therefore try to keep a little real estate between us.

It was Charles's concept of Gracchus in this scene that the moral paradox he expresses is played straight; that Gracchus recognizes no paradox at all and is quite serious in his view of himself as a moral man. This frustrates your lewd scheme to bounce one of his babes on your knee. Similarly, some of the Gracchus lines you cut or replaced were lines that Charles had already approved of, so back they went and out went yours.

I send you also a scene between Batiatus and Gracchus upon Batiatus' return from the battlefield. This scene approaches the throne tomorrow morning. When approval is bestowed, it takes its little place in this remarkably unstable script.

However if there are any of your lines in either of these two scenes

[29] Ustinov was one of the stars of *Spartacus*.

you wish to cut, enlarge, alter, improve, or fuck up, please feel free to do so and shoot them to me as soon as convenient by phone or otherwise. I will then route them through channels as official corrections.

As you will note, I snatched a line you'd used in the first enclosed scene and slipped it into the second. Your other lines not used I've squirreled away for flavoring still other scenes.

I hear they had Kirk [Douglas] in one of those training scenes running so fast in such tight circles that he collided with his own spoor. Keep out of the way. And say a word at vespers for your poor friend who started out to be a baker and didn't have the guts to stick.

I.H.S.V.,
SAM, *the quiet American*

10.

"Once in a While When God Smiles"

On January 19, 1960, Otto Preminger announced to the press that he had hired Dalton Trumbo to write the screenplay for Leon Uris' novel *Exodus*. Preminger thus cannily made himself the herald of the end of the blacklist and essentially outmaneuvered Kirk Douglas and Edward Lewis for whom Trumbo had already written *Spartacus* and who had long been preparing to give the writer screen credit.

Yet accolades such as "champion of the blacklistee' or "first to hire a blacklisted writer" cannot justifiably be awarded to Preminger, Douglas or any other single individual. For the blacklist had run its course; it had failed, and everyone in Hollywood knew it was essentially over. Trumbo was the first to come out in the open, he insists, not because of cleverness or talent, but simply because he had "more hooks in the sea" and was writing six scripts to everybody else's one.

There was no loud announcement that the blacklist was dead, nor is it likely there will ever be an industry declaration. Yet the first disclosure paved the way for those that were to follow, and one by one writers who had continued to practice their craft during the years of the black market and who had developed a degree of skill as screen writers return to work without furor or incident. Trumbo wrote:

Just consider, for a minute, two men like Lardner [*M*A*S*H**] and [Waldo] Salt [*Midnight Cowboy*]: blacklisted in their mid-thirties—blacklisted for over twenty years—both have returned from the darkness in their mid-fifties better writers than they ever were—and each with a film that has enormous appeal to youth! I don't know any of their unblacklisted contemporaries who could have done either job. Such men have both guts and quality, wouldn't you say?

Actors and directors are less fortunate. Actors grow older; their faces change. Directors lose their skill through disuse. "These people," Trumbo laments, "remain bloody victims."

Of the original Ten, fates have been various. Edward Dmytryk returned to work with his appearance before the committee in 1950. Samuel Ornitz died of cancer in 1956. Two have not actively returned to screen work: Alvah Bessie, who had few credits at the time of the blacklist and who never became a part of the black market, worked as stage manager at the Hungry i nightclub in San Francisco and achieved considerable success as a novelist with *The Symbol;* and John Howard Lawson, who has spent much of his recent life in

Europe and has concerned himself with non-dramatic forms of writing, is currently teaching at both Loyola and Hebrew Universities in Los Angeles. Another of the original Ten, Herbert Biberman, gave up film directing for business during the period of the blacklist but has since returned both as director and collaborator on the screenplay for the Theatre Guild's *Slaves*.

As in the case of many Hollywood blacklistees, two of the Ten found favorable climate abroad. Adrian Scott and Lester Cole lived for a time in England where Scott was an executive producer for M-G-M and Cole both wrote and produced. Both have now returned to the West Coast and to film work. Scott has recently produced *The Great Man's Whiskers,* a television special for children, at Universal-International, and Cole (non-credited screen writer for *Born Free*) is currently a lecturer in film at San Francisco State.

Besides Trumbo, Ring Lardner, Jr., and Albert Maltz are writing once more under their own names. Lardner's first screen credit after the blacklist was *The Cincinnati Kid*. Maltz's return was initially retarded by an abortive attempt on the part of Frank Sinatra to hire him for *The Execution of Private Slovak* in 1960. Conditions and circumstances not being propitious to such a move, Sinatra was forced to yield to pressure from the right and buy off Maltz's contract. Maltz has since received credit for *Two Mules for Sister Sara* in 1970.

No such pressures postponed the appearance of Trumbo's name upon the screen. It is true there were minor skirmishes surrounding both *Spartacus* and *Exodus:* picketing by the American Legion and the American Nazi Party in such cities as Boston, Chicago, Los Angeles, Pittsburgh and San Diego. The outbursts of protest were thwarted not only by lack of support but also by the fact that both films were expensive, well publicized and featured outstanding casts who were sure draws at the box office.

So it is that Dalton Trumbo, sometimes longing for the irresponsible days of anonymity, writes completely in the open and turns down far more offers than he can accept. He wrote me in 1965:

. . . although I was ostensibly doing *Will Adams* [for Peter O'Toole], a small crisis came up on *Montezuma* and I had to go to Mexico to pacify the national censorship and threaten them with a withdrawal of the production from Mexico unless they realized that we are engaged in drama rather than history. Back to *Will Adams,* and then *Hawaii* was marvelously revived, and I passed swiftly from *Will Adams* to *Hawaii* and back a dozen times. Then came the rough cut of *The Sandpiper* [with blacklistee Michael Wilson for Elizabeth Taylor and Richard Burton] which filled me with vapors and discontents and took a good deal of time.

Trumbo also wrote the screenplay of the 1968 film, *The Fixer,* and more recently *A Feast of Freedom* and the script of *Sons* from the Evan Hunter novel—both for MGM. His next project will be the direction of his own screenplay for his 1939 novel, *Johnny Got His Gun,* making him, he says, "the oldest new director in Hollywood." 1970 will also see a new paperback edition of *Johnny* by Bantam Books in 150,000 copies (32 years after its first publication) and a hardback edition by Lyle Stuart. Indeed, Dalton Trumbo's unique career has come full circle: he is once again one of the most important writers in Hollywood.

1. Wire to President of Western Union

Los Angeles, California
February 22, 1959

On Saturday morning at 2 a.m. I received 103 rings trying to get Western Union by telephone. Tonight, approximately midnight on Sunday, I have rung 118 times. You are a public utility. If you cannot service your clientele, and if you will not employ sufficient persons at an adequate salary to perform your public function, notify me within six days or expect to find my complaint for your disgraceful attitude toward the public need filed through my attorney with the proper authorities in Washington, D.C. In the meanwhile, as a victim of your tragic negligence, I beg you to inform me of the existence of a competitor who has a decent regard for his business obligations, through whom I may send a message which may reasonably be expected to reach its recipient more swiftly than by carrier pigeon.

DALTON TRUMBO

2. To Ingo Preminger

Los Angeles, California
January 2, 1960

Dear Ingo: [1]

Now that . . . Otto [Preminger] . . . has cut his last lifeline to Mexico City, he would appear to be entirely dependent on me [for the *Exodus* script]. I enjoy such situations only when I can use them for a good purpose. I propose to take advantage of this one by putting him through a small character-strengthening campaign. Nat-

[1] Ingo Preminger, Otto's brother, was a successful Hollywood agent. In 1970 he made his debut as a producer with *M*A*S*H**. Throughout the entire McCarthy period Ingo Preminger's principal pleasure lay in representing the work of such blacklisted writers as Trumbo, Hal Smith, Ned Young, Hugo Butler, Michael Wilson and others.

urally, I don't want to do it directly—that's your job. Hence I request you, as delicately as you can, to drop a few hints in his general direction.

In the first place, we must try to get him genuinely *interested* in this film.[2] Granted that our first act is thin as a nun's hymen, still and all it's the best we can manage until he gets some *enthusiasm* for the project. He must constantly be reminded that we still have two acts to go. God knows *where* they'll go, but unless I can get Otto pushing, I can't see any direction but down hill straight to the fade.

Actually, I don't think it's possible for anyone—no matter how talented—to handle more than one project at a time. As for jumping around between three and four simultaneous projects—well, it can only end up tragically. While I clamor for him to read scenes and do a little thinking about *Exodus,* he's off in the wild blue yonder. Somebody gave him a telephone credit card, and he seems crazed with its possibilities. It's nothing but London, Paris, Salt Lake City, New York until you'd think I was operating the Third International out of this joint.

For one thing, he's really making a fool of himself over that silly murder story he shot somewhere out in the Midwest.[3] He pesters people from one ocean to the other about getting a local theatre for it, and by God, I think he's *serious.* If it isn't the last picture that diverts him, it's the next one—never *Exodus*—that commands his attention. For example, these ads for *Advise and Consent* distract him constantly, and he's always telling people that he knows better

---

[2] The film referred to is *Exodus.* Trumbo was signed to do the screenplay in December of 1959. Recalling the period of *Exodus'* composition, during which this letter was written, Trumbo said:

With contracts signed and actors employed to begin shooting *Exodus* in March, Otto found himself with a script he considered unshootable. He telephoned me from New York on December 10, commanding me to read the book and prepare myself to write a completely new one. He arrived in Los Angeles on December 16 1959. We worked together at my house from 7 a.m. to 7 p.m., Saturdays and Sundays, Christmas Eve and Christmas Day, New Years Eve and New Years Day, for 44 straight days. Otto left with the completed script in January, and the film went into production in Israel in late March, on schedule.

Otto was on a straight steak diet. 16 oz. of beef for lunch, very rare, each day. I called it the 44 carniverous days. The butcher, I'm sure, thought I was keeping a pet lion in the house—and so I was. I respect O.P. very much; more than that, I have affection for him, and he, I feel, also has for me.

Although when he announced, in January, my authorship of the script, it *did* break on page 1, *New York Times,* and got much publicity, it has never entered my mind, nor I think his, that he gave me credit because of the publicity that was bound to attend such a move. He gave it because he strongly opposed the hypocrisy of the blacklist as a matter of principle.

[3] *Anatomy of a Murder.*

than they how to exploit the book. Then he sits and broods over the best-seller lists, checking on his bets like a damned tout. Or else he's busy hiring limousines to ferry actors to and from a theatre in which he actually thinks he's going to put on a play that isn't even written yet. If not that, he gets hysterical and tells people three thousand miles away to go fuck themselves, while I can't even sneak a decent erection into the script that should concern him most. And now when I *need* him—right in the middle of a very dank script, mind you!—he's running away to London or Israel to oversee the building of a cow trail that any deformed halfwit could clear in four days with a team of mules and one drag plow.

The only way I can explain such scatterbrained conduct on the part of an otherwise rational man is that he's stuck with a commitment and has thrown *Exodus* in, catch-as-catch-can, to work it off. Fair enough, fair enough; we're both stuck. But until we get this poor little thing wobbling about on its own two feet, he should forget *Anatomy* and *Advise and Consent* and *Bunny Lake* and that rough-draft hunch for a play somebody fobbed off on him. He should also forget about *Coin*. In fact, let him forget that one first. The problem—you must explain to him—is *Exodus, Exodus* and *Exodus*!

Also, I think you should let him know it's no bed of roses for me. Working, so to speak, against the competition of all his other projects, and getting so little of his attention, means that I have practically no time even for so primitive a matter as personal hygiene. I took my last bath the day before Christmas. By now I stink worse than the script. Cleo, who is a fastidious woman, sprays me once in a while with something called Stag, but the minute I begin sweating again, it's as bad as ever. Otto notices it too. Only today he asked me whether I showered or tubbed, which *he* may have thought a subtle way to bring the subject up, but which I considered downright indelicate. The smell is so bad down here he keeps the windows open all day long, and the winds howl through, and it's like camping out on a glacier.

Cleo has other complaints, too, and the divorce court is not beyond her at this point. She doesn't mind not seeing me very often (on the contrary), but in those rare moments when we *are* together, it infuriates her when I converse exclusively with shrugs, questions when statements are called for, and quaint Middle-European jokes. Whatever capacity I may once have had to write straight English dialogue has vanished altogether. I'm fifth-rate Shalom Aleichem. In one of the retakes at U.I., everyone was puzzled when the Senate told [Laurence] Olivier that if he didn't march against Spartacus, Rome herself would fall. Olivier lifted his brows and replied, "Nu?" They shot it anyhow, but it's not going to help *me*.

Something also is happening to my psyche. Either by reference or in fact, I've baited, bullied, beaten, burned, cursed, kicked, cuffed and killed so many Jews I'm turning callous—I'm losing all human feeling for the bastards. That, of course, is a first step along the road to anti-Semitism. I hate to see it happen to anybody, and especially to me, because when I pick up a cause I run with it, and you know the stories *I'll* have to tell. Add to this the fact that the only place on earth I'm positively *not* blacklisted is in the Arabian countries, and you can see that I have sacrified a great deal in what I'm trying to convince Otto is his emergency as well as mine.

On the other hand, I like him very much. He's a charming man, and unlike most directors, full of protein instead of shit. I *like* keeping him supplied with his favorite food, despite the fact that prime horse sirloins are up to 65c per pound these days. The only thing that troubles me is our local pet-food dealer, who has spread a story around the block that I've got a lion locked up here. But even that I don't mind, since it compels neighborhood mothers to keep their children behind locked doors during the holiday season. Result: I haven't caught one neighborhood kid pilfering his way across our hill in nine days.

The whole point of my appeal, Ingo, is this: I'm willing to give this script everything I have. I'm willing to ruin what I used to call my style in English dialogue, and hopelessly compromise what has jocosely been referred to as my "career." I'm willing even to risk that ultimate and final exposure which Otto leeringly holds over my head whenever my spirit flags. All of this I shall do if only he will get *interested*; if only we can stimulate his *enthusiasm*; if only he will give me some of his *time*.

Do talk to him, won't you?

Affectionately,
D.T.

Postscript: I'm asking him to give this to you the next time he sees you, feeling it'll be faster than the mails. On the other hand, there's no point in letting *him* know it. We had a mailman in jail down in Ashland, Kentucky. His problem was this: his mail route included his own house, and his wife was cuckolding him with a local sport, and the sport was writing her daily love letters which her poor cuckoldee had to deliver with his own hand—and finally he opened one. The instant he demanded of that tricky slut his rights as a husband, he lost his rights as a citizen. Because you just can't open other people's mail—especially if you're the mailman. He only got three years, and his dream of the future was the other side of the coin (to mint a phrase)—he decided to become a milkman.

3. To Ingo Preminger

Los Angeles, California
January 14, 1960

Dear Ingo:

This is a delicious situation,[4] and I'm sure you know already that I'm going to savor it to the last drop—even though you sweat a bit. You see, I am just a stupid screen writer. I'm no businessman. I don't know what current prices are in the writing market because I've so long been isolated from others in it. Such a naive fellow, in this complicated situation, would be a fool to set a price on his services. He would, on the contrary, seek out the most expert advice, and follow it rigidly, and pay for it.

Thinking about experts, it occurs to me that determining the value of writers and their services is the precise business of a very good friend of mine—Ingo Preminger. He is one of the country's leading specialists in that sort of thing. He also happens, in this instance, to be my agent.

I fall upon that happy coincidence with shouts of joy. It's perfect! You, therefore, shall be the one to determine the value of your client-friend's services to your producer-brother. And if you lose a little sleep wrestling with the problem—well, that laughter you hear at the moment of dozing off will be mine.

I will show you how various my prices and deals have been these two years, so you can measure them against the present circumstances and have something to go by. *Spartacus:* it now comes to $100,000 for interminable treatment, three drafts, and re-writes. *Camp-followers,* as you know, I was willing to do for $50,000; and [*The Other Side of the*] *Coin* for $60,000. So you see I'm a pliable fellow who understands that circumstances alter prices.

When you estimate the value of the present job, I take it that we are agreed that the total working time, be it small or large, has utterly no affect upon the value of the finished product—except that, in this instance, speed may be accounted an extra virtue.

Another reason I wished to delay until now is that I honestly had no way of knowing how much work the script would require. I now report to you, dear agent, that the job involves a complete re-write. Also that the script is approximately twice the length of a normal script. Moreover, this is not one draft of a script; it is a first draft and a final draft, the first draft scenes being immediately re-written into final scenes as we go along. So we speak of a finished screenplay, ready to go before the cameras.

. . . .

[4] After Trumbo had been working on *Exodus* for about three weeks, Ingo Preminger asked Trumbo what price should be asked of producer Otto Preminger.

There. I wash my hands of this whole ugly business. I've got to get back to my writing. I cannot be troubled at this moment by talk about money. Torment yourself, old friend! And think of me from time to time, calmly at peace, accepting in advance any arrangement you choose to make.[5]

Hah!
DALTON

4. To A. C. Spectorsky

Los Angeles, California
January 17, 1960

Dear Mr. Spectorsky:

More god-damned problems: Got out of the hospital alive—which is rare—then had to go back for a couple of days, Also, sick picture problems. I'll have the piece, but please check all who-whoms, which-thats, subjects without verbs, verbs without subjects, misspellings and clichés.[6]

From 1941 to 1952 I was in *Who's Who*, and that material is correct. They hurled me later, but they weren't the first. *Johnny Got His Gun* has just been republished 20 years after it first appeared. It sells slowly, but then it never *did* sell fast. The other novels were not much good.

I am, of course, the Robert Rich who wrote the original story and screenplay of a simple—if not simple-minded—little film called *The Brave One*, for which young Rich was awarded an Oscar. He hasn't got it yet, and neither have I. However, it's just as well, for although those statues look like gold, I'm told they're nothing but pot-metal inside.

I had a play on Broadway around 1950 or '51 called *The Biggest Thief in Town*. It got even worse reviews than Dore Schary's *The Highest Tree*. Later it played for two years in London; everybody liked it, the royal family came, I was a big man. I wasn't able to enjoy that moment of tinsel triumph because the first year I was being Federally Corrected down at Ashland, Kentucky, at the tax-payers' expense, and during the second year Mrs. Shipley of the passport office found the most extraordinary reasons for confining me to the continental boundaries of the U.S.A. She was afraid that, having

---

[5] He was paid $50,000. for the script.

[6] Spectorsky, associate publisher of *Playboy* Magazine, had been impressed with Trumbo's October 24, 1959, *Nation* article, "Hail, Blithe Spirit," and had requested one for *Playboy* along with biographical material which Trumbo here supplies. The article, titled "The Oscar Syndrome," appeared in the April, 1960, issue of *Playboy*.

failed to overthrow the American government, I might mess up the international scene by actually *doing* it to the British.

I have two pleasant children in college—one at the University of Colorado (does *she* have fun!) and the other at Columbia. He was pensive on his return home for Christmas vacation. I think he misses [Charles] Van Doren. I have a third child—a blonde who is urgently beautiful—in high school, and the only woman I ever married is still at my side. She brings in extra money as a photographer, so we eat well and love each other rather more than we did on that day twenty-two years ago when each confronted the other, with justifiable suspicion, under the benign eyes of Judge Ben Lindsay, who swore us to that terrible oath never *never* to———

There's really nothing more. I think the *average* Hollwood screenplay is better written, constructed, and conceived than most Broadway hits; I like my work here and do a lot of it; toward the latter part of 1960 my name is going to appear, for the first time in 12 years, on a screenplay I've written. This, in Hollywood, will be an almost unparalleled example of freedom, truth, and virtue.

I respect every institution in America—even those not yet established—and I think that *all* members of Congress are wise, witty, and noble. My wife and I oath ourselves each morning before brushing our teeth. At a recent school saturnalia under the auspices of the PTA, I pledged allegiance twice, saluted four times, and was on my feet in solemn tribute most of the evening. Practically nobody at the school can spell, but God almighty, they're loyal. That's what counts.

I am, sir,

Suspiciously yours,
DALTON TRUMBO

5. Wire to Carl Sandburg

Los Angeles, California
January 26, 1960

Last week Mr. Otto Preminger, who produced and directed the current film *Anatomy of a Murder*, announced in a front page story in *The New York Times* that he had openly employed me to do the screenplay of *Exodus*, his next film, and that credit would be given me on the screen for the first time in 13 years of the Hollywood blacklist. *The New York Times,* New York *Post* and other papers and columnists have lauded his stand. The New York *Daily News* and *Counter-Attack* have condemned it. If you can find it in your heart to write him a letter or send him a wire approving the idea that American writers should be permitted to sign their true names to their own work, many people, including, of course, myself, will be most grateful to you. His address is: Otto Preminger, Columbia Studio, 1438 North Gower, Hollywood, California. Mr. Preminger does not know I have addressed this wire to you.

Sincerely,
DALTON TRUMBO

6. To Edward Lewis

Los Angeles, California
[c. January, 1960]
Saturday night

Dear Eddie:

This note is charged to me, not Bryna. I haven't called you because no one has called me, and I assume affairs are too hectic and complicated for much conversation . . . about what it was W[alter] W[inchell] said in the Friday *Mirror*. . . . The item read: "Dalton Trumbo, once banned by Hollywood studios for being pro-Red, doing the new script for *Spartacus*. His fee is $50,000."

It does not say that I am banned, but that I was; it does not call me a "Commie"; it does not attack me nor the people who employed me. It is as straight and objective as recent stories about me in *Newsweek, Time,* and *The New York Times* have been. That is the new atmosphere in which we're living.

The long note I sent this afternoon, based on what Winchell might have said, now becomes a fact; he has said it. WW, although I'm not his greatest admirer, is a man who hangs onto a story when he knows he's got one. He is not Mike Connelly,[7] whom everybody can and does ignore with perfect safety. . . . If you acknowledge his scoop at once, you can get him into your corner. If you deny it, he will hit you every day because he must, whether he's got mere rumor to back him or absolute proof. If he has the proof (or gets it), he's not above challenging you to put up $1,000,000 for a charity to see whether he's right or not. His attack will inevitably center on Kirk [Douglas], not on political grounds, but on the grounds Kirk has denied a news story WW knows to be true. Instant announcement of the truth, done by personal contact with Winchell, will bring him stoutly onto your side.

If a Douglas-Winchell feud develops, the whole press will naturally join in it. They will pester your cast; they will badger your two directors[8] and you; they will pursue Kirk; they will, over a

---

[7] A columnist for the *Hollywood Reporter,* now deceased.

[8] Anthony Mann who directed the first two weeks of *Spartacus* had been replaced by Stanley Kublick.

period of months, absolutely demoralize your cast. Kirk is bound to look bad, because his denial will not be believed, and will make it appear as if he has actually been engaged in dirty business.

If you deny this story, you will have a fight on your hands. Kirk's enemies will add fuel to that fight. And your fight will have a nasty look about it, not only because you're denying the truth, but because your denial implies that you are doing something wrong, nasty, criminal, underhanded—which, of course, you are not. You cannot win the fight because you cannot stop the rumor. All of you will suffer loss of prestige, of dignity by it, and it's downright stupid to suffer such losses when the other course is open.

Has Kirk deceived Laughton, Olivier, Ustinov, his two directors? Of course not. They willingly associated with his writer. They must therefore be protected, as Kirk must be, by a decisive end to any thought of deception or underhandedness.

Forget my interests, forget my desires: the objective conditions surrounding this mess-that-can-be-converted-into-a-triumph would continue to exist if I had no interest or desires. You have a simple choice: (1) You can drag this story out for as long as the film is in production [9] and *never* be believed, or (2) You can end it Monday morning with a dignified statement of the truth. Any other course is impossible because (1) it will degrade you, (2) it will prolong the crisis interminably, (3) it will not work, and (4) you will lose.

But not, I hasten to add, because of any action of mine. I will act in your behalf in good faith no matter what you decide. But remember, that's easy for me. I can't be hurt. And despite my own yearning for the sunshine, I am actually more concerned (for your own future and personal dignity as well as mine) that you act immediately in the only way that logic permits.

Sympathy and fidelity always—
SAM

7. Wire to Cedars of Lebanon Hospital, Hollywood, California

Los Angeles, California
February 6, [1960]

I wish to inform you that Saturday night between 9:25 and 9:36 I called three times asking to be connected with Mrs. Elizabeth Fincher who is my mother-in-law, who has been in your hospital

---

[9] *Spartacus* was still in post-production and Preminger had not yet announced the authorship of *Exodus*.

intermittently since May of 1959, and who has been in it, in a private room, steadily since before Christmas. On each of my three telephone calls I was informed that no such person existed in your slaughter house, and was referred to your admissions desk. I do not wish to be admitted to your hospital, and I would never again enter a dog into it. I have paid all bills regularly, and I insist that this woman be listed [with] your telephone operators, as, at least a temporary resident of the death house which you operate so expensively. If I ever call again and am told that she is not there, I shall give you all the trouble that murderers deserve. Mistakes are to be forgiven but stupidity is a crime.[10]

DALTON TRUMBO

8. Wire to Michael Wilson

Los Angeles, California
December 9, 1960

Dear Mike:

The big film [*Spartacus*] suffering from organized party cancellations and mailing and press attacks all aimed at me. Attack underway on second film [*Exodus*] opening next week including cancellations by Jewish organizations. This plus business recession has studio alarmed. Employment restrictions tighter than in last three years. Committee reported preparing for closed hearings. Pressure is on me for statement that can be used to halt organized campaign. If these films are economically damaged by my name the ban against everyone will be absolute. Kirk in London this week told by Sam Spiegel that Spiegel has protective letter from you and urges Kirk for his own good to get one from me. Will you cable me immediately Spiegel has or has not letter and write such details as will assist me.[11]

Love,
DALTON

[10] Both Elizabeth Fincher and Maud Trumbo were hospitalized, Mrs. Fincher at Cedars of Lebanon and Mrs. Trumbo at Huntington Memorial in Pasadena. Trumbo's medical expenses in 1959–1960 amounted to more than $75,000.
[11] Wilson immediately wired that he had written no such clearance letter. On December 12, Wilson elaborated by mail: he had not written a clearance letter, had no intention of doing so, and encouraged Trumbo to hold out against such an action—one that would negate all of Trumbo's efforts to kill the blacklist. Trumbo, of course, never wrote a clearance letter (See Section 9, footnote 22, pp. 493-494).

9. Extract of a letter to Robert Jennings

Los Angeles, California
December 20, 1961

Anybody connected with this [*Time*] story,[12] of course, has the right to interview anybody and seek opinions as to what my present political affiliations may be. But for myself (since everything relating to present politics at our lunch was, I believe, off the record), I should like to stand on the [notes] attached hereto, which pretty honestly summarize my feelings:

I'll open my political records to any prospective employer on the day he asks me to browse through his income tax returns.

The man who spends his life trying to prove what he isn't has a damned slim chance of ever proving what he is.

I'm perfectly willing to swear what I am, but I'm damned if I'll swear what I'm not. So long as a single witness can be found to equate advocacy with treason—and there are hordes of such witnesses—a wise man will decline to analyze every treasonable thought he didn't think.

Loyalty is what happens at night when the bonded cashier is working all alone and late, and knows the combination.

The ordinary man probably doesn't care one way or another about compulsory loyalty oaths, but they're absolutely indispensable to traitors. The first requirement of any working spy is a notarized certificate of loyalty.

I'll bet every spy we've got in jail oathed himself a dozen times before we caught up with him. As for the CIA, if it has any spies at all in Russia, you can lay your last nickel they've all signed more oaths of loyalty than Khrushchev.

I'm perfectly willing to discuss with friends or casual acquaintances how I voted in any election, but there's a curtain across the booth to keep my employer and particularly my Congressman from peering over my shoulder. It's a criminal offense, even for me, to draw the curtain aside and vote in public. I'm fond of that curtain, and whenever I'm pressured to make public announcement of what went on behind it while I was there, I clam up.

I try to support every underdog, but when he becomes an overdog I like to keep a weather eye on him.

I detest all censors, snoops, and certain cops, specifically including those of the U.S.A. and U.S.S.R. May their whole tribe simmer together in some reasonably humane, equalitarian hell.

I insist on the right of all groups, no matter how crazy, wicked, or wrong-minded they may be, to organize political parties designed

---

[12] Trumbo was featured in *Time* Magazine's "Show Business" section, January 2, 1961. Jennings, who wrote the story, had asked for a series of possible quotations.

to enact their principles into law. I also insist on my right to join them, stand apart from them, or oppose them as I choose.

10. To Robert Jennings

Los Angeles, California
December 21, 1960

Dear Bob:

Please forgive me a few last minute thoughts on the [*Time*] piece. My personal and political position, as now you know, is somewhat complex. With two major studios, simultaneously and for the first time, using my name on the screen, I feel a deep responsibility to do and say nothing that can upset the present delicate balance. My responsibility goes not only to the studios that gambled on me, but to other blacklisted persons less fortunate than I, who may be damaged or helped by what happens to me in the next three crucial months, during which I hope the impotence of the [American] Legion to keep audiences out of theatres that show uncertified films will be demonstrated for all to see. Naturally, I don't want to make the slightest slip that can be seized on by any anti-Trumbo fringe group, or that will reflect in any way on the people who have employed me or the pictures which have resulted.

I do therefore hope there will be no implication of contempt, hostility, or flippancy on my part toward U[nited] A[rtists], U[niversal]-I[nternational], or [Otto] Preminger and [Kirk] Douglas. The officials of U-I, in their multi-million dollar *Spartacus* gamble, have behaved extraordinarily well toward me throughout what has, for them, been a difficult public relations period. I never asked that my name be used on *Spartacus*, and they, by contract, had the right to use any other name they chose or none at all. It was their decision to put my name up, and I think it a decision that honors them. And it certainly was not reached without considerable and justifiable misgivings.

Despite the Legion resolution, and occasional picketing by its satellites, the people at U-I have never once pressured me to reply to political accusations with political denials. On the contrary, their dealings with me continue to this day to be forthright, courteous, and decent. This, in my experiece, is a rare thing. I could not forgive myself if by any inadvertent word or act I should give them cause to regret what they have done, or cause other studios to draw back from dealings with other blacklisted persons.

I don't recall exactly what was on record and what was off, for we rambled widely, since I was trying to give you the entire picture from which we could winnow for the record such parts as suited your purpose. I should like, therefore, to consider as privileged anything I may have told you concerning complications of maneuverings that went on behind the scenes during the writing and filming of *Spartacus* (and *Exodus* also), and particularly anything that would reflect on the integrity and intelligence of Bryna and UA or U-I officials.

Then again—and this is a matter of the writer's attitude toward the material—while I understand that politics and biography can scarcely be separated in my case, I hope that nothing will appear in the piece that can give effective ammunition to organizations or people who would dearly love to gun me down. I don't, of course, want to be whitewashed (who's got that much whitewash anyhow?), and I know that a certain attitude of defiance on my part is inherent in the story. I only hope the defiance will seem amusing rather than grim, not altogether extraordinary, but actually a defiance that comes quite naturally to a normal, healthy American male of my advanced years.

I am, I believe, correct in assuming that (1) there will be no mention of what I told you about the UNO organizational conference in San Francisco, (2) that all inside details about both films are off the record, (3) that if Oscars are mentioned, none but the Rich award be attributed or implied to me, (4) that there was nothing of the warrior-hero in my sixty day tour of the Pacific area in 1945.

It's simply outrageous that I have written this letter. I assure you that I do not really take myself as solemnly as it makes me seem to, and that it does not imply the faintest mistrust of your professional confidence or literary skill. It's simply that fourteen years of handling my own relations with the press during times far more difficult than these have bred in me a caution that perhaps does me small credit. The whole blacklist situation at this moment is in such a delicate state of balance, and the careers of so many people depend on tipping the balance against blacklisting, that I could never forgive myself if an act or word or interview of mine should backfire to the disadvantage of all the others.

D.T.

11. Extract of a letter to Alvah Bessie

Los Angeles, California
January 3, 1961

Although each personal breakthrough,[13] I now reluctantly begin to see, will have to be made individually, *Exodus* and *Spartacus* have proved at least *one* thing that previously would not have been believed by any producer or distributor in the country; both have been the subject of denunciatory national Legion resolutions, both have been picketed (the first films in many years to endure this hazard), and both have been attacked in certain sections of the press—all for the association of my name with the two films. Yet I enclose weekly *Variety*'s most recent "National Boxoffice Survey" (Wednesday, December 28, 1960)—which shows that in terms of cash revenue *Exodus* is number one nationally and *Spartacus* is number two. The two films will shift back and forth between those two positions for many many weeks in the future.

This proves to the banks, the distributors, the studios, and the organizations and press of the right that, ordinarily, good films cannot be financially damaged by political attack, threatened boycott, and actual picketing. Not in today's climate, at least. This *has* to be, in one degree or another, a victory for every blacklisted person, since it knocks the props out from under the principal economic reason for blacklisting him. It cannot hurt him, therefore; it can only make easier his personal struggle to break through. To understand the degree of this, consider what would have happened to blacklisted persons not yet in the daylight, if the campaigns against *Spartacus* and *Exodus* had succeeded in frightening the public away from them, and thereby placed them in the category of financial flops. I, for one, would never have been able to work again, and those who do not yet work openly would have even a slighter chance than I of making it. Instead, the two films that have borne the main attack (and with mixed reviews, to boot!) stand first and second nationally in terms of box-office cash.

Remember, please God, no quotes, no attributions of any of this material. It sounds too damned self-congratulatory and solemn. Nonetheless, it's my view of the truth. . . .

In other words, you have forgotten every personal thing I told you in the course of the past two years about either of these films. You are a journalist, writing independently, writing even (save the mark!) objectively; and I am a writer, a screen writer as it happens,

---

[13] Bessie was writing an article for *Frontier* on *Exodus* and *Spartacus*. He asked Trumbo two questions: first, to account for Trumbo's breakthrough and to analyze why other talented blacklistees had not yet achieved open credits; second, to assess what effect Trumbos breakthrough and the success of the two films in question would have upon the talented black market writers.

whose work you are commenting on just as objectively as if we had never met, just as objectively as if I were Morrie Ryskind.[14] Only then, in my view, can your piece come off as a piece of critical evaluation on the highest level. In this piece you and I are not friends. You are a critic, and I am one of those whose collective work you are criticizing. Tear my ass off where I'm wrong. Make no excuses for me. Then you'll have a piece that will draw respect to you, and help me by indicating wherein I'm good and wherein I'm bad. We're too old to backscratch each other publicly, and we're too widely known as friends to get away with it.

12. To Mr. M. D. Fraider

New York City
March 4, 1961

Dear Mr. Fraider: [15]

I'm terribly sorry the *Time* piece has had the effect of increasing both your and Mr. Sullivan's work.[16] The truth is that the quotation

[14] Ryskind, screen writer and columnist, was one of the right wing, "friendly" witnesses of the 1947 hearings. He is now a columnist for the Hearst papers.

[15] Fraider was a lawyer specializing in tax matters who represented Trumbo during the Federal tax investigation.

[16] This letter can best be explained by Trumbo's note of October 1, 1962: "There are many hazards and losses to which a writer in the black market quickly becomes accustomed. Since the employment is completely secret, there can be no withholding for social security. There can be no state unemployment insurance. All company retirement funds are automatically cancelled. For a period of five or six years, it was next to impossible to purchase life insurance. (Just two months ago, I was written up in rates by my insurance company because of my past political record.)

During the first ten years of the blacklist, when everyone was informing on everyone else, no sane employer in the black market would draw a check to the name of a blacklisted person, lest some bank clerk report passage of the check to trade papers or some friend of the committee. The Motion Picture Alliance for the Preservation of American Ideals, headed by Sam Wood, James K. McGuinness, Morrie Ryskind, Adolphe Menjou, Ward Bond, George Murphy, Hedda Hopper, Lela Rogers (mother of Ginger), John Wayne, and other patriots, had its representatives and informants in every firm in Hollywood that did business of any sort with the studios. It was a happy, happy community.

During this period I used as pseudonyms such names as John Abbott, Doc Abbott, James Bonham, Theodore Flexman, C. F. Demaine, Evelyn Bonham, Sam Jackson, Peter Flint, and various others. In order to cash checks made out to such names, my wife and I opened an account under the names of James and Dorothy Bonham. Then we forged the name of the person to whom the check was made out, endorsed it over to ourselves (James and/or Dorothy about lying, as well as the other quotes with which the piece concluded, was ironically intended; and, like most irony, sought to make its point by turning truth upside down.

As an instance, I have just read Ezra Goodman's new volume entitled *The Fifty-Year Decline and Fall of Hollywood*. On page 28 I find the following paragraph:

Dalton Trumbo once had the fairly final words to say on Hollywood's multifarious awards: "The man doesn't live who can spend a decade in motion pictures without accumulating at least one diplomat-size brief case full of kudos. I've got three gold certificates with blue ribbon, two medals, a bronze plaque and $736,000 in the bank . . . I recommend certificates and citations above holloware (bronze can cost you your life) because they're easy to lift, they pack flat, and you can always run faster with them."

Bonham), deposited it in the Bonham account. Then when we wished to place money in our regular commercial checking account, we withdrew it from the Bonham account, and placed it in our Trumbo account at another bank. Thus there was no connection between Trumbo and the producers in terms of money transactions.

Inevitably such procedure, combined with trade paper rumors of vast sums flowing under the table to blacklisted writers, compelled the interest of the Federal government. Late in 1960, due to a fatuous error on my part, the Treasury Department overnight subpoenaed all records from my two accountants, and summoned me to appear.

It was not to be an ordinary income tax audit. It was a criminal investigation conducted by a special intelligence agent of the Treasury Department. They investigate, I understand, about 3,000 cases a year; indict 1,400 and secure convictions in about 1,200. The instant you are in special intelligence investigation the chances are about 1 in 3 you'll end up in a Federal penitentiary. It is not a happy prospect.

. . . .

Unlike most businessmen, who understand tax matters, I had not destroyed my financial records at the end of every three or six years. I had (and have) them in the greatest detail for the past 22 years. It was the records that saved me—plus at least three months of my own time spent poring over them, trying to remember obscure notes and odd figures seeking to reconstruct my reasons, in 1958, for wiring $2.50 to the County Clerk of Fresno County. The government had a copy of the wire. They concluded it related to hidden real estate. Actually, it was for my wife's birth certificate. Thus it went, an endless mountain of detail to plow through, including a complete audit of the years 1957, 1958, and 1959.

Of the matter, I will say three things.

1. The circumstances which caused my error could never have occurred in the ordinary market, only in the secrecy and fiscal confusion of the black market.
2. Special agent Sullivan, who was assigned the case, and, of course, had worked on it a good time before I knew it was even contemplated, was a serious, courteous, correct and very efficient man. Given the preliminary evidence which he gathered, I, in his position, would have decided, as

That sounds like a direct and recent quotation. Actually, it derives from a satirical piece on the Academy Awards written by me some ten years ago and published in *Theatre Arts*. The whole quotation is wildly improbable and was intended to be. Instead of having "$736,000 in the bank" at that time, my best recollection tells me I was broke, unemployed, and several thousand dollars in the hole.

The quotation at issue on lying was taken from a letter which I wrote to my son several years ago, in which I satirized Lord Chesterfield's letters of moral and social advice to his son by giving *my* son immoral and anti-social guidance. I counseled him on four issues: borrowing (always borrow more than you need, since you'll never be able to borrow again from the same person anyhow), lying (as quoted in *Time*), stealing (as also quoted), and girls (how to discover whether or not a girl will date you without directly asking her and thereby risking rejection). The whole letter was so manifestly absurd that my son had copies struck off for his friends. I suspect that I still have one of those copies somewhere around the house.

Somewhat later our daughter spent a year in Europe, and I dispatched to her a long letter in which I detailed the various sexual approaches of European males, and outlined techniques of avoidance by which an American girl could frustrate them all.[17] (Last summer, while I was in Vienna, she sent *me* a letter in the same mocking vein, explaining how a middle-aged American male in Europe could best evade designing foreign females.)

During my son's first year in college, the publisher sent me a

---

he did, that the case warranted criminal investigation. I've never seen such a convincing mass of suspicious details and coincidences. I can feel no ill will toward special agent Sullivan or local officials for what happened.

3. But the regional official in San Francisco who, on the basis of an ironic quotation in a national magazine [In *Time,* January 2, 1961, Trumbo's September 1, 1956 (Section 6, #13, pp. 344-346) letter to Christopher had been quoted, 'On Lying: let the lie be delivered full-face, eye to eye, and without scratching of the scalp, but let it, for all its simplicity, contain one fantastical element of creative ingenuity!'] overruled the Los Angeles office's recommendation to drop the case, ordered the investigation to be reopened, and then was "reluctantly" obliged to terminate it—this fellow had something more than taxes on his mind. He had politics and personal opinions also, and he should not have. He is rather a high official in the regional offices of the revenue department (I don't know who he is, and I fancy he will not forget my name. Hence I can expect special treatment from him whenever he is in a position to administer it.)

P.S. Many producers paid only in cash. I received $26,000 in cash on one occasion, $10,00 on another, and many lesser sums. Cash excites the feds.

[17] See letter of September 3, 1956, to Nikola (Section 6, #14, pp. 346-352).

complimentary copy of *Sex Without Guilt* by Albert Ellis, Ph.D. I promptly labeled it a "manual on masturbation," wrote a long review of it in the style of Nabokov's *Lolita*, and mailed it to my son.[18] Or—in another vein—when my wife and I returned a couple of years ago from a session with the Mayo Brothers, we received a letter from the Franklin Hotel, at which we stayed while in Rochester, thanking us for our patronage and politely hoping that our stay with the hotel was a comfortable one. I shot off eight full pages informing them in great detail that our stay had *not* been comfortable, analyzing all the specific discomforts to which I alleged the hotel had submitted us during our stay.[19]

In other words, I fear that writers are somewhat like actors; they utter words which in no way reflect their personal feelings—words which are designed merely to be entertaining, or amusing, or shocking, or absurd. If I really believed that lying was admirable, I should myself be a liar, and a practicing one at that. As such, I would go to great lengths to conceal my moral deficiency, rather than expose it as the *Time* piece does.

I just remember that last week I gave an interview here in which I was asked to summarize my philosophy of life. I answered, "If you can't join 'em, beat 'em," which is an opposite of sorts. I also said, "I ask very little of life, and the trouble is, I'm getting it." But those I promise you will be the last—at least until we get this tax mess straightened out.

Cordially,
DALTON TRUMBO

13. To Otto Preminger

Los Angeles, California
May 7, 1961

Dear Otto:

I came home, bearing my two copies of *Bunny* [*Lake Is Missing*]. I put them on my desk and left them there for four or five days. Friday I opened the top copy and read it carefully from beginning to end. I took a nap. I awakened and read it again. My first feelings were confirmed. The script is no good. We have wasted our time.

The script is not *about* anything. Perhaps it *could* have been

[18] See letter of November 8, 1958, to Christopher (Section 8, #14, pp. 443-451).

[19] See letter of December 9, 1958, to Mr. William Hunt of the Franklin Hotel (Section 8, #16, pp. 455-464).

about the cruelty of society, conscious or unconscious, toward a young woman who has had the misfortune to give birth to an illegitimate child. Perhaps it *could* have been about the dangers and stupidities of amateur psychiatry, since we live in a time when everyone fancies himself a psychiatrist and does not hesitate to pass judgments and give advice based upon this half-knowledge we all seem to think we possess—judgments and advice which are dangerous and sometimes vicious. Then we could have had a young woman, surrounded and almost destroyed by this miasmatic tide of ignorance, clinging to reality—herself the only normal person of the lot. Or perhaps it could have been something inestimably better. But as matters stand, it is about nothing.[20]

The invention of the characters of Louise, Newhouse and Kendall in their relationships to each other as we presently have them now strikes me as a confession of basic weakness, and an attempt to avoid it which fails. Because there seemed no way to make Blanche herself interesting, we decided to get away from her, to avoid the challenge she presented by inventing other characters who would be interesting. Our evasion did not and does not work, and was in itself primary evidence of our basic error.

. . . .

Examine our individual scenes. There is not a cinema scene among them. They are nothing but talk, each torrent of dialogue conducted against a static set. They are invariably scenes either of exposition or of debate. And that is all they are. The one movie scene we did have—the chase through the dark house—we have replaced with a long, climactic debate. I don't defend the chase scene, but at the very least, it was movie. Now we have not one single movie scene in the whole piece.

. . . .

I think you should postpone this film for at least a year—or, conceivably, drop it altogether. Somehow we should have known that when we found ourselves wrangling patiently over words, over mere lines, something was wrong. Perhaps we trusted each other too much. Perhaps we should not have tried to force the story into our pre-

---

[20] Blanche Lake delivers her illegitimate daughter, Bunny, at Louise Benton's school in the morning. When she goes to claim the child that afternoon, not only is the child not there but the school records disclose that she was never enrolled and never attended. Louise Benton and her psychiatrist lover, Newhouse, think Blanche insane. Newspaper photographer Wilson, however, befriends and believes in Blanche even though no record reveals the birth or existence of the child. Finally, Newhouse, persuaded to help, suspects that Louise Benton's sponsor—rich, five-time divorcé, Kendall Betaincourt—has kidnaped the child from the school. When suspicions are confirmed Blanche confronts Kendall and pleads for Bunny, who, as the women struggle for possession of her, innocently attempts to suffocate herself with a plastic bag in Kendall's locker bathroom. Finally the victorious Blanche rescues her child.

arranged plot. But to hell with perhaps: the stone cold truth is that I have written you a damned bad script, and unless you are absolutely certain that you want to do it, that you can bring to it through direction everything it now so patently lacks—you should not make it. If you do, I think it will be a disaster.

It is bad enough that you and I, working very hard and for a protracted time, should have come up with a bad script; but to go ahead and compound the error by deliberately making a bad picture would be unforgivable.

If you are sure—*if you are absolutely certain*—that you can make a successful film based on all or any part of this script, then I will stick with you till the bitter end; I will write and re-write till the day you begin to shoot, and even after; I will do everything in my power to improve chances which I now think so slim. I will even demand a full card on the screen, with my name in enormous letters, and credit in all advertising, if for no other reason than to inform the world that I am as willing to share a disaster with you as I was to share a success.

Call the scripts in and burn them, cancel or postpone the picture, fire my son,[21] post notices in the press that I have perpetrated an obscenity, circularize the Screen Producers Guild with warnings against me—but do not make this film! [22]

Affectionately,
DALTON

14. To Writers' Service, Los Angeles, California

Los Angeles, California
June 18, 1961

Dear Miss Tatum:

I think perhaps the planets weren't very favorably disposed toward any of us last Friday and Saturday. I mailed three copies of your mimeographed script without reading it. On doing so, I found sixteen pages with typos on them, one of them hilariously Freudian in nature and somewhat disadvantageous to the leading lady.

In any event, I am returning to you all the remaining scripts, the

---

[21] Christopher had worked on *Exodus,* ending up with a screen credit as second assistant director. Preminger had offered a similar job on *Bunny Lake Is Missing.* Christopher has since married and continues working in films as a writer.

[22] Preminger abandoned the film for a time, then had the script rewritten and shot it in London.

one to which this note is attached being the corrected master copy. Pages containing typos are marked "X" in upper right-hand corner, with typo or typos clearly marked where they occur. . . .

I have decided to do a little correction of my own on pages . . . . These pages I have marked with * in upper right-hand corner, with the changes printed in or pasted on the page.

Will you run off the corrected and changed pages as quickly as convenient, insert them in the scripts, and return the batch to me by ABC?

Please don't feel upset about the errors, and don't flog anyone for them. I have a film in current release called *The Last Sunset* which scarcely qualifies me to rebuke anyone for momentary inefficiency. If, by some misfortune, you should blunder into a theatre playing it, you will understand at once why my mood is so forgiving.

Cordially,
DALTON TRUMBO

15. To Joan Lewis[23]

Los Angeles, California

Nineteen Hundred Sixty-One
Aug-13, the day is Sun

Dear Miss Lewis—or may I call you Joan?
I've lately come to love the telephone

Because its GRanite-Ashdale end
Has given me a charming friend,

Who answers instantly I've dialed,
And talks to me—that lovely child!—

As if I were her equal, which I'm not.
(I'm only partly so, or just somewhat.)

And so, before she goes to Mexico,
I thought I'd write and tell her so,

And seal the message with a kiss
To wish her years and years of bliss,

[23] Daughter of Edward Lewis.

And sign the message with regret
That she is such a young coquette,

So young, in fact, that she can never be
A grown-up woman for the man who's me,

While I myself can never hope again
To be—with her—a child of ten.

Trapped thus by time, I'm only what I am—
Her middle-aged admirer,

UNCLE SAM

16. To President John F. Kennedy

Los Angeles, California
September 5, 1961

Dear Mr. President:

I enclose herewith a copy of a letter I've written today to Mr. Konstantin Simonov of the Writers' Union of the U.S.S.R. which expresses the feelings of at least one American about the resumption of nuclear testing by the Soviet Union.

The poise and confidence with which your administration has confronted this terrible event should, and I'm sure does, command the respect and admiration of the entire world.[24]

Sincerely,
DALTON TRUMBO

---

[24] On reading the Kennedy letter, Trumbo suggested that it be cut because "although at the time I think I was not conscious of it, the letter now smacks of ass-kissing and self service." There could, however, have been an additional reason for sending it: at a time when the American Legion and other groups were picketing *Spartacus* in various cities, President Kennedy violated White House tradition by unexpectedly attending a regular Washington showing of the film and commenting favorably on it to the press. Trumbo felt the incident was not accidental, and admired the President for it.

17. To Mr. Konstantin Simonov

Los Angeles, California
September 5, 1961

Dear Mr. Simonov:

During your wartime visit to the United States under the auspices of the State Department it was my pleasure to give you a reception at our house in Beverly Hills. During my subsequent imprisonment in the Federal Correctional Institution at Ashland, Kentucky, I received on New Year's Day of 1951, at the height of the Korean War, a cable from you and nineteen other Soviet Writers thanking me for my part in "the struggle for world peace," and wishing me well in the forthcoming year.

I'm afraid I haven't contributed significantly to the struggle for world peace or anything else, but it is true that during most of my adult life I have spoken frequently and publicly against those policies of the American government with which I found myself in disagreement. Sometimes I spoke wisely and sometimes not, but always I spoke what was in my heart. This I believe to be the obligation of all citizens of all countries and, considering the temper of the times, I've suffered very little from it.

I have, however, never criticized my government while outside its national territories. This springs from a conviction that the most effective criticism of national policy comes from citizens living under the national authority and participating in the life of the national community. Dissent from citizens residing outside the country, or from citizens of other countries, is automatically, and sometimes justifiably, suspect: being suspect, it is ineffective. The primary responsibility of each citizen of every country is the rectitude of his own government.

There are times, however, when the action of a particular government becomes the concern of all other governments and peoples. Recent examples, about which I'm sure we can find a measure of agreement, are the action of the Soviet government against Hungary, of the Anglo-Franco-Israeli governments against Egypt, and of the American government against Cuba. In times of such actions it seems perfectly proper for citizens of one country to communicate their apprehensions to citizens of another, since only the citizens of a given country—and never the citizens of another country—have the right and power to change their government's conduct.

As an American citizen speaking to a Soviet citizen in the month of September, 1961, I refer to the recent decision of the Soviet government to abandon the moratorium on nuclear testing; its announced intention to manufacture a bomb in the power range of 100 megatons; and the two nuclear explosions which occurred so shortly thereafter in Central Asia.

I am aware that the Soviet government was most active in initiating the test ban, for which it won the approbation of the world. I am also aware that the Soviet government and press have consistently warned against the dangers of test resumption, and that Premier Khrushchev only last year warned the world that "the first government to resume tests will bear a grave responsibitly to mankind . . ."

The event has now occurred—a tragedy even as matters presently stand, but a tragedy to be redoubled when the United States feels itself compelled by the inexorable logic of Soviet bombs to resume testing its own. Already the action of the Soviet government has brought the world a step closer to the irreversible genetic degeneration of the human race, or its practical annihilation. Tomorrow the United States may feel itself compelled to take the second step. And then . . . who may take the third and last?

I am bewildered by the Soviet Peace Committee's approval of Soviet nuclear testing as the necessary handmaiden to world peace, and appalled by a statement of the Organization of Soviet Biologists that "renewal of explosions of nuclear weapons under the present conditions is in the interest of . . . the whole progress of mankind."

As an American citizen I have no standing before the Soviet government, and no power to alter its decisions. You, who are a Soviet citizen, do have such standing and such power. Beyond that, you are a writer, and it has always been the honor and burden of our profession to speak out against any action of government which turns its course even momentarily against the just claims of humanity.

For years in the United States, the United Kingdom, and France, men and women of widely different political groupings and religious faiths—writers, scientists, educators, clergymen, artists—have dissented from numerous aspects of their governments' nuclear policies. They have dissented publicly and emphatically, sometimes successfully, and sometimes to no avail. The important thing is that the dissent has been openly made; that the argument has been heard—not decided on, but heard.

For six tense days the world has been waiting once more for the voice of dissent—this time from the Soviet Union. The issue confronting Soviet writers is far more important than the plight of a briefly imprisoned American writer which caused them to speak in unison ten years ago. The issue today is peace or death for mankind. If you and other Soviet writers who cabled me on New Year's Day in 1951 should lift your voices again, this time to the Soviet government in a concert of protest against the resumption of nuclear tests, the course of history might be changed and the peace saved.

In writing to you in this fashion I have denied myself the luxury of denigrating adjectives which should, in any event, be barred from all forms of political discourse. Neither have I attempted to argue my point of view, nor to anticipate those arguments you yourself could present were we to descend to points and feints and debates. No government on earth has been so consistently right these past twenty years that it can charge another with consistent wrong. This letter goes from my concern to your concern—from my heart to yours—and the best answer to it cannot be addressed to me.

> *With all good wishes, I am*
> *Your friend,*
> DALTON TRUMBO

18. To *The Saturday Evening Post,* Philadelphia, Pennsylvania

> *Los Angeles, California*
> *September 14, 1961*

Re: Ring Lardner Jr. Article
Gentlemen:

I presume there will be some brief identification beneath the photo your representative has just taken.[25] I hope it will not be pejorative in nature, since my position, in the sense of public relations, is quite delicate.

Actually, I consider myself a thorough non-odd ball, and am always surprised when others think differently. I've earned my living as a writer for the past thirty years: four novels, one of which (*Johnny Got His Gun*) won a National Booksellers Award; about fifty movies, one of which (*The Brave One*) won an Academy Award for Robert Rich, alias me; a play that flopped here and hit in England; and a new movie (*Lonely Are the Brave*) in the can and due for winter release. That does it.

I date all of my trouble from the day I first began to sell. That was in 1936, when the *Post* published my first short story.[26] So the whole damned mess is your fault. Since I'm thus established as your baby, if you can't be proud, at least be merciful.

> *Cordially,*
> DALTON TRUMBO

[25] An article by Ring Lardner, Jr., "My Life on the Blacklist," appeared in *The Saturday Evening Post,* October 14, 1961. Trumbo was pictured and identified as the once mysterious Robert Rich.
[26] Trumbo refers to "Darling Bill—."

19. Extract of a letter to Otto Preminger

Los Angeles, California
September 19, 1961

I see you've found youself a former senator to play that somnolent old cocker who always votes nay, thereby neatly casting me out of your goddam picture.[27] It's just as well, because I've got too much principle to let you exploit me on the screen without proper billing. I'm much hotter than Lew Ayers and I know it, so that's the way the billing would have had to be. I'll make no charge for all those hours I've sat before my mirror rehearsing how to wake up and holler no. I finally got it right by trying to imagine I was genial old gelatinous Charley Laughton. Have you ever tried to imagine being Charles Laughton? Has he?

20. To Melissa Trumbo

Los Angeles, California
October 4, 1961

Sing hymns, ring bells, beat drum and tambourine!
Bring laurels, musk, seed-pearls, and serpentine!
Cheer fiercely at the ascent of our newest family queen,
Whose reign of terror opened on the day she turned sixteen!

I gladly cheer, but tell me—is she sweet, or is she mean?
Is she gluttonous at table—is she lean?
Is there a glow when she appears—or just a sheen?
Is her adolescent mind a little dull—or is it keen?
Does her walk reveal some inner grace—or does she only preen?
Does seeing please her somewhat more than merely being seen?
Are her secret little private thoughts impure, or just obscene?
And regardless of her morals, does she smell good, is she clean?

Do you dig me, chick?
Do you glean
What I mean?

— POP

The briefer lines that just precede my name
May indicate to stupid folk the purpose of my game

---

[27] The picture referred to is Preminger's *Advise and Consent,* in which Preminger had threatened to cast Trumbo as a somnolent, dissenting senator.

Is to tell you that you do not wash—in short, that you are dirty;

But they're fools,
Or, more conceivably, they're ghouls—

Because, although you're sadly squirty,
And there's no doubt that you're flirty,
And voluminously skirty,
And conceivably and probably subverty . . .
You were never never *never* never never never dirty!

21. To Nelson Algren, c/o *The Nation*

Los Angeles, California
Nov. 8, 1961

Dear Nelson:

Your piece on Hemingway did the job. You're a good man and getting better every day, as good men always do.

The seasonal shit seems a lot runnier than it used to be. I remember when kids molded their own father-images from the stuff. Now it's only fit for finger-painting.

How the hell are you? and where?

Sincereliestly yours,
DALTON TRUMBO

22. To Nikola Trumbo

Los Angeles, California
November 11, 1961

Dear Nikola:

I'm hideously engaged at the moment completing a rewrite of *Montezuma*, a first draft of *The Walls of Jolo*, and starting a first draft of *Hawaii*. Simultaneously, I'm appalled to say. This note will, in consequence, be hasty, although it has not been hastily conceived.

I'm thoroughly opposed to your idea of remaining on in Boulder after you've completed your present (and degree) term. Wherever in the world you may be in June, you'll be only one day's flight from Boulder, and we can all foregather there for the ceremony. I see no point at all in wasting the first four months of your twenty-third year in a town and community which now belongs entirely to the past, working at starvation wages in a profession you plainly do not intend to make your own.

You are now an adult. You should be looking forward to an independent life of work and social pleasure among the sort of people to whom you are accustomed—very few of whom are to be found in such backwashes of the country as Boulder, Denver, or, indeed, any other Rocky Mountain community. During the next few years of your life (which should be the most exciting and stimulating also) you should be at the center of things, not on the periphery.

I feel that as soon as you have completed the present semester you should cut all emotional and geographical ties with undergraduate life and ways. You should be eager to leave the last phase of your life behind and to embrace the next one. You should be making positive and decisive plans for your future in advance of completing your studies, rather than vacillating for no discernible reason at all between work in a Denver telephone company and instructing on the local campus.

I can understand why you would not wish to live in Los Angeles under the parental eye, even though separately domiciled. But I cannot believe you would be reluctant to strike out on your own in a city like New York, and do not understand why you have not made efforts in that direction.

In New York, for example, you will find many family friends to bridge the gulf between girlhood and womanhood. You will, moreover, soon discover on your own, or through present friends, all sorts of active, stimulating, creative contemporaries. You have a good background for any sort of creative enterprise, plus an education. In many employment areas your name will be advantageous rather than the contrary. You should have no difficulty in finding work— even though at first it be no more important than that of receptionist —in the general field of books and magazines; theatrical, literary, and advertising agencies; film and theatrical management and production offices; and a dozen other places.

You should have a small apartment of your own (not luxurious, I'm afraid) in which you live your own life. You should resolve to live within the limits of your income (although at the outset we can supplement it until you have matters leveled off), arrange your own budget, pay your own bills, and, in all general ways, enter the grownup stage of living for which you are now excellently prepared.

It is our desire also that you live *alone* for a substantial time. It is the only way to live truly free, and it is an excellent way to savor your own resources. You would be living in one of the great world centers of art, music, literature, and theatre. Each evening there is an incredible variety of choices and with forethought and attention to cheap seats, a good many will be within your budget—not to mention the presence in the neighborhood of young men who may take it into their foolish heads to dine and free-seat you from time to time. For cost-free idle hours there's a dazzling galaxy of libraries, museums, universities—enough to fill the surplus minutes of a dozen lives, much less of your own necessarily short one. You must grab that life now, and use it to the fullest.

In your new state of self-sufficiency and ultimately self-support, you will win a completely new circle of friends, all engaged in the actual work of a career (or toward marriage), as you will also be. You will, in a word, be independent. Also happy. In Boulder you will only vegetate, serenely and expensively, with a friend and a cat. That's for old age, child—not for youth.[28]

Much, much love,
DADDY

23. To Christopher Trumbo

Los Angeles, California
November 27, 1961

Dear old boy—
. . . .

For your next semester at Columbia I am going to make it an absolute requirement of your education that you see *every* Broadway and *Off Broadway* show that lasts more than two weeks. After you've done this a while, you'll be able to sniff out in advance, and attend the shows that are worthy of success (or at least attention) but will fail before two weeks.

You are missing so *much* of a city about which you now know a great deal! The terms I intend to *try* to impose on you in the future will be much less monastic than those you have thus far imposed on yourself.

Love—
POP

[28] Nikola moved to San Francisco.

24. To Albert Maltz

Los Angeles, California
[*c. late 1961 or early 1962*]

There are a number of reasons why that *Variety* ploy won't and can't work.[29]

1. *Spartacus* (cost $10.5 million) did $19 million world-wide in only 528 theatres. Its mass distribution hasn't even happened yet.

2. *Exodus* (cost $3.5 million) did $14 million in under 400 houses, world-wide.

3. It seems probable that these two films, costing $14 million will, by the time they've ended their runs, have brought into the box-office somewhere between $40 and $50 million.

4. To those who really feel that they *need* my work and services, the figures above prove that the rather consistent picketing by the Legion, the Nazi Party, and Youth for Freedom groups, cannot and does not hurt a film the public wishes to see, regardless of my name. Conversely, the economic success of the two films proves to them that such wide-spread acceptance indicates that far more Legionnaires went to those films than were persuaded not to go.

5. The few who are willing to employ me do so because my name seems to them to be a guarantee of financial success. Even that abomination, *The Last Sunset,* will not lose money, as it deserves to. It won't make, but it won't lose—so even my flops, they feel, do not make red ink for them.

6. I was employed for *Hawaii* because they were desperate, and they felt I could cure their problem. If they had felt anyone else could do it better than I, they would not have risked the unpleasantness of my name, and the inconvenience of public attack. They are shrewd men; they took the risk calculatingly, in full knowledge of what could happen.

7. One reason they will not be intimidated is that they want the script I'm writing for them. A second reason is that if they do fire me, they will still have to pay my full fee.

8. Their attorney was at *Variety* next morning raising hell. In other words, their attorney now fights for me rather than against me.

9. [Fred] Zinnemann prepared and gave out a statement which was firm and completely unapologetic.

10. Not one trade paper, not one Los Angeles paper, not one news service touched the story. Weekly *Variety* ran it, as it was almost obliged to, in briefer form, but I know of no other publication in the country that gave it the slightest notice. So the story flopped on the day it was born.

11. *Since* the story broke, I have been signed for two pictures

[29] The American Legion had attempted a renewed attack on Trumbo's politics in *Variety.*

to one of the big independents, full salary for each plus 25% of the *negative* each.

12. *Since* the story broke, I have been talking deal with one of the biggest stars (male) in the business (a new one for me), and he wants to make the deal now, and I have declined, saying I prefer to do the script on my own from my own story, and then if he wants it he may have it.

13. *The Lonely and the Brave* [sic] is ready now, will be released in the spring, and in my opinion it's a lovely, simple, moving job. That will help, because I think people will like it a good deal.

14. I have still to do, for UA after *Hawaii*, one more film, as contracted for.

15. Plus two other films, one to be released by U-I, the other by Columbia.

16. In other words *Lonely Are the Brave* is ready for release, *Hawaii* is in progress, *Montezuma* [30] is almost ready to go; and after them, I hold iron-clad contracts for five additional films, with one or two extra as distinct possibilities. The body of product in release, ready for release, and in work (all of it contracted for in full knowledge of the risks involved in my name), plus the five future commitments, constitute too much money and too large a number of films to be easily knocked over by some jerk who is merely a tenth ranking officer in but one of the fifty American Legion state organizations.

I was offered a debate with the Legion and turned it down. I was offered my own show for my own purposes and turned it down. To debate with the Legion now, or at any other time, would, in my opinion, revert the dialogue to the level of 1947, which would be a great step backward. To defend myself against an attack which had no power and no effective distribution would have been, in this instance, to publicize for the Legion what they, without my assistance, could not have publicized. The attack infected only a few people; to have defended myself against something the overwhelming majority of people had never read would [have] served the Legion purpose of infecting hundreds of thousands, or even millions.

The situation in the country today, which of course affects the situation of blacklistees, is so curious that I think one almost has to live in it, to smell and sniff it daily, to get the hang of it. I see it this way:

The extreme right, in all its varied and wonderful forms, is no longer *fundamentally* interested in Communists, ex-Communists, crypto-Communists, etc. It knows perfectly well that the Communists have been smashed, that they have not one iota of influence on any even small segment of American society, that the sup-

---

[30] *Montezuma* was never made.

port or endorsement of any progressive movement or objective by Communists is the worst thing that can happen to it.

The attack against Communists and so-called Communists, once specific, is now merely general. The specific attack now is directed against 'liberals'—a term which includes most Democrats, not a few Republicans, all artists and all intellectuals. At their large public rallies these people don't attack Elizabeth Curley Flynn, they attack Eleanor Roosevelt. They don't want to lynch Ben Davis, they want to impeach Chief Justice Warren. They make no mention of Gus Hall, they take out after Stevenson and Bowles and Kennedy. They bow low before the international Communist conspiracy, but their specific attack is on the United Nations.

This time they are not merely after the Democratic administration, they are after the government of the United States itself. They want to take possession of that government for themselves, and then to change or subvert it from constitutional democracy to constitutional autocracy. Their ends are revolutionary, and the government against which their revolution is aimed is the United States of America.

In such circumstances, the 'liberals'—i.e., the government, the universities, the establishment, so to speak—must defend themselves or, in very large areas, go under. In the course of their own self-defense, the basic law which protects such rights as I still may have must be defended also.

Therefore, I have no intention of defending myself if, through some fluke, some of them were temporarily diverted from the main target to a side-swipe at me which might, for all I know, destroy me. I have defended certain rights until I am powerless to defend them further. The main attack has swept by me, and now is aimed straight for the major target. Therefore those now under attack must defend themselves and, whether they like it or not, me too, since any defense of such constitutional liberties as still exist—and they are considerable—is also a defense of my liberty. It's their job, not mine.

Of course if a sudden, and improbable, concentration were made on me, I would fight—but fight or not, I should probably lose unless the establishment were simultaneously fighting in defense of itself. If the establishment chooses to surrender, I'll go down automatically and completely. If the establishment resists, then my resistance will be strengthened.

In the meanwhile, I won't even consider fighting—nor do I think, tactically, should anyone else—unless and until these people are able to mount and sustain a national campaign specifically directed against me or them. This they have tried to do for over two years, plus their picketing, and they have failed to get the thing going.

In fact, up to now, the only way they could really have got press space was for me to give it to them by answering them. It is my defense that makes the controversy, not their attack; it is my anwser that gets the newspaper space for their attack. Without my help they have thus far failed in terms of publicity. I shall withhold that help from them in the future. Only if they are able to get the space on their own—which I doubt—will I think of replying to them. Refusal to reply minimizes the newspaper space they can command.

A year ago Susskind wanted me on Open End with the National Chairman of the Legion. I said to him, "Why don't you put the Chairman on alone? Or with two or three other Legionnaires?" He said, "Because that wouldn't make a show." I said, "Then it is my presence on the show that makes the appearance of the Legion Chairman possible?" He said, "That's right." I said, "Then if I go on the show, I give the Legion Chairman an audience of millions of TV viewers he would not have otherwise?" He said, "That is correct." I said, "Then I will not go on the show. In refusing, I deny him an audience of millions, and that is a thundering victory. If, by appearing myself, I make him a present of a platform and an audience of millions, he has won a victory no matter how the show turns out. I will give him no platforms, no audiences, and no victories. Those he will have to earn for himself."

Susskind thought a moment, and said, "You're absolutely right. From my point of view as a showman, it would make a great show. But from the point of view of yourself and the blacklist, you are correct." We agreed that I would do a show with him in the indefinite future, in either one of two circumstances: (1) if the blacklist were thoroughly smashed, I'd go on a victory show; (2) if the fight became so severe that I felt I had to fight for my life, then I'd take on anybody he chose. But apart from those two circumstances, no show, no defense, no statement, not one damned word from me that will call attention and gain readers for words spoken by my enemies.

Tomorrow may change all, but today I am sitting it out rather coolly, ducking occasionally as missiles fly through the air addressed to far more tempting targets than your friend.

D.T.

P.S. I thought I was through, but I keep thinking of something more, so I'll continue, since by now I may as well run this off on the Thermo and send it to one or two others abroad who may find in it something that bears on their own situations or strategy.

I have watched this rise of the Right, and I think thus far it's hollow as a gourd. I'm not playing down its danger, nor its capacity, in selected spots, to score an occasional hard blow. The rise of conservatism on the campus, for example, doesn't mean there is any larger percentage of conservative students than there always was. It means only that they have a Conservative campus organization where formerly they didn't. Nor does their organization on each campus attract all or the majority of conservative youngsters in the school. It attracts only itself, a minority within a minority. And the extremist minority of the conservative minority on campus is generally organized, directed, and financed by some middle-aged Bircher, which means that the organization is basically a front, that its members are generally obedient and hence unimaginative, that the group doesn't think for itself, doesn't act in its own behalf, doesn't make its own policy, doesn't raise its own funds, and hence is really not viable.

Now organizations, "schools," institutes, and projects of the extreme right are springing up all over the place, but they suffer from their very diversity. With the exception of the John Birch Society (insofar as I know) most of them are almost fatally flawed at the outset in that they do not rise from any spontaneous need of the community or demand from it; they are, on the contrary, organized *to make money*. If a man has any reputation at all, and can deliver a good spell-binding speech, he can now make a damned good living by sponsoring and encouraging the formation of such outfits, and speaking for them and lecturing to them for a fee. Their speeches, books and pamphlets are all strictly for profit, and this fact alone works strongly against the permanence of the various organizations they establish. They hit a community like a circus troup, ballyhoo the show, run for three or four days, pick up the swag, and hit the road again.

As for the crowds they draw, do not be deceived. First, they are not as large as they are reported by the sponsors; and secondly, if they were as large as reported they still would not necessarily indicate massive support in the community or the country.

I remember the Henry Wallace campaign in 1948. In Los Angeles, for example, neither the Republicans nor the Democrats could even think of trying to fill Gilmore Stadium for their respective presidential candidates. They didn't even try because they knew they couldn't do it. But Henry Wallace and the Progressive party filled it till people were standing in the aisles. If getting out the crowds bore any relation to getting the votes, Wallace would have been elected in a landslide; but when the shooting match was over the Progressive party didn't even represent a healthy political splinter. Those people in that stadium represented only themselves. They were busy as hell organizing each other and making noise, but when you counted noses at a Progressive rally you were actually counting the full Progressive vote of the district. Not so with the majority parties.

Yet these massive campaigns of the right, and their great rallies, simply do not attract even the sort of crowds the Progressives used to. They took the Shrine, had 30 stars on hand, a Senator on the program, a tremendous build-up in the press—and they drew 12,000 people. They just had a five-day school of some sort, lectures round the clock at $10 for the full course. Culminating event was a mass meeting in the Shrine Auditorium. Result: 3,500 persons in a hall whose capacity is 6,500. Financial result of the five-day "school"— $20,000 loss. General Walker, who resigned to save the country, has been taken up by big Texas money. He's a bright man, a hell of a speaker, and has a first-rate military record behind him. They held his kick-off rally in Dallas the other day, his national debut, so to speak. Capacity of hall: 10,000. Seats filled: 5,400.

The main problem of those people, as I see it, is that they have too many organizations with too many different objectives; that they are organized for money-making, and hence compete with each other; and that, try though they may, they have not yet achieved the faintest aura of intellectual respectability. Most of the great Republican papers, while reporting their activities, find the racket too embarrassing to support. Thus they do not get the good press one would expect for them, and often, as when a local speaker urged that Warren be hanged, they draw sharp opposition editorials from unexpected sources.

The Birch Society, which infiltrates them all and directs many of them, is quite another thing. It has money and power. When *Life* Magazine jumped our Australian messiah, Schwarts or whatever his name is, the magazine suddenly found $8,500,000 in advertisements turning elsewhere. *Life* backtracked. When a local TV newscaster, sponsored by a building and loan association, did an exposé of the Birch Society on his show, depositors in the sponsoring loan association withdrew $130,000 in three days. That sort of delivered power talks. But it cannot yet deliver mass people-power, and I doubt that it ever will.

When they find a uniform, a slogan, and one simple cause—then's when the danger will come. But I don't see much sign of it yet.

Coming back again to me, to us, to the blacklist, I have the feeling that it will continue to open up, but only as each individual finds, sometimes through blind luck, that unique situation which he can exploit for the acceptance of his own name. For myself, one thing could really hurt: another ticket from the committee. I'd stand a better than even chance of going under, and probably would go under. Barring that, and barring a really dramatic upsurge of the right and a careful concentration on me, the situation here looks relatively stable.

D.T.

25. Extract of a letter to Frank King[31]

Los Angeles, California
April 28, 1962

1. *I am rich* . . . (The widow who's suing is poor. I shall appear therefore as a rich writer who has robbed the grave of a poor writer.)

2. *I am Hollywood.* (And therefore . . . not quite respectable. It can be assumed I drink, lech, and seduce two-thirds of the time.)

3. *I have written scores of successful scripts.* (Therefore, say we, I had no need to steal. But, says the jury in its mind, precisely because he is successful and did not have to steal, the fact that he *did* steal becomes absolutely unforgivable. A man who steals from hunger can be understood: a man who steals out of sheer acquisitive greed should be shot at sunrise.)

4. *I have used many pseudonyms and many bank accounts under different names.* (Try as we may to explain the black list and the black market, it is too far in the past, and too complex for a jury to understand. To a jury there is something dishonest about pseudonyms and phony bank accounts, something secret and conspiratorial. An honest man [like all members of the jury] will work under his own name and bank money in his own open account. The man who conceals his identity and his bank account must have dark reason for con-

---

[31] This humorous self-analysis was written in a lengthy note to the King Brothers, trying to persuade them to settle a particular plagiarism case out of court. In explanation of the case itself, Trumbo wrote the following note:

Court action, whether criminal or civil, is the constant ghost that haunts the ghost in black market work.

Here is an example of a plagiarism suit that was settled out of court . . . When "Robert Rich" won the Oscar—and didn't exist—11 persons stepped forth from the shadows to contend for the statuette. Five of them actually began legal proceedings for plagiarism. There was no reason not to sue. The King Brothers were stuck with a script and couldn't produce an author to testify he'd written it.

Later, at their request, I announced I had written the script to scare off the free-loaders. It did scare them off.

But not the woman in the action which follows because she was not a free-loader. She was a sincere woman with an honest conviction supported by an amazing sequence of events and similarities. (The plot of *The Brave One* is as old as the first story ever told about a child and an animal.)

My reaction was instant when I saw the value of her case: settle. In urging settlement I was concerned not with justice, but expediency. I had never read her script nor heard of it, but to convince a jury's another matter. I do not altogether trust juries. Their honesty I would rarely question: but their capacity for objective judgment I do question—particularly when such emotional issues as mother, God, country intrude in the course of trial.

Hence—I'm glad o say—a settlement of $12,500 was made to plantiff. The defendents could afford it (I paid nothing) and the plaintiff needed it. Not just for herself, but as emotional vindication of her deceased husband's work. Good enough! God works in mysterious . . .

cealment: viz., he is a furtive, suspicious, and probably dishonest character. Testimony from such a man is not to be believed.)

5. *I have been before the House Un-American Activities Committee, and refused to testify.* (Hence, to the jury, I am a Communist —and if you think that will add to their belief in my testimony you are wrong, because:——)

6. *I am an ex-convict.* (Which means, in the jury's mind, no matter how carefully all the differences and legalities are explained, that I am not only a convicted Communist but a convicted traitor, and conceivably a spy to boot. In addition to this, if they wish to go back to about 1949 or '50, they will be able to bring out, from my own lips or from the record, the fact that:——)

7. *I was arrested for drunkenness.* (Jailed, released on bail, forfeited bail. The whole thing was an outrageous fraud, but there it is. Your . . . key witness is therefore a drunk.)

8. *I am the object of widespread public hostility and contempt.* (For 12 years my name has been blasted in headlines, in the trade press, in movie columns, in newspaper gossip columns, in magazines. Anyone who has read Parsons, Hopper, Winchell, Skolsky, Sullivan, Riesel, or the Hearst press with any degree of regularity is bound to consider me unreliable at best, and a traitor at worst. I am regularly condemned by resolution at each California and National American Legion convention. In the last year my films have been picketed by the Legion and by front groups of the Birch Society. If we try to exclude Legionnaires and Birchites from the jury, we shall be inviting a political trial in advance. If they are not excluded, just one good Legionnaire on the jury, just one secret Birchite—or, for that matter, just one decent, gullible person who believes what he reads— *and we cannot fail to lose.*)

Let's summarize, now, your . . . key witness: a rich Hollywood writer who stole a dead man's work not out of necessity, but out of sheer greed; a man who used aliases, kept secret bank accounts, shunned his own name; a public drunk, an ex-convict, a Communist and a traitor.

26. To Cleo Trumbo

Los Angeles, California
July 17, 1962

Dear Cleo:

Sixty is not
 quite as old
  as you think,

                    And fifty is not
                        quite as young.
                    For myself,
                        I've a fix,
                    On the age
                        Forty-six,
                    When the song
                        of your life
                            on the tip
                                of your tongue
                    Hasn't really had
                        time to
                            begin to
                                be sung.
        I know I sign it "love," but which follows—

                                    DALTON? or—TRUMBO? [32]

27. Wire to Kirk Douglas

Los Angeles, California
[c. August], 1962

Dear Kirk:

Once in a while when God smiles and the table is tilted just slightly in our favor, something happens. It comes from inside and reveals what we really are. I think it happened with you in *Cowboy*.[33] I think they are going to leave the theatre saying, "that is what I really am. Or at least it is what I want to be in my finest hour." You did it. You showed the heart of a man. Do you dig me, Amigo? Old Sam is grateful and sends you love.

[32] Mrs. Trumbo has always called her husband by his last name.
[33] Douglas was the star of *Lonely Are the Brave* (formerly titled *The Brave Cowboy*) which has achieved the status of an underground classic. Eight years after its production it led off the U.C.L.A. annual film festival.

28. Extract of a letter to Derrick John Taylor

Los Angeles, California
December 4, 1962

Nikola [34] is a strong, healthy girl, fierce in her loyalties, and good to have at one's side in a fight. You'll find her handier with a monkey-wrench than a skillet, but that's a small deficiency, since the gift of wrenches comes from God alone, while cooking is only an art, and can be learned.

Having already over-compensated us by the joy of her birth and the charm of her existence, she arrives at her new address entirely free of gratitude's unpleasant debt. The major claim which thus far we have had upon her life is now surrendered unconditionally to you.

I hesitate to wish you a lifetime's happiness because I doubt there is such a thing, even were the meanings of happiness not as various as the people who seek it. Instead—and much more modestly—I wish you contentment with each other in days of triumph, and in defeat the kind of unfailing refuge one never has to ask for: it's simply there, waiting and wanting to be used.

I send my love to both of you.

D.T.

[34] Nikola married San Francisco artist and sculptor Derrick John Taylor in the Trumbo home on December 23, 1962. Their son, Dominic Trumbo Taylor, was born in 1964 on February 6—a date which prompted Trumbo to dub him "Child of Epiphany."

Postscript

On March 13, 1970 the Trumbos' thirty-second wedding anniversary, Trumbo received the Writers' Guild annual Laurel Award "for that member of the Guild who has advanced the literature of the motion picture through the years and who has made outstanding contributions to the profession of the screenwriter." Trumbo accepted the award, feeling that it offered a chance to summarize his conclusions about the blacklist.

Shortly after I joined this organization in 1936 the Producers Association offered its members a simple choice: resign from the Guild and accept a company union or get off the lot. Within a single month our membership diminished from several hundred to less than forty. I remember the four years it required to recover from that blow—four years of evidence-gathering, affidavits, house meetings, planning sessions, legal briefings, recruiting parties, none of which was secret, but all of which were certainly as private as they could be kept, not because their purpose was shameful, but because at that time it was not possible to organize a guild or union *without* privacy.

I remember the houses in which those meetings were held and the names of most of their owners—Lester Cole, Oliver Garrett, Sheridan Gibney, Dashiell Hammett, Lillian Hellman, Jack Lawson, Mary McCall, Dudley Nichols, Sam Ornitz, Ted Paramore, Dorothy Parker, Ernest Pascal, Wells Root, Donald Ogden Stewart, Jo Swerling, Nathanael West, and, of course, others. Over half of them are dead by now, and some of them are in retirement, but without their devotion, their work, their money, their passion, their principled and sometimes almost clandestine conspiracies, this Guild would not today be preparing, openly and confidently and legally, for a new round of contract negotiations with the producers of American films.

I remember the years immediately following recognition during which 277 members of the Guild entered the armed services (as I did not) to fight what then was called a war against fascism. Five of them did not come back. Within six years, forty-three of those who *did* return were denounced as un-American, stripped of their names and passports, and blacklisted from the profession to which they had so recently returned. Men who left the screen in their early thirties return to it today in their fifties.

I presume that over half of our members have no memory of that blacklist because they were children when it began, or not yet born. To them I would say only this: that the blacklist was a time of evil, and that no one on either side who survived it came through untouched by evil. Caught in a situation that had passed beyond the control of mere individuals, each person reacted as his nature, his needs, his convictions, and his particular circumstances compelled him to. There was bad faith and good, honesty and dishonesty, courage and cowardice, selflessness and opportunism, wisdom and stupidity, good and bad on both sides; and almost every individual involved, no matter where he stood, combined some or all of these antithetical qualities in his own person, in his own acts.

When you who are in your forties or younger look back with curiosity on that dark time, as I think occasionally you should, it will do no good to search for villains or heroes or saints or devils because there were none; there were only victims. Some suffered less than others, some grew and some diminished, but in the final tally we were *all* victims because almost without exception each of us felt compelled to say things he did not want to say, to do things he did not want to do, to deliver and receive wounds he truly did not want to exchange. That is why none of us—right, left, or center —emerged from that long nightmare without sin.

I said "almost without exception" because those who were killed in World War II escaped the blacklist altogether, and therefore lay beyond its reach. In July of 1947 the Guild published the names of its five war dead and established, in memory of all of them, an annual honor which it called the Robert Meltzer Award. Lieutenant Robert Meltzer, whose last published work appeared in *Collier's* on September 23, 1944, served with a specially trained, specially equipped volunteer attack group called the Rangers. He survived the Normandy landings only to be killed while leading a later assault on the fortress of Brest, leaving behind an infant christened Jo Victory, which is a nice name for a soldier's daughter to bear.

During the 1951–52 hearings of the House Committee on Un-American Activities reference was made to the existence of a Meltzer club or branch or cell of the Communist Party in Hollywood. The last Meltzer Award was presented in 1952; the first Laurel Award was announced and given in 1953. As its eighteenth recipient I ask your permission to accept it in the names of Robert Meltzer and those forgotten writers who died with him and for us three wars ago—Frederick Faust, Arch Heath, Edward de Melcher, and David Silverstein.

I assure you—I assure you most sincerely—that what I have said here is not intended to be hurtful to anyone: it is intended rather to repair a hurt, to heal a wound which years ago we inflicted on each other, and on ourselves most of all. I beg you to understand my feelings when I tell you that it was not emotionally possible for me to accept this award, as gladly and proudly I do, in any words but those I have just used. Thank you.

Index

571